A GUIDE TO CRITICAL REVIEWS

Part I: *American Drama, 1900-1969.* 2d ed. 1973.

Part II: *The Musical, 1909-1974.* 2d ed. 1976.

Part III: *British and Continental Drama.* 1968.

Part IV: *The Screenplay from "The Jazz Singer to Dr. Strangelove."* 2 vols. 1971.

A Guide to Critical Reviews:

Part II:
The Musical, 1909-1974

Second edition

by

JAMES M. SALEM

The Scarecrow Press, Inc.
Metuchen, N.J.   1976

Library of Congress Cataloging in Publication Data   (Revised)

Salem, James M
    A guide to critical reviews.

    CONTENTS: pt. 1. American drama, 1909-1969. pt. 2.
The musical, 1909-1974.
    1. Theater--Reviews--Indexes. 2. Moving-pictures--Reviews
--Indexes. I. Title.
Z5782. S342   016. 809'2   73-3120
ISBN 0-8108-0608-8 (v. 1)
ISBN 0-8108-0959-1 (v. 2)

To Tim

TABLE OF CONTENTS

FOREWORD

The purpose of Part II of A Guide to Critical Reviews (second edition) is to provide a bibliography of critical reviews of the musical on the New York stage from 1909 to the 1973-74 theater season. The productions listed are, for the most part, Broadway productions, though Off-Broadway and Off-Off-Broadway presentations have been included when accurate statistical data could be obtained.

The key source for twentieth century American theater research of this kind is, of course, The Best Plays of the Year series (New York: Dodd, Mead and Co.) begun by Burns Mantle and currently directed by Otis L. Guernsey, Jr. In addition, I have found the following books valuable for statistical, historical, and general reference information on the musical play:

Baral, Robert. Revue: A Nostalgic Reprise of the Great Broadway Period. New York: Fleet Publishing Co., 1962.

Engel, Lehman. The American Musical Theater/A Consideration by Lehman Engel. New York: The Macmillan Co., 1967.

Ewen, David. Complete Book of the American Musical Theater. New York: Henry Holt, 1958.

_____. The Story of America's Musical Theater. Philadelphia and New York: The Chilton Co., 1961.

Green, Stanley. The World of Musical Comedy (Revised). South Brunswick and New York: A. S. Barnes and Co., 1968.

Smith, Cecil. Musical Comedy in America. New York: Theatre Arts Books, 1960.

Musical revues have been included in this volume, and musical extravaganzas, spectacles, burlesques--even a musical described as a "Fragment from France in two explosions, seven splinters and a short gas attack" (The Better 'Ole, Season of 1918-19). I have,

vii

however, excluded most operas and operettas, though <u>Porgy and Bess</u> is here along with the works of Marc Blitzstein and Gian-Carlo Menotti.

The reviews cited in this volume are those which appeared in general circulation American and Canadian periodicals and in the <u>New York Times.</u> With the exception of some now defunct dramatic magazines like <u>Dramatic Mirror</u> and the <u>New York Clipper</u>, most of the reviews should be available in college and public libraries. Reviews in other New York newspapers have not been indexed, but <u>New York Theatre Critics' Reviews</u>, which currently reprints reviews from the <u>New York Daily News</u>, <u>Post</u>, <u>Wall Street Journal</u>, <u>Women's Wear Daily</u>, <u>Christian Science Monitor</u>, and the three major television networks, has been cited for plays produced since that publication began in 1940.

The organization of this volume is alphabetical, by title, with liberal cross-referencing. The three indexes at the end will enable the user to track down Authors, Composers, and Lyricists; Directors, Designers, and Choreographers; and the titles and original authors of novels, plays, movies, comic strips, and stories upon which many musical plays are based.

I have used two symbols throughout to indicate incomplete data. For early plays, the number of performances enclosed by parentheses denotes that the play may in fact have had a longer run than the performances given. For the most recent productions, an asterisk [*] denotes that the musical was still running on June 1, 1975.

The revised version of this book would still be in the talking and promising stage had it not been for the willingness of my three older children to lend a hand--to cut, paste, alphabetize, track things down, and learn how to type. The traditional debt of gratitude, then, goes to Children Power--to Tim and Betsy and Jennifer who helped make this book. Also to Donna, who helped me turn the house, for a whole summer, into a book factory.

University, Alabama
September, 1975

MUSICALS

À La Broadway (Presented with Hello, Paris, 1911)
  book: William Le Baron
  music: Harold Orlob
  lyrics: William Le Baron and M. H. Hollins
Productions:
  Opened September 22, 1911 for 8 performances
Reviews:
  Life (New York) 96:35, Dec 5, 1930

À La Carte
  book: Rosalie Stewart
  sketches: George Kelly
  music: Herman Hupfeld, Louis Atter, Norma Gregg,
                   Paul Lanin and Creamer and Johnson
  staging: George Kelly
Productions:
  Opened August 17, 1927 for 45 performances
Reviews:
  Life (New York) 90:19, Sep 8, 1927
  Theatre Magazine 46:23, Oct 1927
  Vogue 70:97, Oct 15, 1927

Above the Clouds
  book: Will B. Johnstone
  music: Tom Johnston
  lyrics: Will B. Johnstone
Productions:
  Opened January 9, 1922 for 89 performances
No Reviews.

Absolutely Free
  music/lyrics: Frank Zappa
Productions:
  (Off-Broadway) Opened May 24, 1967 for 208 performances
Reviews:
  New York Times page 58, May 25, 1967

Adele
  book: Paul Herve; English version by Adolf Philipp
                   and Edward A. Paulton
  music: Jean Briquet
  staging: Ben Teal

1

Productions:
    Opened August 28, 1913 for 196 performances
Reviews:
    Dramatic Mirror 70:6, Sep 3, 1913; 70:2+, Oct 22, 1913
    Green Book 10:769-70, Nov 1913; 11:524, Mar 1914
    Munsey 50:290-3, Nov 1913
    New York Dramatic News 58:20-1, Sep 6, 1913
    New York Times page 9, Aug 29, 1913
                III, page 4, Jun 14, 1914
    Theatre Arts 18:xi, Oct 1913; 18:117, Oct 1913
    Theatre Magazine 18:127, Oct 1913; 20:283, Dec 1914

Adolph Green   (see A Party with Betty Comden and Adolph Green)

Adrienne
    book: A. Seymour Brown; from a story by Frances
                       Bryant and William Stone
    music: Albert Von Tilzer
    lyrics: A. Seymour Brown
    staging: Edgar J. MacGregor
Productions:
    Opened May 28, 1923 for (24) performances
Reviews:
    Life (New York) 81:18, Jun 21, 1923
    New York Clipper 71:14, Jun 6, 1923
    New York Times page 10, May 29, 1923
    Theatre Magazine 38:16, Aug 1923

Aesop's Fables
    book: Jon Swan; based on Aesop's Fables
    music: William Russo
    lyrics: Jon Swan
    staging: William Russo
    sets: Vanessa James
Productions:
    (Off-Broadway) Opened August 16, 1972 for 58 performances
No Reviews.

Afgar
    book: Fred Thompson and Worton David
    music: Charles Cuvillier
    lyrics: Douglass Furher
    staging: Frank Collins
Productions:
    Opened November 8, 1920 for 171 performances
Reviews:
    Dramatic Mirror page 895, Nov 13, 1920
                    page 1218, Dec 25, 1920
    Life (New York) 76:960, Nov 25, 1920
    New York Clipper 68:page 3, Nov 17, 1920
    New York Times page 13, Nov 9, 1920
                    VI, page 1, Nov 14, 1920
    Theatre Magazine 33:11+, Jan 1921; 33:74, Jan 1921

Africana

music:	Donald Heyward
lyrics:	Donald Heyward
staging:	Louis Douglas

Productions:
    Opened July 11, 1927 for 72 performances
Reviews:
    Life (New York) 90:19, Aug 18, 1927
    New York Times page 29, Jul 12, 1927
                 VII, page 1, Sep 4, 1927

Ain't Supposed to Die a Natural Death (Tunes from Blackness)

book:	Melvin Van Peebles
music:	Melvin Van Peebles
lyrics:	Melvin Van Peebles
staging:	Gilbert Moses
sets:	Kert Lundell
costumes:	Bernard Johnson

Productions:
    Opened October 20, 1971 for 325 performances
Reviews:
    Nation 213:476-7, Nov 8, 1971
    New York Theatre Critics' Reviews 1971:229
    New York Times page 55, Oct 21, 1971; II, page 3, Oct 31,
            1971; II, page 1, Nov 7, 1971; II, page 28, Apr 16,
            1972; page 13, Jul 29, 1972
    New Yorker 47:101-2, Oct 30, 1971
    Newsweek 78:85-6, Nov 1, 1971
    Saturday Review 54.10+, Nov 13, 1971
    Time 98:95, Nov 1, 1971

Alive and Kicking

sketches:	Ray Golden, I. A. Diamond, Henry Morgan, Jerome Chodorov, Joseph Stein, Will Glickman, Mike Stuart
music:	Hal Borne, Irma Jurist and Sammy Fain
lyrics:	Paul Francis Webster and Ray Golden
additional music and lyrics:	Sonny Burke, Leonard Gershe, Billy Kyle, Sid Kuller
special music and lyrics:	Harold Rome
staging:	Robert H. Gordon
sets:	Raoul Pene du Bois
costumes:	Raoul Pene du Bois
choreography:	Jack Cole

Productions:
    Opened January 17, 1950 for 46 performances
Reviews:
    New York Theatre Critics' Reviews 1950:390+
    New York Times page 25, Jan 18, 1950
    Newsweek 35:66, Jan 30, 1950
    Theatre Arts 34:16, Mar 1950

Time 55:40, Jan 30, 1950

All Aboard
book:	Mark Swan
music:	E. Ray Goetz and Malvin Franklin
lyrics:	E. Ray Goetz
staging:	William J. Wilson and W. H. Post

Productions:
Opened June 5, 1913 for 108 performances
Reviews:
Blue Book 17:876-80, Sep 1913
Book News 32:255-6, Jan 1914
Dramatic Mirror 69:15, Jun 11, 1913
Green Book 10:433-5, Sep 1913
New York Dramatic News 57:18, Jun 14, 1913
New York Times page 11, Jun 6, 1913
Theatre Magazine 18:xx, Jul 1913

All American
book:	Mel Brooks, based on Robert Lewis Taylor's Professor Fodorski
music:	Charles Strouse
lyrics:	Lee Adams
staging:	Joshua Logan
sets:	Jo Mielziner
costumes:	Patton Campbell
choreography:	Danny Daniels

Productions:
Opened March 19, 1962 for 86 performances
Reviews:
America 107:278-9, May 19, 1962
New York Theatre Critics' Reviews 1962:318+
New York Times page 44, Mar 20, 1962; page 29, May 24, 1962
New Yorker 38:104-6, Mar 31, 1962
Newsweek 59:58, Apr 2, 1962
Theatre Arts 46:58, May 1962
Time 79:46, Mar 30, 1962

All By Myself
sketches:	Anna Russell
music/lyrics:	Anna Russell
staging:	Kurt Cerf
sets:	Robert E. Darling
costumes:	Stephanya

Productions:
(Off-Broadway) Opened June 15, 1964 for 40 performances
Reviews:
New York Times page 47, Jun 16, 1964

All for Love
sketches:	Max Shulman and others
music/lyrics:	Allan Roberts and Lester Lee
staging:	Edward Reveaux

sets: Edward Gilbert
costumes: Billy Livingston
choreography: Eric Victor
Productions:
Opened January 22, 1949 for 141 performances
Reviews:
Commonweal 49:447, Feb 11, 1949
New York Theatre Critics' Reviews 1949:377+
New York Times page 16, Jan 24, 1949
New Yorker 24:42, Jan 29, 1949
Newsweek 33:71, Jan 31, 1949
Time 53:44, Jan 31, 1949; 53:63-4, May 2, 1949

All for the Ladies
book: Henry Blossom
music: Alfred C. Robyn
lyrics: Henry Blossom
costumes: Melville Ellis
Productions:
Opened December 30, 1912 for 112 performances
Reviews:
Blue Book 16:1137-40, Apr 1913
Book News 32:180, Nov 1913
Dramatic Mirror 69:6, Jan 8, 1913
Red Book 21:317+, Jun 1913
Theatre Magazine 17:34+, Feb 1913; 17:xii, Feb 1913

All in Fun
book: Virginia Faulkner and Everett Marcy
music and
lyrics: Baldwin Bergerson, June Sillman, John Rox,
                    Irvin Graham, Will Irwin, Pembroke Davenport,
                    S. K. Russell
staging: Leonard Sillman
sets: Edward Gilbert
costumes: Irene Sharaff
choreography: Marjorie Fielding
Productions:
Opened December 27, 1940 for 3 performances
Reviews:
New York Theatre Critics' Reviews 1940:167+
New York Times page 26, Nov 22, 1940
              page 11, Dec 28, 1940
Stage 1:6, Dec 1940

All In Love
book: Bruce Geller, based on Sheridan's The Rivals
music: Jacques Urbont
lyrics: Bruce Geller
staging: Tom Brennan
sets: Charles Lisanby
costumes: Charles Lisanby

choreography: Jack Beaber
Productions:
   (Off-Broadway)   Opened November 10, 1961 for 141 performances
   (Off-Broadway)   Opened Season of 1966-1967 for 14 performances
      (Equity Theatre)
Reviews:
   Commonweal 75:389, Jan 5, 1962
   New York Times page 15, Nov 11, 1961
   New Yorker 37:96+, Nov 18, 1961

All In One   (see Trouble in Tahiti)

All Kinds of Giants
   book: Tom Whedon
   music: Stan Pottle
   lyrics: Tom Whedon
   staging: Peter Conlow
Productions:
   (Off Broadway)   Opened December 18, 1961 for 16 performances
Reviews:
   New York Times page 40, Dec 19, 1961
   New Yorker 37:58-9, Jan 6, 1962

All Star Gambol   (see Marie Dressler's All Star Gambol)

All the King's Horses
   book: Frederick Herendeen
   music: Edward A. Horan
   lyrics: Frederick Herendeen
   staging: Jose Ruben
   sets: Herbert Ward
Productions:
   Opened January 30, 1934 for 120 performances
Reviews:
   Catholic World 138:734, Mar 1934
   New Outlook 163:32, Mar 1934
   New York Times page 21, Jan 31, 1934
   Review of Reviews 89:58, Apr 1934

All the King's Men
   book: Vinnette Carroll; adapted from Robert Penn War-
                      ren's novel
   music: Malcolm Dodds
   lyrics: Malcolm Dodds
   staging: Vinnette Carroll
Productions:
   (Off-Off-Broadway)   Opened May 14, 1974 (Urban Arts Corps.)
No Reviews.

Allah Be Praised!
   book: George Marion, Jr.
   music: Don Walker and Baldwin Bergersen
   lyrics: George Marion, Jr.

staging: Robert H. Gordon and Jack Small
sets: George Jenkins
costumes: Miles White
choreography: Jack Cole
Productions:
Opened April 20, 1944 for 20 performances
Reviews:
New York Theatre Critics' Reviews 1944:207+
New York Times page 14, Apr 21, 1944
New Yorker 20:46, Apr 29, 1944
Newsweek 23:78, May 1, 1944
Time 43:58, May 1, 1944

Allegro
book: Oscar Hammerstein II
music: Richard Rodgers
lyrics: Oscar Hammerstein II
staging: Lawrence Langner and Theresa Helburn
sets: Jo Mielziner
costumes: Lucinda Ballard
choreography: Agnes de Mille
Productions:
Opened October 10, 1947 for 315 performances
Reviews:
Catholic World 166:167, Nov 1947
Collier's 120:20-1+, Oct 25, 1947
Commonweal 47:70-1, Oct 31, 1947
Forum 109:23-4, Jan 1948
Life 23:70-2, Oct 13, 1947
Nation 165:567-8, Nov 22, 1947
New Republic 117:35, Oct 27, 1947
New York Theatre Critics' Reviews 1947:300+
New York Times II, page 2, Oct 5, 1947
                page 10, Oct 11, 1947
                II, page 1, Nov 2, 1947
                II, page 6, Nov 9, 1947
                II, page 1, Nov 16, 1947
                II, page 3, Jan 18, 1948
                page 36, Sep 18, 1952
New Yorker 23:55-6, Oct 18, 1947
Newsweek 30:86, Oct 20, 1947
Saturday Review 30:30-3, Nov 8, 1947
                30:59, Nov 29, 1947
School and Society 67:476, Jun 26, 1948
Theatre Arts 31:23, Oct 1947
                31:13-15, Nov 1947
Time 50:66-8+, Oct 20, 1947
Vogue 110:191, Nov 15, 1947

Allez-Oop
sketches: J. P. McEvoy
music: Charig and Richard Myers
lyrics: Leo Robin

staging: Carl Hemmer
Productions:
Opened August 2, 1927 for 120 performances
Reviews:
Life (New York) 90:10, Aug 18, 1927
New York Times page 29, Aug 3, 1927
Theatre Magazine 46:23, Oct 1927
Vogue 70:84-5, Oct 1, 1927

Alma, Where Do You Live?
book: George V. Hobart; from the French of Paul
                  Herve
music: Jean Briquet
staging: Joe Weber
Productions:
Opened September 26, 1910 for 232 performances
Reviews:
Blue Book 12:652-3, Feb 1911
Life 56:565, Oct 6, 1910
Metropolitan Magazine 33:402-3, Dec 1910
Stage 13:58, Aug 1936
Theatre Magazine 12:159, Nov 1910

Almanac (1929) (see Murray Anderson's Almanac)

Almanac (1953) (see John Murray Anderson's Almanac)

Almost Crazy
sketches: James Shelton, Hal Hackady, and Robert A.
                  Bernstein
music: Portia Nelson, Raymond Taylor and James
                  Shelton
lyrics: Portia Nelson, Raymond Taylor and James
                  Shelton
staging: Lew Kesler
sets: John Robert Lloyd
costumes: Stanley Simmons
choreography: William Skipper
Productions:
Opened June 20, 1955 for 16 performances
Reviews:
America 93:378-9, Jul 9, 1955
New York Theatre Critics' Reviews 1955:298+
New York Times page 37, June 21, 1955
Theatre Arts 39:16, Sep 1955

Along Fifth Avenue
sketches: Charles Sherman and Nat Hiken
music: Gordon Jenkins
lyrics: Tom Adair
additional
  music and
  lyrics: Richard Stutz, Milton Pascal, Nat Hiken

sets: Oliver Smith
costumes: David Ffolkes
choreography: Robert Sidney
Productions:
Opened January 13, 1949 for 180 performances
Reviews:
Catholic World 168:481, Mar 1949
New Republic 120:29, Jan 31, 1949
New York Theatre Critics' Reviews 1949:392+
New York Times page 28, Jan 14, 1949
New Yorker 24:44, Jan 22, 1949
Newsweek 33:70, Jan 24, 1949
Time 53:52, Jan 24, 1949
Theatre Arts 33:16-17+, Mar 1949

Always You
    book: Oscar Hammerstein II
    music: Herbert P. Stothart
    lyrics: Oscar Hammerstein II
Productions:
Opened January 5, 1920 for 66 performances
Reviews:
Dramatic Mirror 82:57, Jan 15, 1920
New York Clipper 67:25, Jan 14, 1920
New York Times page 18, Jan 6, 1920
Theatre Magazine 31:184, Mar 1920

Ambassador
    book: Don Ettllnger and Anna Marie Barlow; based on
                 Henry James' novel The Ambassadors
    music: Don Gohman
    lyrics: Hal Hackady
    staging: Stone Widney
    sets: Peter Rice
    costumes: Peter Rice
    choreography: Joyce Trisler
Productions:
Opened November 19, 1972 for 19 performances
Reviews:
New York Theatre Critics' Reviews 1972:177
New York Times page 46, Nov 20, 1972
              page 53, Nov 28, 1972
New Yorker 48:123, Dec 2, 1972

The Amber Express
    book: Marc Connelly
    music: Zoel Parenteau
    lyrics: Marc Connelly
    staging: George Marion
Productions:
Opened September 19, 1916 for 15 performances
Reviews:
Dramatic Mirror 76:7, Sep 30, 1916

Munsey 59:498, Dec 1916
New York Dramatic News 63:2, Sep 30, 1916
New York Times page 7, Sep 20, 1916
Theatre Magazine 24:281-2, Nov 1916

America
    conceived: Arthur Voegtlin
    music: Manuel Klein
    lyrics: Manuel Klein
    staging: William J. Wilson
Productions:
    Opened August 30, 1913 for 360 performances
Reviews:
    Dramatic Mirror 70:7, Sep 3, 1913
                    70:2, Dec 24, 1913
    Leslie's Weekly 117:275, Sep 18, 1913
    New York Dramatic News 58:20, Sep 6, 1913
    Theatre Magazine 18:xiv, Oct 1913
                    18:129, Oct 1913

The American Ballad Singers
    arranged: Elsie Siegmeister
    staging: Elsie Siegmeister
Productions:
    Opened February 6, 1944 for 2 performances
No Reviews.

American Legend
    book: Paul Green's "Saturday Night" and E. P.
                    Conkle's "Minnie Field"
    staging: Baldwin Bergersen
    sets: John Pratt and Hugh Laing
    choreography: Agnes de Mille
Productions:
    (Off-Broadway) Opened April 28, 1941
No Reviews.

Americana (1926)
    book: J. P. McEvoy
    music: Con Conrad and Henry Souvaine; additional
                    music by George Gershwin, Philip Charig,
                    Ira Gershwin and Morrie Ryskind
    staging: Allen Dinehart and Larry Ceballos
Productions:
    Opened July 26, 1926 for 224 performances
Reviews:
    Life (New York) 88:21, Sep 9, 1926
    New York Times page 15, Jul 27, 1926
    Theatre Magazine 44:14-15, Oct 1926
    Vogue 68:124, Oct 1, 1926
    Woman's Home Companion 54:130, Feb 1927

Americana (1928)

book: J. P. McEvoy
music: Roger Wolfe Kahn
lyrics: J. P. McEvoy and Irving Caesar
staging: J. P. McEvoy
Productions:
   Opened October 30, 1928 for 12 performances
Reviews:
   New York Times X, page 1, Oct 14, 1928
                   page 28, Oct 31, 1928
                   page 34, Nov 6, 1928

Americana (1932)
   book: J. P. McEvoy
   music: Jay Gorney, Harold Arlen, Herman Hupfeld,
                 Richard Meyers
   lyrics: E. Y. Harburg
   staging: Harold Johnsrud
   sets: Albert R. Johnson
Productions:
   Opened October 5, 1932 for 77 performances
Reviews:
   Catholic World 136:210, Nov 1932
   New York Times IX, page 1, Sep 23, 1932
                    page 19, Oct 6, 1932
   Stage 10:49, Dec 15, 1932
   Theatre Arts 16:863+, Nov-Dec 1932

America's Sweetheart
   book: Herbert Fields
   music: Richard Rodgers
   lyrics: Lorenz Hart
   staging: Bobby Connelly and Monty Woolley
Productions:
   Opened February 10, 1931 for 135 performances
Reviews:
   New York Times VIII, page 2, Jan 25, 1931
                     page 23, Feb 11, 1931
   Theatre Magazine 53:25, Apr 1931
   Vogue 77:116, Apr 1, 1931

The Amorous Flea
   book: Jerry Devine; based on Moliere's School for
                 Wives
   music: Bruce Montgomery
   lyrics: Bruce Montgomery
   staging: Jack Sydow
   sets: Bill Hargate
   costumes: Donald Brooks
Productions:
   (Off Broadway) Opened February 17, 1964 for 93 performances
Reviews:
   New York Times page 26, Feb 18, 1964
                  page 34, May 4, 1964

New Yorker 40:108-9, Feb 29, 1964

...And in This Corner
    conceived: Michael McWhinney and Rod Warren
    staging: Jonathon Lucas
    costumes: Baba
Productions:
    (Off-Broadway) Opened February 12, 1964 for 410 performances
No Reviews.

Anderson, John Murray (see John Murray Anderson and Murray
    Anderson)

André Charlot's Revue of 1924
    book: André Charlot and R. Jeans
    staging: André Charlot
Productions:
    Opened January 9, 1924 for (173) performances
Reviews:
    New Republic 38:73, Mar 12, 1924
    New York Times page 18, Jan 10, 1924
                   page 22, Mar 20, 1924
    Theatre Magazine 39:16, Mar 1924
                       39:18, Mar 1924

Angel Face
    book: Harry B. Smith
    music: Victor Herbert
    lyrics: Robert B. Smith
    staging: George W. Lederer
    choreography: Julian Alfred
Productions:
    Opened December 29, 1919 for 57 performances
Reviews:
    Dramatic Mirror 82:7, Jan 8, 1920
    New York Clipper 67:12, Jan 7, 1920
    New York Times page 18, Dec 30, 1919
    Theatre Magazine 31:101+, Feb 1920

Angel in the Wings
    sketches: Ted Luce, Hank Ladd, Grace Hartman,
                  Paul Hartman
    music: Carl Sigman
    lyrics: Bob Hilliard
    staging: John Kennedy
    sets: Donald Oenslager
    costumes: Julia Sze
    choreography: Edward Noll
Productions:
    Opened December 11, 1947 for 300 performances
Reviews:
    Catholic World 166:456, Feb 1948
    Commonweal 47:277, Dec 26, 1947

Forum 109:155, Mar 1948
Life 24:35-7, Jan 5, 1948
New Republic 117:37, Dec 29, 1947
New York Theatre Critics' Reviews 1947:238+
New York Times page 36, Dec 12, 1947
         II, page 3, Dec 21, 1947
         II, page 2, Feb 8, 1948
         II, page 1, Aug 29, 1948
New Yorker 23:48, Dec 20, 1947
Newsweek 30:76, Dec 22, 1947
Time 50:72, Dec 22, 1947
Vogue 111:151+, Apr 1, 1948

Animal Crackers
     book: George S. Kaufman and Morrie Ryskind
     music: Harry Ruby
     lyrics: Bert Kalmar
Productions:
     Opened October 23, 1928 for 191 performances
Reviews:
     Life (New York) 92:14, Nov 16, 1928
     New Republic 56:351-2, Nov 14, 1928
     New York Times page 26, Oct 24, 1928
                    page 26, Apr 7, 1929
     Theatre Magazine 52:47, Nov 1930

Ankles Aweigh
     book: Guy Bolton and Eddie Davis
     music: Sammy Fain
     lyrics: Dan Shapiro
     staging: Fred F. Finklehoffe
     sets: George Jenkins
     costumes: Miles White
     choreography: Tony Charmoli
Productions:
     Opened April 18, 1955 for 176 performances
Reviews:
     Catholic World 181:228, Jun 1955
     Commonweal 62:330, Jul 1, 1955
     New York Theatre Critics' Reviews 1955:329+
     New York Times page 27, Apr 19, 1955
     New Yorker 31:71-2, Apr 30, 1955
     Theatre Arts 39:16, 88, Jul 1955
     Time 65:78, May 2, 1955

Anna Russell's Little Show
     music: Anna Russell
     lyrics: Anna Russell
     staging: Arthur Klein
Productions:
     Opened September 7, 1953 for 16 performances
Reviews:
     America 89:629, Sep 26, 1953

American Magazine 155:55, Apr 1953
Commonweal 58:634, Oct 2, 1953
New York Theatre Critics' Reviews 1953:289
New Yorker 29:75, Sep 19, 1953
Theatre Arts 37:20, Nov 1953

Anne of Green Gables
   adapted: Donald Harron; from the novel by L. M.
                  Montgomery
   music: Norman Campbell
   lyrics: Donald Harron and Norman Campbell
   staging: Alan Lund
   costumes: Marie Day
   choreography: Alan Lund
Productions:
   Opened December 21, 1971 for 16 performances
Reviews:
   New York Times page 30, Dec 22, 1971
           II, page 1, Jan 2, 1972

Annie Dear
   book: Clare Kummer
   music: Sigmund Romberg and Clare Kummer
   lyrics: Clifford Grey and Clare Kummer
   staging: Edward Royce
Productions:
   Opened November 4, 1924 for 103 performances
Reviews:
   New York Times page 25, Nov 5, 1924
   Theatre Magazine 41:22, Jan 1925

Annie Get Your Gun
   book: Herbert Fields and Dorothy Fields
   music: Irving Berlin
   lyrics: Irving Berlin
   staging: Joshua Logan
   sets: Jo Mielziner
   costumes: Lucinda Ballard
   choreography: Helen Tamiris
Productions:
   Opened May 16, 1946 for 1,147 performances
   Opened February 19, 1958 for 16 performances
   Opened May 31, 1966 for 47 performances
   Opened September 21, 1966 for 78 performances
Reviews:
   America 98:677, Mar 8, 1958
        114:882, Jun 25, 1966
   Catholic World 163:359, Jul 1946
        187:146-7, May 1958
   Commonweal 84:393-4, Jun 24, 1966
   Dance Magazine 40:27+, Jul 1966
   Life 20:89-94, Jun 3, 1946
       60:47, Jun 10, 1966

Modern Music 23 no. 2:144, Apr 1946
New York Theatre Critics' Reviews 1946:382+
New York Times page 18, Mar 29, 1946
              page 14, May 17, 1946
              II, page 1, May 26, 1946
              II, page 1, Jul 21, 1946
              II, page 1, Sep 29, 1946
              VI, page 25, Sep 29, 1946
              II, page 3, Dec 15, 1946
              page 63, Jun 8, 1947
              page 26, Jun 9, 1947
              page 10, Oct 4, 1947
              page 35, May 11, 1949
              page 35, May 3, 1950
              page 18, Feb 28, 1957
              page 18, Aug 31, 1957
              page 15, Mar 9, 1957
              page 29, Feb 20, 1958
              page 42, Jun 1, 1966
              page 40, Jul 1, 1966
              page 59, Nov 21, 1966
              page 63, Mar 20, 1967
New Yorker 22:42+, May 25, 1946
Newsweek 27:84-5, May 27, 1946
Saturday Review 29:30-2, Jun 15, 1946
Time 47:66, May 27, 1946

Another Evening with Harry Stoones
    sketches: Jeff Harris
    music: Jeff Harris
    lyrics: Jeff Harris
    staging: G. Adam Jordon
Productions:
    (Off-Broadway) Opened October 21, 1961 for one performance
Reviews:
    New York Times page 22, Oct 23, 1961
                   page 31, Oct 25, 1961
    New Yorker 37:132, Nov 4, 1961

Antiques
    music: Alan Greene and Laura Manning
    lyrics: Alan Greene and Laura Manning
    special
      material: Dore Schary
    staging: Marco Martone
    sets: Bruno C. Scordino
    costumes: William Christians
    choreography: Jeffrey K. Neill
Productions:
    (Off-Broadway) Opened June 19, 1973 for 8 performances
Reviews:
    New York Times page 33, Jun 20, 1973
                   page 83, Jun 21, 1973

Anyone Can Whistle
```
    book:          Arthur Laurents
    music:         Stephen Sondheim
    lyrics:        Stephen Sondheim
    staging:       Arthur Laurents
    sets:          William and Jean Eckart
    costumes:      Theoni V. Aldredge
    choreography:  Herbert Ross
```
Productions:
Opened April 4, 1964 for 9 performances
Reviews:
New York Theatre Critics' Reviews 1964:301+
New York Times page 36, Apr 6, 1964
           page 17, Apr 11, 1964

Anything Goes
```
    book:          Guy Bolton, P. G. Wodehouse, Howard Lindsay
                   and Russel Crouse
    music:         Cole Porter
    lyrics:        Cole Porter
    staging:       Howard Lindsay
    sets:          Donald Oenslager
    choreography:  Robert Alton
```
Productions:
Opened November 21, 1934 for 420 performances
(Off-Broadway) Opened May 15, 1962 for 239 performances
Reviews:
Catholic World 140:469-70, Jan 1935
Dance Magazine 36:26, Jul 1962
Literary Digest 118:18, Dec 8, 1934
New Republic 81:131, Dec 12, 1934
New York Times IX, page 1, Nov 18, 1934
           page 26, Nov 22, 1934
           IX, page 3, Nov 25, 1934
           page 20, Jun 15, 1935
           X, page 1, Jul 28, 1935
           IX, page 1, Aug 18, 1935
           IX, page 1, Sep 15, 1935
           page 23, Aug 17, 1937
           page 24, Aug 26, 1937
           page 35, May 16, 1962
New Yorker 38:92-3, May 26, 1962
Newsweek 4:23, Dec 1, 1934
Theatre Arts 19:19, Jan 1935
           46:59, Aug 1962
Time 24:24, Dec 3, 1934

Aphrodite
```
    book:          Pierre Frondaie and George C. Hazleton;
                   adapted from Pierre Louys' novel
    music:         Henri Fevrier and Anselm Goetzl
    staging:       E. Lyall Swete
```
Productions:

Opened November 24, 1919 for 148 performances
Reviews:
    Dramatic Mirror 80:1901+, Dec 11, 1919
    Dramatist 11:1000-1, Apr 1920
    Forum 63:111-12, Jan 1920
    Life (New York) 74:1024, Dec 18, 1919
    New York Times IV, page 7, Oct 26, 1919
                page 11, Dec 2, 1919
                IX, page 2, Dec 7, 1919
    Theatre Magazine 31:16, Jan 1920
                31:61, Jan 1920

Applause

    book: Betty Comden and Adolph Green; based on the film All About Eve and the original story by Mary Orr
    music: Charles Strouse
    lyrics: Lee Adams
    staging: Ron Field
    sets: Robert Randolph
    costumes: Ray Aghayan
    choreography: Ron Field
Productions:
    Opened March 30, 1970 for 896 performances
Reviews:
    Commentary 51:79, Feb 1971
    Dance Magazine 44:84-5, Jun 1970
    Life 68:54A-54D, Apr 3, 1970
    Nation 210:473-4+, Apr 20, 1970
    New Republic 162:20+, May 23, 1970
    New York Theatre Critics' Reviews 1970:316
    New York Times II, page 1, Mar 22, 1970
                page 35, Mar 31, 1970
                page 36, Apr 1, 1970
                II, page 1, Apr 26, 1970
                page 24, Jul 27, 1971
                II, page 1, Aug 22, 1971
                page 53, May 24, 1972
                page 42, Nov 17, 1972
    New Yorker 46:81, Apr 11, 1970
    Newsweek 75:83, Apr 13, 1970
    Saturday Review 53:26, Apr 18, 1970
    Time 95:97, Apr 18, 1970

Apple Blossoms

    book: William Le Baron
    music: Fritz Kreisler and Victor Jacobi
    lyrics: William Le Baron
Productions:
    Opened October 7, 1919 for 256 performances
Reviews:
    Dramatic Mirror 80:1652, Oct 23, 1919
    New York Times page 22, Oct 8, 1919

Theatre Magazine 30:350, Nov 1919

The Apple Tree
    book: Sheldon Harnick and Jerry Bock; based on
                     The Diary of Adam and Eve by Mark Twain,
                     The Lady or the Tiger? by Frank R. Stockton,
                     and Passionella by Jules Feiffer; additional book
                     material by Jerome Coppersmith
    music: Jerry Bock
    lyrics: Sheldon Harnick
    staging: Mike Nichols
    sets: Tony Walton
    costumes: Tony Walton
    choreography: Lee Theodore
Productions:
    Opened Oct 18, 1966 for 463 performances
Reviews:
    America 115:786, Dec 10, 1966
    Christian Century 84:144, Feb 1, 1967
    Commonweal 85:167, Nov 11, 1966
    Dance Magazine 41:22, Feb 1967
    Nation 203:493-4, Nov 7, 1966
    New York Theatre Critics' Reviews 1966:262
    New York Times page 53, Oct 19, 1966
                   II, page 1, Oct 30, 1966
                   page 56, Oct 12, 1967
                   page 61, Nov 4, 1967
                   page 61, Nov 10, 1967
    New Yorker 42:95, Oct 29, 1966
    Newsweek 68:98, Oct 31, 1966
    Saturday Review 49:47, Nov 5, 1966
    Time 88:90, Oct 28, 1966
    Vogue 148:161, Dec 1966

Arabesque
    book: Cloyd Head and Eunice Tietjens
    music: Ruth Warfield
    staging: Norman-Bel Geddes
Productions:
    Opened October 20, 1925 for 23 performances
Reviews:
    New Republic 44:305-6, Nov 11, 1925
    New York Times page 20, Oct 21, 1925
    Theatre Arts 10:33-4, Jan 1926
    Theatre Magazine 42:44, Dec 1925
                   43:32, Mar 1926

The Arcadians
    book: Mark Ambient and A. M. Thompson
    music: Lionel Monckton and Howard Talbot
    lyrics: Arthur Wimperis
    staging: Thomas Reynolds
Productions:

Opened January 17, 1910 for 136 performances
Reviews:
    American Mercury 70:110, May 1910
    Burr McIntosh Monthly 22:322, Apr 1910
    Everybody's 22:700, May 1910
    Hampton 24:566-7, Apr 1910
    Leslie's Weekly 110:591, Jun 18, 1910
                    110:640, Jun 30, 1910
    Metropolitan Magazine 32:256-7, May 1910
    Munsey 41:902-5, Sep 1909
    New York Dramatic News 63:6, Jan 29, 1910
    Theatre Magazine 11:xi, Mar 1910
                     11:70, Mar 1910
                     11:94, Mar 1910
                     11:96, Mar 1910
                     12:74, Sep 1910
                     12:114, Oct 1910

Are You With It?
    book: Sam Perrin and George Balzer, adapted from
                   George Malcolm-Smith's Slightly Perfect
    music: Harry Revel
    lyrics: Arnold B. Horwitt
    staging: Edward Reveaux
    sets: George Jenkins
    costumes: Raoul Pene du Bois
Productions:
    Opened November 10, 1945 for 267 performances
Reviews.
    Catholic World 162:359, Jan 1946
    Collier's 117:14-15, Feb 2, 1946
    Commonweal 43:169, Nov 30, 1945
    Life 19:97-100, Nov 26, 1945
    Nation 161:604, Dec 1, 1945
    New York Theatre Critics' Reviews 1945:113+
    New York Times page 17, Nov 12, 1945
                    II, page 1, Feb 3, 1946
                    II, page 1, Apr 28, 1946
    New Yorker 21:50+, Nov 24, 1945
    Newsweek 26:96, Nov 26, 1945
    Theatre Arts 30:14, Jan 1946
    Time 46:64, Nov 19, 1945
    Vogue 106:145, Dec 1, 1945

Ari
    book: Leon Uris; based on his novel Exodus
    music: Walt Smith
    lyrics: Leon Uris
    staging: Lucia Victor
    sets: Robert Randolf
    costumes: Sara Brock
    choreography: Talley Beatty
Productions:

Opened January 15, 1971 for 19 performances
Reviews:
New York Theatre Critics' Reviews 1971:386
New York Times page 16, Jan 16, 1971
                  page 29, Jan 27, 1971
New Yorker 46:66, Jan 23, 1971

Arlen, Harold (see Harold Arlen)

Arms and the Girl
    book: Herbert and Dorothy Fields, Rouben Mamoulian,
                     based on Lawrence Langner and Armina Mar-
                     shall's play The Pursuit of Happiness
    music: Morton Gould
    lyrics: Dorothy Fields
    staging: Rouben Mamoulian
    sets: Horace Armistead
    costumes: Audre
Productions:
Opened February 2, 1950 for 134 performances
Reviews:
    Catholic World 171:67, Apr 1950
    New York Theatre Critics' Reviews 1950:356+
    New York Times II, page 1, Jan 28, 1950
                     page 28, Feb 3, 1950
    New Yorker 25:46-7, Feb 11, 1950
    Newsweek 35:80, Feb 13, 1950
    Theatre Arts 34:17, Apr 1950
    Time 55:53-4, Feb 13, 1950

Around the Map
    book: C. M. S. McLellan
    music: Herman Finck
    lyrics: C. M. S. McLellan
    staging: Herbert Gresham
    choreography: Julian Mitchell
Productions:
Opened November 1, 1915 for 104 performances
Reviews:
    Dramatic Mirror 74:8, Nov 6, 1915
                    74:2, Nov 20, 1915
                    74:2, Dec 4, 1915
    Green Book 15:26, Jan 1916
    Munsey 56:617, Jan 1916
           57:324, Mar 1916
    New York Dramatic News 61:17, Nov 6, 1915
    New York Times page 11, Nov 2, 1915
                   VI, page 8, Nov 7, 1915
    Opera Magazine 2:28-30, Dec 1915
    Theatre Magazine 22:278-9+, Dec 1915

Around the World (1911)
    book: Carroll Fleming

```
        music:              Manuel Klein
        lyrics:             Manuel Klein
        staging:            Carroll Fleming
Productions:
    Opened September 2, 1911 for 445 performances
Reviews:
    Theatre Magazine 14:125, Oct 1911
                     14:128, Oct 1911
```

Around the World (1946)
```
        book:               Orson Welles from Jules Verne's Around the
                            World in Eighty Days
        music:              Cole Porter
        lyrics:             Cole Porter
        staging:            Orson Welles
        sets:               Robert Davison
        costumes:           Alvin Colt
        choreography:       Nelson Barclift
Productions:
    Opened May 31, 1946 for 75 performances
Reviews:
    Catholic World 163:359-60, Jul 1946
    Commonweal 44:238, Jun 21, 1946
    Life 20:74-6, Jun 17, 1946
    New York Theatre Critics' Reviews 1946:375+
    New York Times page 9, Jun 1, 1946
                     II, page 1, Jun 9, 1946
    New Yorker 22:48+, Jun 8, 1046
    Newsweek 27:87, Jun 10, 1946
    Theatre Arts 30:473, Aug 1946
    Time 47:64, Jun 3, 1946
         47:67, Jun 10, 1946
```

Around the World in 80 Days
```
        book:               Sig Herzig; based on the novel by Jules Verne
        music:              Sammy Fain; additional music by Victor Young
        lyrics:             Harold Adamson
        production
          supervised:       Arnold Spector
        staging:            June Taylor
        sets:               George Jenkins
        costumes:           Winn Morton
        choreography:       June Taylor
Productions:
    (Off-Broadway) Opened June 22, 1963 for 73 performances
    (Off-Broadway) Opened June 27, 1964 for 70 performances
Reviews:
    America 109:122, Aug 3, 1963
    New York Times page 22, Jun 24, 1963
                     page 33, Jun 29, 1964
```

Artists and Models (1923)
```
        staging:            Larry Wagstaff Gribble and Francis Weldon
```

Productions:
    Opened August 20, 1923 for 312 performances
Reviews:
    New York Times page 12, Aug 21, 1923

Artists and Models (1924)
        sketches: Harry Wagstaff Gribble
        music: Sigmund Romberg and J. Fred Coots
        lyrics: Clifford Grey and Sam Coslow
        staging: J. J. Shubert
Productions:
    Opened October 15, 1924 for 261 performances
Reviews:
    New York Times page 33, Oct 16, 1924
                    page 16, Jun 17, 1925
                    page 16, Jun 25, 1925
    Theatre Magazine 40:64, Dec 1924

Artists and Models (1925)
        sketches: Harold Atteridge and Harry Wagstaff Gribble
        music: Alfred Goodman, J. Fred Coots, and Maurice
                         Rubens
        lyrics: Clifford Grey
        staging: J. J. Shubert
Productions:
    Opened June 24, 1925 for 411 performances
Reviews:
    New York Times page 16, Jun 17, 1925
                    page 16, Jun 25, 1925
    Survey 55:632, Mar 1, 1926
    Theatre Magazine 42:3, Sep 1925
                     42:15, Sep 1925

Artists and Models (1927)
        music: Harry Akst and Maurie Rubens
        lyrics: Benny Davis; additional lyrics by J. Keirn
                         Brennan, Jack Osterman and Ted Lewis
        staging: J. C. Huffman
Productions:
    Opened November 15, 1927 for 151 performances
Reviews:
    Life (New York) 90:21, Dec 8, 1927
    New Republic 54:246-7, Apr 11, 1928
    New York Times page 28, Nov 16, 1927
    Theatre Magazine 47:40, Feb 1928

Artists and Models (1930)
        book: adapted from the English musical comedy
                         Dear Love
        music: Harold Stern
        lyrics: Ernie Golden
        staging: Frank Smithson and Pal'mere Brandeaux
Productions:

Opened June 10, 1930 for 55 performances
Reviews:
Life (New York) 95:16, Jul 11, 1930
New York Times page 33, Jun 11, 1930
Theatre Magazine 52:25, Aug 1930

Artists and Models (1943)
    assembled: Lou Walters
    dialogue: Lou Walters, Don Ross, Frank Luther
    music: Dan Shapiro, Milton Pascal, Phil Charig
    lyrics: Dan Shapiro, Milton Pascal, Phil Charig
    staging: Lou Walters
    sets: Watson Barratt
    costumes: Kathryn Kuhn
    choreography: Natalie Kamarova and Laurette Jefferson
Productions:
Opened November 5, 1943 for 28 performances
Reviews:
New York Theatre Critics' Reviews 1943:239+
New York Times page 16, Nov 6, 1943
    II, page 1, Nov 21, 1943

As the Girls Go
    book: William Roos
    music: Jimmy McHugh
    lyrics: Harold Adamson
    staging: Howard Bay
    sets: Howard Bay
    costumes: Oleg Cassini
    choreography: Hermes Pan
Productions:
Opened November 13, 1938 for 420 performances
Reviews:
Catholic World 168:324, Jan 1949
Commonweal 49:231, Dec 10, 1948
Life 25:89-90+, Nov 29, 1948
New Republic 119:37, Dec 6, 1948
New York Theatre Critics' Reviews 1948:159+
New York Times page 21, Nov 15, 1948
    II, page 2, Jan 2, 1949
New Yorker 24:58, Nov 20, 1948
Newsweek 32:80, Nov 22, 1948
Theatre Arts 33:18, Jan 1949
Time 52:85, Nov 22, 1948
Vogue 113:114, Jan 1949

As Thousands Cheer
    book: Irving Berlin and Moss Hart
    music: Edward Heyman and Richard Meyers
    lyrics: Edward Heyman and Richard Meyers
    staging: Hassard Short
    sets: Albert Johnson
    choreography: Charles Weidman

Productions:
    Opened September 30, 1933 for 400 performances
Reviews:
    Canadian Forum 15:274, Apr 1935
    Catholic World 138:337, Dec 1933
    Collier's 94:17+, Aug 18, 1934
    Commonweal 18:591-2, Oct 20, 1933
    Literary Digest 116:18, Oct 21, 1933
    New Outlook 162:42, Nov 1933
    New Republic 76:279, Oct 18, 1933
    New York Times II, page 5, Sep 10, 1933
                    page 22, Oct 2, 1933
                    IX, page 1, Oct 15, 1933
                    page 26, Mar 20, 1934
                    page 24, Jul 10, 1934
                    IX, page 1, Nov 11, 1934
    Review of Reviews 89:40, Feb 1934
    Stage 11:12-17, Oct 1933
          11:13, Nov 1933
    Theatre Arts 17:919, Dec 1933
    Time 22:27, Oct 9, 1933
    Vanity Fair 41:42, Dec 1933

As You Like It
    book: Dran and Tani Seitz, adapted from Shakespeare's
                  comedy
    music: John Balamos
    lyrics: Dran and Tani Seitz
    staging: Val Forslund
    choreography: Joe Nelson
Productions:
    (Off-Off-Broadway) Opened October 27, 1964 for 1 performance
No Reviews.

As You Wait
    book: Arthur Williams and Lois Dengrove
    music: Jay Woody
Productions:
    (Off-Off-Broadway) Season of 1973-1974 (New York Theatre
    Ensemble).
No Reviews.

As You Were
    book: Arthur Wimperis
    music: Herman Darewski
Productions:
    Opened January 27, 1920 for 143 performances
Reviews:
    Forum 63:317-2, Mar 1920
    New York Clipper 67:25, Feb 4, 1920
    New York Times page 22, Jan 28, 1920
                    VIII, page 2, Feb 8, 1920
    Theatre Magazine 31:185, Mar 1920

At Home Abroad
    dialogue: Thomas Mitchell
    songs: Howard Dietz and Arthur Schwartz
    staging: Vincente Minnelli
    sets: Vincente Minnelli
    choreography: Gene Snyder and Harry Losee
Productions:
Opened September 19, 1935 for 198 performances
Reviews:
    Catholic World 142:472, Jan 1936
    Literary Digest 120:18, Nov 2, 1935
    Nation 141:392, Oct 2, 1935
    New York Times page 22, Sep 4, 1935
                    IX, page 1, Sep 8, 1935
                    page 17, Sep 20, 1935
                    XI, page 2, Oct 6, 1935
                    IX, page 1, Oct 27, 1935
                    IX, page 8, Oct 27, 1935
    Newsweek 6:28-9, Sep 28, 1935
    Stage 12:16-17, Sep 1935
           13:57, Oct 1935
           14:61-3, Dec 1936
    Theatre Arts 19:818+, Nov 1935
    Time 26:22, Sep 30, 1935
    Vanity Fair 45:69, Nov 1935
    Vogue 86:57, Nov 15, 1935

At Home at the Palace (see Judy Garland at Home at the Palace)

At Home with Ethel Waters
    songs: W. C. Handy, Hoagy Carmichael, Irving Berlin,
                    Ira and George Gershwin, and others
    staging: Richard Barr
    sets: Oliver Smith
    costumes: Robert Mackintosh
Productions:
Opened September 22, 1953 for 23 performances
Reviews:
    America 90:54, Oct 10, 1953
    Catholic World 178:148, Nov 1953
    Commonweal 59:38, Oct 16, 1953
    Nation 177:298, Oct 10, 1953
    New Republic 129:20, Oct 26, 1953
    New York Times page 36, Sep 23, 1953
    New Yorker 29:80, Oct 3, 1953
    Saturday Review 36:30-2, Oct 10, 1953
    Theatre Arts 37:22-3, Nov 1953
    Time 62:78, Oct 5, 1953

The Athenian Touch
    book: Arthur Goodman and J. Albert Fracht
    music: Willard Straight
    lyrics: David Eddy

```
      staging:        Alex Palermo
      sets:           Robert T. Williams
      costumes:       Don Foote
      choreography:   Alex Palermo
```
Productions:
   (Off-Broadway) Opened January 14, 1964 for one performance
Reviews:
   New York Times page 25, Jan 15, 1964
                   page 30, Jan 30, 1964

The Atlantic Crossing
```
      book:           Charles Mingus III
      songs:          Charles Mingus III and Paul Jeffrey
      music:          Gunter Hampel
      staging:        Lee Kissman
```
Productions:
   (Off-Off-Broadway) Opened July 27, 1972 (Theatre for the
   New City)
No Reviews.

Atta Boy
```
      by:             F. Tinney, J. B. Walsh, B. Macdonald, N.
                      Osborne
      staging:        Jack Mason
```
Productions:
   Opened December 23, 1918 for 24 performances
Reviews:
   Dramatic Mirror 80:9, Jan 4, 1919
   New York Times page 7, Dec 24, 1918

Audition
```
      book:           Steven Holt
      music:          John Braden
      staging:        Suzanna Foster
```
Productions:
   (Off-Off-Broadway) Opened November 8, 1972 (La Mama Ex-
   perimental Theatre Club)
No Reviews.

Autumn's Here!
```
      book:           Norman Dean; based on Washington Irving's
                      Legend of Sleepy Hollow
      music:          Norman Dean
      lyrics:         Norman Dean
      staging:        Hal LeRoy
      sets:           Robert Conley
      costumes:       Eve Henriksen
      choreography:   Hal LeRoy
```
Productions:
   (Off-Broadway) Opened October 25, 1966 for 80 performances
Reviews:
   New York Times page 40, Oct 26, 1966
                   page 18, Dec 29, 1966

Aznavour, Charles (see Charles Aznavour)

- B -

Babes in Arms
    book: Lorenz Hart
    music: Richard Rodgers
    lyrics: Lorenz Hart
    staging: Robert Sinclair
    sets: Raymond Sovey
    costumes: Helene Pons
    choreography: George Balanchine
Productions:
    Opened April 14, 1937 for 289 performances
    (Off-Broadway) Season of 1950-51 (Equity Theatre)
    (Off-Broadway) Opened October 20, 1967 for 15 performances
Reviews:
    Catholic World 145:343, Jun 1937
    Commonweal 26:48, May 7, 1937
    New York Times page 18, Apr 15, 1937
               page 7, Mar 10, 1951
    Newsweek 9:20+, Apr 24, 1937
    Theatre Arts 21:424-5, Jun 1937
    Time 29:26+, Apr 26, 1937

Babes in the Wood
    book, music,
    and lyrics: Rick Besoyan; adapted from Shakespeare's
                  A Midsummer Night's Dream
    staging: Rick Besoyan
    sets: Paul Morrison
    costumes: Howard Barker
    choreography: Ralph Beaumont
Productions:
    (Off-Broadway) Opened December 28, 1964 for 45 performances
Reviews:
    New York Times page 21, December 29, 1964
    New Yorker 40:84, Jan 9, 1965
    Time 85:32, Jan 8, 1965

The Bachelor Belles
    words: Harry B. Smith
    music: Raymond Hubbell
    staging: Julian Mitchell
Productions:
    Opened November 7, 1910 for 32 performances
Reviews:
    Blue Book 12:657-60, Feb 1911
    Metropolitan Magazine 33:668-9, Feb 1911
    Munsey 44:562, Jan 1911
    Theatre Magazine 12:xxi, Dec 1910

Bad Habits of 1926
    music: Manning Sherwin
    lyrics: Arthur Herzog
Productions:
    Opened April 30, 1926 for 19 performances
Reviews:
    New York Times page 11, May 1, 1926
    Theatre Magazine 44:16, Jul 1926

Bagels and Yox
    songs: Sholom Secunda and Hy Jacobson
Productions:
    Opened September 12, 1951 for 208 performances
Reviews:
    Catholic World 174:149, Nov 1951
    Commonweal 54:596, Sep 28, 1951
    New Republic 125:21, Oct 1, 1951
    New York Theatre Critics' Reviews 1951:238
    New York Times page 38, Sep 13, 1951
    Theatre Arts 35:6, Nov 1951

Bajour
    book: Ernest Kinoy, based on Joseph Mitchell's
                     New Yorker stories
    music: Walter Marks
    lyrics: Ernest Kinoy
    staging: Lawrence Kasha
    sets: Oliver Smith
    costumes: Freddy Wittop
    choreography: Peter Gennaro and Wally Seibert
Productions:
    Opened November 23, 1964 for 232 performances
Reviews:
    America 112:25, Jan 2, 1965
    Commonweal 81:422-3, Dec 18, 1964
    Dance Magazine 39:19-20, Jan 1965
    New York Theatre Critics' Reviews 1964:132+
    New York Times page 42, Nov 24, 1964
    New Yorker 40:88, Dec 5, 1964
    Newsweek 64:94, Dec 7, 1964
    Time 84:88, Dec 4, 1964

Baker, Josephine (see Josephine Baker)

Baker Street
    book: Jerome Coopersmith, adapted from Sir Arthur
                     Conan Doyle's stories
    music: Marion Grudeff and Raymond Jessel
    lyrics: Marion Grudeff and Raymond Jessel
    staging: Harold Prince
    sets: Oliver Smith
    costumes: Motley
    choreography: Lee Becker Theodore

Productions:
    Opened February 16, 1965 for 311 performances
Reviews:
    America 112:589, Apr 17, 1965
    Commonweal 82:21-2, Mar 26, 1965
    Dance Magazine 39:18-19, Apr 1965
    Life 58:133-4, Apr 2, 1965
    National Review 17:561, Jun 29, 1965
    New York Theatre Critics' Reviews 1965:374+
    New York Times page 36, Feb 17, 1965
                    II, page 1, Feb 28, 1965
    New Yorker 41:94+, Feb 27, 1965
    Newsweek 65:84, Mar 1, 1965
    Saturday Review 48:22, Mar 6, 1965
    Time 85:78, Feb 26, 1965
    Vogue 145:100, Apr 1, 1965

Baker's Dozen
    conceived: Julius Monk
    staging: Frank Wagner
    costumes: Bill Belew
    choreography: Frank Wagner
Productions:
    (Off-Broadway) Opened January 9, 1964 for 469 performances
Reviews:
    Newsweek 63:57, Jan 20, 1964

The Balkan Princess
    book: Frederick Lonsdale and Frank Curzon
    music: Paul A. Rubens
    lyrics: Paul A. Rubens and Arthur Wimperis
Productions:
    Opened February 9, 1911 for 108 performances
Reviews:
    Blue Book 13:25-7, May 1911
    Columbian 4:349+, May 1911
    Dramatic Mirror 65:15, Jan 25, 1911
                    65:10, Feb 15, 1911
                    65:2, May 31, 1911
                    67:2, Jan 31, 1912
    Green Book Album 5:694-5, Apr 1911
    Metropolitan Magazine 34:221-2, May 1911
    Stage 13:58, Aug 1936
    Theatre Magazine 13:ix, Mar 1911
                    13:74, Mar 1911

Ballad for a Firing Squad
    book: Jerome Coopersmith
    music: Edward Thomas
    lyrics: Martin Charnin
    staging: Martin Charnin
    sets: James Tilton
    costumes: Theoni V. Aldredge

        choreography: Alan Johnson
Productions:
    (Off-Broadway) Opened December 13, 1968 for 7 performances
Reviews:
    New York Times page 44, Oct 4, 1968
                    page 64, Dec 12, 1968
                    page 56, Dec 18, 1968
    New Yorker 44:65, Dec 21, 1968

Ballad for Bimshire
    book: Irving Burgie and Loften Mitchell
    music: Irving Burgie
    lyrics: Irving Burgie
    staging: Ed Cambridge
    sets: Donald Ryder
    costumes: Mozelle Forte
    choreography: Talley Beatty
Productions:
    (Off-Broadway) Opened October 15, 1963 for 74 performances
Reviews:
    America 109:643, Nov 16, 1963
    New York Times page 54, Oct 15, 1963
    New Yorker 39:113-14, Oct 26, 1963

The Ballad of Johnny Pot
    book: Carolyn Richter
    music: Clinton Ballard
    lyrics: Carolyn Richter
    staging: Joshua Shelly
    sets: Lloyd Burlingame
    costumes: Alvin Colt
    choreography: Jay Norman
Productions:
    (Off-Broadway) Opened April 26, 1971 for 16 performances
Reviews:
    New York Times page 52, Apr 27, 1971

Ballet Ballads (Susanna and the Elders, Willie the Weeper, and
                The Eccentricities of Davy Crockett)
    music: Jerome Moross
    lyrics: John Latouche
    staging: Mary Hunter
    choreography: Katherine Litz, Paul Godkin, Hanya Holm
Productions:
    Opened May 9, 1948 for 69 performances
Reviews:
    Life 24:135-6+, Jun 7, 1948
    Musical Courier 138:20, Jul 1948
    New Republic 118:34, May 31, 1948
    New York Times page 25, May 10, 1948
                    II, page 1, May 16, 1948
                    II, page 1, Jun 6, 1948
    Saturday Review 31:28-30, Jun 5, 1948

School and Society 67:476-7, Jun 26, 1948
Theatre Arts 32:16, Summer of 1948

Ballet of Niagra   (see The International Cup, the Ballet of Niagra
and the Earthquake)

Ballyhoo (1930)
    book: Harry Ruskin and Leighton K. Brill
    music: Louis Alter
    lyrics: Harry Ruskin and Leighton K. Brill
    staging: Reginald Hammerstein
    choreography: Earl Lindsey
Productions:
Opened December 22, 1930 for 68 performances
Reviews:
    Nation 132:24-5, Jan 7, 1931
    New York Times IX, page 3, Dec 14, 1930
                     page 24, Dec 23, 1930
                     page 26, Jan 9, 1931
    Theatre Magazine 53:26, Feb 1931
    Vogue 77:102, Feb 15, 1931

Ballyhoo of 1932
    book: Norman B. Anthony
    music: Lewis E. Gensler
    lyrics: E. Y. Harburg
    staging: Norman B. Anthony, Lewis E. Gensler,
                  Bobby Connelly, Russell Patterson
    sets: Russell Patterson
Productions:
Opened September 6, 1932 for 95 performances
Reviews:
    Nation 135:266, Sep 21, 1932
    New York Times page 14, Sep 7, 1932
                   page 23, Nov 29, 1932
    Stage 10:10-11, Oct 1932
    Vogue 80:100, Oct 15, 1932

Bamboola
    book: D. Frank Marcus
    music: D. Frank Marcus and Bernard Maltin
    lyrics: D. Frank Marcus
    staging: Sam Rose
Productions:
Opened June 26, 1929 for 34 performances
Reviews:
    New York Times page 17, Jun 27, 1929

The Band Wagon
    book: George S. Kaufman and Howard Dietz
    music: Arthur Schwartz
    lyrics: George S. Kaufman and Howard Dietz
    staging: Hassard Short

    choreography: Albertina Rasch
Productions:
Opened June 3, 1931 for 260 performances
Reviews:
    Bookman 73:633-4, Aug 1931
    Catholic World 133:463-4, Jul 1931
    Life (New York) 97:18, Jun 19, 1931
    New York Times VIII, page 3, May 17, 1931
                    page 31, Jun 4, 1931
                    VIII, page 8, Jun 7, 1931
                    VIII, page 1, Jun 14, 1931
                    VIII, page 2, Jun 14, 1931
                    page 28, Dec 21, 1931
    Outlook 158:219, Jun 17, 1931
    Theatre Arts 15:625+, Aug 1931
    Theatre Guild Magazine 8:18-19, Aug 1931

Banjo Eyes
    book: Joe Quillan and Izzy Elinson from John Cecil
                    Holm and George Abbott's Three Men on a
                    Horse
    music: Vernon Duke
    lyrics: John LaTouche and Harold Adamson
    staging: Hassard Short
    sets: Harry Horner
    costumes: Irene Sharaff
    choreography: Charles Walters
Productions:
Opened December 25, 1941 for 126 performances
Reviews:
    Catholic World 154:731, Mar 1942
    Life 12:62-3, Feb 23, 1942
    New York Theatre Critics' Reviews 1941:164+
    New York Times page 10, Nov 8, 1941
                    page 20, Dec 26, 1941
                    page 17, Apr 16, 1942
    New Yorker 17:28, Jan 3, 1942
    Theatre Arts 26:155, Mar 1942
    Time 39:47, Jan 5, 1942

The Banker's Daughter
    book: Edward Eliscu; based on Boucicault's
                    Streets of New York
    music: Sol Kaplan
    lyrics: Edward Eliscu
    staging: David Brooks
    sets: Kim Swados
    costumes: Peter Joseph
Productions:
    (Off-Broadway) Opened January 21, 1962 for 68 performances
Reviews:
    America 106:633, Feb 10, 1962
    New York Times page 37, Jan 23, 1962

                    page 42, Mar 20, 1962
    New Yorker 37:70+, Feb 3, 1962

The Bar That Never Closes
    book: Louisa Rose
    sketches: Marco Vassi
    music: Tom Mandel
    lyrics: Louisa Rose
    staging: John Braswell
    sets: Susan Haskins
Productions:
    (Off-Broadway) Opened December 3, 1972 for 33 performances
Reviews:
    New York Times page 55, Dec 4, 1972
    (Also see Everything for Anybody)

Bare Facts of 1926
    sketches: Stuart Hamill
    music: Charles M. Schwab
    lyrics: Henry Myers
    staging: Kathleen Kirkwood
Productions:
    Opened July 16, 1926 for 107 performances
Reviews:
    New York Times page 7, Jul 17, 1926
                    page 13, Jul 19, 1926
                    page 27, Aug 17, 1927

Barefoot Boy with Cheek
    book: Max Shulman, from his novel Barefoot Boy
                       with Cheek
    music: Sidney Lippman
    lyrics: Sylvia Dee
    staging: George Abbott
    sets: Jo Mielziner
    costumes: Alvin Colt
    choreography: Richard Barstow
Productions:
    Opened April 3, 1947 for 108 performances
Reviews:
    Catholic World 165:169, May 1947
    Commonweal 46:16, Apr 18, 1947
    New Republic 116:37, Apr 21, 1947
    New York Theatre Critics' Reviews 1947:402+
    New York Times page 20, Apr 4, 1947
                    II, page 1, May 4, 1947
    New Yorker 23:46, Apr 12, 1947
    Newsweek 29:86, Apr 14, 1947
    Theatre Arts 31:41, Jun 1947
    Time 49:70, Apr 14, 1947

Barnes, Billie (see Billie Barnes and Billy Barnes)

34   Baron Trenck

Baron Trenck
    libretto: A. M. Wilner and R. Rodansky; English version
                           by Henry Blossom
    music: Felix Albini
    lyrics: Frederick F. Schrader
    staging: Al Holbrook
Productions:
    Opened March 11, 1912 for 40 performances
Reviews:
    Blue Book 15:26-8, May 1912
    Dramatic Mirror 67:7, Mar 13, 1912
    Green Book 7:1100-3+, Jun 1912
    Hampton 28:295, May 1912
    New York Dramatic News 55:14, Mar 16, 1912
    Theatre Magazine 15:xiii, Apr 1912
                          15:105, Apr 1912

The Barrier
    book: Langston Hughes
    music: Jan Meyerowitz
    lyrics: Langston Hughes
    staging: Doris Humphrey
    sets: H. A. Condell
    choreography: Charles Weidman and Doris Humphrey
Productions:
    Opened November, 1950 for 4 performances
    (Off-Broadway) Season of 1952-53 (Circle in the Square)
Reviews:
    Christian Science Monitor Magazine page 8, Nov 11, 1950
    Commonweal 53:172, Nov 24, 1950
    Musical America 70:244, Feb 1950
    New York Theatre Critics' Reviews 1950:218+
    New York Times page 34, Jan 19, 1950
                    page 32, Nov 3, 1950
                    page 24, Mar 9, 1953
    New Yorker 25:71, Jan 28, 1950
              26:79-81, Nov 11, 1950
    Newsweek 35:68, Jan 30, 1950
    School and Society 71:120, Feb 25, 1950
    Theatre Arts 35:12, Jan 1951
    Time 55:68+, Jan 30, 1950

Battling Buttler
    adapted by: Ballard MacDonald; from the original of
                           Brightman, Melford and Furber
    music: Walter L. Rosemont
    staging: Guy Bragdon
Productions:
    Opened October 8, 1923 for (288) performances
Reviews:
    New York Times page 17, Oct 9, 1923

Be Yourself

book:	George S. Kaufman and Marc Connelly
music:	Lewis Gensler and Milton Schwarzwald
staging:	William Collier

Productions:
Opened September 3, 1924 for 93 performances
Reviews:
New York Times page 13, Sep 4, 1924
                page 24, Oct 1, 1924
Theatre Magazine 40:19, Nov 1924

The Beast in Me

conceived by:	Haila Stoddard, based on James Thurber's Fables for our Time
book:	adapted by James Costigan
music:	Don Elliott
lyrics:	James Costigan
staging:	John Lehne
sets:	Jean Rosenthal
costumes:	Leo Van Witsen
choreography:	John Butler

Productions:
Opened May 16, 1963 for 4 performances
Reviews:
New York Theatre Critics' Reviews 1963:324+
New York Times II, page 1, May 12, 1963
                page 29, May 17, 1963
New Yorker 39:57, May 25, 1963
Newsweek 61:93, May 27, 1963

Beat the Band

book:	George Marion, Jr. and George Abbott
music:	Johnny Green
lyrics:	George Marion, Jr. and George Abbott
staging:	George Abbott
sets:	Sam Leve
costumes:	Freddy Wittop
choreography:	David Lichine

Productions:
Opened October 14, 1942 for 68 performances
Reviews:
Catholic World 156:337, Dec 1942
Nation 155:458, Oct 31, 1942
New York Theatre Critics' Reviews 1942:204+
New York Times VIII, page 8, Oct 4, 1942
                page 26, Oct 15, 1942
Newsweek 20:87, Oct 26, 1942
Theatre Arts 26:742, Dec 1942
Time 40:54, Oct 26, 1942

Beautiful Dreamer

book:	William Engvick; based on the life of Stephen Foster
music:	William Engvick

      lyrics: William Engvick
Productions:
      (Off-Broadway) Season of 1960-1961
Reviews:
      New York Times page 22, Dec 28, 1960

The Beauty and the Beast
      book: Oswald Rodriquez; adapted from the fairy tale
      music: Joseph Blunt
      staging: Oswald Rodriquez
Productions:
      (Off-Off-Broadway) Opened January 4, 1973 (La Mama Experi-
      mental Theatre Club)
No Reviews.

The Beauty Shop
      book: Channing Pollock and Rennold Wolf
      music: Charles J. Gebest
      lyrics: Channing Pollock and Rennold Wolf
      staging: R. H. Burnside
Productions:
      Opened April 13, 1914 for 88 performances
Reviews:
      Blue Book 18:426-9, Jan 1914
      Dramatic Mirror 71:13, Apr 15, 1914
      Green Book 12:106, Jul 1914
      New York Dramatic News 59:20, Apr 8, 1914
      New York Times page 11, Apr 14, 1914
      Theatre Magazine 19:282, Jun 1914
                          19:289, Jun 1914

Becaud, Gilbert (see Gilbert Becaud)

Beg, Borrow or Steal
      book: Bud Freeman, from a story by Marvin Seiger
                          and Bud Freeman
      music: Leon Prober
      lyrics: Bud Freeman
      staging: Billy Matthews
      sets: Carter Morningstar
      costumes: Carter Morningstar
      choreography: Peter Hamilton
Productions:
      Opened February 10, 1960 for 5 performances
Reviews:
      New York Theatre Critics' Reviews 1960:370+
      New York Times page 39, Feb 11, 1960
                          page 22, Feb 12, 1960
      New Yorker 36:101-2, Feb 20, 1960

Beggar's Holiday
      book: John Latouche, adapted from John Gay's The
                          Beggar's Opera

```
music:            Duke Ellington
lyrics:           John Latouche
staging:          Nicholas Ray
sets:             Oliver Smith
costumes:         Walter Florell
choreography:     Valerie Bettis
```
Productions:
Opened December 26, 1936 for 108 performances
Reviews:
Catholic World 164:455-6, Feb 1947
Commonweal 45:351-2, Jan 17, 1947
Life 22:75, Feb 24, 1947
New York Theatre Critics' Reviews 1946:204+
New York Times II, page 3, Dec 22, 1946
                 page 13, Dec 27, 1946
                 II, page 1, Jan 26, 1947
                 II, page 3, Feb 2, 1947
New Yorker 22:46-7, Jan 4, 1947
Newsweek 29:64, Jan 6, 1947
School and Society 65:252, Apr 5, 1947
Theatre Arts 31:16-17, Mar 1947
             31:27, Mar 1947
Time 49:57, Jan 6, 1947

Bei Mir Bist Du Schoen
```
    book:             Louis Freiman
    music:            Sholom Secunda
    lyrics:           Jacob Jacobs
    staging:          Leo Fuchs
```
Productions:
(Off-Broadway) Opened October 21, 1961 for 88 performances
Reviews:
New York Times page 22, Oct 23, 1961
                page 17, Dec 26, 1961

The Believers
```
    book:             Josephine Jackson and Joseph A. Walker
    music and
     lyrics:          Benjamin Carter, Dorothy Dinroe, Josephine
                      Jackson, Anje Ray and Ron Steward
    staging:          Barbara Ann Teer
    sets:             Joseph A. Walker
    costumes:         Robert Pusilo
```
Productions:
(Off-Broadway) Opened May 9, 1968 for 310 performances
Reviews:
New York Times page 57, May 10, 1968
                page 33, Jul 15, 1968
New Yorker 44:75, May 18, 1968

Bella
```
    book:             Tom O'Malley and Lance Barklie
    music:            Jane Douglas
```

lyrics: Tom O'Malley
staging: Richard C. Shank
Productions:
(Off-Broadway) Opened November 16, 1961 for 6 performances
Reviews:
New York Times page 40, Nov 17, 1961
                page 14, Nov 18, 1961
New Yorker 37:95-6, Nov 25, 1961

The Belle of Bond Street
book: Owen Hall and Harold Atteridge, based on
                   The Girl from Kay's
music: Ivan Caryll and Lionel Monckton
lyrics: Adrian Ross and Claude Aveling
staging: Edwin T. Emery
Productions:
Opened March 30, 1914 for 48 performances
Reviews:
Dramatic Mirror 71:13, Apr 1, 1914
                71:2, Apr 15, 1914
Green Book 11:1020, Jun 1914
           12:94-6, Jul 1914
Life (New York) 63:655, Apr 9, 1914
New York Dramatic News 59:21, Apr 4, 1914
New York Times page 11, Mar 31, 1914
Theatre Magazine 19:261, May 1914
                 19:279, Jun 1914
                 19:298, Jun 1914

The Belle of Brittany
book: Leedham Bantock, P. J. Barron and Percy
                   Greenbank
music: Howard Talbot and Marie Horne
staging: Frank Smithson
Productions:
Opened November 8, 1909 for 72 performances
Reviews:
Hampton 24:134-5, Jan 1910
Harper's Weekly 53:24, Dec 4, 1909
Leslie's Weekly 109:545, Dec 2, 1909
Metropolitan Magazine 31:826-7, Mar 1910
New York Dramatic News page 5, Nov 20, 1909
Theatre Magazine 10:v, Dec 1909
                 10:vii, Dec 1909

La Belle Paree
book: Edgar Smith
music: Jerome Kern and Frank Tours
lyrics: Edward Madden
Productions:
Opened March 1910 for 104 performances
Reviews:
Blue Book 13:700-2+, Aug 1911

Dramatic Mirror 65:2, May 31, 1911

Bells Are Ringing
   book: Betty Comden and Adolph Green
   music: Jule Styne
   lyrics: Betty Comden and Adolph Green
   staging: Jerome Robbins
   sets: Raoul Pene du Bois
   costumes: Raoul Pene du Bois
   choreography: Jerome Robbins and Bob Fosse
Productions:
   Opened November 29, 1956 for 924 performances
Reviews:
   America 96:742, Mar 30, 1957
   Catholic World 184:386-7, Feb 1957
   Commonweal 65:408, Jan 18, 1957
   Life 42:69-70+, Feb 11, 1957
   Nation 183:526, Dec 15, 1956
   New York Theatre Critics' Reviews 1956:182+
   New York Times VI, page 29, Sep 16, 1956
                  VI, page 29, Nov 4, 1956
                  page 18, Nov 30, 1956
                  II, page 3, Dec 16, 1956
                  page 37, Nov 15, 1957
   New Yorker 32:88+, Dec 1956
   Newsweek 48:77, Dec 10, 1956
   Reporter 16:35, Jan 24, 1957
   Saturday Review 39:25, Dec 29, 1956
   Theatre Arts 40:76-8, Dec 1956
                41:15-16, Feb 1957
                41:27-8+, Mar 1957
   Time 68:70, Dec 10, 1956

Belmont Varieties
   book: Helen and Nolan Leary and Sam Bernard II
   music and
   lyrics: Serge Walter, Alvin Kaufman, Charles Kenny,
                    Henry Lloyd, Mildred Kaufman, Robert Burk
   staging: Max Scheck and Sam Bernard II
Productions:
   Opened September 26, 1932 for 8 performances
No Reviews.

Below the Belt
   conceived: Rod Warren
   staging: Sandra Devlin
Productions:
   (Off-Broadway) Opened June 21, 1966 for 186 performances
No Reviews.

Ben Franklin in Paris
   book: Sidney Michaels
   music: Mark Sandrich, Jr.

        lyrics: Sidney Michaels
        staging: Michael Kidd
        sets: Oliver Smith
        costumes: Motley
        choreography: Michael Kidd
Productions:
    Opened October 27, 1964 for 215 performances
Reviews:
    America 111:758, Dec 5, 1964
    Commonweal 81:423, Dec 18, 1964
    Dance Magazine 38:16, Dec 1964
    New York Theatre Critics' Reviews 1964:181+
    New York Times page 52, Oct 28, 1964
    Newsweek 64:92, Nov 9, 1964
    Saturday Review 47:53, Nov 14, 1964
    Senior Scholastic 86:21, Mar 4, 1965
    Time 84:52, Nov 6, 1964

Berlin to Broadway with Kurt Weill
        music: Kurt Weill
        lyrics: Maxwell Anderson, Marc Blitzstein, Bertolt
                           Brecht, Jacques Deval, Michael Feingold, Ira
                           Gershwin, Paul Green, Langston Hughes, Alan
                           Jay Lerner, Ogden Nash, George Tabori and
                           Arnold Weinstein
        staging: Donald Saddler
        sets: Herbert Senn and Helen Pond
        costumes: Frank Thompson
Productions:
    (Off-Broadway) Opened October 1, 1972 for 152 performances
Reviews:
    America 127:323, Oct 21, 1972
    Dance Magazine 46:78, Nov 1972
    New Republic 167:18+, Nov 11, 1972
    New York Theatre Critics' Reviews 1972:170
    New York Times page 43, Oct 2, 1972
                           II, page 1, Oct 8, 1972
    New Yorker 48:125, Oct 14, 1972
    Time 100:56, Oct 16, 1972

Bernstein, Leonard (see Leonard Bernstein)

Best Foot Forward
        book: John Cecil Holm
        music: Hugh Martin and Ralph Blane
        lyrics: Hugh Martin and Ralph Blane
        staging: George Abbott
        sets: Jo Mielziner
        costumes: Miles White
        choreography: Gene Kelly
Productions:
    Opened October 1, 1941 for 326 performances
    (Off-Broadway) Opened April 2, 1963 for 224 performances

Reviews:
    America 108:594, Apr 20, 1963
    Catholic World 154:213, Nov 1941
    Life 11:91-2+, Oct 12, 1941
           12:63, Feb 23, 1942
    New York Theatre Critics' Reviews 1941:286+
    New York Times page 24, Sep 12, 1941
                 page 28, Oct 2, 1941
                 IX, page 1, Oct 26, 1941
                 page 43, Apr 3, 1963
                 VI, page 104, May 5, 1963
    New Yorker 17:44, Oct 11, 1941
              39:140, Apr 13, 1963
    Newsweek 18:68, Oct 13, 1941
    Players Magazine 18:14, Feb 1942
    Theatre Arts 25:868+, Dec 1941
              26:18, Jan 1942
              47:12-13+, Jun 1963
    Time 38:67, Oct 13, 1941

Betsy (1911)
    book: H. Kellett Chambers, based on An American
                     Widow
    music: Alexander Johnstone
    lyrics: W. B. Johnstone
    staging: Edward Elsner
Productions:
    Opened December 11, 1911 for 32 performances
Reviews:
    Dramatic Mirror 66:7, Dec 13, 1911
                   66:8, Dec 27, 1911
    Life (New York) pp. 1134-5, Dec 21, 1911
    New York Times page 9, Dec 12, 1911
    Theatre Magazine 15:xii, Jan 1912

Betsy (1926)
    book: Irving Caesar and David Freedman
    music: Richard Rodgers
    lyrics: Lorenz Hart
    staging: William Anthony McGuire and Sammy Lee
Productions:
    Opened December 28, 1926 for 39 performances
Reviews:
    New York Times page 24, Dec 29, 1926

The Better 'Ole
    book: Captain Bruce Bairnsfather and Captain Arthur
                     Elliott
    music: Herman Darewski and Percival Knight
    staging: Percival Knight
Productions:
    Opened October 19, 1918 for 353 performances
Reviews:

Dramatic Mirror 79:651, Nov 2, 1918
                79:827, Dec 7, 1918
New York Dramatic News 65:6, Dec 28, 1918
New York Times page 13, Oct 21, 1918
              IV, page 2, Oct 27, 1918
Theatre Magazine 28:344-5, Dec 1918

Better Times
    book: R. H. Burnside
    music: Raymond Hubbell
    staging: R. H. Burnside
Productions:
    Opened September 2, 1922 for 409 performances
Reviews:
    Current Opinion 73:625, Nov 1922
    New York Times page 14, Sep 4, 1922
    Theatre Magazine 36:377, Dec 1922
                     36:383, Dec 1922

Betty
    book: Frederick Lonsdale and Gladys Unger
    music: Paul A. Rubens
    lyrics: Adrian Ross and Paul A. Rubens
    staging: Edward Royce
Productions:
    Opened October 3, 1916 for 63 performances
Reviews:
    Dramatic Mirror 76:7, Oct 14, 1916
    Green Book 16:976+, Dec 1916
    Life (New York) 68:272-3, Oct 19, 1916
    Munsey 59:668, Jan 1917
    New York Dramatic News 63:11, Oct 7, 1916
    New York Times page 11, Oct 4, 1916
    Opera Magazine 3:26-7, Nov 1916
    Theatre Magazine 24:284, Nov 1916

Betty Be Good
    book: Harry B. Smith; adapted from a French vaude-
                     ville by Scribe
    music: Hugo Reisenfeld
    lyrics: Harry B. Smith
    staging: David Bennett
Productions:
    Opened May 4, 1920 for 31 performances
Reviews:
    Dramatic Mirror 82:311, Feb 21, 1920
                    82:889, May 8, 1920
    New York Clipper 68:17, May 12, 1920
    New York Times page 14, May 5, 1920
    Theatre Magazine 31:505, Jun 1920
                     31:525, Jun 1920

Betty Lee

    book: Otto Harbach
    music: Louis Hirsch and Con Conrad
    lyrics: Irving Ceaser and Otto Harbach
    staging: David Bennett
Productions:
    Opened December 25, 1924 for 111 performances
Reviews:
    New York Times page 18, Dec 26, 1924

Betty Comden and Adolph Green (see A Party with Betty Comden
    and Adolph Green)

Between the Devil
    book: Howard Dietz
    music: Arthur Schwartz
    lyrics: Howard Dietz
    staging: Hassard Short and John Hayden
    sets: Albert Johnson
    costumes: Kiviette
    choreography: Robert Alton
Productions:
    Opened December 22, 1937 for 93 performances
Reviews:
    Nation 146:754, Jan 1, 1938
    New York Times page 19, Oct 15, 1937
                   XI, page 2, Oct 24, 1937
                   page 24, Dec 23, 1937
    One Act Play Magazine 1:849, Jan 1938
    Stage 15:52-3, Feb 1938
    Time 31:22, Jan 3, 1938

The Bible Salesman (with The Oldest Trick in the World, billed as
    Double Entry)
    book: Jay Thompson
    music: Jay Thompson
    lyrics: Jay Thompson
    staging: Bill Penn
    sets: Howard Becknell
Productions:
    (Off-Broadway) Opened February 20, 1961 for 56 performances
Reviews:
    New York Times page 40, Feb 21, 1961
    New Yorker 37:115-16, Mar 11, 1961

Biff! Bang!
    book: Philip Dunning, Robert Cohen, and William
                   Israel
    music: William Schroeder
Productions:
    Opened May 30, 1918 for 16 performances
Reviews:
    New York Times page 15, May 31, 1918
                   page 9, Jun 3, 1918

                        page 11, June 4, 1918
        Theatre Magazine 28:23-4, Jul 1918
                        28:96, Aug 1918

Big Boy
        book: Harold Atteridge
        music: James F. Hanley and Joseph Meyer
        lyrics: Bud G. DeSylva
        staging: J. C. Huffman
Productions:
        Opened January 7, 1925 for 48 performances
        Opened August 24, 1925 for 120 performances
Reviews:
        New York Times page 28, Jan 8, 1925
                        page 9, Jan 10, 1925
                        page 15, Jan 12, 1925
                        page 19, Jan 21, 1925
                        page 17, Jan 26, 1925
                        page 20, Feb 10, 1925
                        page 17, Mar 16, 1925
                        page 14, Aug 18, 1925
                        page 12, Aug 25, 1925
                        page 16, Jan 27, 1926
                        page 13, Feb 7, 1926
                        page 20, Feb 10, 1926
        Theatre Magazine 40:19, Mar 1925
                        40:62, Mar 1925

The Big Show
        book: R. H. Burnside
        music: Raymond Hubbell
        lyrics: John L. Golden
        staging: R. H. Burnside
Productions:
        Opened August 31, 1916 for 425 performances
Reviews:
        New York Times page 7, Sep 1, 1916
        Theatre Magazine 24:246, Oct 1916
                        24:275, Nov 1916

Big Time Buck White   (see Buck White)

Billie
        book: George M. Cohan, adapted from his play
                             Broadway Jones
        music: George M. Cohan
        lyrics: George M. Cohan
        staging: Edward Royce and Sam Forrest
Productions:
        Opened October 1, 1928 for 112 performances
Reviews:
        New York Times page 34, Oct 2, 1928
        Theatre Magazine 49:60, Jan 1929

The Billie Barnes People
    sketches: Bob Rodgers
    music: Billy Barnes
    lyrics: Billy Barnes
    staging: Bob Rodgers
    sets: Spencer Davies
    costumes: Grady Hunt
Productions:
    Opened June 13, 1961 for 7 performances
Reviews:
    New York Theatre Critics' Reviews 1961:276+
    New York Times page 10, Jun 14, 1961

Billion Dollar Baby
    book: Betty Comden and Adolph Green
    music: Morton Gould
    lyrics: Betty Comden and Adolph Green
    staging: George Abbott
    sets: Oliver Smith
    costumes: Irene Sharaff
    choreography: Jerome Robbins
Productions:
    Opened December 21, 1945 for 220 performances
Reviews:
    Catholic World 162:458, Feb 1946
    Harpers 80:106, Jan 1946
    Life 20:67+, Jan 21, 1946
    Modern Music 23 no. 2:145, Apr 1946
    New York Theatre Critics' Reviews 1945:61+
    New York Times page 17, Dec 22, 1945
                    II, page 1, Dec 30, 1945
                    II, page 1, Feb 10, 1946
    New Yorker 21:40, Jan 5, 1946
    Newsweek 26:78, Dec 31, 1945
    Theatre Arts 30:80-1, Feb 1946
    Time 46:64, Dec 31, 1945
    Vogue 107:170-1, Feb 1, 1946

Billy
    book: Stephen Glassman; suggested by Herman Mel-
                     ville's Billy Budd
    music: Ron Dante and Gene Allan
    lyrics: Ron Dante and Gene Allan
    staging: Arthur A. Seidelman
    sets: Ming Cho Lee
    costumes: Theoni V. Aldredge
    choreography: Grover Dale
Productions:
    Opened March 22, 1969 for one performance
Reviews:
    New York Theatre Critics' Reviews 1969:316
    New York Times page 56, Mar 24, 1969
    New Yorker 45:99, Mar 29, 1969

46

Billy Barnes Revue
    sketches: Bob Rodgers
    dialogue: Bob Rodgers
    music: Billy Barnes
    lyrics: Billy Barnes
    staging: Bob Rodgers
    sets: Glen Holse
    costumes: Peggy Morrison
Productions:
    Opened August 4, 1959 for 87 performances
    (Off-Broadway) Season of 1959-60
Reviews:
    Dance Magazine 33:13, Sep 1959
    New York Times page 42, Jun 10, 1959
                    page 21, Jul 22, 1959
                    II page 1, Aug 30, 1959
                    page 47, Oct 15, 1959
                    page 19, Nov 25, 1959
    Saturday Review 42:33, Oct 10, 1959

Billy Noname
    book: William Wellington Mackey
    music: Johnny Brandon
    lyrics: Johnny Brandon
    staging: Lucia Victor
    sets: Jack Brown
    costumes: Pearl Somner
    choreography: Talley Beatty
Productions:
    (Off-Broadway) Opened March 2, 1970 for 48 performances
Reviews:
    Dance Magazine 44:89-91, May 1970
    New York Theatre Critics' Reviews 1970:285
    New York Times page 37, Mar 3, 1970
    New Yorker 46:122, Mar 14, 1970

Billy Rose's Crazy Quilt
    assembled by: Billy Rose
    music: Harry Warren, Ned Lehak, Louis Alter
    lyrics: Bud Green, Edward Eliscu, Billy Rose, Mort
                   Dixon, E. Y. Harburg
    staging: Billy Rose
Productions:
    Opened May 19, 1931 for 79 performances
Reviews:
    New York Times VIII, page 2, May 3, 1931
                    VIII, page 2, May 31, 1931
    Stage 9:13, May 1932

Bits and Pieces XIV
    conceived: Julius Monk
    staging: Julius Monk
    costumes: Bill Belew

        choreography: Frank Wagner
Productions:
    (Off-Broadway) Opened October 6, 1964 for 426 performances
No Reviews.

The Black Light Theater of Prague
        book: Jiri Srnec and Frantisek Kratochvil
        music: Jiri Srnec
        lyrics: Jiri Srnec and Frantisek Kratochvil
        staging: Jiri Srnec
        sets: Jiri Srnec and Frantisek Kratochvil
Productions:
    Opened September 27, 1971 for 10 performances
Reviews:
    New York Theatre Critics' Reviews 1971:251

Black Nativity
        book: Langston Hughes
        music: Langston Hughes
        lyrics: Langston Hughes
        staging: Vinnette Carroll
Productions:
    (Off-Broadway) Opened December 11, 1961 for 57 performances
Reviews:
    New York Times page 54, Dec 12, 1961
                    page 38, Jan 23, 1962
                    page 37, Aug 15, 1962
    New Yorker 37:57, Dec 23, 1961

Black Rhythm
        book: Donald Heywood
        music: Donald Heywood
        lyrics: Donald Heywood
        staging: Earl Dancer and Donald Heywood
Productions:
    Opened December 19, 1936 for 6 performances
Reviews:
    New York Times page 19, Dec 21, 1936

Blackberries of 1932
        assembled by: Lee Posner
        book: Eddie Green
        music: Donald Heywood and Tom Peluso
        lyrics: Donald Heywood and Tom Peluso
        staging: Ben Bernard
Productions:
    Opened April 4, 1932 for 24 performances
Reviews:
    New York Times page 27, Apr 5, 1932

Blackbirds (see Lew Leslie's Blackbirds)

Blackouts of 1949 (see Ken Murray's Blackouts of 1949)

48   Bless You All

Bless You All
    sketches: Arnold Auerbach
    music: Harold Rome
    lyrics: Harold Rome
    staging: John C. Wilson
    sets: Oliver Smith
    costumes: Miles White
    choreography: Helen Tamiris
Productions:
    Opened December 14, 1950 for 84 performances
Reviews:
    Catholic World 172:387, Feb 1951
    Christian Science Monitor Magazine page 7, Dec 23, 1950
    Commonweal 53:327, Jan 5, 1951
    Life 30:58+, Jan 22, 1951
    Nation 171:709, Dec 30, 1950
    New Republic 124:22, Jan 8, 1951
    New York Theatre Critics' Reviews 1950:170+
    New York Times VI, page 62, Dec 10, 1950
                    page 42, Dec 15, 1950
    New Yorker 26:40, Dec 23, 1950
    Newsweek 36:59, Dec 25, 1950
    Theatre Arts 35:18, Feb 1951
    Time 56:47, Dec 25, 1950

Blitzstein!
    music: Marc Blitzstein
    lyrics: Marc Blitzstein
    staging: Ellen Pahl
    sets: Cynthia Bernardi
Productions:
    (Off-Broadway) Opened November 30, 1966 for 7 performances
Reviews:
    New York Times page 37, Nov 11, 1966
                    page 58, Dec 1, 1966
                    page 54, Dec 7, 1966

The Blonde Sinner
    book: Leon De Costa
    staging: Edwin Vail
Productions:
    Opened July 14, 1926 for 173 performances
Reviews:
    New York Times page 21, Jul 15, 1926

Blood Red Roses
    book: John Lewin
    music: Michael Valenti
    lyrics: John Lewin
    staging: Alan Schneider
    sets: Ed Wittstein
    costumes: Deidre Cartier

Bloomer Girl

choreography: Larry Fuller
Productions:
Opened March 22, 1970 for one performance
Reviews:
New York Theatre Critics' Reviews 1970:332
New York Times page 48, Mar 23, 1970
page 20, Mar 27, 1970
New Yorker 46:82+, Mar 28, 1970

Bloomer Girl
book: Sig Herzig and Fred Saidy, based on a play by
             Lilith and Dan James
music: Harold Arlen
lyrics: E. Y. Harburg
staging: E. Y. Harburg
sets: Lemuel Ayers
costumes: Miles White
choreography: Agnes de Mille
Productions:
Opened October 5, 1944 for 654 performances
Opened January 6, 1947 for 48 performances
Reviews:
Catholic World 160:168, Nov 1944
164:455, Feb 1947
Collier's 114:12-13+, Dec 9, 1944
Commonweal 41:37, Oct 27, 1944
Harper's 78:81, Dec 1944
Life 17:67-70, Nov 6, 1944
Nation 159:483, Oct 21, 1944
New Republic 111:521, Oct 23, 1944
New York Theatre Critics' Reviews 1944:118+
New York Times VI, page 16, Sep 24, 1944
page 18, Oct 6, 1944
II, page 1, Oct 8, 1944
VI, page 52, Nov 19, 1944
II, page 6, Dec 17, 1944
II, page 1, Feb 24, 1946
II, page 3, Jan 5, 1947
page 33, Jan 7, 1947
page 19, Feb 15, 1947
New York Times Magazine pages 16-17, Sep 24, 1944
New Yorker 20:41, Oct 14, 1944
Newsweek 24:85-6, Oct 16, 1944
Theatre Arts 28:643-5, Nov 1944
29:78, Feb 1945
29:652, Nov 1945
Time 44:52, Oct 16, 1944

Blossom Time
book: Dorothy Donnelly, adapted from the German
             Das Dreimädlerhaus
music: Sigmund Romberg, derived from Franz Schubert
             themes

lyrics: Dorothy Donnelly
Productions:
Opened September 29, 1921 for 592 performances
Opened May 19, 1924 for 24 performances
Opened March 8, 1926 for 16 performances
Opened March 4, 1931 for 29 performances
Opened December 26, 1938 for 19 performances
Opened September 4, 1943 for 47 performances
Reviews:
Dramatic Mirror 84:520, Oct 8, 1921
Life (New York) 78:18, Oct 20, 1921
New York Clipper 69:17, Oct 12, 1921
New York Theatre Critics' Reviews 1943:286+
New York Times page 10, Sep 30, 1921
             VI, page 1, Oct 9, 1921
             page 26, Aug 8, 1922
             page 14, May 22, 1923
             page 22, May 16, 1924
             page 15, May 20, 1924
             VIII, page 8, Mar 7, 1926
             page 32, Mar 5, 1931
             VIII, page 4, Mar 22, 1931
             page 12, Dec 27, 1938
             page 21, Sep 6, 1943
Theatre Magazine 34:367, Dec 1921
             34:388, Dec 1921

The Blue Bird   (see Seeniaya Ptitza)

Blue Eyes
book: LeRoy Clemens and Leon Gordon
music: I. B. Kornblum and Z. Meyers
lyrics: LeRoy Clemens and Leon Gordon
staging: Clifford Brooke
Productions:
Opened February 21, 1921 for 56 performances
Reviews:
Dramatic Mirror 83:385-8, Feb 26, 1921
New York Clipper 69:19, Mar 2, 1921
New York Times page 11, Feb 22, 1921
Theatre Magazine 33:340-41, May 1921

Blue Holiday
songs: Duke Ellington, E. Y. Harburg, Earl Robinson
music: Al Moritz
lyrics: Al Moritz
staging: Moe Hack
sets: Perry Watkins
choreography: Katherine Dunham
Productions:
Opened May 21, 1945 for 8 performances
Reviews:
New York Theatre Critics' Reviews 1945:216

New York Times page 13, May 22, 1945

The Blue Kitten
    book: Otto Harbach and William Cary Duncan, adapted
                    from Le Chassear de Chez Maxim's
    music: Rudolf Friml
    lyrics: Otto Harbach and William Cary Duncan
    staging: Edgar Selwyn, Leon Errol, Julian Mitchell
Productions:
    Opened January 13, 1922 for 140 performances
Reviews:
    Dramatic Mirror 95:63, Mar 1922
    Life (New York) 79:18, Feb 2, 1922
    New York Clipper 69:20, Jan 11, 1922
    New York Times page 9, Jan 14, 1922
    Theatre Magazine 35:264, Apr 1922

The Blue Paradise
    book: Edgar Smith; based on a Viennese operetta by
                    Leo Stein and Bela Jenbasch
    music: Edmund Eysler; additional numbers by Sigmund
                    Romberg
    lyrics: Herbert Reynolds
    staging: J. H. Benrimo
    choreography: Ed Hutchinson
Productions:
    Opened August 5, 1915 for 356 performances
Reviews:
    Dramatic Mirror 74:8, Aug 11, 1915; 74:2, Sep 1, 1915;
                    75:1, Apr 1, 1916
    Green Book 14:623, Oct 1915
    Nation 101:212, Aug 12, 1915
    Opera Magazine 2:25+, Oct 1915
    Theatre Magazine 22:113+, Sep 1915

Blues, Ballads, and Sin-Songs (see Libby Holman's Blues, Ballads,
    and Sin-Songs)

The Blushing Bride
    book: Cyrus Wood, based on a play by Edward Clark
    music: Sigmund Romberg
    lyrics: Cyrus Wood
    staging: Frank Smithson
Productions:
    Opened February 6, 1922 for 144 performances
Reviews:
    New York Clipper 70:20, Feb 15, 1922
    New York Times page 12, Feb 7, 1922
    Theatre Magazine 35:262, Apr 1922

The Body Beautiful
    book: Joseph Stein and Will Glickman
    music: Jerry Bock

    lyrics: Sheldon Harnick
    staging: George Schaefer
    sets: Jean and Willian Eckart
    costumes: Noel Taylor
    choreography: Herbert Ross
Productions:
    Opened January 23, 1958 for 60 performances
Reviews:
    America 98:677, Mar 8, 1958
    Catholic World 187:70, Apr 1958
    Dance Magazine 32:15, Mar 1958
    New York Theatre Critics' Reviews 1958:386+
    New York Times page 15, Jan 24, 1958
    New Yorker 33:54-6, Feb 1, 1958
    Newsweek 51:55, Feb 3, 1958
    Saturday Review 41:28, Feb 15, 1958
    Theatre Arts 42:17-18, Apr 1958
    Time 71:78, Feb 3, 1958

Body Indian
    book: Hanay Geoigamah
    music: Ed Wapp
Productions:
    (Off-Off-Broadway) Opened October 25, 1972 (La Mama Experi-
      mental Theater Club)
Reviews:
    New York Times page 69, Oct 29, 1972

Bombo
    book: Harold Atteridge
    music: Sigmund Romberg
    lyrics: Harold Atteridge
    staging: J. C. Huffman
Productions:
    Opened October 6, 1921 for 219 performances
Reviews:
    Dramatic Mirror 84:556, Oct 15, 1921
    New York Clipper 69:26, Oct 12, 1921
    New York Times page 20, Oct 7, 1921
                       VI, page 1, Oct 30, 1921
                       page 22, May 15, 1923
    Theatre Magazine 34:424, Dec 1921

Boom Boom
    book: Fanny Todd Mitchell, adapted from Louis
                       Verneuil's Mlle. Ma Mere
    music: Werner Janssen
    lyrics: Mann Holiner and J. Keirn Brennan
    staging: George Marion
Productions:
    Opened January 28, 1929 for 72 performances
Reviews:
    New York Times page 26, Jan 29, 1929

Theatre Magazine 49:47, May 1929

Borge, Victor (see Comedy in Music)

Borscht Capades
    staging: Mickey Katz
    sets: Charles Elson
Productions:
    Opened September 17, 1951 for 99 performances
Reviews:
    Catholic World 174:149, Nov 1951
    New Republic 125:21, Oct 1, 1951
    New York Theatre Critics' Reviews 1951:235
    New York Times page 38, Sep 18, 1951
    New Yorker 27:64, Sep 29, 1951
    Theatre Arts 35:8, Nov 1951

Bottomland
    book: Clarence Williams
    music: Clarence Williams
Productions:
    Opened June 27, 1927 for 21 performances
Reviews:
    New York Times page 29, Jun 28, 1927

The Boy Friend
    book: Sandy Wilson
    music: Sandy Wilson
    lyrics: Sandy Wilson
    staging: Vida Hope
    sets: Reginald Woolley
    costumes: Reginald Woolley
    choreography: John Heawood
Productions:
    Opened September 30, 1954 for 485 performances
    (Off-Broadway) Season of 1957-58
    (Off-Broadway) Opened February 4, 1966 for 17 performances
    Opened April 14, 1970 for 119 performances
Reviews:
    America 92:138, Oct 30, 1954
            122:54-5, May 9, 1970
    Catholic World 180:226, Dec 1954
    Commonweal 61:93, Oct 29, 1954
    Dance Magazine 32:17, May 1958
            44:84, Jun 1970
    Life 37:113-14+, Oct 25, 1954
    Mademoiselle 40:142, Nov 1954
    Nation 179:349, Oct 16, 1954
          210:574, May 11, 1970
    New Republic 131:23, Nov 1, 1954
    New York Theatre Critics' Reviews 1954:299+
                             1970:277
    New York Times II, page 1, Sep 26, 1954

                    page 20, Oct 1, 1954
                    II, page 1, Oct 10, 1954
                    VI, page 33, Nov 21, 1954
                    II, page 5, Dec 23, 1956
                    page 24, Jan 27, 1958
                    II, page 1, Jan 25, 1959
                    page 54, Apr 15, 1970
                    II, page 5, Apr 26, 1970
                    page 18, Jul 17, 1970
        New Yorker 29:69, Feb 6, 1954
                    30:58+, Oct 9, 1954
                    46:95, Apr 25, 1970
        Newsweek 44:56, Oct 11, 1954
                    75:64, Apr 27, 1970
        Saturday Review 37:24, Sep 18, 1954
                    37:29, Oct 16, 1954
        Theatre Arts 38:18-19+, Dec 1954
        Time 64:93, Oct 11, 1954
                    95:59, Apr 27, 1970
        Vogue 124:125, Oct 1, 1954

Boys and Girls Together
        book: Ed Wynn and Pat C. Flick
        music: Sammy Fain
        lyrics: Jack Yellen and Irving Kahal
        staging: Ed Wynn
        sets: William Oden Waller
        costumes: Irene Sharaff and Veronica
        choreography: Albertina Rasch
Productions:
        Opened October 1, 1940 for 191 performances
Reviews:
        Catholic World 152:218-19, Nov 1940
        Life 9:57-8+, Oct 7, 1940
        Nation 151:345, Oct 12, 1940
        New Republic 103:526, Oct 14, 1940
        New York Theatre Critics' Reviews 1940:266+
                                          1941:475+
        New York Times page 28, Sep 5, 1940
                        IX, page 1, Sep 15, 1940
                        page 19, Oct 2, 1940
                        IX, page 1, Oct 13, 1940
        Newsweek 16:74, Oct 14, 1940
        Stage 1:8, Nov 1940
                1:42-3, Nov 1940
                1:7, Dec 1940
        Theatre Arts 24:773-4, Nov 1940
        Time 36:62, Oct 4, 1940

The Boys from Syracuse
        book: George Abbott, based on Shakespeare's The
                        Comedy of Errors
        music: Richard Rodgers

lyrics: Lorenz Hart
staging: George Abbott
sets: Jo Mielziner
costumes: Irene Sharaff
choreography: George Balanchine
Productions:
Opened November 23, 1938 for 235 performances
(Off-Broadway) Opened April 15, 1963 for 469 performances
Reviews:
Catholic World 148:474-6, Jan 1939
Commonweal 29:190, Dec 9, 1938
Life 5:43-4, Dec 12, 1938
Nation 147:638, Dec 10, 1938
New Republic 97:173, Dec 14, 1938
New York Times IX, page 2, Nov 13, 1938
                page 36, Nov 24, 1938
                X, page 5, Dec 4, 1938
                page 31, Apr 16, 1963
                VI, page 106, May 5, 1963
                II, page 1, Jun 2, 1963
                page 14, Nov 9, 1963
                page 37, Jun 19, 1964
New Yorker 39:84, Apr 27, 1963
North American Review 247 no. 1:159-60, Mar 1939
Saturday Review 46:33, Aug 10, 1963
Theatre Arts 23:10-11, Jan 1939
             47:13, Jun 1963
             47:14-15, Jun 1963
Time 32:35, Sep 26, 1938
     32:44, Dec 5, 1938

Bravo Giovanni
book: A. J. Russell, adapted from Howard Shaw's
                 The Crime of Giovanni Venturi
music: Milton Schafer
lyrics: Ronny Graham
staging: Stanley Prager
sets: Robert Randolph
costumes: Ed Wittstein
choreography: Carol Haney and Buzz Miller
Productions:
Opened May 19, 1962 for 76 performances
Reviews:
America 107:429-30, Jun 23, 1962
Commonweal 76:304, Jun 15, 1962
New York Theatre Critics' Reviews 1962:276+
New York Times page 41, May 21, 1962
                II, page 1, May 27, 1962
                page 34, Sep 12, 1962
New Yorker 38:91-2, May 26, 1962
Newsweek 59:65, Jun 4, 1962
Saturday Review 45:24, Jun 2, 1962
Theatre Arts 46:67-9, Jul 1962

Time 79:83, Jun 1, 1962

Brel, Jacques   (see Jacques Brel)

Brigadoon
    book: Alan Jay Lerner
    music: Frederick Loewe
    lyrics: Alan Jay Lerner
    staging: Robert Lewis
    sets: Oliver Smith
    costumes: David Ffolkes
    choreography: Agnes de Mille
Productions:
    Opened March 13, 1947 for 581 performances
    Opened May 2, 1950 for 24 performances
    Opened March 27, 1957 for 47 performances
    Opened May 30, 1962 for 16 performances
    Opened January 30, 1963 for 16 performances
    Opened December 23, 1964 for 17 performances
    Opened December 13, 1967 for 23 performances
Reviews:
    Catholic World 165:73, Apr 1947
                185:227, Jun 1957
    Commonweal 45:593, Mar 28, 1947
            66:128, May 3, 1957
    Harpers 81:174, May 1947
    Life 23:57-60, Jul 21, 1947
    New Republic 116:38, Mar 31, 1947
    New York Theatre Critics' Reviews 1947:427+
                            1957:305+
    New York Times II, page 1, Mar 9, 1947
                 VI, page 32, Mar 9, 1947
                 page 28, Mar 14, 1947
                 II, page 1, Mar 23, 1947
                 II, page 1, Apr 6, 1947
                 II, page 1, Jun 22, 1947
                 page 11, Apr 16, 1949
                 page 36, May 3, 1950
                 II, page 3, May 21, 1950
                 II, page 1, Dec 31, 1950
                 page 37, Mar 28, 1957
                 II, page 1, Apr 7, 1957
                 page 21, May 31, 1962
                 page 6, Feb 1, 1963
                 page 9, Dec 24, 1964
                 page 59, Dec 14, 1967
    New Yorker 23:54+, Mar 22, 1947
    Newsweek 29:84, Mar 24, 1947
    Saturday Review 30:24-6, Apr 5, 1947
    School and Society 66:245-7, Sep 27, 1947
                 68:386, Dec 4, 1948
    Theatre Arts 31:21, May 1947
               31:41, Jun 1947

41:18, Jun 1957
46:58-9, Aug 1962
47:64-5, Mar 1963
Time 49:66, Mar 24, 1947

Bright Eyes
    book: Charles Dickson; adapted from Mistakes Will
                     Happen by Charles Dickson and Grant Stewart
    music: Karl Hoschna
    lyrics: Otto A. Hauerbach
Productions:
    Opened February 28, 1910 for 40 performances
Reviews:
    Cosmopolitan 49:81, Jun 1910
    Dramatic Mirror 63:6, Mar 12, 1910
    Hampton 24:700-1, May 1910
    Metropolitan Magazine 32:404, Jun 1910
    Theatre Magazine 11:127, Apr 1910

Bright Lights of 1944
    book: Norman Anthony and Charles Sherman (additional
                     dialogue by Joseph Erens)
    music: Jerry Livingston
    lyrics: Mack David
    staging: Dan Eckley
    sets: Perry Watkins
    costumes: Perry Watkins
    choreography: Truly McGee
Productions:
    Opened September 16, 1943 for 4 performances
Reviews:
    New York Theatre Critics' Reviews 1943:276+
    New York Times page 27, Sep 17, 1943
                    II, page 1, Sep 26, 1943
    Theatre Arts 27:647-8, Nov 1943

Bringing Up Father
    book: Nat Leroy; based on George McManus's cartoon
    music: Seymour Furth
    lyrics: R. F. Carroll
    staging: Richard F. Carroll
Productions:
    Opened April 6, 1925 for 24 performances
No Reviews.

Broadway Nights
    music: Sam Timberg, Lee David, Maurice Rubens
    lyrics: Moe Jaffe
    staging: Busby Berkeley and Stanley Logan
Productions:
    Opened July 15, 1929 for 40 performances
Reviews:
    New York Times page 23, Jul 16, 1929

Outlook 152:595, Aug 7, 1929
Theatre Magazine 50:41, Sep 1929

Broadway Sho-Window
    sketches: Eugene Conrad
    lyrics: Eugene Conrad
    sets: Clark Robinson
    choreography: Bill Powers
Productions:
    (Off-Broadway) Opened April 12, 1936
Reviews:
    New York Times page 14, Apr 13, 1936

Broadway to Paris
    book: George Bronson Howard and Harold Atteridge
    music: Max Hoffman; additional numbers by Anatol
                 Friedland
    lyrics: George Bronson Howard and Harold Atteridge
    staging: Ned Wayburn
Productions:
    Opened November 20, 1912 for 77 performances
Reviews:
    Theatre Magazine 17:5, Jan 1913
                    17:6, Jan 1913

The Broadway Whirl
    music: Harry Tierney and George Gershwin
    lyrics: Joseph McCarthy, Richard Carle, Bud de Silva
                 and John Henry Mears
Productions:
    Opened June 8, 1921 for (8) performances
Reviews:
    New York Clipper 69:29, Jun 15, 1921
    New York Times page 10, Jun 9, 1921
    Theatre Magazine 34:98, Aug 1921

A Broken Idol
    book: Hal Stephens
    music: Egbert Van Alsteyne
    lyrics: Harry Williams
    staging: Gus Sohlke
Productions:
    Opened August 16, 1909 for 40 performances
Reviews:
    Dramatic Mirror 62:7, Aug 28, 1909
    Metropolitan Magazine 31:128-9, Oct 1909
    Theatre Magazine 19:iii+, Oct 1909

Brown Buddies
    book: Carl Rickman
    music: Joe Jordan and Millard Thomas
    lyrics: Carl Rickman
Productions:

Opened October 7, 1930 for 111 performances
Reviews:
New York Times page 29, Oct 8, 1930

Brown, Oscar (see Worlds of Oscar Brown)

Buck White
book: Oscar Brown Jr.; based on the play Big Time Buck White by Joseph Dolan Tuotti
music: Oscar Brown Jr.
lyrics: Oscar Brown Jr.
staging: Oscar Brown Jr. and Jean Pace
sets: Edward Burbridge
costumes: Jean Pace
Productions:
Opened December 2, 1969 for 7 performances
Reviews:
New York Theatre Critics' Reviews 1969:170
New York Times page 56, Oct 30, 1969
II, page 1, Nov 23, 1969
page 42, Nov 29, 1969
VI, page 32, Nov 30, 1969
page 63, Dec 3, 1969
page 54, Dec 5, 1969
II, page 5, Dec 7, 1969

Buddies
book: George V. Hobart
music: B. C. Hilliam
lyrics: B. C. Hilliam
Productions:
Opened October 27, 1919 for 259 performances
Reviews:
Independent 101:86, Jan 17, 1920
New York Times page 11, Oct 29, 1919
Theatre Magazine 31:18, Jan 1920

Buddy Hackett (see Eddie Fisher-Buddy Hackett at the Palace)

The Bunch and Judy
book: Anne Caldwell and Hugh Ford
music: Jerome Kern
lyrics: Anne Caldwell
staging: Fred G. Latham
Productions:
Opened November 28, 1922 for 63 performances
Reviews:
New York Clipper 70:20, Dec 6, 1922
New York Times VIII, page 6, Nov 12, 1922
page 20, Nov 29, 1922
Theatre Magazine 37:20, Feb 1923

Bunk of 1926

```
     sketches:        Gene Lockhart and Percy Waxman
     music:           Gene Lockhart
     lyrics:          Gene Lockhart and Percy Waxman
Productions:
     Opened February 16, 1926 for 104 performances
Reviews:
     Life (New York) 87:21, Jun 24, 1926
     New York Times page 12, Feb 17, 1926
                     page 25, Apr 23, 1926
     Theatre Magazine 43:14, May 1926
                      43:18, May 1926
```

Buttrio Square
```
     book:            Billy Gilbert and Gen Genovese, based on a play
                      by Hal Cranton from an original story by Gen
                      Genovese
     music:           Arthur Jones and Fred Stamer
     lyrics:          Gen Genovese
     staging:         Eugene Loring
     sets:            Samuel Leve
     costumes:        Sal Anthony
     choreography:    Eugene Loring
Productions:
     Opened October 14, 1952 for 7 performances
Reviews:
     New York Theatre Critics' Reviews 1952:238+
     New York Times page 40, Oct 15, 1952
     New Yorker 28:30, Oct 25, 1952
     Time 60:76, Oct 27, 1952
```

Buy Bonds, Buster!
```
     book:            Jack Holmes; based on an original concept by
                      Bob Miller and Billy Conklin
     music:           Jack Holmes
     lyrics:          M. B. Miller
     staging:         John Bishop
     sets:            William Pitkin
     choreography:    Bick Goss
Productions:
     (Off-Broadway) Opened June 4, 1972 for 1 performance
Reviews:
     New York Times page 41, Jun 5, 1972
```

By Jupiter
```
     book:            Richard Rodgers and Lorenz Hart, based on
                      Julian F. Thompson's The Warrior's Husband
     music:           Richard Rodgers
     lyrics:          Lorenz Hart
     staging:         Joshua Logan
     sets:            Jo Mielziner
     costumes:        Irene Sharaff
     choreography:    Robert Alton
Productions:
```

Opened June 3, 1942 for 427 performances
(Off-Off-Broadway) Opened February 12, 1965 for 14 per-
    formances (Equity Library Theatre)
(Off-Broadway) Opened January 19, 1967 for 118 performances
Reviews:
    America 116:264, Feb 18, 1967
    Catholic World 155:472-3, Jul 1942
    Commonweal 36:255-6, Jul 3, 1942
    Independent Woman 22:155, May 1943
    Life 12:82-5, Jun 1, 1942
    Nation 154:693, Jun 13, 1942
    New York Theatre Critics' Reviews 1942:274+
    New York Times page 22, Jun 4, 1942
                        VIII, page 1, Aug 30, 1942
                        page 28, Jan 20, 1967
                        page 52, Apr 20, 1967
    New Yorker 18:36, Jun 13, 1942
              42:46+, Jan 28, 1967
    Newsweek 19:70-1, Jun 15, 1942
    Theatre Arts 26:607, Oct 1942
    Time 39:66, Jun 15, 1942

By the Beautiful Sea
    book: Herbert and Dorothy Fields
    music: Arthur Schwartz
    lyrics: Dorothy Fields
    staging: Marshall Jamison
    sets: Jo Mielziner
    costumes: Irene Sharaff
    choreography: Helen Tamiris
Productions:
    Opened April 8, 1954 for 270 performances
Reviews:
    America 91:171-2, May 8, 1954
    Catholic World 179:225, Jun 1954
    Commonweal 60:95-6, Apr 30, 1954
    Life 36:109-10, May 17, 1954
    Mademoiselle 38:125, Apr 1954
    Nation 178:370, Apr 24, 1954
    New York Theatre Critics' Reviews 1954:335+
    New York Times page 20, Apr 9, 1954
                        II, page 1, Apr 18, 1954
    New Yorker 30:64-6, Apr 17, 1954
    Newsweek 43:66, Apr 19, 1954
    Saturday Review 37:32, May 1, 1954
    Theatre Arts 38:18-19, Jun 1954
    Time 63:85, Apr 19, 1954

By the Way
    book: Ronald Jeans and Harold Simpson
    music: Vivian Ellis
    lyrics: Graham John
    staging: Jack Hulburt

Productions:
    Opened December 28, 1925 for 176 performances
Reviews:
    New York Times page 20, Dec 29, 1925
                    VIII, page 1, Apr 4, 1926
                    page 20, Apr 16, 1926

Bye, Bye, Barbara
    book: Sidney Toler and Alonzo Price
    music: Carlo and Sanders
Productions:
    Opened August 25, 1924 for 16 performances
Reviews:
    New York Times page 6, Aug 26, 1924

Bye Bye Birdie
    book: Michael Stewart
    music: Charles Strouse
    lyrics: Lee Adams
    staging: Gower Champion
    sets: Robert Randolph
    costumes: Miles White
    choreography: Gower Champion
Productions:
    Opened April 14, 1960 for 607 performances
Reviews:
    Life 48:143+, May 23, 1960
    Nation 190:390, Apr 30, 1960
    New York Theatre Critics' Reviews 1960:296+
    New York Times VI, page 90, Mar 27, 1960
                    page 13, Apr 15, 1960
                    page 13, Jun 17, 1960
    New Yorker 36:116-18, Apr 23, 1960
    Newsweek 55:100, Apr 25, 1960
    Saturday Review 43:26, Apr 30, 1960
    Time 75:50, Apr 25, 1960

Bye, Bye, Bonnie
    book: Louis Simon and Bide Dudley
    staging: Edgar McGregor
Productions:
    Opened January 13, 1927 for 125 performances
Reviews:
    New York Times page 15, Jan 14, 1927

                        - C -

Cabalgata (A Night in Spain)
    material: Iberian folksongs
    staging: Daniel Cordoba
    sets: Luis Marquez
    costumes: Daniel Cordoba

Productions:
    Opened July 7, 1949 for 76 performances
Reviews:
    Catholic World 169:467, Sep 1949
    New York Theatre Critics' Reviews 1949:284
    New York Times page 14, Jul 8, 1949
                II, page 1, Aug 28, 1949

Cabaret
    book: Joe Masteroff; based on John Van Druten's play
                      I Am a Camera and stories by Christopher
                      Isherwood
    music: John Kander
    lyrics: Fred Ebb
    staging: Harold Prince
    sets: Boris Aronson
    costumes: Patricia Zipprodt
    choreography: Ronald Field
Productions:
    Opened November 20, 1966 for 1,165 performances
Reviews:
    America 116:25, Jan 7, 1967
    Christian Century 84:1071-2, Aug 23, 1967
    Commonweal 85:326, Dec 16, 1967
    Dance Magazine 41:26+, Jan 1967
    Life 62:16, Jan 13, 1967
        62:82-3, Jan 13, 1967
    Look 31:72-4+, Mar 7, 1967
    Mademoiselle 64:186-7, Mar 1967
    Nation 203:651-2, Dec 12, 1966
    New York Theatre Critics' Reviews 1966:240
    New York Times VI, page 128, Nov 20, 1966
                  page 62, Nov 21, 1966
                  II, page 5, Dec 4, 1966
                  II, page 1, Feb 26, 1967
                  page 19, Jan 12, 1968
                  page 32, Mar 1, 1968
                  page 74, Feb 2, 1969
                  page 30, Sep 5, 1969
    New Yorker 42:155-6, Dec 3, 1966
    Newsweek 68:96, Dec 5, 1966
    Reporter 36:49, Mar 9, 1967
    Saturday Review 49:64, Dec 10, 1966
    Time 88:84, Dec 2, 1966
    Vogue 149:52, Jan 1, 1967

Cabin in the Sky
    book: Lynn Root
    music: Vernon Duke
    lyrics: John La Touche
    staging: George Balanchine
    sets: Boris Aronson
    costumes: Boris Aronson

Productions:
    Opened October 25, 1940 for 156 performances
    (Off-Broadway) Opened January 21, 1964 for 47 performances
Reviews:
    America 110:239, Feb 15, 1964
    Catholic World 152:333-4, Dec 1940
    Commonweal 33:80, Nov 8, 1940
    Life 9:63+, Dec 9, 1940
    Nation 151:458, Nov 9, 1940
    New Republic 103:661, Nov 11, 1940
    New York Theatre Critics' Reviews 1940:242+
                                        1941:463+
    New York Times page 19, Oct 26, 1940
                    IX, page 3, Nov 10, 1940
                    page 32, Jan 22, 1964
                    page 12, Feb 29, 1964
    Newsweek 16:62, Nov 4, 1940
    Stage 1:24-5, Dec 1940
    Theatre Arts 24:841-2+, Dec 1940
    Time 36:51, Nov 4, 1940

Cafe Crown
        book: Hy Kraft, based on his play
        music: Albert Hague
        lyrics: Marty Brill
        staging: Jerome Eskow
        sets: Sam Leve
        costumes: Ruth Morley
        choreography: Ronald Field
Productions:
    Opened April 17, 1964 for 3 performances
Reviews:
    Dance Magazine 38:26-7, May 1964
    New York Theatre Critics' Reviews 1964:284+
    New York Times page 32, Apr 18, 1964
                    page 83, Apr 19, 1964
    New Yorker 40:130, Apr 25, 1964

Call Me Charlie
        book: Michael Moran
        music: Sam Burtis and Jane Blackstone
        lyrics: Sam Burtis and Jane Blackstone
Productions:
    (Off-Off-Broadway) Opened April 1974 (La Mama Experimental
        Theater Club)
    (Off-Off-Broadway) Opened May 11, 1974 (The Performing
        Garage)
Reviews:
    New York Times page 46, Apr 2, 1974

Call Me Madam
        book: Howard Lindsay and Russel Crouse
        music: Irving Berlin

lyrics: Irving Berlin
staging: George Abbott
sets: Raoul Pene du Bois
costumes: Raoul Pene du Bois
choreography: Jerome Robbins
Productions:
    Opened October 12, 1950 for 644 performances
    (Off-Off-Broadway) Opened November 8, 1973 (Equity Library
        Theatre)
Reviews:
    Catholic World 172:225, Dec 1950
    Christian Science Monitor Magazine page 6, Oct 21, 1950
    Collier's 126:22-3+, Oct 21, 1950
    Commonweal 53:94, Nov 3, 1950
    Life 29:117-18+, Oct 30, 1950
    Nation 171:370, Oct 21, 1950
    New Republic 123:23, Nov 6, 1950
    New York Theatre Critics' Reviews 1950:243+
    New York Times II, page 1, Sep 3, 1950
                    VI, page 24, Oct 1, 1950
                    II, page 1, Oct 8, 1950
                    page 25, Oct 13, 1950
                    II, page 1, Oct 22, 1950
                    II, page 1, Apr 29, 1951
                    page 84, Mar 16, 1952
                    page 17, Mar 17, 1952
                    II, page 3, Apr 13, 1952
                    page 35, May 6, 1952
                    page 44, Dec 16, 1952
    New Yorker 26:55, Oct 21, 1950
    Newsweek 36:84, Oct 23, 1950
    Saturday Review 33:49-50, Sep 30, 1950
                    33:42-4, Oct 28, 1950
    Theatre Arts 34:16-17, Nov 1950
                 34:15, Dec 1950
    Time 56:58, Oct 23, 1950

Call Me Mister
    book: Arnold Auerbach and Arnold B. Horwitt
    music: Harold Rome
    lyrics: Harold Rome
    staging: Robert H. Gordon
    sets: Lester Polokov
    costumes: Grace Houston
    choreography: John Wray
Productions:
    Opened April 18, 1946 for 734 performances
Reviews:
    Catholic World 163:264, Jun 1946
    Collier's 117:22-3, May 18, 1946
    Commonweal 44:72, May 3, 1946
    Forum 105:938-9, Jun 1946
    Life 20:131-2+, May 27, 1946

Modern Music 23 No. 3:223, Jul 1946
New Republic 114:662, May 6, 1946
New York Theatre Critics' Reviews 1946:403+
New York Times VI, page 26, Apr 7, 1946
                    page 26, Apr 19, 1946
                    II, page 1, Apr 14, 1946
                    II, page 1, Apr 18, 1946
                    II, page 1, Aug 4, 1946
                    II, page 3, Apr 13, 1947
                    II, page 1, Jun 29, 1947
                    II, page 1, Oct 12, 1947
                    II, page 3, Dec 14, 1947
New York Times Magazine pages 26-7, Apr 7, 1946
New Yorker 22:42, Apr 27, 1946
Newsweek 27:80, Apr 29, 1946
Saturday Review 29:24-6, May 18, 1946
Theatre Arts 30:322, Jun 1946
Time 47:68+, Apr 29, 1946
        47:70, May 6, 1946

Calling All Stars
    sketches: Lew Brown
    music: Harry Akst
    lyrics: Lew Brown
    staging: Lew Brown and Thomas Mitchell
    sets: Nat Karson
    choreography: Sara Mildred Strauss
Productions:
    Opened December 13, 1934 for 36 performances
Reviews:
    New York Times page 28, Dec 14, 1934
    Time 24:13, Dec 24, 1934

Cambridge Circus
    sketches: Tim Brooke-Taylor, Graham Chapman, John
                     Cleese, David Hatch, Jo Kendall, Jonathan
                     Lynn, Bill Oddie, and others
    music: Bill Oddie, Hugh MacDonald, David Palmer
    staging: Humphrey Barclay
    sets: Stephen Mullin
    costumes: Judy Birdwood
Productions:
    Opened October 6, 1964 for 23 performances
Reviews:
    Dance Magazine 38:16-17, Dec 1964
    Nation 199:286, Oct 26, 1964
    New York Theatre Critics' Reviews 1964:201+
    New York Times page 53, Oct 7, 1964
                    page 44, Oct 27, 1964
    Time 84:77, Oct 16, 1964

Camelot
    book: Alan Jay Lerner, based on T. H. White's The

Once and Future King
music: Frederick Loewe
lyrics: Alan Jay Lerner
staging: Moss Hart
sets: Oliver Smith
costumes: Adrian and Tony Duquette
choreography: Hanya Holm
Productions:
Opened December 3, 1960 for 873 performances
Reviews:
America 104:546, Jan 21, 1961
Commonweal 74:379, Jul 7, 1961
Coronet 50:15, May 1961
Dance Magazine 35:16, Feb 1961
Horizon 3:102-4, May 1961
Life 49:90-3, Dec 19, 1960
Musical America 81:264, Jan 1961
Nation 191:510, Dec 24, 1960
National Review 10:224-5, Apr 8, 1961
New York Theatre Critics' Reviews 1960:154+
New York Times VI, page 4, Oct 2, 1960
                page 35, Oct 3, 1960
                VI, page 68, Oct 16, 1960
                II, page 1, Nov 27, 1960
                page 42, Dec 5, 1960
                II, page 5, Dec 11, 1960
                VI, pages 26-27, Dec 11, 1960
                page 20, Aug 7, 1961
                VI, page 34, Dec 3, 1961
                page 5, Jan 5, 1963
                page 34, Aug 20, 1964
New York Times Magazine pages 18-19, Sep 18, 1960
New Yorker 36:95, Dec 10, 1960
Newsweek 56:94, Dec 12, 1900
        56:104-5, Dec 5, 1960
Saturday Review 43:30, Dec 24, 1960
Theatre Arts 44:25-6, Dec 1960
        45:8-9, Feb 1961
Time 76:78, Oct 17, 1960
        76:64-6+, Nov 14, 1960
        76:63, Dec 19, 1960
Vogue 137:116-17, Feb 15, 1961

Can-Can
book: Abe Burrows
music: Cole Porter
lyrics: Cole Porter
staging: Abe Burrows
sets: Jo Mielziner
costumes: Motley
choreography: Michael Kidd
Productions:
Opened May 7, 1953 for 892 performances

Opened May 16, 1962 for 16 performances
Reviews:
America 89:228, May 23, 1953
              107:361, Jun 2, 1962
Catholic World 177:308-9, Jul 1953
Commonweal 58:200, May 29, 1953
Life 34:59-60+, Jun 1, 1953
Look 17:36-8, May 19, 1953
Nation 176:441-2, May 23, 1953
New York Theatre Critics' Reviews 1953:304+
New York Times VI, page 68, Apr 26, 1953
                      page 28, May 8, 1953
                      II, page 1, May 17, 1953
                      II, page 3, Oct 24, 1954
                      page 32, May 17, 1962
New York Times Magazine pages 68-9, Apr 26, 1953
New Yorker 29:59, May 16, 1953
Newsweek 42:60, Dec 21, 1953
Saturday Review 36:28, May 23, 1953
Theatre Arts 37:14, Jul 1953
Time 61:69, May 18, 1953
Vogue 121:86-7, Apr 15, 1953

The Canary
    book: based on the French of Georges Barr and
                     Louis Vernevil
    music: Ivan Caryll, Irving Berlin and Harry Tierney
    staging: Fred G. Latham and Edward Royce
Productions:
Opened November 4, 1918 for 152 performances
Reviews:
Dramatic Mirror 79:507, Oct 5, 1918
                79:795, Nov 30, 1918
                79:899, Dec 21, 1918
New York Dramatic News 65:10, Nov 9, 1918
New York Times page 11, Nov 5, 1918
Theatre Magazine 28:378, Dec 1918
                 29:37, Jan 1919

Canary Cottage
    book: Oliver Morosco and Elmer Harris
    music: Earl Carroll
    lyrics: Earl Carroll
    choreography: Frank Stammers and Frank Rainger
Productions:
Opened February 5, 1917 for 112 performances
Reviews:
Dramatic Mirror 75:16, Jun 10, 1916
                77:7+, Feb 10, 1917
                77:9, Feb 24, 1917
Green Book 17:592-3, Apr 1917
Life (New York) 69:268, Feb 15, 1917
New York Dramatic News 63:6, Feb 10, 1917

New York Times page 9, Feb 5, 1917
Theatre Magazine 25:150, Mar 1917
                25:153, Mar 1917

Candide
book:	Lillian Hellman, based on Voltaire's satire
music:	Leonard Bernstein
lyrics:	Richard Wilbur, John LaTouche, Dorothy Parker
staging:	Tyrone Guthrie
sets:	Oliver Smith
costumes:	Irene Sharaff

Productions:
Opened December 1, 1956 for 73 performances
(Off-Off-Broadway) Opened December 11, 1973 for 48 per-
    formances
Opened March 10, 1974 for 519 performances
Reviews:
America 130:262, Apr 6, 1974
Catholic World 184:384-5, Feb 1957
Commentary 57:78, Jun 1974
Commonweal 65:333-4, Dec 28, 1956
Dance Magazine 49:91, Apr 1975
High Fidelity 24:MA 31, Apr 1974
Musical America 76:26, Dec 15, 1956
Nation 183:527, Dec 15, 1956
National Review 26:1049, Sep 13, 1974
New Republic 135:30-1, Dec 17, 1956
            170:16+, Mar 30, 1974
New York Theatre Critics' Reviews 1956:176+
                                1973:138
New York Times VI, page 28, Nov 4, 1956
            II, page 1, Nov 18, 1956
            page 40, Dec 3, 1956
            II, page 5, Dec 9, 1956
            II, page 9, Dec 16, 1956
            page 47, Dec 21, 1973
            II, page 1, Dec 30, 1973
            page 34, Mar 12, 1974
New Yorker 32:52+, Dec 15, 1956
Newsweek 48:77, Dec 10, 1956
Opera News 38:33, Feb 9, 1974
Reporter 16:35, Jan 24, 1957
Saturday Review 39:34, Dec 22, 1956
Time 68:70, Dec 10, 1956
        103:75, Mar 25, 1974

Canterbury Tales
book:	Martin Starkie and Nevill Coghill; based on the work by Geoffrey Chaucer
music:	Richard Hill and John Hawkins
lyrics:	Nevill Coghill
staging:	Martin Starkie
sets:	Derek Cousins

costumes: Loudon Saintill
choreography: Sammy Bayes and Bert Michaels
Productions:
Opened February 3, 1969 for 121 performances
Reviews:
America 120:316, Mar 15, 1969
Dance Magazine 43:26+, May 1969
National Review 21:918, Sep 9, 1969
New York Theatre Critics' Review 1969:368
New York Times page 34, Feb 4, 1969
                      II, page 10, Feb 16, 1969
                      page 19, May 17, 1969
New Yorker 44:90, Feb 15, 1969
Newsweek 73:113, Feb 17, 1969
Time 91:68, Apr 12, 1968
      93:62, Feb 14, 1969
Vogue 153:42, Mar 15, 1969

Canticle
book: Michael Champagne
music: William Penn
lyrics: Michael Champagne
Productions:
(Off-Off Broadway) Season of 1973-1974 (Central Arts Cabaret
Theatre)
No Reviews

Cape Cod Follies
book: Stewart Baird
music: Alexander Fogarty
lyrics: Stewart Baird
staging: Stewart Baird
choreography: John Lonergan
Productions:
Opened September 18, 1929 for 30 performances
Reviews:
New York Times page 37, Sep 19, 1929
Outlook 153:192, Oct 2, 1929

Captain Jinks
book: Frank Mandel and Laurence Schwab; based on
                 the play by Clyde Fitch
music: Lewis E. Gensler and Stephen Jones
lyrics: B. G. DeSylva
staging: Edgar MacGregor
Productions:
Opened September 8, 1925 for 167 performances
Reviews:
New York Times page 22, Sep 9, 1925
Theatre Magazine 42:16, Nov 1925

Carib Song
book: William Archibald

music: Baldwin Bergersen
lyrics: William Archibald
staging: Katherine Dunham and Mary Hunter
sets: Jo Mielziner
costumes: Motley
choreography: Katherine Dunham
Productions:
Opened September 27, 1945 for 36 performances
Reviews:
Catholic World 162:167, Nov 1945
Commonweal 43:17, Oct 19, 1945
New York Theatre Critics' Reviews 1945:157+
New York Times page 17, Sep 28, 1945
New Yorker 21:50, Oct 6, 1945
Theatre Arts page 29:624+, Nov 1945
Time 46:78, Oct 8, 1945

Caribbean Carnival
book: Samuel L. Manning and Adolph Thenstead
music: Samuel L. Manning and Adolph Thenstead
lyrics: Samuel L. Manning and Adolph Thenstead
staging: Samuel L. Manning and John Hirshman
costumes: Lou Eisele
choreography: Pearl Primus and Claude Marchant
Productions:
Opened December 5, 1947 for 11 performances
Reviews:
New York Theatre Critics' Reviews 1947:246+
New York Times page 12, Dec 6, 1947
              page 34, Dec 15, 1947

Carmen Jones
book: Oscar Hammerstein II, based on Meilhac and
                  Halevy's adaptation of Prosper Merimee's
                  Carmen (Georges Bizet and Prosper Merimee)
music: Georges Bizet, arranged by Robert Russell
lyrics: Oscar Hammerstein II
staging: Hassard Short
sets: Howard Bay
costumes: Raoul Pene du Bois
choreography: Eugene Loring
Productions:
Opened December 2, 1943 for 503 performances
Opened May 2, 1945 for 21 performances
Opened April 7, 1946 for 32 performances
Opened May 31, 1956 for 24 performances
Reviews:
America 95:290-2, Jun 16, 1956
Catholic World 158:394, Jan 1944
              183:311, Jul 1956
Collier's 113:14-15+, Jan 15, 1944
Commonweal 39:231-2, Dec 17, 1943
Life 15:111-12+, Dec 20, 1943

16:70-4, May 8, 1944
Nation 157:740, Dec 18, 1943
New Republic 109:885, Dec 20, 1943
New York Theatre Critics' Reviews 1943:207+
New York Times page 17, Oct 20, 1943
                page 29, Oct 28, 1943
                II, page 1, Nov 28, 1943
                page 26, Dec 3, 1943
                II, page 3, Dec 12, 1943
                II, page 9, Dec 19, 1943
                II, page 1, Jun 18, 1944
                page 26, May 3, 1945
                II, page 1, Apr 7, 1946
                page 32, Apr 8, 1946
                page 8, Sep 22, 1951
                page 28, Jun 1, 1956
                II, page 1, Jun 10, 1956
                page 25, Aug 18, 1959
Newsweek 22:91-2, Dec 13, 1943
Theatre Arts 28:69-73, Feb 1944
            28:154-63, Mar 1944
            40:19, Aug 1956
Time 42:44, Dec 13, 1943
Vogue 103:80-1, Mar 15, 1944

Carmilla
    music: Ben Johnston
    staging: Wilford Leach and John Braswell
Productions:
    (Off-Off-Broadway) Opened February 2, 1973 (La Mama Experimental Theater Club)
No Reviews.

Carnival!
    book: Michael Stewart, based on material by Helen Deutsch
    music: Bob Merrill
    lyrics: Bob Merrill
    staging: Gower Champion
    sets: Will Steven Armstrong
    costumes: Freddy Wittop
    choreography: Gower Champion
Productions:
    Opened April 13, 1961 for 719 performances
    Opened December 12, 1968 for 30 performances
Reviews:
    America 105:410, Jun 3, 1961
    Catholic World 193:271-2, Jul 1961
    Commonweal 74:327-8, Jun 23, 1961
    Coronet 50:10, Aug 1961
    Dance Magazine 35:15, Jun 1961
    Life 50:85-6+, May 5, 1961
    Musical America 81:25-6, Jul 1961

Nation 192:378, Apr 29, 1961
New York Theatre Critics' Reviews 1961:304+
New York Times II, page 1, Apr 9, 1961
        page 22, Apr 14, 1961
        II, page 1, Apr 23, 1961
        VI, page 16, Apr 23, 1961
        page 37, Jun 6, 1962
        page 5, Jan 5, 1963
        page 58, Dec 13, 1968
New Yorker 37:116+, Apr 22, 1961
Newsweek 57:90, Apr 24, 1961
Saturday Review 44:22, Apr 29, 1961
Theatre Arts 45:29+, Jun 1961
Time 77:60, Apr 21, 1961

Carnival in Flanders
    book: Preston Sturges, based on La Kermesse Heroique by C. Spaak, J. Feyder and B. Zimmer
    music: James Van Heusen
    lyrics: Johnny Burke
    staging: Preston Sturges
    sets: Oliver Smith
    costumes: Lucinda Ballard
    choreography: Helen Tamiris
Productions:
    Opened September 8, 1953 for 6 performances
Reviews:
    America 89:629, Sep 26, 1953
    Commonweal 58:634, Oct 2, 1953
    New York Theatre Critics' Reviews 1953:286+
    New York Times page 38, Sep 9, 1953
    New Yorker 29:74, Sep 19, 1953
    Theatre Arts 37:18, Nov 1953

Caroline
    book: Harry B. Smith and E. Kunneke; adapted from the original by Herman Haller and Edward Rideamus
    music: Edward Rideamus and Alfred Goodman
    staging: Charles Sinclair
Productions:
    Opened January 31, 1923 for (149) performances
Reviews:
    New York Clipper 71:14, Feb 7, 1923
    New York Times page 13, Feb 1, 1923
    Theatre Magazine 37:19, Apr 1923

Carousel
    book: Benjamin F. Glazer and Oscar Hammerstein II, adapted from Ferenc Molnar's play Liliom
    music: Richard Rodgers
    lyrics: Oscar Hammerstein II

staging: Rouben Mamoulian
sets: Jo Mielziner
costumes: Miles White
choreography: Agnes de Mille
Productions:
Opened April 19, 1945 for 890 performances
Opened June 2, 1954 for 79 performances
Opened September 11, 1957 for 24 performances
(Off-Broadway) Season of 1959-60 (Equity Library Theatre)
Opened August 10, 1965 for 48 performances
Opened December 15, 1966 for 22 performances
(Off-Off-Broadway) Opened June 22, 1973 (Jones Beach Marine
    Theatre)
(Off-Off-Broadway) Opened February 7, 1974 (Equity Library
    Theatre)
Reviews:
America 91:367, Jul 3, 1954
        98:27, Oct 5, 1957
        113:266-7, Sep 11, 1965
Catholic World 161:260, Jun 1945
        168:481, Mar 1949
        179:308, Jul 1954
Christian Science Monitor Magazine page 7, Jun 24, 1950
Collier's 115:18-19+, May 26, 1945
Commonweal 42:70, May 4, 1945
Dance Magazine 39:16-17, Oct 1965
        41:25, Feb 1967
Life 18:67-70+, May 14, 1945
Nation 160:525, May 5, 1945
        178:550, Jun 26, 1954
New Republic 112:644, May 7, 1945
New York Theatre Critics' Reviews 1945:226+
New York Times II, page 1, Apr 15, 1945
        page 24, Apr 20, 1945
        II, page 1, Apr 29, 1945
        II, page 1, May 6, 1945
        II, page 1, Apr 7, 1946
        II, page 11, Dec 29, 1946
        page 28, Jan 26, 1949
        page 14, Jan 31, 1949
        II, page 1, Feb 6, 1949
        page 37, Jun 8, 1950
        page 85, Oct 14, 1951
        page 38, May 6, 1953
        II, page 3, May 30, 1954
        page 32, Jun 3, 1954
        II, page 1, Jun 13, 1954
        page 38, Sep 12, 1957
        page 39, Aug 11, 1965
        page 56, Dec 16, 1966
        page 68, Jun 27, 1973
New Yorker 21:38, Apr 28, 1945
        24:52, Feb 5, 1949

Newsweek 25:87, Apr 30, 1945
Saturday Review 28:18-19, May 5, 1945
Theatre Arts 29:328-30, Jun 1945
        30:41, Jan 1946
        41:18-19, Nov 1957
Time 45:56, Apr 30, 1945

Carroll, Earl (see Earl Carroll)

Castles in the Air
    book: Raymond W. Peck
    music: Percy Wenrich
    lyrics: Raymond W. Peck
    staging: James W. Elliott
    choreography: John Boyle
Productions:
    Opened September 6, 1926 for 160 performances
Reviews:
    Life (New York) 88:23, Oct 7, 1926
    New York Times page 19, Sep 7, 1926
    Theatre Magazine 44:68, Nov 1926

The Cat and the Fiddle
    book: Otto Harbach
    music: Jerome Kern
    lyrics: Otto Harbach
    staging: Jose Ruben
Productions:
    Opened October 15, 1931 for 395 performances
Reviews:
    Catholic World 134:335-6, Dec 1931
    Life 98:18, Nov 6, 1931
    New Statesman 3:330-1, Mar 12, 1932
    New York Times VIII, page 3, Sep 27, 1931
                   page 26, Oct 16, 1931
                   VIII, page 2, Oct 18, 1931
                   page 17, Aug 4, 1932
    Vogue 78:102, Dec 15, 1931

Catch A Star !
    sketches: Danny and Neil Simon
    music: Sammy Fain and Phil Charig
    lyrics: Paul Webster and Ray Golden
    staging: Ray Golden
    sets: Ralph Alswang
    costumes: Thomas Becher
    choreography: Lee Sherman
Productions:
    Opened September 6, 1955 for 23 performances
Reviews:
    America 93:629, Sep 24, 1955
    New York Theatre Critics' Reviews 1955:290+
    New York Times page 35, Sep 7, 1955

New Yorker 31:72+, Sep 17, 1955
Theatre Arts 39:17, Nov 1955
Time 66:52, Sep 19, 1955

Caviar
　　book:　　　　　　Leo Randole
　　music:　　　　　　Harden Church
　　lyrics:　　　　　　Edward Heyman
　　staging:　　　　　Clifford Brooke
　　sets:　　　　　　　Steele Savage
　　choreography:　　John Lonergan
Productions:
Opened June 7, 1934 for 20 performances
Reviews:
New York Times page 19, Jun 8, 1934

Celebration
　　book:　　　　　　Tom Jones
　　music:　　　　　　Harvey Schmidt
　　lyrics:　　　　　　Tom Jones
　　staging:　　　　　Tom Jones
　　sets:　　　　　　　Ed Wittstein
　　costumes:　　　　Ed Wittstein
　　choreography:　　Vernon Lusby
Productions:
Opened January 22, 1969 for 109 performances
Reviews:
America 120:315, Mar 15, 1969
Dance Magazine 43:71, Mar 1969
Life 66:82-4+, Mar 14, 1969
New York Theatre Critics' Reviews 1969:383
New York Times page 55, Jan 23, 1969
　　　　　　　　　　II, page 3, Feb 2, 1969
New Yorker 44:49, Feb 1, 1969
Time 93:72, Jan 31, 1969

The Century Girl
　　music:　　　　　　Victor Herbert and Irving Berlin
Productions:
Opened November 6, 1916 for 200 performances
Reviews:
Dramatic Mirror 76:7, Nov 18, 1916
Green Book 17:13+, Jan 1917
Leslie's Weekly 124:128, Feb 1, 1917
Life (New York) 68:904, Nov 23, 1916
New Republic 9:154, Dec 9, 1916
New York Times page 9, Nov 7, 1916
Theatre Magazine 24:392, Dec 1916
　　　　　　　　　　25:10, Jan 1917
　　　　　　　　　　25:12, Jan 1917

A Certain Party
　　book:　　　　　　Robert Hood Bowers

staging: William Collier
Productions:
    Opened April 24, 1911 for 24 performances
Reviews:
    Dramatic Mirror 65:7, Apr 26, 1911
                    65:2+, May 3, 1911
    Green Book Album 6:20-3, Jul 1911
    Harper's Weekly 55:19, May 13, 1911
    Red Book 17:573+, Jul 1911
    Theatre Magazine 12:10, Jul 1910
                    13:183, Jun 1911
                    13:196, Jun 1911

Change Your Luck
    book: Garland Howard
    music: J. C. Johnson
    lyrics: Garland Howard
    staging: Cleon Throckmorton
    choreography: Lawrence Deas and Speedy Smith
Productions:
    Opened June 6, 1930 for 17 performances
Reviews:
    New Republic 63:150-1, Jun 25, 1930
    New York Times page 10, Jun 7, 1930

The Charity Girl
    libretto: Edward Peple; added lyrics by Melville
                       Alexander
    music: Victor Hallaender
    staging: George W. Lederer
Productions:
    Opened October 2, 1912 for 21 performances
Reviews:
    Blue Book 15:1138-43, Oct 1912
    Dramatic Mirror 68:10, Jul 31, 1912
                    68:11, Aug 7, 1912
                    68:7, Oct 9, 1912
    Harper's Weekly 56:20, Oct 12, 1912
    New York Dramatic News 56:18, Aug 10, 1912
                            56:25, Oct 12, 1912
    Theatre Magazine 16:xii, Nov 1912

Charles Aznavour
    songs by: Charles Aznavour
Productions:
    Opened February 4, 1970 for 23 performances
Reviews:
    New York Times page 32, Feb 5, 1970

Charles Aznavour   (see The World of Charles Aznavour)

Charlot, André   (see André Charlot's Revue of 1924)

Chauve-Souris 1943
    assembled: M. Nikita Balieff
    music: Gleb Yellin
    lyrics: (English) Irving Florman
    staging: Michel Michon
    sets: Serge Soudeikine
    costumes: Serge Soudeikine
    choreography: Vecheslav Swoboda and Boris Romanoff
Productions:
    Opened August 12, 1943 for 12 performances
Reviews:
    New York Theatre Critics' Reviews 1943:298
    New York Times page 13, Aug 13, 1943
    Newsweek 22:86, Aug 23, 1943
    Time 42:64, Aug 23, 1943

Chee-Chee
    book: Lew Fields
    music: Richard Rodgers
    lyrics: Lorenz Hart
    staging: Alexander Leftwich and Jack Haskell
Productions:
    Opened September 25, 1928 for 31 performances
Reviews:
    Life (New York) 92:19, Oct 28, 1928
    New York Times page 25, Sep 26, 1928

Cheer Up
    book: R. H. Burnside
    music: Raymond Hubbell
    lyrics: John L. Golden
    staging: R. H. Burnside
Productions:
    Opened August 23, 1917 for 456 performances
Reviews:
    Dramatic Mirror 77:7, Sep 1, 1917
                77:7, Sep 22, 1917
    Life (New York) 70:424, Sep 13, 1917
    New Republic 13:23, Nov 3, 1917
    New York Dramatic News 64:2, Sep 1, 1917
    New York Times page 9, Aug 24, 1917
               IV, page 5, Sep 2, 1917
    Theatre Magazine 26:242, Oct 1917
               26:287, Nov 1917

Cherry Blossoms
    book: Harry B. Smith, adapted from Benrimo and
               Harrison Rhodes' The Willow Tree
    music: Sigmund Romberg
    lyrics: Harry B. Smith
    staging: Lew Morton
Productions:
    Opened March 28, 1927 for 56 performances

Reviews:
    New York Times page 22, Mar 29, 1927

Chevalier, Maurice   (see Maurice Chevalier)

The Chiffon Girl
        book: George Murray
        music: Carlo and Sanders
        lyrics: Carlo and Sanders
Productions:
    Opened February 19, 1924 for 103 performances
Reviews:
    New York Times page 15, Feb 26, 1924

Chin-Chin
        book: Anne Caldwell and R. H. Burnside
        music: Ivan Caryll
        lyrics: Anne Caldwell and James O'Dea
        staging: R. H. Burnside
Productions:
    Opened October 20, 1914 for 295 performances
Reviews:
    Colliers 54:14-15, Jan 2, 1915
    Dramatic Mirror 72:9, Oct 28, 1914
    Green Book 13:123-4, Jan 1915
    New York Dramatic News 60:17, Oct 13, 1914
    New York Times page 11, Oct 21, 1914
                     VII, page 8, Nov 8, 1914
                     page 13, Jun 2, 1915
                     page 9, Aug 17, 1915
    Theatre Magazine 20:265, Dec 1914
                     20:304, Dec 1914
                     21:238-9, May 1915
                     21:305, Jun 1915

Chinese Love
        book: Clare Kummer
        staging: W. L. Gilmore
Productions:
    Opened February 28, 1921 for 5 matinees
Reviews:
    Dramatic Mirror 83:408+, Mar 5, 1921
    New York Times page 18, Mar 1, 1921
    Theatre Magazine 33:342, May 1921

The Chocolate Dandies
        book: Noble Sissle and Lew Payton
        music: Noble Sissle and Eubie Blake
        lyrics: Noble Sissle and Eubie Blake
Productions:
    Opened September 1, 1924 for 96 performances
Reviews:
    New York Times page 22, Sept 2, 1924

Theatre Magazine 40:70, Nov 1924

Christine
    book: Pearl S. Buck and Charles K. Peck, Jr.,
                        adapted from Hilda Wernher's My Indian Family
    music: Sammy Fain
    lyrics: Paul Francis Webster
    sets: Jo Mielziner
    costumes: Alvin Colt
    choreography: Hanya Holm
Productions:
    Opened April 28, 1960 for 12 performances
Reviews:
    America 103:267; May 14, 1960
    New York Theatre Critics' Reviews 1960:272+
    New York Times page 27, Apr 29, 1960
    New Yorker 36:114+, May 7, 1960
    Saturday Review 43:28, May 14, 1960
    Time 75:56, May 9, 1960

Christmas Rappings
    text: Al Carmines, adapted from the New Testament
    music: Al Carmines
    staging: Al Carmines
Productions:
    (Off-Off-Broadway) Opened December 15, 1972 (Judson Poets'
        Theatre)
    (Off-Broadway) Season of 1971-1972 (Judson Poets' Theatre)
Reviews:
    New York Times page 22, Dec 18, 1971

Chu Chin Chow
    book: Oscar Asche
    music: Frederick Norton
    staging: E. Lyle Swete
Productions:
    Opened October 22, 1917 for 208 performances
Reviews:
    Dramatic Mirror 77:7, Nov 3, 1917
                    77:4, Dec 29, 1917
    Green Book 19:12-16, Jan 1918
    Hearst 33:118-20+, Feb 1918
    Nation 103:448, Nov 9, 1916
    New York Dramatic News 64:7, Oct 27, 1917
    New York Times page 14, Oct 23, 1917
                    VIII, page 6, Oct 28, 1917
    Theatre Magazine 26:198+, Oct 1917
                    27:337, Dec 1917
                    27:392, Dec 1917
                    41:36+, May 1925

Cinderella on Broadway
    book: Harold Atteridge

    music: Bert Grant and Al Goodman
    staging: J. C. Huffman
Productions:
    Opened June 24, 1920 for 126 performances
Reviews:
    Dramatic Mirror page 9, Jul 3, 1920
    New York Clipper 68:19, Jun 30, 1920
    New York Times page 18, Jun 25, 1920
    Theatre Magazine 32:106, Sep 1920

Cinders
    book: Edward Clark
    music: Rudolf Friml
    lyrics: Edward Clark
    staging: Edward Royce
Productions:
    Opened April 3, 1923 for 31 performances
Reviews:
    New York Clipper 71:14, Apr 11, 1923
    New York Times page 22, Apr 4, 1923

Cindy
    book: Joe Sauter and Mike Sawyer
    music: Johnny Brandon
    lyrics: Johnny Brandon
    staging: Marvin Gordon
    sets: Robert T. Williams
    costumes: Patricia Quinn Stuart
    choreography: Marvin Gordon
Productions:
    (Off-Broadway) Opened March 19, 1964 for 110 performances
    (Off-Broadway) Opened September 24, 1964 for 94 performances
    (Off-Broadway) Opened January 19, 1965 for 114 performances
Reviews:
    New York Times page 24, Mar 20, 1964
                    page 33, Sep 25, 1964
    New Yorker 40:136, Mar 28, 1964

The Circus Princess
    music: Emmerich Kalman
    staging: J. C. Huffman
Productions:
    Opened April 25, 1927 for 192 performances
Reviews:
    Bookman 65:576, Jul 1927
    Life (New York) 89:23, May 19, 1927
    Theatre Magazine 46:20, Jul 1927
    Vanity Fair 28:76, Jun 1927
    Vogue 69:100, Jun 15, 1927

The City Chap
    book: James Montgomery, adapted from Winchell
                        Smith's The Fortune Hunter

music: Jerome Kern
lyrics: Anne Caldwell
staging: R. H. Burnside
Productions:
Opened October 26, 1925 for 72 performances
Reviews:
New York Times page 21, Oct 27, 1925

City of Light
conceived: John Dodd
music: John Herbert McDowell and Terence Thomas
staging: John Dodd
Productions:
(Off-Off-Broadway) Opened January 5, 1973 (La Mama Experimental Theater Club)
No Reviews.

The Clinging Vine
book: Zelda Sears
music: Harold Levey
staging: Ira Hards
Productions:
Opened December 25, 1922 for 184 performances
Reviews:
New York Clipper 70:20, Jan 3, 1923
New York Times page 20, Dec 25, 1922
                VII, page 1, Dec 31, 1922
Theatre Arts 32:40, Fall 1948
Theatre Magazine 37:19, Mar 1928
                40:24, Sep 1924
Woman's Home Companion 51:48, Feb 1924

El Coca-Cola Grande (see El Grande de Coca-Cola)

Coco
book: Alan Jay Lerner
music: Andre Previn
lyrics: Alan Jay Lerner
staging: Michael Benthall
sets: Cecil Beaton
costumes: Cecil Beaton
choreography: Michael Bennett
Productions:
Opened December 18, 1969 for 332 performances
Reviews:
America 122:54-5, Jan 17, 1970
Commonweal 91:558-9, Feb 20, 1970
Dance Magazine 44:84-5, Mar 1970
                44:72-8, Feb 1970
Life 68:12, Jan 30, 1970
Nation 210:61, Jan 19, 1970
National Review 22:370-1, Apr 7, 1970
New York Theatre Critics' Reviews 1969:151

The Cocoanuts 83

New York Times page 28, Aug 6, 1969
                page 52, Oct 14, 1969
                page 36, Oct 15, 1969
                page 50, Nov 25, 1969
                page 59, Dec 19, 1969
                page 66, Dec 19, 1969
                II, page 1, Dec 28, 1969
                page 38, Jul 16, 1970
                page 28, Aug 7, 1970
                page 52, Oct 1, 1970
New Yorker 45:38, Dec 27, 1969
Newsweek 74:75-9, Nov 10, 1969
          74:58, Dec 29, 1969
Saturday Review 53:88, Jan 10, 1970
Time 94:86-7, Nov 7, 1969
     94:35, Dec 26, 1969

The Cocoanuts
     book: George S. Kaufman
     music: Irving Berlin
     lyrics: Irving Berlin
     staging: Sammy Lee and Oscar Eagle
Productions:
     Opened December 8, 1925 for 377 performances
Reviews:
     Dial 80:166-7, Feb 1926
     New York Times page 30, Dec 9, 1925
                     IX, page 1, Dec 13, 1925
                     VIII, page 1, Apr 18, 1926
                     page 27, May 17, 1927
     Vogue 67:61+, Feb 1, 1926

The Cohan Revue of 1916
     book: George M. Cohan
     music: George M. Cohan
     lyrics: George M. Cohan
     staging: George M. Cohan
     choreography: James Gorman
Productions:
     Opened February 9, 1916 for 165 performances
Reviews:
     Dramatic Mirror 75:8, Feb 19, 1916
                     75:2, Feb 26, 1916
                     75:2, Mar 4, 1916
     Green Book 15:658+, Apr 1916
     Harper's Weekly 62:206, Feb 26, 1916
     Life (New York) 67:352-3, Feb 24, 1916
     Munsey 58:314, Jul 1916
     New York Dramatic News 62:17, Feb 19, 1916
     New York Times page 9, Feb 10, 1916
                     II, page 7, Feb 20, 1916
     Theatre Magazine 23:124, Mar 1916
                      23:164, Mar 1916

The Cohan Revue of 1918
        book: George M. Cohan
        music: Irving Berlin and George M. Cohan
        lyrics: Irving Berlin and George M. Cohan
        staging: George M. Cohan
        choreography: Jack Mason and James Gorman
Productions:
    Opened December 31, 1917 for 96 performances
Reviews:
    Dramatic Mirror 78:7, Jan 12, 1918
    New York Times page 15, Jan 1, 1918
                    IV, page 6, Jan 27, 1918
    Theatre Magazine 27:87, Feb 1918
                    27:137, Mar 1918
                    27:235, Apr 1918

Cole Porter   (see The Decline and Fall of the Entire World as
    Seen through the Eyes of Cole Porter) (Also see New Cole
    Porter Revue)

Colette
        book: Elinor Jones; adapted from Earthly Paradise,
                           the Robert Phelps collection of Colette's auto-
                           biographical writings
        music: Harvey Schmidt
        lyrics: Tom Jones
        staging: Gerald Freedman
        sets: David Mitchell
        costumes: Theoni V. Aldredge
Productions:
    (Off-Broadway) Opened May 6, 1970 for 101 performances
    (Off-Broadway) Opened October 14, 1970 for 7 performances
Reviews:
    New York Theatre Critics' Reviews 1970:228
    New York Times page 60, May 7, 1970
                    II, page 1, May 17, 1970
                    page 34, Jun 2, 1970
                    page 58, Oct 15, 1970
                    page 40, Oct 21, 1970

Comden, Betty   (see A Party with Betty Comden and Adolph Green)

Come Along
        book: Bide Dudley
        music: John L. Nelson
        lyrics: John L. Nelson
        staging: Edward Royce
Productions:
    Opened April 8, 1919 for 47 performances
Reviews:
    New York Times page 9, Apr 9, 1919
    Theatre Magazine 29:276+, May 1919

Come Summer

book:	Will Holt; based on Rainbow on the Road by Esther Forbes
music:	David Baker
lyrics:	Will Holt
staging:	Agnes de Mille
sets:	Oliver Smith
costumes:	Stanley Simmons
choreography:	Milton Rosenstock

Productions:
Opened March 18, 1969 for 7 performances
Reviews:
New York Theatre Critics' Reviews 1969:319
New York Times page 43, Mar 19, 1969
           page 43, Mar 21, 1969
New Yorker 45:99, Mar 29, 1969

Come to Bohemia

book:	George S. Chappell
music:	Kenneth M. Murchinson
lyrics:	George S. Chappell
staging:	Jacques Coini

Productions:
Opened April 27, 1916 for 20 performances
Reviews:
Dramatic Mirror 75:8, May 6, 1916
                75:2, May 20, 1916
Life (New York) 67:602-3, May 11, 1916
New York Dramatic News 62:7, May 6, 1916
Theatre Magazine 23:329, Jun 1916
                  23:366, Jun 1916

Comedy in Music (Victor Borge's One-Man Show)

material:	Victor Borge

Productions:
Opened October 2, 1953 for 849 performances
Reviews:
American Magazine 158:50, Sep 1954
Catholic World 178:230, Dec 1953
Commonweal 59:119, Nov 6, 1953
Coronet 35:29-34, Apr 1954
Cosmopolitan 137:110-17, Oct 1954
Etude 73:9+, Feb 1955
Holiday 16:56-7, Sep 1954
House and Garden 106:116-17+, Dec 1954
Life 35:87, Dec 7, 1953
Nation 177:337-8, Oct 24, 1953
New York Times page 15, Oct 3, 1953
           page 10, Oct 1, 1955
New Yorker 29:34-5, Nov 7, 1953
Newsweek 41:94, Mar 23, 1953
          44:82, Oct 4, 1954
Saturday Review 36:37, Oct 17, 1953

37:5-8, Apr 24, 1954
Theatre Arts 37:17, Dec 1953
Time 62:49, Oct 12, 1953

Comedy in Music, Opus 2
     created: Victor Borge
     sets: Ralph Alswang
Productions:
     Opened November 9, 1964 for 192 performances
Reviews:
     America 111:758, Dec 5, 1964
     Commonweal 81:354, Dec 4, 1964
     New York Theatre Critics' Reviews 1964:164
     New York Times II, page 3, Nov 8, 1964
                   page 54, Nov 10, 1964
     Saturday Review 48:32, Jan 2, 1965
     Time 84:81, Nov 20, 1964

Company
     book: George Furth
     music: Stephen Sondheim
     lyrics: Stephen Sondheim
     staging: Harold Prince
     sets: Boris Aronson
     costumes: D. D. Ryan
     choreography: Michael Bennett
Productions:
     Opened April 26, 1970 for 705 performances
Reviews:
     America 122:568, May 23, 1970
     Commentary 51:79, Feb 1971
     Dance Magazine 44:85-6+, Jun 1970
     Life 68:20, Jun 26, 1970
     National Review 22:905-6, Aug 25, 1970
     Nation 210:572-3, May 11, 1970
     New Republic 162:20, May 23, 1970
     New York Theatre Critics' Reviews 1970:260
     New York Times page 40, Apr 27, 1970
                  page 50, Apr 28, 1970
                  II, page 1, May 3, 1970
                  II, page 1, May 10, 1970
                  page 31, Jul 29, 1970
                  II, page 21, Nov 1, 1970
                  II, page 1, Jun 27, 1971
                  page 21, Dec 29, 1971
                  page 22, Jan 24, 1972
     New Yorker 46:83, May 22, 1970
     Newsweek 75:79, May 11, 1970
     Saturday Review 53:4-5, May 9, 1970
     Time 95:62, May 11, 1970

A Connecticut Yankee
     book: Herbert Fields, adapted from Mark Twain's

                              novel A Connecticut Yankee in King Arthur's
                              Court
      music: Richard Rodgers
      lyrics: Lorenz Hart
      staging: Alexander Leftwich
Productions:
      Opened November 3, 1927 for 418 performances
      Opened November 17, 1943 for 135 performances
Reviews:
      Catholic World 158:395, Jun 1944
      Life (New York) 90:23, Nov 24, 1927
      New York Theatre Critics' Reviews 1943:219+
      New York Times VIII, page 1, Oct 9, 1927
                        page 24, Nov 4, 1927
                        VIII, page 2, Jun 10, 1928
                        page 30, Nov 18, 1943
                        II, page 1, Nov 21, 1943
      Theatre Arts 28:17-18, Jan 1944
      Theatre Magazine 47:49, Feb 1928

The Conquering Hero
      book: Larry Gelbart, based on Preston Sturges'
                              Hail, The Conquering Hero
      music: Moose Charlap
      lyrics: Norman Gimbel
      sets: Jean Rosenthal and William Pitkin
      costumes: Patton Campbell
Productions:
      Opened January 16, 1961 for 8 performances
Reviews:
      New York Theatre Critics' Reviews 1961:388+
      New York Times page 40, Jan 17, 1961
                        page 29, Jan 18, 1961
      New Yorker 36:64, Jan 28, 1961

The Consul
      book: Gian-Carlo Menotti
      music: Gian-Carlo Menotti
      lyrics: Gian-Carlo Menotti
      staging: Gian-Carlo Menotti
      sets: Horace Armistead
      costumes: Grace Houston
      choreography: John Butler
Productions:
      Opened March 15, 1950 for 269 performances
      Opened March 17, 1966 for 3 performances
      Opened October 6, 1966 for 2 performances
Reviews:
      Catholic World 171:148, May 1950
      Christian Science Monitor Magazine page 5, Mar 25, 1950
      Commonweal 51:677, Apr 7, 1950
      Life 28:61-3, Apr 10, 1950
      Musical America 70:7, Mar 1950

                          71:90, Apr 1951
                          71:6, Oct 1951
                          72:12, Jul 1952
Musical Quarterly 36:447-50, Jul 1950
Nation 170:305, Apr 1, 1950
          170:557-8, Jun 3, 1950
New Republic 122:21-2, Apr 10, 1950
New York Theatre Critics' Reviews 1950:329+
New York Times page 32, Mar 2, 1950
                          II, page 1, Mar 12, 1950
                          page 41, Mar 16, 1950
                          II, page 1, Mar 26, 1950
                          II, page 7, Apr 2, 1950
                          II, page 1, May 21, 1950
                          page 24, Jan 23, 1951
                          II, page 7, Jan 28, 1951
                          page 26, Feb 8, 1951
                          page 9, Sep 8, 1951
                          page 40, Oct 9, 1952
                          page 41, Oct 30, 1952
                          page 30, Apr 17, 1953
New Yorker 26:54+, Mar 25, 1950
                  28:149, Oct 18, 1952
Saturday Review 33:28-30, Apr 22, 1950
School and Society 72:183, Sep 16, 1950
Theatre Arts 34:28-9, Mar 1950
                  34:17, May 1950

Continental Varieties
      material: A. Selwyn and H. B. Franklin
Productions:
      Opened October 3, 1934 for 77 performances
Reviews:
      New York Times page 18, Oct 4, 1934
                          page 24, Nov 15, 1934
      Stage 12:9-10, Nov 1934

The Contrast
      book: Anthony Stimac; based on the play by Royall
                        Tyler
      music: Don Pippin
      lyrics: Steve Brown
      staging: Anthony Stimac
      sets: David Chapman
      costumes: Robert Pusilo
      choreography: Bill Guske
Productions:
      (Off-Broadway) Opened November 28, 1972 for 24 performances
Reviews:
      Nation 215:637, Dec 18, 1972
      New York Times page 51, Nov 28, 1972
                          II, page 7, Dec 24, 1972

Cooler Near the Lake
      music: Fred Kaz
      staging: Barnard Sahlins
      choreography: Mel Spinney
Productions:
    (Off-Broadway) Opened February 7, 1971 for 26 performances
No Reviews.

Copper and Brass
      book: Ellen Violett and David Craig
      music: David Baker
      lyrics: David Craig
      staging: Marc Daniels
      sets: William and Jean Eckart
      costumes: Alvin Colt
      choreography: Anna Sokolow
Productions:
    Opened October 17, 1957 for 36 performances
Reviews:
    Dance Magazine 31:13, Dec 1957
    Nation 185:310, Nov 2, 1957
    New York Theatre Critics' Reviews 1957:216+
    New York Times VI, page 20, Aug 25, 1957
                  page 19, Oct 18, 1957
    New Yorker 33:98-100, Oct 26, 1957
    Theatre Arts 41:26-7, Dec 1957
    Time 70:92, Oct 28, 1957

Corn
      book: Charles Ludlam
      music: Virgil Young
      lyrics: Virgil Young
      staging: Charles Ludlam
Productions:
    (Off-Off-Broadway) Opened November 23, 1972 (The Ridiculous
    Theatrical Co.)
Reviews:
    New York Times page 43, Nov 24, 1972

Cosmo Vanities (see Belmont Varieties)

Count Me In
      book: Walter Kerr, Leo Brady, Nancy Hamilton
      music: Ann Ronell and Will Irwin
      lyrics: Walter Kerr, Leo Brady, Nancy Hamilton
      staging: Robert Ross
      sets: Howard Bay
      costumes: Irene Sharaff
      choreography: Robert Alton
Productions:
    Opened October 8, 1942 for 61 performances
Reviews:
    New York Theatre Critics' Reviews 1942:214+

90 The Count of Luxembourg

New York Times page 24, Oct 9, 1942
Newsweek 20:76, Oct 19, 1942
Theatre Arts 26:742, Dec 1942

The Count of Luxembourg
    book: Glen MacDonough, adapted from the original of
                        Willner and Bodansky
    music: Franz Lehar
    lyrics: Adrian Ross and Basil Hood
    staging: Herbert Gresham
Productions:
    Opened September 16, 1912 for 120 performances
    Opened February 17, 1930 for 16 performances
Reviews:
    Blue Book 16:474-7, Jan 1913
    Dramatic Mirror 68:7, Sep 18, 1912
                  68:2, Oct 9, 1912
    Green Book 8:936-8+, Dec 1912
    Harper's Weekly 56:21, Oct 12, 1912
    Munsey 48:353, Nov 1912
    New York Dramatic News 56:19, Aug 31, 1912
                       56:13, Sep 21, 1912
                       57:29, Dec 28, 1912
    New York Times page 28, Feb 18, 1930
    Red Book 20:508-12, Jan 1913
    Theatre Magazine 16:xiii-iv, Oct 1912
                 16:157, Nov 1912
                 51:74, Apr 1930

Countess Maritza
    book: Harry B. Smith, adapted from the original of
                        Julius Brammer and Alfred Grunwald
    music: Emmerich Kalman
    lyrics: Harry B. Smith
    staging: J. J. Shubert
Productions:
    Opened September 18, 1926 for 318 performances
    Opened April 9, 1928 for 16 performances
Reviews:
    Life (New York) 88:23, Oct 27, 1916
    Nation 23:330, Oct 6, 1926
    New York Times page 28, Sep 19, 1926
                   page 21, Sep 20, 1926
                   page 32, Apr 10, 1928
    Theatre Magazine 44:15+, Nov 1926
    Vanity Fair 27:56, Nov 1926
    Vogue 68:110, Nov 15, 1926

A Country Girl
    book: James T. Tanner
    lyrics: Adrian Ross; additional lyrics and numbers by
                        Paul Rubens
Productions:

Opened May 29, 1911 for 32 performances
Reviews:
    Blue Book 13:905-7, Sep 1911
    Dramatic Mirror 65:7, Jun 7, 1911
                  65:9, Jun 14, 1911
                  65:4, Jun 21, 1911
    Green Book Album 6:237-40, Aug 1911
    New York Times page 11, May 30, 1911
    Red Book 17:765-8, Aug 1911
    Theatre Magazine 14:iii, Jul 1911

Courtin' Time
    book: William Roos, based on Eden Phillpott's play
                      The Farmer's Wife
    music: Don Walker
    lyrics: Jack Lawrence
    staging: Alfred Drake
    sets: Ralph Alswang
    costumes: Saul Bolsani
    choreography: George Balanchine
Productions:
    Opened June 13, 1951 for 37 performances
Reviews:
    Catholic World 173:386-7, Aug 1951
    Commonweal 54:285, Jun 29, 1951
    Nation 172:594, Jun 23, 1951
    New York Theatre Critics' Reviews 1951:254+
    New York Times page 30, Jun 14, 1951
                  II, page 1, Jun 17, 1951
                  II, page 1, Jul 1, 1951
                  II, page 9, Jul 1, 1951
    New Yorker 27:45, Jun 23, 1951
    Newsweek 37:72, Jun 25, 1951
    Theatre Arts 35:6, Sep 1951
    Time 57:73, Jun 25, 1951

Coward, Noel (see Noel Coward)

The Cowgirl and the Tiger
    book: Wallace Gray
    music: Hank Beebe
    lyrics: Hank Beebe
    staging: Howard Lipson
Productions:
    (Off-Off-Broadway) Opened 1973-1974 (Thirteenth Street
    Repertory Co.)
No Reviews.

The Cradle Will Rock
    book: Marc Blitzstein
    music: Marc Blitzstein
    lyrics: Marc Blitzstein
    staging: Marc Blitzstein

Productions:
    Opened January 3, 1938 for 108 performances
    (Off-Broadway) Season of 1936-37
    (Off-Broadway) Season of 1937-38 for 19 performances
    (Off-Broadway) Season of 1938-39 for one performance
    (Off-Broadway) Opened January 15, 1939
    Opened November 24, 1947 for 2 performances
    Opened December 26, 1947 for 21 performances
    (Off-Broadway) Season of 1959-60
    (Off-Broadway) Opened November 8, 1964 for 82 performances
Reviews:
    Catholic World 146:598-9, Feb 1938
    Commonweal 47:350, Jan 16, 1948
    Current History 48:53, Apr 1938
    Forum 109:156, Mar 1948
    Literary Digest 125:34, Jan 1, 1938
    Magazine of Art 32:356-7+, Jun 1939
    Nation 146:107, Jan 22, 1938
        190:236, Mar 12, 1960
    New Republic 93:310, Jan 19, 1938
        117:35-6, Dec 22, 1947
    New York Theatre Critics' Reviews 1947:229+
    New York Times page 19, Dec 6, 1937
               page 19, Jan 4, 1938
               II, page 7, Nov 23, 1947
               page 38, Nov 25, 1947
               II, page 9, Feb 7, 1960
               page 23, Feb 12, 1960
               II, page 9, Feb 21, 1960
               page 40, Nov 9, 1964
               page 35, Jan 6, 1965
    New Yorker 23:45, Jan 10, 1948
        36:142-3, Feb 20, 1960
    Newsweek 10:20-1, Jul 3, 1937
        30:78, Dec 7, 1948
        64:102, Nov 23, 1964
    Reporter 30:46+, May 21, 1964
    Saturday Review 31:22-4, Jan 17, 1948
    Scribner's Magazine 103:70-1, Mar 1938
    Stage 15:54, Feb 1938
    Theatre Arts 22:98-9, Feb 1938
    Time 29:46+, Jun 28, 1937
        30:57, Dec 13, 1937
        51:64, Jan 5, 1948

Cranks
    book: John Cranko
    music: John Addison
    lyrics: John Cranko
    staging: John Cranko
Productions:
    Opened November 26, 1956 for 40 performances
Reviews:

Christian Century 74:172, Feb 6, 1957
Nation 183:526, Dec 15, 1956
New York Theatre Critics' Reviews 1956:185+
New York Times page 23, May 14, 1956
                page 32, Nov 27, 1956
New Yorker 32:90-1, Dec 8, 1956
          32:25, Dec 15, 1956
Saturday Review 39:26, Dec 15, 1956
Theatre Arts 41:19, Feb 1957
Time 68:70, Dec 10, 1956

Crazy Now
    book: Richard Smithies and Maura Cavanagh
    music: Norman Sachs
    lyrics: Richard Smithies and Maura Cavanagh
    staging: Voight Kempson
    choreography: Voight Kempson
Productions:
    (Off-Broadway) Opened September 17, 1972 for 1 performance
Reviews:
    New York Times page 45, Sep 11, 1972

Crazy Quilt   (see Billy Rose's Crazy Quilt)

Crazy with the Heat
    sketches: Sam E. Werris, Arthur Sheekman, Mack Davis,
                     Max Liebman, Don Herold
    music: Irvin Graham, Dana Suesse, Rudi Revil
    lyrics: Irvin Graham, Dana Suesse, Rudi Revil
    staging: Kurt Kasznar
    sets: Albert Johnson
    costumes: Lester Polakov and Marie Humans
    choreography: Catherine Littlefield
Productions:
    Opened January 14, 1941 for 99 performances
Reviews:
    Catholic World 152:728, Mar 1941
    Nation 152:137, Feb 1, 1941
    New York Theatre Critics' Reviews 1941:410+
    New York Times page 18, Jan 15, 1941
                    page 25, Jan 16, 1941
                    page 15, Jan 31, 1941
    Theatre Arts 25:257+, Apr 1941

The Crinoline Girl
    book: Otto Harbach
    music: Percy Wenrich
    lyrics: Julian Eltinge
    staging: John Emerson
Productions:
    Opened March 16, 1914 for 88 performances
Reviews:
    Dramatic Mirror 71:6, Mar 18, 1914

71:2, Apr 1, 1914
Green Book 11:976, Jun 1914
11:1019-20, Jun 1914
New York Dramatic News 59:14, Mar 21, 1914
New York Times page 11, Mar 17, 1914
Theatre Magazine 19:227, May 1914
19:240, May 1914

Criss Cross
book: Otto Harbach and Anne Caldwell
music: Jerome Kern
lyrics: Otto Harbach and Anne Caldwell
staging: R. H. Burnside
Productions:
Opened October 12, 1926 for 206 performances
Reviews:
New York Times page 20, Oct 13, 1926

Croesus and the Witch
music: Micki Grant; based on a fable
lyrics: Micki Grant
staging: Vinnette Carroll
sets: Richard A. Miller
choreography: Talley Beatty
Productions:
(Off-Broadway) Opened August 24, 1971 (Urban Arts Corps.)
Reviews:
New York Times page 18, Aug 27, 1971
New Yorker 47:54, Sep 4, 1971

Cross My Heart
book: Daniel Kusell
music: Harry Tierney
lyrics: Joseph McCarthy
staging: Sammy Lee
Productions:
Opened September 17, 1928 for 64 performances
Reviews:
New York Times page 32, Sep 18, 1928
Theatre Magazine 48:48, Nov 1928

The Crucible
book: Based on the play by Arthur Miller
music: Robert Ward
lyrics: Bernard Stambler
words: Bernard Stambler
staging: Allen Fletcher
sets: Paul Sylbert
costumes: Ruth Morley
Productions:
(Off-Broadway) Opened October 26, 1961 for 3 performances
No Reviews.

Cry For Us All
    book: William Alfred and Albert Marre; based on
                     William Alfred's play Hogan's Goat
    music: Mitch Leigh
    lyrics: William Alfred and Phyllis Robinson
    staging: Albert Marre
    sets: Howard Bay
    costumes: Robert Fletcher
    choreography: Todd Bolender
Productions:
    Opened April 8, 1970 for 9 performances
Reviews:
    New York Theatre Critics' Reviews 1970:304
    New York Times page 48, Apr 9, 1970
    New Yorker 46:79-80, Apr 18, 1970
    Time 95:51, Apr 20, 1970

The Crystal Heart
    book: William Archibald
    music: Baldwin Bergersen
    lyrics: William Archibald
    staging: William Archibald
    sets: Richard Casler
    costumes: Ted Van Griethuysen
    choreography: William Archibald
Productions:
    (Off-Broadway) Opened February 15, 1960 for 9 performances
Reviews:
    New York Times page 31, Feb 16, 1960
                   page 40, Feb 24, 1960
    New Yorker 36:104-6, Feb 27, 1960

Curley McDimple
    book: Mary Boylan and Robert Dahdah
    music: Robert Dahdah
    lyrics: Robert Dahdah
    staging: Robert Dahdah
    sets: Richard Jackson
    costumes: John Hirsch
    choreography: Larry Stevens
Productions:
    (Off-Broadway) Opened November 22, 1967 for 931 performances
Reviews:
    New York Times page 59, Nov 23, 1967
                   page 52, May 9, 1968
                   page 53, Nov 14, 1968
                   page 53, Nov 25, 1969

Cybele
    book: Mario Fratti; based on Sundays and Cybele
    music: Paul Dick
    lyrics: Paul Dick
    staging: Amy Saltz

Productions:
    (Off-Broadway)   Opened 1971-1972 (The Workshop of the Play-
    ers' Art)
No Reviews.

Cyrano
    book: Anthony Burgess; adapted from Edmund Ros-
                         tand's Cyrano de Bergerac
    music: Michael J. Lewis
    lyrics: Anthony Burgess
    staging: Michael Kidd
    sets: John Jenson
    costumes: Desmond Heeley
Productions:
    Opened May 13, 1973 for 49 performances
Reviews:
    America 128:538, Jun 9, 1973
    Harper's 106:153, Mar 1973
             106:98+, Apr 1973
    Nation 216:731, Jun 4, 1973
    New York Theatre Critics' Reviews 1973:272
    New York Times page 37, May 14, 1973
                    page 52, May 17, 1973
                    II, page 1, May 20, 1973
    New Yorker 49:54, May 26, 1973
    Newsweek 81:83, May 28, 1973
    Time 101:55, May 28, 1973

                              - D -

Daffy Dill
    book: Guy Bolton and Oscar Hammerstein II
    music: Herbert Stothart
    lyrics: Oscar Hammerstein II
    staging: Julian Mitchell
Productions:
    Opened August 22, 1922 for 71 performances
Reviews:
    New York Clipper 70:20, Aug 30, 1922
    New York Times page 14, Aug 23, 1922
    Theatre Magazine 36:228, Oct 1922

Dakota
    book: Tom Hill
    music: Frances Ziffer, Hortense Belson and Hardy
                         Wieder
Productions:
    (Off-Broadway)   Opened 1952-1953 (Originals Only)
No Reviews.

Dames at Sea
    book: George Haimsohn and Robin Miller

music: Jim Wise
lyrics: George Haimsohn and Robin Miller
staging: Neal Kenyon
sets: Peter Harvey
costumes: Peter Harvey
choreography: Neal Kenyon
Productions:
   (Off-Broadway) Opened December 20, 1968 for 575 performances
   (Off-Broadway) Opened September 23, 1970 for 170 per-
    formances
Reviews:
   Commonweal 89:735-6, Mar 14, 1969
   Dance Magazine 43:70-1, Mar 1969
   Life 66:8, Mar 7, 1969
   Nation 208:109, Feb 10, 1969
   New York Theatre Critics' Reviews 1968:126
   New York Times page 46, Dec 21, 1968
             II, page 1, Jan 5, 1969
             II, page 3, Feb 9, 1969
             page 24, Aug 29, 1969
             page 46, Jan 5, 1970
             page 44, Aug 27, 1970
             page 60, Sep 24, 1970
   New Yorker 44:60-1, Jan 4, 1969
   Newsweek 73:86, Jan 13, 1969
   Saturday Review 52:74, Jan 11, 1969
   Time 93:65, Jan 3, 1969

Damn Yankees
   book: George Abbott and Douglass Wallop, based on
               Douglass Wallop's novel The Year the Yankees
               Lost the Pennant
   music: Richard Adler and Jerry Ross
   lyrics: Richard Adler and Jerry Ross
   staging: George Abbott
   sets: William and Jean Eckart
   costumes: William and Jean Eckart
   choreography: Bob Fosse
Productions:
   Opened May 5, 1955 for 1,019 performances
   (Off-Broadway) Season of 1966-67 for 14 performances
    (Equity Theatre)
Reviews:
   America 93:278, Jun 4, 1955
   Catholic World 181:307, Jul 1955
   Commonweal 62:329, Jul 1, 1955
   Life 38:163-71, May 16, 1955
   Look 19:64+, Jul 12, 1955
   Nation 180:449, May 21, 1955
   New York Theatre Critics' Reviews 1955:310+
   New York Times VI, page 67, Apr 17, 1955
             II, page 1, May 1, 1955
             page 17, May 6, 1955

II, page 1, Apr 1, 1956
II, page 1, May 13, 1956
page 15, Mar 29, 1957
New York Times Magazine page 67, Apr 17, 1955
New Yorker 31:132+, May 14, 1955
Newsweek 45:96, May 16, 1955
Saturday Review 38:44, May 21, 1955
                    39:12, Sep 15, 1956
Theatre Arts 39:20-2, Jul 1955
Time 65:104, May 16, 1955
Vogue 125:77, May 15, 1955

Dance Me a Song
    sketches: Jimmy Kirkwood and Lee Goodman, George
                     Oppenheimer and Vincente Minnelli, Marya
                     Mannes, Robert Anderson, James Shelton and
                     Wally Cox
    songs: James Shelton, Herman Hupfeld, Albert Hague,
                     Maurice Valency and Bud Gregg
    staging: James Shelton
    sets: Jo Mielziner
    costumes: Irene Sharaff
    choreography: Robert Sidney
Productions:
    Opened January 20, 1950 for 35 performances
Reviews:
    New York Theatre Critics' Reviews 1950:380+
    New York Times page 10, Jan 21, 1950
    New Yorker 25:48, Jan 28, 1950
    Newsweek 35:66, Jan 30, 1950
    Theatre Arts 34:19, Mar 1950
    Time 55:40, Jan 30, 1950

Dancing Around
    dialogue: Harold Atteridge
    music: Sigmund Romberg and Harry Carroll
    lyrics: Harold Atteridge
    staging: J. C. Huffman
    choreography: Jack Mason
Productions:
    Opened October 10, 1914 for 145 performances
Reviews:
    Dramatic Mirror 72:8, Oct 21, 1914
                    72:2, Nov 11, 1914
    Munsey 53:558, Dec 1914
    New York Times III, page 3, Oct 11, 1914
    Theatre Magazine 20:255, Nov 1914
                     20:259, Dec 1914

The Dancing Duchess
    book: C. V. Kerr and R. H. Burnside
    music: Milton Lusk
    lyrics: C. V. Kerr and R. H. Burnside

    staging: R. H. Burnside
Productions:
    Opened August 19, 1914 for 13 performances
Reviews:
    Dramatic Mirror 72:6, Aug 26, 1914
    Green Book 12:901, Nov 1914
    New York Times page 9, Aug 21, 1914
    Theatre Magazine 20:95, Sep 1914

The Dancing Girl
    book: Harold Atteridge
    music: Sigmund Romberg and Alfred Goodman
    lyrics: Harold Atteridge
    staging: J. C. Huffman
Productions:
    Opened January 24, 1923 for 126 performances
Reviews:
    New York Clipper 71:14, Feb 7, 1923
    New York Times page 16, Jan 25, 1923

Dark of the Moon
    book: Howard Richardson and William Berney
    music: Walter Hendl
    staging: Robert E. Perry
    sets: George Jenkins
    choreography: Esther Junger
Productions:
    Opened March 14, 1945 for 320 performances
Reviews:
    Life 17:55-7, Sep 11, 1944
    Musical Courier 132:13, Oct 15, 1945
    Nation 160:370, Mar 31, 1945
    New Republic 112:447, Apr 2, 1945
    New York Theatre Critics' Reviews 1945:252
    New York Times VI, page 24, Mar 11, 1945
                     page 27, Mar 15, 1945
                     II, page 1, Mar 25, 1945
    Newsweek 25:88, Mar 26, 1945
    Player's Magazine 22:14, Nov-Dec 1945
    Theatre Arts 29:262+, May 1945
    Time 45:70, Mar 26, 1945

Darling of the Day
    book: Nunnally Johnson; based on Arnold Bennett's
                      Buried Alive
    music: Jule Styne
    lyrics: E. Y. Harburg
    staging: Noel Willman
    sets: Oliver Smith
    costumes: Raoul Péne du Bois
    choreography: Lee Theodore
Productions:
    Opened January 27, 1968 for 33 performances

Reviews:
  Dance Magazine 42:27-8, Apr 1968
  New York Theatre Critics' Reviews 1968:359
                                    1968:370
  New York Times page 26, Jan 29, 1968
                  II, page 3, Feb 11, 1968
                  page 45, Feb 23, 1968
                  page 42, Feb 26, 1968
  New Yorker 43:77-8, Feb 3, 1968

Darwin's Theories
  book: Darwin Venneri
  music: Darwin Venneri
  lyrics: Darwin Venneri
Productions:
  (Off-Broadway) Season of 1960-1961
Reviews:
  New York Times page 40, Sep 6, 1960
                  page 53, Oct 19, 1960
                  page 28, Oct 21, 1960

The Day Before Spring
  book: Alan Jay Lerner
  music: Frederick Loewe
  lyrics: Alan Jay Lerner
  staging: John C. Wilson
  sets: Robert Davison
  costumes: Miles White
  choreography: Antony Tudor
Productions:
  Opened November 22, 1945 for 165 performances
Reviews:
  Catholic World 162:360, Jan 1946
  Commonweal 43:238, Dec 14, 1945
  Harpers 79:128, Dec 1945
  Life 19:85-6+, Dec 17, 1945
  New York Theatre Critics' Reviews 1945:92+
  New York Times page 27, Nov 23, 1945
                  II, page 1, Dec 2, 1945
  New Yorker 21:52, Dec 1, 1945
  Newsweek 26:92, Dec 3, 1945
  Theatre Arts 30:14, Jan 1946
  Time 46:68, Dec 3, 1945

A Day in the Life of Just About Everyone
  book: Earl Wilson Jr.; additional dialogue by Michael
                 Sawyer
  music: Earl Wilson Jr.
  lyrics: Earl Wilson Jr.
  staging: Tom Panko
  sets: Andrew Greenhut
  costumes: Miles White
Productions:

(Off-Broadway) Opened March 9, 1971 for 8 performances
Reviews:
New York Times page 31, Mar 10, 1971
New Yorker 47:96, Mar 20, 1971

The Deacon and the Lady
book: George Totten Smith
music: Alfred E. Aarons
staging: Alfred E. Aarons
Productions:
Opened October 4, 1910 for 16 performances
Reviews:
Blue Book 12:443-5, Jan 1911
Metropolitan Magazine 33:530, Jan 1911
Theatre Magazine 12:x, Nov 1910

Dear Oscar
book: Caryl Gabrielle Young, based on the life of
               Oscar Wilde
music: Addy O. Fieger
lyrics: Caryl Gabrielle Young
staging: John Allen
sets: William Pitkin
costumes: Mary McKinley
Productions:
Opened November 16, 1972 for 5 performances
Reviews:
New York Theatre Critics' Reviews 1972:179
New York Times page 37, Nov 17, 1972

Dear Sir
book: Edgar Selwyn
music: Jerome Kern
lyrics: Howard Dietz
Productions:
Opened September 23, 1924 for 15 performances
Reviews:
New York Times page 21, Sep 24, 1924

Dear World
book: Jerome Lawrence and Robert E. Lee; based on
               The Madwoman of Chaillot by Jean Giraudoux,
               as adapted by Maurice Valency
music: Jerry Herman
lyrics: Jerry Herman
staging: Joe Layton
sets: Oliver Smith
costumes: Freddy Wittop
choreography: Dorothea Freitage
Productions:
Opened February 6, 1969 for 132 performances
Reviews:

America 120:512, Apr 26, 1969
Christian Century 86:483-4, Apr 9, 1969
Dance Magazine 43:20+, Apr 1969
New York Theatre Critics' Reviews 1969:363
New York Times page 33, Feb 7, 1969
                 II, page 1, Feb 16, 1969
                 II, page 25, May 11, 1969
                 page 19, May 17, 1969
New Yorker 44:90, Feb 15, 1969
Newsweek 73:113, Feb 17, 1969

Dearest Enemy
    book: Herbert Fields
    music: Richard Rodgers
    lyrics: Lorenz Hart
    staging: John Murray Anderson
Productions:
    Opened September 18, 1925 for 286 performances
Reviews:
    Literary Digest 87:31-2, Oct 19, 1925
    New York Times page 9, Sep 19, 1925
    Theatre Magazine 42:44, Dec 1925

The Decameron
    book: Yvonne Tarr, based on Boccaccio
    music: Edward Earle
    lyrics: Yvonne Tarr
Productions:
    (Off-Broadway) Season of 1960-1961
Reviews:
    New York Times page 32, Apr 13, 1961

The Decline and Fall of the Entire World as Seen through the Eyes
    of Cole Porter, revisited
    continuity: Bud McCreery
    songs: Cole Porter
    staging: Ben Bagley
    sets: Shirley Kaplan
    costumes: Charles Fatone
Productions:
    (Off-Broadway) Opened March 30, 1965 for 273 performances
Reviews:
    Life 59:12, Jul 30, 1965
    National Review 17:561, Jun 25, 1965
    New York Times page 24, Mar 31, 1965
                     page 20, Dec 23, 1965
    Newsweek 65:98, Apr 12, 1965
    Saturday Review 48:44, Apr 17, 1965

Deep Harlem
    book: Salem Whitney and Homer Tutt
    music: Joe Jordan
    lyrics: Homer Tutt and Henry Creamer

staging: Henry Creamer
Productions:
   Opened January 7, 1929 for 8 performances
No Reviews.

Deep River
   book: Laurence Stallings
   music: Frank Harling
   lyrics: Laurence Stallings
   staging: Arthur Hopkins
Productions:
   Opened October 4, 1926 for 32 performances
Reviews:
   American Mercury 9:500-01, Dec 1926
   Dial 81:524, Dec 1926
   Life (New York) 88:23, Oct 21, 1926
   Literary Digest 91:26-7, Oct 23, 1926
   Musical Courier 93:24, Oct 14, 1926
   Nation 123:409, Oct 20, 1926
   Theatre Arts 10:814-15, Dec 1926
   Theatre Magazine 44:18, Dec 1926
   Vogue 68:78-9, Dec 15, 1926

A Delightful Season
   book, music
   and lyrics: Don Allan Clayton, based on Oscar Wilde's
                Lady Windermere's Fan
Productions:
   (Off-Broadway) Season of 1960-1961
Reviews:
   New York Times page 30, Sep 29, 1960
                page 49, Oct 4, 1960

Delmar's Revels
   sketches: William K. Wells
   music: Jimmy Monaco, Jesse Greer and Lester Lee
   lyrics: Billy Rose and Ballard MacDonald
   staging: Harry Delmar
Productions:
   Opened November 28, 1927 for 112 performances
No Reviews.

The Desert Song
   book: Otto Harbach, Oscar Hammerstein II, and
                Frank Mandel
   music: Sigmund Romberg
   staging: Arthur Hurley and Robert Connelly
Productions:
   Opened November 30, 1926 for 471 performances
   Opened January 8, 1946 for 45 performances
   Opened September 5, 1973 for 15 performances
Reviews:
   Bookman 65:73-4, Mar 1927

Life (New York) 88:19, Dec 16, 1926
New York Theatre Critics' Reviews 1973:236
New York Times VII, page 1, May 8, 1927
                VIII, page 4, Feb 5, 1928
                II, page 1, Jan 6, 1946
                page 20, Jan 9, 1946
                page 56, Aug 12, 1973
                page 44, Sep 6, 1973
                II, page 1, Sep 16, 1973
                page 38, Sep 19, 1973
New Yorker 21:46, Jan 26, 1946
Newsweek 82:90, Sep 17, 1973
Theatre Magazine 49:28, Feb 1929
Vogue 69:73, Feb 1, 1927

Design for Laughter
    book: William Michkin and John Francis
    music: Alexander Maissel
Productions:
    (Off-Broadway)   Opened November 29, 1944
No Reviews.

Destry Rides Again
    book: Leonard Gershe, based on a story by Max Brand
    music: Harold Rome
    lyrics: Harold Rome
    staging: Michael Kidd
    sets: Oliver Smith
    costumes: Alvin Colt
    choreography: Michael Kidd
Productions:
    Opened April 23, 1959 for 472 performances
Reviews:
    America 101:479, Jun 27, 1959
    Catholic World 189:320, Jul 1959
    Commonweal 70:328, Jun 26, 1959
    Dance Magazine 33:17, Jun 1959
    Life 46:49-54, May 25, 1959
    New Republic 140:20, May 11, 1959
    New York Theatre Critics' Reviews 1959:314+
    New York Times II, page 1, Apr 19, 1959
                    page 24, Apr 24, 1959
                    II, page 1, May 3, 1959
                    page 37, Jun 16, 1960
    New Yorker 35:95-7, May 2, 1959
    Newsweek 53:57, May 4, 1959
    Saturday Review 42:22, May 9, 1959
    Theatre Arts 43:22-4, Jun 1959
                43:9-10, Jul 1959
    Time 73:74, May 4, 1959

The Devil and Daniel Webster
    book: Douglas Moore, based on Stephen Vincent

                          Benet's short story
     music: Douglas Moore
     lyrics: Douglas Moore
     staging: John Houseman
     sets: Robert Edmund Jones
     choreography: Eugene Loring
Productions:
Opened May 18, 1939 for 6 performances
Reviews:
     Commonweal 30:160, Jun 2, 1939
     Life 6:37-8+, Jun 12, 1939
     Musical Courier 119:7, Jun 1, 1939
     New Republic 99:131, Jun 7, 1939
     New York Times page 26, May 19, 1939
                          X, page 1, May 21, 1939
     Newsweek 13:34, Jun 5, 1939
     Saturday Review 20:10, May 20, 1939
                          20:8, May 27, 1939
     Time 33:40, May 29, 1939

Dew Drops Inn
     book: Walter DeLeon and Edward Delaney Dunn
     music: Alfred Goodman
     lyrics: Cyrus Wood
     staging: J. J. Shubert
Productions:
Opened May 17, 1923 for (37) performances
Reviews:
     New York Clipper 71:14, May 23, 1923
     New York Times page 26, May 18, 1923
                          page 12, Jul 31, 1923
     Theatre Magazine 38:16, Jul 1923

Different Times
     book: Michael Brown
     music: Michael Brown
     lyrics: Michael Brown
     staging: Michael Brown
     sets: David Guthrie
     costumes: David Guthrie
     choreography: Tod Jackson
Productions:
Opened May 1, 1972 for 24 performances
Reviews:
     New York Theatre Critics' Reviews 1972:286
     New York Times page 50, May 2, 1972
                          page 19, May 20, 1972

The Difficult Woman
     book: Adapted and translated by Ruth C. Gillespie
                          and Malcolm Stuart Boylan; based on a play by
                          Conrado Nale Roxlo
     music: Dick Frietas

lyrics: Morty Neff and George Mysels; additional ma-
                     terial and dialogue by Maurice Alevy
staging: Maurice Alevy
Productions:
(Off-Broadway) Opened April 25, 1962 for 3 performances
Reviews:
New York Times page 22, Apr 26, 1962

Digging for Apples
    book: James E. Butler and Robert Bowers
    music: James E. Butler and Robert Bowers
    lyrics: James E. Butler and Robert Bowers
    staging: James E. Butler and Robert Bowers
    sets: Gerald E. Proctor
    choreography: Gretchen Vanaken and Bob Cotton
Productions:
(Off-Broadway) Opened September 27, 1962 for 28 performances
Reviews:
New York Times page 29, Sep 28, 1962

Dime A Dozen
    conceived: Julius Monk
    staging: Frank Wagner
    costumes: Donald Brooks
    choreography: Frank Wagner
Productions:
(Off-Broadway) Opened October 18, 1962 for 728 performances
No Reviews.

The Disposal
    book: William Inge
    music: Anthony Caldarella
    lyrics: Judith Gero
    staging: Barry Feinstein
Productions:
(Off-Off-Broadway) Opened September 22, 1973 (Greenwich
    Mews Theater)
No Reviews.

Dixie to Broadway
    book: Walter DeLeon, Tom Howard, Lew Leslie and
                     Sidney Lazarus
    music: George W. Meyer and Arthur Johnstone
    lyrics: Grant Clarke and Roy Turk
Productions:
Opened October 29, 1924 for 77 performances
Reviews:
New York Times page 22, Oct 30, 1924

Do I Hear a Waltz?
    book: Arthur Laurents, based on his play The Time
                     of the Cuckoo
    music: Richard Rodgers

Do It Again!

lyrics:	Stephen Sondheim
staging:	John Dexter
sets:	Beni Montresor
costumes:	Beni Montresor
choreography:	Herbert Ross

Productions:
Opened March 18, 1965 for 220 performances
Reviews:
America 112:590-1, Apr 17, 1965
Commonweal 82:85-6, Apr 9, 1965
Dance Magazine 39:28-9, May 1965
New York Theatre Critics' Reviews 1965:357+
New York Times page 29, Nov 6, 1964
              page 40, Feb 16, 1965
              page 28, Mar 19, 1965
              II, page 1, Mar 28, 1965
New Yorker 41:144, Mar 27, 1965
Newsweek 65:82, Mar 29, 1965
Saturday Review 48:36, Apr 3, 1965
Time 85:60, Mar 26, 1965

Do It Again!

conceived:	Bert Convy
music:	George Gershwin
lyrics:	Ira Gershwin
staging:	Bert Convy
sets:	Barry Arnold

Productions:
(Off-Broadway) Opened February 18, 1971 for 14 performances
Reviews:
New York Times page 27, Feb 19, 1971

Do Re Mi

book:	Garson Kanin
music:	Jule Styne
lyrics:	Betty Comden and Adolph Green
staging:	Garson Kanin
sets:	Boris Aronson
costumes:	Irene Sharaff
choreography:	Marc Breaux and Deedee Wood

Productions:
Opened December 26, 1960 for 400 performances
Reviews:
America 104:549, Jan 21, 1961
Commonweal 73:509, Feb 10, 1961
Coronet 49:16, Apr 1961
Dance Magazine 35:16-17, Feb 1961
Life 50:53-4+, Feb 10, 1961
Nation 192:39, Jan 14, 1961
New York Theatre Critics' Reviews 1960:129+
New York Times II, page 3, Dec 25, 1960
              page 23, Dec 27, 1960
              II, page 1, Jan 8, 1961

                              page 27, Oct 13, 1961
              New Yorker 36:68, Jan 14, 1961
              Newsweek 57:52, Jan 9, 1961
              Saturday Review 44:28, Jan 14, 1961
              Time 77:51, Jan 6, 1961

Dr. DeLuxe
      book: Otto Hauerbach and Karl Hoschna
      staging: Frank Smithson
Productions:
      Opened April 17, 1911 for 32 performances
Reviews:
      Blue Book 13:695-8, Aug 1911
      Dramatic Mirror 65:7, Apr 19, 1911
                        65:2, Apr 26, 1911
                        65:4, May 10, 1911
                        67:31, Jan 31, 1912
      Green Book Album 6:16-18, Jul 1911
      Leslie's Weekly 112:507, May 4, 1911
      Life (New York) 57:286, May 4, 1911
      Red Book 17:572+, Jul 1911
      Theatre Magazine 13:x, May 1911
                        13:144, May 1911

Dr. Magico   (see The Magic Show of Dr. Magico)

Doctor Selavy's Magic Theater (The Mental Cure)
      conceived: Richard Foreman
      music: Stanley Silverman
      lyrics: Tom Hendry
      staging: Richard Foreman
Productions:
      (Off-Broadway) Opened November 23, 1972 for 144 per-
      formances
Reviews:
      High Fidelity 23:ma 27-8, Mar 1973
      Nation 215:597, Dec 11, 1972
      New York Times page 20, Aug 8, 1972
                        II, page 1, Aug 20, 1972
                        page 47, Nov 24, 1972
                        II, page 32, Dec 3, 1972
                        II, page 21, Dec 17, 1972
                        II, page 15, Jan 21, 1973
                        II, page 18, Jan 21, 1973
      New Yorker 48:109, Dec 9, 1972
      Newsweek 80:70, Dec 4, 1972

Doing Our Bit
      dialogue: Harold Atteridge
      music: Sigmund Romberg and Herman Timberg
      lyrics: Harold Atteridge
      staging: J. C. Huffman and J. J. Shubert
Productions:

Opened October 18, 1917 for 130 performances
Reviews:
Dramatic Mirror 77:7, Oct 27, 1917
Green Book 19:5+, Jan 1918
New York Dramatic News 64:7, Oct 27, 1917
New York Times page 11, Oct 19, 1917
Theatre Magazine 26:343, Dec 1917
26:392, Dec 1917

The Doll Girl
book: Leo Stein and A. M. Willner; English version
by Harry B. Smith
music: Leo Fall
Productions:
Opened August 25, 1913 for 88 performances
Reviews:
Dramatic Mirror 70:6, Aug 27, 1913
70:4, Sep 3, 1913
Munsey 50:288-90, Nov 1913
New York Times page 19, Aug 26, 1913
Theatre Magazine 18:xiii, Oct 1913
18:114, Oct 1913

The Dollar Princess
book: Messrs. Willner and Grunbaum; adapted by
George Grossmith Jr.
music: Leo Fall
staging: A. E. Malone
Productions:
Opened September 6, 1909 for 288 performances
Reviews:
American Mercury 70:105, May 1910
Green Book Album 2:1017, Nov 1909
Hampton 23:694-5, Nov 1909
Harper's Weekly 54:24, Apr 30, 1910
Leslie's Weekly 109:318, Sep 20, 1909
110:136, Feb 10, 1910
109:391, Oct 21, 1909
Metropolitan Magazine 31:260-1, Nov 1909
Theatre Magazine 10:xii, Sep 1909
10:157, Oct 1909
10:163, Oct 1909
Vanity Fair 6:198-9, Nov 1909

Donnybrook!
book: Robert E. McEnroe, based on Maurice Walsh's
The Quiet Man
music: Johnny Burke
lyrics: Johnny Burke
staging: Jack Cole
sets: Rouben Ter-Arutunian
costumes: Rouben Ter-Arutunian
choreography: Jack Cole

Productions:
    Opened May 18, 1961 for 68 performances
Reviews:
    America 105:532, Jul 15, 1961
    Dance Magazine 35:20, Jul 1961
    New York Theatre Critics' Reviews 1961:292+
    New York Times II, page 1, May 14, 1961
                    page 23, May 19, 1961
                    II, page 1, May 28, 1961
                    page 26, Jul 10, 1961
                    page 13, Jul 14, 1961
    New Yorker 37:72+, May 27, 1961
    Saturday Review 44:51, Jun 17, 1961
    Theatre Arts 45:9-10, Jul 1961
    Time 77:79, May 26, 1961

Don't Bother Me, I Can't Cope
    conceived: Vinnette Carroll
    songs: Micki Grant and others
    sketches: Micki Grant and others
    staging: Vinnette Carroll
    sets: Richard A. Miller
    costumes: Edna Watson
    choreography: George Faison
Productions:
    Opened April 19, 1972 for 1,065 performances
Reviews:
    America 126:515, May 13, 1972
    Ebony 28:100-2+, Feb 1973
    Nation 214:604, May 8, 1972
    New York Theatre Critics' Reviews 1972:304
    New York Times page 51, Apr 20, 1972
                    II, page 30, Apr 30, 1972
                    II, page 1, May 7, 1972
                    page 147, Dec 3, 1972
    New Yorker 48:104, Apr 29, 1972
    Time 99:75, May 8, 1972

Don't Play Us Cheap!
    book: Melvin Van Peebles
    music: Melvin Van Peebles
    lyrics: Melvin Van Peebles
    staging: Melvin Van Peebles
    sets: Kert Lundell
    costumes: Bernard Johnson
Productions:
    Opened May 16, 1972 for 164 performances
Reviews:
    New York Theatre Critics' Reviews 1972:279
    New York Times page 39, May 17, 1972
                    II, page 1, May 28, 1972
    New Yorker 48:82, May 27, 1972
    Newsweek 79:75, May 29, 1972

Don't Walk on the Clouds
    book: Marvin Gordon
    music: John Aman
    lyrics: John Aman
Productions:
    (Off-Broadway) Season of 1971-1972 (St. Clement's)
Reviews:
    New York Times page 83, Dec 5, 1971

Doodle Dandy of the U.S.A.
    book: Saul Lancourt
    music: Elsie Siegmeister
    staging: Saul Lancourt
    choreography: Elsie Siegmeister
Productions:
    (Off-Broadway) Opened December 26, 1942
Reviews:
    New York Times page 15, Oct 19, 1942
                   page 26, Dec 21, 1942
                   page 36, Dec 27, 1942
                   page 22, Dec 30, 1942
    Newsweek 20:74, Dec 28, 1942

Double Entry (see The Bible Salesman and The Oldest Trick in the
    World)

Down in the Valley
    libretto: Arnold Sundgaard
    music: Kurt Weill
    costumes: Bobb Nichols
Productions:
    (Off-Broadway) Opened Season of 1952-53 (Circle in the Square)
    (Off-Broadway) Opened June 5, 1962 for 16 performances
    (Off-Broadway) Opened April 23, 1965 for 14 performances
        (Equity Library Theatre)
No Reviews.

Drat!
    book: Fred Bluth
    music: Steven Metcalf
    lyrics: Fred Bluth
    staging: Fred Bluth
    sets: Christian Thee
    costumes: Tamianne Wiley
Productions:
    (Off-Broadway) Opened October 18, 1971 for one performance
Reviews:
    New York Times page 53, Oct 19, 1971

Drat! The Cat!
    book: Ira Levin
    music: Milton Schafer
    lyrics: Ira Levin

    staging: Joe Layton
    sets: David Hays
    costumes: Fred Voelpel
    choreography: Joe Layton
Productions:
    Opened October 10, 1965 for 8 performances
Reviews:
    Dance Magazine 39:138, Dec 1965
    New York Theatre Critics' Reviews 1965:319
    New York Times page 54, Oct 11, 1965
    Saturday Review 48:74, Oct 30, 1965

The Dream Girl
    book: Rida Johnson Young and Harold Atteridge
    music: Victor Herbert
    lyrics: Rida Johnson Young and Harold Atteridge
Productions:
    Opened August 20, 1924 for 117 performances
Reviews:
    New York Times page 12, Aug 21, 1924
    Theatre Magazine 40:16, Oct 1924

Dream with Music
    book: Sidney Sheldon, Dorothy Kilgallen, Ben Roberts
    music: Clay Warnick
    lyrics: Edward Eager
    staging: Richard Kollmar
    sets: Stewart Chaney
    costumes: Miles White
    choreography: George Balanchine and Henry LeTang
Productions:
    Opened May 18, 1944 for 28 performances
Reviews:
    Commonweal 40:156, Jun 2, 1944
    Nation 158:688, Jun 10, 1944
    New York Theatre Critics' Reviews 1944:188+
    New York Times page 15, May 19, 1944
    New Yorker 20:40, May 27, 1944
    Newsweek 23:91, May 29, 1944

Dressler, Marie (see Marie Dressler)

The Drunkard
    book: Bro Herrod; based on the play by W. H. S.
                    Smith
    music: Barry Manilow
    lyrics: Barry Manilow
    staging: Bro Herrod
    costumes: Carol Luiken
    choreography: Carveth Wells
Productions:
    (Off-Broadway) Opened April 13, 1970 for 48 performances
Reviews:

New York Times page 54, Apr 14, 1970
New Yorker 46:97, Apr 25, 1970

DuBarry Was a Lady
　　book:　　　　　B. G. DeSylva and Herbert Fields
　　music:　　　　Cole Porter
　　lyrics:　　　　Cole Porter
　　staging:　　　Edgar McGregor
　　sets:　　　　　Raoul Pene duBois
　　costumes:　　Raoul Pene duBois
　　choreography: Robert Alton
Productions:
　　Opened December 6, 1939 for 408 performances
　　(Off-Broadway) Opened May 4, 1972 (Equity Library Theatre)
Reviews:
　　Commonweal 31:227, Dec 29, 1939
　　Life 7:58-63, Dec 11, 1939
　　Nation 149:716, Dec 23, 1939
　　New York Theatre Critics' Reviews 1940:439+
　　New York Times X, page 3, Nov 19, 1939
　　　　　　　　　　　page 34, Dec 7, 1939
　　　　　　　　　　　IX, page 1, Dec 24, 1939
　　　　　　　　　　　page 29, Apr 10, 1941
　　　　　　　　　　　VIII, page 2, Nov 1, 1942
　　　　　　　　　　　page 27, May 12, 1972
　　Newsweek 14:35, Dec 18, 1939
　　Theatre Arts 24:39-49, Jan 1940
　　　　　　　　　24:92-3, Feb 1940
　　Time 34:45, Dec 18, 1939

The Duchess
　　book:　　　　　Joseph Herbert and Harry B. Smith
　　music:　　　　Victor Herbert
　　staging:　　　J. C. Huffman
Productions:
　　Opened October 16, 1911 for 24 performances
Reviews:
　　Dramatic Mirror 66:10, Oct 18, 1911
　　Theatre Magazine 14:xiv, Dec 1911

The Duchess Misbehaves
　　book:　　　　　Gladys Shelly
　　music:　　　　Frank Black
　　lyrics:　　　　Gladys Shelly
　　staging:　　　Martin Manulis
　　sets:　　　　　A. A. Ostrander
　　costumes:　　Willa Kim
　　choreography: George Tapps
Productions:
　　Opened February 13, 1946 for 5 performances
Reviews:
　　New York Theatre Critics' Reviews 1946:456+
　　New York Times page 32, Feb 14, 1946

                    page 10, Feb 16, 1946
     New Yorker 22:44+, Feb 23, 1946

Dude (The Highway Life)
     book: Gerome Ragni
     music: Galt MacDermot
     lyrics: Gerome Ragni
     staging: Tom O'Horgan
     sets: Roger Morgan
     costumes: Randy Barcelo
Productions:
     Opened October 9, 1972 for 16 performances
Reviews:
     Nation 215:410, Oct 30, 1972
     New York Theatre Critics' Reviews 1972:222
     New York Times page 24, Aug 1972
                    page 54, Oct 22, 1972
                    II, page 1, Oct 1972
                    page 39, Oct 26, 1972
                    II, page 7, Nov 12, 1972
     Newsweek 80:111, Oct 30, 1972
     New Yorker 48:30, Sep 23, 1972
                48:76, Oct 21, 1972
     Time 100:81, Oct 23, 1972
     Vogue 160:86-7, Oct 15, 1972

Dynamite Tonite
     libretto: Arnold Weinstein
     music: William Bolcom
     staging: Paul Stills and Arnold Weinstein
     sets: Willa Kim
Productions:
     (Off-Broadway) Opened March 15, 1967 for 7 performances
Reviews:
     Commonweal 86:126, Apr 14, 1967
                86:152-4, Apr 21, 1967
     New York Times page 52, Mar 16, 1967

                         - E -

Earl Carroll Sketch Book (1929)
     book: Eddie Cantor and E. Y. Harburg
     music: Jay Gorney and Vincent Rose
     lyrics: E. Y. Harburg, Charles and Harry Tobias
     staging: Earl Carroll, Edgar MacGregor, Leroy Prinz
Productions:
     Opened July 1, 1929 for 400 performances
Reviews:
     New Republic 59:262, Jul 24, 1929
     New York Times page 33, Jul 2, 1929
     Outlook 152:471, Jul 17, 1929
     Theatre Magazine 50:39, Sep 1929

Earl Carroll Sketch Book (1935)
   sketches: Eugene Conrad and Charles Sherman
   music and
     lyrics: Charles Tobias, Murray Mencher, Charles New-
                man, Norman Zeno, Will Irwin
   staging: Earl Carroll
   sets: Clark Robinson
   choreography: Boots McKenna
Productions:
   Opened June 4, 1935 for 207 performances
Reviews:
   Nation 140:724, Jun 19, 1935
   New York Times page 22, Jun 5, 1935

Earl Carroll Vanities (1923)
   songs: Earl Carroll
   staging: Earl Carroll
   costumes: Paul Arlington and R. Reid MacQuire
   choreography: Sammy Lee and Renoff
Productions:
   Opened July 5, 1923 for 204 performances
Reviews:
   New York Clipper 71:14, Jul 11, 1923
   New York Times page 8, Jul 6, 1923
               VIII, page 2, Oct 14, 1923
   Theatre Magazine 38:15, Sep 1923

Earl Carroll Vanities (1924)
   songs: Earl Carroll and others
   staging: Earl Carroll
   sets: Max Ree
   choreography: Sammy Lee
Productions:
   Opened September 10, 1924 for 133 performances
Reviews:
   Life (New York) 84:20, Oct 2, 1924
   New York Times page 23, Sep 11, 1924

Earl Carroll Vanities (1925)
   dialogue: William A. Grew; additional sketches by Jimmy
                Duffy, Arthur ("Bugs") Baer, Blanche Merrill
                and others
   songs: Clarence Gaskill, Ray Klages, Louis Alter,
                Fred Phillips, Irving Bilbo, Owen Murphy, Jay
                Gorney
   staging: Earl Carroll
   sets: Willy Pogany
   costumes: Charles LeMaire
   choreography: Dave Bennett and Sonia Gluck
Productions:
   Opened July 6, 1925 for 390 performances
Reviews:
   New York Times page 24, Jul 27, 1925

                    page 10, Aug 24, 1926
                    page 19, Aug 25, 1926
         Theatre Magazine 42:15, Sep 1925

Earl Carroll Vanities (1926-1927)
         sketches: Stanley Rauh and Wm. A. Grew
         music: Grace Henry and Morris Hamilton
         lyrics: Grace Henry and Morris Hamilton
         staging: Earl Carroll
         choreography: David Bennett
Productions:
         Opened August 24, 1926 for 440 performances
Reviews:
         Life (New York) 88:21, Sep 9, 1926
                          89:19, Feb 3, 1927
         New York Times page 10, Aug 24, 1926
                          page 19, Aug 25, 1926
                          page 18, Jan 5, 1927
                          page 19, Feb 22, 1927
         Vogue 68:142, Oct 15, 1926

Earl Carroll Vanities (1928)
         assembled by: Earl Carroll
         music: Louis Alter, Jesse Greer, Richard Whiting
         lyrics: Ray Klages and Joe Burke
         staging: Earl Carroll
Productions:
         Opened August 6, 1928 for 203 performances
Reviews:
         Life (New York) 92:12, Aug 23, 1928
         New Republic 56:21-2, Aug 22, 1928
         New York Times page 25, Aug 7, 1928
         Outlook 149:670, Aug 22, 1928
         Vogue 72:66, Sep 29, 1928

Earl Carroll Vanities (1930)
         assembled by: Earl Carroll
         music: Harold Arlen and Ted Koehler
         lyrics: E. Y. Harburg
         staging: Earl Carroll, Priestly Morrison, LeRoy Prinz
Productions:
         Opened July 1, 1930 for 215 performances
Reviews:
         New York Times page 28, Jul 2, 1930
         Theatre Magazine 52:24, Aug 1930

Earl Carroll Vanities (1931)
         sketches: Ralph Spence and Eddie Welch
         music: Burton Lane
         lyrics: Harold Adamson
         staging: Earl Carroll
Productions:
         Opened August 27, 1931 for 278 performances

Reviews:
    New Republic 68:127-8, Sep 16, 1931
    New York Times page 28, Aug 11, 1931
                 VIII, page 1, Aug 16, 1931
                 page 18, Aug 28, 1931
                 VIII, page 1, Sep 6, 1931
    Outlook 159:55, Sep 9, 1931
           159:570, Dec 30, 1931
    Vogue 78:79+, Oct 15, 1931

Earl Carroll Vanities (1932)
    book: Jack McGowan
    music: Harold Arlen
    lyrics: Ted Koehler
    staging: Earl Carroll
    sets: Vincente Minnelli
Productions:
Opened September 27, 1932 for 87 performances
Reviews:
    Nation 135:375, Oct 19, 1932
    New Outlook 161:46, Dec 1932
    New York Times IX, page 2, Sep 18, 1932
                 page 22, Sep 28, 1932

Earl Carroll Vanities (1940)
    assembled by: Earl Carroll
    music: Charles Rosoff and Peter deRose
    lyrics: Dorcas Cochran and Mitchell Parrish
    staging: Earl Carroll
    sets: Jean LeSeyeux
    costumes: Jean LeSeyeux
    choreography: Eddie Prinz
Productions:
Opened January 13, 1940 for 25 performances
Reviews:
    New York Theatre Critics' Reviews 1940:418+
    New York Times page 1, Jan 15, 1940

Earl of Ruston
    book: C. C. Courtney and Ragan Courtney
    music: Peter Link
    lyrics: C. C. Courtney and Ragan Courtney
    staging: C. C. Courtney
    sets: Neil Peter
Productions:
Opened May 5, 1971 for 5 performances
Reviews:
    New York Theatre Critics' Reviews 1971:289
    New York Times page 38, Apr 27, 1971
                 page 55, May 6, 1971
                 II, page 14, May 16, 1971
    New Yorker 47:102+, May 15, 1971

Early to Bed
    book: George Marion, Jr.
    music: Thomas Waller
    lyrics: George Marion, Jr.
    staging: Alfred Bloomingdale
    sets: George Jenkins
    costumes: Miles White
    choreography: Robert Alton
Productions:
Opened June 17, 1943 for 382 performances
Reviews:
    Catholic World 157:522, Aug 1943
    Commonweal 38:274, Jul 2, 1943
    Life 15:54, Aug 30, 1943
    New York Theatre Critics' Reviews 1943:314+
    New York Times page 16, Jun 18, 1943
    New Yorker 19:33, Jun 26, 1943
    Newsweek 21:108+, Jun 28, 1943
    Theatre Arts 27:573, Oct 1943
    Time 41:94, Jun 28, 1943

Earthlight
    book: Allan Mann and the Earthlight Ensemble
    music: Pure Love and Pleasure
    staging: Allan Mann
    sets: Ron Tannis
    choreography: Peggy Chiereska
Productions:
(Off-Broadway) Opened January 17, 1971 for 56 performances
Reviews:
    New York Times page 38, Nov 4, 1970
                  page 27, Jan 21, 1971

Earthquake (see The International Cup, the Ballet of Niagra and
   the Earthquake)

East Wind
    book: Oscar Hammerstein II and Frank Mandel
    music: Sigmund Romberg
    lyrics: Oscar Hammerstein II
    staging: Oscar Hammerstein II
    choreography: Bobby Connelly
Productions:
Opened October 27, 1931 for 23 performances
Reviews:
    New York Times page 18, Oct 28, 1931

The Eccentricities of Davy Crockett (see Ballet Ballads)

The Echo
    book: William Le Baron
    music: Deems Taylor
    staging: Fred G. Latham

Productions:
    Opened August 17, 1910 for 53 performances
Reviews:
    Cosmopolitan 49:736, Nov 1910
                50:62, Dec 1910
    Dramatic Mirror 64:7, Aug 27, 1910
    Life (New York) 56:398, Sep 8, 1910
    Metropolitan Magazine 33:116-17, Oct 1910
    Munsey 44:136, Oct 1910
    Theatre Magazine 12:xiii, Oct 1910

Ed Wynn Carnival
    dialogue: Ed Wynn
    songs: Ed Wynn
Productions:
    Opened April 5, 1920 for 64 performances
Reviews:
    New York Clipper 68:14, Apr 14, 1920
    New York Times page 18, Apr 6, 1920
                    VI, page 2, Apr 18, 1920
    Theatre Magazine 31:403+, May 1920

Eddie Fisher at the Winter Garden
    songs: Gordon Jenkins, Sammy Cahn and Jimmy Van
                     Heusen, and others
    staging: John Fearnley
    sets: Oliver Smith
    choreography: Tony Charmoli
Productions:
    Opened October 2, 1962 for 40 performances
Reviews:
    New York Theatre Critics' Reviews 1962:264
    New York Times page 47, Oct 3, 1962

Eddie Fisher-Buddy Hackett at the Palace
    staging: Colin Romoff
Productions:
    Opened August 28, 1967 for 42 performances
Reviews:
    New York Times page 54, Mar 15, 1967
                    page 26, Aug 29, 1967

Edith Piaf
    assembled: Edith Piaf
    staging: Edward Lewis
Productions:
    Opened October 30, 1947 for 44 performances
Reviews:
    New Republic 117:33, Nov 17, 1947
    New Yorker 23:52+, Nov 8, 1947
              23:26-7, Nov 15, 1947
    Newsweek 30:76, Nov 10, 1947

The Education of H*Y*M*A*N K*A*P*L*A*N
    book: Benjamin Bernard Zavin; based on the stories
                       by Leo Rosten
    music: Paul Nassau and Oscar Brand
    lyrics: Paul Nassau and Oscar Brand
    staging: George Abbott
    sets: William and Jean Eckart
    costumes: Winn Morton
    choreography: Jaime Rogers
Productions:
    Opened April 4, 1968 for 28 performances
Reviews:
    Dance Magazine 42:29, Jun 1968
    New York Theatre Critics' Reviews 1968:307+
    New York Times page 57, Apr 5, 1968
                    II, page 1, Apr 14, 1968
                    page 38, Apr 26, 1968
    New Yorker 44:114, Apr 13, 1968
    Time 91:68, Apr 12, 1968

Elsa Lanchester--Herself
Productions:
    (Off-Broadway) Season of 1960-1961
Reviews:
    New York Times page 28, Feb 6, 1961
                    page 29, Apr 3, 1961

Elsie
    book: Charles W. Bell
    music: Sissle and Blake, Carlo and Sanders
    lyrics: Sissle and Blake, Carlo and Sanders
    staging: Edgar MacGregor
Productions:
    Opened April 2, 1923 for 40 performances
Reviews:
    New York Clipper 71:14, Apr 11, 1923
    New York Times page 26, Apr 3, 1923

Elsie Janis and her Gang
    book: Elsie Janis
    songs: William Kernell, Richard Fechheimer, B. C.
                       Hilliam and Elsie Janis
    staging: Elsie Janis
    costumes: Charles LeMaire
Productions:
    Opened December 1, 1919 for 55 performances
Reviews:
    New York Clipper 69:20, Jan 25, 1922
    New York Times page 11, Dec 2, 1919

Enchanted Isle
    book: Ida Hoyt Chamberlain
    music: Ida Hoyt Chamberlain

lyrics: Ida Hoyt Chamberlain
staging: Oscar Eagle
Productions:
Opened September 19, 1927 for 32 performances
Reviews:
New York Times page 33, Sep 20, 1927

Enchanting Melody
book: Itzik Manger
music: Henock Kon
staging: David Licht
sets: Marvin Gingold
costumes: Dina Harris
choreography: Yehudith and Felix Fibich
Productions:
(Off-Broadway) Opened November 24, 1964 for 84 performances
Reviews:
New York Times page 40, Nov 25, 1964

The Enchantress
book: Fred DeGresac and Harry B. Smith
music: Victor Herbert
lyrics: Fred DeGresac and Harry B. Smith
staging: Frederick G. Latham
Productions:
Opened October 19, 1911 for 72 performances
Reviews:
Blue Book 14:683-5, Feb 1912
Delineator 79:174, Mar 1912
Dramatic Mirror 66:7+, Oct 25, 1911
                  67:2, Jan 3, 1912
Green Book 7:8-9+, Jan 1912
Leslie's Weekly 113:529, Nov 9, 1911
Munsey 46:430, Dec 1911
Red Book 18:573-6, Jan 1912
Theatre Magazine 14:xiv, Dec 1911
                  14:217, Dec 1911

Ernest in Love
book: Anne Croswell; based on Oscar Wilde's The
                   Importance of Being Earnest
music: Lee Pockriss
lyrics: Anne Croswell
staging: Harold Stone
sets: Peter Dahanos
costumes: Ann Roth
choreography: Frank Derbas
Productions:
(Off-Broadway) Opened May 4, 1960 for 103 performances
(Off-Off-Broadway) Opened November 20, 1964 (Equity Library
    Theatre)
Reviews:
New York Times page 39, May 5, 1960

122   The Establishment

New Yorker 36:117, May 21, 1960
Time 75:70, Jun 6, 1960

The Establishment (1962-1963)
    written: Peter Cook and others
    music and
      lyrics: Christopher Logue, Stanley Myers, John Bird,
                        Patrick Gowers and Tony Kinsey
    staging: Nicholas Garland
Productions:
    (Off-Broadway) Opened January 19, 1963 for 192 performances
Reviews:
    America 108:237, Feb 16, 1963
    Nation 196:186-7, Mar 2, 1963
    New Republic 148:28-9, Feb 23, 1963
    Reporter 28:48+, Feb 14, 1963

The Establishment (1963-1964)
    written: Peter Cook, Peter Shaffer, Peter Lewis, John
                        Brine and Charles Lawson
    songs: Stephen Vinaver
    music: Carl Davis
    staging: Peter Cook and Bill Francisco
    costumes: Robert Leader
Productions:
    (Off-Broadway) Opened October 31, 1963 for 260 performances
Reviews:
    Newsweek 62:76, Nov 11, 1963

Ethel Waters   (see At Home with Ethel Waters)

Eva
    book: Glen MacDonough; based upon the original of
                       Willner and Bodansky
    music: Franz Lehar
    staging: Herbert Gresham
    choreography: Julian Mitchell
Productions:
    Opened December 30, 1912 for 24 performances
Reviews:
    Dramatic Mirror 69:2, Jan 1, 1913
                    69:6, Jan 8, 1913
    Green Book 9:499, Mar 1913
    Harper's Weekly 57:19, Jan 8, 1913
    New York Dramatic News 57:20, Jan 4, 1913
    Theatre Magazine 17:xxii, Jan 1913
                     17:34+, Feb 1913

An Evening with Max Morath at the Turn of the Century
    compiled: Max Morath
    staging: Max Morath
    sets: Dennis Dougherty

Productions:
      (Off-Broadway) Opened February 17, 1969 for 140 performances
Reviews:
      New York Times page 38, Jun 13, 1969
      New Yorker 45:96-7, Mar 8, 1969

An Evening with Sue and Pugh
      songs: Sue Lawless and Ted Pugh
      sketches: Sue Lawless and Ted Pugh
Productions:
      (Off-Broadway) Opened January 16, 1967 for 3 performances
      (Equity Library Informal)
No Reviews.

An Evening with the Times Square Two
      music: Mycroft Partner and Andrew i.
      staging: Saul Gottlieb
Productions:
      (Off-Broadway) Opened May 19, 1967 for 10 performances
No Reviews.

An Evening with Yves Montand
      staging: Y. Montand
Productions:
      Opened October 24, 1961 for 55 performances
Reviews:
      New York Theatre Critics' Reviews 1961:202
      New York Times page 30, Oct 25, 1961
                      page 39, Nov 17, 1961
      Newsweek 58:69, Nov 6, 1961
      Theatre Arts 46:15, Jan 1962
      Time 78:44, Nov 3, 1961

Everybody's Welcome
      book: Harold Atteridge, based on Frances Goodrich
                         and Albert Hackett's Up Pops the Devil
      music: Sammy Fain
      lyrics: Irving Kahal
      staging: William Mollison
Productions:
      Opened October 13, 1931 for 139 performances
Reviews:
      New York Times VIII, page 3, Sep 20, 1931
                      page 26, Oct 14, 1931

Everyman at La Mama
      written: Geraldine Fitzgerald and Brother Jonathan
      music: Jimmy Justice
      staging: Geraldine Fitzgerald and Brother Jonathan
Productions:
      (Off-Off-Broadway) Opened September 7, 1972 (La Mama
      Experimental Theatre Club)
No Reviews.

Everything
     book: R. H. Burnside
     music: John Philip Sousa, Irving Berlin and others
     lyrics: John L. Golden and others
     staging: R. H. Burnside
Productions:
     Opened August 22, 1918 for 461 performances
Reviews:
     Dramatic Mirror 79:360, Sep 7, 1918
     New York Times page 7, Aug 23, 1918
                       page 5, Sep 7, 1918
                       page 11, Jan 27, 1919
     Theatre Magazine 28:199, Oct 1918
                       28:212, Oct 1918

Everything for Anybody (The Bar That Never Closes)
     book: Louisa Rose
     fables: Marco Vassi
     music: Tommy Mandel
     staging: John Broswell
Productions:
     (Off-Off-Broadway) Opened September 9, 1972 (La Mama Ex-
     perimental Theatre Club)
Reviews:
     New York Times page 65, Sep 19, 1972
(Also see The Bar That Never Closes)

Exchange
     dialogue: Eric Levy
     music and
      lyrics: Mike Brandt, Michael Knight and Robert J.
                        Lowery
     staging: Sondra Lee
     sets: Peter Harvey
     costumes: Stanley Simmons
Productions:
     (Off-Broadway) Opened February 8, 1970 for one performance
Reviews:
     New York Times page 47, Feb 9, 1970

Experience
     book: George V. Hobart
     music: Max Bendix
     songs: Silvio Hein
     staging: George V. Hobart
Productions:
     Opened October 27, 1914 for 255 performances
     Opened January 22, 1918 for 23 performances
Reviews:
     American Playwright 3:377-8, Nov 1914
     Book News 34:525-6, Aug 1916
     Bookman 40:417, Dec 1914
     Dramatic Mirror 72:8-9, Nov 4, 1914

F. Jasmine Addams   125
73:2, Feb 17, 1915
                    73:1, Mar 10, 1915
Green Book 13:107-8+, Jan 1915
Hearst 27:198-205, Feb 1915
Life (New York) 64:860, Nov 12, 1914
Munsey 53:795-9, Jan 1915
Nation 99:561, Nov 5, 1915
New England Magazine 53:239, Sep 1915
New York Dramatic News 60:16, Nov 7, 1914
                    61:4, Apr 3, 1915
New York Times page 13, Oct 28, 1914
                    VIII, page 9, Nov 1, 1914
Strand 49:414-5, Apr 1915
Theatre Magazine 20:264-6, Dec 1914

                        - F -

F. Jasmine Addams
    book: Carson McCullers, G. Wood and Theodore
                    Mann; based on Carson McCullers' The Member
                    of the Wedding
    music: G. Wood
    lyrics: G. Wood
    staging: Theodore Mann
    sets: Marsha Louis Eck
    costumes: Joseph G. Aulisi
    choreography: Patricia Birch
Productions:
    (Off-Broadway) Opened October 27, 1971 for 6 performances
Reviews:
    America 125:427, Nov 20, 1971
    New York Times page 49, Oct 28, 1971
                    II, page 6, Nov 7, 1971
    New Yorker 47:115-16, Nov 6, 1971

Face the Music
    book: Moss Hart
    music: Irving Berlin
    lyrics: Irving Berlin
    staging: Hassard Short and George S. Kaufman
    choreography: Albertina Rasch
Productions:
    Opened February 17, 1932 for 165 performances
    Opened January 31, 1933 for 32 performances
Reviews:
    Arts and Decoration 36:45+, Apr 1932
    Bookman 74:666, Mar 1932
    Catholic World 135:75-6, Apr 1932
    Commonweal 15:495, Mar 2, 1932
    Nation 134:294, Mar 9, 1932
    New Outlook 161:48, Mar 1933
    New Republic 70:97, Mar 9, 1932

New York Times page 25, Feb 4, 1932
                page 24, Feb 18, 1932
                VIII, page 1, Mar 20, 1932
                page 13, Feb 1, 1933
Outlook 160:189, Mar 1932
Theatre Guild Magazine 9:28-30, Mar 1932
                        9:23, Apr 1932
Vogue 79:56+, Apr 15, 1932

Fade Out--Fade In
    book: Betty Comden and Adolph Green
    music: Jule Styne
    lyrics: Betty Comden and Adolph Green
    staging: George Abbott
    sets: William and Jean Eckart
    costumes: Donald Brooks
    choreography: Ernest Flatt
Productions:
Opened May 26, 1964 for 271 performances
Reviews:
    America 111:114-15, Aug 1, 1964
    Dance Magazine 38:17, Aug 1964
    Life 57:30, Sep 25, 1964
    Nation 198:611, Jun 15, 1964
    New York Theatre Critics' Reviews 1964:248+
    New York Times page 45, May 27, 1964
                    page 42, May 28, 1964
                    II, page 1, Jun 7, 1964
                    page 56, Nov 10, 1964
                    page 34, Apr 14, 1965
    Newsweek 63:69, Jun 8, 1964
    Saturday Review 47:28, Jun 20, 1964
    Time 83:75, Jun 5, 1964

Fads and Fancies
    book: Glen MacDonough
    music: Raymond Hubbell
    lyrics: Glen MacDonough
    staging: Herbert Gresham
    choreography: Julian Mitchell
Productions:
Opened March 8, 1915 for 48 performances
Reviews:
    Dramatic Mirror 73:8, Mar 17, 1915
                    73:2, Mar 24, 1915
    Green Book 13:1150-1, Jun 1915
    Life (New York) 65:467, Mar 18, 1915
    Munsey 55:111, Jun 1915
    New York Dramatic News 60:17, Mar 13, 1915
    New York Times page 9, Mar 9, 1915
    Theatre Magazine 21:167, Apr 1915
                    21:170, Apr 1915

The Faggot
    words: Al Carmines
    music: Al Carmines
    staging: Al Carmines
    sets: T. E. Mason
    costumes: T. E. Mason
    choreography: David Vaughan
Productions:
    (Off-Off-Broadway) Opened April 13, 1973 (Judson Poets'
       Theatre)
    (Off-Broadway) Opened June 18, 1973 for 182 performances
Reviews:
    National Review 25:1125-6, Oct 12, 1973
    New Republic 169:20+, Aug 11, 1973
    New York Theatre Critics' Reviews 1973:247
    New York Times page 50, Apr 16, 1973
                    page 30, Jun 19, 1973
                    II, page 1, Jul 1, 1973
                    II, page 1, Jul 22, 1973
                    II, page 12, Jul 29, 1973

A Family Affair
    book: James Goldman, John Kander, William Goldman
    music: James Goldman, John Kander, William Goldman
    lyrics: James Goldman, John Kander, William Goldman
    staging: Harold Prince
    sets: David Hays
    costumes: Robert Fletcher
    choreography: John Butler
Productions:
    Opened January 27, 1962 for 65 performances
Reviews:
    America 106:737, Mar 3, 1962
    New York Theatre Critics' Reviews 1962:374+
    New York Times page 17, Jan 29, 1962
                    page 36, Mar 26, 1962
    Theatre Arts 46:58-9, Apr 1962
    Time 79:61, Feb 9, 1962

Fancy Free
    book: Dorothy Donnelly and Edgar Smith
    music: Augustus Barratt
    lyrics: Augustus Barratt
    staging: J. C. Huffman
Productions:
    Opened April 11, 1918 for 116 performances
Reviews:
    Dramatic Mirror 78:549, Apr 20, 1918
                    78:584, Apr 27, 1918
    Green Book 20:200+, Aug 1918
    Life (New York) 71:682, Apr 25, 1918
    New York Times page 11, Apr 12, 1918
    Theatre Magazine 27:316, May 1918

Fanny
    book: S. N. Behrman and Joshua Logan, based on
                     Marcel Pagnol's "Marius," "Fanny," and
                     "Cesar"
    music: Harold Rome
    lyrics: Harold Rome
    staging: Joshua Logan
    sets: Jo Mielziner
    costumes: Alvin Colt
    choreography: Helen Tamiris
Productions:
Opened November 4, 1954 for 888 performances
Reviews:
    America 92:305, Dec 11, 1954
    Catholic World 180:307-8, Jan 1955
    Commonweal 61:288, Dec 10, 1954
    Life 37:117-20, Nov 29, 1954
    Look 18:56-60, Nov 16, 1954
    Mademoiselle 40:142, Nov 1954
    Nation 179:451, Nov 20, 1954
    New Republic 131:22-3, Nov 29, 1954
    New York Theatre Critics' Reviews 1954:256+
    New York Times VI, page 64, Oct 31, 1954
                      page 16, Nov 5, 1954
                      II, page 1, Nov 21, 1954
                      VI, page 23, Jan 16, 1955
                      II, page 1, Oct 30, 1955
                      page 19, Dec 17, 1955
                      page 17, Nov 17, 1956
                      II, page 3, Dec 2, 1956
    New York Times Magazine pages 64-5, Oct 31, 1954
    New Yorker 30:104, Nov 13, 1954
    Newsweek 44:98, Nov 15, 1954
    Saturday Review 37:30, Nov 20, 1954
                      38:5, 23, Jan 8, 1955
                      38:23, Feb 5, 1955
                      39:13, Sep 15, 1956
    Theatre Arts 39:17-18, 20-1, Jan 1955
    Time 64:62, Nov 15, 1954

A Fantastic Fricassee
    staging: Andre Chotin
Productions:
Opened September 11, 1922 for 112 performances
Reviews:
    New York Clipper 70:20, Sep 27, 1922
    New York Times page 24, Sep 12, 1922

The Fantasticks
    book: Tom Jones; based on Edmund Rostand's Les
                     Romantiques
    music: Harvey Schmidt
    lyrics: Tom Jones

staging: Word Baker
sets: Ed Wittstein
Productions:
  (Off-Broadway) Opened May 3, 1960 for 6,281 performances
Reviews:
  Catholic World 194:128, Nov 1961
  Life 57:75-6+, Oct 16, 1964
  New York Times page 55, May 4, 1960
                  page 36, Sep 8, 1961
                  page 15, Nov 24, 1962
                  page 14, Feb 1, 1964
                  II, page 3, May 3, 1964
                  II, page 19, Oct 18, 1964
                  page 67, Oct 19, 1964
                  page 41, May 3, 1965
                  page 50, May 3, 1966
                  II, page 3, Jul 31, 1966
                  page 23, Aug 4, 1966
                  page 21, Nov 5, 1966
                  page 20, Jan 7, 1967
                  page 32, Jan 7, 1967
                  page 32, Jan 19, 1968
                  page 42, May 3, 1968
                  page 73, May 20, 1968
                  page 53, May 5, 1969
                  page 49, May 4, 1970
                  II, page 24, May 2, 1971
                  page 50, May 1, 1973
  New Yorker 36:96-7, May 14, 1960
  Saturday Review 43:33, May 21, 1960
  Theatre Arts 46:9, Nov 1962

Farina, Richard (see Richard Farina)

The Fascinating Widow
    book: Otto Hauerbach
    staging: George Marion
Productions:
    Opened September 11, 1911 for 56 performances
Reviews:
    Blue Book 12:648-51, Feb 1911
    Dramatic Mirror 66:13, Sep 13, 1911
    Green Book Album 5:246-8+, Feb 1911
    Munsey 46:282-3, Nov 1911
    Theatre Magazine 14:113, Oct 1911

Fashion
    book: Anthony Stimac; based on the play by Anna
                  Cora Mowatt
    music: Don Pippin
    lyrics: Steve Brown
    staging: Anthony Stimac
Productions:

(Off-Off-Broadway) Opened December 6, 1973 (Greenwich
    Mews Theatre)
(Off-Broadway) Opened February 18, 1974 for 94 performances
Reviews:
    New York Theatre Critics' Reviews 1974:294
    New York Times page 61, Dec 6, 1973
                    II, page 3, Mar 3, 1974
    New Yorker 50:68-9, Mar 4, 1974
    Time 103:104, Mar 11, 1974

Fashions of 1924
    music: Ted Snyder
    lyrics: Harry B. Smith
    staging: Alexander Leftwich
Productions:
    Opened July 18, 1923 for 13 performances
Reviews:
    Life (New York) 82:18, Aug 8, 1923
    New York Times page 18, Jul 19, 1923
                    page 12, Jul 31, 1923
    Theatre Magazine 38:15, Sep 1923

Fast and Furious
    assembled by: Forbes Randolph
    music: Joe Jordan and Harry Revel
    lyrics: Rosamond Johnson, Mack Gordon, Harold
                    Adamson
    staging: Forbes Randolph
Productions:
    Opened September 15, 1931 for 7 performances
Reviews:
    New York Times page 15, Sep 16, 1931

Feunte Ovehuna
    book: Lope de Vega
    music: Guy Strobel
    staging: Alan Holzman
Productions:
    (Off-Off-Broadway) Opened October 12, 1972 (La Mama Ex-
    perimental Theatre Club)
No Reviews.

Fiddler on the Roof
    book: Joseph Stein, based on the stories of Sholom
                    Aleichem
    music: Jerry Bock
    lyrics: Sheldon Harnick
    staging: Jerome Robbins
    sets: Boris Aronson
    costumes: Patricia Zipprodt
    choreography: Jerome Robbins
Productions:
    Opened September 22, 1964 for 3,242 performances

Reviews:
   America 112:25, Jan 2, 1965
   Commentary 38:73-5, Nov 1964
           39:12+, Apr 1965
   Commonweal 81:100, Oct 16, 1964
   Dance Magazine 38:24-5+, Nov 1964
   Life 57:104-5+, Dec 4, 1964
   Nation 199:229-30, Oct 12, 1964
   New Republic 151:31+, Oct 17, 1964
   New York Theatre Critics' Reviews 1964:214+
   New York Times page 10, Aug 8, 1964
               page 56, Sep 23, 1964
               page 47, Sep 24, 1964
               II, page 1, Oct 4, 1964
               page 36, Oct 6, 1964
               page 14, Jan 23, 1965
               page 40, Jun 9, 1965
               II, page 2, Aug 15, 1965
               page 35, Jan 23, 1966
               page 39, Sep 2, 1966
               page 54, Sep 22, 1966
               page 40, Dec 22, 1966
               page 50, Feb 17, 1967
               page 29, Jun 30, 1967
               page 25, Sep 4, 1967
               page 50, Sep 7, 1967
               page 59, Sep 28, 1967
               page 61, Nov 16, 1967
               page 28, Feb 2, 1968
               page 36, Feb 22, 1968
               page 36, Feb 26, 1969
               page 47, Jun 26, 1969
               page 82, Nov 16, 1969
               page 20, Feb 28, 1970
               page 34, Jul 8, 1970
               page 39, Sep 22, 1970
               II, page 40, Dec 27, 1970
               II, page 16, Apr 18, 1971
               II, page 3, Jul 18, 1971
               page 16, Jul 21, 1971
               page 35, Aug 23, 1971
               page 54, Dec 7, 1971
               page 47, Jan 13, 1972
               II, page 14, Jan 16, 1972
               page 28, Jun 17, 1972
               page 1, Jun 18, 1972
               page 7, Jul 3, 1972
               page 11, May 29, 1973
  New Yorker 40:96, Oct 3, 1964
  Newsweek 64:106, Oct 5, 1964
  Saturday Review 47:33, Oct 10, 1964
  Time 84:82, Oct 2, 1964
  Vogue 144:66, Nov 1, 1964

Fiesta in Madrid
    book: Tito Capobianco; adapted from Thomas Breton's
                   La Verbena de La Paloma
    music: Tito Capobianco
    lyrics: Tito Capobianco
    staging: Tito Capobianco
    sets: Jose Varona
    costumes: Jose Varona
    choreography: Teresa
Productions:
    Opened May 28, 1969 for 23 performances
Reviews:
    Dance Magazine 43:71, Aug 1969
    New York Times page 49, May 29, 1969
    Newsweek 73:95-6, Jun 9, 1969
    Saturday Review 52:46, Jun 14, 1969

Fifty-Fifty, Ltd.
    book: Margaret Michael and William Lennox; based
                   on William Gillette's All the Comforts of Home
    music: Leon De Costa
    lyrics: Leon De Costa
Productions:
    Opened October 27, 1919 for 40 performances
Reviews:
    New York Times page 14, Oct 28, 1919
                     VIII, page 2, Oct 19, 1919

Fifty Million Frenchmen
    book: Herbert Fields
    music: Cole Porter
    lyrics: Cole Porter
    staging: Edgar M. Wooley (Monty Wooley)
    choreography: Larry Ceballos
Productions:
    Opened November 27, 1929 for 254 performances
Reviews:
    Nation 129:756-8, Dec 18, 1929
    New York Times page 34, Nov 28, 1929
                  X, page 1, Dec 8, 1929
                  VIII, page 1, Jan 5, 1930
    Theatre Magazine 51:49, Jan 1930
    Vogue 75:100, Jan 18, 1930

The Fig Leaves Are Falling
    book: Allan Sherman
    music: Albert Hague
    lyrics: Allan Sherman
    staging: George Abbott
    sets: William and Jean Eckart
    costumes: Robert Mackintosh
    choreography: Eddie Gasper
Productions:

Opened January 2, 1969 for 4 performances
Reviews:
New York Theatre Critics' Reviews 1969:397
New York Times page 19, Jan 3, 1969
           page 32, Jan 4, 1969
New Yorker 44:56, Jan 11, 1969
Newsweek 73:86, Jan 13, 1969

Fine and Dandy
     book: Donald Ogden Stewart
     music: Kay Swift
     lyrics: Paul James
     staging: Morris Green, Frank McCoy, Dave Gould,
                   Tom Nip
Productions:
Opened September 23, 1930 for 255 performances
Reviews:
Bookman 72:411, Dec 1930
Commonweal 12:583, Oct 8, 1930
Life (New York) 96:18, Oct 10, 1930
Nation 131:422, Oct 15, 1930
New York Times IX, page 2, Sep 7, 1930
               page 26, Sep 24, 1930
               IX, page 1, Oct 5, 1930
Outlook 156:233, Oct 8, 1930
Theatre Magazine 52:64, Dec 1930
Vogue 76:116, Nov 10, 1930

Finian's Rainbow
     book: E. Y. Harburg and Fred Saidy
     music: Burton Lane
     lyrics: E. Y. Harburg
     staging: Bretaigne Windust
     sets: Jo Mielziner
     costumes: Eleanor Goldsmith
     choreography: Michael Kidd
Productions:
Opened January 10, 1947 for 725 performances
(Off-Broadway) Season of 1952-53 (Equity Library Theatre)
Opened May 18, 1955 for 18 performances
(Off-Broadway) Season of 1959-60
Opened April 27, 1960 for 27 performances
Opened April 5, 1967 for 23 performances
Reviews:
Catholic World 164:453-4, Feb 1947
                181:308, Jul 1955
Collier's 120:14-15, Aug 2, 1947
Commonweal 45:446, Feb 14, 1947
Dance Magazine 41:26, May 1967
Harper's 81:174, May 1947
Life 22:76-7, Feb 24, 1947
New Republic 116:43, Feb 3, 1947
New York Theatre Critics' Reviews 1947:486+

                                        1960:279+
New York Times VI, page 28, Jan 5, 1947
                    page 23, Jan 11, 1947
                    II, page 1, Jan 26, 1947
                    II, page 3, Feb 2, 1947
                    II, page 1, Apr 6, 1947
                    II, page 1, Jul 13, 1947
                    II, page 1, Aug 17, 1947
                    page 38, Oct 22, 1947
                    II, page 3, Nov 9, 1947
                    II, page 1, Aug 29, 1948
                    page 36, Oct 19, 1949
                    page 13, Mar 17, 1953
                    page 19, Sep 25, 1953
                    page 25, May 17, 1955
                    page 31, Apr 28, 1960
                    page 44, Apr 6, 1967
New Yorker 22:46+, Jan 18, 1947
Newsweek 29:84, Jan 20, 1947
            30:78, Nov 3, 1947
Saturday Review 30:28-30, Feb 15, 1947
Theatre Arts 31:8, 15, 23, Mar 1947
            32:49, Feb 1948
Time 49:69, Jan 20, 1947
Vogue 109:148, Feb 15, 1947

Fiorello!
    book: Jerome Weidman and George Abbott
    music: Jerry Bock
    lyrics: Sheldon Harnick
    staging: George Abbott
    sets: William and Jean Eckart
    costumes: William and Jean Eckart
    choreography: Peter Gennaro
Productions:
    Opened November 23, 1959 for 795 performances
    Opened June 13, 1962 for 16 performances
Reviews:
    America 102:594, Feb 13, 1960
    Christian Century 76:1506, Dec 23, 1959
    Commonweal 71:422, Jan 8, 1960
    Life 48:55-7, Jan 18, 1960
    Nation 189:475, Dec 19, 1959
    New York Theatre Critics' Reviews 1959:219+
    New York Times VI, page 18, Nov 8, 1959
                    II, page 1, Nov 22, 1959
                    page 45, Nov 24, 1959
                    page 19, Nov 25, 1959
                    II, page 1, Nov 29, 1959
                    page 12, Oct 28, 1961
                    page 24, Jun 14, 1962
                    page 60, Oct 10, 1962
    New Yorker 35:95-7, Dec 5, 1959

Newsweek 54:96, Dec 7, 1959
Saturday Review 42:26-7, Dec 12, 1959
                43:75, Jan 16, 1960
Time 74:54+, Dec 7, 1959

Fioretta
    book: Earl Carroll, adapted by Charlton Andrews
    music: George Babgy and G. Romilli
    lyrics: George Babgy and G. Romilli
    staging: Earl Carroll
Productions:
Opened February 5, 1929 for 111 performances
Reviews:
    Life (New York) 93:24, Mar 15, 1929
    New York Times VIII, page 4, Jan 6, 1929
                    page 30, Feb 6, 1929
    Theatre Magazine 49:46, Apr 1929

The Firebrand of Florence
    book: Edwin Justus Mayer and Ira Gershwin, based
                    on The Firebrand by Edwin Justus Mayer
    music: Kurt Weill
    lyrics: Edwin Justus Mayer and Ira Gershwin
    staging: John Murray Anderson
    sets: Jo Mielziner
    costumes: Raoul Pene du Bois
    choreography: Catherine Littlefield
Productions:
Opened March 22, 1945 for 43 performances
Reviews:
    Catholic World 161:167, May 1945
    New York Theatre Critics' Reviews 1945:241+
    New York Times page 13, Mar 23, 1945
    New Yorker 21:42, Mar 3, 1945
    Newsweek 25:84, Apr 2, 1945
    Theatre Arts 29:271, May 1945
    Time 45:60, Apr 2, 1945

The Firefly
    book: Otto Hauerbach
    music: Rudolf Friml
    lyrics: Otto Hauerbach
    staging: Frederick G. Latham
Productions:
Opened December 30, 1912 for 120 performances
Opened November 30, 1931 for 8 performances
Reviews:
    Dramatic Mirror 68:6, Dec 4, 1912
                    68:2, Dec 18, 1912
    Green Book 9:196-7+, Feb 1913
    Harper's Weekly page 18, Feb 1, 1913
    Munsey 48:844, Feb 1913
    New York Dramatic News 56:19, Dec 7, 1912

Red Book 20:894-6, Mar 1913
Theatre Magazine 17:3, Jan 1913

The Fireman's Flame
    book: John Van Antwerp
    music: Richard Lewine
    lyrics: Ted Fetter
    staging: John and Jerrold Krimsky
    sets: Eugene Dunkel
    costumes: Kermit Love
    choreography: Morgan Lewis
Productions:
    Opened October 9, 1937 for 204 performances
Reviews:
    Life 3:62-5, Dec 27, 1937
    New York Times XI, page 3, Oct 3, 1937
                    page 26, Oct 10, 1937

First Impressions
    book: Abe Burrows, based on Jane Austen's Pride and
                   Prejudice and the play by Helen Jerome
    music: Robert Goldman, Glenn Paxton, George Weiss
    lyrics: Robert Goldman, Glenn Paxton, George Weiss
    staging: Abe Burrows
    sets: Peter Larkin
    costumes: Alvin Colt
    choreography: Jonathan Lucas
Productions:
    Opened March 19, 1959 for 92 performances
Reviews:
    Catholic World 189:241-2, Jun 1959
    Commonweal 70:57-8, Apr 10, 1959
    Dance Magazine 33:16, Jun 1959
    New York Theatre Critics' Reviews 1959:336+
    New York Times page 28, Mar 20, 1959
                    II, page 1, Mar 29, 1959
                    page 31, May 26, 1959
    New Yorker 35:89, Mar 28, 1959
    Saturday Review 42:28, Apr 4, 1959
    Theatre Arts 42:23-4, May 1959
    Time 73:43, Mar 30, 1959

First Reader   (see Gertrude Stein's First Reader)

Fisher, Eddie   (see Eddie Fisher)

5 O'Clock Girl
    book: Guy Bolton and Fred Thompson
    music: Bert Kalmar and Harry Ruby
    lyrics: Bert Kalmar and Harry Ruby
    staging: Philip Goodman
Productions:
    Opened October 10, 1927 for 280 performances

Reviews:
   Life (New York) 90:23, Nov 3, 1927
   New York Times page 26, Oct 11, 1927
   Vogue 70:116, Dec 15, 1927

Flahooley
      book: E. Y. Harburg and Fred Saidy
      music: Sammy Fain
      lyrics: E. Y. Harburg
      staging: E. Y. Harburg and Fred Saidy
      sets: Howard Bay
      costumes: David Ffolkes
      choreography: Helen Tamiris
Productions:
   Opened May 14, 1951 for 40 performances
   (Off-Off-Broadway) Opened April 25, 1964 for 8 performances
      (Equity Library Theatre)
Reviews:
   Catholic World 173:307, Jul 1951
   Commonweal 54:189, Jun 1, 1951
   New York Theatre Critics' Reviews 1951:264+
   New York Times II, page 1, May 13, 1951
                    page 39, May 15, 1951
                    II, page 1, May 20, 1951
                    page 17, Aug 13, 1952
   New Yorker 27:48+, May 26, 1951
   Newsweek 37:58, May 28, 1951
   Theatre Arts 35:5, Sep 1951
   Time 57:78, May 28, 1951

Flo-Flo
      book: Fred de Gresac
      music: Silvio Hein
      lyrics: E. Paulton and Fred de Gresac
      staging: Walter Brooks
Productions:
   Opened December 20, 1917 for 220 performances
Reviews:
   Dramatic Mirror 77:7, Dec 29, 1917
   Green Book 20:208-10, Aug 1918
   Life (New York) 71:22, Jan 3, 1918
   New York Times page 9, Dec 20, 1917
   Theatre Magazine 27:87, Feb 1918
                    27:93, Feb 1918

Flora, the Red Menace
      book: George Abbott and Robert Russell, based on
                       Lester Atwell's Love Is Just Around the Corner
      music: John Kander
      lyrics: Fred Ebb
      staging: George Abbott
      sets: William and Jean Eckart
      costumes: Donald Brooks

  choreography: Lee Theodore
Productions:
  Opened May 11, 1965 for 87 performances
Reviews:
  America 113:121-2, Jul 31, 1965
  Dance Magazine 39:23, Jul 1965
  National Review 17:561-2, Jun 29, 1965
  New York Theatre Critics' Reviews 1965:330+
  New York Times page 31, Mar 2, 1965
              page 41, May 12, 1965
  New Yorker 41:114, May 22, 1965
  Newsweek 65:99, May 24, 1965
  Saturday Review 48:50, May 8, 1965
  Time 85:69, May 21, 1965
  Vogue 146:38, Jul 1965

Floradora
  book: Owen Hall
  music: Leslie Stuart
  lyrics: E. Boyd Jones and Paul Rubens
  staging: Lewis Morton
Productions:
  Opened April 5, 1920 for 64 performances
Reviews:
  Dramatic Mirror 82:572-3, Mar 27, 1920
                  82:680, Apr 10, 1920
  Green Book 8:102-10, Jul 1912
  Life (New York) 75:752, Apr 22, 1920
  New York Clipper 68:14, Apr 14, 1920
  New York Times page 18, Apr 6, 1920
                  VI, page 2, Apr 18, 1920
  Stage 14:88, Aug 1937
  Theatre Arts 29:456, Aug 1945
  Theatre Magazine 31:573, Jun 1920
                   40:52, Oct 1924

Florida Girl
  book: Paul Porter, Benjamin Hapgood Burt and
                 William A. Grew
  music: Milton Suskind
  lyrics: Paul Porter, Benjamin Hapgood Burt and
                 William A. Grew
  staging: Frederick Stanhope
Productions:
  Opened November 2, 1925 for 40 performances
Reviews:
  New York Times page 34, Nov 3, 1925

Flossie
  book: Armand Robi
  music: Armand Robi
  lyrics: Ralph Murphey
Productions:

Opened June 3, 1924 for (16) performances
Reviews:
New York Times page 25, Jun 4, 1924
Theatre Magazine 40:15, Aug 1924

Flower Drum Song
book: Oscar Hammerstein II and Joseph Fields,
                 based on the novel by C. Y. Lee
music: Richard Rodgers
lyrics: Oscar Hammerstein II
staging: Gene Kelly
sets: Oliver Smith
costumes: Irene Sharaff
choreography: Carol Haney
Productions:
Opened December 1, 1958 for 600 performances
Reviews:
America 100:438, Jan 10, 1959
Catholic World 188:420, Feb 1959
Commonweal 70:426-7, Apr 14, 1959
Dance Magazine 33:16-17, Jan 1959
Life 45:77-8+, Dec 22, 1958
New Republic 139:23, Dec 22, 1958
New York Theatre Critics' Reviews 1958:187+
New York Times VI, pages 16-17, Nov 23, 1958
                page 44, Dec 2, 1958
                II, page 5, Dec 7, 1958
                page 20, Mar 25, 1960
New Yorker 34:104+, Dec 13, 1958
Newsweek 52:53-6, Dec 1, 1958
         52:63, Dec 15, 1958
Saturday Review 41:33, Dec 20, 1958
Theatre Arts 43:10, Feb 1959
Time 72:44, Dec 15, 1958
     72:42-4+, Dec 22, 1958
Vogue 133:95, Jan 1, 1959

Fly Blackbird
book: C. Jackson and James Hatch
music: C. Jackson and James Hatch
lyrics: C. Jackson and James Hatch
staging: Jerome Eskow
sets: Robert Soule
costumes: Robby Campbell
choreography: Talley Beatty
Productions:
(Off-Broadway) Opened February 5, 1962 for 127 performances
Reviews:
America 106:773-4, Mar 10, 1962
Nation 194:201, Mar 3, 1962
New York Times page 26, Feb 6, 1962
New Yorker 37:94-5, Feb 17, 1962
Theatre Arts 46:61-3, May 1962

Flying Colors
    book: Howard Dietz
    music: Arthur Schwartz
    lyrics: Howard Dietz
    staging: Howard Dietz
    sets: Norman Bel-Geddes
Productions:
Opened September 15, 1932 for 188 performances
Reviews:
    Arts and Decoration 38:45+, Nov 1932
    Catholic World 136:210-11, Nov 1932
    New Outlook 161:47, Jan 1933
    Nation 135:318, Oct 5, 1932
    New York Times page 24, Sep 16, 1932
    Stage 10:11, Oct 1932
          10:18-21, Nov 1932
    Theatre Arts 16:873, Nov 1932
    Vogue 80:89, Nov 1, 1932

Flying High
    book: B. G. DeSylva, John McGowan
    music: Ray Henderson
    lyrics: B. G. DeSylva and Lew Brown
    staging: Edward Clark Lilley
    choreography: Bobby Connelly
Productions:
Opened March 3, 1930 for 357 performances
Reviews:
    Life (New York) 95:18, Mar 28, 1930
    New York Times VIII, page 4, Feb 9, 1930
                 page 24, Mar 4, 1930
                 VIII, page 4, Mar 30, 1930
    Outlook 155:29, May 7, 1930
    Theatre Magazine 51:43, May 1930
    Vogue 75:126, May 10, 1930

Folies Bergère
    book: Paul Derval
    music: Henri Betti, additional music by Phillippe
                  Gerard
    staging: Michel Gyarmathy
    sets: Michel Gyarmathy
    costumes: Michel Gyarmathy
    choreography: George Reich
Productions:
Opened June 2, 1964 for 191 performances
Reviews:
    New York Theatre Critics' Reviews 1964:242+
    New York Times page 52, May 13, 1964
                   II, page 1, May 31, 1964
                   page 36, Jun 3, 1964
                   II, page 1, Jun 21, 1964
                   page 53, Sep 17, 1964

page 18, Sep 19, 1964

Follies (1971)
book:	James Goldman
music:	Stephen Sondheim
lyrics:	Stephen Sondheim
staging:	Harold Prince and Michael Bennett
sets:	Boris Aronson
costumes:	Florence Klotz
choreography:	Michael Bennett

Productions:
   Opened April 4, 1971 for 521 performances
Reviews:
   America 124:615, Jun 12, 1971
   Commonweal 94:239-40, May 14, 1971
   Dance Magazine 45:81-2, Jun 1971
   National Review 23:1129-30, Oct 8, 1971
   Nation 212:509-10, Apr 19, 1971
   New Republic 164:24+, May 8, 1971
   New York Theatre Critics' Reviews 1971:309
   New York Times II, page 1, Apr 4, 1971
                     page 44, Apr 5, 1971
                     page 20, Apr 9, 1971
                     II, page 1, Apr 11, 1971
                     II, page 1, Apr 25, 1971
                     page 26, May 16, 1971
                     II, page 32, Nov 14, 1971
   New Yorker 47:67, Apr 10, 1971
   Newsweek 77:121, Apr 12, 1971
   Saturday Review 54:16+, May 1, 1971
   Time 97:78, Apr 12, 1971
        97:70-4, May 3, 1971
   Vogue 157:154-5, May 1971

Follies   (see Ziegfeld Follies)

Follies Burlesque '67
book:	Stanley Richman
music:	Sol Richman
lyrics:	Sol Richman
staging:	Dick Richards
costumes:	S. Binder
choreography:	Paul Morokoff

Productions:
   (Off-Broadway) Opened May 3, 1967 for 16 performances
No Reviews.

Follow Me
book:	Based on the original of Felix Doermann and Leo Ascher
music:	Sigmund Romberg
lyrics:	Robert B. Smith
staging:	J. H. Benrimo

        choreography: Jack Mason and Allen K. Foster
Productions:
    Opened November 29, 1916 for 78 performances
Reviews:
    Dramatic Mirror 76:7-8, Dec 9, 1916
                     77:4, Jan 13, 1917
    New York Times page 11, Nov 30, 1916
    Theatre Magazine 25:20, Jan 1917
                     25:24, Jan 1917

Follow the Girl
    book: Henry Blossom and Zoel Parenteau
    staging: J. C. Huffman
Productions:
    Opened March 2, 1918 for 25 performances
Reviews:
    Dramatic Mirror 78:5, Mar 16, 1918
    New York Times page 9, Mar 4, 1918
    Theatre Magazine 27:216, Apr 1918
                     27:220, Apr 1918

Follow the Girls
    book: Guy Bolton and Eddie Davis, with dialogue by
                       Fred Thompson
    music: Dan Shapiro, Milton Pascal, Phil Charig
    lyrics: Dan Shapiro, Milton Pascal, Phil Charig
    staging: Harry Delmar
    sets: Howard Bay
    costumes: Lou Eisele
    choreography: Catherine Littlefield
Productions:
    Opened April 8, 1944 for 882 performances
Reviews:
    Commonweal 40:38-9, Apr 28, 1944
    Life 16:115-18+, Apr 24, 1944
    New York Theatre Critics' Reviews 1944:222+
    New York Times page 15, Apr 10, 1944
                     II, page 1, Apr 16, 1944
    Newsweek 23:106, Apr 17, 1944

Follow Thru
    book: Laurence Schwab and B. G. DeSylva
    music: Ray Henderson
    lyrics: B. G. DeSylva and Lew Brown
    staging: Edgar MacGregor and Donald Oenslager
Productions:
    Opened January 9, 1929 for 403 performances
Reviews:
    Theatre Magazine 49:51, Mar 1929
    Vogue 73:72, Mar 2, 1929

Footlights
    book: Roland Oliver

staging: Bunny Weldon
Productions:
    Opened August 19, 1927 for 43 performances
Reviews:
    Life (New York) 90:19, Sep 8, 1927
    New York Times page 8, Aug 20, 1927

For Goodness Sake
    book: Fred Jackson
    music: William Daly and Paul Lannin
    lyrics: Arthur Jackson
    staging: Priestly Morrison and Allan K. Foster
Productions:
    Opened February 20, 1922 for 103 performances
Reviews:
    New York Clipper 70:22, Mar 8, 1922
    New York Times page 13, Feb 22, 1922
    Theatre Magazine 35:334, May 1922

Forbidden Melody
    book: Otto Harbach
    music: Sigmund Romberg
    lyrics: Otto Harbach
    staging: Macklin Megley
    sets: Sergei Soudeikine
    costumes: Ten Eyck
Productions:
    Opened November 2, 1936 for 32 performances
Reviews:
    New York Times page 30, Oct 13, 1936

Fortuna
    book: Arnold Weinstein; adapted from a drama by
                       Eduardo de Filippo and Armando Curcio
    music: Francis Thorne
    lyrics: Arnold Weinstein
    staging: Glen Tetley
Productions:
    (Off-Broadway) Opened January 3, 1962 for 5 performances
Reviews:
    New York Times page 26, Jan 4, 1962
                   page 12, Jan 6, 1962
    New Yorker 37:67, Jan 13, 1962

45 Minutes from Broadway
    book: George M. Cohan
    music: George M. Cohan
    lyrics: George M. Cohan
    staging: George M. Cohan
Productions:
    Opened January 1, 1906 for 90 performances
    Opened March 14, 1912 for 36 performances
Reviews:

Blue Book 15:228-32, Jun 1912
Dramatic Mirror 67:6, Mar 20, 1912
                  67:4, Apr 10, 1912
Theatre Magazine 6:26+, Feb 1906

Four Saints in Three Acts
book:	Gertrude Stein
music:	Virgil Thomson
lyrics:	Gertrude Stein
staging:	Maurice Grosser
sets:	Paul Morison
costumes:	Paul Morison
choreography:	William Dollar

Productions:
Opened April 16, 1952 for 15 performances
Reviews:
Catholic World 178:228, Jun 1952
Commonweal 56:116, May 9, 1952
Musical America 72:7, May 1952
New York Theatre Critics' Reviews 1952:312
New York Times page 35, Apr 17, 1952
New Yorker 28:122-4, Apr 26, 1952
Newsweek 39:52, Apr 28, 1952
Saturday Review 35:33, May 3, 1952
School and Society 75:393-4, Jun 21, 1952
Theatre Arts 36:19, Jun 1952
Time 59:42, Apr 28, 1952

4th Avenue North
sketches:	George Allan, Michael Batterberry, Shippen Geer, Murray Grand, Cy Walter and others
music, lyrics:	George Allan, Michael Batterberry, Shippen Geer, Murray Grand, Cy Walter and others
staging:	Michael Batterberry

Productions:
(Off-Broadway) Opened September 27, 1961 for 2 performances
Reviews:
New York Times page 50, Sep 28, 1961

Foxy
book:	Ian McLellan Hunter and Ring Lardner, Jr., suggested by Ben Jonson's Volpone
music:	Robert Emmett Dolan
lyrics:	Johnny Mercer
staging:	Robert Lewis
sets:	Robert Randolph
costumes:	Robert Fletcher
choreography:	Jack Cole

Productions:
Opened February 16, 1964 for 72 performances
Reviews:
America 110:465, Mar 28, 1964

Commonweal 79:723, Mar 13, 1964
New York Theatre Critics' Reviews 1964:349+
New York Times page 26, Feb 17, 1964
                page 30, Mar 20, 1964
                page 33, Apr 14, 1964
New Yorker 40:106, Feb 29, 1964
Newsweek 63:56, Mar 2, 1964
Saturday Review 47:23, Mar 7, 1964
Time 83:61, Feb 28, 1964

Frank Merriwell, or Honor Challenged
    book: Skip Redwine, Larry Frank and Heywood Gould
    music: Skip Redwine and Larry Frank
    lyrics: Skip Redwine and Larry Frank
    staging: Neal Kenyon
    sets: Tom John
    costumes: Frank Thompson
    choreography: Neal Kenyon
Productions:
Opened April 24, 1971 for 1 performance
Reviews:
New York Theatre Critics' Reviews 1971:296
New York Times II, page 1, Mar 14, 1971
                page 40, Apr 26, 1971
                II, page 1, May 9, 1971
New Yorker 47:94, May 1, 1971

Frankie and Johnny
    book: John Huston
    songs: Hilda Taylor and Eddie Safranski
    incidental
      music: Irwin A. Bazelon
Productions:
    (Off-Broadway) Opened October 28, 1952 for 2 performances
Reviews:
New York Times page 37, Oct 29, 1952

Free for All
    book: Oscar Hammerstein II and Laurence Schwab
    music: Richard A. Whiting
    lyrics: Oscar Hammerstein II
    staging: Oscar Hammerstein II
    choreography: Bobby Connelly
Productions:
Opened September 8, 1931 for 15 performances
Reviews:
Arts and Decoration 36:73, Nov 1931
New York Times VIII, page 1, Aug 16, 1931
Outlook 159:119, Sep 23, 1931

Freedom
    book: C. Lewis Hind and E. Lyall Swete
    music: Norman O'Neill

Productions:
  Opened October 19, 1918 for 33 performances
Reviews:
  Dramatic Mirror 79:687, Nov 9, 1918
  New York Times page 9, Oct 28, 1918
                 page 11, Dec 9, 1918
  Theatre Magazine 28:339, Dec 1918
                   28:345, Dec 1918

Frère Jacques
  music: Gerard Singer
  staging: Richard Balin
Productions:
  (Off-Broadway)   Opened June 6, 1968 for 13 performances
Reviews:
  New York Times page 23, Jun 8, 1968

Frivolities of 1920
  sketches: William Anthony McGuire
  music: William B. Friedlander
  lyrics: William B. Friedlander
  additional
    songs: Harry Auracher and Tom Johnstone
Productions:
  Opened January 8, 1920 for 61 performances
Reviews:
  New York Clipper 67:25, Jan 14, 1920
  New York Times page 22, Jan 9, 1920

From A to Z
  sketches: Woody Allen, Herbert Farjeon, Mark Epstein
                    and Christopher Hewett, Nina Warner Hook
  music and
    lyrics: Jerry Herman, Jay Thompson, Dickson Hughes
                    and Everett Sloane, Jack Holmes, Mary Rod-
                    gers and Marshall Barer, Paul Klein and Fred
                    Ebb, Fred Ebb and Norma Martin, William
                    Dyer and Don Parks, Paul Klein and Lee Gold-
                    smith and Fred Ebb, Charles Zwar and Alan
                    Melville
  staging: Christopher Hewett
  sets: Fred Voelpel
  costumes: Fred Voelpel
  choreography: Ray Harrison
Productions:
  Opened April 20, 1960 for 22 performances
Reviews:
  New York Theatre Critics' Reviews 1960:284+
  New York Times page 23, Apr 21, 1960
  New Yorker 36:84+, Apr 30, 1960

From Israel with Love
  staging: Avi David

    choreography: Yakov Kalusky
Productions:
    Opened October 2, 1972 for 8 performances
Reviews:
    New York Times page 41, Oct 3, 1972

From Nowhere
    book: Bill Solly
    music: Bill Solly
    lyrics: Bill Solly
    choreography: Brian MacDonald
Productions:
    (Off-Off-Broadway) Opened December 4, 1973 (Thirteenth St.
    Repertory Co.)
No Reviews.

From the Second City
    sketches: Howard Alk, Severn Darden, Barbara Harris,
                   Paul Sand, Alan Arkin, Andrew Duncan, Mina
                   Kolb, Eugene Troobnick
    music: William Mathieu
    staging: Paul Sills
    sets: Frederick Fox
Productions:
    Opened September 26, 1961 for 87 performances
Reviews:
    Commonweal 75:94, Oct 20, 1961
    Nation 193:255, Oct 14, 1961
           194:127, Feb 10, 1962
    New York Theatre Critics' Reviews 1961:259+
    New York Times page 32, Sep 27, 1961
                II, page 1, Oct 8, 1961
                page 49, Dec 5, 1961
                page 47, Dec 15, 1961
                page 30, Jan 12, 1962
    New Yorker 37:129, Oct 7, 1961
    Reporter 25:44+, Nov 23, 1961
    Saturday Review 44:78, Oct 14, 1961

From Vienna
    sketches: Lothar Metzl, Werner Michel, Hans Weigel,
                   Jura Soyfer, Peter Hammerschlag, David
                   Gregory; adaptations by John LaTouche, Eva
                   Frankin, Hugo Hauff
    music: Werner Michel, Walter Drix, Otto Andreas,
                   Jimmy Berg
    lyrics: Lothar Metzl, Werner Michel, Hans Weigel,
                   Jura Soyfer, Peter Hammerschlag, David
                   Gregory; adaptations by John LaTouche, Eva
                   Frankin, Hugo Hauff
    staging: Herbert Berghof
    sets: Donald Oenslager
    costumes: Irene Sharaff

Productions:
    Opened June 20, 1939 for 79 performances
Reviews:
    Life 7:32-3, Jul 17, 1939
    Nation 149:109, Jul 22, 1939
    New York Times page 26, Jun 21, 1939
                 IX, page 1, Jun 25, 1939
                 IX, page 1, Jul 2, 1939
    Newsweek 14:24, Jul 19, 1939
    Time 34:43, Jul 3, 1939

Fun City
    sketches: David Rogers
    special
      material: Fred Silver, Nelson Garringer, Jay Jeffries,
                       Franklin Underwood, Norman Martin, David
                       Rogers and James Reed Lawlor
    staging: David Rogers
    sets: Sal Tinnerello and Richard Burnside
    costumes: Frank Page
Productions:
    (Off-Broadway) Opened March 6, 1968 for 31 performances
Reviews:
    New York Times page 53, Mar 7, 1968
                   page 37, Apr 3, 1968

Fun to Be Free
    book: Ben Hecht and Charles MacArthur
    music: Kurt Weill
    staging: Brett Warren
Productions:
    (Off-Broadway) Opened October 5, 1941
No Reviews.

Funny Face
    book: Fred Thompson and Paul Gerard Smith
    music: George Gershwin
    lyrics: Ira Gershwin
Productions:
    Opened November 22, 1927 for 244 performances
Reviews:
    New York Times page 28, Nov 23, 1927
                X, page 2, Dec 4, 1927
                page 22, Nov 9, 1928
    Theatre Magazine 47:58, Feb 1928
    Vogue 71:118, Jan 15, 1928

Funny Girl
    book: Isobel Lennart
    music: Jule Styne
    lyrics: Bob Merrill
    staging: Garson Kanin
    sets: Robert Randolph

    costumes: Irene Sharaff
    choreography: Carol Haney
Productions:
    Opened March 26, 1964 for 1,348 performances
Reviews:
    America 111:114, Aug 1, 1964
    Commonweal 80:147, Apr 24, 1964
    Life 56:10, Apr 17, 1964
    Nation 198:384, Apr 13, 1964
    New York Theatre Critics' Reviews 1964:314+
    New York Times II, page 3, Mar 22, 1964
                   page 15, Mar 27, 1964
                   II, page 3, Apr 5, 1964
                   page 24, Dec 11, 1965
                   II, page 14, Apr 24, 1966
                   page 47, Jun 22, 1967
    New Yorker 40:76, Apr 4, 1964
    Newsweek 63:76-7, Apr 6, 1964
    Saturday Review 47:34, Apr 11, 1964
    Time 83:54, Apr 3, 1964

A Funny Thing Happened on the Way to the Forum
    book: Burt Shevelove and Larry Gelbart, based on
                   Plautus' plays
    music: Stephen Sondheim
    lyrics: Stephen Sondheim
    staging: George Abbott
    sets: Tony Walton
    costumes: Tony Walton
    choreography: Jack Cole
Productions:
    Opened May 8, 1962 for 964 performances
    Opened March 30, 1972 for 156 performances
Reviews:
    America 107:360-1, Jun 2, 1962
            126:405-6, Apr 15, 1972
    Commonweal 76:279, Jun 8, 1962
    Dance Magazine 36:27, Jul 1962
    Life 53:93-5, Jul 20, 1962
    Nation 195:60, Aug 11, 1962
           214:509, Apr 17, 1972
    New Republic 146:28-30, May 28, 1962
    New York Theatre Critics' Reviews 1962:290+
                                      1972:348
    New York Times page 49, May 9, 1962
                   II, page 1, May 20, 1962
                   page 22, Jul 6, 1962
                   page 83, Oct 14, 1962
                   page 14, May 11, 1963
                   page 20, Aug 6, 1964
                   page 14, Aug 7, 1964
                   page 13, Mar 31, 1972
                   II, page 1, Apr 9, 1972

II, page 11, Apr 16, 1972
New Yorker 38:103, May 19, 1962
              48:108, Apr 15, 1972
Newsweek 59:85, May 21, 1962
              79:50, Apr 24, 1972
Saturday Review 45:22, May 26, 1962
Theatre Arts 46:66-8, Jul 1962
Time 79:76, May 18, 1962
        99:73, Apr 17, 1972

Furs and Frills
      book: Edward Clark
      music: Silvio Hein
      lyrics: Edward Clark
      staging: Edward Clark and Arthur Hammerstein
Productions:
      Opened October 9, 1917 for 32 performances
Reviews:
      Dramatic Mirror 77:7, Oct 20, 1917
      New York Dramatic News 64:6, Oct 13, 1917
      New York Times page 9, Oct 10, 1917
      Theatre Magazine 26:275, Nov 1917
                       26:349, Dec 1917

The Future
      book: Al Carmines
      music: Al Carmines
      lyrics: Al Carmines
      staging: Al Carmines
      choreography: Dan Wagoner
Productions:
      (Off-Off-Broadway) Opened March 25, 1974 (Judson Poets'
      Theatre)
Reviews:
      New York Times page 37, Mar 27, 1974
      New Yorker 50:106, Apr 15, 1974

- G -

Gaby
      book: Harry B. and Robert B. Smith
      lyrics: Harry B. and Robert B. Smith
      staging: George Marion
Productions:
      Opened April 27, 1911 for 92 performances
Reviews:
      Green Book Album 6:231-6, Aug 1911
      Theatre Magazine 13:183, Jun 1911

Gaieties 1919 (see Shubert Gaieties 1919)

The Game Is Up

conceived: Rod Warren
music: Rod Warren and others
lyrics: Rod Warren and others
staging: Jonathon Lucas
Productions:
    (Off-Broadway) Opened September 29, 1964 for 620 performances
No Reviews.

The Game Is Up (New Edition)
    book: Rod Warren
    music and
      lyrics: Rod Warren, Alan Friedman, Linda Ashton,
                Michael Cohen, Michael McWhinney, Lesley
                Davidson, Kenny Solms, Gayle Parent
    staging: Sandra Devlin
Productions:
    (Off-Broadway) Opened June 15, 1965 for 228 performances
No Reviews.

The Gang's All Here
    book: Russel Crouse, Oscar Hammerstein II, Morrie
                Ryskind
    music: Lewis E. Gensler
    lyrics: Owen Murphy and Robert A. Simon
    staging: Oscar Hammerstein II
    choreography: Dave Gould and Tilly Losch
Productions:
    Opened February 18, 1931 for 23 performances
Reviews:
    New York Times page 21, Feb 19, 1931
    Theatre Magazine 53:27, Mar 1931
                    53:36, Apr 1931

Gantry
    book: Peter Bellwood; based on the novel Elmer
                Gantry by Sinclair Lewis
    music: Stanley Lebowsky
    lyrics: Fred Tobias
    staging: Onna White
    sets: Robin Wagner
    costumes: Ann Roth
    choreography: Onna White and Patrick Cummings
Productions:
    Opened February 14, 1970 for one performance
Reviews:
    New York Theatre Critics' Reviews 1970:370
    New York Times page 48, Jan 5, 1970
                    page 44, Feb 16, 1970
                    page 34, Feb 17, 1970
    New Yorker 46:62+, Feb 21, 1970
    Saturday Review 53:61, Feb 28, 1970

Garland, Judy (see Judy Garland)

Garrick Gaieties (1925)
    sketches: Benjamin Kaye, Louis Sorin, Sam Jaffe, New-
                     man Levy, Morrie Ryskind
    music: Richard Rodgers
    lyrics: Lorenz Hart
    additional
    lyrics: Benjamin Kaye, Louis Sorin, Sam Jaffe, New-
                     man Levy, Morrie Ryskind
    staging: Philip Loeb
    choreography: Herbert Fields
Productions:
    Opened June 8, 1925 for 211 performances
Reviews:
    Nation 121:77, Jul 8, 1925
    New York Times page 12, May 18, 1925
                     page 16, Jun 9, 1925
    Theatre Magazine 44:15, Aug 1926

Garrick Gaieties (1926)
    sketches: Benjamin Kaye, Newman Levy, Herbert Fields,
                     Philip Loeb
    music: Richard Rodgers
    lyrics: Lorenz Hart
    staging: Philip Loeb
    choreography: Herbert Fields
Productions:
    Opened May 10, 1926 for 174 performances
Reviews:
    Bookman 63:588-9, Jul 1926
    New York Times page 25, May 11, 1926
                     VII, page 1, Jun 13, 1926
    Theatre Magazine 44:15, Aug 1926

Garrick Gaieties (1930)
    sketches: H. Alexander, Carroll Carroll, Ruth Chorpen-
                     ning, Leopoldine Damrosch, Gretchen Dam-
                     rosch Finletter, Landon Herrick, Sterling Hol-
                     loway, Benjamin M. Kaye, Newman Levy,
                     Dorian Otvos, Louis M. Simon
    music: Marc Blitzstein, Aaron Copland, Vernon Duke,
                     Basil Fomeen, Harold Goldman, William Irwin,
                     Ned Lehak, Everett Miller, Peter Nolan,
                     Willard Robison, Charles M. Schwab, Kay
                     Swift
    lyrics: Allen Boretz, Ruth Chorpenning, Ira Gershwin,
                     E. Y. Harburg, Sterling Holloway, Paul James,
                     Ronald Jeans, Malcolm McComb, John Mercer,
                     Henry Myers, Louis M. Simon, Josiah Titzell
    staging: Philip Loeb and Olin Howard
Productions:
    Opened June 4, 1930 for 158 performances
Reviews:
    Life (New York) 95:16, Jun 27, 1930

New Republic 63:127-8, Jun 18, 1930
New York Times page 29, Jun 5, 1930
              VIII, page 1, Jun 22, 1930
Theatre Magazine 52:24, Aug 1930

Gay Divorce
    book: Dwight Taylor, based on J. Hartley Manners'
                     unproduced play. Musical adaptation by Kenneth
                     Webb and Samuel Hoffenstein
    music: Cole Porter
    lyrics: Cole Porter
    staging: Howard Lindsay
    sets: Jo Mielziner
Productions:
    Opened November 29, 1932 for 248 performances
    (Off-Broadway) Season of 1959-60
Reviews:
    New Outlook 161:47, Jan 1933
    New Republic 73:89, Dec 28, 1932
    New York Times page 23, Nov 30, 1932
                    page 15, Apr 19, 1933
                    IX, page 3, Nov 19, 1933
                    page 37, Apr 4, 1960
    New Yorker 36:136, Apr 16, 1960

The Gay Life
    book: Fay and Michael Kanin, suggested by Arthur
                     Schnitzler's Anatol
    music: Arthur Schwartz
    lyrics: Howard Dietz
    staging: Gerald Freedman
    sets: Oliver Smith
    costumes: Lucinda Ballard
    choreography: Herbert Ross
Productions:
    Opened November 18, 1961 for 113 performances
Reviews:
    America 106:737, Mar 3, 1962
    Dance Magazine 36:13-14, Jan 1962
    Life 52:49-51, Jan 19, 1962
    New York Theatre Critics' Reviews 1961:168+
    New York Times II, page 1, Nov 12, 1961
                     page 38, Nov 18, 1961
    New Yorker 37:118, Dec 2, 1961
    Newsweek 58:79, Dec 4, 1961
    Theatre Arts 46:11-12, Feb 1962
    Time 78:64, Dec 1, 1961

Gay Paree
    sketches: Harold Atteridge
    music: Alfred Goodman, Maurie Rubens and J. Fred
                     Coots
    lyrics: Clifford Grey

154   The Geisha

staging: J. J. Shubert
Productions:
Opened August 18, 1925 for 190 performances
Reviews:
New York Times page 14, Aug 19, 1925
Theatre Magazine 42:70, Oct 1925

The Geisha
libretto: Owen Hall
music: Sidney Jones
lyrics: Harry Greenbank
staging: Edwin T. Emery
Productions:
Opened March 27, 1913 for 52 performances
Opened October 5, 1931 for 16 performances
Reviews:
Dramatic Mirror 69:6, Apr 2, 1913
                69:2, Apr 16, 1913
                69:2, Apr 23, 1913
                69:2, May 7, 1913
Harper's Weekly 57:20, Apr 19, 1913
Life (New York) 61:734, Apr 10, 1913
New York Times page 15, Mar 28, 1913
Theatre Magazine 17:xii, May 1913
                17:129, May 1913
                17:133, May 1913

Gentlemen, Be Seated!
book: Jerome Moross and Edward Eager
music: Jerome Moross
lyrics: Edward Eager
staging: Robert Turoff
sets: William Pitkin
costumes: Henry Heymann
choreography: Paul Draper
Productions:
(Off-Broadway) Opened October 10, 1963 for 3 performances
No Reviews.

Gentlemen Prefer Blondes
book: Joseph Fields and Anita Loos, based on a col-
                lection of stories by Anita Loos
music: Jule Styne
lyrics: Leo Robin
staging: John C. Wilson
sets: Oliver Smith
costumes: Miles White
choreography: Agnes De Mille
Productions:
Opened December 8, 1949 for 740 performances
Reviews:
Catholic World 170:387, Feb 1950
Commonweal 51:342, Dec 30, 1949

Life 27:68-71, Dec 26, 1949
Nation 169:629, Dec 24, 1949
New Republic 122:21, Jan 2, 1950
New York Theatre Critics' Reviews 1949:198+
New York Times II, page 5, Dec 4, 1949
                page 35, Dec 9, 1949
                II, page 3, Dec 18, 1949
                II, page 3, Jan 8, 1950
New Yorker 25:50+, Dec 17, 1949
Newsweek 34:72, Dec 19, 1949
Saturday Review 32:28-9, Dec 31, 1949
Theatre Arts 34:13, Feb 1950
Time 54:62, Dec 19, 1949
        55:50-2+, Jan 9, 1950

George M!
    book: Michael Stewart and John and Fran Pascal
    music: George M. Cohan; revised by Mary Cohan
    lyrics: George M. Cohan; revised by Mary Cohan
    staging: Joe Layton
    sets: Tom John
    costumes: Freddy Wittop
    choreography: Joe Layton
Productions:
    Opened April 10, 1968 for 427 performances
Reviews:
    America 118:651, May 11, 1968
    Dance Magazine 42:29+, Jun 1968
    Nation 206:581, Apr 29, 1968
    New York Theatre Critics' Reviews 1968:302
    New York Times page 48, Apr 11, 1968
                    II, page 1, Apr 21, 1968
    New Yorker 44:156, Apr 20, 1968
    Newsweek 71:105, Apr 22, 1968
    Saturday Review 51:26, Apr 27, 1968
    Time 91:64, Apr 19, 1968

George White's Music Hall Varieties
    book: William K. Wells and George White
    music and
     lyrics: Irving Caesar and others
    staging: George White and Russell Markert
Productions:
    Opened November 22, 1932 for 72 performances
Reviews:
    New Outlook 161:47, Jan 1933
    New York Times page 15, Nov 15, 1932
                    page 19, Jan 3, 1933
    Vogue 81:73, Jan 15, 1933
          81:88, Mar 1, 1933

George White's Scandals (1919)
    book: Arthur Jackson and George White

    songs: Richard Whiting, Herbert Spencer, Arthur
                        Jackson
    staging: George White
    sets: Herbert Ward
Productions:
    Opened June 2, 1919 for 128 performances
Reviews:
    New York Times page 9, Jun 3, 1919
    Theatre Magazine 30:11+, Jul 1919

George White's Scandals (1920)
    book: Andy Rice and George White
    music: George Gershwin
    lyrics: Arthur Jackson
    staging: George White
    sets: Law Studios
Productions:
    Opened June 7, 1920 for 318 performances
Reviews:
    New York Clipper 68:25, Jun 2, 1920
                     68:18, Jun 9, 1920
    New York Times page 9, Jun 8, 1920
    Theatre Magazine 32:19+, Jul-Aug 1920

George White's Scandals (1921)
    book: "Bugs" Baer and George White
    music: George Gershwin
    lyrics: Arthur Jackson
    staging: George White
Productions:
    Opened July 11, 1921 for 97 performances
Reviews:
    Life (New York) 78:18, Jul 28, 1921
    New York Clipper 69:25, Jul 20, 1921
    New York Times page 14, Jul 12, 1921

George White's Scandals (1922)
    book: George White, W. C. Fields, Andy Rice
    music: George Gershwin
    lyrics: B. G. DeSylva and Ray Goetz
    staging: George White
Productions:
    Opened August 28, 1922 for 88 performances
Reviews:
    New York Clipper 70:20, Sep 6, 1922
    New York Times page 10, Aug 29, 1922

George White's Scandals (1923)
    book: George White and W. K. Wells
    music: George Gershwin
    lyrics: B. G. DeSylva, Ray Goetz, Ballard McDonald
    staging: George White
Productions:

Opened June 18, 1923 for 168 performances
Reviews:
Life (New York) 82:20, Jul 12, 1923
New York Clipper 71:14, Jun 27, 1923
New York Times page 22, Jun 19, 1923
Theatre Magazine 38:15, Aug 1923

George White's Scandals (1924)
book: William K. Wells and George White
music: George Gershwin
lyrics: B. G. DeSylva
staging: George White
Productions:
Opened June 30, 1924 for 171 performances
Reviews:
Life (New York) 84:18, Jul 31, 1924
New York Times page 16, Jul 1, 1924
Theatre Magazine 40:15, Sep 1924

George White's Scandals (1926)
sketches: George White and William K. Wells
music: Ray Henderson
lyrics: B. G. DeSylva and Lew Brown
staging: George White
Productions:
Opened June 14, 1926 for 424 performances
Reviews:
Life (New York) 88:21, Jul 8, 1926
New York Times page 23, Jun 15, 1926
                 VII, page 1, Jul 3, 1927
Theatre Magazine 44:15, Aug 1926
Vogue 68:71+, Sep 1, 1926

George White's Scandals (1928)
sketches: William K. Wells and George White
music: Ray Henderson
lyrics: B. G. DeSylva and Lew Brown
staging: George White
Productions:
Opened July 2, 1928 for 230 performances
Reviews:
Life (New York) 92:16, Jul 19, 1928
New York Times page 19, Jul 3, 1928
Outlook 149:467, Jul 18, 1928
Theatre Magazine 48:36, Sep 1928
                 48:41, Oct 1928
Vogue 72:74-5, Sep 1, 1928

George White's Scandals (1929)
book: W. K. Wells and George White
music: Cliff Friend, George White, Irving Caesar
lyrics: Cliff Friend, George White, Irving Caesar

staging: George White
choreography: Florence Wilson
Productions:
Opened September 23, 1929 for 161 performances
Reviews:
Life (New York) 94:26, Oct 18, 1929
New York Times page 29, Sep 24, 1929
                      page 21, Dec 25, 1929
Theatre Magazine 50:70, Nov 1929

George White's Scandals (1931)
sketches: George White, Lew Brown, Irving Caesar
music: Ray Henderson
lyrics: Lew Brown
staging: George White
Productions:
Opened September 14, 1931 for 202 performances
Reviews:
New York Times page 28, Aug 11, 1931
                      VIII, page 1, Aug 16, 1931
                      page 30, Sep 15, 1931
                      page 26, Feb 10, 1932
Vogue 78:55+, Nov 15, 1931

George White's Scandals (1935)
sketches: George White, William K. Wells, Howard A.
                   Shiebler
music: Ray Henderson
lyrics: Jack Yellen
staging: George White
sets: Russell Patterson and Walter Jagemann
costumes: Charles LeMaire
choreography: Russell Markert
Productions:
Opened December 25, 1935 for 110 performances
Reviews:
Nation 142:56, Jan 8, 1936
New York Times page 20, Dec 26, 1935
                      page 17, Mar 30, 1936
Newsweek 7:25, Jan 4, 1936
Time 27:24, Jan 6, 1936

George White's Scandals (1939)
sketches: Matt Brooks, Eddie Davis, George White
music: Sammy Fain
lyrics: Jack Yellen
staging: George White
sets: Albert Johnson
costumes: Charles LeMaire
Productions:
Opened August 28, 1939 for 120 performances
Reviews:
New York Times IX, page 2, Aug 20, 1939

page 17, Aug 29, 1939
IX, page 1, Sep 3, 1939
Newsweek 14:40-1, Sep 11, 1939
Time 34:55, Sep 11, 1939

Georgy
book: Tom Mankiewicz; based on a novel by Margaret
                 Forster and a screenplay by Margaret Forster
                 and Peter Nichols
music: George Fischoff
lyrics: Carole Bayer
staging: Peter Hunt
sets: Jo Mielziner
costumes: Patricia Zipprodt
choreography: Howard Jeffrey
Productions:
Opened February 26, 1970 for 4 performances
Reviews:
New York Theatre Critics' Reviews 1970:354
New York Times page 26, Feb 27, 1970
             page 20, Feb 28, 1970
New Yorker 46:83, Mar 7, 1970

Gertrude Stein's First Reader
words: Gertrude Stein
music: Ann Sternberg
staging: Herbert Machiz
sets: Kendall Shaw
Productions:
(Off-Broadway) Opened December 15, 1969 for 40 performances
Reviews:
New York Times II, page 33, Dec 14, 1969
             page 56, Dec 16, 1969
New Yorker 45:39, Dec 27, 1969

Gest, Morris (see Morris Gest)

Get Thee to Canterbury
book: Jan Steen and David Secter; adapted from
                 Chaucer's The Canterbury Tales
music: Paul Hoffert
lyrics: David Secter
staging: Jan Steen
sets: James F. Gohl
costumes: Jeanne Button
choreography: Darwin Knight
Productions:
(Off-Broadway) Opened January 25, 1969 for 20 performances
Reviews:
New York Times page 74, Jan 26, 1969

Getout
book: Joseph Renard

```
    music:              Joseph Blunt
    lyrics:             Joseph Renard
    staging:            Joseph Renard
    choreography:       Joaquin La Habana
Productions:
    (Off-Off-Broadway)  Opened February 24, 1974 (La Mama Ex-
    perimental Theatre Club)
No Reviews.
```

Gilbert Becaud on Broadway
```
    music:              Gilbert Becaud
    lyrics:             Pierre Delanoe, Louis Amade, Maurice Vidalin,
                        Charles Aznavour, Jean Broussolle, Mack
                        David, Gilbert Becaud
    staging:            Raymond Bernard
    sets:               Ralph Alswang
Productions:
    Opened October 31, 1966 for 19 performances
Reviews:
    New York Times page 35, Nov 1, 1966
                    page 46, Nov 8, 1966
```

Gilbert Becaud Sings Love
```
    music:              Gilbert Becaud
    lyrics:             Pierre Delanoe, Louis Amade, Maurice Vidalin,
                        Charles Aznavour, Jean Broussolle, Mack
                        David, Carl Sigman and Gilbert Becaud
    staging:            Raymond Bernard
    sets:               Ralph Alswang
Productions:
    Opened October 6, 1968 for 24 performances
No Reviews.
```

Ginger
```
    book:               Harold Orlob and H. I. Phillips
Productions:
    Opened October 16, 1923 for 38 performances
Reviews:
    New York Times page 14, Oct 17, 1923
```

The Gingham Girl
```
    book:               Daniel Kusell
    music:              Albert Van Tilzer
    lyrics:             Neville Fleeson
Productions:
    Opened August 28, 1922 for 422 performances
Reviews:
    New York Clipper 70:20, Sep 6, 1922
    New York Times page 15, Apr 29, 1922
    Theatre Magazine 36:377, Dec 1922
                     36:387, Dec 1922
```

The Girl and the Wizard

    book: J. Hartley Manners
    music: Julian Edwards
    lyrics: Robert B. Smith and Edward Madden
    staging: Ned Wayburn
Productions:
    Opened September 27, 1909 for 96 performances
Reviews:
    Cosmopolitan 48:202, Jan 1910
    Dramatic Mirror 62:6, Oct 9, 1909
    Hampton 23:823, Dec 1909
    Harper's Weekly 53:25, Oct 16, 1909
    Leslie's Weekly 109:370, Oct 14, 1909
                     109:391, Oct 21, 1909
    Life (New York) 54:517, Oct 14, 1909
    Metropolitan Magazine 31:390-1, Dec 1909
    Theatre Magazine 10:137, Nov 1909
                     10:141, Nov 1909

The Girl Behind the Counter   (see Step This Way)

The Girl Behind the Gun
    book: Guy Bolton and P. G. Wodehouse
    music: Ivan Caryll
    lyrics: Guy Bolton and P. G. Wodehouse
    staging: Edgar MacGregor and Julian Mitchell
Productions:
    Opened September 16, 1918 for 160 performances
Reviews:
    Dramatic Mirror 79:435, Sep 21, 1918
                    79:472-3, Sep 28, 1918
                    79:647, Nov 2, 1918
                    79:683, Nov 9, 1918
                    79;755, Nov 23, 1918
                    79:827, Dec 7, 1918
    Green Book 20:949+, Dec 1918
    New York Times page 11, Sep 1, 1918
                    IV, page 2, Sep 22, 1918
    Theatre Magazine 28:271, Nov 1-18

Girl Crazy
    book: Guy Bolton and John McGowan
    music: George Gershwin
    lyrics: Ira Gershwin
    staging: Alexander Leftwich
    choreography: George Hale
Productions:
    Opened October 14, 1930 for 272 performances
Reviews:
    Life (New York) 96:16, Nov 7, 1930
    Nation 131:479, Oct 29, 1930
    New York Times IX, page 4, Oct 5, 1930
                    page 27, Oct 15, 1930
    Theatre Magazine 52:64, Dec 1930

Vogue 76:136, Dec 8, 1930

The Girl Friend
    book: Herbert Fields
    music: Richard Rodgers
    lyrics: Lorenz Hart
    staging: Lew Fields
Productions:
Opened March 17, 1926 for 409 performances
Reviews:
    New York Times page 26, Mar 18, 1926
                    page 8, Dec 14, 1927
    Theatre Magazine 43:50, Jun 1926

The Girl from Brazil
    book: Edgar Smith; from the original of Julius Bram-
                        mer and Alfred Grunwald
    music: Robert Winterberg and Sigmund Romberg
    staging: J. H. Benrimo
    choreography: Allen K. Foster
Productions:
Opened August 30, 1916 for 61 performances
Reviews:
    Dramatic Mirror 76:8, Sep 9, 1916
    Life (New York) 68:450, Sep 14, 1916
    Munsey 59:278, Nov 1916
    New York Times page 7, Aug 31, 1916
                    page 8, Sep 5, 1916
                    page 7, Sep 13, 1916
    Theatre Magazine 24:204b, Oct 1916
                        24:280, Nov 1916

The Girl from Brighton
    book: Jean C. Havez and Aaron Hoffman
    music: William Backer
    lyrics: Jean C. Havez and Aaron Hoffman
    staging: Jack Mason
Productions:
Opened August 31, 1912 for 49 performances
Reviews:
    Dramatic Mirror 68:7, Sep 11, 1912
    New York Dramatic News 56:12, Sep 14, 1912

The Girl from Home
    book: Frank Craven; based on the Richard Harding
                        Davis farce
    music: Silvio Hein
    lyrics: Frank Craven
    staging: R. H. Burnside
Productions:
Opened May 3, 1920 for 24 performances
Reviews:
    Dramatic Mirror 82:889, May 8, 1920

New York Clipper 68:17, May 12, 1920
New York Times page 9, May 4, 1920
Theatre Magazine 32:505, Jun 1920

The Girl from Nantucket
    book: Paul Stamford and Harold M. Sherman from a
                       story by Fred Thompson and Berne Giler
    music: Jacques Belasco
    lyrics: Kay Twomey
    staging: Edward Clarke Lilley
    sets: Albert Johnson
    costumes: Lou Eisele
    choreography: Val Raset and Van Grona
Productions:
    Opened November 8, 1945 for 12 performances
Reviews:
    New York Theatre Critics' Reviews 1945:121+
    New York Times page 17, Nov 9, 1945
    Time 46:64, Nov 19, 1945

The Girl from Utah
    book: James T. Tanner
    music: Paul Rubens and Sydney Jones; additional num-
                       bers by Jerome D. Kern
    staging: J. A. E. Malone
Productions:
    Opened August 24, 1914 for 120 performances
Reviews:
    Dramatic Mirror 72:8, Sep 2, 1914
    Everybody's 31:698-9, Nov 1914
    Green Book 12:893, Nov 1914
    New York Times page 9, Aug 25, 1914
    Theatre Magazine 20:157-8+, Oct 1914
                       20:167, Oct 1914

The Girl in Pink Tights
    book: Jerome Chodorov and Joseph Fields
    music: Sigmund Romberg
    lyrics: Leo Robin
    staging: Shepard Traube
    sets: Eldon Elder
    costumes: Miles White
    choreography: Agnes de Mille
Productions:
    Opened March 5, 1954 for 115 performances
Reviews:
    America 91:79, Apr 17, 1954
    Catholic World 179:149, May 1954
    Commonweal 60:95-6, Apr 30, 1954
    Life 36:67-8+, Mar 29, 1954
    Mademoiselle 38:124, Apr 1954
    Musical America 74:7, Jun 1954
    Nation 178:246, Mar 20, 1954

New York Theatre Critics' Reviews 1954:354+
New York Times II, page 1, Feb 21, 1954
                page 13, Mar 6, 1954
New Yorker 30:71, Mar 13, 1954
Newsweek 43:63, Mar 15, 1954
Theatre Arts 38:24-5, Apr 1954
                38:16-17, May 1954
Time 63:87, Mar 15, 1954

The Girl in the Spotlight
    book: Richard Bruce (Robert B. Smith)
    music: Victor Herbert
    lyrics: Richard Bruce (Robert B. Smith)
    staging: George W. Lederer
Productions:
Opened July 12, 1920 for 56 performances
Reviews:
    Dramatic Mirror page 97, Jul 17, 1920
    Independent 103:97, Jul 24, 1920
    New York Clipper 68:23, Jul 21, 1920
    New York Times page 9, Jul 13, 1920
    Theatre Magazine 32:105, Sep 1920

The Girl in the Taxi
    book: Anthony Mars; adapted by Stanislaus Stange
    staging: Carter DeHaven
Productions:
Opened October 24, 1910 for 48 performances
Reviews:
    Dramatic Mirror 64:7, Oct 26, 1910
                    64:8, Nov 2, 1910
    Life (New York) 56:762, Nov 3, 1910
    Metropolitan Magazine 32:676-7, Aug 1910

Girl o' Mine
    book: Philip Bartholomae
    music: Frank Tours
    lyrics: Philip Bartholomae
    staging: Clifford Brooke and E. P. Temple
Productions:
Opened January 28, 1918 for 48 performances
Reviews:
    Dramatic Mirror 78:35, Jan 12, 1918
                    78:5, Feb 9, 1918
    Green Book 19:785-6, May 1918
    New York Dramatic News 65:6, Feb 2, 1918
    New York Times page 13, Jan 29, 1918
    Theatre Magazine 27:151, Mar 1918
                    27:231, Apr 1918

The Girl of Montmartre
    book: Georges Feydeau and Rudolph Schanzer;
                   American version by Harry B. and Robert B.

Smith
    music: Henry Bereny and Jerome D. Kern
Productions:
    Opened August 5, 1912 for 64 performances
No Reviews.

The Girl of My Dreams
    book: Wilbur Nesbit and Otto Hauerbach
    music: Karl Haschna
    staging: Frank Smithson
Productions:
    Opened August 7, 1911 for 40 performances
Reviews:
    Dramatic Mirror 66:4, Jul 26, 1911
                  66:4, Aug 2, 1911
                  66:12, Aug 9, 1911
                  66:2, Sep 20, 1911
    Green Book Album 6:984, Nov 1911
    Hampton 27:519, Oct 1911
    Leslie's Weekly 113:138, Aug 3, 1911
                 113:278, Sep 7, 1911
    New York Times page 9, Aug 8, 1911
    Red Book 17:1145-6+, Oct 1911
    Theatre Magazine 14:79, Sep 1911
                 14:89, Sep 1911

The Girl on the Film
    book: James T. Tanner; from the German of Rudolph
                  Schanzer
    music: Walter Kollo, Willy Bredschneider and Albert
                  Sirmay
    lyrics: Adrian Ross
Productions:
    Opened December 29, 1913 for 64 performances
Reviews:
    Blue Book 18:1054-6, Apr 1914
    Dramatic Mirror 70:6, Dec 31, 1913
                 71:5, Jan 7, 1914
                 71:2, Jan 21, 1914
    Munsey 49:596-7, Jul 1913
    New York Times page 9, Dec 31, 1913
    Theatre Magazine 19:59-60+, Feb 1914
                 19:69, Feb 1914

The Girl Who Came to Supper
    book: Harry Kurnitz, based on Terence Rattigan's
                  play The Sleeping Prince
    music: Noel Coward
    lyrics: Noel Coward
    staging: Joe Layton
    sets: Oliver Smith
    costumes: Irene Sharaff
Productions:

Opened December 8, 1963 for 112 performances
Reviews:
America 110:26, Jan 4, 1964
New York Theatre Critics' Reviews 1963:178+
New York Times VI, pages 64, 67, Nov 24, 1963
                      II, page 5, Dec 8, 1963
                      page 49, Dec 9, 1963
                      page 54, Dec 10, 1963
New Yorker 39:62, Dec 21, 1963
Saturday Review 47:52, Jan 11, 1964
Time 82:81, Dec 20, 1963
Vogue 143:62, Feb 1, 1964

The Girl Who Smiles
        book: Paul Herve and Jean Briquet; English version
                   .   by Adolf Philipp and Edward A. Paulton
        staging: Ben Teal
Productions:
Opened August 9, 1915 for 104 performances
Reviews:
Dramatic Mirror 74:8, Aug 11, 1915
                74:4, Aug 25, 1915
                74:2, Oct 6, 1915
New York Times VI, page 2, Sep 5, 1915
Opera Magazine 2:25-6, Oct 1915
Theatre Magazine 22:113, Sep 1915
                22:170, Oct 1915

Girlies
        book: George V. Hobart
        music: Williams and Van Alstyne
        lyrics: Williams and Van Alstyne
Productions:
Opened June 13, 1910 for 88 performances
Reviews:
Cosmopolitan 49:613, Oct 1910
Dramatic Mirror 63:6, Jun 25, 1910
Leslie's Weekly 111:11, Jul 7, 1910
Metropolitan Magazine 32:666-7, Aug 1910
Theatre Magazine 12:x, Jul 1910
                12:42, Aug 1910

The Girls Against the Boys
        sketches: Arnold B. Horwitt
        music: Richard Lewine (additional music by Albert
                         Hague)
        lyrics: Arnold B. Horwitt
        staging: Aaron Ruben
        sets: Ralph Alswang
        costumes: Sal Anthony
        choreography: Boris Runanin
Productions:
Opened November 2, 1959 for 16 performances

Reviews:
New York Theatre Critics' Reviews 1959:239+
New York Times page 26, Nov 3, 1959
                II, page 1, Nov 8, 1959
                page 56, Nov 10, 1959
New Yorker 35:121-2, Nov 14, 1959
Newsweek 54:108, Nov 16, 1959
Time 74:57, Nov 16, 1959

Glorianna
        book: Catherine Chisholm Cushing
        music: Rudolf Friml
        lyrics: Catherine Chisholm Cushing
        staging: Clifford Brooke
Productions:
Opened October 28, 1918 for 96 performances
Reviews:
Dramatic Mirror 79:688, Nov 9, 1918
New York Times page 9, Oct 29, 1918
Theatre Magazine 38:339, Dec 1918
                38:378, Dec 1918

Glory
        book: James Montgomery
        music: Maurice de Packh and Harry Tierney
        lyrics: James Dyrenforth and Joseph McCarthy
Productions:
Opened December 25, 1922 for 64 performances
Reviews:
New York Clipper 70:14, Jan 17, 1923
New York Times page 10, Dec 26, 1922

Go Easy, Mabel
        book: Charles George
        staging: Bertram Harrison and Julian Alfred
Productions:
Opened May 8, 1922 for 16 performances
Reviews:
New York Clipper 70:20, May 17, 1922
New York Times page 22, May 9, 1922
Theatre Magazine 36:32, Jul 1922

Go Fight City Hall
        book: Harry Kalmanowich
        music: Murray Rumshinsky
        lyrics: Bella Mysell
        staging: Menachem Rubin
Productions:
(Off-Broadway) Opened November 2, 1961 for 77 performances
Reviews:
New York Times page 28, Nov 3, 1961

Go-Go

        book: Harry L. Cort and George E. Stoddard
        music: C. Luckyeth Roberts
        lyrics: Alex Rogers
Productions:
    Opened March 12, 1923 for (102) performances
Reviews:
    Life (New York) 81:20, Apr 12, 1923
    New York Clipper 71:14, Mar 21, 1923
    New York Times page 19, Mar 13, 1923

God Bless Coney
        book: John Glines
        music: John Glines
        lyrics: John Glines
        staging: Bob Schwartz
        sets: Don Tirrell
        costumes: Margaretta Mazanini
Productions:
    (Off-Broadway) Opened May 3, 1972 for 3 performances
Reviews:
    New York Times page 55, May 4, 1972
                    page 31, May 5, 1972

God Is a (Guess What?)
        book: Ray McIver
        music: Coleridge-Taylor Perkinson
        staging: Michael A. Schultz
        sets: Edward Burbridge
        costumes: Bernard Johnson
        choreography: Louis Johnson
Productions:
    (Off-Broadway) Opened December 17, 1968 for 32 performances
Reviews:
    New York Theatre Critics' Reviews 1968:129
    New York Times page 56, Dec 18, 1968
                    page 63, Dec 19, 1968
                    II, page 3, Dec 29, 1968

The Goddess of Liberty
        book: Adams and Hough
        music: Joseph E. Howard
        staging: Ned Wayburn and Percy Leach
Productions:
    Opened December 22, 1909 for 29 performances
Reviews:
    Cosmopolitan 48:621, Apr 1910
    Leslie's Weekly 110:35, Jan 13, 1910
    Theatre Magazine 11:xvi, Feb 1910

Godspell
        book: John-Michael Tebelak; based on the Gospel ac-
                         cording to St. Matthew
        music: Stephen Schwartz

```
    lyrics:            Stephen Schwartz
    staging:           John-Michael Tebelak
    costumes:          Susan Tzu
Productions:
    (Off-Broadway)  Opened May 17, 1971 for 1,684 performances
Reviews:
    America 125:516-17, Dec 11, 1971
              127:542-4, Dec 23, 1972
    Christian Century 88:938, Aug 4, 1971
                        89:785-6, Jul 19, 1972
    Commonweal 95:447, Feb 11, 1972
    Christianity Today 15:36-7, Aug 27, 1971
    Life 73:20, Aug 4, 1972
    New York Theatre Critics' Reviews 1971:264
    New York Times page 45, May 18, 1971
                   II, page 1, May 30, 1971
                   page 81, Nov 21, 1971
                   page 47, May 1, 1973
                   page 34, May 14, 1973
    New Yorker 47:56, May 29, 1971
```

Gogo Loves You
```
    book:            Anita Loos; adapted from the French comedy
                     L' Ecole des Cocottes
    music:           Claude Leveillee
    lyrics:          Gladys Shelley
    staging:         Fred Weintraub
    sets:            Kert Lundell
    costumes:        Alfred Lehman
    choreography:    Marvin Gordon
Productions:
    (Off-Broadway)  Opened October 9, 1964 for 2 performances
Reviews:
    New York Times page 10, Oct 10, 1964
```

Going Up
```
    book:            Otto Hauerbach
    music:           Louis A. Hirsch
    lyrics:          Otto Hauerbach
    staging:         Edward Royce and James Montgomery
Productions:
    Opened December 25, 1917 for 351 performances
Reviews:
    Dramatic Mirror 78:4+, Jan 5, 1918
                     78:729, May 25, 1918
    Green Book 19:397+, Mar 1918
    New York Times page 7, Dec 26, 1917
    Theatre Magazine 27:88, Feb 1918
                     27:93, Feb 1918
```

The Golden Age
```
    devised:         Richard Johnson; from words and music of the
                     Elizabethan Age
```

staging: Douglas Campbell
Productions:
    Opened November 18, 1963 for 7 performances
Reviews:
    New York Theatre Critics' Reviews 1963:191
    New York Times page 17, Nov 16, 1963
                    page 49, Nov 19, 1963

The Golden Apple
    book: John Latouche
    music: Jerome Moross
    lyrics: John Latouche
    staging: Norman Lloyd
    sets: William and Jean Eckart
    costumes: Alvin Colt
    choreography: Hanya Holm
Productions:
    Opened March 11, 1954 for 125 performances
    (Off-Broadway) Season of 1960-61 (Equity Library Theatre)
    (Off-Broadway) Opened February 12, 1962 for 112 performances
Reviews:
    America 91:24-5+, Apr 3, 1954
    Catholic World 179:148, May 1954
    Commonweal 60:95, Apr 30, 1954
                76:210, May 18, 1962
    Harper's 208:91-2, May 1954
    Life 36:163-4+, Apr 12, 1954
    Musical America 74:7, Jun 1954
    Nation 178:265-6, Mar 27, 1954
    New York Theatre Critics' Reviews 1954:346+
    New York Times page 15, Mar 12, 1954
                    II, page 1, Mar 21, 1954
                    page 38, Feb 13, 1962
                    page 47, May 9, 1962
    New Yorker 30:60+, Mar 20, 1954
    Saturday Review 37:23, Mar 27, 1954
    Theatre Arts 38:80, May 1954
                38:23, Jun 1954
                38:22-5, Aug 1954
                46:59-61, Apr 1962
    Time 63:96+, Mar 22, 1954

Golden Bat
    book: Yutaka Higashi
    music: Itsuro Shimoda
    lyrics: Yutaka Higashi
    staging: Yutaka Higashi and Kazuko Oshima
    sets: Kenkichi Sato
    costumes: Kiyoko Chiba
Productions:
    (Off-Broadway) Opened July 21, 1970 for 152 performances
Reviews:
    Commonweal 93:278, Dec 11, 1970

Dance Magazine 44:81, Nov 1970
Nation 211:285, Sep 28, 1970
New York Times page 18, Jun 27, 1970
                    II, page 1, Aug 16, 1970
New Yorker 46:59, Aug 1, 1970
Newsweek 76:77, Aug 31, 1970
Saturday Review 53:53, Sep 19, 1970
Time 96:68-9, Aug 3, 1970

Golden Boy
    book: Clifford Odets and William Gibson, based on
                     Odets' play
    music: Charles Strouse
    lyrics: Lee Adams
    staging: Arthur Penn
    sets: Tony Walton
    costumes: Tony Walton
    choreography: Donald McKayle, Jaime Rogers
Productions:
    Opened October 20, 1964 for 568 performances
Reviews:
    America 111:639, Nov 14, 1964
    Commonweal 81:287-9, Nov 20, 1964
    Dance Magazine 38:16, Dec 1964
    Life 57:84A-85+, Nov 13, 1964
    Nation 199:340-1, Nov 9, 1964
    New York Theatre Critics' Reviews 1964:185+
    New York Times II, page 3, Oct 18, 1964
                     page 56, Oct 21, 1964
                     II, page 1, Nov 1, 1964
    Newsweek 64:94-5, Nov 2, 1964
    New Yorker 40:129, Oct 31, 1964
    Saturday Review 47:29, Nov 7, 1964
    Time 84:79, Oct 30, 1964

Golden Dawn
    book: Otto Harbach and Oscar Hammerstein II
    music: Emmerich Kalman and Herbert Stothart
    lyrics: Otto Harbach and Oscar Hammerstein II
    staging: Dave Bennett and Reginald Hammerstein
Productions:
    Opened November 30, 1927 for 184 performances
Reviews:
    New York Times VIII, page 4, Oct 2, 1927
                     page 32, Dec 1, 1927

Golden Rainbow
    book: Ernest Kinoy; based on a play by Arnold
                     Schulman
    music: Walter Marks
    lyrics: Walter Marks
    staging: Arthur Storch
    sets: Robert Randolph

172   The Golden Screw

    costumes: Alvin Colt
    choreography: Tom Panko
Productions:
    Opened February 4, 1968 for 383 performances
Reviews:
    America 118:356-7, Mar 16, 1968
    Dance Magazine 42:30-1, Apr 1968
    New York Theatre Critics' Reviews 1968:350
                                       1968:355
    New York Times page 27, Feb 5, 1968
                    II, page 3, Mar 3, 1968
    New Yorker 43:88, Feb 10, 1968

The Golden Screw
    book: Tom Sankey
    music: Tom Sankey
    lyrics: Tom Sankey
    staging: David Eliscu
    sets: C. Murawski
Productions:
    (Off-Broadway) Opened January 30, 1967 for 40 performances
Reviews:
    New York Times page 52, Jan 31, 1967
    New Yorker 42:116+, Feb 11, 1967

Goldilocks
    book: Walter and Jean Kerr
    music: Leroy Anderson
    lyrics: Joan Ford, Walter and Jean Kerr
    staging: Walter Kerr
    sets: Peter Larkin
    costumes: Castillo
    choreography: Agnes de Mille
Productions:
    Opened October 11, 1958 for 161 performances
Reviews:
    America 100:255, Nov 22, 1958
    Catholic World 188:333, Jan 1959
    Christian Century 75:1338, Nov 19, 1958
    Dance Magazine 32:16-17, Nov 1958
    New Republic 139:22, Oct 27, 1958
    New York Theatre Critics' Reviews 1958:273+
    New York Times page 33, Oct 13, 1958
                    II, page 1, Oct 19, 1958
                    page 25, Feb 21, 1959
    New Yorker 34:55, Oct 18, 1958
    Reporter 19:37-8, Nov 13, 1958
    Theatre Arts 42:12, Dec 1958
    Time 72:100, Oct 20, 1958
    Vogue 132:104, Nov 15, 1958

Good Boy
    book: Otto Harbach, Oscar Hammerstein II, Henry

                        Myers
       music: Herbert Stothart and Harry Ruby
       lyrics: Bert Kalmar
       staging: Reginald Hammerstein
       choreography: Busby Berkeley
Productions:
    Opened September 5, 1928 for 235 performances
Reviews:
    Life (New York) 92:17, Sep 28, 1928
    New York Times page 23, Sep 6, 1928
    Theatre Magazine 48:78, Dec 1928

Good Evening
    written: Peter Cook and Dudley Moore
    staging: Jerry Adler
    sets: Robert Randolph
Productions:
    Opened November 14, 1973 for 438 performances
Reviews:
    Nation 217:603, Dec 3, 1973
    New Republic 169:34, Dec 15, 1973
    New York Theatre Critics' Reviews 1973:186
    New York Times page 58, Nov 15, 1973
                        II, page 1, Dec 2, 1973
                        page 30, Mar 19, 1974
    New Yorker 49:80, Nov 26, 1973
    Newsweek 82:113, Nov 26, 1973
    Time 102:114, Dec 3, 1973

Good Luck
    book: Chaim Tauber and Louis Freiman
    music: Sholom Secunda
    lyrics: Jacob Jacobs
    staging: Max Perlman
    sets: Arthur Aronson
Productions:
    (Off-Broadway) Opened October 17, 1964 for 117 performances
Reviews:
    New York Times page 38, Oct 19, 1964

Good Morning Dearie
    book: Anne Caldwell
    music: Jerome Kern
    lyrics: Anne Caldwell
    staging: Edward Royce
Productions:
    Opened November 1, 1921 for 265 performances
Reviews:
    Dramatic Mirror 84:665, Nov 5, 1921
    Life (New York) 78:18, Nov 17, 1921
    New York Clipper 69:20, Nov 9, 1921
    New York Times page 20, Nov 2, 1921
                        VI, page 1, Nov 27, 1921

Theatre Magazine 35:32, Jan 1922

Good Morning, Judge
    book: Fred Thompson; based on Sir Arthur Wing
                        Pinero's The Magistrate
    music: Lionel Monckton and Howard Talbot
    staging: Wybert Stamford
Productions:
    Opened February 6, 1919 for 140 performances
Reviews:
    Dramatic Mirror 80:268, Feb 22, 1919
    New York Dramatic News 65:8, Feb 8, 1919
    New York Times page 15, Feb 7, 1919
                  IV, page 2, Feb 16, 1919
    Theatre Magazine 29:144, Mar 1919
                 29:163 Mar 1919

Good News
    book: Laurence Schwab and B. G. DeSylva
    music: Ray Henderson
    lyrics: B. G. DeSylva and Lew Brown
    staging: Edgar MacGregor
Productions:
    Opened September 6, 1927 for 551 performances
Reviews:
    New York Times VII, page 2, Aug 14, 1927
                  page 35, Sep 7, 1927
                  IX, page 4, Apr 1, 1928
    Theatre Magazine 48:39, Aug 1928
    Vogue 70:124, Nov 1, 1927

Good Night, Paul
    book: Roland Oliver and Charles Dickson
    music: Harry B. Olsen
    lyrics: Roland Oliver and Charles Dickson
Productions:
    Opened September 3, 1917 for 40 performances
Reviews:
    Dramatic Mirror 77:7, Sep 15, 1917
    New York Times page 9, Sep 4, 1917
    Theatre Magazine 26:203, Oct 1917
                 26:207, Oct 1917

Good Times
    book: R. H. Burnside
    music: Raymond Hubbell
Productions:
    Opened August 9, 1920 for 456 performances
Reviews:
    Dramatic Mirror page 1208, Dec 25, 1920
    New York Times page 10, Aug 10, 1920
    Theatre Magazine 32:242, Oct 1920

Goodbye Tomorrow
      book: Sue Brock
      music: Carl Friberg
      lyrics: Sue Brock
      staging: Anthony Stimac
Productions:
     (Off-Off-Broadway) Opened March 23, 1973 (Central Arts
     Cabaret)
No Reviews.

The Grab Bag
      book: Ed Wynn
      music: Ed Wynn
      lyrics: Ed Wynn
      staging: Ed Wynn
Productions:
     Opened October 6, 1924 for 184 performances
Reviews:
     New York Times page 26, Oct 7, 1924
                         page 7, Feb 17, 1925
     Theatre Magazine 40:70, Dec 1924

Graham Crackers
      conceived: Ronny Graham
      devised: Ronny Graham
      choreography: Lee Becker
Productions:
     (Off-Broadway) Opened January 23, 1963 for 286 performances
No Reviews.

The Grand Music Hall of Israel
      conceived: Jonathon Karmon
      staging: Jonathon Karmon
      costumes: Hovav Kruvi
      choreography: Jonathon Karmon
Productions:
     Opened February 6, 1968 for 64 performances
     (Off-Broadway) Opened January 4, 1973 for 15 performances
Reviews:
     New York Times page 42, Feb 7, 1968
                         page 39, Feb 8, 1968

Grand Street Follies (1925)
      book: Agnes Morgan
      music: Lily Hyland
      lyrics: Agnes Morgan
Productions:
     Opened June 18, 1925 for 148 performances
Reviews:
     Nation 121:77, Jul 8, 1925
     New York Times page 24, Jun 19, 1925
     Theatre Magazine 42:15, Sep 1925
                         42:21, Sep 1925

Grand Street Follies (1926)
    book: Agnes Morgan
    music: Lily Hyland, Arthur Schwartz, and Randall
                  Thompson
    lyrics: Agnes Morgan
    staging: Agnes Morgan
Productions:
    Opened June 15, 1926 for 53 performances
Reviews:
    Bookman 64:85-6, Sep 1926
    Independent 117:133, Jul 31, 1926
    Life (New York) 88:21, Jul 8, 1926
    New York Times page 23, Jun 16, 1926
    Theatre Magazine 44:15, Aug 1926
                   44:19, Sep 1926

Grand Street Follies (1927)
    book: Agnes Morgan
    music: Max Ewing
    lyrics: Agnes Morgan
    staging: Agnes Morgan
Productions:
    Opened May 19, 1927 for 148 performances
Reviews:
    Nation 124:616-17, Jun 1, 1927
    New Republic 51:70, Jun 8, 1927
    New York Times page 22, May 20, 1927
                  page 24, Jun 1, 1927
                  VII, page 1, Jul 3, 1927
    Vogue 70:98, Jul 15, 1927

Grand Street Follies (1928)
    book: Agnes Morgan
    music: Max Ewing, Lily Hyland and Serge Walter
    lyrics: Agnes Morgan
    staging: Agnes Morgan
Productions:
    Opened May 28, 1928 for 144 performances
Reviews:
    Life (New York) 92:12, Jul 12, 1928
    Nation 126:675, Jun 13, 1928
    New Republic 55:95, Jun 15, 1928
    New York Times page 16, May 29, 1928
                  VIII, page 1, Jun 3, 1928
                  page 7, Jun 23, 1928
    Outlook 149:345, Jun 27, 1928
    Theatre Arts 12:537-8, Aug 1928
    Vogue 72:56+, Aug 1, 1928

Grand Street Follies (1929)
    book: Agnes Morgan
    music: Arthur Schwartz and Max Ewing, additional
                  numbers by William Irwin and Serge Walter

lyrics: Agnes Morgan
staging: Agnes Morgan
choreography: Dave Gould
Productions:
Opened May 1, 1929 for 93 performances
Reviews:
Bookman 64:85-6, Sep 1926
Independent 117:133, Jul 31, 1926
Life (New York) 88:21, Jul 8, 1926
                 93:20, May 31, 1929
Nation 121:77, Jul 8, 1925
       124:616-17, Jun 1, 1927
       128:594-5, May 15, 1929
New Republic 51:70, Jun 8, 1927
             59:24-5, May 22, 1929
New York Times IX, page 2, Apr 18, 1929
               page 20, May 2, 1929
               IX, page 1, May 12, 1929
               page 34, Jun 19, 1929
Outlook 152:191, May 29, 1929
Theatre Magazine 42:15+, Sep 1925
                 50:42, Jul 1929
Vogue 70:98, Jul 15, 1927
      74:92+, Jul 6, 1929

El Grande de Coca-Cola (El Coca-Cola Grande)
    conceived: Ron House and Diz White
    written: Ron House, Diz White and others
    choreography: Anna Nygh
Productions:
    (Off-Broadway) Opened February 13, 1973 for 1,114 per-
    formances
Reviews:
    New York Theatre Critics' Reviews 1973:311
    New York Times page 26, Feb 14, 1973
                   II, page 16, Apr 8, 1973
    New Yorker 49:81, Feb 24, 1973
    Newsweek 81:90, Feb 26, 1973
    Time 101:68, Feb 26, 1973

The Grass Harp
    book: Kenward Elmslie; based on the novel by Truman
                    Capote
    music: Claibe Richardson
    lyrics: Kenward Elmslie
    staging: Ellis Rabb
    sets: James Tilton
    costumes: Nancy Potts
    choreography: Rhoda Levine
Productions:
    Opened November 2, 1971 for 7 performances
Reviews:
    America 125:427, Nov 20, 1971

New York Theatre Critics' Reviews 1971:196
New York Times page 56, Oct 7, 1971
                page 41, Nov 3, 1971
New Yorker 47:66, Nov 13, 1971

The Grass Widow
book: Channing Pollock and Rennold Wolf; adapted
                 from Le Peril Jaune by Bisson and St. Albin
music: Louis A. Hirsch
lyrics: Channing Pollock and Rennold Wolf
staging: George Marion
Productions:
Opened December 3, 1917 for 48 performances
Reviews:
Dramatic Mirror 77:31, Oct 20, 1917
                77:5, Dec 15, 1917
Green Book 19:196+, Feb 1918
New York Times page 11, Dec 4, 1917

Grease
book: Jim Jacobs and Warren Casey
music: Jim Jacobs and Warren Casey
lyrics: Jim Jacobs and Warren Casey
staging: Tom Moore
sets: Douglas W. Schmidt
costumes: Carrie F. Robbins
choreography: Patricia Birch
Productions:
Opened February 14, 1972 for 1,375* performances
Reviews:
Dance Magazine 49:90, Apr 1975
New York Theatre Critics' Reviews 1972:336
New York Times page 27, Feb 15, 1972
                page 11, Feb 27, 1972
                II, page 1, Jun 4, 1972
New Yorker 48:68, Feb 26, 1972
Newsweek 79:95, Feb 28, 1972
Saturday Review 55:64, Jul 15, 1972
Time 99:56, May 29, 1972

Great Day
book: William Cary Duncan and John Wells
music: Vincent Youmans
lyrics: William Rose
staging: R. H. Burnside and Frank M. Gillespie
choreography: LeRoy Prinz
Productions:
Opened October 17, 1929 for 36 performances
Reviews:
New York Times VIII, page 1, Jun 9, 1929
                page 24, Oct 18, 1929
                IX, page 1, Nov 3, 1929
Theatre Magazine 50:16, Oct 1929

Great Lady
    book: Earle Crooker and Lowell Brentano
    music: Frederick Loewe
    lyrics: Earle Crooker and Lowell Brentano
    staging: Bretaigne Windust
    sets: Albert R. Johnson
    costumes: Lucinda Ballard and Scott Wilson
    choreography: William Dollar
Productions:
    Opened December 1, 1938 for 20 performances
Reviews:
    Catholic World 148:477-8, Jan 1939
    New York Times page 26, Dec 2, 1938
    Time 32:32, Dec 12, 1938

The Great Magician
    book: Lawrence Carra
    music: Wenner Laise
    staging: Edward Padula
Productions:
    (Off-Broadway) Opened April 1939
No Reviews.

Great Scot!
    book: Mark Conradt and Gregory Dawson
    music: Dan McAfee
    lyrics: Nancy Leeds
    staging: Charles Tate
    sets: Herbert Senn and Helen Pond
    costumes: Patton Campbell
Productions:
    (Off-Broadway) Opened November 10, 1965 for 38 performances
Reviews:
    New York Times page 50, Nov 9, 1965
                  page 56, Nov 12, 1965

Great Temptations
    book: Harold Atteridge
    music: Maurice Rubens
    lyrics: Clifford Grey
    staging: J. J. Shubert
Productions:
    Opened May 18, 1926 for 197 performances
Reviews:
    Bookman 63:691-3, Aug 1926
    Nation 122:616, Jun 2, 1926
    New York Times page 29, May 19, 1926
                    VIII, page 1, May 23, 1926
                    VIII, page 1, May 30, 1926
                    page 13, Jun 26, 1926
    Theatre Magazine 44:15, Aug 1926
                     44:19, Aug 1926

Great to Be Alive
    book: Walter Bullock and Sylvia Regan
    music: Abraham Ellstein
    lyrics: Walter Bullock
    staging: Mary Hunter
    sets: Stewart Chaney
    costumes: Stewart Chaney
    choreography: Helen Tamiris
Productions:
Opened March 23, 1950 for 52 performances
Reviews:
    Catholic World 171:149, May 1950
    New York Theatre Critics' Reviews 1950:324+
    New York Times page 28, Mar 24, 1950
    New Yorker 26:46+, Apr 1, 1950
    Newsweek 35:73, Apr 3, 1950
    Theatre Arts 34:18, May 1950
    Time 55:51, Apr 3, 1950

The Great Waltz
    book: Moss Hart, based on libretti by Dr. A. M.
                     Willner, Heinz Reichert, Ernst Marischka,
                     Caswell Garth
    music: Johann Strauss, father and son
    lyrics: Desmond Carter
    staging: Hassard Short
    sets: Albert Johnson
    choreography: Albertina Rasch
Productions:
Opened September 22, 1934 for 298 performances
Opened August 5, 1935 for 49 performances
Reviews:
    Catholic World 140:213, Nov 1934
    Golden Book Magazine 20:508+, Nov 1934
    Literary Digest 118:19, Oct 6, 1934
    New Republic 81:131, Dec 12, 1934
    New York Times page 14, Sep 23, 1934
                    IX, page 1, Sep 30, 1934
                    IX, page 1, Aug 4, 1935
                    page 20, Aug 6, 1935
                    IX, page 2, Sep 8, 1935
    Newsweek 4:27, Sep 29, 1934
            4:23, Dec 1, 1934
    Stage 12:3+, Nov 1934
    Theatre Arts 18:819-20, Nov 1934
                19:19, Jan 1935
    Time 24:34, Oct 1, 1934

Green, Adolph (see A Party with Betty Comden and Adolph Green)

Green Fruit (see The Madcap)

Greenwich Village Follies (1919)

book: Philip Bartholomae and John Murray Anderson
music: A. Baldwin Sloane
lyrics: Philip Bartholomae and John Murray Anderson
staging: John Murray Anderson
sets: Pieter Myer and Charles Ellis
costumes: Pieter Myer and Charles Ellis
Productions:
Opened July 15, 1919 for 232 performances
Reviews:
Dramatic Mirror 80:1165, Jul 29, 1919
New York Times page 14, Jul 16, 1919
Theatre Magazine 30:152-3, Sep 1919

The Greenwich Village Follies (1920)
dialogue: Thomas J. Gray
music: A. Baldwin Sloane
lyrics: John Murray Anderson and Arthur Swanstrom
sets: Robert Locher and James Reynolds
costumes: Robert Locher and James Reynolds
Productions:
Opened August 30, 1920 for 192 performances
Reviews:
Dramatic Mirror page 415, Sep 4, 1920
Forum 64:234, Sep-Oct 1920
New York Clipper 68:28-9, Sep 8, 1920
New York Times page 7, Aug 31, 1920
Theatre Magazine 32:259, Nov 1920
                 32:279, Nov 1920
                 32:375, Dec 1920

Greenwich Village Follies (1921)
music: Carey Morgan
lyrics·   Arthur Swanstrom and J. M. Anderson
staging: John Murray Anderson
sets: Robert Locher and James Reynolds
costumes: Robert Locher and James Reynolds
Productions:
Opened August 31, 1921 for 167 performances
Reviews:
New York Clipper 69:22, Sep 7, 1921
New York Times page 18, Sep 1, 1921
Theatre Magazine 34:314, Nov 1921

Greenwich Village Follies (1922)
book: George V. Hobart
music: Louis A. Hirsch
lyrics: John Murray Anderson and Irving Caesar
sets and
   costumes: Howard Greer, Erté of Paris, Ingeborg Hansell,
                 Cleon Throckmorten, Earl Payne Franke,
                 Blanding Sloan, Georgianna Brown, Alice
                 O'Neill, Reginald Marsh, Dorothy Armstrong,
                 Pieter Myer, James Reynolds

182   Greenwich Village Follies

choreography: Carl Randall
Productions:
    Opened September 12, 1922 for 216 performances
Reviews:
    Forum 68:1034-7, Dec 1922
    New Republic 32:175-6, Oct 11, 1922
                33:21-4, Nov 29, 1922
    New York Times page 18, Sep 13, 1922
    Theatre Magazine 36:299, Nov 1922

Greenwich Village Follies (1923)
    music: Louis A. Hirsch and Con Conrad
    lyrics: Irving Caesar and John M. Anderson
    sketches: Lew Fields
    staging: John Murray Anderson
    sets: Howard Greer, Ingeborg Hansell, James Reynolds
    costumes: Howard Greer, Ingeborg Hansell, James Reynolds
    choreography: Larry Ceballos and Michio Itow
Productions:
    Opened September 20, 1923 for 140 performances
Reviews:
    Life 82:18, Oct 18, 1923
    New York Times page 4, Sep 21, 1923
                page 21, Oct 16, 1923
    Theatre Magazine 38:54, Nov 1923

Greenwich Village Follies (1924)
    music: Cole Porter
    lyrics: Cole Porter, Irving Caesar, John Murray Ander-
                  son
    staging: John Murray Anderson
Productions:
    Opened September 16, 1924 for 180 performances
Reviews:
    Life (New York) 84:18, Oct 9, 1924
    New York Times page 19, Feb 11, 1924
                page 16, Sep 17, 1924
                VII, page 1, Sep 21, 1924
                VIII, page 1, Sep 28, 1924
    Theatre Magazine 40:64, Nov 1924

Greenwich Village Follies (1925)
    music: Harold Levey and Owen Murphy
    lyrics: Harold Levey and Owen Murphy
    staging: Hassard Short
    sets: Clark Robinson
    costumes: Mark Mooring, Charles LeMaire, Gilbert Adrian
    choreography: Larry Ceballos and Alexander Gabrilov
Productions:
    Opened December 24, 1925 for 180 performances
Reviews:
    Life (New York) 87:18, Jan 28, 1926
    New York Times page 23, Dec 25, 1925

VII, page 1, Jan 10, 1926
page 22, Mar 16, 1926
Theatre Magazine 43:18, Mar 1926
44:25, Jul 1926

Greenwich Village Follies (1928)
sketches: Harold Atteridge
music: Ray Perkins and Maurie Rubens
lyrics: Max and Nathaniel Lief
staging: J. C. Huffman, Chester Hale and Ralph Reader
sets: Watson Barratt
costumes: Ernest Schraps
Productions:
Opened April 9, 1928 for 158 performances
Reviews:
New York Times page 32, Apr 10, 1928
Outlook 149:185, May 30, 1928
Vogue 71:79, Jun 1, 1928

Greenwich Village USA
sketches: Frank Gehrecke
music: Jeanne Bargy
lyrics: Jeanne Bargy
Productions:
(Off-Broadway) Opened Season of 1960-61
Reviews:
New York Times page 30, Sep 29, 1960
page 56, Dec 7, 1960
New Yorker 36:97-8, Oct 8, 1960

Greenwillow
book: Lesser Samuels and Frank Loesser, based on
the novel by B. J. Chute
music: Frank Loesser
lyrics: Frank Loesser
staging: George Roy Hill
sets: Peter Larkin
costumes: Alvin Colt
choreography: Joe Layton
Productions:
Opened March 8, 1960 for 97 performances
(Off-Broadway) Season of 1970-71 (Equity Library Theatre)
Reviews:
Commonweal 72:16, Apr 1, 1960
New York Theatre Critics' Reviews 1960:325+
New York Times II, page 3, Feb 28, 1960
page 38, Mar 9, 1960
II, page 1, Mar 20, 1960
page 26, May 13, 1960
page 60, Dec 8, 1970
New Yorker 36:117, Mar 19, 1960
Newsweek 55:116, Mar 21, 1960
Time 75:74, Mar 21, 1960

Grenfell, Joyce (see Joyce Grenfell)

La Grosse Valise
    book: Robert Dhery
    music: Gerard Calvi
    lyrics: Harold Rome
    staging: Robert Dhery
    sets: Jacques Dupont and Frederick Fox
    costumes: Jacques Dupont and Frederick Fox
    choreography: Colette Brosset and Tom Panko
Productions:
    Opened December 14, 1965 for 7 performances
Reviews:
    Dance Magazine 40:14-15+, Feb 1966
    New York Theater Critics' Reviews 1965:218
    New York Times page 52, Dec 15, 1965
                  page 64, Dec 16, 1965
    New Yorker 41:50, Dec 25, 1965

Guys and Dolls
    book: Jo Swerling and Abe Burrows, based on a story
                  and characters of Damon Runyon
    music: Frank Loesser
    lyrics: Frank Loesser
    staging: George S. Kaufman
    sets: Jo Mielziner
    costumes: Alvin Colt
    choreography: Michael Kidd
Productions:
    Opened November 24, 1950 for 1,200 performances
    Opened April 20, 1955 for 31 performances
    Opened April 28, 1965 for 15 performances
    Opened June 8, 1966 for 23 performances
Reviews:
    America 93:192, May 14, 1955
    Catholic World 172:309, Jan 1951
               181:228, Jun 1955
    Christian Science Monitor Magazine page 13, Dec 2, 1950
    Commonweal 53:252, Dec 15, 1950
    Dance Magazine 40:59, Jul 1966
    Holiday 20:75+, Oct 1956
    Life 29:64-5, Dec 25, 1950
         60:18, Jun 17, 1966
    Nation 171:515, Dec 2, 1950
    New Republic 123:22, Dec 25, 1950
              132:22, May 2, 1955
    New York Theatre Critics' Reviews 1950:185+
    New York Times page 32, Oct 24, 1950
                 II, page 1, Nov 12, 1950
                 page 11, Nov 25, 1950
                 II, page 1, Dec 3, 1950
                 VI, page 63, Dec 10, 1950
                 II, page 1, Dec 17, 1950

                    page 20, Mar 26, 1951
                    page 34, Apr 4, 1951
                    II, page 1, Oct 7, 1951
                    page 17, May 29, 1953
                    II, page 1, Jun 7, 1953
                    page 32, Apr 21, 1955
                    page 22, Jul 22, 1959
                    page 39, Apr 29, 1965
                    page 55, Jun 9, 1966
    New Yorker 26:77, Dec 2, 1950
    Newsweek 36:75, Dec 4, 1950
    Saturday Review 33:27-8, Dec 23, 1950
                    33:38+, Dec 30, 1950
    Theatre Arts 35:13+, Feb 1951
                    35:32+, Jul 1951
                    39:88, Jul 1955
    Time 56:63, Dec 4, 1950

Gypsy
    book: Arthur Laurents, suggested by the memoirs of
                    Gypsy Rose Lee
    music: Jule Styne
    lyrics: Stephen Sondheim
    staging: Jerome Robbins
    sets: Jo Mielziner
    costumes: Raoul Pene du Bois
    choreography: Jerome Robbins
Productions:
    Opened May 21, 1959 for 702 performances
Reviews:
    America 101:438, Jun 13, 1959
    Coronet 46:12, Oct 1959
    Dance Magazine 33:12-13, Jul 1959
    Life 47:63-4, Jul 27, 1959
    Nation 188:521, Jun 6, 1959
    New York Theatre Critics' Reviews 1959:300+
    New York Times II, page 1, May 17, 1959
                    page 31, May 22, 1959
                    II, page 1, May 31, 1959
                    VI, pages 12-13, May 31, 1959
                    II, page 1, Jun 7, 1959
    New Yorker 35:65-7, May 30, 1959
    Newsweek 53:58, Jun 1, 1959
    Saturday Review 42:29, Jun 6, 1959
    Theatre Arts 43:9+, Aug 1959
                    43:18-20, May 1959
    Time 73:84+, Jun 1, 1959
    Vogue 134:60-1, Jul 1959

Gypsy Blonde
    book: Kenneth Johns, based on Michael Balfe's opera
                    Bohemian Girl
    music: Michael Balfe

lyrics: Frank Gabrielson
staging: Dmitri Ostrov
sets: Karl Amend
choreography: Vaughn Godfrey
Productions:
Opened June 25, 1934 for 24 performances
Reviews:
New York Times page 22, Jun 26, 1934

- H -

Hackett, Buddy (see Buddy Hackett)

Hair
book: Gerome Ragni and James Rado
music: Galt MacDermot
lyrics: Gerome Ragni and James Rado
staging: Tom O'Horgan
sets: Robin Wagner
costumes: Nancy Potts
Productions:
(Off-Broadway) Opened October 29, 1967 for 94 performances
Opened April 29, 1968 for 1,750 performances
Reviews:
America 118:759-60, Jun 8, 1968
Commonweal 88:268, May 17, 1968
Dance Magazine 41:28-9, Dec 1967
                42:24-5+, Jul 1968
Ebony 25:120-2+, May 1970
English Journal 60:626-8, May 1971
High Fidelity 19:108, Jul 1969
Harper's 237:107-9, Sep 1968
Life 68:83-6, Apr 17, 1970
National Review 20:519, May 21, 1968
                22:319, Mar 24, 1970
New Republic 157:38-9, Nov 18, 1967
New York Theatre Critics' Reviews 1968:280
                                   1968:288
New York Times page 55, Oct 30, 1967
              page 50, Nov 14, 1967
              II, page 1, Nov 19, 1967
              page 25, Jan 23, 1968
              II, page 1, Apr 28, 1968
              page 40, Apr 30, 1968
              page 41, May 1, 1968
              II, page 1, May 19, 1968
              II, page 3, May 19, 1968
              page 76, Sep 29, 1968
              page 36, Feb 5, 1969
              II, page 1, May 11, 1969
              page 53, Jun 2, 1969
              page 26, Jun 7, 1969

                            page 13, Jun 8, 1969
                            page 52, Jun 10, 1969
                            page 30, Sep 13, 1969
                            II, page 3, Sep 14, 1969
                            page 62, Nov 3, 1969
                            page 64, Dec 10, 1969
                            page 39, Jan 13, 1970
                            page 44, Jun 29, 1970
                            page 10, Sep 5, 1970
                            II, page 1, Sep 27, 1970
                            page 17, Mar 13, 1971
                            page 26, May 10, 1971
                            VI, page 14, Jan 2, 1972
                            page 41, May 8, 1972
                            page 42, May 17, 1972
        New Yorker 43:128+, Nov 11, 1967
                   44:84-5, May 11, 1968
                   45:102, Jun 14, 1969
        Newsweek 70:124, Nov 13, 1967
                 71:110, May 13, 1968
                 74:94, Jul 7, 1969
        Opera News 34:8-13, Dec 20, 1969
        Reporter 33:36+, Apr 4, 1968
        Saturday Evening Post 241:66-9, Aug 10, 1968
        Saturday Review 51:95, Jan 13, 1968
                        51:26, May 11, 1968
        Time 91:72, May 10, 1968
             94:76, Dec 12, 1969

Hairpin Harmony
    book: Harold Orlob
    music: Harold Orlob
    lyrics: Harold Orlob
    staging: Dora Maugham
    sets: Donald Oenslager
    costumes: Mahieu
Productions:
    Opened October 1, 1943 for 3 performances
Reviews:
    New York Theatre Critics' Reviews 1943:269
    New York Times page 18, Oct 2, 1943

Half a Sixpence
    book: Beverly Cross, based on H. G. Wells's Kipps
    music: David Heneker
    lyrics: David Heneker
    staging: Gene Saks
    sets: Loudon Sainthill
    costumes: Loudon Sainthill
    choreography: Onna White and Tom Panko
Productions:
    Opened April 25, 1965 for 511 performances
Reviews:

America 113:63, Jul 10, 1965
Commonweal 82:383-4, Jun 11, 1965
Dance Magazine 39:22-3, Jul 1965
New York Theatre Critics' Reviews 1965:346+
New York Times page 38, Apr 26, 1965
           II, page 12, Aug 29, 1965
New Yorker 41:120, May 8, 1965
Newsweek 65:100, May 10, 1965
Saturday Review 48:24, May 15, 1965
Time 85:88, May 7, 1965

Half a Widow
    book: Harry B. Smith and Frank Dupree
    music: Shep Camp
    lyrics: Harry B. Smith and Frank Dupree
    staging: Lawrence Marston and Edwin T. Emery
Productions:
    Opened September 12, 1927 for 8 performances
Reviews:
    New York Times page 37, Sep 13, 1927
    Theatre Magazine 46:24+, Nov 1927

The Half Moon
    book: William Le Baron
    music: Victor Jacobi
    lyrics: William Le Baron
    staging: Fred G. Latham
Productions:
    Opened November 1, 1920 for 48 performances
Reviews:
    Dramatic Mirror page 847, Nov 6, 1920
    Life (New York) 76:960-1, Nov 25, 1920
    New York Clipper 68:31, Nov 17, 1920
    New York Times page 15, Nov 2, 1920
    Theatre Magazine 33:30-31, Jan 1921

Half-Past Wednesday
    book: Anna Marie Barlow
    music: Robert Colby
    lyrics: Robert Colby and Nita Jonas
    staging: Hal Raywin
    sets: Lloyd Burlingame
    costumes: Robert Fletcher
    choreography: Gene Bayliss
Productions:
    (Off-Broadway) Opened April 6, 1962 for 2 performances
Reviews:
    New York Times page 16, Apr 7, 1962
                page 34, Apr 9, 1962

Hallelujah, Baby!
    book: Arthur Laurents
    music: Julie Styne

lyrics: Betty Comden and Adolph Green
staging: Burt Shevelove
sets: William and Jean Eckart
costumes: Irene Sharaff
choreography: Kevin Carlisle, William Guske, and Marie Lake
Productions:
Opened April 26, 1967 for 293 performances
Reviews:
America 116:879, Jun 24, 1967
Christian Century 84:1106, Aug 30, 1967
Commonweal 86:342-5, Jun 9, 1967
Dance Magazine 41:78-9, Jun 1967
National Review 19:976-7, Sep 5, 1967
New York Theatre Critics' Reviews 1967:312
New York Times page 51, Apr 27, 1967
                II, page 1, May 7, 1967
                page 41, Jan 5, 1968
New Yorker 43:150, May 6, 1967
Newsweek 69:116, May 8, 1967
Saturday Review 50:66, May 13, 1967
Time 89:58, May 5, 1967

Hammerstein's 9 O'Clock Revue
book: Harold Simpson and Morris Harvey
Productions:
Opened October 4, 1923 for 12 performances
Reviews:
New York Times page 22, Oct 5, 1923
                VIII, page 1, Oct 14, 1923

A Hand Is on the Gate
arranged: Roscoe Lee Brown
staging: Ivor David Balding, Peter Cook and Joseph E.
                 Levine
Productions:
Opened September 21, 1966 for 21 performances
Reviews:
New York Theatre Critics' Reviews 1966:298
New York Times page 54, Sep 22, 1966
                page 58, Sep 29, 1966

Hands Up
book: Edgar Smith
music: E. Ray Goetz and Sigmund Romberg
lyrics: E. Ray Goetz
staging: J. H. Benrimo
choreography: Jack Mason
Productions:
Opened July 22, 1915 for 52 performances
Reviews:
Dramatic Mirror 74:8, Jul 28, 1915
Green Book 14:615, Oct 1915
Theatre Magazine 22:139, Sep 1915

Hang Down Your Head and Die
     book: David Wright
     staging: Braham Murray
     sets: Fred Voelpel
     choreography: Braham Murray
Productions:
     (Off-Broadway) Opened October 18, 1964 for 1 performance
Reviews:
     New York Times page 38, Oct 19, 1964
                     page 42, Oct 20, 1964

Hanky Panky
     book: Edgar Smith
     music: A. Baldwin Sloane
     lyrics: E. Ray Goetz
     staging: Gus Sohlke
Productions:
     Opened August 5, 1912 for 104 performances
Reviews:
     Blue Book 16:29-32, Nov 1912
     Dramatic Mirror 68:11, Aug 7, 1912
     Green Book 8:568-70, Oct 1912
     Theatre Magazine 16:xi, Sep 1912

The Happiest Girl in the World
     book: Fred Saidy and Henry Myers, based on
                      Aristophanes' Lysistrata and Bullfinch's stories
                      of Greek mythology
     music: Jacques Offenbach
     lyrics: E. Y. Harburg
     staging: Cyril Ritchard
     sets: William and Jean Eckart
     costumes: Robert Fletcher
     choreography: Dania Krupska
Productions:
     Opened April 3, 1961 for 96 performances
Reviews:
     America 105:410, Jun 3, 1961
     Dance Magazine 35:13-14, May 1961
     Nation 192:358, Apr 22, 1961
     New York Theatre Critics' Reviews 1961:314+
     New York Times II, page 1, Apr 2, 1961
                     page 42, Apr 4, 1961
     Newsweek 57:69, Apr 17, 1961
     New Yorker 37:76, Apr 15, 1961
     Theatre Arts 45:32, Jun 1961
     Time 77:106+, Apr 14, 1961

Happy
     book: Vincent Lawrence and McElbert Moore
     music: Frank Grey
     lyrics: Earle Crooker and McElbert Moore
     staging: Walter Brooks

Productions:
    Opened December 5, 1927 for 80 performances
Reviews:
    New York Times page 26, Dec 6, 1927
                    page 30, Feb 7, 1928
    Theatre Magazine 47:40, Feb 1928

Happy as Larry
    book: Donagh MacDonagh
    music: Mescha and Wesley Portnoff
    lyrics: Donagh MacDonagh
    staging: Burgess Meredith
    sets: Motley
    costumes: Motley
    choreography: Anna Sokolow
Productions:
    Opened January 6, 1950 for 3 performances
Reviews:
    New York Theatre Critics' Reviews 1950:394+
    New York Times page 11, Jan 7, 1950
    New Yorker 25:48, Jan 14, 1950
    Newsweek 35:74, Jan 16, 1950
    Theatre Arts 34:14, Mar 1950
    Time 55:45, Jan 16, 1950

Happy Birthday
    book: Anita Loos
    songs: Richard Rodgers, Oscar Hammerstein II, James
                     Livingston
    incidental
      music: Robert Russell Bennett
    staging: Joshua Logan
    sets: Jo Mielziner
    costumes: Lucinda Ballard
Productions:
    Opened October 31, 1946 for 564 performances
Reviews:
    Catholic World 164:261, Dec 1946
    Commonweal 45:116, Nov 15, 1946
    Life 21:79-82, Nov 18, 1946
    Nation 163:565, Nov 16, 1946
    New Republic 115:662, Nov 18, 1946
    New York Theatre Critics' Reviews 1946:280
    New York Times VI, page 27, Sep 22, 1946
                   VI, page 30, Oct 27, 1946
                   page 31, Nov 1, 1946
                   II, page 1, Nov 10, 1946
                   II, page 1, Jan 26, 1947
                   II, page 1, Apr 20, 1947
                   II, page 1, Oct 26, 1947
    New Yorker 22:55, Nov 9, 1946
    Newsweek 28:92, Nov 11, 1946
    Saturday Review 29:23, Dec 21, 1946

School and Society 66:327-8, Oct 25, 1947
Theatre Arts 31:18-19+, Jan 1947
Time 48:56, Nov 11, 1946

Happy Days
    words: R. H. Burnside and Raymond Hubbell
    music: R. H. Burnside and Raymond Hubbell
    staging: R. H. Burnside
Productions:
Opened August 23, 1919 for 452 performances
Reviews:
    New York Times page 8, Aug 25, 1919
    Theatre Magazine 34:217, Jul 1921

Happy Go Lucky
    book: Helena Phillips Evans
    music: Lucien Denni
    lyrics: Helena Phillips Evans
    staging: Fred G. Latham
Productions:
Opened September 30, 1926 for 52 performances
Reviews:
    New York Times page 13, Aug 6, 1926
    Theatre Magazine 44:18, Dec 1926

Happy Hunting
    book: Howard Lindsay and Russel Crouse
    music: Harold Karr
    lyrics: Matt Dubey
    staging: Abe Burrows
    sets: Jo Mielziner
    costumes: Irene Sharaff
    choreography: Alex Romero and Bob Herget
Productions:
Opened December 6, 1956 for 412 performances
Reviews:
    America 96:743, Mar 30, 1957
    Catholic World 184:386, Feb 1957
    New York Theatre Critics' Reviews 1956:166+
    New York Times VI, page 29, Sep 16, 1956
                    VI, page 29, Nov 4, 1956
                    page 30, Dec 7, 1956
                    II, page 3, Dec 16, 1956
    New Yorker 32:54+, Dec 22, 1956
    Newsweek 48:66, Dec 17, 1956
    Reporter 16:35, Jan 24, 1957
    Saturday Review 39:25, Dec 29, 1956
    Theatre Arts 41:20-1, Feb 1957
    Time 68:62+, Dec 17, 1956
    Vogue 128:111, Dec 1956

The Happy Hypocrite
    book: Edward Eager; based on the short story by

                              Max Beerbohm
    music: James Bredt; additional material by Tony Tanner
    lyrics: Edward Eager
    staging: Tony Tanner
    sets: Michael Horen
    costumes: Deidre Cartier
Productions:
    (Off-Broadway) Opened September 5, 1968 for 17 performances
Reviews:
    New York Times page 38, Sep 6, 1968
    New Yorker 44:129-30, Sep 14, 1969

The Happy Time
    book: N. Richard Nash; based on the play by Samuel
                      Taylor and the book by Robert L. Fontaine
    music: John Kander
    lyrics: Fred Ebb
    staging: Gower Champion
    sets: Peter Wexler
    costumes: Freddy Wittop
    choreography: Gower Champion
Productions:
    Opened January 18, 1968 for 285 performances
Reviews:
    America 118:356, Mar 16, 1968
    Dance Magazine 42:27, Apr 1968
    Nation 206:186+, Feb 5, 1968
    New York Theatre Critics' Reviews 1968:375
                                       1968:378
    New York Times page 32, Jan 19, 1968
                    II, page 3, Jan 28, 1968
                    page 36, Sep 14, 1968
    New Yorker 43:84+, Jan 27, 1968
    Newsweek 71:76, Jan 29, 1968
    Saturday Review 51:45, Feb 3, 1968

Happy Town
    book: Max Hampton
    music: Gordon Duffy (additional music by Paul Nassau)
    lyrics: Harry M. Haldane (additional lyrics by Paul
                      Nassau)
    staging: Allan A. Buckhantz
    sets: Curt Nations
    costumes: J. Michael Travis
    choreography: Lee Scott
Productions:
    Opened October 7, 1959 for 5 performances
Reviews:
    New York Theatre Critics' Reviews 1959:279+
    New York Times page 49, Oct 8, 1959
                    page 22, Oct 9, 1959
    New Yorker 35:134, Oct 17, 1959

Hard Job Being God
       book: Based on the Old Testament
       music: Tom Martel
       lyrics: Tom Martel
       staging: Bob Yde
       sets: Ray Wilke
       costumes: Mary Whitehead
       choreography: Lee Theodore
Productions:
       Opened May 15, 1972 for 6 performances
Reviews:
       New York Times page 49, May 16, 1972
       New Yorker 48:82+, May 27, 1972

Harlem Cavalcade
       assembled: Ed Sullivan
       staging: Ed Sullivan and Noble Sissle
       costumes: Veronica
       choreography: Leonard Harper
Productions:
       Opened May 1, 1942 for 49 performances
Reviews:
       New York Theatre Critics' Reviews 1942:296
       New York Times page 11, May 2, 1942
                    VIII, page 1, May 17, 1942

The Harold Arlen Songbook
       conceived: Robert Elston
       music: Harold Arlen
       lyrics: Truman Capote, Harold Arlen, Dorothy Fields,
                        Ira Gershwin, E. Y. Harburg, Ted Koehler,
                        Dory Langdon, Johnny Mercer, Leo Robin and
                        Billy Rose
       staging: Robert Elston
Productions:
       (Off-Broadway) Opened February 28, 1967 for 41 performances
Reviews:
       New York Times page 48, Mar 1, 1967
                        page 37, Mar 29, 1967

Harry Stoones   (see Another Evening with Harry Stoones)

Hassard Short's Ritz Revue
       staging: Hassard Short
Productions:
       Opened September 17, 1924 for 109 performances
Reviews:
       New York Times page 19, Sep 18, 1924
       Theatre Magazine 40:70, Nov 1924

Hats Off to Ice
       assembled: Sonja Henie and Arthur M. Wirtz
       music: James Littlefield and John Fortis

Have a Heart

        lyrics: James Littlefield and John Fortis
        staging: William H. Burke and Catherine Littlefield
        sets: Bruno Maine
        costumes: Grace Houston
        choreography: Catherine Littlefield and Dorothie Littlefield
Productions:
    Opened June 22, 1944 for 889 performances
Reviews:
    Catholic World 159:459, Aug 1944
    Commonweal 40:279, Jul 7, 1944
    New York Times page 15, Jun 23, 1944
    Time 44:70, Jul 3, 1944

Have a Heart
        book: Guy Bolton and P. G. Wodehouse
        music: Jerome Kern
        lyrics: Guy Bolton and P. G. Wodehouse
        staging: Edward Royce
Productions:
    Opened January 11, 1917 for 76 performances
Reviews:
    Dramatic Mirror 77:7, Jan 13, 1917
                    77:10, Jan 20, 1917
                    77:8, Feb 17, 1917
                    77:9, Mar 10, 1917
    Green Book 17:590+, Apr 1917
    Leslie's Weekly 124:327, Mar 22, 1917
    National Magazine 46:121-4, Oct-Nov 1917
    New York Dramatic News 63:22, Jan 13, 1917
                            63:22, Jan 20, 1917
    New York Times page 11, Jan 12, 1917
    Theatre Magazine 25:84, Feb 1917
                     25:128, Feb 1917

Have I Got One for You
        book: Jerry Blatt and Lonnie Burstein
        music: Jerry Blatt
        lyrics: Jerry Blatt and Lonnie Burstein
        staging: Roberta Sklar
        sets: John Conklin
        costumes: John Conklin
Productions:
    (Off-Broadway) Opened January 7, 1968 for 1 performance
Reviews:
    New York Times page 32, Jan 8, 1968
                     page 36, Jan 9, 1968

Hayride
        book: Based on folk material
        music: Based on folk music
        sets: Art Guild, Jack Woodson and Jack Derrenberger
Productions:
    Opened September 13, 1954 for 24 performances

Reviews:
America 92:25, Oct 2, 1954
New York Theatre Critics' Reviews 1954:319
New York Times page 24, Sep 14, 1954
Theatre Arts 38:13+, Nov 1954

Hazel Flagg
book: Ben Hecht, based on a story by James Street
                 and the film Nothing Sacred
music: Jule Styne
lyrics: Bob Hilliard
staging: David Alexander
sets: Harry Horner
costumes: Miles White
choreography: Robert Alton
Productions:
Opened February 11, 1953 for 190 performances
Reviews:
America 88:661, Mar 14, 1953
Catholic World 177:70, Apr 1953
Commonweal 57:552, Mar 6, 1953
Dance Magazine 27:12-15+, Mar 1953
Life 34:102-4+, Mar 9, 1953
Look 17:20, Mar 24, 1953
Nation 176:193, Feb 28, 1953
New York Theatre Critics' Reviews 1953:362+
New York Times page 22, Feb 12, 1953
                 II, page 3, Sep 13, 1953
New Yorker 29:58, Feb 21, 1953
Newsweek 41:62, Feb 23, 1953
Saturday Review 36:38, Feb 28, 1953
Theatre Arts 37:14-15, Feb 1953
                 37:15, May 1953
Time 61:86, Feb 23, 1953

He Came from Milwaukee
book: Mark Swan
music: Ben M. Jerome and Louis A. Hirsch
lyrics: Edward Madden
staging: Sidney Ellison
Productions:
Opened September 21, 1910 for 117 performances
Reviews:
Blue Book 12:644-7, Feb 1911
Dramatic Mirror 64:7, Sep 28, 1910
Green Book Album 5:254-5+, Feb 1911
Hampton 25:680, Nov 1910
Leslie's Weekly 111:403, Oct 20, 1910
Metropolitan Magazine 33:400-1, Dec 1910
Theatre Magazine 12:xiv, Nov 1910
                 12:153, Nov 1910
Woman's Home Companion 38:43, Feb 1911

He Didn't Want to Do It
    book: George Broadhurst
    music: Silvio Hein
    lyrics: George Broadhurst
    staging: Clifford Brooke
Productions:
Opened August 20, 1918 for 23 performances
Reviews:
    Dramatic Mirror 79:360, Sep 7, 1918
                    79:399, Sep 14, 1918
    Life (New York) 72:344, Sep 5, 1918
    New York Times page 7, Aug 21, 1918
    Theatre Magazine 28:242, Oct 1918

Head over Heels
    book: Edgar Allan Woolf; suggested by Lee Arthur's
                       dramatization of Nalbro Bartley's Shadows
    music: Jerome Kern
    lyrics: Edgar Allan Woolf
    staging: George Marion
Productions:
Opened August 29, 1918 for 100 performances
Reviews:
    Dramatic Mirror 78:802, Jun 8, 1918
                    79:434, Sep 21, 1918
    National Magazine 47:461-2, Sep 1918
    New York Times page 9, Aug 30, 1918
    Theatre Magazine 28:11, Jul 1918
                    28:212, Oct 1918

Heads Up
    book: John McGowan and Paul Gerard Smith
    music: Richard Rodgers
    lyrics: Lorenz Hart
    staging: George Hale
Productions:
Opened November 11, 1929 for 114 performances
Reviews:
    New York Times page 34, Nov 12, 1929
                    IX, page 14, Nov 17, 1929
    Outlook 153:513, Nov 27, 1929
    Theatre Magazine 51:49, Jan 1930
    Vogue 75:60+, Jan 18, 1930

Heathen!
    book: Robert Helpman and Eaton Magoon Jr.
    music: Eaton Magoon Jr.
    lyrics: Eaton Magoon Jr.
    staging: Lucia Victor
    sets: Jack Brown
    costumes: Bruce Harrow
    choreography: Sammy Bayes and Dan Siretta
Productions:

Opened May 21, 1972 for one performance
Reviews:
New York Theatre Critics' Reviews 1972:276
New York Times page 43, May 22, 1972
New Yorker 48:84, May 27, 1972

Heaven On Earth
    book: Barry Trivers
    music: Jay Gorney
    lyrics: Barry Trivers
    staging: John Murray Anderson
    sets: Raoul Pene du Bois
    costumes: Raoul Pene du Bois
    choreography: Nick Castle
Productions:
Opened September 16, 1948 for 12 performances
Reviews:
New York Theatre Critics' Reviews 1948:240+
New York Times page 29, Sep 17, 1948
            II, page 1, Sep 26, 1948
New Yorker 24:53, Sep 25, 1948
Newsweek 32:79, Sep 27, 1948
Time 52:63, Sep 27, 1948

Helen of Troy, New York
    book: George Kaufman and Marc Connelly
    music: Bert Kalmar and Harry Ruby
    lyrics: Bert Kalmar and Harry Ruby
    staging: Bertram Harrison and Bert French
Productions:
Opened June 19, 1923 for 191 performances
Reviews:
Life (New York) 82:20, Jul 12, 1923
New York Clipper 71:14, Jun 27, 1923
New York Times page 22, Jun 20, 1923
Stage 15:28, Aug 1938
Theatre Arts 32:44, Fall 1948
Theatre Magazine 38:15, Aug 1923

Hell
    book: Rennold Wolf
    lyrics: Rennold Wolf
Productions:
Opened April 27, 1911 for 92 performances
Reviews:
Theatre Magazine 13:183, Jun 1911

Hello Alexander
    book: Edgar Smith and Emily Young
    music: Jean Schwartz
    lyrics: Alfred Bryan
Productions.
Opened October 7, 1919 for 56 performances

Reviews:
    Dramatic Mirror 80:1612, Oct 16, 1919
    New York Times page 22, Oct 8, 1919
    Theatre Magazine 30:354, Nov 1919

Hello Broadway
    words: George M. Cohan
    music: George M. Cohan
Productions:
    Opened December 25, 1914 for 123 performances
Reviews:
    American Mercury 79:42, May 1915
    Current Opinion 58:98, Feb 1915
    Dramatic Mirror 72:8, Dec 30, 1914
                    73:2, Jan 27, 1915
                    73:2, Mar 31, 1915
    Green Book 13:476-7, Mar 1915
              13:576, Mar 1915
    Life (New York) 65:24, Jan 7, 1915
    Munsey 54:330, Mar 1915
          54:537, Apr 1915
    New York Times page 7, Dec 26, 1914
    Smart Set 45:287-8, Mar 1915
    Theatre Magazine 21:52+, Feb 1915
                    21:101, Feb 1915
                    25:272, May 1917

Hello Charlie
    book: H. Kalmanowitch
    music: Maurice Rauch
    lyrics: Jacob Jacobs
    staging: Max Perlman
    sets: Arthur Aaronson
    choreography: Michael Aubrey
Productions:
    (Off-Broadway) Opened October 23, 1965 for 129 performances
Reviews:
    New York Times page 47, Oct 25, 1965

Hello Daddy
    book: Herbert Fields
    music: Jimmy McHugh
    lyrics: Dorothy Fields
    staging: John Murray Anderson
Productions:
    Opened December 26, 1928 for 198 performances
Reviews:
    Life (New York) 93:21, Jan 25, 1929
    New York Times page 26, Dec 27, 1928

Hello Dolly!
    book: Michael Stewart, suggested by Thornton
                    Wilder's The Matchmaker

music: Jerry Herman
lyrics: Jerry Herman
staging: Gower Champion
sets: Oliver Smith
costumes: Freddy Wittop
choreography: Gower Champion
Productions:
Opened January 16, 1964 for 2,844 performances
Reviews:
America 110:552, Apr 18, 1964
         118:20, Jan 6, 1968
Christian Century 85:118, Jan 24, 1968
Ebony 23:83-9, Jan 1968
Harper's 236:112, Apr 1968
Life 56:107-9, Apr 3, 1964
     63:128-30+, Dec 8, 1967
Mademoiselle 59:56, May 1964
New York Theatre Critics' Reviews 1964:384+
New York Times II, page 1, Jan 12, 1964
              page 22, Jan 17, 1964
              II, page 1, Jan 26, 1964
              page 28, Feb 5, 1964
              II, page 1, Jan 10, 1965
              II, page 8, Aug 8, 1965
              page 17, Aug 10, 1965
              page 43, Dec 3, 1965
              II, page 7, Dec 12, 1965
              page 79, Feb 8, 1966
              page 47, Mar 9, 1966
              II, page 1, Jun 26, 1966
              page 40, Jan 19, 1967
              page 34, Feb 16, 1967
              page 19, Feb 18, 1967
              page 56, Feb 21, 1967
              page 30, Mar 2, 1967
              page 55, Jun 6, 1967
              page 56, Jun 12, 1967
              page 38, Jun 14, 1967
              page 12, Jul 29, 1967
              page 40, Oct 25, 1967
              page 56, Nov 5, 1967
              page 61, Nov 13, 1967
              II, page 3, Nov 26, 1967
              page 21, May 31, 1968
              page 36, Nov 13, 1968
              page 43, Nov 16, 1968
              page 42, Jun 3, 1969
              page 32, Oct 31, 1968
              page 70, Jan 25, 1970
              page 52, Mar 30, 1970
              II, page 1, Apr 12, 1970
              II, page 1, Sep 6, 1970
              page 44, Sep 8, 1970

                    pages 51-53, Sep 9, 1970
                    page 61, Sep 10, 1970
                    II, page 38, Nov 29, 1970
                    II, page 40, Dec 27, 1970
                    page 38, Dec 28, 1970
        New Yorker 39:72, Jan 25, 1964
        Newsweek 63:59, Jan 27, 1964
                    70:105, Nov 27, 1967
        Saturday Review 47:22, Feb 8, 1964
                    50:24, Dec 2, 1967
        Time 83:44, Jan 24, 1964
                    90:56, Nov 24, 1967

Hello, Lola!
     book: Dorothy Donnelly
     music: William B. Kernell
     lyrics: Dorothy Donnelly
     staging: Seymour Felix
Productions:
     Opened January 12, 1926 for 47 performances
Reviews:
     New York Times page 30, Jan 13, 1926

Hello, Paris (1911)
     dialogue: William Le Baron
     music: J. Rosamond Johnson
     lyrics: J. L. Hill
     staging: Ned Wayburn
Productions:
     Opened September 22, 1911 for 8 performances
No Reviews.

Hello, Paris (1930)
     book: Edgar Smith, adapted from Homer Croy's novel
     music: Russell Tarbox and Michael Cleary
     lyrics: Edgar Smith
     staging: Ben Holmes
Productions:
     Opened November 15, 1930 for 33 performances
Reviews:
     Life (New York) 96:35, Dec 5, 1930
     New York Times page 29, Nov 19, 1930

Hello, Solly!
     staging: Al Hausman
Productions:
     Opened April 4, 1967 for 68 performances
Reviews:
     New York Times page 44, Apr 6, 1967
                    page 54, May 26, 1967

Hello Yourself
     book: Walter De Leon

        music: Richard Myers
        lyrics: Leo Robin
        staging: Clarke Silvernail
Productions:
    Opened October 30, 1928 for 87 performances
Reviews:
    New York Times page 28, Oct 31, 1928
    Theatre Magazine 49:60, Jan 1929

Hellzapoppin
    assembled by: Ole Olson and Chic Johnson
        music: Sammy Fain
        lyrics: Charles Tobias
        staging: Edward Duryea Dowling
Productions:
    Opened September 22, 1938 for 1, 404 performances
Reviews:
    Catholic World 148:215, Nov 1938
    Collier's 102:16-17+, Dec 10, 1938
    Commonweal 31:227, Dec 29, 1939
    Life 5:30-3, Oct 24, 1938
    New York Theatre Critics' Reviews 1940:493+
                                       1941:495+
    New York Times page 34, Sep 23, 1938
                    IX, page 1, Oct 2, 1938
                    X, page 1, Sep 17, 1939
                    page 36, Dec 12, 1939
                    page 14, Sep 20, 1940
                    page 39, Jan 19, 1941
                    IX, page 2, Mar 2, 1941
                    IX, page 1, Aug 3, 1941
                    VIII, page 2, Feb 15, 1942
    Newsweek 12:28, Oct 10, 1938
             14:28, Dec 25, 1939
    Stage 16:20-2, Jan 1939
    Theatre Arts 22:783, Nov 1938
                 24:93-4, Feb 1940
    Time 32:30, Oct 3, 1938
         34:24, Dec 25, 1939

The Hen-Pecks
        words: Glen MacDonough
        notes: A. Baldwin Sloane
        rhymes: E. Ray Goetz
        staging: Ned Wayburn
Productions:
    Opened February 4, 1911 for 137 performances
Reviews:
    Blue Book 13:12-15, May 1911
    Dramatic Mirror 65:7, Feb 8, 1911
                    65:9, Feb 22, 1911
                    65:2, Jun 7, 1911
                    67:26, Jan 31, 1912

Green Book Album 5:682-3, Apr 1911
Munsey 45:134, Apr 1911
New York Dramatic News 56:31, Sep 21, 1912
Red Book 16:1149+, Apr 1911
Stage 13:59, Aug 1936
Theatre Magazine 13:xi, Mar 1911
                    13:71, Mar 1911

Henry, Sweet Henry
    book: Nunnally Johnson; based on the novel The World
                     of Henry Orient by Nora Johnson
    music: Bob Merrill
    lyrics: Bob Merrill
    staging: George Roy Hill
    sets: Robert Randolph
    costumes: Alvin Colt
    choreography: Michael Bennett
Productions:
    Opened October 23, 1967 for 80 performances
Reviews:
    America 117:624, Nov 18, 1967
    New York Theatre Critics' Reviews 1967:241
                                      1967:244
    New York Times page 51, Oct 24, 1967
                    page 39, Oct 25, 1967
                    II, page 3, Nov 5, 1967
                    page 25, Dec 28, 1967
    Newsweek 70:89A, Nov 6, 1967
    Saturday Review 50:26, Nov 11, 1967

Her Family Tree
    book: Al Weeks and "Bugs" Baer
    staging: Hassard Short
Productions:
    Opened December 27, 1920 for 98 performances
Reviews:
    Dramatic Mirror 83:11+, Jan 1, 1921
    Life (New York) 77:100, Jan 20, 1921
    New York Clipper 69:30, Jan 5, 1921
    New York Times page 9, Dec 28, 1920
    Theatre Magazine 33:159, Mar 1921
                     33:180, Mar 1921

Her First Roman
    book: Ervin Drake; based on George Bernard Shaw's
                     Caesar and Cleopatra
    music: Ervin Drake
    lyrics: Ervin Drake
    staging: Derek Goldby
    sets: Michael Annals
    costumes: Michael Annals
    choreography: Dania Krupska
Productions:

Opened October 20, 1968 for 17 performances
Reviews:
New York Theatre Critics' Reviews 1968:183
1968:200
New York Times page 53, Oct 21, 1968
page 53, Oct 29, 1968
II, page 1, Nov 3, 1968
New Yorker 44:139-40, Oct 26, 1968
Newsweek 72:118, Nov 4, 1968

Her Little Highness
book: Channing Pollock and Rennold Wolf; based on
Such a Little Queen by Channing Pollock
music: Reginald De Koven
staging: George Marion
Productions:
Opened October 13, 1913 for 16 performances
Reviews:
Dramatic Mirror 70:6-7, Oct 15, 1913
Green Book 11:161, Jan 1914
New York Dramatic News 58:14, Oct 18, 1913
New York Times page 13, Oct 14, 1913
Theatre Magazine 18:xxii+, Nov 1913

Her Soldier Boy
book: Victor Leon; adapted by Rida Johnson Young
music: Emmerich Kalman and Sigmund Romberg
staging: J. J. Shubert
Productions:
Opened December 6, 1916 for 198 performances
Reviews:
Dramatic Mirror 76:4, Dec 9, 1916
76:4+, Dec 16, 1916
Munsey 59:501, Dec 1916
New York Dramatic News 63:6, Dec 16, 1916
New York Times page 11, Dec 7, 1916
Theatre Magazine 25:24, Jan 1917

Here Goes the Bride
book: Peter Arno
music: John W. Green and Richard Myers
lyrics: Peter Arno
staging: Edward Clarke Lilley
choreography: Russell Markert
Productions:
Opened November 3, 1931 for 7 performances
Reviews:
New York Times page 31, Nov 4, 1931
page 22, Nov 9, 1931

Here's Howe
book: Fred Thompson and Paul Gerard Smith
music: Roger Wolfe Kahn and Joseph Meyer

    lyrics: Irving Caesar
Productions:
    Opened May 1, 1928 for 71 performances
Reviews:
    New York Times page 19, May 2, 1928
    Outlook 149:305, Jun 30, 1928
    Theatre Magazine 48:39, Jul 1928
    Vogue 72:92, Jul 1, 1928

Here's Love
    book: Meredith Willson, based on Valentine Davies
                     and George Seaton's screen play Miracle on
                     34th Street
    music: Meredith Willson
    lyrics: Meredith Willson
    staging: Stuart Ostrow
    sets: William and Jean Eckart
    costumes: Alvin Colt
    choreography: Michael Kidd
Productions:
    Opened October 3, 1963 for 334 performances
Reviews:
    America 109:642-3, Nov 16, 1963
    New York Theatre Critics' Reviews 1963:258+
    New York Times page 24, Aug 6, 1963
                    page 28, Sep 20, 1963
                    VI, page 51, Sep 22, 1963
                    II, page 3, Sep 29, 1963
                    page 28, Oct 4, 1963
                    page 28, Jul 2, 1964
    Newsweek 62:72, Oct 14, 1963
    Saturday Review 46:18, Nov 2, 1963
    Theatre Arts 48:11, Jan 1964
    Time 82:72, Oct 11, 1963

Here's Where I Belong
    book: Alex Gordon; based on the novel East of Eden
                     by John Steinbeck
    music: Robert Waldman
    lyrics: Alfred Uhry
    staging: Michael Kahn
    sets: Ming Cho Lee
    costumes: Ruth Morley
    choreography: Tony Mordente
Productions:
    Opened March 3, 1968 for one performance
Reviews:
    New York Theatre Critics' Reviews 1968:331
    New York Times page 32, Mar 4, 1968
                    page 35, Mar 5, 1968
    New Yorker 44:132, Mar 9, 1968

A Hero Is Born

    book: Theresa Helburn, based on a fairy tale by
                     Andrew Lang
    music: A. Lehman Engel
    lyrics: Agnes Morgan
    staging: Agnes Morgan
    sets: Tom Adrian Cracraft
    costumes: Alexander Saron
Productions:
    Opened October 1, 1937 for 50 performances
Reviews:
    Catholic World 146:218, Nov 1937
    New York Times page 18, Oct 2, 1937
    Time 30:54, Oct 11, 1937

Hey Nonny Nonny!
    book: Max and Nathaniel Lief
    music: Michael H. Cleary
    lyrics: Max and Nathaniel Lief
    staging: Alexander Leftwich
Productions:
    Opened June 6, 1932 for 32 performances
Reviews:
    Nation 134:708, Jun 22, 1932
    New York Times page 22, Jun 7, 1932

Hey, You
    music: Norman Meranus
    lyrics: June Carroll
Productions:
    (Off-Broadway) Opened Season of 1952-53 (American Lyric
    Theatre)
No Reviews.

Hi, Paisano!
    book: Ernest Chambers
    music: Robert Holton
    lyrics: June Carroll
    staging: Vassili Lambrinos
Productions:
    (Off-Broadway) Opened September 30, 1961 for 3 performances
Reviews:
    New York Times page 36, Oct 2, 1961
    New Yorker 37:131-2, Oct 7, 1961

High Button Shoes
    book: Stephen Longstreet, adapted from his novel
                     The Sisters Liked Them Handsome
    music: Jule Styne
    lyrics: Sammy Cahn
    staging: George Abbott
    sets: Oliver Smith
    costumes: Miles White
    choreography: Jerome Robbins

Productions:
    Opened October 9, 1947 for 727 performances
Reviews:
    Catholic World 166:172, Nov 1947
    Commonweal 47:71, Oct 31, 1947
    Life 23:102-4, Nov 10, 1947
    New Republic 117:35, Oct 27, 1947
    New York Theatre Critics' Reviews 1947:304+
    New York Times II, page 3, Oct 5, 1947
                    page 32, Oct 10, 1947
                    II, page 6, Nov 9, 1947
                    II, page 3, Nov 30, 1947
                    II, page 1, Nov 23, 1947
                    page 23, Dec 23, 1948
                    page 10, Mar 12, 1955
    New Yorker 23:56+, Oct 18, 1947
    Newsweek 30:86+, Oct 20, 1947
    Theatre Arts 31:15-16, Nov 1947
    Time 50:73, Oct 20, 1947
    Vogue 110:190, Nov 15, 1947

High Jinks
    book: Leo Ditrichstein and Otto Hauerbach
    music: Rudolph Friml
    lyrics: Leo Ditrichstein and Otto Hauerbach
    staging: Frank Smithson
Productions:
    Opened December 10, 1913 for 213 performances
Reviews:
    Dramatic Mirror 70:6, Dec 17, 1913
    Life (New York) 62:1155, Dec 25, 1913
    New York Times page 11, Dec 11, 1913
    Theatre Magazine 19:46, Jan 1914

High Kickers
    book: George Jessel, from a suggestion by Sid Silvers
    music: Harry Ruby
    lyrics: Bert Dalmar
    staging: Edward Sobel
    sets: Nat Karson
    choreography: Carl Randall
Productions:
    Opened October 31, 1941 for 171 performances
Reviews:
    New York Theatre Critics' Reviews 1941:246+
    New York Times page 54, Oct 12, 1941
                    page 21, Nov 1, 1941
    Theatre Arts 26-8, Jan 1942
    Time 38:55, Nov 10, 1941

High Spirits
    book: Hugh Martin and Timothy Gray, based on Noel
                    Coward's play Blithe Spirit
    music: Hugh Martin

<pre>
    lyrics: Timothy Gray
    staging: Noel Coward
    sets: Robert Fletcher
    costumes: Robert Fletcher and Valentina Rasch
    choreography: Danny Daniels
</pre>
Productions:
    Opened April 7, 1964 for 375 performances
Reviews:
    America 111:114, Aug 1, 1964
    Life 56:9, May 1, 1964
        56:125-7, May 15, 1964
    Look 28:87-91, Mar 10, 1964
    National Review 16:546-7, Jun 30, 1964
    New York Theatre Critics' Reviews 1964:292+
    New York Times page 34, Apr 8, 1964
                   page 46, Nov 4, 1964
    New Yorker 40:108, Apr 18, 1964
    Time 83:65, Apr 17, 1964

Higher and Higher
<pre>
    book: Gladys Hurlbut and Joshua Logan, based on
                   an idea by Irvin Pincus
    music: Richard Rodgers
    lyrics: Lorenz Hart
    staging: Joshua Logan
    sets: Jo Mielziner
    costumes: Lucinda Ballard
    choreography: Robert Alton
</pre>
Productions:
    Opened April 4, 1940 for 84 performances
    Opened August 5, 1940 for 24 performances
Reviews:
    Life 8:42+, Apr 15, 1940
    New York Theatre Critics' Reviews 1940:337+
    New York Times X, page 2, Mar 17, 1940
                   page 24, Apr 5, 1940
                   page 15, Aug 6, 1940
                   IX, page 1, Aug 11, 1940
    Time 35:76, Apr 15, 1940

The Highway of Life   (see Dude)

Hilarities
<pre>
    sketches: Sidney Zelinka, Howard Harris, Morey Amster-
                   dam
    music: Buddy Kaye, Carl Lampl
    lyrics: Stanley Arnold
</pre>
Productions:
    Opened September 9, 1948 for 14 performances
Reviews:
    New Republic 119:38, Sep 27, 1948
    New York Theatre Critics' Reviews 1948:250+
    New York Times page 20, Sep 10, 1948

Hip-Hip-Hooray
    book: R. H. Burnside
    music: Raymond Hubbell
    lyrics: John L. Golden
    staging: R. H. Burnside
Productions:
Opened September 30, 1915 for 425 performances
Reviews:
Current Opinion 59:326-7, Nov 1915
Dramatic Mirror 74:8, Oct 6, 1915
Green Book 14:986-7, Dec 1915
New York Times page 11, Oct 1, 1915
              VI, page 6, Oct 3, 1915
              page 11, May 2, 1916
Opera Magazine 3:29-31, Jan 1916
Theatre Magazine 22:221, Nov 1915
                 23:15, Jan 1916
                 23:84, Feb 1916

His Honor, the Barber
    book: Edwin Hanaford
    music: James Brymm
    staging: S. H. Dudley
Productions:
Opened May 8, 1911 for 16 performances
Reviews:
Dramatic Mirror 65:7, May 10, 1911
New York Times page 11, May 9, 1911

His Little Widows
    book: Rida Johnson Young and William Cary Duncan
    music: William Schroeder
    lyrics: Rida Johnson Young and William Cary Duncan
    staging: Frank Stammers
    choreography: David Bennett
Productions:
Opened April 30, 1917 for 72 performances
Reviews:
Dramatic Mirror 77:7, May 12, 1917
Green Book 18:4-5+, Jul 1917
New York Dramatic News 64:18, May 12, 1917
New York Times page 11, May 1, 1917
Public 69:816-17, May 10, 1917
Theatre Magazine 25:340+, Jun 1917

Hit the Deck
    book: Herbert Fields, adapted from the play Shore
               Leave
    music: Vincent Youmans
    lyrics: Leo Robin and Clifford Grey
    staging: Lew Fields, Seymour Felix, Alexander
               Leftwich
Productions:

Opened April 25, 1927 for 352 performances
Reviews:
    Life (New York) 89:23, May 19, 1927
    New York Times page 32, Apr 26, 1927
                      page 8, Dec 14, 1927
                      IX, page 4, Apr 1, 1928
                      IX, page 2, Apr 29, 1928
    Theatre Magazine 46:18, Jul 1927
    Vogue 69:75+, Jun 15, 1927

Hit the Trail
    book: Frank O'Neill
    music: Frederico Valerio
    lyrics: Elizabeth Miele
    staging: Charles W. Christenberry Jr. and Byrle Cass
    sets: Leo Kerz
    costumes: Michi
    choreography: Gene Bayliss
Productions:
    Opened December 2, 1954 for 4 performances
Reviews:
    New York Theatre Critics' Reviews 1954:228+
    New York Times page 31, Dec 3, 1954
    New Yorker 30:98, Dec 11, 1954
    Theatre Arts 39:16, 92, Feb 1955

Hitchy-Koo (1917)
    book: Harry Grattan, Glen MacDonough and E. Ray
                     Goetz
    music: E. Ray Goetz
    lyrics: Harry Grattan, Glen MacDonough and E. Ray
                     Goetz
    staging: Julian Mitchell and Leon Errol
Productions:
    Opened June 7, 1917 for 220 performances
Reviews:
    Dramatic Mirror 77:7, Jun 16, 1917
                    77:7, Jun 30, 1917
                    77:4, Jul 7, 1917
    New York Times page 9, Jun 8, 1917
                    VIII, page 5, Jun 10, 1917
                    VIII, page 5, Jun 17, 1917
    Theatre Magazine 26:22, Jul 1917
                     26:83, Jul 1917

Hitchy-Koo (1918)
    book: Glen MacDonough and Raymond Hubbell
    staging: Leon Errol
Productions:
    Opened June 6, 1918 for 68 performances
Reviews:
    Dramatic Mirror 78:847, Jun 15, 1918
    Green Book 20:204-5+, Aug 1918

New York Times page 11, Jun 7, 1918
Theatre Magazine 28:23, Jul 1918

Hitchy-Koo (1919)
    book: George V. Hobart
    music: Cole Porter
    lyrics: Cole Porter
Productions:
    Opened October 6, 1919 for 56 performances
Reviews:
    Dramatic Mirror 80:1612, Oct 16, 1919
    New York Times page 22, Oct 7, 1919

Hitchy-Koo (1920)
    book: Glen MacDonough and Anne Caldwell
    music: Jerome Kern
    lyrics: Glen MacDonough and Anne Caldwell
    staging: Ned Wayburn
Productions:
    Opened October 19, 1920 for 71 performances
Reviews:
    Dramatic Mirror page 777, Oct 23, 1920
    New York Clipper 68:28, Oct 27, 1920
    New York Times page 11, Oct 20, 1920
    Theatre Magazine 33:29, Jan 1921

Hobo
    book: John Dooley
    music: John Dooley
    lyrics: John Dooley
Productions:
    (Off-Broadway) Opened Season of 1960-61
Reviews:
    New York Times page 41, Apr 11, 1961
                    page 33, Apr 19, 1961
    New Yorker 37:118-19, Apr 22, 1961

Hokey-Pokey and Bunty, Bulls and Strings
    music: John Stromberg, A. Baldwin Sloane and W. T.
                    Francis
    lyrics: Edgar Smith and E. Ray Goetz
    staging: Gus Sohlke
Productions:
    Opened February 8, 1912 for 108 performances
Reviews:
    Blue Book 15:8-11, May 1912
    Dramatic Mirror 67:4, Mar 6, 1912
                    67:2, Apr 3, 1912
                    67:7, May 1912
    Everybody's 26:689, May 1912
    Theatre Magazine 15:xii, Mar 1912

Hold Everything

    book: B. G. DeSylva and John McGowan
    music: Ray Henderson
    lyrics: B. G. DeSylva, Lew Brown
    choreography: Jack Haskell and Sam Rose
Productions:
    Opened October 10, 1928 for 413 performances
Reviews:
    Life (New York) 92:21, Nov 2, 1928
    New York Times page 24, Oct 11, 1928
    Theatre Magazine 49:60, Jan 1929

Hold It!
    book: Matt Brooks and Art Arthur
    music: Gerald Marks
    lyrics: Sam Lerner
    staging: Robert E. Perry
    sets: Edward Gilbert
    costumes: Julia Sze
    choreography: Irma Jurist
Productions:
    Opened May 5, 1948 for 46 performances
Reviews:
    New York Theatre Critics' Reviews 1948:274+
    New York Times page 31, May 6, 1948
    New Yorker 24:48, May 15, 1948
    Newsweek 31:89, May 17, 1948
    Theatre Arts 32:14+, Jun 1948

Hold on to Your Hats
    book: Guy Bolton, Matt Brooks, Eddie Davis
    music: Burton Lane
    lyrics: E. Y. Harburg
    staging: Edgar MacGregor
    sets: Raoul Pene du Bois
    choreography: Catherine Littlefield
Productions:
    Opened September 11, 1940 for 158 performances
Reviews:
    Catholic World 152:218-19, Nov 1940
    Life 9:60-2, Jul 29, 1940
    Nation 151:281, Sep 28, 1940
    New York Theatre Critics' Reviews 1940:278+
                                        1941:481+
    New York Times page 25, Jul 17, 1940
                    IX, page 1, Jul 21, 1940
                    page 30, Sep 12, 1940
                    IX, page 3, Oct 20, 1940
    Stage 1:12, Nov 1940
          1:12, Dec 1940
    Theatre Arts 24:770-1+, Nov 1940
    Time 36:41, Sep 23, 1940

Hold Your Horses

    book: Russel Crouse and Corey Ford, based on a
                       play by Crouse, Ford, and Charles Beahan
    music and
    lyrics: Russell Bennett, Robert A. Simon, Louis Alter,
                       Arthur Swanstrom, Ben Oakland, Owen Murphy
    staging: Russell Patterson
    choreography: Robert Alton and Harriet Hoctor
Productions:
    Opened September 25, 1933 for 88 performances
Reviews:
    Catholic World 138:218, Nov 1933
    Commonweal 18:592, Oct 20, 1933
    New Outlook 162:43, Nov 1933
    New York Times page 20, Aug 31, 1933
                    X, page 1, Sep 10, 1933
                    page 26, Sep 26, 1933
                    IX, page 2, Oct 29, 1933
    Stage 11:9-11, Oct 1933

Holka Polka
    book: Bert Kalmar and Harry Ruby, adapted from the
                       European success by W. Walzer
    music: Will Ortman
    lyrics: Gus Kahn and Raymond B. Eagan
    staging: Oscar Eagle
Productions:
    Opened October 14, 1925 for 21 performances
Reviews:
    New York Times page 27, Oct 15, 1925

Holman, Libby (see Libby Holman)

Hollywood Ice Revue
    assembled: Sonja Henie
    staging: Catherine Littlefield
    sets: Bruno Maine
    costumes: Billy Livingston
    choreography: Catherine Littlefield
Productions:
    (Off-Broadway) Opened January 18, 1943
    (Off-Broadway) Opened January 18, 1944
    (Off-Broadway) Opened January 17, 1945 for 18 performances
    (Off-Broadway) Opened January 23, 1947
    (Off-Broadway) Opened February 3, 1947
    (Off-Broadway) Opened January 22, 1948
Reviews:
    Collier's 119:76-7, Jan 25, 1947
             122:20-21, Dec 4, 1948
    Life 20:50-55, May 20, 1946
    Time 48:50, Jul 1, 1946

Hollywood Pinafore
    book: George S. Kaufman, based on Gilbert and Sul-

                              livan's H. M. S. Pinafore
    music: Original Sullivan score
    lyrics: George S. Kaufman
    staging: George S. Kaufman
    sets: Jo Mielziner
    costumes: Kathryn Kuhn and Mary Percy Schenck
    choreography: Antony Tudor and Douglas Coudy
Productions:
    Opened May 31, 1945 for 53 performances
Reviews:
    Catholic World 161:351, Jul 1945
    Commonweal 42:213, Jun 15, 1945
    Nation 160:705, Jun 23, 1945
    New York Theatre Critics' Reviews 1945:203+
    New York Times page 20, Jun 1, 1945
                              II, page 1, Jun 10, 1945
                              II, page 4, Jun 17, 1945
                              page 14, Jul 9, 1945
    New Yorker 21:38, Jun 9, 1945
    Newsweek 25:93, Jun 11, 1945
    Saturday Review 28:24-5, Jun 16, 1945
    Theatre Arts 29:389, Jul 1945
    Time 45:58, Jun 11, 1945

Home Movies (Presented with Softly, and Consider the Nearness)
    book: Rosalyn Drexler
    music: Al Carmines
    lyrics: Rosalyn Drexler
    staging: Lawrence Kornfeld
    sets: Larry Siegel
    costumes: Judith Berkowitz
Productions:
    (Off-Broadway) Opened May 11, 1964 for 72 performances
Reviews:
    New York Times page 32, May 12, 1964
    New Yorker 40:134, May 23, 1964

Honey Girl
    book: Edward Clark; based on Henry Blossom's
                              Checkers
    music: Albert von Tilzer
    lyrics: Neville Fleeson
    staging: Bert French and Sam Forrest
Productions:
    Opened May 3, 1920 for 32 performances
Reviews:
    Dramatic Mirror 82:889, May 8, 1920
    Life (New York) 75:946, May 20, 1920
    New York Clipper 68:17, May 12, 1920
    New York Times page 9, May 4, 1920
    Theatre Magazine 31:505, Jun 1920
                              31:521, Jun 1920
                              31:527, Jun 1920

Honeydew
    book: Joseph Herbert
    music: Efrem Zimbalist
    lyrics: Joseph Herbert
    staging: Hassard Short
Productions:
Opened September 6, 1920 for (231) performances
Reviews:
    Dramatic Mirror page 459, Sep 11, 1920
    Life (New York) 76:542-3, Sep 23, 1920
    Musical Courier 81:12, Sep 9, 1920
    New York Clipper 68:19, Sep 15, 1920
    New York Times page 20, Sep 7, 1920
    Theatre Magazine 32:281, Nov 1920
                     32:332, Nov 1920

The Honeymoon Express
    book: Joseph W. Herbert and Harold Atteridge
    music: Jean Schwartz
    lyrics: Joseph W. Herbert and Harold Atteridge
    staging: Ned Wayburn
Productions:
Opened February 6, 1913 for 156 performances
Reviews:
    Blue Book 17:656-8, Aug 1913
    Dramatic Mirror 69:6, Feb 12, 1913
                     69:2, Apr 2, 1913
    Life (New York) 61:375, Feb 20, 1913
    Munsey 49:148-9, Apr 1913
    New York Dramatic News 57:20, Feb 15, 1913
    New York Times page 11, Feb 17, 1913
    Theatre Magazine 17:66-7, Mar 1913
                     17:147, Mar 1913

Honeymoon Lane
    book: Eddie Dowling and James Hanley
    music: Eddie Dowling and James Hanley
    lyrics: Eddie Dowling and James Hanley
    staging: Edgar MacGregor
Productions:
Opened September 20, 1926 for 364 performances
Reviews:
    New York Times page 32, Sep 21, 1926
    Theatre Magazine 44:15, Nov 1926

Honor Challenged   (see Frank Merriwell, or Honor Challenged)

Hooray for What!
    book: Howard Lindsay and Russel Crouse (conceived
                      by E. Y. Harburg)
    music: Harold Arlen
    lyrics: E. Y. Harburg
    staging: Howard Lindsay

     sets: Vincente Minnelli
     costumes: Raoul Pene du Bois
     choreography: Robert Alton
Productions:
     Opened December 1, 1937 for 200 performances
Reviews:
     Catholic World 146:470, Jan 1938
     Commonweal 27:220, Dec 17, 1937
     Life 3:44-6, Dec 20, 1937
     Literary Digest 124:34-5, Dec 25, 1937
     Nation 145:698, Dec 18, 1937
     New Republic 93:198, Dec 22, 1937
     New York Times XI, page 2, Nov 7, 1937
                    page 32, Dec 2, 1937
                    X, page 3, Jan 9, 1938
     Stage 15:51-3, Dec 1937
     Time 30:57, Dec 13, 1937

Hooray! It's a Glorious Day ... and All That
     book: Maurice Teitelbaum and Charles Grodin
     music: Arthur Gordon
     lyrics: Ethel Bieber, Messrs. Teitelbaum and Charles
                      Grodin
     staging: Charles Grodin
     sets: Peter Harvey
     costumes: Peter Harvey
     choreography: Sandra Devlin
Productions:
     (Off-Broadway) Opened March 9, 1966 for 15 performances
Reviews:
     New York Times page 28, Mar 10, 1966
     New Yorker 42:163-4, Mar 19, 1966

Hop o' My Thumb
     book: George R. Sims, Frank Dix and Arthur Col-
                      lins; American version by Sydney Rosenfeld
     music: Manuel Klein
     lyrics: Ernest D'Auban
Productions:
     Opened November 26, 1913 for 46 performances
Reviews:
     Blue Book 18:838-40, Mar 1914
     Collier's 52:30, Jan 10, 1914
     Dramatic Mirror 70:6, Dec 3, 1913
     New York Times page 13, Nov 27, 1913
     Theatre Magazine 19:9, Jan 1914
                      19:46, Jan 1914

Horseman, Pass By
     book: Rocco Bufano and John Duffy; based on
                      writings of W. B. Yeats
     music: John Duffy
     staging: Rocco Bufano

     sets: Dennis Dougherty
     costumes: Nancy Potts
     choreography: Rhoda Levine
Productions:
     (Off-Broadway) Opened January 15, 1969 for 37 performances
Reviews:
     New York Times page 46, Jan 16, 1969
     New Yorker 44:77-8, Jan 25, 1969

Hot and Cold Heros
     conceived: Joe Jakubowitz
     staging: Joe Jakubowitz
     sets: R. Thomas Finch
     costumes: Fran Caruso
     choreography: Ivan Todd
Productions:
     (Off-Broadway) Opened May 9, 1973 for 16 performances
Reviews:
     New York Times page 27, May 11, 1973

Hot-Cha!
     book: Lew Brown, Ray Henderson, Mark Hellinger,
                      H. S. Kraft
     music: Ray Henderson
     lyrics: Lew Brown
     staging: Edgar McGregor
     choreography: Bobby Connelly
Productions:
     Opened March 8, 1932 for 119 performances
Reviews:
     Bookman 75:77, Apr 1932
     New York Times VIII, page 2, Feb 21, 1932
                    page 17, Mar 9, 1932
                    VIII, page 1, Mar 20, 1932
     Outlook 160:229, Apr 1932
     Vogue 79:60+, May 1, 1932

Hot Chocolates
     book: Andy Razaf
     music: Thomas Waller and Harry Brooks
     staging: Leonard Harper
Productions:
     Opened June 20, 1929 for 219 performances
Reviews:
     New York Times page 17, Jun 21, 1929
     Outlook 152:553, Jul 31, 1929
     Theatre Magazine 50:43, Aug 1929

Hot Rhythm
     sketches: Ballard McDonald, Will Morrissey, Edward
                      Hurley
     music: Porter Grainger and Donald Heywood
     lyrics: Porter Grainger and Donald Heywood

staging: Will Morrissey and Nat Cash
Productions:
Opened August 21, 1930 for 68 performances
Reviews:
Life (New York) 96:16, Sep 12, 1930
New York Times page 18, Aug 22, 1930

Hot Spot
    book: Jack Weinstock and Willie Gilbert
    music: Mary Rodgers
    lyrics: Martin Charnin
    sets: Rouben Ter-Arutunian
    costumes: Rouben Ter-Arutunian
Productions:
Opened April 19, 1963 for 43 performances
Reviews:
Commonweal 78:225, May 17, 1963
New York Theatre Critics' Reviews 1963:336+
New York Times II, page 1, Apr 14, 1963
                 page 17, Apr 20, 1963
                 page 26, May 21, 1963
New Yorker 39:82, Apr 27, 1963
Newsweek 61:54, Apr 29, 1963
Theatre Arts 47:66, Jun 1963
Time 81:58, Apr 26, 1963

The Hotel Mouse
    book: Adapted from a French source by Guy Bolton
    music: Armand Vecsey and Ivan Caryll
    lyrics: Clifford Grey
Productions:
Opened March 13, 1922 for 88 performances
Reviews:
New York Clipper 70:20, Mar 22, 1922
New York Times page 11, Mar 14, 1922
Theatre Magazine 35:283, May 1922
                       35:334, May 1922

Hotel Passionato
    book: Jerome J. Schwartz
    music: Philip Springer
    lyrics: Joan Javits
    staging: Michael Ross
    sets: Paul Barnes
    costumes: Robert Mackintosh
Productions:
(Off-Broadway) Opened October 22, 1965 for 11 performances
Reviews:
New York Times page 16, Oct 23, 1965
New Yorker 41:116, Nov 6, 1965

House of Flowers
    book: Truman Capote

    music: Harold Arlen
    lyrics: Truman Capote and Harold Arlen
    staging: Peter Brook
    sets: Oliver Messel
    costumes: Oliver Messel
    choreography: Herbert Ross
Productions:
    Opened December 30, 1954 for 165 performances
    (Off-Broadway) Opened January 28, 1968 for 57 performances
Reviews:
    Catholic World 180:469, Mar 1955
    Commonweal 61:454-5, Jan 28, 1955
    Dance Magazine 42:28+, Apr 1968
    Mademoiselle 40:142, Nov 1954
    Nation 180:106, Jan 29, 1955
    New York Theatre Critics' Reviews 1954:189+
    New York Times page 75, Dec 19, 1954
                     page 11, Dec 31, 1954
                     page 39, Jan 24, 1968
                     page 26, Jan 29, 1968
                     page 50, Mar 14, 1968
    New Yorker 30:62, Jan 8, 1955
    Newsweek 45:62, Jan 10, 1955
    Saturday Review 38:31, Jan 15, 1955
    Theatre Arts 39:30-1+, Jan 1955
                 39:20-1+, Mar 1955
    Time 65:34, Jan 10, 1955
         91:75, Feb 9, 1968
    Vogue 125:125, Jan 1955

The House of Leather
    book: Frederick Gaines
    music: Dale F. Menten
    lyrics: Dale F. Menten and Frederick Gaines
    staging: H. Wesley Balk
    sets: David F. Segal
    costumes: Judith Cooper and James K. Shearon
Productions:
    (Off-Broadway) Opened March 18, 1970 for one performance
Reviews:
    New York Times page 56, Mar 19, 1970
    New Yorker 46:86+, Mar 28, 1970

How Come?
    book: Eddie Hunter
    staging: Sam H. Grisman
Productions:
    Opened April 16, 1923 for 32 performances
Reviews:
    New York Clipper 71:14, Apr 25, 1923
    New York Times page 26, Apr 17, 1923

How Now, Dow Jones

    book: Max Shulman; based on an original idea by
                       Carolyn Leigh
    music: Elmer Bernstein
    lyrics: Carolyn Leigh
    staging: George Abbott
    sets: Oliver Smith
    costumes: Robert Mackintosh
    choreography: Gillian Lynne
Productions:
    Opened December 7, 1967 for 220 performances
Reviews:
    America 118:330, Mar 9, 1968
    Christian Century 85:269, Feb 28, 1968
    Dance Magazine 42:29+, Feb 1968
    Nation 206:28, Jan 1, 1968
    New York Theatre Critics' Reviews 1967:190
                                       1967:198
    New York Times page 60, Nov 10, 1967
                    page 53, Dec 8, 1967
                    page 38, Jun 18, 1968
    New Yorker 43:97, Dec 16, 1967
    Newsweek 70:94+, Dec 18, 1967

How to Be a Jewish Mother
    book: Seymour Vall; based on the book by Dan Green-
                       burg
    music: Michael Leonard
    lyrics: Herbert Martin
    staging: Avery Schreiber
    sets: Robert Randolph
    costumes: Michael Travis
Productions:
    Opened December 28, 1967 for 21 performances
Reviews:
    New York Theatre Critics' Reviews 1967:187
    New York Times page 18, Dec 29, 1967
                    page 32, Jan 15, 1968

How to Steal an Election
    book: William F. Brown
    music: Oscar Brand
    lyrics: Oscar Brand
    staging: Robert H. Livingston
    sets: Clarke Dunham
    costumes: Mopsy
Productions:
    (Off-Broadway) Opened October 13, 1968 for 89 performances
Reviews:
    New York Times page 56, Oct 14, 1968
                    page 39, Dec 19, 1968
    New Yorker 44:142, Oct 26, 1968
    Newsweek 72:121, Nov 11, 1968

How to Succeed in Business without Really Trying

book:	Abe Burrows, Jack Weinstock, Willie Gilbert, based on Shepherd Mead's novel
music:	Frank Loesser
lyrics:	Frank Loesser
staging:	Abe Burrows
sets:	Robert Randolph
costumes:	Robert Fletcher
choreography:	Hugh Lambert

Productions:
Opened October 14, 1961 for 1, 417 performances
Opened April 20, 1966 for 23 performances
(Off-Off-Broadway) Opened November 9, 1972 (Equity Library Theatre)

Reviews:
America 106:632, Feb 10, 1962
Business Week pages 30-1, Oct 21, 1961
Christian Century 79:234, Feb 21, 1962
Commonweal 75:154, Nov 3, 1961
Dance Magazine 35:23, Dec 1961
              36:12-13, Jan 1962
              40:22, Jun 1966
Life 51:192-4, Nov 17, 1961
    60:18, Jun 17, 1966
National Review 12:31-3, Jan 16, 1962
Nation 193:361-2, Nov 4, 1961
New Republic 145:23, Nov 6, 1961
New York Theatre Critics' Reviews 1961:224+
New York Times II, page 1, Oct 8, 1961
              page 34, Oct 16, 1961
              II, page 3, Sep 2, 1962
              page 5, Mar 30, 1963
              page 43, Oct 11, 1963
              page 30, Feb 12, 1964
              II, page 7, Mar 8, 1964
              page 10, Jul 18, 1964
              page 45, Apr 21, 1966
              page 45, Nov 12, 1972
New Yorker 37:129, Oct 21, 1961
Newsweek 58:50-3, Nov 27, 1961
        58:62, Oct 23, 1961
Reporter 25:58, Nov 9, 1961
Saturday Evening Post 235:24-7, Jun 23, 1962
Saturday Review 44:33, Oct 28, 1961
Theatre Arts 45:8-9, Dec 1961
Time 78:79, Oct 27, 1961
    80:38, Dec 14, 1962

Howdy, Mr. Ice!

assembled:	Sonja Henie and Arthur M. Wirtz
music:	Al Stillman and Alan Moran
lyrics:	Al Stillman and Alan Moran
staging:	Catherine Littlefield

    sets: Bruno Maine
    costumes: Billy Livingston and Katherine Kuhn
Productions:
    Opened June 24, 1948 for 406 performances
Reviews:
    Catholic World 167:459, Aug 1948
    Commonweal 48:308, Jul 9, 1948
    New Republic 119:27, Jul 12, 1948
    New York Times page 28, Jun 25, 1948
    Theatre Arts 32:40, Oct 1948
    Time 52:42, Jul 5, 1948

Howdy, Mr. Ice of 1950!
    assembled: Sonja Henie and Arthur M. Wirtz
    music: Al Stillman and Alan Moran
    lyrics: Al Stillman and Alan Moran
    staging: Catherine Littlefield
    sets: Bruno Maine
    costumes: Grace Huston, Billy Livingston and Katherine
                     Kuhn
Productions:
    Opened May 26, 1949 for 430 performances
Reviews:
    New York Times page 24, May 27, 1949

Humming Sam
    book: Eileen Nutter
    music: Alexander Hill
    staging: Carey and Davis
Productions:
    Opened April 8, 1933 for one performance
Reviews:
    New York Times page 8, Apr 10, 1933

Hurry, Harry
    book: Jeremiah Morris, Lee Kalcheim and Susan
                     Perkins
    music: Bill Weeden
    lyrics: David Finkle
    staging: Jeremiah Morris
    sets: Fred Voelpel
    costumes: Sara Brook
    choreography: Gerald Teijelo
Productions:
    Opened October 12, 1972 for 2 performances
Reviews:
    New York Theatre Critics' Reviews 1972:220

                            - I -

I Can Get It for You Wholesale
    book: Jerome Weidman, based on his novel

music: Harold Rome
lyrics: Harold Rome
staging: Arthur Laurents
sets: Will Steven Armstrong
costumes: Theoni V. Aldredge
choreography: Herbert Ross
Productions:
Opened March 22, 1962 for 300 performances
Reviews:
Dance Magazine 36:18, May 1962
Life 52:103-4, May 18, 1962
Nation 194:338, Apr 14, 1962
New York Theatre Critics' Reviews 1962:314+
New York Times page 29, Mar 23, 1962
Newsweek 59:58, Apr 2, 1962
Saturday Review 45:28, Apr 14, 1962
Theatre Arts 46:58+, May 1962
Time 79:46, Mar 30, 1962

I Do! I Do!
book: Tom Jones; based on Jan de Hartog's play
                  The Fourposter
music: Harvey Schmidt
lyrics: Tom Jones
staging: Gower Champion
sets: Oliver Smith
costumes: Freddy Wittop
Productions:
Opened December 5, 1966 for 560 performances
Reviews:
America 116:263, Feb 18, 1967
Christian Century 84:144, Feb 1, 1967
Commonweal 85:402-3, Jan 13, 1967
Life 62:16, Jan 13, 1967
     62:82-5, Jan 13, 1967
Nation 204:29-30, Jan 2, 1967
New York Theatre Critics' Reviews 1966:217
New York Times page 58, Dec 6, 1966
              II, page 3, Dec 18, 1966
              page 54, Nov 28, 1967
              page 38, Jun 18, 1968
New Yorker 42:117, Dec 17, 1966
Newsweek 68:106, Dec 19, 1966
Saturday Review 49:61+, Dec 24, 1966
Time 88:87, Dec 16, 1966

I Dreamt I Dwelt in Bloomingdale's
book: Jack Ramer
music: Ernest McCarty
lyrics: Jack Ramer and Ernest McCarty
staging: David Dunham
sets: Ed Wittstein
choreography: Bick Goss

Productions:
    (Off-Broadway) Opened February 12, 1970 for 6 performances
Reviews:
    New York Times page 26, Feb 13, 1970
    New Yorker 46:67, Feb 21, 1970

I Feel Wonderful
    sketches: Barry Alan Grael
    music: Jerry Herman
    lyrics: Jerry Herman
Productions:
    (Off-Broadway) Opened Season of 1954-1955 (Theater de Lys)
Reviews:
    Catholic World 180:228, Dec 1954
    New York Times page 22, Oct 19, 1954
    Saturday Review 37:38, Nov 6, 1954

I Had a Ball
    book: Jerome Chodorov
    music: Jack Lawrence and Stan Freeman
    lyrics: Jack Lawrence and Stan Freeman
    staging: Lloyd Richards
    sets: Will Steven Armstrong
    costumes: Ann Roth
    choreography: Onna White and Tom Panko
Productions:
    Opened December 15, 1964 for 199 performances
Reviews:
    America 112:335-6, Mar 6, 1965
    New York Theatre Critics' Reviews 1964:107+
    New York Times page 50, Dec 16, 1964
    New Yorker 40:50, Dec 26, 1964
    Newsweek 64:57, Dec 28, 1964
    Saturday Review 48:32, Jan 2, 1965
    Time 84:62, Dec 25, 1964

I Married an Angel
    book: Richard Rodgers and Lorenz Hart, adapted from
                    John Veszary's Hungarian play
    music: Richard Rodgers
    lyrics: Lorenz Hart
    staging: Joshua Logan
    sets: Jo Mielziner
    costumes: John Hambleton
    choreography: George Balanchine
Productions:
    Opened May 11, 1938 for 338 performances
Reviews:
    Catholic World 147:474-5, Jul 1938
    Commonweal 28:133, May 27, 1938
    Life 4:48-9, May 30, 1938
    New York Times page 26, May 12, 1938
                    XI, page 1, May 22, 1938

IX, page 8, Jul 17, 1938
Newsweek 11:20, May 23, 1938
Stage 15:13-15, Jun 1938
Theatre Arts 22:464, Jul 1938
Time 31:20, May 23, 1938

I Want You
    book: Stefan Kanfer and Jess J. Korman
    music: Stefan Kanfer, Jess J. Korman and Joseph
                 Grayhon
    lyrics: Stefan Kanfer, Jess J. Korman and Joseph
                 Grayhon
    staging: Theodore J. Flicker
Productions:
    (Off-Broadway) Opened September 14, 1961 for 4 performances
Reviews:
    New York Times page 29, Sep 15, 1961
                    page 10, Sep 16, 1961

Ice Follies of 1942
Productions:
    (Off-Broadway) Opened December 1941
No Reviews.

Icetime of 1948
    assembled: Sonja Henie and Arthur M. Wirtz
    music: James Littlefield and John Fortis
    lyrics: James Littlefield and John Fortis
    songs: Al Stillman and Paul McGrane
    staging: Catherine Littlefield
    sets: Bruno Maine and Edward Gilbert
    costumes: Lou Eisele, Billy Livingston, Katherine Kuhn
    choreography: Catherine Littlefield and Dorothie Littlefield
Productions:
    Opened May 28, 1947 for 422 performances
Reviews:
    Life 24:120-21, Mar 8, 1948
    New York Times page 28, May 29, 1947
                 II, page 3, Nov 9, 1947
    Newsweek 32:86, Oct 25, 1948
    Time 49:54, Jun 9, 1947

I'd Rather Be Right
    book: George S. Kaufman and Moss Hart
    music: Richard Rodgers
    lyrics: Lorenz Hart
    staging: George S. Kaufman
    sets: Donald Oenslager
    costumes: Irene Sharaff
    choreography: Charles Weidman
Productions:
    Opened November 2, 1937 for 290 performances
Reviews:

Catholic World 146:339-40, Dec 1937
Commonweal 27:106, Nov 19, 1937
Independent Woman 16:351, Nov 1937
Life 3:27-9, Oct 25, 1937
Literary Digest 1:35, Nov 20, 1937
New Republic 93:44, Nov 17, 1937
New York Times page 27, Oct 12, 1937
                IX, page 2, Oct 17, 1937
                page 18, Oct 26, 1937
                page 28, Nov 3, 1937
                XI, page 2, Nov 7, 1937
Newsweek 10:24-6, Oct 25, 1937
          10:29, Nov 15, 1937
Scholastic 31:2, Oct 30, 1937
Scribner's Magazine 103:70, Jan 1938
Stage 15:52-4, Nov 1937
      15:94, Nov 1937
      15:56-9, Dec 1937
Theatre Arts 21:924+, Dec 1937
Time 30:45, Oct 25, 1937
     30:25, Nov 15, 1937
Vogue 90:108+, Dec 1, 1937

If the Shoe Fits
    book: June Carroll and Robert Duke
    music: David Raksin
    lyrics: June Carroll and Robert Duke
    staging: Eugene Bryden
    sets: Edward Gilbert
    costumes: Kathryn Kuhn
    choreography: Charles Weidman
Productions:
    Opened December 5, 1946 for 21 performances
Reviews:
    New York Theatre Critics' Reviews 1946:226+
    New York Times II, page 1, Dec 1, 1946
                    page 29, Dec 6, 1946
    New Yorker 22:64, Dec 14, 1946

I'll Say She Is
    book: Will B. Johnstone
    music: Tom Johnstone
    lyrics: Will B. Johnstone
    staging: Eugene Sanger and Vaughan Godfrey
Productions:
    Opened May 19, 1924 for (32) performances
Reviews:
    New York Times page 15, May 20, 1924
    Theatre Magazine 40:16, Aug 1924

The Illustrator's Show
    assembled by: The Society of Illustrators, edited by Tom
                  Weatherly

music:	Frank Loesser and Irving Actman
lyrics:	Frank Loesser and Irving Actman
staging:	Tom Weatherly
sets:	Arne Lundborg
costumes:	Carl Sidney
choreography:	Carl Randall

Productions:
Opened January 22, 1936 for 5 performances
Reviews:
New York Times page 25, Jan 23, 1936

Illya Darling
book:	Jules Dassin; based on the movie Never on
	Sunday
music:	Manos Hadjidakis
lyrics:	Joe Darion
staging:	Jules Dassin
sets:	Oliver Smith
costumes:	Theoni V. Aldredge
choreography:	Onna White and Tommy Panko

Productions:
Opened April 11, 1967 for 318 performances
Reviews:
America 116:737-8, May 13, 1967
Commonweal 86:342-5, Jun 9, 1967
Dance Magazine 41:38, Jun 1967
New York Theatre Critics' Reviews 1967:328
New York Times page 37, Apr 12, 1967
              II, page 1, Apr 30, 1967
              page 58, Nov 2, 1967
              page 50, Jan 3, 1968
Newsweek 69:107, Apr 24, 1967
Saturday Review 50·47, Apr 29, 1967
Time 89:83, Apr 21, 1967

I'm Solomon
book:	Anne Croswell and Dan Almagor; based on the
	play King Solomon and the Cobbler by Sammy
	Gronemann
music:	Ernest Gold
lyrics:	Anne Croswell
staging:	Michael Benthall
sets:	Rouben Ter-Arutunian
choreography:	Dorothea Freitag

Productions:
Opened April 23, 1968 for 7 performances
Reviews:
New York Theatre Critics' Reviews 1968:297
New York Times page 51, Apr 24, 1968
              page 42, Apr 30, 1968
New Yorker 44:129, May 4, 1968

In Hayti

    book: John J. McNally
    music: Jerome and Schwartz
    lyrics: Jerome and Schwartz
    staging: Julian Alfred
Productions:
    Opened August 30, 1909 for 56 performances
Reviews:
    Dramatic Mirror 62:5, Sep 11, 1909
    Theatre Magazine 10:xv, Oct 1909

In the Nick of Time
    contributors: Barbara Fried, Charles Appel, Herb Suffrin,
                     Leni Stern, Sue Lawless and Ted Pugh
    staging: Earl Durham
Productions:
    (Off-Broadway) Opened June 1, 1967 for 22 performances
Reviews:
    Commonweal 86:394, Jun 23, 1967
    New York Times page 36, Jun 2, 1967

Inner City
    conceived: Tom O'Horgan; based on the book The Inner
                     City Mother Goose, by Eve Merriam
    music: Helen Miller
    lyrics: Eve Merriam
    staging: Tom O'Horgan
    sets: Robin Wagner
    costumes: Joseph G. Aulisi
Productions:
    Opened December 19, 1971 for 97 performances
Reviews:
    Nation 214:61, Jan 10, 1972
    New York Theatre Critics' Reviews 1971:147
    New York Times page 40, Sep 15, 1971
                    page 48, Dec 20, 1971
                    II, page 1, Dec 26, 1971
                    II, page 18, Feb 13, 1972

Innocent Eyes
    book: Harold Atteridge
    music: Sigmund Romberg and Jean Schwartz
    lyrics: Harold Atteridge and Tot Seymour
Productions:
    Opened May 20, 1924 for 126 performances
Reviews:
    New York Times page 22, May 21, 1924
                    page 8, Aug 22, 1924
    Theatre Magazine 40:15, Aug 1924

Inside U.S.A.
    sketches: Arnold Auerbach, Moss Hart, Arnold B. Hor-
                     witt, suggested by John Gunther's book
    music: Arthur Schwartz

The International

```
    lyrics:          Howard Dietz
    staging:         Victor Samrock
    sets:            Lemuel Ayers
    costumes:        Eleanor Goldsmith and Castillo
    choreography:    Helen Tamiris
Productions:
    Opened April 30, 1948 for 399 performances
Reviews:
    Catholic World 167:265, Jun 1948
    Collier's 121:24-5+, May 15, 1948
    Commonweal 48:100, May 14, 1948
    Harper 196:478-80, May 1948
    Life 24:135-6+, May 17, 1948
    New Republic 118:35-6, May 17, 1948
    New York Theatre Critics' Reviews 1948:279+
    New York Times page 27, Mar 30, 1948
                    page 19, May 1, 1948
                    II, page 1, May 23, 1948
                    II, page 6, Jun 13, 1948
                    II, page 1, Aug 29, 1948
                    page 34, Jun 9, 1949
    New Yorker 24:52+, May 8, 1948
    Newsweek 31:76, May 10, 1948
    Saturday Review 31:25, May 22, 1948
    Theatre Arts 32:14-15+, Jun 1948
    Time 51:80, May 10, 1948
    Vogue 111:137, May 1, 1948
```

The International
```
    book:            John Howard Lawson
    music:           Edward A. Ziman
    staging:         John Howard Lawson
Productions:
    Opened January 12, 1928 for 27 performances
Reviews:
    Life (New York) 92:21, Feb 2, 1928
    Nation 126:130, Feb 1, 1928
```

The International Cup, the Ballet of Niagra and the Earthquake
```
    written:         R. H. Burnside
    music:           Manuel Klein
    lyrics:          Manuel Klein
    staged:          R. H. Burnside
Productions:
    Opened September 3, 1910 for 333 performances
Reviews:
    Theatre Magazine 12:110, Oct 1910
```

The International Revue
```
    book:            Nat N. Dorfman and Lew Leslie
    music:           Jimmy McHugh
    lyrics:          Dorothy Fields
    staging:         Lew Leslie and E. C. Lilley
```

    choreography: Busby Berkeley and Harry Crosley
Productions:
    Opened February 25, 1930 for 95 performances
Reviews:
    Life (New York) 95:18, Mar 28, 1930
    New York Times VIII, page 4, Feb 9, 1930
                    page 22, Feb 26, 1930
    Outlook 155:109, May 21, 1930

Iole
    book: Robert W. Chambers and Ben Teal
    music: William Frederick
    lyrics: Robert W. Chambers and Ben Teal
    staging: Ben Teal
Productions:
    Opened December 29, 1913 for 24 performances
Reviews:
    Blue Book 18:1046-7, Apr 1914
    Dramatic Mirror 70:6-7, Dec 31, 1913
                    71:2, Jan 7, 1914
    Green Book 11:521, Mar 1914
    Leslie's Weekly 118:107, Jan 29, 1914
    New York Life 63:110, Jan 15, 1914
    New York Dramatic News 58:20, Jan 3, 1914
    New York Times page 11, Dec 9, 1913
                    VII page 6, Dec 28, 1913
    Theatre Magazine 19:55+, Feb 1914
                    19:106, Feb 1914

Ionescopade
    conceived: Robert Allan Ackerman, adapted from the works
                   of Eugene Ionesco
    music: Mildred Kayden
    lyrics: Mildred Kayden
    staging: Robert Allan Ackerman
    sets: David Sackeroff
    costumes: Patricia Adshead
    choreography: Merry Lynn Katis
Productions:
    (Off-Off-Broadway) Opened July 26, 1973 (New Phoenix
       Repertory Co.)
    (Off-Broadway) Opened April 25, 1974 for 14 performances
Reviews:
    New York Times page 16, Jul 28, 1973
                    page 29, Apr 26, 1974
    New Yorker 50:76-7, May 6, 1974

Irene (1919)
    book: James Montgomery
    music: Harry Tierney
    lyrics: Joe McCarthy
Productions:
    Opened November 18, 1919 for 228 performances

Reviews:
     Dramatic Mirror 80:1861, Dec 4, 1919
     New York Times page 11, Nov 19, 1919

Irene (1973)
          book: Hugh Wheeler and Joseph Stein; from an
                                adaption by Harry Rigby of the original 1919
                                musical
          music: Harry Tierney (original)
          lyrics: Joe McCarthy (original)
          additional
             music: Charles Gaynor and Otis Clements
          additional
             lyrics: Charles Gaynor and Otis Clements
          staging: Gower Champion
          sets: Raoul Pene du Bois
          costumes: Raoul Pene du Bois
          choreography: Peter Gennaro
Productions:
     Opened March 13, 1973 for 590* performances
Reviews:
     America 128:336, Apr 14, 1973
     Dance Magazine 47:58D-59+, Jun 1973
     Nation 216:444-5, Apr 2, 1973
     National Review 25:473-4, Apr 27, 1973
     New York Theatre Critics' Reviews 1973:328
     New York Times II, page 1, Feb 25, 1973
                        page 28, Mar 14, 1973
                        page 16, Feb 8, 1974
     New Yorker 49:74, Mar 24, 1973
     Newsweek 81:56, Mar 26, 1973
     Saturday Evening Post 246:52-3, Apr 1974
     Time 101:101, Mar 26, 1973

Irma La Douce
          book: Julian More, David Heneker and Monty Norman,
                                English version of the original book by Alexandre
                                Breffort
          music: Marguerite Monnot
          lyrics: Julian More, David Heneker and Monty Norman,
                                English version of the original lyrics by
                                Alexandre Breffort
          staging: Peter Brook
          sets: Rolf Gerard
          costumes: Rolf Gerard
          choreography: Onna White
Productions:
     Opened September 29, 1960 for 524 performances
Reviews:
     America 104:130+, Oct 22, 1960
     Commonweal 73:152, Nov 4, 1960
     Coronet 49:14, Jan 1961
     Dance Magazine 34:32, Dec 1960

Life 49:53+, Nov 14, 1960
Nation 188:462, May 16, 1959
        191:253, Oct 15, 1960
New Republic 143:21-2, Oct 17, 1960
New York Theatre Critics' Reviews 1960:230+
New York Times II, page 3, Sep 25, 1960
                    page 31, Sep 30, 1960
                    II, page 1, Oct 16, 1960
                    II, page 1, Oct 30, 1960
New Yorker 36:95, Oct 8, 1960
Newsweek 56:65, Oct 10, 1960
Saturday Review 43:36, Oct 15, 1960
Time 76:84, Oct 10, 1960

It Happens on Ice
    assembled: Sonja Henie and Arthur Wirtz
    lyrics: Al Stillman
    songs: Vernon Duke, Fred E. Ahlert and Peter de Rose
    staging: Leon Leonidoff
    sets: Norman Bel Geddes
    costumes: Norman Bel Geddes
    choreography: Catherine Littlefield and Robert Linden
Productions:
    Opened October 10, 1940 for 180 performances
    Opened April 4, 1941 for 96 performances
    Opened July 15, 1941 for 386 performances
Reviews:
    New York Theatre Critics' Reviews 1940:259
                                      1941:340
                                      1941:472
    New York Times page 24, Oct 11, 1940
                    II, page 1, Nov 3, 1940
                    page 13, Apr 5, 1941
                    IX, page 1, Aug 31, 1941
                    page 25, Feb 17, 1942
                    page 18, Apr 6, 1942
    Scholastic 37:36, Jan 13, 1941
    Stage 1:12, Nov 1940
    Theatre Arts 24:847-8+, Dec 1940
    Time 36:71, Oct 21, 1940

It's a Bird It's a Plane It's SUPERMAN
    book: David Newman and Robert Benton; based on the
                    comic strip "Superman"
    music: Charles Strouse
    lyrics: Lee Adams
    staging: Harold Prince
    sets: Robert Randolph
    costumes: Florence Klotz
    choreography: Betty Walberg
Productions:
    Opened March 29, 1966 for 129 performances
Reviews:

America 114:704, May 14, 1966
Commonweal 84:156, Apr 22, 1966
Dance Magazine 40:25, May 1966
Life 60:25, Mar 11, 1966
New York Theatre Critics' Reviews 1966:310
New York Times II, page 1, Mar 27, 1966
                              page 34, Mar 30, 1966
                              page 15, Jul 16, 1966
New Yorker 42:81, Apr 9, 1966
Newsweek 67:94, Apr 11, 1966
Saturday Review 49:62, Apr 16, 1966
Time 78:81, Apr 8, 1966

It's About Time
   sketches: Peter Barry, Arnold Horwitt, Arthur Elmer,
                        Sam Locke, David Gregory, and Reuben Shipp
   music: Will Lorin, Al Moss and Genevieve Pitot
   lyrics: David Gregory
   sets: William Martin and Walter Ketchum
Productions:
   (Off-Broadway) Opened March 28, 1942
Reviews:
   New York Times page 28, Mar 31, 1942

It's up to You
   book: Augustin MacHugh, Douglas Leavitt, Edward
                        Paulton and Harry Clarke
   lyrics: Augustin MacHugh, Douglas Leavitt, Edward
                        Paulton and Harry Clarke
   staging: Frank Stammers
Productions:
   Opened March 24, 1921 for 24 performances
Reviews:
   Dramatic Mirror 83:601, Apr 2, 1921
   New York Life 77:536, Apr 14, 1921
   New York Clipper 69:19, Apr 6, 1921
   New York Times page 20, Mar 29, 1921
   Theatre Magazine 33:460, Jun 1921

I've Got the Tune
   book: Mark Blitzstein
   music: Mark Blitzstein
   lyrics: Mark Blitzstein
Productions:
   (Off-Broadway) Opened April 1939
   (Off-Broadway) Opened June 24, 1939
No Reviews.

- J -

Jack and Jill
   book: Frederick Isham and Otto Harbach

music: John Murray Anderson and A. Barratt
lyrics: John Murray Anderson and A. Barratt
Productions:
    Opened March 22, 1923 for 92 performances
Reviews:
    Life (New York) 81:20, Apr 12, 1923
    New York Clipper 71:14, Mar 28, 1923
    New York Times page 17, Mar 23, 1923
    Theatre Magazine 37:16, May 1923
                        38:18, Sep 1923

Jack O'Lantern
    book: Anne Caldwell and R. H. Burnside
    music: Ivan Caryll
    staging: R. H. Burnside
Productions:
    Opened October 16, 1917 for 265 performances
Reviews:
    Dramatic Mirror 77:7, Oct 27, 1917
    Green Book 19:8+, Jan 1918
    Life (New York) 70:714, Nov 1, 1917
    Munsey 64:430, Jul 1918
    New York Dramatic Mirror 64:6, Oct 27, 1917
    New York Times page 13, Oct 17, 1917
    Theatre Magazine 26:392, Dec 1917

Jackpot
    book: Guy Bolton, Sidney Sheldon, Ben Roberts
    music: Vernon Duke
    lyrics: Howard Dietz
    staging: Roy Hargrave
    sets: Raymond Sovey and Robert Edmund Jones
    costumes: Kiviette
    choreography: Lauretta Jefferson and Charles Weidman
Productions:
    Opened January 13, 1944 for 69 performances
Reviews:
    New York Theatre Critics' Reviews 1944:284+
    New York Times page 15, Jan 14, 1944
                    II, page 1, Jan 30, 1944
    New Yorker 19:34+, Jan 22, 1944
    Theatre Arts 28:142, Mar 1944

Jacques Brel Is Alive and Well and Living in Paris
    music: Jacques Brel
    lyrics: Eric Blau and Mort Shuman; based on lyrics
                  and commentary by Jacques Brel
    staging: Moni Yakim
    sets: Henry E. Scott III
    costumes: Ilka Suarez
Productions:
    (Off-Broadway) Opened January 22, 1968 for 1,847 per-
        formances

Opened September 15, 1972 for 51 performances
(Off-Broadway) Opened May 17, 1974 for 125 performances
Reviews:
   Nation 206:318, Mar 4, 1968
   New York Theatre Critics' Reviews 1972:248
   New York Times page 25, Jan 23, 1968
                  page 43, Jan 27, 1972
                  page 39, Feb 28, 1972
                  page 39, May 20, 1974
   Newsweek 80:98, Oct 30, 1972
   Saturday Review 51:26, Apr 27, 1968

Jamaica
   book: E. Y. Harburg and Fred Saidy
   music: Harold Arlen
   lyrics: E. Y. Harburg
   staging: Robert Lewis
   sets: Oliver Smith
   costumes: Miles White
   choreography: Jack Cole
Productions:
   Opened October 31, 1957 for 555 performances
Reviews:
   America 98:436, Jan 11, 1958
   Catholic World 186:304-5, Jan 1958
   Dance Magazine 31:13, Dec 1957
   Life 43:112+, Nov 18, 1957
   Nation 185:394, Nov 23, 1957
   New York Theatre Critics' Reviews 1957:196+
   New York Times VI, page 28, Aug 25, 1957
                     page 32, Nov 1, 1957
                     II, page 1, Nov 10, 1957
   New York Times Magazine pages 72-3, Oct 13, 1957
   New Yorker 33:103, Nov 9, 1957
   Newsweek 50:83, Nov 11, 1957
   Saturday Review 40:48, Nov 16, 1957
   Theatre Arts 41:73-4+, Oct 1957
               42:17, Jan 1958
   Time 70:93, Nov 11, 1957

The James Joyce Memorial Liquid Theatre
   conceived: Steven Kent
   music: Jack Rowe, Robert Walker and Lance Larsen
   staging: Steven Kent
   sets: Donald Harris
Productions:
   (Off-Broadway) Opened October 11, 1971 for 189 performances
Reviews:
   New York Theatre Critics' Reviews 1971:210
   New York Times page 44, Aug 26, 1971
                  page 51, Oct 12, 1971
                  II, page 1, Oct 17, 1971

Janis, Elsie (see Elsie Janis)

Jennie
    book: Arnold Schulman, suggested by Marguerite
                   Courtney's biography Laurette
    music: Arthur Schwartz
    lyrics: Howard Dietz
    staging: Vincent J. Donehue
    sets: George Jenkins
    costumes: Irene Sharaff
    choreography: Matt Mattox
Productions:
    Opened October 17, 1963 for 82 performances
Reviews:
    America 109:644, Nov 16, 1963
    New York Theatre Critics' Reviews 1963:234+
    New York Times II, page 1, Oct 13, 1963
                    page 35, Oct 18, 1963
                    page 21, Dec 20, 1963
    New Yorker 39:113, Oct 26, 1963
    Newsweek 62:91, Oct 28, 1963
    Saturday Review 46:18, Nov 2, 1963
    Theatre Arts 48:67, Jan 1964
    Time 82:75, Oct 25, 1963

Jesus Christ Superstar
    conceived: Tom O'Horgan, for the stage; based on the last
                   seven days in the life of Jesus of Nazareth
    music: Andrew Lloyd Webber
    lyrics: Tim Rice
    staging: Tom O'Horgan
    sets: Robin Wagner
    costumes: Randy Barcelo
Productions:
    Opened October 12, 1971 for 720 performances
Reviews:
    America 125:352-3, Oct 30, 1971
    Business Week pages 46-7, Sep 11, 1971
    Catholic World 213:217-21, Aug 1971
    Christian Century 88:1333-4, Nov 10, 1971
                     89:785-6, Jul 19, 1972
    Christianity Today 16:42-3, Dec 3, 1971
    Commentary 52:36, Dec 1971
    Commonweal 95:447-9, Feb 11, 1972
    Life 70:20 B-26, May 28, 1971
    Mademoiselle 74:102-5, Dec 1971
    Nation 213:444, Nov 1, 1971
    New Republic 165:24, Nov 6, 1971
    New York Theatre Critics' Reviews 1971:239
    New York Times II, page 1, May 30, 1971
                    page 46, Sep 1, 1971
                    page 48, Oct 12, 1971
                    page 40, Oct 13, 1971

II, page 1, Oct 24, 1971
II, page 1, Oct 31, 1971
VI, page 14, Jan 2, 1972
II, page 18, Mar 26, 1972
New Yorker 47:109, Oct 23, 1971
Newsweek 78:84-5, Oct 25, 1971
Saturday Review 54:38, Oct 30, 1971
                    54:65-7+, Oct 30, 1971
Senior Scholastic 99:10-11, Dec 13, 1971
Seventeen 30:156-7+, Mar 1971
Time 98:64-8+, Oct 25, 1971
Vogue 158:102-3, Dec 1971

Jim Jam Jems
    book: Harry L. Cort and George E. Stoddard
    music: James Hanley
    staging: Edward J. McGregor
Productions:
    Opened October 4, 1920 for 105 performances
Reviews:
    Dramatic Mirror page 664, Oct 9, 1920
    New York Clipper 68:29, Oct 13, 1920
    New York Times page 12, Oct 5, 1920
    Theatre Magazine 33:76, Jan 1921

Jimmie
    book: Otto Harbach, Oscar Hammerstein II and
                   Frank Mandel
    music: Herbert Stothart
Productions:
    Opened November 17, 1920 for 71 performances
Reviews:
    New York Times page 15, Nov 18, 1920
    Theatre Magazine 33:74, Jan 1921

Jimmy
    book: Melville Shavelson; based on Gene Fowler's
                   novel Beau James
    music: Bill and Patti Jacob
    lyrics: Bill and Patti Jacob
    staging: Joseph Anthony
    sets: Oliver Smith
    costumes: W. Robert Lavine
    choreography: Peter Gennaro
Productions:
    Opened October 23, 1969 for 84 performances
Reviews:
    America 121:544-5, Nov 29, 1969
    Commonweal 91:382-3, Dec 26, 1969
    New York Theatre Critics' Reviews 1969:192
                                      1969:218
    New York Times page 38, Oct 24, 1969
                    II, page 3, Nov 9, 1969

                              page 20, Jan 3, 1970
              New Yorker 45:128, Nov 1, 1969
              Newsweek 74:94, Nov 3, 1969

Jo
    book: Don Parks and William Dyer; based on Little
                       Women by Louisa May Alcott
    music: William Dyer
    lyrics: Don Parks and William Dyer
    staging: John Bishop
    sets: Gordon Micunis
    costumes: Evelyn Norton Anderson
    choreography: Chele Abel and Gerald Teijelo
Productions:
    (Off-Broadway) Opened February 12, 1964 for 63 performances
Reviews:
    America 110:322, Mar 7, 1964
    New York Times page 25, Feb 13, 1964
    New Yorker 40:92+, Feb 22, 1964

Joan
    book: Al Carmines
    music: Al Carmines
    lyrics: Al Carmines
    staging: Al Carmines
    sets: Earl Eidman
    costumes: Ira Siff and Joan Kilpatrick
    choreography: Gus Solomons, Jr. and David Vaughan
Productions:
    (Off-Broadway) Opened Season of 1971-1972 (Judson Poets'
        Theatre)
    (Off-Broadway) Opened June 19, 1972 for 64 performances
Reviews:
    America 127:292-3, Oct 4, 1972
    New York Theatre Critics' Reviews 1972:235
    New York Times page 33, Jun 20, 1972
                   II, page 1, Jun 25, 1972
    New Yorker 47:101, Dec 11, 1971
    Saturday Review 55:72, Jul 8, 1972
    Time 100:72, Jul 10, 1972

John Henry
    book: Roark Bradford
    music: Jaques Wolfe
    lyrics: Roark Bradford
    staging: Anthony Brown and Charles Friedman
    sets: Albert Johnson
    costumes: John Hambleton
Productions:
    Opened January 10, 1940 for 7 performances
Reviews:
    Catholic World 150:598-9, Feb 1940
    Collier's 105:15+, Jan 13, 1940

New York Theatre Critics' Reviews 1940:421+
New York Times IX, page 1, Jan 7, 1940
           page 18, Jan 11, 1940
Newsweek 15:33, Jan 22, 1940
Theatre Arts 24:166-7, Mar 1940
Time 35:49, Jan 22, 1940

John Murray Anderson's Almanac
    sketches: Jean Kerr, Summer Locke-Elliot, Arthur
                      Macrae, Herbert Farjeon, Lauri Wylie, Billy
                      K. Wells
    music and
    lyrics: Richard Adler, Jerry Ross, Cy Coleman,
                      Michael Grace, Joseph McCarthy, Jr., Henry
                      Sullivan, John Rox, Bart Howard
    staging: John Murray Anderson
    sets: Raoul Pene du Bois
    costumes: Thomas Becher
    choreography: Donald Saddler
Productions:
    Opened December 10, 1953 for 229 performances
Reviews:
    America 90:366, Jan 2, 1954
    Catholic World 178:390, Feb 1954
    Commonweal 59:353, Jan 8, 1954
    Life 35:72-3, Dec 28, 1953
    Nation 177:574, Dec 26, 1953
    New Republic 130:21, Jan 4, 1954
    New York Theatre Critics' Reviews 1953:191+
    New York Times page 42, Dec 11, 1953
                    page 51, Dec 14, 1953
                    II, page 1, Jan 3, 1954
    New Yorker 29:75, Dec 19, 1953
    Newsweek 42:60, Dec 21, 1953
    Saturday Review 37:30, Jan 9, 1954
    Theatre Arts 38:76-8, Jan 1954
                38:22-3, Feb 1954
    Time 62:57, Dec 21, 1953

Johnny Doodle
    by: Jane McLeod and Alfred Saxe
    staging: Lan Adomian
Productions:
    (Off-Broadway) Opened March 18, 1942
Reviews:
    New York Times page 28, Mar 19, 1942

The Jolly Bachelors
    words: Glen MacDonough
    music: Raymond Hubbell
    staging: Ned Wayburn
Productions:
    Opened January 6, 1910 for 84 performances

Reviews:
    Dramatic Mirror 63:5, Jan 15, 1910
    Hampton 204:409, Mar 1910
    Harper's Weekly 54:24, Feb 5, 1910
    Life (New York) 55:20, Jan 20, 1910
    Metropolitan Magazine 32:123-4+, Apr 1910
    Theatre Magazine 11:xiv, Feb 1910

Jonica
    book: Dorothy Heyward and Moss Hart
    music: Joseph Meyer
    lyrics: William Moll
    staging: William B. Friedlander
    choreography: Pal'mere Brandeaux
Productions:
    Opened April 7, 1930 for 40 performances
Reviews:
    New York Times VIII, page 2, Mar 30, 1930
                              page 27, Apr 8, 1930
    Outlook 154:671, Apr 23, 1930

Josephine Baker
    songs: Josephine Baker
    staging: Felix G. Gerstman
    costumes: Christian Dior, Pierre Balmain, House of Lan-
                              vin, Balenciaga
    choreography: Geoffrey Holder
Productions:
    Opened February 4, 1964 for 16 performances
    Opened March 31, 1964 for 24 performances
Reviews:
    New York Times page 37, Feb 7, 1964
    Newsweek 63:90, Feb 17, 1964

The Journey of Snow White
    music: Al Carmines
    staging: Gus Solomons Jr.
Productions:
    (Off-Broadway) Season of 1970-1971 (Judson Poets' Theatre)
Reviews:
    New York Times page 39, Mar 22, 1971

Joy
    sketches: Oscar Brown, Jr.
    songs: Oscar Brown, Jr. and others
Productions:
    (Off-Broadway) Opened January 27, 1970 for 208 performances
Reviews:
    New York Times page 50, Jan 28, 1970
    Newsweek 75:95, Feb 9, 1970
    Time 95:63, Mar 30, 1970

Joyce Grenfell

    monologues: Joyce Grenfell
    songs: Joyce Grenfell
    music: Richard Addinsell
    costumes: Victor Stiebel
Productions:
    Opened April 7, 1958 for 24 performances
Reviews:
    Christian Century 75:533, Apr 30, 1958
    New York Times page 32, Apr 8, 1958
    Time 71:76, Apr 21, 1958

Joyce Grenfell Requests the Pleasure...
    book: Joyce Grenfell
    music: Richard Addinsell
    lyrics: Joyce Grenfell
    staging: Laurier Lister
    sets: Paul Morrison
    choreography: Wendy Toye, John Heathwood, and others
Productions:
    Opened October 10, 1955 for 65 performances
Reviews:
    America 94:138, Oct 29, 1955
    Catholic World 182:224, Dec 1955
    Commonweal 63:116-7, Nov 18, 1955
    New York Times page 48, Oct 11, 1955
    New Yorker 31:90-92, Oct 22, 1955
                  31:41-2, Nov 19, 1955
    Newsweek 46:54, Oct 24, 1955
    Saturday Review 38:20, Oct 29, 1955
    Theatre Arts 39:20, Dec 1955
    Time 66:86, Oct 24, 1955

Joyce, James (see James Joyce Memorial Liquid Theatre)

A Joyful Noise
    book: Edward Padula; based on Borden Deal's novel
                   The Insolent Breed
    music: Oscar Brand and Paul Nassau
    lyrics: Oscar Brand and Paul Nassau
    staging: Edward Padula
    sets: Peter Wexler
    costumes: Peter Joseph
    choreography: Michael Bennett, Leland Palmer, Jo Jo Smith
Productions:
    Opened December 15, 1966 for 12 performances
Reviews:
    Dance Magazine 41:23, Feb 1967
    New York Theatre Critics' Reviews 1966:202
    New York Times page 41, Jul 5, 1966
                   II, page 4, Nov 27, 1966
                   page 57, Dec 16, 1966
                   page 10, Dec 24, 1966
    New Yorker 42:45, Dec 24, 1966

Newsweek 68:45, Dec 26, 1966

Jubilee
    book: Moss Hart
    music: Cole Porter
    lyrics: Cole Porter
    staging: Hassard Short
    sets: Jo Mielziner
    costumes: Irene Sharaff and Connie de Pinna
    choreography: Albertina Rasch
Productions:
    Opened October 12, 1935 for 169 performances
Reviews:
    Catholic World 142:340, Dec 1935
    Commonweal 22:642, Oct 1935
    Nation 141:548, Nov 6, 1935
    New York Times IX, page 2, Sep 15, 1935
                   page 20, Sep 23, 1935
                   X, page 1, Sep 29, 1935
                   page 20, Oct 14, 1935
                   X, page 3, Oct 20, 1935
                   IX, page 1, Oct 27, 1935
                   IX, page 8, Nov 24, 1935
    Newsweek 6:26-7, Oct 19, 1935
    Stage 13:30-1, Oct 1935
          13:33-4, Dec 1935
    Theatre Arts 19:901-2, Dec 1935
    Time 26:51, Oct 21, 1935
    Vanity Fair 45:68, Dec 1935

Judy
    book: Mark Swan
    staging: Bobby Connolly
Productions:
    Opened February 7, 1927 for 96 performances
Reviews:
    New York Times page 20, Feb 8, 1927
    Theatre Magazine 45:19, Apr 1927

Judy Forgot
    book: Avery Hopwood; based on The Winking Princess
    music: Silvio Hein
    lyrics: Avery Hopwood
    staging: Daniel V. Arthur
Productions:
    Opened October 6, 1910 for 44 performances
Reviews:
    Blue Book 12:427-30, Jan 1911
    Dramatic Mirror 64:9, Oct 19, 1910
    Green Book Album 5:476-7, Mar 1911
    Hampton 25:830, Dec 1910
    Leslie's Weekly 111:461, Nov 3, 1910
    Life (New York) 56:660, Oct 20, 1910

Metropolitan Magazine 33:522-3, Jan 1911
Munsey 44:413, Dec 1910
Theatre Magazine 12:130, Nov 1910
                  12:133, Nov 1910

Judy Garland at Home at the Palace
    staging: Richard Barstow
    costumes: Bill Smith Travilla
Productions:
Opened July 31, 1967 for 24 performances
Reviews:
    America 117:208, Aug 26, 1967
    Ladies Home Journal 84:64-5+, Aug 1967
    New York Times page 23, Aug 1, 1967
                    page 45, Dec 26, 1967
    Saturday Review 50:66, Sep 30, 1967
    Time 90:40, Aug 18, 1967

Jumbo
    book: Ben Hecht and Charles MacArthur
    music: Richard Rodgers
    lyrics: Lorenz Hart
    staging: John Murray Anderson
    sets: Albert Johnson
    costumes: Raoul Pene du Bois and James Reynolds
    choreography: Allan K. Foster and Marjery Fielding
Productions:
Opened November 16, 1935 for 233 performances
Reviews:
    Literary Digest 120:18-19, Nov 30, 1935
    Nation 141:660, Dec 4, 1935
    New Republic 85:134, Dec 11, 1935
    New York Times page 12, Aug 8, 1935
                    IX, page 1, Aug 11, 1935
                    page 20, Nov 18, 1935
                    IX, page 1, Nov 24, 1935
                    IX, page 4, Dec 22, 1935
    Newsweek 6:30-2, Nov 23, 1935
    Stage 13:49-51, Jan 1936
    Theatre Arts 20:12+, Jan 1936
    Time 26:47, Nov 25, 1935
    Vanity Fair 45:57, Jan 1936

Jumping Jupiter
    book: Richard Carle and Sydney Rosenfeld
    music: Karl Hoschna
    staging: Richard Carle
Productions:
Opened March 6, 1911 for 24 performances
Reviews:
    Dramatic Mirror 65:7, Mar 8, 1911
    Life (New York) 57:581, Mar 23, 1911
    Pearson 25:671, May 1911

Theatre Magazine 13:xiii, Apr 1911

June Days
    book: Cyrus Wood; based on a play by Alice Duer
                      Miller and Robert Milton
    music: J. Fred Coots
    lyrics: Clifford Grey
    staging: J. J. Shubert
Productions:
Opened August 6, 1925 for 84 performances
Reviews:
    New York Times page 12, Aug 7, 1925
                VII, page 4, Aug 7, 1925
                VII, page 1, Aug 23, 1925

June Love
    book: Otto Harbach and W. H. Post, adapted from a
                      story by Charlotte Thompson
    music: Rudolph Friml
    lyrics: Brian Hooker
    staging: George Vivian
Productions:
Opened April 25, 1921 for 50 performances
Reviews:
    Dramatic Mirror 83:733, Apr 30, 1921
    Life (New York) 77:688, May 12, 1921
    New York Clipper 69:19, Apr 27, 1921
    New York Times page 20, Apr 26, 1921
    Theatre Magazine 34:30, Jul 1921

Juno
    book: Joseph Stein, based on Sean O'Casey's play
                      Juno and the Paycock
    music: Marc Blitzstein
    lyrics: Marc Blitzstein
    staging: Jose Ferrer
    sets: Oliver Smith
    costumes: Irene Sharaff
    choreography: Agnes de Mille
Productions:
Opened March 9, 1959 for 16 performances
Reviews:
    Dance Magazine 33:22, Apr 1959
    New Republic 140:20, Mar 30, 1959
    New York Theatre Critics' Reviews 1959:351+
    New York Times II, page 1, Mar 1, 1959
                page 41, Mar 10, 1959
                II, page 1, Mar 15, 1959
                page 42, Mar 17, 1959
    New Yorker 35:97, Mar 21, 1959
    Newsweek 53:76, Mar 23, 1959
    Theatre Arts 43:65-6, May 1959
    Time 73:60, Mar 23, 1959

Just a Minute (1919)
    by: Harry L. Cort, George E. Stoddard, Harold
                     Orlob
Productions:
    Opened October 27, 1919 for 40 performances
Reviews:
    New York Times page 11, Oct 29, 1919
    Theatre Magazine 30:391, Dec 1919
                   30:426, Dec 1919

Just a Minute (1928)
    book: H. C. Greene
    music: Harry Archer
    lyrics: Walter O'Keefe
    staging: H. C. Greene
Productions:
    Opened October 8, 1928 for 80 performances
Reviews:
    New York Times page 34, Oct 9, 1928

Just Because
    book: Anne Wynne O'Ryan and Helen S. Woodruff
    music: Madelyn Sheppard
    lyrics: Anne Wynne O'Ryan and Helen S. Woodruff
    staging: Oscar Eagle
Productions:
    Opened March 22, 1922 for 46 performances
Reviews:
    New York Clipper 70:20, Mar 29, 1922
    New York Times page 11, Mar 23, 1922
    Theatre Magazine 35:379, Jun 1922

Just Fancy
    book: Joseph Santley and Gertrude Purcell; based on
                     a play by A. E. Thomas
    music: Joseph Meyer and Philip Charig
    lyrics: Leo Robin
    staging: Joseph Santley
Productions:
    Opened October 11, 1927 for 79 performances
Reviews:
    Life (New York) 90:23, Nov 3, 1927
    New York Times page 30, Oct 12, 1927
    Theatre Magazine 47:38, Jan 1928

Just for Love
    book: Jill Showell and Henry Comor
    music: Michael Valenti
    lyrics: Jill Showell and Henry Comor
    staging: Henry Comor
    sets: Jack Blackmon
    costumes: Sara Brook
Productions:

(Off-Broadway) Opened October 17, 1968 for 6 performances
Reviews:
New York Times page 40, Oct 18, 1968

Just for Openers
    conceived: Rod Warren
    sketches: Rod Warren and others
    songs: Rod Warren and others
    staging: Sandra Devlin
Productions:
(Off-Broadway) Opened November 3, 1965 for 395 performances
No Reviews.

- K -

Kaboom!
    book: Ira Wallach
    music: Doris Schwerin
    lyrics: Ira Wallach
    staging: Don Price
    sets: Peter Harvey
    costumes: Lohr Wilson
Productions:
(Off-Broadway) Opened May 1, 1974 for 1 performance
Reviews:
New York Times page 64, May 2, 1974

Katinka
    book: Otto Hauerbach
    music: Rudolf Friml
    lyrics: Otto Hauerbach
    staging: Frank Smithson
Productions:
Opened December 23, 1915 for 220 performances
Reviews:
Dramatic Mirror 75:8, Jan 1, 1916
               75:2, Feb 5, 1916
Green Book 15:447, Mar 1916
Munsey 57:512, Apr 1916
New York Dramatic News 62:18, Jan 1, 1916
Opera Magazine 3:31-2, Feb 1916
Theatre Magazine 23:65-6, Feb 1916

Kean
    book: Peter Stone, based on Jean Paul Sartre's play
                and Alexandre Dumas' play
    music: Robert Wright and George Forrest
    lyrics: Robert Wright and George Forrest
    staging: Jack Cole
    sets: Ed Wittstein
    costumes: Ed Wittstein
    choreography: Jack Cole

Productions:
Opened November 2, 1961 for 92 performances
Reviews:
Commonweal 75:389, Jan 5, 1962
Dance Magazine 35:23, Dec 1961
Nation 193:438, Nov 25, 1961
New York Theatre Critics' Reviews 1961:180+
New York Times page 28, Nov 3, 1961
II, page 1, Nov 12, 1961
New Yorker 37:117, Nov 11, 1961
Newsweek 58:94, Nov 13, 1961
Theatre Arts 45:17-24, Dec 1961
46:11-12, Jan 1962
Time 78:66, Nov 10, 1961

Keep 'em Laughing
assembled: Clifford C. Fischer
sketches: Arthur Pierson and Eddie Davis
staging: Clifford Fischer
sets: Frank W. Stevens
Productions:
Opened April 24, 1942 for 77 performances
Reviews:
New York Theatre Critics' Reviews 1942:306
New York Times page 9, Apr 25, 1942
page 24, May 20, 1942
Time 39:70, May 4, 1942
(Also see Top-Notchers)

Keep It Clean
book: Jimmy Duffy and Will Morrissey
music: Lester Lee, Jimmy Duffy, Harry Archer,
                Benny Ryan, James Hanley, Clarence Gaskill,
                Violinsky, Charles Tobias, Harry Converse
staging: Will Morrissey and Russell Markert
Productions:
Opened June 24, 1929 for 16 performances
Reviews:
New York Times page 35, Jun 25, 1929

Keep Kool
book: Paul Gerard Smith
music: Jack Frost
lyrics: Paul Gerard Smith
staging: Earl Lindsay
Productions:
Opened May 22, 1924 for (28) performances
Reviews:
New York Times page 16, May 23, 1924
Theatre Magazine 40:15, Aug 1924

Keep Moving
sketches: Newman Levy and Jack School

    music: Max Rich
    lyrics: Newman Levy and Jack School
    staging: George Rosener and Harry Losee
    sets: Clark Robinson
Productions:
    Opened August 23, 1934 for 20 performances
Reviews:
    New York Times page 10, Aug 24, 1934

Keep off the Grass
    book: Mort Lewis, Parke Levy, Alan Lipscott, S. J.
                      Kaufman, Reginald Beckwith, Panama and Frank
    music: James McHugh
    lyrics: Al Dubin and Howard Dietz
    staging: Fred deCordova
    sets: Nat Carson
    costumes: Nat Carson
    choreography: George Balanchine
Productions:
    Opened May 23, 1940 for 44 performances
Reviews:
    Catholic World 151:471-2, Jul 1940
    Commonweal 32:212, Jun 18, 1940
    Life 9:52-4, Jul 8, 1940
    Nation 150:716, Jun 8, 1940
    New York Theatre Critics' Reviews 1940:302+
    New York Times X, page 1, May 5, 1940
                     page 22, May 24, 1940
                  IX, page 1, Jun 16, 1940
    Newsweek 15:44, Jun 3, 1940
    Time 35:52, Jun 3, 1940

Keep Shufflin'
    book: Flourney Miller and Aubrey Lyles
    music: Jimmy Johnson, "Fats" Waller and Clarence
                      Todd
    lyrics: Henry Creamer and Andy Razaf
    staging: Con Conrad
Productions:
    Opened February 27, 1928 for 104 performances
Reviews:
    New York Times page 18, Feb 28, 1928
    Theatre Magazine 47:41+, May 1927
    Vogue 71:136, May 1, 1928

Kelly
    book: Eddie Lawrence
    music: Moose Charlap
    lyrics: Eddie Lawrence
    staging: Herbert Ross
    sets: Oliver Smith
    costumes: Freddy Wittop
    choreography: Herbert Ross

Productions:
    Opened February 6, 1965 for one performance
Reviews:
    New York Theatre Critics' Reviews 1965:382+
    New York Times page 28, Feb 8, 1965
                  page 42, Feb 9, 1965
    New Yorker 40:76, Feb 13, 1965
    Saturday Evening Post 238:32-4+, Apr 24, 1965
    Time 85:64, Feb 19, 1965

Ken Murray's Blackouts of 1949
    music: Charles Henderson and Ray Foster
    lyrics: Charles Henderson and Ray Foster
    sets: Ben Tipton
Productions:
    Opened September 6, 1949 for 51 performances
Reviews:
    Life 27:12-13, Oct 3, 1949
    New Republic 121:29, Sep 26, 1949
    New York Theatre Critics' Reviews 1949:273+
    New York Times page 39, Sep 7, 1949
    New Yorker 25:56, Sep 17, 1949
    Newsweek 34:79, Sep 19, 1949
    Saturday Evening Post 222:38-9+, Sep 10, 1949
    Theatre Arts 33:8, Oct 1949
    Time 54:70, Sep 19, 1949

Kid Boats
    book: William Anthony McGuire and Otto Harbach
    music: Harry Tierney
    lyrics: Joseph McCarthy
Productions:
    Opened December 31, 1923 for (192) performances
Reviews:
    New York Times IX, page 2, Dec 16, 1923
                  page 21, Jan 1, 1924
    Theatre Magazine 39:70, Mar 1924
                  39:17, Apr 1924

The King and I
    book: Oscar Hammerstein II, based on Margaret
                  Landon's novel Anna and the King of Siam
    music: Richard Rodgers
    lyrics: Oscar Hammerstein II
    staging: John Van Druten
    sets: Jo Mielziner
    costumes: Irene Sharaff
    choreography: Jerome Robbins
Productions:
    Opened March 29, 1951 for 1,246 performances
    Opened April 18, 1956 for 23 performances
    (Off-Broadway) Season of 1959-60
    Opened May 11, 1960 for 24 performances

Opened June 12, 1963 for 15 performances
Opened July 6, 1964 for 40 performances
Opened May 23, 1968 for 22 performances
(Off-Off-Broadway) Opened June 28, 1972 (Jones Beach
   Marine Theatre)
Reviews:
   America 95:147, May 5, 1956
          111:143-4, Aug 8, 1964
   Catholic World 173:145-6, May 1951
          183:229, Jun 1956
          183:311, Jul 1956
   Colliers 127:24-5+, Apr 7, 1951
   Commonweal 54:12, Apr 13, 1951
          64:299, Jun 22, 1956
   Dance Magazine 42:19, Aug 1968
   Harper's 203:99-100, Sep 1951
   Life 30:79-80+, Apr 23, 1951
   Nation 172:353, Apr 14, 1951
   New Republic 124:29, Apr 16, 1951
   New York Theatre Critics' Reviews 1951:304+
                       1960:267+
   New York Times II, page 1, Mar 25, 1951
              page 26, Mar 30, 1951
              II, page 1, Apr 8, 1951
              II, page 1, Oct 5, 1952
              page 33, Oct 9, 1953
              II, page 3, Oct 18, 1953
              page 33, May 17, 1955
              page 35, Apr 19, 1956
              page 40, May 12, 1960
              II, page 1, May 22, 1960
              I, page 22, Mar 19, 1961
              page 30, Jun 13, 1963
              page 20, Jul 6, 1964
              page 26, Jul 7, 1964
              page 39, Jul 8, 1964
              page 27, Jul 9, 1964
              page 39, May 24, 1968
              page 24, Jun 30, 1972
   New Yorker 27:70+, Apr 7, 1951
   Newsweek 37:78, Apr 9, 1951
   Saturday Review 34:32, Mar 31, 1951
          34:44-6, Apr 14, 1951
          47:18, Jul 25, 1964
   Theatre Arts 35:30-1, Jul 1951
          40:19, Jun 1956
   Time 57:78, Apr 9, 1951

The King of Cadonia
   book: Frederick Lonsdale
   music: Sidney Jones and Jerome D. Kern
   lyrics: Adrian Ross and M. E. Rourke
   staging: Joseph Herbert

Productions:
    Opened January 10, 1910 for 16 performances
Reviews:
    American Mercury 70:109, May 1910
    Cosmopolitan 48:619, Apr 1910
    Dramatic Mirror 63:5, Jan 22, 1910
    Munsey 41:902-3, Sep 1909
    Theatre Magazine 11:iii, Feb 1910
                       11:38, Feb 1910

King of the Whole Damn World
    book: George Panetta
    music: Robert Larimer
    lyrics: Robert Larimer
    staging: Jack Ragotzy
    sets: Jack Cornwell
    costumes: Rachel Mehr
    choreography: Zachary Solov
Productions:
    (Off-Broadway) Opened April 14, 1962 for 43 performances
Reviews:
    New York Times page 32, Apr 16, 1962
                    page 30, May 22, 1962
    New Yorker 38:97, Apr 28, 1962
    Saturday Review 45:29, May 5, 1962

Kismet
    book: Charles Lederer and Luther Davis, based on
                   the play by Edward Knoblock
    music: Alexander Borodin, adapted by Robert Wright
                   and George Forrest
    lyrics: Robert Wright and George Forrest
    staging: Albert Marre
    sets: Lemuel Ayers
    costumes: Lemuel Ayers
    choreography: Jack Cole
Productions:
    Opened December 3, 1953 for 583 performances
    (Off-Off-Broadway) Opened November 16, 1963 for 8 per-
        formances (Equity Library Theatre)
    Opened June 22, 1965 for 48 performances
Reviews:
    America 90:366, Jan 2, 1954
            113:122, Jul 31, 1965
    Catholic World 178:388, Feb 1954
    Colliers 133:78-9, Jan 8, 1954
    Commonweal 59:353, Jan 8, 1954
    Dance Magazine 39:24, Aug 1965
    Life 35:25-8, Dec 21, 1953
    Nation 177:555, Dec 19, 1953
    New York Theatre Critics' Reviews 1953:198+
    New York Times page 2, Dec 4, 1953
                    page 51, Dec 14, 1953

II, page 1, Jun 20, 1965
                            page 45, Jun 23, 1965
New Yorker 29:85-7, Dec 12, 1953
Newsweek 42:61, Dec 14, 1953
                    42:60, Dec 21, 1953
Saturday Review 36:28-9, Dec 26, 1953
Theatre Arts 38:18-19, Feb 1954
Time 62:94, Dec 14, 1953

The Kiss Burglar
    book: Glen MacDonough
    music: Raymond Hubbell
    lyrics: Glen MacDonough
    staging: Julian Mitchell and Edgar MacGregor
Productions:
    Opened May 9, 1918 for 100 performances
    Opened March 17, 1919 for 24 performances
Reviews:
    Dramatic Mirror 78:730, May 25, 1918
                    78:801, Jun 8, 1918
    Green Book 20:10, Jul 1918
    Life (New York) 71:842, May 23, 1918
    New York Times page 9, May 10, 1918
                    page 9, Mar 18, 1919
    Theatre Magazine 27:356-8, Jun 1918

Kiss Me
    book: Adapted by Derick Wulff and Max Simon
    music: Winthrop Cortelyou
    lyrics: Derick Wulff
Productions:
    Opened July 18, 1927 for 32 performances
Reviews:
    New York Times page 17, Jul 22, 1927

Kiss Me, Kate
    book: Bella Spewack and Samuel Spewack, based on
                    Shakespeare's The Taming of the Shrew
    music: Cole Porter
    lyrics: Cole Porter
    staging: John C. Wilson
    sets: Lemuel Ayers
    costumes: Lemuel Ayers
    choreography: Hanya Holm
Productions:
    Opened December 30, 1948 for 1, 070 performances
    Opened January 8, 1952 for 8 performances
    (Off-Broadway) Season of 1953-54 (Equity Library Theatre)
    Opened May 9, 1956 for 23 performances
    Opened May 12, 1965 for 23 performances
Reviews:
    America 95:252, Jun 2, 1956
    Catholic World 168:402-3, Feb 1949

                        193:311, Jul 1956
        Commonweal 49:376, Jan 21, 1949
        Good Housekeeping 139:4+, Dec 1949
        Life 26:99-100+, Feb 7, 1949
        New Republic 120:25, Jan 24, 1949
        New York Theatre Critics' Reviews 1948:91+
        New York Times page 10, Dec 31, 1948
                        II, page 1, Jan 9, 1949
                        II, page 1, Jan 16, 1949
                        VI, page 20, Jan 16, 1949
                        II, page 6, Jan 30, 1949
                        page 30, Mar 9, 1951
                        II, page 3, Apr 15, 1951
                        page 31, Jul 17, 1951
                        page 24, Jan 9, 1952
                        page 23, Jan 31, 1952
                        page 13, Mar 27, 1954
                        page 19, Dec 17, 1955
                        page 27, Feb 15, 1956
                        page 94, Feb 19, 1956
                        page 27, May 10, 1956
                        page 24, Aug 10, 1959
                        page 184, Dec 1, 1963
                        page 31, May 13, 1965
        New Yorker 24:50-2, Jan 8, 1949
                        41:130+, Jun 12, 1965
        Newsweek 33:72, Jan 10, 1949
        Saturday Review 32:34-5, Jan 22, 1949
                        39:24, May 26, 1956
        Theatre Arts 33:17+, Mar 1949
                        39:32, Jan 1955
                        40:78-80+, Jun 1956
                        40:21, Jul 1956
        Time 53:36+, Jan 10, 1949
                53:40-4, Jan 31, 1949
                67:47, Mar 5, 1956

Kiss Now
        book: Maxine Klein
        music: William S. Fischer
        lyrics: Maxine Klein
        staging: Maxine Klein
        sets: Richard Devin
        costumes: Nancy Adzima
        choreography: Sandra Caprin
Productions:
        (Off-Broadway) Opened April 20, 1971 for 4 performances
No Reviews.

Kissing Time
        book: George V. Hobart; based on the French of A.
                        Philipp and E. Paulton
        music: Ivan Caryll

lyrics: Philander Johnson
staging: Edward Royce
Productions:
Opened October 11, 1920 for 72 performances
Reviews:
Dramatic Mirror page 693, Oct 16, 1920
New York Clipper 68:21, Aug 18, 1920
                68:20, Oct 20, 1920
New York Times page 18, Oct 12, 1920
Theatre Magazine 32:414, Dec 1920

Kittiwake Island
book: Arnold Sundgaard
music: Alec Wilder
lyrics: Arnold Sundgaard
staging: Lawrence Carra
sets: Romaine Johnston
costumes: Al Lehman
choreography: Peter Hamilton
Productions:
(Off-Broadway) Opened October 12, 1960 for 7 performances
Reviews:
New York Times page 43, Oct 13, 1960
                page 46, Oct 18, 1960
New Yorker 36:93, Oct 22, 1960

Kitty Darlin'
book: Otto Hauerbach
music: Rudolf Friml
lyrics: Otto Hauerbach
staging: Edward Royce
Productions:
Opened November 7, 1917 for 14 performances
Reviews:
Dramatic Mirror 77:31, Sep 22, 1917
                77:5, Nov 17, 1917
New York Times page 13, Nov 8, 1917

Kitty's Kisses
book: Philip Bartholomae and Otto Harbach; based on
                Little Miss Brown
music: Con Conrad
lyrics: Gus Kahn
staging: John Cronwell and Bobby Connolly
Productions:
Opened May 6, 1926 for 170 performances
Reviews:
New York Times page 12, May 7, 1926
Theatre Magazine 44:16, Jul 1926

Knickerbocker Holiday
book: Maxwell Anderson
music: Kurt Weill

    lyrics: Maxwell Anderson
    staging: Joshua Logan
    sets: Jo Mielziner
    costumes: Frank Bevan
    choreography: Carl Randall and Edwin Denby
Productions:
    Opened October 19, 1938 for 168 performances
Reviews:
    Catholic World 148:343-4, Dec 1938
    Commonweal 29:48, Nov 4, 1938
    Life 5:27, Nov 21, 1938
    Modern Music 16:54-6, Nov 1938
    Nation 147:488-9, Nov 5, 1938
            147:673, Dec 17, 1938
    New Republic 97:18, Nov 9, 1938
    New York Times IX, page 1, Sep 25, 1938
                   IX, page 3, Oct 2, 1938
                   page 26, Oct 20, 1938
                   IX, page 1, Nov 20, 1938
    Newsweek 12:29, Oct 31, 1938
    North American Review 246 no2:374-6, Dec 1938
    Theatre Arts 22:862, Dec 1938
    Time 32:55, Oct 31, 1938

Knights of Song
    book: Glendon Allvine, based on a story by Glendon
                       Allvine and Adele Gutman Nathan
    music: excerpts from Gilbert and Sullivan operettas
    lyrics: excerpts from Gilbert and Sullivan operettas
    staging: Oscar Hammerstein and Avalon Collard
    sets: Raymond Sovey
    costumes: Kate Lawson
Productions:
    Opened October 17, 1938 for 16 performances
Reviews:
    Commonweal 29:48, Nov 4, 1938
    Musical Courier 118:11, Aug 15, 1938
    New York Times page 29, Oct 18, 1938
    Time 32:54, Oct 31, 1938

Kosher Kitty Kelly
    book: Leon DeCosta
    staging: A. H. Van Buren
Productions:
    Opened June 15, 1925 for one performance
Reviews:
    New York Times page 24, Jun 16, 1925

The Kumquat in the Persimmon Tree
    sketches: William C. Curtis
    music: Bruce Haack and Ted Pandel
    staging: George Lanin
    sets: Charles Copenhaver

    choreography: Mamie Jones
Productions:
    (Off-Broadway) Opened June 18, 1962 for 11 performances
Reviews:
    New York Times page 27, Jun 19, 1962

Kurt Weill (see Berlin to Broadway with Kurt Weill) (Also see
  The World of Kurt Weill in Song)

Kwamina
    book: Robert Alan Aurthur
    music: Richard Adler
    lyrics: Richard Adler
    staging: Robert Lewis
    sets: Will Steven Armstrong
    costumes: Motley
    choreography: Agnes de Mille
Productions:
    Opened October 23, 1961 for 32 performances
Reviews:
    America 106:257, Nov 18, 1961
    Dance Magazine 35:23, Dec 1961
    New Republic 145:23, Nov 6, 1961
    New York Theatre Critics' Reviews 1961:206+
    New York Times II, page 3, Oct 22, 1961
                page 42, Oct 24, 1961
              II, page 1, Nov 12, 1961
    New Yorker 37:126, Nov 4, 1961
    Newsweek 58:69, Nov 6, 1961
    Saturday Review 44:39, Nov 18, 1961
    Theatre Arts 46:13-14, Jan 1962
    Time 78:44, Nov 3, 1961

- L -

La, La, Lucille
    book: Fred Jackson
    music: George Gershwin
    lyrics: Arthur J. Jackson and B. G. De Sylva
    staging: Herbert Gresham and Julian Alfred
Productions:
    Opened May 26, 1919 for 104 performances
Reviews:
    New York Times page 15, May 27, 1919
    Theatre Magazine 30:7+, Jul 1919

Labor Sings
    script: Alfred Hayes
    music: George Kleinsinger
    sets: Sointu Syrjala
    choreography: Lily Mehlmann
Productions:

(Off-Broadway) Opened October 5, 1940 for 2 performances
No Reviews.

Lace Petticoat
    book: Stewart St. Clair
    music: Emil Gerstenberger and Carl Carlton
    lyrics: Howard Johnson
    staging: Carl Carlton
Productions:
    Opened January 4, 1927 for 15 performances
Reviews:
    New York Times page 18, Jan 5, 1927
    Theatre Magazine 45:21, Mar 1927

Ladies First
    book: Harry B. Smith; based on A Contented Woman
    music: A. Baldwin Sloane
    lyrics: Harry B. Smith
    staging: Frank Smithson
Productions:
    Opened October 24, 1918 for 164 performances
Reviews:
    Dramatic Mirror 79:688, Nov 9, 1918
    New York Times page 11, Oct 25, 1918
    Theatre Magazine 28:378, Dec 1918

Lady Audley's Secret
    book: Douglas Seale, adapted from the novel by Mary
                     Elizabeth Braddon
    music: George Goehring
    lyrics: John Kuntz
    staging: Douglas Seale
    sets: Alicia Finkel
    costumes: Alicia Finkel
    choreography: George Bunt
Productions:
    (Off-Broadway) Opened October 3, 1972 for 7 performances
Reviews:
    New York Times page 40, Oct 4, 1972
    Saturday Review 54:33, Aug 7, 1971

Lady Be Good
    book: Guy Bolton and Fred Thompson
    music: George Gershwin
    lyrics: Ira Gershwin
Productions:
    Opened December 1, 1924 for 330 performances
Reviews:
    Canadian Magazine 64:164-6, Jul 1925
    New York Times page 23, Dec 2, 1924
                   VII, page 1, Dec 28, 1924
    Theatre Magazine 41:16, Feb 1925

Lady Billy
        book: Zelda Sears
        music: Harold A. Levey
        lyrics: Zelda Sears
        staging: John McKee
Productions:
        Opened December 14, 1920 for 188 performances
Reviews:
        Dramatic Mirror page 1155, Dec 18, 1920
                        83:249, Feb 5, 1921
        New York Clipper 68:18, Dec 29, 1920
        New York Times page 18, Dec 15, 1920
        Theatre Magazine 33:107, Feb 1921

Lady Butterfly
        book: Clifford Grey; adapted from a farce by Mark
                         Swan and James T. Powers
        music: Werner Janssen
        staging: Walter Wilson
Productions:
        Opened January 22, 1923 for 128 performances
Reviews:
        Life (New York) 81:18, Feb 15, 1923
        New York Clipper 70:14, Jan 31, 1923

The Lady Comes Across
        book: Fred Thompson and Dawn Powell
        music: Vernon Duke
        lyrics: John Latouche
        staging: Romney Brent
        sets: Stewart Chaney
        costumes: Stewart Chaney
        choreography: George Balanchine
Productions:
        Opened January 9, 1942 for 3 performances
Reviews:
        New York Theatre Critics' Reviews 1942:388+
        New York Times page 10, Jan 10, 1942
                        IX, page 3, Jan 11, 1942

Lady Day: A Musical Tragedy
        book: Aishah Rahman; based on the career of Billie
                         Holiday
        music: Archie Shepp; additional music by Stanley
                         Cowell and Cal Massey
        staging: Paul Carter Harrison
        sets: Robert U. Taylor
        costumes: Randy Barcelo
Productions:
        (Off-Broadway) Opened October 17, 1972 for 24 performances
Reviews:
        New York Theatre Critics' Reviews 1972:165
        New York Times page 39, Oct 26, 1972

II, page 5, Nov 5, 1972
New Yorker 48:105-6+, Nov 4, 1972
Newsweek 80:133-4, Nov 6, 1972

Lady Do
      book: Jack McClellan and Albert Cowles
      music: Abel Baer
      lyrics: Sam M. Lewis and Joe Young
      staging: Edgar J. Macgregor
Productions:
Opened April 18, 1927 for 56 performances
Reviews:
New York Times page 24, Apr 19, 1927

Lady Fingers
      book: Eddie Buzzell, based on Owen Davis's Easy
                       Come, Easy Go
      music: Joseph Meyer
      lyrics: Edward Eliscu
      staging: Lew Levenson
Productions:
Opened January 31, 1929 for 132 performances
Reviews:
New York Times VIII, page 2, Jan 13, 1929
                page 22, Feb 1, 1929

The Lady in Ermine
      book: Frederick Lonsdale and Cyrus Wood; adapted
                       from the book by Rudolph Schanzer and Ernest
                       Welisch
      music: Jean Gilbert and Alfred Goodman
      lyrics: Harry Graham and Cyrus Wood
      staging: Charles Sinclair and Allan K. Foster
Productions:
Opened October 2, 1922 for 232 performances
Reviews:
New York Clipper 70:20, Oct 11, 1922
New York Times page 22, Oct 3, 1922

The Lady in Red
      book: Anne Caldwell
      music: Robert Winterberg
      lyrics: Anne Caldwell
      staging: Frank Smithson
Productions:
Opened May 12, 1919 for 48 performances
Reviews:
Forum 61:755-6, Jun 1919
Life (New York) 73:904-5, May 22, 1919
New York Dramatic News 65:6, May 17, 1919
New York Times page 18, May 13, 1919

Lady in the Dark

    book: Moss Hart
    music: Kurt Weill
    lyrics: Ira Gershwin
    staging: Hassard Short and Moss Hart
    sets: Harry Horner
    costumes: Irene Sharaff and Hattie Carnegie
    choreography: Albertina Rasch
Productions:
    Opened January 23, 1941 for 162 performances
    Opened September 2, 1941 for 305 performances
    Opened February 27, 1943 for 83 performances
Reviews:
    Catholic World 152:726-7, Mar 1941
    Commonweal 33:401, Feb 7, 1941
                   37:542, Mar 19, 1943
    Life 10:43, Feb 17, 1941
    Nation 152:164, Feb 8, 1941
    New Republic 104:179, Feb 10, 1941
    New York Theatre Critics' Reviews 1941:400+
    New York Times page 18, Dec 31, 1940
                     IX, page 1, Jan 5, 1941
                     page 14, Jan 24, 1941
                     IX, page 1, Feb 2, 1941
                     IX, page 3, Apr 6, 1941
                     page 26, Sep 3, 1941
                     IX, page 1, Sep 7, 1941
                     page 14, Mar 1, 1943
                     II, page 1, Mar 7, 1943
    New Yorker 16:27, Feb 1, 1941
    Newsweek 17:59, Feb 3, 1941
    Stage 1:26-7, Feb 1941
    Theatre Arts 25:177-8+, Mar 1941
                 25:265-75, Apr 1941
    Time 37:53-4, Feb 3, 1941
    Vogue 97:72-3, May 15, 1941

Lady Luxury
    book: Rida Johnson Young
    music: William Schroeder
    lyrics: Rida Johnson Young
    staging: J. H. Benrimo
Productions:
    Opened December 25, 1914 for 35 performances
Reviews:
    Dramatic Mirror 72:8, Dec 30, 1914
                    73:2, Jan 20, 1915
    Green Book 13:574-5, Mar 1915
    Nation 99:783-4, Dec 31, 1914
    New York Times page 7, Dec 26, 1914
    Theatre Magazine 21:60, Feb 1915

The Lady of the Slipper
    book: Anne Caldwell and Lawrence McCarty; based on

                              the Cinderella story
        music: Victor Herbert
        lyrics: James O'Dea
        staging: R. H. Burnside
Productions:
        Opened October 28, 1912 for 232 performances
Reviews:
        Collier's 50:15, Jan 25, 1913
        Dramatic Mirror 68:6, Oct 30, 1912
        Green Book 9:4-6+, Jan 1913
                          9:182, Jan 1913
        Harper's Weekly 56:20, Nov 9, 1912
        Munsey 48:530, Dec 1912
        New York Dramatic News 56:11, Oct 26, 1912
                                56:21-2, Nov 2, 1912
        Red Book 20:702-4, Feb 1913
        Theatre Magazine 16:193, Dec 1912
                         17:3, Mar 1913
                         17:79, Mar 1913

A Lady Says Yes
        book: Clayton Ashley (Dr. Maxwell Maltz) and Stanley
                              Adams
        music: Fred Spielman and Arthur Gershwin
        lyrics: Clayton Ashley and Stanley Adams
        sets: Watson Barratt
        costumes: Lou Eisele
        choreography: Boots McKenna and Natalie Kamarova
Productions:
        Opened January 10, 1945 for 87 performances
Reviews:
        Nation 160:136, Feb 3, 1945
        New York Theatre Critics' Reviews 1945:294+
        New York Times page 18, Jan 11, 1945
        Time 45:63, Jan 22, 1945

Laffing Room Only
        book: Ole Olsen, Chic Johnson, Eugene Conrad
        music: Burton Lane
        lyrics: Burton Lane
        staging: John Murray Anderson
        sets: Stewart Chaney
        costumes: Billy Livingston
        choreography: Robert Alton
Productions:
        Opened December 23, 1944 for 233 performances
Reviews:
        Life 18:76, Apr 9, 1945
        New York Theatre Critics' Reviews 1944:52+
        New York Times page 15, Dec 25, 1944
                        page 31, Sep 20, 1945
        Theatre Arts 29:142+, Mar 1945
        Time 45:67, Jan 8, 1945

The Land of Joy (La Tierra de la Alegria)
      book: J. F. Elizondo and E. Velasco
      adapted: Ruth Boyd Ober
      music: J. Valverde
      lyrics: Ruth Boyd Ober
Productions:
      Opened October 31, 1917 for 86 performances
Reviews:
      Dramatic Mirror 77:7, Nov 10, 1917
      Green Book 19:218-20, Feb 1918
      Life (New York) 70:795, Nov 15, 1917
      New York Dramatic News 64:10, Nov 10, 1917
      New York Times page 13, Nov 2, 1917
                     VIII, page 6, Nov 11, 1917
      Theatre Magazine 27:9, Jan 1918
                       27:23, Jan 1918
                       27:78, Feb 1918

Lassie
      book: Catherine Chisolm Cushing; based on Kitty
                         MacKaye
      music: Hugo Felix
      lyrics: Catherine Chisolm Cushing
      staging: Edward Royce
Productions:
      Opened April 6, 1920 for 63 performances
Reviews:
      Dramatic Mirror 82:680, Apr 10, 1920
      New York Clipper 68:14, Mar 17, 1920
      New York Times page 9, Apr 7, 1920
      Theatre Magazine 31:401-2, May 1920
                       31:407, May 1920

The Last Savage
      book: Gian Carlo Menotti; translated by George Meade
      music: Gian Carlo Menotti
      lyrics: Gian Carlo Menotti
      staging: Gian Carlo Menotti
      sets: Beni Montresor
      costumes: Beni Montresor
Productions:
      Opened January 23, 1964 for 7 performances
Reviews:
      Life 56:66 A-66B, Feb 14, 1964
      New Yorker 39:198-200, Nov 2, 1963
                 39:60+, Feb 1, 1964
      Newsweek 63:77, Feb 3, 1964
      Opera News 28:24-5, Feb 8, 1964
                 28:28-30, Dec 7, 1963
                 28:13-15, Feb 8, 1964
                 28:27-8, Feb 8, 1964
      Saturday Review 47:27-8, Feb 8, 1964
                      48:22, Jan 16, 1965

Time 82:63, Nov 1, 1963
      83:33, Jan 31, 1964

The Last Sweet Days of Isaac
    book: Gretchen Cryer
    music: Nancy Ford
    lyrics: Gretchen Cryer
    staging: Word Baker
    sets: Ed Wittstein
    costumes: Caley Summers
Productions:
    (Off-Broadway) Opened January 26, 1970 for 485 performances
Reviews:
    Nation 210:284, Mar 9, 1970
    New York Theatre Critics' Reviews 1970:292
    New York Times page 49, Jan 27, 1970
                    II, page 1, Feb 8, 1970
                    II, page 1, Feb 15, 1970
                    page 34, Mar 3, 1970
                    II, page 17, Jun 28, 1970
                    page 17, Jan 9, 1971
                    II, page 24, May 2, 1971
    New Yorker 45:73-4+, Feb 7, 1970
    Newsweek 75:95, Feb 9, 1970

The Last Waltz
    book: Julius Brammer and Alfred Grunwald; adapted by
                     Harold Atteridge and Edward Delaney Dunn
    music: Oscar Straus
    staging: J. C. Huffman and Frank Smithson
Productions:
    Opened May 10, 1921 for (43) performances
Reviews:
    Dramatic Mirror 83:817, May 14, 1921
    Life (New York) 77:760, May 26, 1921
    New York Clipper 69:23, May 18, 1921
    New York Times page 20, May 11, 1921
    Theatre Magazine 34:64, Jul 1921
                     34:101, Aug 1921
    Woman's Home Companion 48:61, Sep 1921

The Laugh Parade
    book: Ed Wynn and Ed Preble
    music: Harry Warren
    lyrics: Mort Dixon and Joe Young
    staging: Ed Wynn
    choreography: Albertina Rasch
Productions:
    Opened November 2, 1931 for 231 performances
Reviews:
    Catholic World 134:471, Jan 1932
    Nation 133:582, Nov 25, 1931
    New York Times VIII, page 3, Sep 20, 1931

page 31, Nov 3, 1931
VIII, page 1, Dec 6, 1931

The Laughing Husband
book: Julius Brammer and Alfred Grunwald; adapted
      by Arthur Wimperis
music: Edmund Eysler
staging: Edward Royce
Productions:
Opened February 2, 1914 for 48 performances
Reviews:
Dramatic Mirror 71:7, Feb 4, 1914
      71:4, Feb 11, 1914
      71:2, Mar 18, 1914
Green Book 11:605-6, Apr 1914
    11:702, Apr 1914
Life (New York) 63:277, Feb 12, 1914
New York Dramatic News 59:20, Feb 7, 1914
New York Times page 9, Jan 13, 1914
      page 11, Feb 3, 1914
Theatre Magazine 19:113, Mar 1914
      19:156, Mar 1914

Laughs and Other Events
songs and
 monologues: Stanley Holloway
staging: Tony Charmoli
sets: John Robert Lloyd
Productions:
Opened October 10, 1960 for 8 performances
Reviews:
New York Theatre Critics' Reviews 1960:213
New York Times page 57, Oct 11, 1960
      page 41, Oct 13, 1960

Lawless, Sue (see An Evening with Sue and Pugh)

Leave It to Jane
book: Guy Bolton and P. G. Wodehouse; based on
      George Ade's The College Widow
music: Jerome Kern
lyrics: Guy Bolton and P. G. Wodehouse
staging: Edward Royce
Productions:
Opened August 28, 1917 for 167 performances
(Off-Broadway) Season of 1959-60
Reviews:
Dance Magazine 33:12, Sep 1959
Dramatic Mirror 77:31, Aug 11, 1917
      77:32, Sep 1, 1917
      77:8, Sep 8, 1917
      77:7, Dec 22, 1917
Independent 92:602, Dec 29, 1917

New York Dramatic News 64:2, Sep 1, 1917
New York Times page 7, Aug 29, 1917
              page 30, May 26, 1959
              II, page 7, Oct 25, 1959
New Yorker 35:120, Jun 6, 1959
Saturday Review 42:29, Jun 13, 1959
Theatre Magazine 26:203, Oct 1917
              26:242, Oct 1917

Leave It to Me
    book: Bella and Samuel Spewack
    music: Cole Porter
    lyrics: Cole Porter
    staging: Samuel Spewack
    sets: Albert Johnson
    costumes: Raoul Pene du Bois
    choreography: Robert Alton
Productions:
    Opened November 9, 1938 for 307 performances
    Opened September 4, 1939 for 16 performances
Reviews:
    Catholic World 148:477, Jan 1939
    Commonweal 29:132, Nov 25, 1938
    Life 5:53-5, Nov 7, 1938
    Nation 147:572-3, Nov 26, 1938
    New Republic 97:100, Nov 30, 1938
    New York Times IX, page 3, Oct 23, 1938
                   page 32, Nov 10, 1938
                   IX, page 1, Nov 20, 1938
                   IX, page 3, Nov 20, 1938
                   page 25, Sep 5, 1939
                   IX, page 1, Sep 10, 1939
                   page 20, Sep 16, 1939
                   page 27, Jan 18, 1940
    Newsweek 12:24, Nov 21, 1938
    North American Review 247 no2:369, (Jun) 1939
    Stage 16:10-11, Nov 1938
          16:12-15, Dec 1938
    Theatre Arts 23:6+, Jan 1939
    Time 32:39, Nov 7, 1938
         32:66, Nov 21, 1938

Leaves of Grass
    book: adapted by Stan Harte, Jr.; based on the
                     writings of Walt Whitman
    music: Stan Harte, Jr.
    staging: Stan Harte, Jr. and Bert Michaels
    sets: David Chapman
    choreography: Bert Michaels
Productions:
    (Off-Broadway) Opened September 12, 1971 for 49 performances
Reviews:
    New York Theatre Critics' Reviews 1971:217

New York Times page 47, Sep 13, 1971

Lemmings   (see National Lampoon's Lemmings)

Lend An Ear
    sketches: Charles Gaynor, additional sketches by Joseph
                   Stein and Will Glickman
    music: Charles Gaynor
    lyrics: Charles Gaynor
    staging: Gower Champion
    sets: Raoul Pene du Bois
    costumes: Raoul Pene du Bois
    choreography: Gower Champion
Productions:
    Opened December 16, 1948 for 460 performances
    (Off-Broadway) Season of 1959-60
    (Off-Broadway) Opened October 16, 1969 for 19 performances
Reviews:
    Catholic World 168:403, Feb 1949
    Commonweal 49:306, Dec 31, 1948
    Life 26:79-80+, Feb 28, 1949
    Nation 168:25, Jan 1, 1949
    New Republic 120:29-31, Jan 3, 1949
    New York Theatre Critics' Reviews 1948:122+
    New York Times page 38, Dec 17, 1948
                   II, page 3, Sep 20, 1959
                   page 20, Sep 25, 1959
                   page 48, Dec 1, 1959
                   page 32, Oct 29, 1969
    New Yorker 24:32, Dec 25, 1948
    Newsweek 32:65, Dec 27, 1948
    Theatre Arts 32:22, Aug 1948
               33:56, Mar 1949
    Time 52:46, Dec 27, 1948
    Vogue 113:214, Feb 1, 1949
          113:90, Feb 15, 1949

Leonard Bernstein's Theater Songs
    music: Leonard Bernstein
    lyrics: Stephen Sondheim, Betty Comden, Adolph Green,
                   Richard Wilbur, Lillian Hellman, Leonard Bern-
                   stein
    staging: Will Holt
Productions:
    Opened June 28, 1965 for 88 performances
Reviews:
    America 113:122, Jul 31, 1965
    Life 59:12, Jul 30, 1965
    New York Times page 49, Jun 16, 1965
                  page 27, Jun 29, 1965
                  page 29, Sep 1, 1965

Leonard Sillman's New Faces of 1968

conceived: Leonard Sillman
staging: Frank Wagner
sets: Winn Morton
costumes: Winn Morton
choreography: Frank Wagner
Productions:
Opened May 2, 1968 for 52 performances
Reviews:
New York Theatre Critics' Reviews 1968:279
                                  1968:282
New York Times page 43, May 3, 1968
              II, page 3, May 12, 1968
              page 54, Jun 6, 1968

Leslie, Lew   (see Lew Leslie)

Let 'em Eat Cake
    book: George S. Kaufman and Morrie Ryskind
    music: George Gershwin
    lyrics: Ira Gershwin
    staging: George S. Kaufman
    sets: Albert R. Johnson
    choreography: Van Grona and Ned McGurn
Productions:
Opened October 21, 1933 for 90 performances
Reviews:
Catholic World 138:338, Dec 1933
Commonweal 19:47, Nov 10, 1933
Nation 137:550, Nov 8, 1933
New Outlook 162:47, Dec 1933
New York Times page 16, Apr 17, 1933
              page 26, Oct 3, 1933
              X, page 2, Oct 8, 1933
              page 18, Oct 23, 1933
              IX, page 1, Nov 12, 1933
Stage 11:9-10, Dec 1933
Time 22:29-30, Oct 30, 1933

Let Freedom Sing
    book: Sam Locke
    music and
    lyrics: Harold Rome, Earl Robinson, Marc Blitzstein,
                   Lou Cooper, Roslyn Harvey, Walter Kent, John
                   Latouche, Hy Zaret, Lewis Allan
    staging: Joseph Pevney and Robert H. Gordon
    sets: Herbert Andrews
    costumes: Paul DuPont
    choreography: Dan Eckley
Productions:
Opened October 5, 1942 for 8 performances
Reviews:
New York Theatre Critics' Reviews 1942:216+
New York Times page 18, Oct 6, 1942

Let It Ride
    book: Abram S. Grimes, based on John Cecil Holm
                        and George Abbott's Three Men on a Horse
    music: Jay Livingston and Ray Evans
    lyrics: Jay Livingston and Ray Evans
    staging: Stanley Prager
    sets: William and Jean Eckart
    costumes: Guy Kent
    choreography: Onna White
Productions:
    Opened October 12, 1961 for 68 performances
Reviews:
    Commonweal 75:154, Nov 3, 1961
    Dance Magazine 35:22, Dec 1961
    New York Theatre Critics' Reviews 1961:230+
    New York Times page 27, Oct 13, 1961
                    page 49, Dec 4, 1961
    New Yorker 37:129, Oct 21, 1961
    Theatre Arts 45:13, Dec 1961
    Time 78:64, Oct 20, 1961

Let My People Come
    music: Earl Wilson, Jr.
    lyrics: Earl Wilson, Jr.
    staging: Phil Oesterman
    choreography: Ian Naylor
Productions:
    (Off-Broadway) Opened January 8, 1974 for 194* performances
Reviews:
    New York Times page 52, May 7, 1974
                 II, page 3, Sep 15, 1974

Let's Face It
    book: Herbert and Dorothy Fields, based on Russell
                        Medcraft and Norma Mitchell's play The Cradle
                        Snatchers
    music: Cole Porter
    lyrics: Cole Porter
    staging: Edgar MacGregor
    sets: Harry Horner
    costumes: John Harkrider
    choreography: Charles Walters
Productions:
    Opened October 29, 1941
    Reopened August 17, 1942 for a total of 547 performances
Reviews:
    Catholic World 154:601-2, Feb 1942
    Cosmopolitan 115:98, Nov 1943
    Harper's Bazaar 75:77, Nov 1941
    Life 11:114-16+, Nov 10, 1941
    New York Theatre Critics' Reviews 1941:249+
    New York Times page 27, Oct 10, 1941
                    page 26, Oct 30, 1941

IX, page 1, Nov 16, 1941
    page 11, Feb 15, 1943
    page 23, Mar 2, 1943
New Yorker 17:36, Nov 8, 1941
Theatre Arts 26:6-8, Jan 1942
Time 38:54, Nov 10, 1941
Vogue 98:90, Dec 1, 1941

Let's Make an Opera
    book: Eric Crozier
    music: Benjamin Britten
    lyrics: Eric Crozier
    staging: Marc Blitzstein
    sets: Ralph Alswang
    costumes: Aline Bernstein
Productions:
    Opened December 13, 1950 for 5 performances
Reviews:
    Commonweal 53:328, Jan 5, 1951
    Home and Garden 98:122-3, Dec 1950
    Musical America 69:34, Dec 1, 1949
                    70:16+, Apr 1950
    Nation 171:682, Dec 23, 1950
    New York Theatre Critics' Reviews 1950:173
    New York Times II, page 7, Dec 10, 1950
                    page 50, Dec 14, 1950
    New Yorker 26:40+, Dec 23, 1950
    Newsweek 36:58, Dec 25, 1950
    Theatre Arts 35:17, Feb 1951
    Time 53:39, Jun 27, 1949
        56:47, Dec 25, 1950

Let's Sing Yiddish
    music: Renee Solomon
    lyrics: Itsik Manger, Mordecai Geloirtig, Morris
                     Rosenfield, M. Nudelman and Wolf Younin
    staging: Mina Bern and Felix Fibich
    choreography: Felix Fibich and Judith Fibich
Productions:
    Opened November 9, 1966 for 107 performances
Reviews:
    Dance Magazine 41:25, Jan 1967
    New York Times page 63, Nov 10, 1966

Letty Pepper
    book: Oliver Morosco and George V. Hobart; based
                     on a comedy Maggie Pepper by Charles Klein
    music: Werner Janssen
    staging: George V. Hobart
Productions:
    Opened April 10, 1922 for 32 performances
Reviews:
    New York Clipper 70:20, Apr 12, 1922

New York Times page 22, Apr 11, 1922

Lew Leslie's Blackbirds of 1928
    music: Jimmy McHugh
    lyrics: Dorothy Fields
    staging: Lew Leslie
Productions:
    Opened May 9, 1928 for 518 performances
Reviews:
    Life (New York) 92:12, Jul 12, 1928
    New York Times page 31, May 10, 1928
                  IX, page 4, Oct 28, 1928
                  page 22, Mar 1, 1929
    Theatre Magazine 48:39, Jul 1928
    Vogue 72:92, Jul 1, 1928

Lew Leslie's Blackbirds (1930)
    book: Flourney Miller
    music: Eubie Blake
    lyrics: Andy Razaf
    staging: Lew Leslie
Productions:
    Opened October 22, 1930 for 57 performances
Reviews:
    Bookman 72:409-10, Dec 1930
    Life (New York) 96:17, Nov 14, 1930
    New York Times page 34, Oct 23, 1930

Lew Leslie's Blackbirds of 1933
    book: Nat N. Dorfman, Mann Holiner, Lew Leslie
    music and
      lyrics: Mann Holiner, Alberta Nichols, Joseph Young,
                  Ned Washington, Victor Young
    staging: Lew Leslie
    sets: Mabel A. Buell
Productions:
    Opened December 2, 1933 for 25 performances
Reviews:
    New York Times page 32, Dec 4, 1933
                  II, page 6, Aug 26, 1934

Lew Leslie's Blackbirds of 1939
    assembled by: Lew Leslie
    music: Rube Bloom and others
    lyrics: Johnny Mercer and others
    staging: Lew Leslie
    sets: Mable A. Buell
    costumes: Frances Feist
Productions:
    Opened February 11, 1939 for 9 performances
Reviews:
    New York Times IX, page 2, Nov 13, 1938
                     page 12, Feb 13, 1939

The Liar
    book: Edward Eager and Alfred Drake, based on the
                         Carlo Goldoni play
    music: John Mundy
    lyrics: Edward Eager
    staging: Alfred Drake
    sets: Donald Oenslager
    costumes: Motley
    choreography: Hanya Holm
Productions:
Opened May 18, 1950 for 12 performances
Reviews:
    Christian Science Monitor Magazine page 6, May 27, 1950
    New York Theatre Critics' Reviews 1950:296+
    New York Times page 30, May 19, 1950
    New Yorker 26:49, May 27, 1950
    Newsweek 35:69, May 29, 1950
    Theatre Arts 34:17, Jul 1950

Libby Holman's Blues, Ballads, and Sin-Songs
    songs: Libby Holman
    sets: Gerald Cook
    costumes: Mainbocher, and Frank Stanley
Productions:
Opened October 4, 1954 for 12 performances
Reviews:
    New York Times II, page 1, Oct 3, 1954
                     page 23, Oct 5, 1954
    Time 64:76, Oct 18, 1954

Life Begins at 8:40
    book: David Freedman
    music: Harold Arlen
    lyrics: Ira Gershwin and E. Y. Harburg
    staging: John Murray Anderson and Philip Loeb
    sets: Albert Johnson
    choreography: Robert Alton and Charles Weidman
Productions:
Opened August 27, 1934 for 237 performances
Reviews:
    Catholic World 140:88, Oct 1934
    Literary Digest 118:20, Sep 8, 1934
    New York Times page 20, Aug 7, 1934
                   IX, page 1, Aug 12, 1934
                   page 24, Aug 28, 1934
                   IX, page 1, Sep 2, 1934
    Stage 12:8-9, Oct 1934
    Time 24:30, Sep 10, 1934

A Life in the Day of a Secretary
    book: Alfred Hayes and Jay Williams
    music: George Kleinsinger
    lyrics: Alfred Hayes and Jay Williams

    staging: Peter Frye
Productions:
    (Off-Broadway) Season of 1938-1939
    (Off-Broadway) Opened June 24, 1939
No Reviews.

The Life of Man
    book: Al Carmines
    music: Al Carmines
    lyrics: Al Carmines
    staging: Al Carmines
Productions:
    (Off-Off-Broadway) Opened September 29, 1972 (Judson Poets'
    Theatre)
Reviews:
    Craft Horizon 32:10+, Dec 1972
    New York Times page 40, Oct 4, 1972
    New Yorker 48:125, Oct 14, 1972
    Saturday Review 55:85, Oct 21, 1972

Light, Lively and Yiddish
    book: A. Shulman, Wolf, Sylvia Younin
    music: Eli Rubinstein
    lyrics: A. Shulman, Wolf, Sylvia Younin
    staging: Mina Bern
    sets: Josef Ijaky
    costumes: Sylvia Friedlander
    choreography: Felix Fibich
Productions:
    Opened October 27, 1970 for 88 performances
Reviews:
    New York Times page 58, Oct 28, 1970
                    page 17, Jan 9, 1971

Li'l Abner
    book: Norman Panama and Melvin Frank, based on
                    characters created by Al Capp
    music: Gene de Paul
    lyrics: Johnny Mercer
    staging: Michael Kidd
    sets: William and Jean Eckart
    costumes: Alvin Colt
    choreography: Michael Kidd
Productions:
    Opened November 15, 1956 for 693 performances
Reviews:
    America 96:398, Jan 5, 1957
    Catholic World 184:307, Jan 1957
    Commonweal 65:408, Jan 18, 1957
    Life 42:81-3, Jan 14, 1957
    Nation 183:485, Dec 1, 1956
    New York Theatre Critics' Reviews 1956:202+
    New York Times VI, page 29, Sep 16, 1956

VI, page 28, Nov 4, 1956
II, page 1, Nov 11, 1956
page 24, Nov 16, 1956
II, page 1, Nov 25, 1956
II, page 3, Dec 16, 1956
New Yorker 32:114+, Dec 1, 1956
Newsweek 48:73, Nov 26, 1956
Saturday Review 39:50, Dec 1, 1956
Theatre Arts 41:28-9, Jan 1957
Time 68:58, Nov 26, 1956

The Lilac Domino
    book: Emerich Von Gatti and Bela Jenbach; English
                       adaption by Harry B. Smith
    lyrics: English lyrics by Robert B. Smith
    staging: Sydney Ellison
Productions:
    Opened October 28, 1914 for 109 performances
Reviews:
    Dramatic Mirror 72:8, Nov 4, 1914
                    72:2, Nov 25, 1914
    Green Book 13:376-7, Feb 1915
    Harper's Weekly 59:518, Nov 28, 1914
    Nation 99:562, Nov 15, 1914
    New York Dramatic News 60:17, Nov 7, 1914
                           63:25, Aug 19, 1916
    New York Times page 11, Oct 7, 1914
                    VII, page 8, Nov 8, 1914
    Theatre Magazine 20:267, Dec 1914
                     21:7, Jan 1915

Linger Longer Letty
    music: Alfred Goodman
    lyrics: Bernard Grosman
Productions:
    Opened November 20, 1919 for 69 performances
Reviews:
    Dramatic Mirror 80:1861, Dec 4, 1919
    New York Times page 14, Nov 21, 1919
    Theatre Magazine 31:20, Jan 1920

Listen Lester
    book: Harry L. Cort and George E. Stoddard
    music: Harold Orlob
    staging: Robert Marks
Productions:
    Opened December 23, 1918 for 272 performances
Reviews:
    Dramatic Mirror 79:831, Dec 17, 1918
                    80:9, Jan 4, 1919
    New York Times page 7, Dec 24, 1918
    Theatre Magazine 29:80, Feb 1919
                     29:87, Feb 1919

The Little Blue Devil
    book: Harold Atteridge, based on Clyde Fitch's The
                     Blue Mouse
    music: Harry Carroll
    lyrics: Harold Atteridge
Productions:
    Opened November 3, 1919 for 75 performances
Reviews:
    Dramatic Mirror 80:1756, Nov 13, 1919
    New York Times page 18, Nov 4, 1919
    Theatre Magazine 30:424+, Dec 1919

The Little Cafe
    book: C. M. S. McLellan; based on Tristan Bernard's
                     La Petit Café
    music: Ivan Caryll
    lyrics: C. M. S. McLellan
Productions:
    Opened November 10, 1913 for 144 performances
Reviews:
    Blue Book 18:628-30, Feb 1914
    Dramatic Mirror 70:6, Nov 12, 1913
                     70:2, Nov 19, 1913
                     70:2, Dec 17, 1913
                     70:1, Dec 31, 1913
    Everybody's 30:254-5, Feb 1914
    Green Book 11:188-90, Feb 1914
                11:345-6, Feb 1914
    Leslie's Weekly 118:59, Jan 15, 1914
    Munsey 50:725, Jan 1914
    New York Dramatic News 58:18, Nov 15, 1913
                           58:1, Dec 20, 1913
    New York Times page 13, Nov 11, 1913
    Theatre Magazine 18:xii+, Dec 1913

Little Jessie James
    book: Harlan Thompson
    music: Harry Archer
    staging: Ernest Cutting
Productions:
    Opened August 15, 1923 for (453) performances
Reviews:
    New York Times page 10, Aug 16, 1923
    Theatre Magazine 38:52, Oct 1923

Little Mary Sunshine
    book: Rick Besoyan
    music: Rick Besoyan
    lyrics: Rick Besoyan
    staging: Ray Harrison
    sets: Howard Barker
    costumes: Howard Barker
    choreography: Ray Harrison

Productions:
    (Off-Broadway) Opened November 18, 1959 for 1, 143 per-
    formances
    (Off-Broadway) Opened February 12, 1970 for 19 performances
Reviews:
    Dance Magazine 34:20-1, Feb 1960
    New York Times page 49, Nov 19, 1959
                  page 27, Nov 21, 1959
                   II, page 1, Nov 29, 1959
                   II, page 3, Dec 20, 1959
                   page 35, May 18, 1962
                   page 18, Jul 31, 1962
    New Yorker 35:110-12, Nov 28, 1959
    Newsweek 55:95, Feb 22, 1960
    Saturday Review 42:29, Dec 5, 1959
    Time 75:70, Jun 6, 1960

Little Me
    book: Neil Simon, based on the novel by Patrick
                  Dennis
    music: Cy Coleman
    lyrics: Carolyn Leigh
    staging: Cy Feuer and Bob Fosse
    sets: Robert Randolph
    costumes: Robert Fletcher
    choreography: Bob Fosse
Productions:
    Opened November 17, 1962 for 257 performances
Reviews:
    America 107:1258, Dec 15, 1962
    Commonweal 77:280, Dec 7, 1962
    Dance Magazine 37:24+, Jan 1963
    Life 53:113-15, Nov 30, 1962
    Nation 195:411, Dec 8, 1962
    New York Theatre Critics' Reviews 1962:196+
    New York Times page 58, Oct 10, 1962
                  page 41, Nov 19, 1962
                   II, page 1, Dec 2, 1962
    New York Times Magazine pages 75-6, Nov 4, 1962
    New Yorker 38:118+, Dec 1, 1962
    Newsweek 60:51-4, Nov 26, 1962
    Reporter 27:43-4, Dec 20, 1962
    Saturday Review 45:51, Dec 8, 1962
    Theatre Arts 46:17-19+, Nov 1962
                  47:12, Jan 1963
    Time 80:53, Nov 30, 1962

The Little Millionaire
    book: George M. Cohan
    staging: George M. Cohan
Productions:
    Opened September 25, 1911 for 192 performances
Reviews:

Blue Book 14:463-5, Jan 1912
Dramatic Mirror 66:11, Sep 27, 1911
        66:4, Oct 4, 1911
        66:2, Oct 18, 1911
        66:2, Dec 13, 1911
        67:2, Jan 3, 1912
        67:1, Jan 31, 1912
Green Book Album 6:1146-8, Dec 1911
        6:1195-6, Dec 1911
Harper's Weekly 55:18, Oct 21, 1911
Leslie's Weekly 113:409, Oct 12, 1911
        113:467, Oct 26, 1911
Life (New York) 58:618, Oct 12, 1911
Munsey 46:426, Dec 1911
New York Times page 9, Sep 26, 1911
Theatre Magazine 14:xvi, Nov 1911
        14:174, Nov 1911

Little Miss Charity

    book: Edward Clark
    music: S. R. Henry and M. Savin
    staging: Alfred Hickman and C. A. de Lima
Productions:
    Opened September 2, 1920 for 77 performances
Reviews:
    Dramatic Mirror page 459, Sep 11, 1920
    New York Clipper 68:14, Mar 24, 1920
             68:19, Sep 8, 1920
    New York Times page 6, Sep 3, 1920

Little Miss Fix-It

    book: William J. Hurlbut and Harry B. Smith
    staging: Gustav Von Seyffertitz
Productions:
    Opened April 3, 1911 for 56 performances
Reviews:
    Blue Book 13:227+, Jun 1911
    Dramatic Mirror 65:2, Apr 5, 1911
             65:7, Aug 5, 1911
    Green Book Album 5:1133-5, Jun 1911
    Leslie's Weekly 112:451+, Apr 20, 1911
    Pearson 25:782-3, Jun 1911
    Red Book 17:369+, Jun 1911
    Stage 13:57, Aug 1936
    Theatre Magazine 13:ix, May 1911
             13:145, May 1911

Little Nellie Kelly

    book: George M. Cohan
    staging: George M. Cohan and Julian Mitchell
Productions:
    Opened November 13, 1922 for (248) performances
Reviews:

National Magazine 52:37+, Jun 1923
New York Clipper 70:20, Nov 29, 1922
New York Times page 16, Nov 14, 1922

A Little Night Music
    book: Hugh Wheeler; suggested by Ingmar Bergman's
                    film Smiles of a Summer Night
    music: Stephen Sondheim
    lyrics: Stephen Sondheim
    staging: Harold Prince
    sets: Boris Aronson
    costumes: Florence Klotz
    choreography: Patricia Birch
Productions:
Opened February 25, 1973 for 600 performances
Reviews:
    America 128:243, Mar 17, 1973
    Dance Magazine 47:60-1, Jun 1973
    Harper's 106:153, Mar 1973
    High Fidelity 23:70-1+, Jul 1973
    Nation 216:379, Mar 19, 1973
    New York Theatre Critics' Reviews 1973:348
    New York Times page 26, Feb 26, 1973
                 II, page 1, Mar 4, 1973
    New Yorker 49:78+, Mar 3, 1973
    Newsweek 81:88, Mar 12, 1973
    Saturday Review (Arts) 1:77, Apr 1973
    Time 101:86+, Mar 12, 1973
    Vogue 161:180-1, Apr 1973

A Little Racketeer
    book: Harry Clarke, adapted from the German of
                    F. Kalbfuss and R. Wilde
    music: Haskell Brown
    lyrics: Edward Eliscu
    staging: William Caryl
    choreography: Albertina Rasch
Productions:
Opened January 18, 1932 for 48 performances
Reviews:
    New York Times VIII, page 4, Oct 18, 1931
                   page 24, Jan 19, 1932
                   page 13, Feb 15, 1932

The Little Show (1929)
    book: Howard Dietz
    music: Arthur Schwartz; additional songs by Kay Swift
                    and Ralph Rainger
    lyrics: Howard Dietz
    staging: Dwight Deere Wiman
    choreography: Danny Dare
Productions:
Opened April 30, 1929 for 321 performances

Reviews:
    Life (New York) 93:22, May 24, 1929
    Nation 131:331, Sep 24, 1930
    New Republic 59:25, May 22, 1929
    New York Times page 28, May 1, 1929
                IX, page 1, May 12, 1929
                IX, page 2, May 12, 1929
                IX, page 7, Jul 14, 1929
    Theatre Magazine 50:42, Jul 1929
    Vogue 74:57+, Jul 6, 1929

Little Show (1953) (see Anna Russell's Little Show)

Little Simplicity
    book: Rida Johnson Young
    music: Augustus Barratt
    lyrics: Rida Johnson Young
    staging: Edward P. Temple
Productions:
    Opened November 4, 1918 for 112 performances
Reviews:
    Dramatic Mirror 79:723, Nov 16, 1918
    New York Dramatic News 65:11, Nov 9, 1918
    New York Times page 11, Nov 5, 1918
    Theatre Magazine 28:347, Dec 1918
                29:15, Jan 1919

The Little Whopper
    book: Otto A. Harbach; adapted from the movie
                    Miss Geo. Washington, Jr.
    music: Rudolf Friml
    lyrics: Bide Dudley and Otto A. Harbach
Productions:
    Opened October 13, 1919 for 224 performances
Reviews:
    Dramatic Mirror 80:1654, Oct 23, 1919
    New York Times page 20, Oct 16, 1919
    Theatre Magazine 30:391, Dec 1919

The Littlest Revue
    conceived by: Ben Bagley
    sketches: Nat Hiken, Billy Friedberg, Eudora Welty, Mike
                   Stewart, George Baxt, Bud McCreery, Allan
                   Manings, Bob Van Scoyk
    music and
    lyrics: Ogden Nash, Vernon Duke, John Latouche,
                   Sheldon Harnick, Lee Adams, Charles Strouse,
                   Sidney Shaw, Sammy Cahn, Michael Brown
    staging: Paul Lammers
    sets: Klaus Holm
    costumes: Alvin Colt
    choreography: Charles Weidman
Productions:

Opened May 22, 1956 for 32 performances
Reviews:
America 95:290-2, Jun 16, 1956
Catholic World 183:311, Jul 1956
Commonweal 64:299, Jun 22, 1956
Nation 182:497, Jun 9, 1956
New York Theatre Critics' Reviews 1956:297+
New York Times page 37, May 23, 1956
New Yorker 32:58, Jun 2, 1956
Saturday Review 39:27, Jun 9, 1956
Theatre Arts 40:73, Aug 1956
Time 67:95, Jun 4, 1956

Livin' the Life
    book: Dale Wasserman and Bruce Geller, based on
                    Mark Twain's Mississippi River stories
    music: Jack Urbont
    lyrics: Bruce Geller
    staging: David Alexander
    sets: William and Jean Eckart
    costumes: Alvin Colt
    choreography: John Butler
Productions:
Opened April 27, 1957 for 25 performances
Reviews:
America 97:270, May 25, 1957
Nation 184:427, May 11, 1957
New York Theatre Critics' Reviews 1957:281+
New York Times II, page 1, Apr 21, 1957
                 page 20, Apr 29, 1957
New Yorker 33:142, May 4, 1957
Theatre Arts 41:18, Jul 1957

Liza (1922)
    book: Irvin C. Miller
    music: Maceo Pinkard
    lyrics: Maceo Pinkard; special lyrics by Nat Vincent
    staging: Walter Brooks
Productions:
Opened November 27, 1922 for 169 performances
Reviews:
New York Clipper 70:20, Dec 6, 1922
New York Times page 24, Nov 28, 1922

Liza (1974)
    written: Fred Ebb; original musical material by Fred Ebb
                    and John Kander
    staging: Bob Fosse
    choreography: Bob Fosse
Productions:
Opened January 6, 1974 for 23 performances
No Reviews.

Lollipop
    book: Zelda Sears
    music: Vincent Youmans
    lyrics: Zelda Sears and Walter DeLeon
Productions:
    Opened January 21, 1924 for 152 performances
Reviews:
    New York Times page 15, Jan 22, 1924
                 VIII, page 2, Apr 27, 1924
    Theatre Magazine 39:68, Mar 1924

The Long Christmas Dinner
    music: Paul Hindemith
    words: Thornton Wilder
    staging: Christopher West
    sets: Thea Neu
    costumes: Thea Neu
Productions:
    (Off-Broadway) Opened March 13, 1963 for 5 performances
No Reviews.

Long Time Coming and a Long Time Gone   (see Richard Farina:
    Long Time Coming and a Long Time Gone)

A Look at the Fifties
    book: Al Carmines
    staging: Al Carmines
Productions:
    (Off-Broadway) Opened Season of 1971-72 (Judson Poets'
    Theatre)
Reviews:
    New York Times page 53, Apr 20, 1972
    New Yorker 48:105, Apr 29, 1972

Look at Us
    book: Arnold Sundgaard
    music: Lorenzo Fuller
    lyrics: Lorenzo Fuller
staging: Michael Wright
Productions:
    (Off-Broadway) Opened June 5, 1962 for 16 performances
No Reviews.

Look, Ma, I'm Dancin'
    book: Jerome Lawrence and Robert E. Lee
    music: Hugh Martin
    lyrics: Hugh Martin
    staging: George Abbott and Jerome Robbins
    sets: Oliver Smith
    costumes: John Pratt
    choreography: Trude Rittman
Productions:
    Opened January 29, 1948 for 188 performances

Reviews:
    Catholic World 166:553, Mar 1948
    Commonweal 47:447, Feb 13, 1948
    Forum 109:155, Mar 1948
    New Republic 118:32, Feb 16, 1948
    New York Theatre Critics' Reviews 1948:364+
    New York Times page 20, Jan 30, 1948
            II, page 1, Feb 8, 1948
            II, page 2, Feb 8, 1948
    New Yorker 23:40, Feb 7, 1948
    Newsweek 31:70, Feb 9, 1948
    Saturday Review 31:26-7, Feb 21, 1948
    Time 51:55, Feb 9, 1948

Look to the Lilies

book:	Leonard Spigelgass; based on William E. Barrett's novel Lilies of the Field
music:	Jule Styne
lyrics:	Sammy Cahn
staging:	Joshua Logan
sets:	Jo Mielziner
costumes:	Carrie F. Robbins
choreography:	Joyce Trisler

Productions:
    Opened March 29, 1970 for 25 performances
Reviews:
    New York Theatre Critics' Reviews 1970:322
    New York Times page 59, Mar 30, 1970
            II, page 3, Apr 12, 1970
    New Yorker 46:61-2, Apr 4, 1970
    Time 95:98, Apr 13, 1970

Look Where I'm At

book:	James Leasor and Gib Dennigan; based on Thorne Smith's Rain in the Doorway
lyrics:	Frank Stanton and Murray Semos
staging:	Wakefield Poole
sets:	Robert Guerra
costumes:	Rosemary Heyer
choreography:	Wakefield Poole

Productions:
    (Off-Broadway) Opened March 5, 1971 for 5 performances
Reviews:
    New York Times page 20, Mar 6, 1971

Look Who's Here

book:	Frank Mandel
music:	Silvio Hein
lyrics:	Edward Paulson and Cecil Lean

Productions:
    Opened March 2, 1920 for 87 performances
Reviews:
    Dramatic Mirror 82:419, Mar 6, 1920

New York Times page 12, Mar 3, 1920
Theatre Magazine 31:309, Apr 1920
                    31:312, Apr 1920

Lorelei
    book: Kenny Solms and Gail Parent; based on the
                       musical Gentlemen Prefer Blondes
    music: Jule Styne
    lyrics: Betty Comden and Adolph Green
    staging: Robert Moore
    sets: John Conklin
    costumes: Alvin Colt
    choreography: Ernest O. Flatt
Productions:
    Opened January 27, 1974 for 321 performances
Reviews:
    Harper's 106:98+, Apr 1973
    Nation 218:222, Feb 16, 1974
    New York Theatre Critics' Reviews 1974:394
    New York Times page 35, Jan 28, 1974
                    II, page 1, Feb 3, 1974
    New Yorker 49:46, Feb 4, 1974
    Newsweek 83:96, Feb 11, 1974

Lost in the Stars
    book: Maxwell Anderson, based on Alan Paton's Cry,
                       the Beloved Country
    music: Kurt Weill
    lyrics: Maxwell Anderson
    staging: Rouben Mamoulian
    sets: George Jenkins
    costumes: Anna Hill Johnstone
Productions:
    Opened October 30, 1949 for 273 performances
    (Off-Broadway) Opened March 22, 1968 for 15 performances
    Opened April 18, 1972 for 39 performances
Reviews:
    America 126:515, May 13, 1972
    American Mercury 70:170-2, Feb 1950
    Catholic World 170:226, Dec 1949
    Commonweal 51:212, Nov 25, 1949
    Forum 112:340, Dec 1949
    Life 27:143-6+, Nov 14, 1949
    Musical America 69:9, Nov 15, 1949
    Nation 169:478, Nov 12, 1949
           186:398-9, May 3, 1958
           214:603-4, May 8, 1972
    New Republic 121:19, Nov 21, 1949
    New York Theatre Critics' Reviews 1949:241
                                      1972:308
    New York Times II, page 3, Oct 30, 1949
                    page 21, Oct 31, 1949
                    II, page 1, Nov 6, 1949

          VI, page 14, Dec 11, 1949
          page 21, Apr 11, 1958
          page 26, May 5, 1958
          page 20, Feb 18, 1972
          page 38, Apr 19, 1972
          II, page 3, Apr 30, 1972
New Yorker 25:64, Nov 5, 1949
          25:58, Nov 12, 1949
          34:138, Apr 19, 1958
          48:103, Apr 29, 1972
Newsweek 34:80, Nov 7, 1949
          51:84, Apr 21, 1958
Saturday Review 32:31-2, Nov 26, 1949
          32:43, Dec 31, 1949
          55:64, May 6, 1972
Theatre Arts 34:11, Jan 1950
Time 54:80, Nov 7, 1949

Lotta
     book: Robert Montgomery
     songs: Robert Montgomery
     staging: David Chambers
     sets: Tom H. John
     costumes: Nancy Adzima
     choreography: Dennis Nahat
Productions:
     (Off-Broadway) Opened October 18, 1973 for 54 performances
Reviews:
     America 129:485, Dec 22, 1973
     New York Theatre Critics' Reviews 1973:168
     New York Times page 42, Nov 23, 1973
          II, page 3, Dec 2, 1973
     New Yorker 49:147, Dec 3, 1973
     Newsweek 82:73, Dec 3, 1973

Louie the 14th
     book: Arthur Wimperis, adapted from the German
     music: Sigmund Romberg
     lyrics: Arthur Wimperis
     staging: Edward Royce
Productions:
     Opened March 3, 1925 for 319 performances
Reviews:
     Life (New York) 85:22, Apr 2, 1925
     New York Times page 17, Mar 4, 1925
     Theatre Magazine 41:32, May 1925

Louisiana Lady
     book: Isaac Green, Jr. and Eugene Berton
     music: Monte Carlo and Alma Sanders
     lyrics: Monte Carlo and Alma Sanders
     staging: Edgar MacGregor
     sets: Watson Barratt

choreography: Felicia Sorel
Productions:
Opened June 2, 1947 for 4 performances
Reviews:
New York Theatre Critics' Reviews 1947:362+
New York Times II, page 1, Jun 1, 1947
                page 35, Jun 3, 1947

Louisiana Purchase
book: Morrie Ryskind, based on a story by B. G.
                 DeSylva
music: Irving Berlin
lyrics: Irving Berlin
staging: Edgar MacGregor
sets: Tom Lee
costumes: Tom Lee
choreography: George Balanchine and Carl Randall
Productions:
Opened May 28, 1940 for 444 performances
Reviews:
Catholic World 151:471, Jul 1940
Commonweal 32:191-2, Jun 21, 1940
Life 8:100-3, Jun 10, 1940
Nation 150:716, Jun 8, 1940
New York Theatre Critics' Reviews 1940:296+
                                  1941:484+
New York Times page 19, May 29, 1940
                IX, page 1, Jun 16, 1940
New Yorker 16:38, Jun 8, 1940
Newsweek 15:43, Jun 10, 1940
Theatre Arts 24:774+, Nov 1940
Time 35:63, Jun 10, 1940

Love and Let Love
book: Based on Twelfth Night by William Shakespeare;
                 adapted by John Lollos
music: Stanley Jay Gelber
lyrics: John Lollos and Don Christopher
staging: John Lollos
sets: Barbara Miller
Productions:
(Off-Broadway) Opened January 3, 1968 for 14 performances
Reviews:
New York Times page 30, Jan 4, 1968
New Yorker 43:58-9, Jan 13, 1968

Love and Maple Syrup
devised: Louis Negin
songs: Gordon Lightfoot and others
sets: Charles L. Dunlop
Productions:
(Off-Broadway) Opened January 7, 1970 for 15 performances
Reviews:

New York Times page 47, Jan 8, 1970
New Yorker 45:52, Jan 17, 1970

Love Birds
    book: Edgar Allen Woolf
    music: Sigmund Romberg
    lyrics: Ballard McDonald
    staging: Edgar MacGregor and Julian Alfred
Productions:
Opened March 15, 1921 for 105 performances
Reviews:
    Dramatic Mirror 83:505+, Mar 19, 1921
    Life (New York) 77:464, Mar 31, 1921
    New York Clipper 69:19, Mar 23, 1921
    New York Times page 12, Mar 16, 1921
    Theatre Magazine 33:342, May 1921

The Love Call
    book: Harry B. Smith and Edward Locke
    music: Sigmund Romberg
    lyrics: Harry B. Smith
    staging: J. C. Huffman
Productions:
Opened October 24, 1927 for 88 performances
Reviews:
    New York Times page 33, Oct 25, 1927
                IX, page 5, Nov 13, 1927

The Love Cure
    book: Oliver Herford; from the German of Leo Stein
                       and Karl Lindau
    music: Edmund Eysler
Productions:
Opened September 1, 1909 for 35 performances
Reviews:
    Dramatic Mirror 62:5-6, Sep 11, 1909
    Hampton 23:695-6, Nov 1909
    Leslie's Weekly 109:299, Sep 23, 1909
                    109:318, Sep 30, 1909
    Metropolitan Magazine 31:256-7, Nov 1909
    Theatre Magazine 10:102, Oct 1909
                      10:111, Oct 1909
    Vanity Fair 6:199, Nov 1909

Love Dreams
    book: Ann Nichols
    music: Werner Janssen
    lyrics: Oliver Morosco
    staging: Oliver Morosco and John McKee
Productions:
Opened October 10, 1921 for 40 performances
Reviews:
    Dramatic Mirror 84:484, Oct 1, 1921

New York Clipper 69:20, Oct 19, 1921
New York Times page 22, Oct 11, 1921
Theatre Magazine 34:416+, Dec 1921

Love in a Garden   (see Prunella, or Love in a Garden)

The Love Letter
    book: William Le Baron; adapted from Franz Molnar's
                     The Phantom Rival
    music: Victor Jacobi
    staging: Edward Royce
Productions:
    Opened October 4, 1921 for 31 performances
Reviews:
    Dramatic Mirror 84:448, Sep 24, 1921
    New York Clipper 69:20, Oct 12, 1921
    New York Times page 20, Oct 5, 1921
    Theatre Magazine 34:388, Dec 1921

Love Life
    book: Alan Jay Lerner
    music: Kurl Weill
    lyrics: Alan Jay Lerner
    staging: Elia Kazan
    sets: Boris Aronson
    costumes: Lucinda Ballard
    choreography: Michael Kidd
Productions:
    Opened October 7, 1948 for 252 performances
Reviews:
    Catholic World 168:161, Nov 1948
    Commonweal 49:94, Nov 5, 1948
    Forum 111:32-3, Jan 1949
    Harper 198:110, Jan 1949
    Musical Courier 138:4, Nov 15, 1948
    New Republic 119:28, Nov 1, 1948
    New York Theatre Critics' Reviews 1948:201+
    New York Times II, page 3, Oct 3, 1948
                    page 31, Oct 8, 1948
    New Yorker 24:52, Oct 16, 1948
    Newsweek 32:89, Oct 18, 1948
    School and Society 68:385-6, Dec 4, 1948
    Theatre Arts 33:18, Jan 1949
    Time 52:82, Oct 18, 1948

Love Me, Love My Children
    book: Robert Swerdlow
    music: Robert Swerdlow
    lyrics: Robert Swerdlow
    staging: Paul Aaron
    sets: Jo Mielziner
    costumes: Patricia Quinn Stuart
    choreography: Elizabeth Swerdlow

Productions:
> (Off-Broadway) Opened November 3, 1971 for 187 performances

Reviews:
> New York Theatre Critics' Reviews 1971:166
> New York Times page 53, Nov 4, 1971
> New Yorker 47:66+, Nov 13, 1971

The Love Mill
> book: Earl Carroll
> music: Alfred Francis
> lyrics: Earl Carroll
> staging: George Marion

Productions:
> Opened February 7, 1918 for 52 performances

Reviews:
> Dramatic Mirror 78:5, Feb 23, 1918
> Life (New York) 71:302, Feb 21, 1918
> New York Times page 13, Feb 9, 1918

Love o' Mike
> book: Thomas Sydney
> music: Jerome Kern
> lyrics: Harry B. Smith
> staging: J. H. Benrimo

Productions:
> Opened January 15, 1917 for 192 performances

Reviews:
> Dramatic Mirror 77:5, Jan 20, 1917
>   77:16, Jan 27, 1917
> New York Dramatic Mirror 63:2, Jan 6, 1917
>   63:22, Jan 20, 1917
> New York Times page 10, Jan 16, 1917
> Theatre Magazine 25:84, Feb 1917
>   25:149, Mar 1917

Lovely Ladies, Kind Gentlemen
> book: John Patrick; based on Vern J. Sneider's book
>   The Teahouse of the August Moon and the play
>   by John Patrick
> music: Stan Freeman and Franklin Underwood
> lyrics: Stan Freeman and Franklin Underwood
> staging: Lawrence Kasha
> sets: Oliver Smith
> costumes: Freddy Wittop
> choreography: Marc Breaux

Productions:
> Opened December 28, 1970 for 16 performances

Reviews:
> Dance Magazine 45:82, Mar 1971
> New York Theatre Critics' Reviews 1970:114
> New York Times page 26, Aug 11, 1970
>   page 38, Dec 29, 1970
>   page 15, Jan 1, 1971

page 17, Jan 9, 1971
II, page 1, Jan 10, 1971
New Yorker 46:51, Jan 9, 1971

Lovely Lady
  book: Gladys Unger and Cyrus Wood; based on the
                     French Déjeuner de Soleil
  music: Dave Stamper and Harold Levey
  lyrics: Cyrus Wood
Productions:
  Opened December 29, 1927 for 164 performances
Reviews:
  New York Times page 22, Dec 30, 1927
  Theatre Magazine 47:56, Mar 1928
                    47:62, Mar 1928

The Loves of Alonzo Fitz Clarence and Rosannah Ethelton
  book: Paul Zakrzewski; based on the short story by
                     Mark Twain
  music: Wally Harper
  lyrics: Paul Zakrzewski
  staging: Paul Zakrzewski
Productions:
  (Off-Off-Broadway) Opened February 6, 1974 (Theatre of the
  Riverside Church)
Reviews:
  New York Times page 44, Feb 7, 1974

Luana
  book: Howard Emmett Rogers, based on Richard
                     Walton Tully's The Bird of Paradise
  music: Rudolf Friml
  lyrics: J. Kiern Brennan
  staging: Arthur Hammerstein, Howard Rogers, Earl
                     Lindsey
Productions:
  Opened September 17, 1930 for 21 performances
Reviews:
  Life (New York) 96:18, Oct 10, 1930
  New York Times page 28, Sep 18, 1930
  Theatre Magazine 52:26, Nov 1930

Luckee Girl
  book: Gertrude Purcell; adapted from the French
                     Un Bon Garcon
  music: Maurice Yvain and Maurie Rubens
  lyrics: Max Lief and Nathaniel Lief
  staging: Lew Morton and Harry Puck
Productions:
  Opened September 15, 1928 for 81 performances
Reviews:
  New York Times page 28, Sep 17, 1928

Lucky
    book: Harry Ruby, Bert Kalmar, Otto Harbach
    music: Harry Ruby and Jerome Kern
    lyrics: Harry Ruby, Bert Kalmar, Otto Harbach
    staging: Hassard Short
Productions:
Opened March 22, 1927 for 71 performances
Reviews:
Life (New York) 89:31, Apr 7, 1927
New Republic 50:196, Apr 6, 1927
New York Times page 24, Mar 25, 1927
Theatre Magazine 45:26, Jun 1927
Vogue 69:118+, May 15, 1927

Lucky Sambo
    book: Porter Grainger and Freddie Johnson
    music: Porter Grainger and Freddie Johnson
    lyrics: Porter Grainger and Freddie Johnson
    staging: Leigh Whipper and Freddie Johnson
Productions:
Opened June 6, 1925 for 9 performances
Reviews:
New York Times page 19, Jun 8, 1925

Lute Song
    book: Sidney Howard and Will Irwin from Chinese
                     classic
    music: Raymond Scott
    lyrics: Bernard Hanighen
    staging: John Houseman
    sets: Robert Edmund Jones
    costumes: Robert Edmund Jones
    choreography: Yeichi Nimura
Productions:
Opened February 6, 1946 for 142 performances
(Off-Broadway) Season of 1958-59 (City Center)
Opened March 12, 1959 for 14 performances
Reviews:
American Mercury 62:587-90, May 1946
Catholic World 162:553, Mar 1946
                 189:159, May 1959
Commonweal 43:479, Feb 22, 1946
Dance Magazine 33:23, Apr 1959
Life 20:53-6, Mar 4, 1946
Modern Music 23no.2:145, Apr 1946
Nation 162:240, Feb 23, 1946
New Republic 114:254, Feb 18, 1946
New York Theatre Critics' Reviews 1946:459+
New York Times page 29, Feb 7, 1946
                II, page 1, Feb 17, 1946
                page 32, Oct 12, 1948
                page 24, Mar 13, 1959
New Yorker 22:48+, Feb 16, 1946

Newsweek 27;92, Feb 18, 1946
Saturday Review 29:28-9, May 2, 1946
Theatre Arts 30:199-200, Apr 1946
                32:67, Feb 1948
                43:67-8, May 1959
Time 47:49, Feb 18, 1946

- M -

Mackey of Appalachia
    book: Walter Cool
    music: Walter Cool
    lyrics: Walter Cool
    staging: Walter Cool
    sets: Allen Edward Klein
    costumes: Alice Merrigal
Productions:
    (Off-Broadway) Opened October 6, 1965 for 54 performances
Reviews:
    America 113:384-5, Oct 2, 1965

The Mad Show
    book: Larry Siegel and Stan Hart; based on Mad
                     Magazine
    music: Mary Rodgers
    lyrics: Marshall Barer, Larry Siegel and Steven Vinaver
    staging: Steven Vinaver
    sets: Peter Harvey
    costumes: Peter Harvey
Productions:
    (Off-Broadway) Opened January 10, 1966 for 871 performances
Reviews:
    Commonweal 84:228, May 13, 1966
    Harper's 232:114-5, May 1966
    Life 60:24-5, Mar 11, 1966
    New Republic 154:36-7, Jan 29, 1966
    New York Times page 16, Jan 10, 1966
                     page 36, Jun 26, 1967
                     page 19, Jul 7, 1967
    Newsweek 67:82, Jan 24, 1966
    Time 37:65+, Feb 18, 1966
    Vogue 147:94, Mar 1, 1966

Madam Moselle
    adapted: Edward A. Paulton
    music: Ludwig Englander and William P. Chase
    staging: George W. Lederer
Productions:
    Opened May 23, 1914 for 9 performances
Reviews:
    Dramatic Mirror 71:8, May 27, 1914
                    71:4, Jun 3, 1914

Green Book 12:94, Jul 1914
New York Times III, page 7, May 24, 1914
Theatre Magazine 20:37, Jul 1914

Madame Aphrodite
    book: Tad Mosel
    music: Jerry Herman
    lyrics: Jerry Herman
    staging: Robert Turoff
    sets: David Ballou
    costumes: Patricia Zipprodt
Productions:
    (Off-Broadway) Opened December 29, 1961 for 13 performances
Reviews:
    New York Times page 13, Dec 30, 1961
    New Yorker 37:66, Jan 11, 1962

Madame Pompadour
    book: Rudolph Schanzer and Ernst Welisch; adapted by
                     Clare Kummer
    music: Leo Fall
    lyrics: Rudolph Schanzer and Ernst Welisch
Productions:
    Opened November 11, 1924 for 80 performances
Reviews:
    New York Times page 20, Nov 12, 1924
    Theatre Magazine 41:19, Jan 1925
                  41:21, Apr 1925

Madame Sherry
    book: Otto Hauerbach; adapted from George Edwarde's
                     English version
    music: Karl Hoschna
    staging: George W. Lederer
Productions:
    Opened August 30, 1910 for 231 performances
Reviews:
    Dramatic Mirror 64:6, Sep 10, 1910
    Leslie's Weekly 111:317, Sep 29, 1910
    Metropolitan Magazine 32:670-1, Aug 1910
    Theatre Magazine 11:179-80, Jun 1910
                  12:74, Sep 1910
                  12:xiv, Oct 1910

The Madcap (Green Fruit)
    book: Gertrude Purcell and Gladys Unger; adapted from
                     the French of Regis Gignoux and Jacques Thery
    music: Maurice Rubens
    staging: Duane Nelson
Productions:
    Opened January 31, 1928 for 103 performances
Reviews:
    New York Times page 31, Feb 1, 1928

Theatre Magazine 47:41, May 1927

Magdalena
    book: Frederick Hazlitt Brennan and Homer Curran
    music: Heitor Villa-Lobos
    lyrics: Robert Wright and George Forrest
    staging: Jules Dassin
    sets: Howard Bay
    costumes: Irene Sharaff
    choreography: Jack Cole
Productions:
Opened September 20, 1948 for 88 performances
Reviews:
    Catholic World 168:158-9, Nov 1948
    Collier's 122:24-5, Nov 20, 1948
    Commonweal 48:618, Oct 8, 1948
    Life 25:106-7, Oct 25, 1948
    New Republic 119:29, Oct 11, 1948
    New York Theatre Critics' Reviews 1948:235+
    New York Times page 27, Jul 28, 1948
                    page 31, Sep 20, 1948
                    II, page 1, Sep 26, 1948
                    II, page 7, Sep 26, 1948
                    II, page 6, Nov 7, 1948
    New Yorker 24:50, Oct 2, 1948
    Newsweek 32:76, Oct 4, 1948
    School and Society 68:301-2, Oct 30, 1948
    Theatre Arts 33:18, Jan 1949
    Time 52:59, Oct 4, 1948
    Vogue 112:183, Dec 1948

Maggie
    book: Hugh Thomas, based on Sir James M. Barrie's
                     play What Every Woman Knows
    music: Hugh Thomas
    lyrics: Hugh Thomas
    staging: Michael Gordon
    sets: Raoul Pene du Bois
    costumes: Raoul Pene du Bois
    choreography: June Graham
Productions:
Opened February 18, 1953 for 5 performances
Reviews:
    Commonweal 57:577, Mar 13, 1953
    New York Theatre Critics' Reviews 1953:351+
    New York Times page 20, Feb 19, 1953
    New Yorker 29:65, Feb 28, 1953
    Newsweek 41:84, Mar 2, 1953
    Saturday Review 36:35, Mar 7, 1953
    Theatre Arts 37:14, Jan 1953
                 37:15, May 1953
    Time 61:77, Mar 2, 1953

Maggie Flynn
  book, music,
    and lyrics: Hugo Peretti, Luigi Creatore and George David
                     Weiss: book in collaboration with Morton Da
                     Costa; based on an idea by John Flaxman
    staging: Morton Da Costa
    sets: William and Jean Eckart
    costumes: W. Robert Lavine
    choreography: Brian Macdonald
Productions:
  Opened October 23, 1968 for 81 performances
Reviews:
  America 119:530, Nov 23, 1969
  Dance Magazine 42:106, Dec 1968
  New York Theatre Critics' Reviews 1968:183
                                    1968:196
  New York Times page 52, Oct 24, 1968
                  II, page 1, Nov 3, 1968
                  page 38, Jan 6, 1969
  New Yorker 44:125, Nov 2, 1968
  Newsweek 72:118, Nov 4, 1968

The Magic Melody
  book: Frederic Arnold Kummer
  music: Sigmund Romberg
  lyrics: Frederic Arnold Kummer
Productions:
  Opened November 11, 1919 for 143 performances
Reviews:
  Dramatic Mirror 80:1792, Nov 20, 1919
  New York Times page 25, Nov 12, 1919
  Theatre Magazine 30:368, Dec 1919
                   31:23, Jan 1920

The Magic Ring
  book: Zelda Sears
  music: Harold Levey
Productions:
  Opened October 1, 1923 for 96 performances
Reviews:
  New York Times page 10, Oct 2, 1923
  Theatre Magazine 38:75, Nov 1923

The Magic Show
  book: Bob Randall
  music: Stephen Schwartz
  lyrics: Stephen Schwartz
  staging: Grover Dale
  sets: David Chapman
  costumes: Randy Barcelo
  choreography: Grover Dale
Productions:
  Opened May 28, 1974 for 422* performances

Reviews:
    Commentary 58:75-6, Nov 1974
    New York Theatre Critics' Reviews 1974:254
    New York Times page 31, Mar 20, 1973
                    page 49, May 29, 1974
    New Yorker 50:64, Jun 10, 1974
    Newsweek 83:84, Jun 10, 1974
    Senior Scholastic 106:33-4, Mar 27, 1975
    Time 103:106, Jun 10, 1974

The Magic Show of Dr. Magico
    book: Jen Bernard and John Vaccaro
    music: Richard Weinstock
    staging: Jen Bernard and John Vaccaro
Productions:
    (Off-Off-Broadway) Opened March 15, 1973 (La Mama Experi-
    mental Theatre Club)
No Reviews.

Magic Theater (see Doctor Selavy's Magic Theater)

The Magnolia Lady
    book: Anne Caldwell
    music: Harold Levey
    lyrics: Anne Caldwell
Productions:
    Opened November 25, 1924 for 47 performances
Reviews:
    New York Times page 17, Nov 26, 1924

Mahagonny
    book: Arnold Weinstein; adapted from Brecht and
                     Weill's opera The Rise and Fall of the City of
                     Mahagonny
    music: Kurt Weill
    lyrics: Bertolt Brecht
    staging: Carmen Capalbo
    sets: Robin Wagner
    costumes: Ruth Morley
Productions:
    (Off-Broadway) Opened April 28, 1970 for 8 performances
Reviews:
    High Fidelity 15:158-9, Sep 1965
                  22:MA 24+, May 1972
                  22:MA 29, Oct 1972
    Nation 201:107, Aug 30, 1965
    New York Theatre Critics' Reviews 1970:235
    New York Times page 38, Jan 14, 1970
                    page 51, Apr 29, 1970
                    page 21, May 21, 1970
                    II, page 3, May 10, 1970
                    II, page 15, 1970
                    page 42, Dec 24, 1972

New Yorker 46:97, May 9, 1970
          48:59-62, Jan 6, 1973
          49:138+, Apr 28, 1973
Newsweek 66:82, Jul 19, 1965
Opera News 30:26, Nov 6, 1965
          34:8-12, Mar 14, 1970
Saturday Review (Education) 1:72, Feb 1973
Time 83:59, Mar 13, 1964

Maid in America
    words: Harold Atteridge and others
    music: Rewritten by Sigmund Romberg and Harry
                  Carroll
    staging: J. C. Huffman
Productions:
    Opened February 18, 1915 for 108 performances
Reviews:
    Dramatic Mirror 73:8, Feb 24, 1915
                 73:2, Mar 10, 1915
    Life (New York) 65:374, Mar 4, 1915
    New York Times page 9, Feb 19, 1915

The Maid of the Mountains
    book: Frederick Lonsdale
    music: Harold Fraser-Simson, James W. Tate and
                  Lieut. Gitz Rice
    lyrics: Harry Graham, Clifford Harris and Valentine
    staging: Capt. J. A. E. Malone
Productions:
    Opened September 11, 1918 for 37 performances
Reviews:
    Dramatic Mirror 79:470, Sep 28, 1918
    Theatre Magazine 28:271, Nov 1918
                 28:280, Nov 1918

Make a Wish
    book: Preston Sturges, based on Ferenc Molnar's
                  The Good Fairy
    music: Hugh Martin
    lyrics: Hugh Martin
    staging: John C. Wilson
    sets: Raoul Pene du Bois
    costumes: Raoul Pene du Bois
    choreography: Gower Champion
Productions:
    Opened April 18, 1951 for 103 performances
Reviews:
    Catholic World 173:228, Jun 1951
    Commonweal 54:88, May 4, 1951
    Life 30:137-8, May 14, 1951
    Musical America 71:7+, Jul 1951
    Nation 172:403, Apr 28, 1951
    New York Theatre Critics' Reviews 1951:294+

New York Times page 38, Apr 19, 1951
New Yorker 27:58, Apr 28, 1951
Newsweek 37:53, Apr 30, 1951
Theatre Arts 35:14, Jun 1951
Time 57:89, Apr 30, 1951

Make It Snappy
    book: Harold Atteridge
    music: Jean Schwartz
    lyrics: Harold Atteridge
    staging: J. C. Huffman and Allan K. Foster
Productions:
Opened April 13, 1922 for (77) performances
Reviews:
New York Clipper 70:20, Apr 19, 1922
New York Times page 20, Apr 14, 1922

Make Mine Manhattan
    book: Arnold B. Horwitt
    music: Richard Lewine
    lyrics: Arnold B. Horwitt
    staging: Hassard Short
    sets: Frederick Fox
    costumes: Morton Haack
    choreography: Lee Sherman
Productions:
Opened January 15, 1948 for 429 performances
Reviews:
Catholic World 166:553-4, Mar 1948
Commonweal 47:399, Jan 30, 1948
Forum 109:155, Mar 1948
Life 24:121-1+, Feb 9, 1948
Look 12:50-51, Mar 30, 1948
New Republic 118:34, Feb 9, 1948
New York Theatre Critics' Reviews 1948:382+
New York Times page 26, Jan 16, 1948
       II, page 2, Feb 8, 1948
New Yorker 23:40, Jan 24, 1948
Newsweek 31:81, Jan 26, 1948
Time 51:62, Jan 26, 1948

The Making of Americans
    libretto: Leon Katz; adapted from Gertrude Stein's novel
    music: Al Carmines
    staging: Lawrence Kornfeld
Productions:
(Off-Off-Broadway) Opened November 10, 1972 (Judson Poets'
Theatre)
Reviews:
New York Times page 34, Nov 29, 1972

La Mama (see Everyman at La Mama)

Mama's Baby Boy
    book: Adapted by Junie McCree
    music: Hans S. Linne; additional numbers by Will H.
                       Becker
    lyrics: Junie McCree
Productions:
    Opened May 25, 1912 for 9 performances
Reviews:
    Dramatic Mirror 67:6, May 29, 1912
    Green Book 8:351, Aug 1912
    New York Dramatic News 55:25, Jun 1, 1912
    Theatre Magazine 16:2, Jul 1912

Mame
    book: Jerome Lawrence and Robert E. Lee; based on
                       Auntie Mame, the novel by Patrick Dennis and
                       the play by Jerome Lawrence and Robert E. Lee
    music: Jerry Herman
    lyrics: Jerry Herman
    staging: Gene Saks
    sets: William and Jean Eckart
    costumes: Robert Mackintosh
    choreography: Onna White and Tom Panko
Productions:
    Opened May 24, 1966 for 1,508 performances
Reviews:
    America 115:79-80, Jul 16, 1966
    Commonweal 84:369-70, Jun 17, 1966
    Dance Magazine 40:25-7, Jul 1966
    Life 60:88-92+, Jun 17, 1966
    New York Theatre Critics' Reviews 1966:302
    New York Times page 16, May 14, 1966
                       page 41, May 25, 1966
                       page 56, May 26, 1966
                       page 55, May 24, 1967
                       page 31, Aug 15, 1967
                       page 25, Apr 20, 1968
                       page 42, May 24, 1968
                       page 19, Jun 29, 1968
                       page 79, Jan 5, 1969
                       page 35, Feb 22, 1969
                       page 36, Jun 20, 1969
                       page 20, Jan 3, 1970
    New Yorker 42:75, Jun 4, 1966
    Newsweek 67:89, Jun 6, 1966
    Saturday Review 49:34, Jun 11, 1966
    Time 87:71, Jun 3, 1966
    Vogue 148:28, Jul 1966

Man Better Man
    book: Errol Hill
    music: Coleridge-Taylor Perkinson
    staging: Douglas Turner Ward

sets: Edward Burbridge
costumes: Bernard Johnson
choreography: Percival Borde
Productions:
(Off-Broadway) Opened July 2, 1969 for 23 performances
Reviews:
New York Times page 22, Jul 3, 1969
                II, page 1, Jul 13, 1969
                II, page 3, Jul 13, 1969
New Yorker 45:58, Jul 12, 1969

The Man from Cook's
    book: Henry Blossom; from the French of M. Ordon-
                     neau
    music: Raymond Hubbell
    staging: Ben Teal
Productions:
Opened March 25, 1912 for 32 performances
Reviews:
Blue Book 15:249-51, Jun 1912
Dramatic Mirror 67:2, Mar 13, 1912
                67:11, Mar 27, 1912
Green Book 7:1091-3+, Jun 1912
Munsey 47:285, May 1912
New York Dramatic News 55:26, Mar 30, 1912
Theatre Magazine 15:xiv+, May 1912

The Man from the East
    music: Stomu Yamash'ta
    words: Stomu Yamash'ta
    staging: Stomu Yamash'ta
    sets: Takeo Adachi and Chuck Murawski
Productions:
(Off-Broadway) Opened October 23, 1973 for 8 performances
Reviews:
New York Times page 18, Sep 22, 1973
                II, page 3, Oct 14, 1973
                page 38, Oct 24, 1973

Man of La Mancha
    book: Dale Wasserman; suggested by the works of
                     Cervantes
    music: Mitch Leigh
    lyrics: Joe Darion
    staging: Albert Marre
    sets: Howard Bay
    costumes: Howard Bay and Patton Campbell
    choreography: Jack Cole
Productions:
Opened November 22, 1965 for 2,328 performances
Opened June 22, 1972 for 140 performances
Reviews:
America 114:53, Jan 8, 1966

Dance Magazine 40:16, Jan 1966
Life 60:47-8+, Apr 8, 1966
Nation 201:484, Dec 13, 1965
National Review 18:1062-3, Oct 18, 1966
New York Theatre Critics' Reviews 1965:251
                                    1972:253
New York Times page 52, Nov 23, 1965
              page 42, Oct 5, 1966
              page 61, Nov 24, 1967
              page 44, Jan 5, 1968
              page 57, Mar 18, 1968
              II, page 27, Nov 17, 1968
              page 61, Dec 12, 1968
              page 40, Apr 2, 1969
              page 38, May 3, 1969
              page 70, Jan 25, 1970
              page 38, Feb 18, 1970
              page 31, Feb 2, 1971
              page 51, May 13, 1971
              page 38, Jun 16, 1971
              page 21, Jun 23, 1972
              page 55, Sep 13, 1972
New Yorker 41:106+, Dec 4, 1965
Saturday Review 48:51, Dec 11, 1965
Time 86:54, Dec 3, 1965
Vogue 147:34, Jan 15, 1966

The Man That Corrupted Hadleyburg
    book: Lewis Gardner; based on the story by Mark
                     Twain
    music: Daniel Paget
    lyrics: Lewis Gardner; based on the story by Mark
                     Twain
    staging: Bert Stimmel
    choreography: Bert Stimmel
Productions:
    (Off-Off-Broadway) Opened August 6, 1963 for 7 performances
    (Barnard-Columbia Summer Theatre Workshop)
No Reviews.

The Man Who Owns Broadway
    book: George M. Cohan
    staging: George M. Cohan
Productions:
    Opened October 11, 1909 for 128 performances
Reviews:
    Cosmopolitan 48:206, Jan 1910
    Dramatic Mirror 62:5, Oct 23, 1909
    Metropolitan Magazine 31:540-1, Jan 1910
    Theatre Magazine 10:xiv, Nov 1909
                     10:134, Nov 1909

Man with a Load of Mischief

book: Ben Tarver; adapted from the play by Ashley
                   Dukes
music: John Clifton
lyrics: John Clifton and Ben Tarver
staging: Tom Gruenewald
sets: Joan Larkey
costumes: Volavkova
choreography: Noel Schwartz
Productions:
   (Off-Broadway) Opened November 6, 1966 for 241 performances
Reviews:
   New York Times page 65, Nov 7, 1966
   New Yorker 42:178+, Nov 19, 1966

Manhattan Mary
   book: B. G. De Sylva, Lew Brown, Ray Henderson,
                   William K. Wells and George White
   music,
     lyrics: B. G. De Sylva, Lew Brown, Ray Henderson,
                   William K. Wells and George White
   staging: George White
Productions:
   Opened September 26, 1927 for 264 performances
Reviews:
   Life (New York) 90:19, Oct 27, 1927
   New York Times VII, page 2, Sep 4, 1927
                   page 35, Sep 6, 1927
                   page 30, Sep 27, 1927
                   page 3, Sep 28, 1927
                   page 26, Sep 29, 1927
                   IX, page 1, Oct 30, 1927
   Theatre Magazine 46:44, Dec 1927

Manhattan Vanities (see Belmont Varieties)

The Manhatters
   sketches: Aline Erlanger and George S. Oppenheimer
   music: Alfred Nathan
   lyrics: George S. Oppenheimer
   staging: Dave Bennett
Productions:
   Opened August 3, 1927 for 68 performances
Reviews:
   New York Times page 27, Jul 19, 1927
                   page 25, Aug 4, 1927
   Vogue 70:85+, Oct 1, 1927

Marching By
   book: Ernst Neubach, adapted by Harry Clarke and
                   Harry B. Smith
   music: Jean Gilbert, Mack Gordon and Harry Revel
   lyrics: Ernst Neubach
   staging: J. C. Huffman

Productions:
Opened March 3, 1932 for 12 performances
Reviews:
New York Times page 17, Mar 4, 1932

Mardi Gras!
book:	Sig Herzig
music:	Carmen Lombardo and John Jacob Loeb
lyrics:	Carmen Lombardo and John Jacob Loeb
staging:	June Taylor
sets:	George Jenkins
costumes:	Winn Morton
choreography:	June Taylor

Productions:
(Off-Broadway) Opened June 26, 1965 for 68 performances
(Off-Broadway) Opened July 8, 1966 for 54 performances
Reviews:
America 113:190, Aug 21, 1965
115:140, Aug 6, 1966
New York Times page 22, Jan 21, 1965
page 33, Jun 28, 1965
page 32, Jul 11, 1966
Saturday Review 49:48, Jul 30, 1966

Marie Dressler's All Star Gambol
arranged:	Marie Dressler
compiled:	Marie Dressler
music:	A. Baldwin Sloane

Productions:
Opened March 10, 1913 for 8 performances
No Reviews.

Maria Golovin
book:	Gian Carlo Menotti
music:	Gian Carlo Menotti
lyrics:	Gian Carlo Menotti
staging:	Gian Carlo Menotti
sets:	Rouben Ter-Arutunian
costumes:	Helene Pons

Productions:
Opened November 5, 1958 for 5 performances
Reviews:
Musical America 78:17, Oct 1958
78:18, Nov 15, 1958
Nation 187:395-6, Nov 22, 1958
New Republic 139:22-3, Nov 17, 1958
New York Theatre Critics' Reviews 1958:215
New York Times II, page 1, Nov 2, 1958
page 43, Nov 6, 1958
II, page 11, Nov 30, 1958
New Yorker 34:200-1, Nov 15, 1958
Newsweek 52:75, Nov 17, 1958
52:54, Sep 1, 1958

Saturday Review 41:43, Nov 22, 1958
Theatre Arts 43:68, Jan 1959
Time 72:40, Sep 1, 1958
    72:54+, Nov 17, 1958

Marinka
    book: George Marion, Jr. and Karl Farkas
    music: Emmerich Kalman
    lyrics: George Marion, Jr. and Karl Farkas
    staging: Hassard Short
    sets: Howard Bay
    costumes: Mary Grant
    choreography: Albertina Rasch
Productions:
    Opened July 18, 1945 for 165 performances
Reviews:
    Catholic World 161:509-10, Sep 1945
    Commonweal 42:381, Aug 3, 1945
    New York Theatre Critics' Reviews 1945:186+
    New York Times page 19, Jul 1945
              II, page 1, Sep 16, 1945
    New Yorker 21:40, Jul 28, 1945
    Newsweek 26:65, Jul 30, 1945
    Saturday Review 28:22-3, Sep 29, 1945
    Theatre Arts 29:551, Oct 1945
    Time 46:72, Jul 30, 1945

Marjolaine
    book: Catherine Chisholm Cushing; based on L. N.
                  Parker's Pomander Walk
    music: Hugo Felix
    lyrics: Brian Hooker
Productions:
    Opened January 24, 1922 for 136 performances
Reviews:
    Dramatic Mirror 95:63, Mar 1922
    Life (New York) 79:18, Feb 16, 1922
    New York Clipper 69:20, Feb 1, 1922
    New York Times page 16, Jan 25, 1922
              page 17, Feb 21, 1922
    Theatre Magazine 35:229, Apr 1922
              35:268, Apr 1922

Marjorie
    book: Fred Thompson, Clifford Grey and Harold
                  Atteridge
    music: Sigmund Romberg, Herbert Stothart, Philip
                  Kulkin and Stephen Jones
Productions:
    Opened August 11, 1924 for 144 performances
Reviews:
    New York Times page 12, Aug 12, 1924
    Theatre Magazine 40:15, Oct 1924

Marjorie Daw
       book: Sally Dixon Weiner
       music: Sally Dixon Weiner
       lyrics: Sally Dixon Weiner
       staging: Miriam Fond
Productions:
       (Off-Off-Broadway) Season of 1973-1974 (Theater at Noon)
No Reviews.

Marlene Dietrich
       staging: Burt Bacharach
Productions:
       Opened October 9, 1967 for 48 performances
       Opened October 3, 1968 for 67 performances
Reviews:
       Life 65:6, Nov 8, 1968
       New York Theatre Critics' Reviews 1967:267
       New York Times page 26, Aug 25, 1967
                        page 55, Sep 26, 1967
                        page 52, Oct 10, 1967
                        page 36, Oct 4, 1968
                        page 36, Dec 1, 1968
       Newsweek 70:113, Oct 23, 1967
       Time 90:84, Oct 20, 1967

Marriage à la Carte
       book: C. M. S. McLellan
       music: Ivan Caryll
       lyrics: C. M. S. McLellan
       staging: Austin Hurgon
Productions:
       Opened January 2, 1911 for 64 performances
Reviews:
       Columbian 3:1080-1, Mar 1911
       Dramatic Mirror 65:7, Jan 4, 1911
                        65:9, Feb 8, 1911
       Everybody's 24:561, Apr 1911
       Green Book Album 5:474-5+, Mar 1911
       New York Times page 12, Jan 3, 1911
       Red Book 16:956-60, Mar 1911
       Theatre Magazine 13:iii, Feb 1911
                        13:xv, Feb 1911
                        13:99, Mar 1911

The Marriage Market
       book: M. Brody and F. Martos; adapted for the
                          English stage by Gladys Unger
       music: Victor Jacobi
       lyrics: Arthur Anderson and Adrian Ross
       staging: Edward Royce
Productions:
       Opened September 22, 1913 for 80 performances
Reviews:

Dramatic Mirror 70:10, Sep 24, 1913
                          70:2, Oct 8, 1913
                          70:2, Nov 5, 1913
Green Book 10:966-7, Dec 1913
Munsey 49:878-79, Aug 1913
              50:476, Dec 1913
New York Dramatic News 58:18-19, Sep 27, 1913
New York Times page 11, Sep 16, 1913
                          page 11, Sep 23, 1913
Theatre Magazine 18:145, Nov 1913
                          18:156, Nov 1913

Mary

book:	Otto Harbach and Frank Mandel
music:	Lou Hirsch
lyrics:	Otto Harbach and Frank Mandel
staging:	George M. Cohan, Julian Mitchell and Sam Forrest

Productions:
Opened October 18, 1920 for 219 performances
Reviews:
Dramatic Mirror 82:733, Apr 17, 1920
                          page 743, Oct 23, 1920
Life (New York) 76:820-1, Nov 4, 1920
New York Clipper 68:19, Oct 27, 1920
New York Times page 12, Oct 19, 1920
Theatre Magazine 33:32-4, Jan 1921

Mary Jane McKane

book:	William Cary Duncan and Oscar Hammerstein II
music:	Herbert Stothart and Vincent Youmans
lyrics:	William Cary Duncan and Oscar Hammerstein II

Productions:
Opened December 25, 1923 for 151 performances
Reviews:
New York Times page 13, Dec 26, 1923
Theatre Magazine 39:19, Mar 1924

Mask and Gown

conceived by:	Leonard Sillman
continuity by:	Ronny Graham and Sidney Carroll
music and lyrics:	Ronny Graham, June Carroll, Arthur Siegel, Dorothea Freitag
staging:	Leonard Sillman
choreography:	Jim Russell

Productions:
Opened September 10, 1957 for 39 performances
Reviews:
New York Theatre Critics' Reviews 1957:259+
New York Times page 29, Sep 11, 1957
Theatre Arts 41:17-18, Nov 1957

Mata Hari   (see Ballad for a Firing Squad)

The Matinee Girl
    book: McElbert Moore and Bide Dudley
    music: Frank Grey
    lyrics: McElbert Moore and Bide Dudley
    staging: Oscar Eagle
Productions:
    Opened February 1, 1926 for 24 performances
Reviews:
    New York Times page 20, Feb 2, 1926

A Matinee Idol
    book: Armand Barnard
    music: Silvio Hein
    lyrics: E. Ray Goetz and Seymour Brown
Productions:
    Opened April 28, 1910 for 68 performances
Reviews:
    Dramatic Mirror 63:8, May 7, 1910
    Harper's Weekly 54:24, May 14, 1910
    Metropolitan Magazine 32:544, Jul 1910
    Theatre Magazine 11:177, Jun 1910

Maurice Chevalier (1932)
Productions:
    Opened February 9, 1932 for 17 performances
Reviews:
    Commonweal 15:470, Feb 24, 1932
    New York Times page 26, Feb 10, 1932

Maurice Chevalier (1947)
Productions:
    Opened March 10, 1947 for 46 performances
Reviews:
    Life 22:94, Apr 14, 1947
        23:67-8, Nov 10, 1947
    Newsweek 29:84, Mar 24, 1947
    Theatre Arts 31:49, Dec 1947
    Time 49:66, Mar 24, 1947

Maurice Chevalier (1948)
Productions:
    Opened February 29, 1948 for 33 performances
Reviews:
    New York Times page 16, Mar 1, 1948

Maurice Chevalier (1963)
    sketches: Maurice Chevalier
    songs: Alan Jay Lerner, Frederick Loewe, George
                     Gershwin, Johnny Mercer, George M. Cohan
                     and others
    staging: Maurice Chevalier

sets: Raoul Pene du Bois
Productions:
    Opened January 28, 1963 for 29 performances
Reviews:
    New York Times page 7, Jan 30, 1963
    Theatre Arts 46:13+, Nov 1962

Maurice Chevalier at 77
    sketches: Maurice Chevalier and others
    songs: Alan Jay Lerner, Frederick Loewe, Cole
                   Porter, Jerry Herman, Johnny Mercer and
                   others
Productions:
    Opened May 1, 1975 for 31 performances
Reviews:
    America 112:590, Apr 17, 1965
    Commonweal 82:155-7, Apr 23, 1965
    New York Theatre Critics' Reviews 1965:354
    New York Times page 26, Apr 2, 1965
    Newsweek 65:100-101, Apr 12, 1965
    Saturday Review 48:44, Apr 17, 1965

Maurice Chevalier in Songs and Impressions
    music: Maurice Chevalier, Fred Freed and others
    lyrics: Maurice Chevalier, Fred Freed and others
Productions:
    Opened September 28, 1955 for 46 performances
Reviews:
    America 94:81, Oct 15, 1955
    Catholic World 182:143, Nov 1955
    Commonweal 63:62-3, Oct 21, 1955
    New York Times page 38, Sep 29, 1955
    New Yorker 31:97, Oct 8, 1955
    Newsweek 46:75, Oct 10, 1955
    Theatre Arts 39:20, Dec 1955
    Time 66:53, Oct 10, 1955

Max Morath   (see An Evening with Max Morath at the Turn of the
    Century)

May Wine
    book: Frank Mandel, adapted from The Happy Alienist
                   by Eric von Stroheim and Wallace Smith
    music: Sigmund Romberg
    lyrics: Oscar Hammerstein II
    staging: Jose Ruben
    sets: Raymond Sovey
    costumes: Kay Morrison
Productions:
    Opened December 5, 1935 for 213 performances
Reviews:
    Catholic World 142:601, Feb 1936
    Commonweal 23:218, Dec 20, 1935

Literary Digest 120:20, Dec 21, 1935
New York Times page 23, Nov 23, 1935
             page 30, Dec 6, 1935
Newsweek 6:38, Dec 14, 1935
Theatre Arts 20:103, Feb 1936
Time 26:61, Dec 16, 1935

Mayflowers
    book: Clifford Grey; from a play by Arthur Richman
    music: Edward Kunneke
    lyrics: Clifford Grey
    staging: William J. Wilson and Joseph Santley
Productions:
    Opened November 24, 1925 for 81 performances
Reviews:
    New York Times page 14, Nov 25, 1925

Maytime
    book: Rida Johnson Young
    music: Sigmund Romberg
    lyrics: Rida Johnson Young
    staging: Edward P. Temple, Allen K. Foster and J. J.
                   Shubert
Productions:
    Opened August 16, 1917 for 492 performances
Reviews:
    Dramatic Mirror 77:8, Aug 25, 1917
    Green Book 20:202+, Aug 1918
    Life (New York) 70:283, Sep 6, 1917
    Munsey 62:305-6, Nov 1917
             64:427, Jul 1918
    New York Times page 7, Aug 17, 1917
                   IX, page 5, Aug 26, 1917
                   IV, page 5, Sep 2, 1917
    Stage 14:68-9, Aug 1937
    Theatre Magazine 26:205+, Oct 1917

Me and Juliet
    book: Oscar Hammerstein II
    music: Richard Rodgers
    lyrics: Oscar Hammerstein II
    staging: George Abbott
    sets: Jo Mielziner
    costumes: Irene Sharaff
    choreography: Robert Alton
Productions:
    Opened May 28, 1953 for 358 performances
    (Off-Broadway) Opened May 7, 1970 for 19 performances
Reviews:
    America 89:305, Jun 13, 1953
    Catholic World 177:308, Jul 1953
    Commonweal 58:273, Jun 19, 1953
    Life 34:89-90+, Jun 15, 1953

Look 17:34-6, Jun 16, 1953
Nation 176:530, Jun 20, 1953
New York Theatre Critics' Reviews 1953:298+
New York Times page 33, Apr 21, 1953
                    II, page 1, May 24, 1953
                    VI, page 28, May 24, 1953
                    page 17, May 29, 1953
                    II, page 1, Jun 7, 1953
                    page 42, May 15, 1970
New York Times Magazine pages 28-9, May 24, 1953
New Yorker 29:64+, Jun 6, 1953
Newsweek 42:60, Dec 21, 1953
              41:72, Jun 8, 1953
Saturday Review 36:37, Jul 11, 1953
                    36:26-7, Jun 13, 1953
Theatre Arts 37:15-16, Aug 1953
                37:28-9, Sep 1953
Time 61:93, Jun 8, 1953
Vogue 121:90-1, Jun 1953

The Me Nobody Knows
   book: Stephen M. Joseph; edited from the book The
                    Me Nobody Knows; and adapted by Robert H.
                    Livingston and Herb Schapiro
   music: Gary William Friedman
   lyrics: Will Holt
   staging: Robert H. Livingston
   sets: Clarke Dunham
   costumes: Patricia Quinn Stuart
   choreography: Patricia Birch
Productions:
   (Off-Broadway) Opened May 18, 1970 for 208 performances
   Opened December 18, 1970 for 586 performances
Reviews:
   America 122:638, Jun 13, 1970
   Commonweal 93:396, Jan 22, 1971
   Dance Magazine 44:80, Sep 1970
   Life 69:34-42, Sep 4, 1970
   Nation 210:701, Jun 8, 1970
   New Republic 162:312, Jun 13, 1970
   New York Theatre Critics' Reviews 1970:203
   New York Times II, page 22, Feb 22, 1970
                    page 42, May 19, 1970
                    II, page 3, May 31, 1970
                    II, page 36, Oct 18, 1970
                    page 48, Dec 18, 1970
                    page 16, Jan 1, 1971
                    page 51, Sep 8, 1971
                    page 58, Nov 12, 1971
   New Yorker 46:70+, May 30, 1970
   Newsweek 75:104, Jun 1, 1970

Mecca

  book: Oscar Asche
  music: Percy E. Fletcher
  staging: E. Lyall Swete
  choreography: Michel Fokine
Productions:
  Opened October 4, 1920 for 128 performances
Reviews:
  Dramatic Mirror page 635, Oct 9, 1920
  New York Clipper 68:19, Oct 13, 1920
  New York Times page 12, Oct 5, 1920
         page 14, Oct 13, 1920
         III, page 8, Oct 24, 1920
         VI, page 1, Oct 24, 1920
  Theatre Magazine 32:349, Dec 1920
         32:369, Dec 1920

The Medium (Presented with The Telephone)
  book: Gian-Carlo Menotti
  music: Gian-Carlo Menotti
  lyrics: Gian-Carlo Menotti
  staging: Gian-Carlo Menotti
  sets: Horace Armistead
  costumes: Horace Armistead
Productions:
  Opened May 1, 1947 for 212 performances
  Opened December 7, 1948 for 40 performances
  Opened July 19, 1950 for 110 performances
Reviews:
  Catholic World 165:265-6, Jun 1947
         171:469, Sep 1950
  Life 22:95-6+, Jun 9, 1947
  Nation 164:637+, May 4, 1947
  New York Theatre Critics' Reviews 1947:379
               1950:280
  New York Times page 28, May 2, 1947
         II, page 2, May 11, 1947
         page 26, Apr 30, 1948
         page 41, Dec 8, 1948
  New Yorker 23:50+, May 10, 1947
  Newsweek 29:76, Mar 3, 1947
  Saturday Review 30:22-4, May 31, 1947
         31:44, Feb 28, 1948
  School and Society 66:66, Jul 26, 1947
         69:86, Jan 29, 1949
  Theatre Arts 31:24, Apr 1947
        31:60, May 1947
  Time 49:69, Jun 30, 1947

Meet My Sister
  book: Harry Wagstaffe Gribble, from the French of
         Berr, Verneuil, and Blum
  music: Ralph Benatsky
  lyrics: Ralph Benatsky

310

staging: William Mollison
choreography: John Pierce
Productions:
Opened December 30, 1930 for 167 performances
Reviews:
Catholic World 132:596, Feb 1931
New York Times page 11, Dec 31, 1930
Theatre Magazine 53:60, Mar 1931

Meet Peter Grant
book: Elliot Arluck; based on Henrik Ibsen's Peer Gynt
music: Ted Harris
lyrics: Elliot Arluck
Productions:
(Off-Broadway) Season of 1960-1961
Reviews:
New York Times page 41, May 11, 1961
New Yorker 37:120, May 29, 1961

Meet the People
assembled: Henry Myers
sketches: Ben and Sol Barzman, Mortimer Offner, Edward
                 Eliscu, Danny Dare, Henry Blankfort, Bert
                 Lawrence, Sid Kuller, Ray Golden, Milt Gross,
                 Mike Quin, Arthur Ross
music: Jay Gorney and George Bassman
staging: Danny Dare
sets: Frederick Stover
costumes: Gerda Vanderneers and Kate Lawson
Productions:
Opened December 25, 1940 for 160 performances
Reviews:
Catholic World 152:598, Feb 1941
Collier's 107:24-5+, Mar 22, 1941
Life 8:39-41, Feb 26, 1940
New York Theatre Critics' Reviews 1940:170+
                                  1941:440+
New York Times IX, page 3, Oct 20, 1940
              page 22, Dec 26, 1940
              IX, page 3, Jan 5, 1941
              IX, page 1, Jan 12, 1941
              II, page 1, Aug 22, 1943
Theatre Arts 25:184, Mar 1941
             28:123, Feb 1944
             39:93, Jun 1955
Time 35:36, Jan 29, 1941

The Megilla of Itzik Manger
book: Schmuel Bunim, adapted from the Israeli ver-
                 sion by Schmuel Bunim, Hayim Hefer, Itzik
                 Manger, and Dov Seltzer
music: Dov Seltzer
staging: Schmuel Bunim

```
        sets:            Schlomo Vitkin
Productions:
    Opened October 9, 1968 for 78 performances
    Opened April 19, 1969 for 12 performances
Reviews:
    New York Times page 60, Oct 10, 1968
                     page 55, Apr 21, 1969
```

Melody
```
        book:            Edward Childs Carpenter
        music:           Sigmund Romberg
        lyrics:          Irving Caesar
        staging:         Bobby Connelly
        sets:            Joseph Urban
        choreography:    Bobby Connelly
Productions:
    Opened February 14, 1933 for 79 performances
Reviews:
    Arts and Decoration 38:59+, Apr 1933
    Catholic World 137:81-2, Apr 1933
    Nation 136:244, Mar 1, 1933
    New Outlook 161:48, Mar 1933
    New York Times page 17, Feb 15, 1933
    Newsweek 1:26, Feb 17, 1933
    Stage 10:16-17, Mar 1933
```

The Melting of Molly
```
        book:            Edgar Smith; from the novel of Maria Thompson
                         Davies
        music:           Sigmund Romberg
        lyrics:          Cyrus Wood
        staging:         Oscar Eagle
Productions:
    Opened December 30, 1918 for 88 performances
Reviews:
    Dramatic Mirror 80:48, Jan 11, 1919
    New York Times page 9, Dec 31, 1918
                     IV, page 2, Jan 5, 1919
    Theatre Magazine 29:80, Feb 1919
                     29:87, Feb 1919
```

Memorial Liquid Theatre (see The James Joyce Memorial Liquid Theatre)

Memphis Bound!
```
        book:            Albert Barker and Sally Benton, a swing version
                         of Gilbert and Sullivan's H. M. S. Pinafore
        music:           Don Walker and Clay Warnick
        lyrics:          Don Walker and Clay Warnick
        staging:         Robert Ross
        sets:            George Jenkins
        costumes:        Lucinda Ballard
        choreography:    Al White
```

Productions:
   Opened May 24, 1945 for 36 performances
Reviews:
   Catholic World 161:350, Jul 1945
   Commonweal 42:191, Jun 8, 1945
   Life 18:57-8+, Jun 25, 1945
   Nation 160:705, Jun 23, 1945
   New York Theatre Critics' Reviews 1945:207+
   New York Times page 23, May 25, 1945
                     II, page 1, Jun 10, 1945
   New Yorker 21:36+, Jun 2, 1945
   Newsweek 25:90, Jun 4, 1945
   Theatre Arts 29:389, Jul 1945
   Time 45:85, Jun 4, 1945

Memphis Store-Bought Teeth
   book: E. Don Alldredge
   music: William Fisher
   lyrics: D. Brian Wallach
   staging: Marvin Gordon
   sets: Robert O'Hearn
   costumes: William Pitkin
Productions:
   (Off-Broadway) Opened December 29, 1971 for one performance
Reviews:
   New York Times page 18, Dec 30, 1971

The Mental Cure   (see Doctor Selavy's Magic Theater)

Mercenary Mary
   book: William B. Friedlander and Isabel Leighton;
                      based on a farce by E. Nyitray and H. H.
                      Winslow
   music: William B. Friedlander and Con Conrad
   lyrics: William B. Friedlander and Con Conrad
   staging: William B. Friedlander
Productions:
   Opened April 13, 1925 for 32 performances
Reviews:
   New York Times page 27, Apr 14, 1925
   Theatre Magazine 42:7, Dec 1925

Mercy Drop
   book: Robert Patrick
   music: Richard Weinstock
   staging: Hugh Gittens
Productions:
   (Off-Off-Broadway) Opened February 4, 1973 (Worshop of the
   Players' Art)
No Reviews.

Merry-Go-Round
   book: Morrie Ryskind and Howard Dietz

Merry Malones

    music: Henry Souvaine and Jay Gorney
    lyrics: Morrie Ryskind and Howard Dietz
    staging: Allan Dinehart
Productions:
    Opened May 31, 1927 for 136 performances
Reviews:
    Bookman 65:705-6, Aug 1927
    New York Times page 25, Jun 1, 1927
                    VII, page 1, Jun 5, 1927
                    page 19, Jul 5, 1927
                    VII, page 1, Jul 10, 1927
    Theatre Magazine 46:18, 1927
    Vogue 70:66, Aug 15, 1927

Merry Malones
    book: George M. Cohan
    staging: Edward Royce
Productions:
    Opened September 26, 1927 for 192 performances
    Opened Season of 1927-28 for 16 performances
Reviews:
    National Magazine 56:87+, Oct 1927
    New York Times VIII, page 1, Sep 11, 1927
                    page 30, Sep 27, 1927
    Theatre Magazine 46:74, Nov 1927

Merry, Merry
    book: Harlan Thompson
    music: Harry Archer
    lyrics: Harlan Thompson
    staging: Harlan Thompson
Productions:
    Opened September 24, 1925 for 176 performance
Reviews:
    New York Times page 24, Sep 25, 1925
    Theatre Magazine 41:16, Feb 1925

The Merry Whirl
    book: Don Roth
    music: Leo Edwards
    choreography: Jack Mason
Productions:
    Opened May 30, 1910 for 24 performances
No Reviews.

The Merry World
    music: Maurice Rubens, J. Fred Coots, Herman Hup-
                        feld and Sam Timber
    lyrics: Clifford Grey
    staging: J. J. Shubert
Productions:
    Opened June 8, 1926 for 85 performances
Reviews:

314 New York Times page 18, Jun 9, 1926
                    VII, page 1, Jun 13, 1926
                    page 15, Jul 30, 1926
Theatre Magazine 44:15, Aug 1926

Messin' Around
    music: Jimmy Johnson
    lyrics: Perry Bradford
    staging: Louis Isquith and Eddie Rector
Productions:
Opened April 22, 1929 for 33 performances
Reviews:
    Life (New York) 93:28, May 17, 1929
    New York Times page 26, Apr 23, 1929
                    page 27, May 23, 1929
    Theatre Magazine 50:41, Jul 1929

Mexican Hayride
    book: Herbert and Dorothy Fields
    music: Cole Porter
    lyrics: Cole Porter
    staging: Hassard Short
    sets: George Jenkins
    costumes: Mary Grant
    choreography: Paul Haakon
Productions:
Opened January 28, 1944 for 481 performances
Reviews;
    Catholic World 158:586, Mar 1944
    Collier's 113:18-21, Feb 5, 1944
    Commonweal 39:446, Feb 18, 1944
    Life 16:83-4+, Feb 21, 1944
    Nation 158:197, Feb 12, 1944
    New York Theatre Critics' Reviews 1944:271+
    New York Times page 9, Jan 29, 1944
                    II, page 1, Feb 6, 1944
                    II, page 8, Mar 26, 1944
                    II, page 1, Jul 2, 1944
    Saturday Review 27:18, Feb 19, 1944
    Theatre Arts 28:202+, Apr 1944
    Time 43:94, Feb 7, 1944

Mexicana
    staging: Celestino Gorostiza
    sets: Julio Castellanos
    costumes: Augustin Lazo
Productions:
Opened April 21, 1939 for 35 performances
Reviews:
    Catholic World 149:346-7, Jun 1939
    Modern Music 16:268-9, May-Jun 1939
    Nation 148:538, May 6, 1939
    New York Times page 14, Apr 22, 1939

X, page 3, May 7, 1939
Theatre Arts 28:404, Jun 1939

Michael Todd's Peep Show
   sketches: Bobby Clark, H. I. Phillips, William Roos,
                         Billy K. Wells
   music and
   lyrics: Bhumibal and Chakraband, Sammy Fain and
                         Herb Magidson, Harold Rome, Raymond Scott,
                         Sammy Stept and Dan Shapiro, Jule Styne and
                         Bob Hilliard
   staging: Hassard Short
   sets: Howard Bay
   costumes: Irene Sharaff
   choreography: James Starbuck
Productions:
   Opened June 28, 1950 for 278 performances
Reviews:
   Life 29:67-70, Jul 10, 1950
   New Republic 123:21, Jul 17, 1950
   New York Theatre Critics' Reviews 1950:285+
   New York Times page 34, Jun 7, 1950
               VI, page 28, Jun 18, 1950
               VI, page 29, Jun 18, 1950
               II, page 2, Jun 25, 1950
               page 37, Jun 29, 1950
               II, page 1, Jul 9, 1950
   New York Times Magazine pages 28-9, Jun 18, 1950
   New Yorker 26:44+, Jul 8, 1950
   Newsweek 36:77, Jul 10, 1950
   Theatre Arts 34:26-31+, Jul 1950
               34:9, Sep 1950
   Time 56:58, Jul 10, 1950
          56:59-60, Jul 17, 1950

The Midnight Girl
   book: Paul Herve; American version by Adolph Philipp
                         and Edward A. Paulton
   music: Jean Briquet and Adolph Philipp
   staging: Ben Teal
Productions:
   Opened February 23, 1914 for 104 performances
Reviews:
   Dramatic Mirror 71:6-7, Feb 25, 1914
                   71:4, Mar 11, 1914
                   71:2, Mar 18, 1914
   Green Book 11:718-19, May 1914
             11:776-7, May 1914
   Munsey 51:581-8, Apr 1914
   New York Times page 12, Feb 24, 1914
   Theatre Magazine 19:182, Apr 1914
                    19:212, Apr 1914

The Midnight Rounders of 1921
    music: Jean Schwartz and Lew Pollack
    lyrics: Alfred Bryan
    staging: J. J. Shubert
Productions:
    Opened February 5, 1921 for 120 performances
Reviews:
    Theatre Magazine 33:264, Apr 1921

Midnight Whirl (see Morris Gest Midnight Whirl)

Milk and Honey
    book: Don Appell
    music: Jerry Herman
    lyrics: Jerry Herman
    staging: Albert Marre
    sets: Howard Bay
    costumes: Miles White
    choreography: Donald Saddler
Productions:
    Opened October 10, 1961 for 543 performances
Reviews:
    America 106:376+, Dec 9, 1961
    Commonweal 75:154, Nov 3, 1961
    Dance Magazine 35:28-30, Nov 1961
    Nation 193:361, Nov 4, 1961
    New York Theatre Critics' Reviews 1961:238+
    New York Times page 52, Oct 11, 1961
    New Yorker 37:130, Oct 21, 1961
    Newsweek 58:60+, Oct 23, 1961
    Saturday Review 44:32, Nov 4, 1961
    Theatre Arts 45:10-11, Dec 1961
    Time 78:64, Oct 20, 1961

The Mimic World
    dialogue: Harold Atteridge, James Hussey and Owen
                     Murphy
    music: Jean Schwartz, Lew Pollack and Owen Murphy
    staging: Allen K. Foster
Productions:
    Opened August 15, 1921 for 27 performances
Reviews:
    New York Times page 22, Aug 14, 1921
                   page 9, Aug 18, 1921
    Theatre Magazine 34:279, Oct 1921

Minnie Field (see American Legend)

Minnie's Boys
    book: Arthur Marx and Robert Fisher; suggested by
                     the life of the Marx Brothers
    music: Larry Grossman
    lyrics: Hal Hackady

    staging: Stanley Prager
    sets: Peter Wexler
    costumes: Donald Brooks
    choreography: Marc Breaux
Productions:
    Opened March 26, 1970 for 76 performances
Reviews:
    Commonweal 92:222, May 15, 1970
    Dance Magazine 44:84, Jun 1970
    New York Theatre Critics' Reviews 1970:325
    New York Times II, page 1, Mar 1, 1970
                    page 27, Mar 27, 1970
                    II, page 3, Apr 5, 1971
                    II, page 16, May 17, 1970
    New Yorker 46:61, Apr 4, 1970
    Newsweek 75:98-9, Apr 6, 1970
    Saturday Review 53:20, Apr 11, 1970
    Time 95:98+, Apr 13, 1970

Miss Daisy
    book: Philip Bartholomae
    music: Silvio Hein
    lyrics: Philip Bartholomae
    staging: Philip Bartholomae
Productions:
    Opened September 9, 1914 for 29 performances
Reviews:
    Dramatic Mirror 72:8, Sep 16, 1914
    Green Book 12:905, Nov 1914
    New York Times page 9, Sep 10, 1914
    Theatre Magazine 20:201, Nov 1914
                     20:206, Nov 1914

Miss Emily Adam
    material: James Lipton and Paul E. Davies; based on
                     Winthrop Palmer's Rosemary and the Planet
Productions:
    (Off-Broadway) Season of 1959-60
Reviews:
    New York Times page 43, Mar 30, 1960
                    page 12, Apr 15, 1960

Miss Information
    book: Paul Dickey and Charles W. Goddard
    music: Jerome Kern
    staging: Robert Milton
Productions:
    Opened October 5, 1915 for 47 performances
Reviews:
    Dramatic Mirror 74:8, Oct 16, 1915
    New York Dramatic News 61:18, Oct 9, 1915
    New York Times page 11, Oct 6, 1915
    Smart Set 47:146-7, Dec 1915

Theatre Magazine 22:223-4+, Nov 1915

Miss Jack
    book: Mark E. Swan
    music: William F. Peters
    lyrics: Mark E. Swan
Productions:
Opened September 4, 1911 for 16 performances
Reviews:
    Dramatic Mirror 66:11, Sep 6, 1911
                  66:4, Sep 13, 1911
    Green Book Album 6:925-7, Nov 1911
                  6:965, Nov 1911
    Life (New York) 58:479, Sep 21, 1911
    Theatre Magazine 14:113, Oct 1911

Miss Liberty
    book: Robert E. Sherwood
    music: Irving Berlin
    lyrics: Irving Berlin
    staging: Moss Hart
    sets: Oliver Smith
    costumes: Motley
    choreography: Jerome Robbins
Productions:
Opened July 15, 1949 for 308 performances
Reviews:
    Catholic World 170:67-8, Oct 1949
    Commonweal 50:414, Aug 5, 1949
    Good Housekeeping 129:121, Dec 1949
    Holiday 6:16-17+, Nov 1949
    Life 27:56-8, Jul 4, 1949
    New Republic 121:27-8, Aug 1, 1949
    New York Theatre Critics' Reviews 1949:279+
    New York Times page 23, Feb 13, 1949
                   VI, page 16, May 29, 1949
                   page 26, Jun 14, 1949
                   page 39, Jun 15, 1949
                   page 6, Jul 16, 1949
                   II, page 6, Aug 7, 1949
    New York Times Magazine pages 16-17, May 29, 1949
                         pages 22-3, Jun 26, 1949
    New Yorker 25:18, Jun 25, 1949
              25:44, Jul 23, 1949
    Newsweek 34:70-1, Jul 25, 1949
    Saturday Review 32:28-9, Aug 13, 1949
    Theatre Arts 33:10, Sep 1949
    Time 54:66, Jul 25, 1949

Miss Millions
    book: R. H. Burnside
    music: Raymond Hubbell
Productions:

Opened December 9, 1919 for 47 performances
Reviews:
    Dramatic Mirror 80:1981, Dec 25, 1919
    New York Times page 11, Dec 10, 1919
                VIII, page 2, Dec 14, 1919

Ms. Nefertiti
    book: Tom Eyen
    music: Ilene Berson and Tom Eyen
    staging: Tom Eyen
Productions:
    (Off-Off-Broadway) Opened February 9, 1973 (La Mama Experimental Theatre Club)
No Reviews.

Miss 1917
    book: Guy Bolton and P. G. Wodehouse
    music: Victor Herbert
    lyrics: Guy Bolton and P. G. Wodehouse
    staging: Ned Wayburn
Productions:
Opened November 5, 1917 for 48 performances
Reviews:
    Dramatic Mirror 77:5, Nov 17, 1917
                 77:5, Dec 8, 1917
    Green Book 19:4+, Jan 1918
    New York Dramatic News 64:11, Nov 10, 1917
    New York Times page 11, Nov 6, 1917
                VIII, page 6, Nov 11, 1917
    Theatre Magazine 27:350-51, Dec 1917

Miss Springtime
    book: Guy Bolton
    music: Emmerich Kalman
    staging: Herbert Gresham
Productions:
Opened September 25, 1916 for 224 performances
Reviews:
    Dramatic Mirror 76:7, Sep 30, 1916
                 76:5, Oct 7, 1916
                 76:1, Oct 14, 1916
    Green Book 16:974-5+, Dec 1916
    Leslie's Weekly 124:327, Mar 22, 1917
    New York Dramatic News 63:3, Sep 30, 1916
    New York Times page 9, Sep 26, 1916
    Theatre Magazine 24:280+, Nov 1916

Mr. Lode of Koal
    book: J. A. Shipp and Alexander Rogers
    music: J. Rosamond and Bert A. Williams
    lyrics: J. A. Shipp and Alexander Rogers
Productions:
Opened November 1, 1909 for 40 performances

No Reviews.

Mr. President
    book: Howard Lindsay and Russel Crouse
    music: Irving Berlin
    lyrics: Irving Berlin
    staging: Joshua Logan
    sets: Jo Mielziner
    costumes: Theoni V. Aldredge
    choreography: Peter Gennaro
Productions:
    Opened October 20, 1962 for 265 performances
Reviews:
    America 107:1230, Dec 8, 1962
    Business Week page 31, Sep 29, 1962
    Commonweal 77:279, Dec 7, 1962
    Dance Magazine 36:98, Dec 1962
    National Review 14:78-9, Jan 29, 1963
    New York Theatre Critics' Reviews 1962:238+
    New York Times page 18, Aug 29, 1962
               page 36, Sep 26, 1962
               II, page 1, Oct 14, 1962
               page 34, Oct 22, 1962
               page 38, May 29, 1963
    New Yorker 38:147, Oct 27, 1962
    Newsweek 60:74, Nov 5, 1962
    Reporter 27:43, Dec 20, 1962
    Saturday Review 45:40, Nov 3, 1962
    Theatre Arts 46:14-16, Nov 1962
             46:14, Dec 1962
    Time 80:62, Sep 7, 1962
         80:82, Nov 2, 1962
    Vogue 140:144-7+, Nov 1, 1962

Mr. Strauss Goes to Boston
    book: Leonard L. Levenson from a story by Alfred
                    Greenwald and Geza Herczeg
    music: Robert Stolz
    lyrics: Robert Sour
    staging: Felix Brentano
    sets: Stewart Chaney
    costumes: Walter Florell
    choreography: George Balanchine
Productions:
    Opened September 6, 1945 for 12 performances
Reviews:
    Catholic World 162:70, Oct 1945
    New York Theatre Critics' Reviews 1945:180+
    New York Times page 20, Sep 7, 1945
               II, page 1, Sep 16, 1945
    New Yorker 21:46, Sep 15, 1945
    Newsweek 26:103, Sep 17, 1945
    Time 46:74, Sep 17, 1945

Mr. Wonderful

book:	Joseph Stein and Will Glickman
music:	Jerry Bock, Larry Holofcener, George Weiss
lyrics:	Jerry Bock, Larry Holofcener, George Weiss
staging:	Jack Donohue
sets:	Oliver Smith
costumes:	Robert Mackintosh
choreography:	Jack Donohue

Productions:
Opened March 22, 1956 for 383 performances
Reviews:
America 95:42, Apr 7, 1956
Catholic World 183:150, May 1956
New York Theatre Critics' Reviews 1956:339+
New York Times page 23, Mar 23, 1956
New Yorker 32:62+, Mar 31, 1956
Saturday Review 39:34, Apr 14, 1956
Theatre Arts 40:14, Jun 1956
Time 67:91, Apr 2, 1956

Mixed Doubles

book:	Rod Warren
music:	Michael Cohen and Edward Morris
lyrics:	Rod Warren
staging:	Robert Audy
choreography:	Robert Audy

Productions:
(Off-Broadway) Opened October 19, 1966 for 428 performances
No Reviews.

Mod Donna

book:	Myrna Lamb
music:	Susan Hulsman Bingham
lyrics:	Myrna Lamb
staging:	Joseph Papp
costumes:	Milo Morrow
choreography:	Ze-eva Cohen

Productions:
(Off-Broadway) Opened April 24, 1970 for 56 performances
Reviews:
Harper's 103:6+, Jul 1970
New York Times page 60, Mar 26, 1970
             page 48, May 4, 1970
             II, page 1, May 10, 1970
New Yorker 46:107, May 16, 1970
Newsweek 75:121, May 18, 1970
Time 95:62, May 25, 1970

A Modern Eve

book:	Adapted by William M. Hough and Benjamin Hapgood Burt
music:	Jean Gilbert and Victor Hallender
choreography:	Julian Alfred

Productions:
    Opened May 3, 1915 for 56 performances
Reviews:
    Dramatic Mirror 73:8, May 5, 1915
                    73:2, May 12, 1915
                    73:2, May 26, 1915
                    73:2, Jun 2, 1915
    Green Book 14:63-4, Jul 1915
               14:192, Jul 1915
    Life (New York) 65:860-1, May 13, 1915
    New York Dramatic News 61:17, May 8, 1915
    Theatre Magazine 21:279+, Jun 1915

A Modern Hamlet
        book: John Guenther
        music: Dennis Deal
        staging: Michael Dennis Moore
Productions:
    (Off-Off-Broadway) Opened April 3, 1973 (Workshop of the
    Players' Art)
No Reviews.

Molly
        book: Louis Garfinkle and Leonard Adelson; based on
                        characters from "The Goldbergs" by Gertrude
                        Berg
        music: Jerry Livingston
        lyrics: Leonard Adelson and Mack David
        staging: Alan Arkin
        sets: Marsha L. Eck
        costumes: Carrie F. Robbins
        choreography: Grover Dale
Productions:
    Opened November 1, 1973 for 68 performances
Reviews:
    New York Theatre Critics' Reviews 1973:206
    New York Times page 45, Jun 11, 1973
                    page 28, Aug 9, 1973
                    page 46, Nov 2, 1973
                    II, page 1, Nov 11, 1973
                    page 21, Dec 28, 1973
    New Yorker 49:114, Nov 12, 1973
    Newsweek 82:81, Nov 12, 1973
    Time 102:97, Nov 19, 1973

Molly Darling
        book: Otto Harbach and William Cary Duncan
        music: Tom Johnstone
        lyrics: Phil Cook
        staging: Julian Mitchell
Productions:
    Opened September 1, 1922 for 99 performances
Reviews:

New York Clipper 70:39, Oct 4, 1922
New York Times page 10, Sep 2, 1922

Money
    book: David Axlerod and Tom Whedon
    music: Sam Pottle
    lyrics: David Axlerod and Tom Whedon
    staging: Ronny Graham
    sets: Peter Harvey
    costumes: Mr. William
Productions:
    (Off-Broadway) Opened July 9, 1963 for 214 performances
No Reviews.

Montand, Yves (see An Evening with Yves Montand)

Monte Cristo, Jr.
    book: Harold Atteridge
    music: Sigmund Romberg and Jean Schwartz
    lyrics: Harold Atteridge
    staging: J. C. Huffman
Productions:
    Opened February 12, 1919 for 254 performances
Reviews:
    Dramatic Mirror 80:305, Mar 1, 1919
    Forum 61:506, Apr 1919
    New York Times page 13, Feb 13, 1919
    Theatre Magazine 29:201, Apr 1919
                       29:208, Apr 1919

Month of Sundays
    book: Romeo Muller; based on his play The Great
                     Git-Away
    music: Maury Laws
    lyrics: Jules Bass
    staging: Stone Widney
    sets: Robert T. Williams
    costumes: Sara Brook
Productions:
    (Off-Broadway) Opened September 16, 1968 for 8 performances
Reviews:
    New York Times page 50, Sep 17, 1968
    New Yorker 44:89, Sep 28, 1968

Moonlight
    book: William Le Baron
    music: Con Conrad
    lyrics: William B. Friedlander
Productions:
    Opened January 30, 1924 for 149 performances
Reviews:
    New York Times page 13, Jan 31, 1924

324   Morath, Max

Morath, Max   (see An Evening with Max Morath at the Turn of the
Century)

Morning Sun
      book: Fred Ebb; based on a story by Mary Deasy
      music: Paul Klein
      lyrics: Fred Ebb
      staging: Daniel Petrie
      sets: Eldon Elder
      costumes: Patricia Zipprodt
      choreography: Donald Saddler
Productions:
   (Off-Broadway) Opened October 6, 1963 for 9 performances
Reviews:
   New York Times page 36, Oct 7, 1963
                        page 34, Oct 14, 1963
   Theatre Arts 48:11+, Jan 1964

Morris Gest Midnight Whirl
      music: George Gershwin
      lyrics: Budd De Sylva and John Henry Mears
      staging: Julian Mitchell
Productions:
   Opened December 27, 1919
Reviews:
   New York Times page 7, Dec 29, 1919

The Most Happy Fella
      book: Frank Loesser, based on Sidney Howard's play
                         They Knew What They Wanted
      music: Frank Loesser
      lyrics: Frank Loesser
      staging: Joseph Anthony
      sets: Jo Mielziner
      costumes: Motley
      choreography: Dania Krupska
Productions:
   Opened May 3, 1956 for 676 performances
   Opened February 10, 1959 for 16 performances
   Opened May 11, 1966 for 15 performances
Reviews:
   America 95:209, May 19, 1956
             100:670, Mar 7, 1959
   Catholic World 183:309, Jul 1956
   Christian Century 73:1453, Dec 12, 1956
   Colliers 138:8, Jul 6, 1956
   Commonweal 64:226, Jun 1, 1956
   Dance Magazine 40:25, Jul 1966
   Holiday 20:75+, Oct 1956
   Life 40:68+, Apr 23, 1956
        60:18, Jun 17, 1966
   Musical America 76:13, Jul 1956
   Nation 182:439, May 19, 1956

New York Theatre Critics' Reviews 1956:308+
New York Times VI, page 62, Apr 22, 1956
                II, page 1, Apr 29, 1956
                page 20, May 4, 1956
                II, page 1, May 13, 1956
                II, page 7, Jun 10, 1956
                page 50, Feb 11, 1959
                page 25, Apr 22, 1960
                page 55, May 12, 1966
New York Times Magazine page 62, Apr 22, 1956
New Yorker 32:84+, May 12, 1956
Newsweek 47:82, May 14, 1956
Reporter 14:34-5, Jun 28, 1956
Saturday Review 39:46, May 19, 1956
                39:39, Aug 25, 1956
Theatre Arts 40:17-19, Jul 1956
              43:67-8, Apr 1959
Time 67:102, May 14, 1956

Mother Earth
    sketches: Ron Thronson
    music: Toni Shearer
    lyrics: Ron Thronson
    staging: Ray Golden
    sets: Alan Kimmel
    costumes: Mary McKinley
    choreography: Lynn Morris
Productions:
    Opened October 19, 1972 for 12 performances
Reviews:
    National Review 23:1481, Dec 31, 1971
    New York Theatre Critics' Reviews 1972:214
    New York Times page 33, Oct 20, 1972
    New Yorker 48:119, Oct 28, 1972
    Time 100:83, Nov 6, 1972

The Motor Girl
    book: Charles J. Campbell and Ralph M. Skinner
    music: Julian Edwards
    lyrics: Charles J. Campbell and Ralph M. Skinner
    staging: Frank Smithson
Productions:
    Opened June 15, 1909 for 95 performances
Reviews:
    Theatre Magazine 10:36, Aug 9, 1909
                     10:63, Aug 9, 1909

The Muffled Report
    material: Peter Cook
Productions:
    (Off-Broadway) Opened April 8, 1964 for 92 performances
No Reviews.

Murder at the Vanities
    book: Earl Carroll and Rufus King
    music and
    lyrics: John Green, Edward Heyman, Richard Meyers,
                     Ned Washington, Victor Young, Herman Hupfeld,
                     John J. Loeb, Paul Francis Webster
    staging: Earl Carroll
Productions:
    Opened September 8, 1933 for 207 performances
Reviews:
    Nation 137:362-3, Sep 27, 1933
    New Outlook 162:49, Oct 1933
    New York Times page 20, Aug 31, 1933
                     page 22, Sep 13, 1933
    Theatre Arts 17:839, Nov 1933

Murray Anderson's Almanac
    book: Noel Coward, Rube Goldberg, Ronald Jeans,
                     Paul Gerard Smith, Harry Ruskin, John McGowan,
                     Peter Arno, Ed Wynn
    music: Milton Agar and Henry Sullivan
    lyrics: Jack Yellen
    staging: John Murray Anderson, William Holbrook, Harry
                     Ruskin
Productions:
    Opened August 14, 1929 for 69 performances
Reviews:
    Life (New York) 94:24, Sep 6, 1929
    New York Times VIII, page 1, Aug 4, 1929
                     page 20, Aug 15, 1929
    Outlook 152:712, Aug 28, 1929
    Theatre Magazine 50:42, Oct 1929

Murray, Ken   (see Ken Murray)

Music Box Revue (1921)
    book: Irving Berlin
    music: Irving Berlin
    lyrics: Irving Berlin
    staging: Hassard Short
    choreography: I. Tarasoff
Productions:
    Opened September 22, 1921 for 440 performances
Reviews:
    Independent 107:856, Dec 31, 1921
    Life (New York) 78:18, Oct 20, 1921
    New York Times page 18, Sep 23, 1921
    Theatre Magazine 34:387, Dec 1921

Music Box Revue (1922)
    book: Irving Berlin
    music: Irving Berlin
    lyrics: Irving Berlin

staging: Hassard Short
choreography: William Seabury
Productions:
Opened October 23, 1922 for 273 performances
Reviews:
Forum 68:1037-8, Dec 1922
New York Times page 18, Oct 24, 1922

Music Box Revue (1923)
book: Irving Berlin
music: Irving Berlin
lyrics: Irving Berlin
staging: Hassard Short
Productions:
Opened September 22, 1923 for 273 performances
Reviews:
New York Times page 5, Sep 24, 1923
Theatre Magazine 38:54, Nov 1923

Music Box Revue (1924)
book: Irving Berlin
music: Irving Berlin
lyrics: Irving Berlin
staging: John Murray Anderson
Productions:
Opened December 1, 1924 for 184 performances
Reviews:
New York Times page 23, Dec 2, 1924
Theatre Magazine 41:19, Feb 1925

Music Hall Varieties   (see George White's Music Hall Varieties)

Music Hath Charms
book: Rowland Leigh, George Rosener, John Shubert
music: Rudolf Friml
lyrics: Rowland Leigh and John Shubert
staging: George Rosener
sets: Watson Barratt
choreography: Alex Yakovleff
Productions:
Opened December 29, 1934 for 29 performances
Reviews:
Catholic World 140:601, Feb 1935
New York Times page 8, Dec 31, 1934

Music in May
book: Fanny Todd Mitchell, adapted from the original
                        by Heinz Merley and Kurt Breuer
music: Emile Berte and Maury Rubens
lyrics: J. Kiern Brennan
staging: Lew Morton and Stanley Logan
Productions:
Opened April 1, 1929 for 80 performances

Reviews:
    New York Times IX, page 1, Jan 7, 1929
                   page 29, Apr 2, 1929

Music in My Heart
    book: Patsy Ruth Miller, based on the life of
                       Tchaikovsky
    music: Franz Steininger, adapted from Tchaikovsky
    lyrics: Forman Brown
    staging: Hassard Short
    sets: Alvin Colt
    costumes: Alvin Colt
    choreography: Ruth Page
Productions:
    Opened October 2, 1947 for 125 performances
Reviews:
    Catholic World 166:171, Nov 1947
    New York Theatre Critics' Reviews 1947:324+
    New York Times II, page 1, Sep 28, 1947
                   page 30, Oct 3, 1947
                   II, page 6, Nov 9, 1947
                   II, page 4, Dec 21, 1947
    New Yorker 23:54, Oct 11, 1947
    Newsweek 30:81, Oct 13, 1947
    School and Society 66:508-9, Dec 27, 1947
    Theatre Arts 31:16, Nov 1947

Music in the Air
    book: Oscar Hammerstein II
    music: Jerome Kern
    lyrics: Oscar Hammerstein II
    staging: Oscar Hammerstein II and Jerome Kern
    sets: Joseph Urban
Productions:
    Opened November 8, 1932 for 342 performances
    Opened October 8, 1951 for 56 performances
Reviews:
    Arts and Decoration 38:50, Jan 1933
    Catholic World 136:462-3, Jan 1933
                  174:228, Dec 1951
    Commonweal 17:131, Nov 30, 1932
                55:62, Oct 26, 1951
    New Republic 125:22, Nov 12, 1951
    New York Theatre Critics' Reviews 1951:215
    New York Times IX, page 3, Oct 23, 1932
                   page 28, Nov 9, 1932
                   IX, page 1, Nov 20, 1932
                   page 11, May 20, 1933
                   II, page 1, Oct 7, 1951
                   page 32, Oct 9, 1951
                   II, page 1, Oct 21, 1951
    New Yorker 27:60+, Oct 20, 1951
    Newsweek 38;93, Oct 22, 1951

Stage 10:32-3, Dec 1932
Theatre Arts 17:4-5, Jan 1933
     35:3+, Dec 1951
Time 58:56, Oct 22, 1951

The Music Man
   book: Meredith Willson
   music: Meredith Willson
   lyrics: Meredith Willson
   staging: Morton Da Costa
   sets: Howard Bay
   costumes: Raoul Pene du Bois
   choreography: Onna White
Productions:
  Opened December 19, 1957 for 1,375 performances
  Opened June 16, 1965 for 15 performances
Reviews:
  America 98:550, Feb 8, 1958
  Catholic World 186:468, Mar 1958
  Dance Magazine 32:17, Jan 1958
         39:24, Aug 1965
  Life 44:103-6, Jan 20, 1958
  Look 22:53-5, Mar 4, 1958
  Nation 186:126, Feb 8, 1959
  New York Theatre Critics' Reviews 1957:146+
  New York Times VI, page 128, Dec 1, 1957
       II, page 3, Dec 15, 1957
       page 31, Dec 20, 1957
       II, page 16, Jan 19, 1958
       page 22, Aug 20, 1958
       II, page 1, Sep 28, 1958
       page 17, Mar 18, 1961
       page 32, Mar 21, 1961
       page 26, Jun 17, 1965
  New Yorker 33:48+, Jan 4, 1958
  Newsweek 50:41, Dec 30, 1957
  Saturday Review 41:21, Jan 4, 1958
  Theatre Arts 42:10-11, Mar 1958
  Time 70:62-4, Dec 30, 1957
     72:42-6, Jul 21, 1958

Music! Music!
   commentary: Alan Jay Lerner
   staging: Martin Charnin
   sets: David Chapman
   costumes: Theoni V. Aldredge
Productions:
  Opened April 11, 1974 for 37 performances
Reviews:
  New York Theatre Critics' Reviews 1974:314
  New York Times page 22, Apr 12, 1974
       II, page 1, Apr 21, 1974
  New Yorker 50:103, Apr 22, 1974

Time 103:84, Apr 22, 1974

A Musical Tragedy   (see Lady Day: A Musical Tragedy)

My Best Girl
    book: Channing Pollock and Rennold Wolf
    music: Clifton Crawford and Augustus Barratt
    lyrics: Channing Pollock and Rennold Wolf
    staging: Sidney Ellison
Productions:
    Opened September 12, 1912 for 68 performances
Reviews:
    Blue Book 16:470-73, Jan 1913
    Dramatic Mirror 68:7+, Sep 18, 1912
                68:2, Sep 25, 1912
    Green Book 8:1005, Dec 1912
    Harper's Weekly 56:21, Oct 1912
    Munsey 48:353-4, Nov 1912
    New York Dramatic News 56:12, Sep 21, 1912
    Red Book 20:381-2+, Dec 1912
    Theatre Magazine 16:iii, Oct 1912
                16:xiv, Oct 1912

My Darlin' Aida
    book: Charles Friedman, based on Verdi's opera
    music: Giuseppe Verdi
    staging: Charles Friedman
    sets: Lemuel Ayers
    costumes: Lemuel Ayers
    choreography: Hanya Holm
Productions:
    Opened October 27, 1952 for 89 performances
Reviews:
    Catholic World 176:228, Dec 1952
    Commonweal 57:164, Nov 21, 1952
    Musical America 72:9, Dec 15, 1952
    New York Theatre Critics' Reviews 1952:218+
    New York Times II, page 1, Oct 26, 1952
                    page 36, Oct 28, 1952
                    II, page 7, Nov 9, 1952
                    II, page 1, Nov 9, 1952
    New Yorker 28:86+, Nov 8, 1952
    Newsweek 40:94-5, Nov 10, 1952
    Theatre Arts 37:24-5, Jan 1953
    Time 60:72, Nov 10, 1952

My Dear Public
    book: Irving Caesar and Chuno Gottesfeld
    songs: Irving Caesar, Sam Lerner, Gerald Marks
    staging: Edgar MacGregor
    sets: Albert Johnson
    costumes: Lucinda Ballard
    choreography: Felicia Sorel and Henry LeTang

Productions:
    Opened September 9, 1943 for 45 performances
Reviews:
    Commonweal 38:562, Sep 24, 1943
    New York Theatre Critics' Reviews 1943:281+
    New York Times page 28, Sep 10, 1943
                    page 10, Oct 18, 1943
    Theatre Arts 27:645-6, Nov 1943

My Fair Lady
    book: Alan Jay Lerner, based on George Bernard
                   Shaw's Pygmalion
    music: Frederick Loewe
    lyrics: Alan Jay Lerner
    staging: Moss Hart
    sets: Oliver Smith
    costumes: Cecil Beaton
    choreography: Hanya Holm
Productions:
    Opened March 15, 1956 for 2,717 performances
    Opened May 20, 1964 for 47 performances
    Opened June 13, 1968 for 22 performances
Reviews:
    America 94:723, Mar 31, 1956
    Business World pages 28-30, Jul 28, 1956
    Catholic World 183:148, May 1956
    Colliers 137:6+, May 25, 1956
    Commonweal 64:95, Apr 27, 1956
    Coronet 41:54-63, Dec 1956
            45:16+, Apr 1959
    Dance Magazine 32:15, Apr 1958
                   38:16, Aug 1964
                   42:18-19, Aug 1968
    Etude 74:57, Jul 1956
    Holiday 20:75+, Oct 1956
    Life 40:58-60+, Mar 26, 1956
    Look 20:47-8+, Apr 17, 1956
    Nation 182:264-5, Mar 31, 1956
    New Republic 134:29-30, Apr 9, 1956
    New York Theatre Critics' Reviews 1956:345+
    New York Times page 30, Feb 13, 1956
                    VI, pages 28-9, Mar 4, 1956
                    II, page 1, Mar 11, 1956
                    page 20, Mar 16, 1956
                    II, page 1, Mar 25, 1956
                    VI, page 24, Apr 1, 1956
                    II, page 17, Apr 29, 1956
                    II, page 1, Jun 3, 1956
                    II, page 1, Aug 12, 1956
                    VI, page 27, Sep 9, 1956
                    II, page 1, Sep 23, 1956
                    page 27, Feb 5, 1957
                    II, page 3, Mar 10, 1957

                    page 33, Mar 20, 1957
                    page 22, Jul 10, 1957
                    II, page 1, Mar 9, 1958
                    VI, page 22, Mar 9, 1958
                    page 34, May 1, 1958
                    II, page 3, May 4, 1958
                    page 26, Jan 27, 1959
                    page 24, Feb 16, 1959
                    page 25, Feb 21, 1959
                    VI, pages 16-17, Mar 15, 1959
                    page 12, Apr 4, 1959
                    page 24, Aug 10, 1959
                    page 35, Aug 12, 1959
                    page 52, Dec 15, 1959
                    page 31, Jan 9, 1961
                    page 24, Jul 13, 1961
                    page 40, Oct 26, 1961
                    page 22, Jan 9, 1962
                    II, page 3, Mar 11, 1962
                    VI, page 55, Mar 11, 1962
                    page 28, Mar 15, 1962
                    page 24, Jun 14, 1962
                    page 27, Sep 11, 1962
                    page 15, Sep 29, 1962
                    page 38, Oct 1, 1962
                    page 34, May 1, 1963
                    page 32, Jun 3, 1963
                    page 8, Jul 4, 1963
                    page 37, Aug 21, 1963
                    page 19, Sep 2, 1963
                    page 13, Sep 21, 1963
                    page 16, Nov 16, 1963
                    page 40, Dec 13, 1963
                    page 24, Feb 20, 1964
                    page 43, May 21, 1964
                    page 29, Oct 31, 1965
                    page 42, Jun 14, 1968
New York Times Magazine pages 28-9, Mar 4, 1956
                        page 27+, Sep 9, 1956
                        page 14+, Mar 10, 1957
                        pages 16-17+, Mar 15, 1959
New Yorker 32:80+, Mar 24, 1956
Newsweek 47:94, Mar 26, 1956
          47:80-1, Apr 2, 1956
          51:94+, May 12, 1958
Reporter 14:34, Jun 28, 1956
Saturday Evening Post 231:34-5+, May 2, 1959
Saturday Review 39:26-7, Mar 31, 1956
Senior Scholastic 85:5, Oct 21, 1964
Theatre Arts 40:14, Nov 1956
             40:18-19, May 1956
             40:68-9, Jun 1956
             40:26-8, Dec 1956

                        41:29+, Mar 1957
                        41:63-4+, Oct 1957
                        42:70-1, May 1958
            Time 67:89, Mar 26, 1956
                 68:42-6, Jul 23, 1956
                 73:44-5, Mar 2, 1959
            Vogue 127:116, Apr 1, 1956
                  127:52-5, Jun 1956
                  144:152-5, Nov 1, 1964

My Girl
        book: Harlan Thompson
        music: Harry Archer
        lyrics: Harlan Thompson
Productions:
        Opened November 24, 1924 for 192 performances
Reviews:
        New York Times page 27, Nov 25, 1924
                        page 24, Apr 1, 1925
        Theatre Magazine 41:64, Jan 1925

My Golden Girl
        book: Frederic Arnold Kummer
        music: Victor Herbert
        lyrics: Frederic Arnold Kummer
Productions:
        Opened February 2, 1920 for 105 performances
Reviews:
        Dramatic Mirror 82:206, Feb 7, 1920
        New York Clipper 68:21, Feb 11, 1920
        New York Times page 18, Feb 3, 1920
        Theatre Magazine 31:220+, Mar 1920

My Little Friend
        book: Harry B. Smith; adapted from the German of
                      Willner and Stein
        music: Oscar Straus
        lyrics: Robert B. Smith
        staging: Herbert Gresham
Productions:
        Opened May 19, 1913 for 24 performances
Reviews:
        Dramatic Mirror 69:6, May 21, 1913
        New York Dramatic News 57:17, May 24, 1913
        New York Times page 11, May 20, 1913
        Theatre Magazine 18:xx, Jul 1913

My Magnolia
        book: Alex C. Rogers and Eddie Hunter
        music: C. Luckey Roberts
        lyrics: Alex C. Rogers
        staging: Alex C. Rogers and Eddie Hunter
Productions:
        Opened July 8, 1926 for 4 performances

Reviews:
    New York Times page 19, Jul 13, 1926

My Maryland
    book: Dorothy Donnelly
    music: Sigmund Romberg
    lyrics: Dorothy Donnelly
    staging: J. J. Shubert
Productions:
    Opened September 12, 1927 for 312 performances
Reviews:
    New York Times page 37, Sep 13, 1927
    Time 49:40, Mar 17, 1947
    Vogue 70:126, Nov 1, 1927

My Romance
    book: Rowland Leigh, based on Edward Sheldon's
                     Romance
    music: Sigmund Romberg
    lyrics: Rowland Leigh
    staging: Rowland Leigh
    sets: Watson Barratt
    costumes: Lou Eisele
    choreography: Fredric N. Kelly
Productions:
    Opened October 19, 1948 for 95 performances
Reviews:
    Catholic World 168:242, Dec 1948
    New Republic 119:26, Nov 8, 1948
    New York Theatre Critics' Reviews 1948:186+
    New York Times page 38, Oct 20, 1948
    New Yorker 24:44, Oct 30, 1948
    Time 52:52, Nov 1, 1948
    Vogue 112:154+, Dec 1948

My Wife and I
    book: Bill Mahoney
    music: Bill Mahoney
    lyrics: Bill Mahoney
    staging: Tom Ross Pather
    sets: Robert Green
Productions:
    (Off-Broadway) Opened October 10, 1966 for 8 performances
Reviews:
    New York Times page 53, Oct 11, 1966

Mystery Moon
    book: Fred Herendeen
    music: Carlo and Sanders
    lyrics: Carlo and Sanders
Productions:
    Opened June 23, 1930 for one performance
Reviews:

New York Times page 23, Jun 24, 1930

- N -

Nash at Nine
    conceived: Martin Charnin
    words: Ogden Nash
    music: Milton Rosenstock
    lyrics: Ogden Nash
    staging: Martin Charnin
    sets: David Chapman
    costumes: Theoni V. Aldredge
Productions:
    Opened May 17, 1973 for 21 performances
Reviews:
    New York Theatre Critics' Reviews 1973:268+
    New York Times page 31, May 18, 1973

National Lampoon's Lemmings
    music: Paul Jacobs and Christopher Guest
    words and
    lyrics: David Axlerod, Anne Beatts, Henry Beard,
                    John Boni, Tony Hendra, Sean Kelly, Doug
                    Kenny, P. G. O'Rourke and the cast
    staging: Tony Hendra
Productions:
    (Off-Broadway) Opened January 25, 1973 for 350 performances
Reviews:
    New York Times page 43, Jan 2, 1973
                   page 46, Jan 26, 1973
                   II, page 3, Feb 4, 1973
                   II, page 1, May 27, 1973
                   II, page 34, Sep 9, 1973
    New Yorker 48:59, Feb 3, 1973
    Time 108:58+, Feb 19, 1973

Naughty Marietta
    book: Rida Johnson Young
    music: Victor Herbert
    lyrics: Rida Johnson Young
Productions:
    Opened November 7, 1910 for 136 performances
    Opened November 16, 1931 for 24 performances
Reviews:
    Blue Book 12:888-9, Mar 1911
             13:1140-41, Oct 1911
    Columbian 3:899, Feb 1911
    Leslie's Weekly 111:541, Nov 24, 1910
    Metropolitan Magazine 33:799, Mar 1911
    Munsey 44:707, Feb 1911
    Musical Courier 106:10, May 27, 1933
    New York Times page 31, Nov 17, 1931

Pearson 25:121, Jan 1911
Stage 13:56, Aug 1936
Theatre Magazine 12:165-6, Dec 1910

Naughty Naught '00
    book: John Van Antwerp
    music: Richard Lewine
    lyrics: Ted Fetter
    staging: Morgan Lewis
    sets: Eugene Dunkel
Productions:
    Opened January 23, 1937 for 173 performances
    Opened October 19, 1946 for 17 performances
Reviews:
    New York Times page 23, Jan 25, 1937
                    page 27, Oct 21, 1946
    Newsweek 9:35, Feb 6, 1937
    Time 48:63, Oct 28, 1946

Naughty Riquette
    book: Harry B. Smith; adapted from the German of
                  R. Schanzer and E. Welisch
    lyrics: Harry B. Smith
    staging: J. J. Shubert
Productions:
    Opened September 13, 1926 for 88 performances
Reviews:
    Life (New York) 88:23, Oct 7, 1926
    New York Times page 25, Sep 14, 1926
                  IX, page 1, Sep 19, 1926
    Theatre Magazine 44:23, Nov 1926

Ned Wayburn's Gambols
    book: Ned Wayburn
    music: Walter G. Samuels
    lyrics: Morrie Ryskind
    staging: Ned Wayburn
Productions:
    Opened January 15, 1929 for 31 performances
Reviews:
    New York Times page 22, Jan 16, 1929

Ned Wayburn's Town Topics
    book: Harry B. Smith, Thomas J. Gray and Robert
                  B. Smith
    music: Harold Orlob
    lyrics: Harry B. Smith, Thomas J. Gray and Robert
                  B. Smith
    staging: Ned Wayburn
Productions:
    Opened September 23, 1915 for 68 performances
Reviews:
    Current Opinion 59:326-7, Nov 1915

Dramatic Mirror 74:8, Sep 29, 1915
                74:2, Oct 6, 1915
                74:2, Oct 16, 1915
Green Book 14:983-6, Dec 1915
Life (New York) 66:662, Oct 7, 1915
New York Dramatic News 61:19, Oct 16, 1915
Opera Magazine 2:29, Oct 1915
Theatre Magazine 22:301, Dec 1915

Nellie Bly
book: Joseph Quillan, based on a story by Jack
                 Emmanuel
music: James Van Heusen
lyrics: Johnny Burke
staging: Edgar McGregor
sets: Nat Karson
choreography: Lee Sherman
Productions:
Opened January 21, 1946 for 16 performances
Reviews:
New York Theatre Critics' Reviews 1946:481+
New York Times page 32, Jan 22, 1946
                II, page 1, Jan 27, 1946
Newsweek 27:80, Feb 4, 1946
Theatre Arts 30:137, Mar 1946
Time 47:63, Feb 4, 1946

The Nervous Set
book: Jay Landesman and Theodore J. Flicker, based
                 on the novel by Jay Landesman
music: Tommy Wolf
lyrics: Fran Landesman
staging: Theodore J. Flicker
sets: Paul Morrison
costumes: Theoni V. Aldredge
Productions:
Opened May 12, 1959 for 23 performances
Reviews:
Nation 188:483, May 23, 1959
New York Theatre Critics' Reviews 1959:306+
New York Times page 43, May 13, 1959
New Yorker 35:72+, May 23, 1959
Reporter 20:35-6, Jun 11, 1959
Saturday Review 42:26, May 30, 1959
Theatre Arts 43:10-11, Jul 1959
Time 73:50, May 25, 1959

The Never Homes
words: Glen MacDonough
rhymes: E. Ray Goetz
music: A. Baldwin Sloane
staging: Ned Wayburn
sets: Arthur Volgtlin

Productions:
    Opened October 5, 1911 for 92 performances
Reviews:
    Blue Book 14:680-2, Feb 1912
    Dramatic Mirror 66:7+, Oct 11, 1911
                        66:2, Oct 25, 1911
                        66:4, Nov 11, 1911
    Green Book Album 6:1126-9, Dec 1911
                        6:1201, Dec 1911
    Leslie's Weekly 113:447, Oct 26, 1911
    Life (New York) 58:662, Oct 19, 1911
    Theatre Magazine 14:ix, Nov 1911
                        14:175, Nov 1911

New Cole Porter Revue
    conceived: Ben Bagley
    songs: Cole Porter
    staging: Ben Bagley
    costumes: Charles Fatone
    choreography: Buddy Schwab
Productions:
    (Off-Broadway) Opened December 22, 1965 for 76 performances
No Reviews.

New Faces (1934)
    sketches: Viola Brothers Shore, Nancy Hamilton, June
                    Sillman
    music: Warburton Guilbert, Donald Honrath, Martha
                    Caples, James Shelton, Morgan Lewis
    lyrics: Viola Brothers Shore, Nancy Hamilton, June
                    Sillman
    staging: Elsie Janis
    sets: Sergei Soudeikine
Productions:
    Opened March 15, 1934 for 149 performances
Reviews:
    Catholic World 139:215, May 1934
    Commonweal 19:609, Mar 30, 1934
    Nation 138:370, Mar 28, 1934
    New Outlook 163:45, Apr 1934
    New York Times page 24, Mar 16, 1934
                    X, page 2, Apr 1, 1934
    Newsweek 3:39, Mar 24, 1934
    Stage 11:10-11, May 1934

New Faces of 1936
    sketches: Mindret Lord and Everett Marcy
    music: Alexander Fogarty and Irvin Graham
    lyrics: June Sillman, Edwin Gilbert, Bickley Reichner
    staging: Leonard Sillman
    sets: Stewart Chaney
    costumes: Stewart Chaney
    choreography: Ned McGurn

Productions:
  Opened May 19, 1936 for 193 performances
Reviews:
  Catholic World 143:474, 602, Jul-Aug 1936
  Commonweal 24:160, Jun 5, 1936
  Literary Digest 121:26, May 30, 1936
  New York Times page 24, May 20, 1936
                  IX, page 2, Jun 21, 1936

New Faces of 1943
  sketches: John Lund, additional sketches by June Carroll
                 and J. B. Rosenberg
  music: John Lund
  lyrics: John Lund, additional lyrics by June Carroll
                 and J. B. Rosenberg
  staging: Leonard Sillman
  choreography: Charles Weidman
Productions:
  Opened December 22, 1942 for 94 performances
Reviews:
  New York Theatre Critics' Reviews 1942:140+
  New York Times page 22, Dec 23, 1942

New Faces of 1952
  sketches: not credited
  music: Francis Lemarque, Sheldon Harnick, Murray
                 Grand, Elisse Boyd, Arthur Siegel, Ronald
                 Graham, Michael Brown
  lyrics: Francis Lemarque, Sheldon Harnick, Murray
                 Grand, Elisse Boyd, June Carroll, Ronald
                 Graham, Michael Brown
  staging: John Murray Anderson
  sets: Raoul Pene du Bois
  costumes: Thomas Becher
  choreography: Richard Barstow
Productions:
  Opened May 16, 1952 for 365 performances
Reviews:
  Catholic World 175:310, Jul 1952
  Commonweal 56:224, Jun 6, 1952
  Life 32:91-2, Jun 2, 1952
  New York Theatre Critics' Reviews 1952:278+
  New York Times page 23, May 17, 1952
                  II, page 1, May 25, 1952
                  II, page 2, Nov 2, 1952
  New Yorker 28:88, May 24, 1952
  Newsweek 39:84, May 26, 1952
  Saturday Review 35:26, May 31, 1952
  Theatre Arts 36:82, Jul 1952
                36:18-21, Aug 1952
  Time 59:56, May 26, 1952

New Faces of '56

              sketches: Paul Lynde, Richard Maury, Louis Botto
              music and
                lyrics: June Carroll, Arthur Siegel, Marshall Barer,
                             Dean Fuller, Murray Grand, Matt Dubey, Harold
                             Karr, Irvin Graham, Paul Nassau, John Rox,
                             Michael Brown
              staging: Paul Lynde
              sets: Peter Larkin
              costumes: Thomas Becher
              choreography: David Tihmar
Productions:
      Opened June 14, 1956 for 220 performances
Reviews:
      America 95:332, Jun 30, 1956
      Catholic World 183:387, Aug 1956
      Commonweal 64:396, Jul 20, 1956
      New York Theatre Critics' Reviews 1956:290+
      New York Times page 32, Jun 15, 1956
      New Yorker 32:62+, Jun 23, 1956
      Saturday Review 39:22, Jun 30, 1956
      Theatre Arts 40:17-18, Aug 1956
      Time 67:86, Jun 25, 1956

New Faces of 1962
              conceived by: Leonard Sillman
              sketches: Ronny Graham, Paul Lynde, Jean Shepherd,
                             Richard Maury, Joey Carter, R. G. Brown,
                             and others
              music and
                lyrics: June Carroll, Arthur Siegel, David Rogers,
                             Mark Bucci, Jack Holmes, Ronny Graham,
                             and others
              staging: Leonard Sillman and Richard Maury
              sets: Marvin Reiss
              costumes: Thomas Becher
              choreography: James Moore and others
Productions:
      Opened February 1, 1962 for 28 performances
Reviews:
      America 106:737, Mar 3, 1962
      New York Theatre Critics' Reviews 1962:366+
      New York Times page 25, Feb 2, 1962
                     page 22, Feb 9, 1962
                     page 21, Feb 22, 1962
      Theatre Arts 46:63, Apr 1962

New Faces of 1968 (see Leonard Sillman's New Faces of 1968)

New Girl in Town
              book: George Abbott, based on Eugene O'Neill's play
                             Anna Christie
              music: Bob Merrill
              lyrics: Bob Merrill

staging: George Abbott
sets: Helene Pons
costumes: Rouben Ter-Arutunian
choreography: Bob Fosse
Productions:
   Opened May 14, 1957 for 431 performances
   (Off-Broadway) Opened February 15, 1963 for 10 performances
      (Equity Library Theatre)
Reviews:
   America 97:311, Jun 8, 1957
   Catholic World 185:307, Jul 1957
   Life 42:109+, Jun 24, 1957
   Nation 184:486, Jun 1, 1957
   New York Theatre Critics' Reviews 1957:268+
   New York Times VI, pages 30-31, Apr 14, 1957
                   II, page 1, May 12, 1957
                   page 50, May 15, 1957
                   II, page 1, May 26, 1957
                   VI, page 25, May 26, 1957
   New York Times Magazine pages 30-1, Apr 14, 1957
                           page 25+, May 26, 1957
   New Yorker 33:82+, May 25, 1957
   Newsweek 49:70, May 27, 1957
   Saturday Review 40:22, Jun 1, 1957
   Theatre Arts 41:25-6, Jun 1957
                41:14-15, Jul 1957
   Time 69:60, May 27, 1957

The New Moon
   book: Oscar Hammerstein II, Frank Mandel, Laurence
                     Schwab
   music: Sigmund Romberg
   lyrics: Oscar Hammerstein II
   staging: Bobby Connelly
   choreography: Bobby Connelly
Productions:
   Opened September 19, 1928 for 509 performances
   Opened August 18, 1942 for 24 performances
   Opened May 17, 1944 for 53 performances
Reviews:
   Life (New York) 92:28, Oct 5, 1928
   New York Times VII, page 4, Sep 2, 1928
                   page 33, Sep 20, 1928
                   IX, page 2, Sep 20, 1928
                   IX, page 2, Sep 15, 1929
                   page 14, Aug 19, 1942
                   page 12, Aug 31, 1942
                   page 16, May 18, 1944
                   page 26, Jul 5, 1950
                   page 13, Jul 1, 1955
   New Yorker 20:40, May 27, 1944
   Theatre Magazine 48:80, Nov 1928
   Vogue 72:100, Nov 10, 1928

The New Music Hall of Israel
    staging: Jonathon Karmon
    costumes: Lydia Pinkus Ganay
    choreography: Jonathon Karmon
Productions:
    Opened October 2, 1969 for 68 performances
Reviews:
    America 121:342, Oct 18, 1969
    New York Times page 40, Oct 3, 1969
    New Yorker 45:88, Oct 11, 1969

New Priorities of 1943
    assembled: Clifford C. Fischer
    music: Lester Lee and Jerry Seelen
    lyrics: Lester Lee and Jerry Seelen
    staging: Jean Le Seyeux
    choreography: Truly McGee
Productions:
    Opened September 15, 1942 for 54 performances
Reviews:
    New York Theatre Critics' Reviews 1942:236
    New York Times page 28, Sep 16, 1942

New York Coloring Book
    music: Jerry Powell
    lyrics: Michael McWhinney
    staging: Bill Penn
    choreography: Bill Miller
Productions:
    (Off-Broadway) Opened April 2, 1963 for 84 performances
No Reviews.

The New Yorkers (1927)
    book: Jo Swerling and Henry Myers
    music: Arthur Schwartz, Edgar Fairchild and Charlie
                        M. Schwab
    lyrics: Jo Swerling and Henry Myers
Productions:
    Opened March 10, 1927 for 52 performances
Reviews:
    New York Times page 24, Mar 11, 1927
    Theatre Magazine 45:21, May 1927

The New Yorkers (1930)
    book: Herbert Fields, suggested by Peter Arno and
                        Ray Goetz
    music: Cole Porter
    lyrics: Cole Porter
    staging: Monty Woolley
    choreography: George Hale
Productions:
    December 8, 1930 for 168 performances
Reviews:

Catholic World 132:596, Feb 1931
Life (New York) 96:18, Dec 26, 1930
New York Times VIII, page 3, Nov 16, 1930
                    page 31, Dec 9, 1930
Outlook 156:671, Dec 24, 1930

The Newcomers
book: Joe Burrows and Will Morrissey
staging: Will Morrissey
Productions:
Opened August 8, 1923 for 21 performances
No Reviews.

Nic Nax of 1926
words: Paul W. Porter, Matt Kennedy and Roger Gray
music: Gitz Rice and Werner Janssen
staging: Paul W. Porter and Jack Conners
Productions:
Opened August 2, 1926 for 13 performances
Reviews:
New York Times page 19, Aug 5, 1926

Nifties of 1923
book: Sam Bernard and William Collier
Productions:
Opened September 25, 1923 for 47 performances
Reviews:
Life (New York) 82:18, Oct 18, 1923
New York Times page 10, Sep 26, 1923
Theatre Magazine 38:54, Nov 1923

The Night Boat
book: Anne Caldwell; adapted from a farce by A.
                 Bisson
music: Jerome Kern
lyrics: Anne Caldwell
Productions:
Opened February 2, 1920 for 148 performances
Reviews:
Dramatic Mirror 82:210, Feb 7, 1920
New York Clipper 68:21, Feb 11, 1920
New York Times page 18, Feb 3, 1920
Theatre Magazine 31:220, Mar 1920
                 31:275, Apr 1920

A Night in Paris
dialogue: Harold Atteridge
music: J. Fred Coots and Maurice Rubens
lyrics: Clifford Grey and McElbert Moore
staging: J. C. Huffman
Productions:
Opened January 5, 1926 for 196 performances
Reviews:

New Republic 46:145, Mar 24, 1926
New York Times page 16, Jan 6, 1926
Theatre Magazine 43:18, Mar 1926
Vogue 68:124+, Oct 1, 1926

Night in Spain (1917)
    assembled: Charles Dillingham and Florenz Ziegfeld
    music: Quinito Valverde
Productions:
Opened December 6, 1917 for 33 performances
Reviews:
    Life (New York) 89:20, May 26, 1927
    Theatre Magazine 46:20, Jul 1927
    Vogue 70:62-3, Jul 1, 1927

A Night in Spain (1927)
    book: Harold Atteridge
    music: Jean Schwartz
    lyrics: Al Bryam
    staging: Gertrude Hoffman and Charles Judels
Productions:
Opened May 3, 1927 for 222 performances
Reviews:
    Life (New York) 89:20, May 26, 1927
    New York Times page 28, May 4, 1927
                   VIII, page 1, May 22, 1927
                   VIII, page 1, Jul 3, 1927
    Theatre Magazine 46:20, Jul 1927
    Vogue 70:62-3, Jul 1, 1927

A Night in Spain (1949) (see Cabalgata)

A Night in Venice
    music: Lee Davis and Maury Rubens
    lyrics: J. Keirn Brennan and Moe Jaffe
    staging: Lew Morton and Thomas A. Hart
    choreography: Busby Berkeley
Productions:
Opened May 21, 1929 for 175 performances
Reviews:
    Life (New York) 93:26, Jun 14, 1929
    New York Times IX, page 1, May 12, 1929
                   page 30, May 22, 1929
    Outlook 152:234, Jun 5, 1929
    Theatre Magazine 50:42, Sep 1929

Night of Love
    book: Rowland Leigh, based on Lili Hatvany's Tonight
                    or Never
    music: Robert Stolz
    lyrics: Rowland Leigh
    staging: Barrie O'Daniels
    sets: Watson Barratt

costumes: Ernest Schraps
Productions:
Opened January 7, 1941 for 7 performances
Reviews:
New York Theatre Critics' Reviews 1941:421+
New York Times page 14, Jan 8, 1941

Night Song
music: Dave Bobrowits
lyrics: Gene Rempel
staging: Andy Thomas and Luba Ash
Productions:
(Off-Off-Broadway) Opened April 3, 1974 (The Cubiculo)
No Reviews.

The Nightingale
book: Guy Bolton and P. G. Wodehouse; based on the
              life of Jenny Lind
music: Armand Vecsey
lyrics: Guy Bolton and P. G. Wodehouse
staging: Lewis Morton
Productions:
Opened January 3, 1927 for 96 performances
Reviews:
Theatre Magazine 45:21, Mar 1927

Nikki
book: John Monk Saunders
music: Philip Charig
lyrics: John Monk Saunders
staging: William B. Friedlander
Productions:
Opened September 29, 1931 for 39 performances
Reviews:
New York Times page 23, Sep 30, 1931

Nina Rosa
book: Otto Harbach
music: Sigmund Romberg
lyrics: Irving Caesar
staging: J. J. Shubert and J. C. Huffman
Productions:
Opened September 20, 1930 for 137 performances
Reviews:
Life (New York) 96:18, Oct 10, 1930
National Magazine 59:107, Nov 1930
New York Times page 13, May 30, 1930
              page 19, May 31, 1930
              page 22, Sep 22, 1930
Theatre Magazine 52:26, Nov 1930
Vogue 76:118, Nov 10, 1930

Nine-Fifteen Revue

    staging: Alexander Leftwich
    choreography: Busby Berkeley and Leon Leonidoff
Productions:
Opened February 11, 1930 for 7 performances
Reviews:
    New York Times page 26, Feb 12, 1930
                        IX, page 4, Feb 16, 1930
                        page 19, Feb 18, 1930

9 O'Clock Revue   (see Hammerstein's 9 O'Clock Revue)

Nine O'Clock Revue
    sketches: Jay Strong, Dorothy Quick, Larry Shaw and
                       Richard Fehr
    music: Arthur Jones and Paul Stackpole
    staging: Mabel Rowland
    sets: John P. Ludlum
Productions:
(Off-Broadway)   Opened June 1936
Reviews:
    New York Times page 14, Jul 8, 1936

90 in the Shade
    book: Guy Bolton
    music: Jerome Kern
    staging: Robert Milton
    choreography: Julian Alfred
Productions:
Opened January 25, 1915 for 40 performances
Reviews:
    Dramatic Mirror 73:8, Feb 3, 1915
                      73:2, Feb 17, 1915
    Green Book 13:766, Apr 1915
    New York Dramatic News 60:17, Jan 30, 1915
    New York Times page 11, Jan 26, 1915
    Theatre Magazine 21:120, Mar 1915
                       21:150, Mar 1915

No Foolin' (Ziegfeld's American Revue of 1926) (Glorifying the
    American Girl)
    sketches: J. P. McEvoy and James Barton
    music: Rudolf Friml and James Hanley
    lyrics: Gene Buck and Irving Caesar
    staging: Florenz Ziegfeld and John Boyle
Productions:
Opened June 24, 1926 for 108 performances
Reviews:
    Bookman 64:86, Sep 1926
    New York Times page 25, Jun 25, 1926
    Theatre Magazine 44:23, Aug 1926
    Vogue 68:122, Sep 1, 1926

No for an Answer

    book: Marc Blitzstein
    music: Marc Blitzstein
    lyrics: Marc Blitzstein
    staging: W. E. Watts
Productions:
    (Off-Broadway) Opened January 5, 1941 for 3 performances
Reviews:
    Modern Music 18:70+, Jan-Feb 1941
    Musical Courier 123:9, Jan 15, 1941
    Theatre Arts 25:183, Mar 1941

No! No! Nanette!
    book: Otto Harbach and Frank Mandel
    music: Vincent Youmans
    lyrics: Otto Harbach and Irving Caesar
    staging: H. H. Frazee
Productions:
    Opened September 16, 1925 for 321 performances
    Opened January 19, 1971 for 861 performances
Reviews:
    Dance Magazine 45:27, Mar 1971
    Life 70:40-1, Feb 19, 1971
    National Review 23:440, Apr 20, 1971
    New York Theatre Critics' Reviews 1971:382
    New York Times page 17, Mar 12, 1925
                     page 28, Nov 17, 1925
                     page 23, Mar 8, 1926
                     page 25, Oct 18, 1926
                     VIII, page 2, Feb 26, 1928
                     page 38, Mar 17, 1970
                     page 56, Jun 25, 1970
                     page 36, Sep 29, 1970
                     II, page 1, Jan 10, 1971
                     page 24, Jan 20, 1971
                     page 26, Jan 21, 1971
                     II, page 1, Jan 31, 1971
                     II, page 1, Feb 21, 1971
                     VI, page 14, Apr 11, 1971
                     page 46, Mar 1, 1972
                     VII, page 29, May 21, 1972
                     page 58, Nov 9, 1972
                     page 25, Jan 30, 1973
    New Yorker 46:54, Jan 30, 1971
    Newsweek 77:73-4, Feb 1, 1971
    Saturday Review 54:62+, Feb 6, 1971
                    54:14, Apr 24, 1971
    Theatre Magazine 44:17, Aug 1926
    Time 47:90, Apr 15, 1946
         97:76, Feb 1, 1971

No Other Girl
    book: Aaron Hoffman
    music: Bert Kalmar and Harry Ruby

lyrics: Bert Kalmar and Harry Ruby
Productions:
Opened August 13, 1924 for 52 performances
Reviews:
New York Times page 10, Aug 14, 1924
Theatre Magazine 40:16, Oct 1924

No Shoestrings
        conceived: Ben Bagley
        staging: Robert Haddad
        costumes: Dick Granger
        choreography: Robert Haddad
Productions:
(Off-Broadway) Opened October 11, 1962 for 66 performances
No Reviews.

No Strings
        book: Samuel Taylor
        music: Richard Rodgers
        lyrics: Richard Rodgers
        staging: Joe Layton
        sets: David Hays
        costumes: Fred Voelpel and Donald Brooks
        choreography: Joe Layton and Buddy Schwab
Productions:
Opened March 15, 1962 for 580 performances
Reviews:
America 106:869, Mar 31, 1962
Christian Century 79:493, Apr 18, 1962
Dance Magazine 36:19-21, May 1962
Ebony 17:40-2+, Jul 1962
Nation 194:337-8, Apr 14, 1962
New Republic 146:26-7+, Apr 9, 1962
New York Theatre Critics' Reviews 1962:328+
New York Times page 24, Mar 16, 1962
                II, page 1, Mar 25, 1962
                page 17, Jan 1, 1964
New Yorker 38:100+, Mar 31, 1962
Newsweek 59:85, Mar 26, 1962
Saturday Review 45:27, Mar 31, 1962
Theatre Arts 46:57-9, May 1962
Time 79:51, Mar 23, 1962

Nobody Home
        book: Guy Bolton and Paul Rubens
        music: Jerome Kern
        staging: J. C. Benrimo
Productions:
Opened April 20, 1915 for 135 performances
Reviews:
Dramatic Mirror 73:8, Apr 28, 1915
                73:2, May 12, 1915
                73:1, Jun 16, 1915

Green Book 14:59-60, Jul 1915
14:191-2, Jul 1915
Life (New York) 65:808, May 16, 1915
Theatre Magazine 21:280, Jun 1915
21:297, Jun 1915

Noel Coward's Sweet Potato
music: Noel Coward
lyrics: Noel Coward
staging: Lee Theodore
sets: Helen Pond and Herbert Senn
costumes: David Toser
choreography: Lee Theodore
Productions:
Opened September 29, 1968 for 44 performances
Reviews:
Dance Magazine 42:106, Dec 1968
New York Theatre Critics' Reviews 1968:232
New York Times page 59, Sep 30, 1968
II, page 5, Oct 13, 1968
page 39, Oct 15, 1968
page 39, Oct 16, 1968
New Yorker 44:97, Oct 5, 1968

Nothing But Love
book: Frank Stammers
music: Harold Orlob
lyrics: Frank Stammers
Productions:
Opened October 14, 1919 for 39 performances
Reviews:
Dramatic Mirror 80:1653, Oct 23, 1919
New York Times page 20, Oct 15, 1919
Theatre Magazine 30:356, Nov 1919

Now
conceived: Marvin Gordon
sketches: George Haimsohn
music: John Aman; additional material by Steve Holden,
              John Kuntz, Sue Lawless and Mart Panzer
lyrics: George Haimsohn
staging: Marvin Gordon
sets: Jack Robinson
costumes: Betsey Johnson, Michael Mott and The Different
              Drummer
Productions:
(Off-Broadway) Opened June 5, 1968 for 22 performances
Reviews:
New York Times page 53, Jun 6, 1968

Now Is the Time for All Good Men
book: Gretchen Cryer
music: Nancy Ford

lyrics: Gretchen Cryer
staging: Word Baker
sets: Holly Haas
costumes: Jeanne Button
Productions:
  (Off-Broadway) Opened September 26, 1967 for 112 per-
    formances
  (Off-Broadway) Opened Season of 1970-1971 (Equity Library
    Theatre)
Reviews:
  America 117:421-2, Oct 14, 1967
  New York Times page 42, Sep 27, 1967
              page 49, Oct 27, 1967
              page 13, Dec 29, 1967
              page 73, May 2, 1971
  New Yorker 43:133-4, Oct 7, 1967

Nowhere to Go But Up

book: James Lipton
music: Sil Berkowitz
lyrics: James Lipton
staging: Sidney Lumet
sets: Peter Larkin
costumes: Robert Fletcher
choreography: Ronald Field
Productions:
  Opened November 10, 1962 for 9 performances
Reviews:
  Dance Magazine 37:24, Jan 1963
               37:28-9, Feb 1963
  New York Theatre Critics' Reviews 1962:209+
  New York Times page 46, Oct 9, 1962
              page 36, Nov 12, 1962
              page 46, Nov 15, 1962
  New Yorker 38:147, Nov 17, 1962
  Theatre Arts 46:15, Dec 1962

- O -

O Marry Me

book: Lola Pergament; based on Goldsmith's She
                  Stoops to Conquer
music: Robert Kessler
lyrics: Lola Pergament
staging: Michael Howard
sets: Herbert Senn and Helen Pond
costumes: Sonia Lowenstein
Productions:
  (Off-Broadway) Opened October 27, 1961 for 21 performances
Reviews:
  New York Times page 13, Oct 28, 1961
              page 42, Nov 13, 1961

O, Oysters!

New Yorker 37:130-2, Nov 4, 1961

O, Oysters!
    book: Eric Blau
    music: Doris Schwerin
Productions:
    (Off-Broadway) Season of 1960-61
Reviews:
    America 104:714, Feb 25, 1961
    New York Times page 23, Jan 31, 1961

O Say Can You See!
    book: Bill Conklin and Bob Miller
    music: Jack Holmes
    lyrics: Bill Conklin and Bob Miller
    staging: Ray Harrison and Cynthia Baer
    sets: Jack H. Cornwell
    costumes: Jane K. Stevens
    choreography: Ray Harrison
Productions:
    (Off-Broadway) Opened October 8, 1962 for 24 performances
Reviews:
    New York Times page 45, Oct 9, 1962
    New Yorker 38:86+, Oct 20, 1962

The O'Brien Girl
    book: Otto Harbach and Frank Mandel
    music: Lou Hirsch
    lyrics: Otto Harbach and Frank Mandel
    staging: Julian Mitchell
Productions:
    Opened October 3, 1921 for 164 performances
Reviews:
    Dramatic Mirror 83:893, May 21, 1921
                     84:520, Oct 8, 1921
    Life (New York) 78:18, Oct 20, 1921
    New York Clipper 69:26, Oct 12, 1921
    New York Times page 10, Oct 4, 1921
                      page 18, Oct 21, 1921
    Theatre Magazine 34:440, Dec 1921

Odds and Ends of 1917
    book: Bide Dudley and John Godfrey
    music: Bide Dudley, John Godfrey and James Byrnes
    lyrics: Bide Dudley, John Godfrey and James Byrnes
    staging: Julian Alfred
Productions:
    Opened November 19, 1917 for 112 performances
Reviews:
    Dramatic Mirror 77:5+, Dec 1, 1917
    Green Book 19:205+, Feb 1918
    New York Times page 11, Nov 20, 1917

Ododo
     book: Joseph A. Walker
     music: Dorothy A. Dinroe
     staging: Joseph A. Walker
     sets: Edward Burbridge
     costumes: Dorothy A. Dinroe
     choreography: Syvilla Fort
Productions:
     (Off-Broadway) Opened November 17, 1970 for 48 performances
Reviews:
     New York Theatre Critics' Reviews 1970:124
     New York Times page 26, Nov 25, 1970
                    II, page 7, Dec 6, 1970
     New Yorker 46:162, Dec 5, 1970

Of Thee I Sing
     book: George S. Kaufman and Morrie Ryskind
     music: George Gershwin
     lyrics: Ira Gershwin
     staging: George S. Kaufman
     choreography: Chester Hale
Productions:
     Opened December 26, 1931 for 441 performances
     Opened May 15, 1933 for 32 performances
     Opened May 5, 1952 for 72 performances
     (Off-Broadway) Opened October 18, 1968 for 15 performances
     (Off-Broadway) Opened March 7, 1969 for 21 performances
Reviews:
     Arts and Decoration 36:39+, Feb 1932
                          37:43+, Sep 1932
     Bookman 74:561-2, Jan 1932
     Catholic World 134:587-8, Feb 1932
                    175:310, Jul 1952
     Commonweal 15:302, Jan 13, 1932
                56:196-7, May 30, 1952
     Harper 205:92, Jul 1952
     Literary Digest 112:18, Jan 16, 1932
     Nation 134:56, Jan 13, 1932
            134:294, Mar 9, 1932
            174:486, May 17, 1952
     New Republic 69:243, Jan 13, 1932
                  70:97, Mar 9, 1932
     New York Theatre Critics' Reviews 1952:289
     New York Times VIII, page 2, Dec 13, 1931
                    VIII, page 1, Mar 20, 1932
                    page 1, May 3, 1932
                    VIII, page 1, May 8, 1932
                    page 28, Jan 2, 1933
                    page 23, Jan 6, 1933
                    page 22, Aug 10, 1937
                    page 14, Aug 18, 1937
                    II, page 1, May 4, 1952
                    page 34, May 6, 1952

II, page 1, May 11, 1952
page 19, Mar 8, 1969
page 39, Mar 25, 1969
New Yorker 28:87, May 17, 1952
Newsweek 39:101, May 19, 1952
Outlook 160:54+, Jan 13, 1932
Saturday Review 9:385-6, Jan 21, 1933
35:30-2, May 24, 1952
Theatre Arts 36:17+, Jul 1952
Theatre Guild Magazine 9:16-20, Feb 1932
9:23, Apr 1932
Time 59:83, May 19, 1952
Vogue 79:73+, Feb 15, 1932

Of V We Sing
sketches: Al Geto, Sam D. Locke, Mel Tolkin
music: Alex North, George Kleinsinger, Ned Lehack,
Beau Bergersen, Lou Cooper and Tony Sacher
lyrics: Alfred Hayes, Lewis Allen, Roslyn Harvey,
Mike Stratton, Bea Goldsmith, Joe Barian and
Arthur Zipser
staging: Perry Bruskin
choreography: Susanne Remos
Productions:
Opened February 11, 1942 for 76 performances
Reviews:
New York Times page 20, Feb 16, 1942

Ogden Nash (see Nash at Nine)

Oh, Boy
book: Guy Bolton and P. G. Wodehouse
music: Jerome Kern
lyrics: Guy Bolton and P. G. Wodehouse
staging: Edward Royce
Productions:
Opened February 20, 1917 for 463 performances
Reviews:
Book News 35:317+, Apr 1917
Dramatic Mirror 77:7, Mar 3, 1917
77:4, Mar 17, 1917
77:9, Mar 31, 1917
77:5, Jun 2, 1917
Green Book 17:785-6+, May 1917
Nation 104:250, Mar 1, 1917
New York Dramatic News 64:11, Feb 24, 1917
New York Times page 7, Feb 20, 1917
Theatre Magazine 25:214-15+, Apr 1917
25:199, Apr 1917
26:157, Sep 1917

Oh, Calcutta!
devised: Kenneth Tynan

      contributors: Samuel Beckett, Jules Feiffer, Dan Greenburg,
                       John Lennon, Jacques Levy, Leonard Melfi,
                       David Newman, Robert Benton, Sam Shepard,
                       Clovis Trouille, Kenneth Tynan and Sherman
                       Yellen
      music: The Open Window
      lyrics: The Open Window
      staging: Jacques Levy
      sets: James Tilton
      costumes: Fred Voelpel
      choreography: Margo Sappington
Productions:
      (Off-Broadway) Opened June 17, 1969
      Moved On Broadway February 26, 1971 for a total run of
      1,314 performances
Reviews:
      America 121:146, Sep 6, 1969
      Commonweal 90:463-4, Jul 25, 1969
      Commentary 48:24+, Nov 1969
      Esquire 72:44, Dec 1969
      Holiday 46:39+, Dec 1969
      New York Theatre Critics' Reviews 1969:208
      New York Times page 54, Apr 9, 1969
                       II, page 1, Jun 15, 1969
                       page 33, Jun 18, 1969
                       II, page 1, Jun 29, 1969
                       page 32, Oct 24, 1969
                       page 30, Jul 29, 1970
                       page 32, Sep 12, 1970
                       page 37, Sep 29, 1970
                       II, page 5, Dec 6, 1970
                       page 40, Feb 8, 1971
                       VI, page 2, Jun 20, 1971
                       page 20, Jul 23, 1971
      New Yorker 45:72+, Jun 28, 1969
      Newsweek 73:107, Jun 16, 1969
                73:81, Jun 30, 1969
      Saturday Review 52:51, Apr 26, 1969
                       52:20, Jul 26, 1969
      Time 93:59, Jun 27, 1969
      Vogue 154:60, Aug 1, 1969

Oh Captain!
      book: Al Morgan and José Ferrer, based on an
                       original screenplay by Alec Coppel
      music: Jay Livingston and Ray Evans
      lyrics: Jay Livingston and Ray Evans
      staging: José Ferrer
      sets: Jo Mielziner
      costumes: Miles White
      choreography: James Starbuck
Productions:
      Opened February 4, 1958 for 192 performances

Reviews:
   America 99:26, Apr 5, 1958
   Catholic World 187:70, Apr 1958
   Dance Magazine 32:15, Mar 1958
   New Republic 138:22-3, Mar 3, 1958
   New York Theatre Critics' Reviews 1958:370+
   New York Times page 21, Feb 5, 1958
   New Yorker 33:55, Feb 15, 1958
   Newsweek 51:66, Feb 17, 1958
   Theatre Arts 42:20-1, Apr 1958
   Time 71:84, Feb 17, 1958

Oh Coward!
   devised: Roderick Cook
   words: Noel Coward
   music: Noel Coward
   staging: Roderick Cook
   sets: Helen Pond and Herbert Senn
Productions:
   (Off-Broadway) Opened October 4, 1972 for 294 performances
Reviews:
   America 127:323-4, Oct 21, 1972
   New York Theatre Critics' Reviews 1972:167
   New York Times page 55, Oct 5, 1972
                   II, page 1, Oct 15, 1972
                   II, page 31, Nov 19, 1972
                   page 37, Jun 6, 1973
   New Yorker 48:125, Oct 14, 1972
   Time 100:80, Oct 23, 1972

Oh, Ernest!
   book: Francis DeWill
   music: Robert Hood Bowers
   lyrics: Francis DeWill
   staging: William J. Wilson
Productions:
   Opened May 9, 1927 for 56 performances
Reviews:
   New York Times page 24, May 10, 1927

Oh Glorious Tintinnabulation
   book: June Havoc
   music: Cathy MacDonald
   lyrics: June Havoc
   staging: June Havoc
Productions:
   (Off-Off-Broadway) Opened May 23, 1974 (The Actors Studio)
No Reviews.

Oh, I Say! (The Wedding Night)
   book: Keroul and Barre; adapted by Sydney Blow and
                   Douglas Hoare
   music: Jerome D. Kern

staging: J. C. Huffman
choreography: Julian Alfred
Productions:
Opened October 30, 1913 for 68 performances
Reviews:
Dramatic Mirror 70:10, Nov 5, 1913
Green Book 11:163-4, Jan 1914
New York Times page 11, Oct 28, 1913
                      page 11, Oct 31, 1913
Theatre Magazine 18:xx, Dec 1913

Oh, Kay
book: Guy Bolton and P. G. Wodehouse
music: George Gershwin
lyrics: Ira Gershwin
staging: John Harwood and Sammy Lee
Productions:
Opened November 8, 1926 for 256 performances
Opened January 2, 1928 for 16 performances
(Off-Broadway) Season of 1959-60
Reviews:
New York Times page 31, Nov 9, 1926
                      page 33, Sep 22, 1927
                      page 29, Jan 3, 1928
                      page 37, Apr 18, 1960
                      page 28, Jun 29, 1960
Vogue 69:100+, Jan 1, 1927

Oh, Lady! Lady!
book: Guy Bolton and P. G. Wodehouse
music: Jerome Kern
lyrics: Guy Bolton and P. G. Wodehouse
staging: Robert Milton and Edward Royce
Productions:
Opened February 1, 1918 for 219 performances
(Off-Off-Broadway) Opened March 13, 1974 (Equity Library
    Theatre)
Reviews:
Dramatic Mirror 78:7, Feb 16, 1918
                      78:7, Mar 2, 1918
                      79:949, Jul 6, 1918
Green Book 19:588+, Apr 1918
Life (New York) 71:262, Feb 14, 1918
New York Times page 7, Feb 1, 1918
                      page 41, Mar 18, 1974
New Yorker 50:108, Mar 25, 1974
Stage 12:29, Oct 1934
Theatre Magazine 27:143, Feb 1918

Oh, Look!
book: Suggested by James Montgomery's Ready Money
music: Harry Carroll
lyrics: Joseph McCarthy

Productions:
Opened March 7, 1918 for 68 performances
Reviews:
Dramatic Mirror 78:5, Mar 16, 1918
Green Book 19:785-7, May 1918
New York Times page 9, Mar 8, 1918
Theatre Magazine 27:216+, Apr 1918

Oh, My Dear!
book: Guy Bolton and P. G. Wodehouse
music: Louis A. Hirsch
lyrics: Guy Bolton and P. G. Wodehouse
staging: Robert Milton and Edward Royce
Productions:
Opened November 27, 1918 for 189 performances
Reviews:
Dramatic Mirror 79:865, Dec 14, 1918
New York Times page 11, Nov 27, 1918
Theatre Magazine 29:37, Jan 1919

Oh! Oh! Delphine
book: C. M. S. McLellan; based on Georges Berr and
                 Marcel Guillemaud's Villa Primrose
music: Ivan Caryll
lyrics: C. M. S. McLellan
staging: Herbert Gresham
Productions:
Opened September 30, 1912 for 248 performances
Reviews:
Blue Book 16:467-9, Jan 1913
Dramatic Mirror 68:6-7, Oct 2, 1912
                 68:2, Nov 6, 1912
                 68:1, Nov 27, 1912
Green Book 8:929-31+, Dec 1912
Harper's Weekly 55:19, Oct 26, 1912
                 57:20, Apr 19, 1913
Life (New York) 60:2005, Oct 17, 1912
Munsey 48:521-5, Dec 1912
New York Dramatic News 56:25, Oct 5, 1912
Theatre Magazine 16:155+, Nov 1912
                 18:71, Apr 1913

Oh! Oh! Oh! Nurse
book: George E. Stoddard
music: Carlo and Sanders
lyrics: Carlo and Sanders
staging: Walter Brooks
Productions:
Opened December 7, 1925 for 32 performances
Reviews:
New York Times page 28, Dec 8, 1925

Oh, Please

book: Otto Harbach and Anne Caldwell, based on a
                 story by Maurice Hennequin and Pierre Veber
music: Vincent Youmans
lyrics: Clifford Grey and Leo Robin
staging: Hassard Short
Productions:
Opened December 17, 1926 for 75 performances
Reviews:
Life (New York) 89:21, Jan 13, 1927
New York Times page 24, Dec 22, 1926

Oh, What a Girl!
book: Edgar Smith and Edward Clark
music: Charles Jules and Jacques Presburg
lyrics: Edgar Smith and Edward Clark
staging: Edward Clark
Productions:
Opened July 28, 1919 for 68 performances
Reviews:
New York Times page 20, Jul 29, 1919
Theatre Magazine 30:151-2, Sep 1919

Oh What a Lovely War
book: The Theatre Workshop, Charles Chilton, and
                 members of the cast
music: The Theatre Workshop, Charles Chilton, and
                 members of the cast
lyrics: The Theatre Workshop, Charles Chilton, and
                 members of the cast
staging: Joan Littlewood
sets: John Bury
costumes: Una Collins
choreography: Bob Stevenson
Productions:
Opened September 30, 1964 for 125 performances
Reviews:
America 111:497-8, Oct 24, 1964
Catholic World 200:131-2, Nov 1964
Commonweal 81:134, Oct 23, 1964
Dance Magazine 38:56-7, Nov 1964
Esquire 60:34+, Dec 1963
Nation 196:450+, May 25, 1963
       199:256, Oct 19, 1964
New Republic 151:26, Oct 24, 1964
New York Theatre Critics' Reviews 1964:209+
New Yorker 39:76-7, Jun 29, 1963
           39:98, Sep 7, 1963
           40:95, Oct 10, 1964
Newsweek 64:104, Oct 12, 1964
Saturday Review 47:29, Oct 17, 1964
Theatre Arts 47:31-2+, Jun 1963
Time 84:92, Oct 9, 1964
Vogue 144:64, Nov 15, 1964

Oklahoma

book:	Oscar Hammerstein II, based on Lynn Riggs' play Green Grow the Lilacs
music:	Richard Rodgers
lyrics:	Oscar Hammerstein II
staging:	Rouben Mamoulian
sets:	Lemuel Ayers
costumes:	Miles White
choreography:	Agnes de Mille

Productions:
Opened March 31, 1943 for 2,212 performances
Opened May 29, 1951 for 100 performances
Opened August 31, 1953 for 40 performances
Opened March 19, 1958 for 16 performances
Opened February 27, 1963 for 15 performances
Opened May 15, 1963 for 15 performances
Opened December 15, 1965 for 24 performances
Opened June 23, 1969 for 88 performances

Reviews:
America 89:609+, Sep 19, 1953
       121:76-7, Aug 2, 1969
Catholic World 157:186-7, May 1943
       173:308, Jul 1951
       178:67, Oct 1953
Commonweal 54:285, Jun 29, 1951
Cosmopolitan 134:24-7, May 1953
Dance Magazine 32:17, May 1958
       37:32-4, Mar 1963
       40:14-15+, Feb 1966
Holiday 20:75+, Oct 1956
Independent Woman 22:144, May 1943
Life 14:56-8+, May 24, 1943
    16:82-5, Mar 6, 1944
Look 17:4, Apr 7, 1953
Mademoiselle 41:125+, May 1955
Nation 156:572, Apr 17, 1943
New Republic 108:508-9, Apr 19, 1943
New York Theatre Critics' Reviews 1943:341+
       1951:257+
       1953:294+
New York Times page 27, Apr 1, 1943
       II, page 1, Apr 11, 1943
       II, page 6, May 9, 1943
       II, page 5, Jun 6, 1943
       VI, page 10, Jul 25, 1943
       II, page 1, Aug 1, 1943
       II, page 2, Sep 5, 1943
       VI, page 39, Jan 21, 1945
       II, page 5, Feb 4, 1945
       VI, page 18, Mar 25, 1945
       page 14, Jul 13, 1945
       II, page 1, Mar 31, 1946
       page 19, Oct 5, 1946

                          II, page 1, Mar 30, 1947
                          page 35, May 1, 1947
                          II, page 3, May 11, 1947
                          page 18, Jun 20, 1947
                          page 31, May 19, 1948
                          II, page 1, Jun 6, 1948
                          page 35, Mar 29, 1950
                          page 23, Sep 5, 1950
                          page 78, Oct 22, 1950
                          page 15, May 30, 1951
                          page 38, Sep 13, 1951
                          II, page 3, Sep 23, 1951
                          page 79, Feb 15, 1953
                          II, page 1, Mar 29, 1953
                          page 22, Aug 31, 1953
                          page 19, Sep 1, 1953
                          II, page 1, Sep 6, 1953
                          page 19, Aug 15, 1955
                          page 15, Mar 8, 1958
                          page 32, Mar 20, 1958
                          page 8, Feb 28, 1963
                          VI, pages 30-31, May 12, 1963
                          page 40, May 16, 1963
                          page 62, Dec 16, 1965
                          page 37, Jun 24, 1969
                          II, page 5, Jul 6, 1969
New York Times Magazine pages 18-19, Mar 25, 1945
                          pages 30-1, May 12, 1963
New Yorker 19:61, May 29, 1943
Newsweek 61:86, Mar 11, 1963
Saturday Review 26:14, Sep 4, 1943
School and Society 67:475, Jun 26, 1948
Theatre Arts 27:329-31, Jun 1943
                          35:5, Sep 1951
                          37:17, Nov 1953
Time 51:75, Apr 12, 1948

Old Bucks and New Wings
        book: Harvey Lasker
        music: Eddie Stuart
        lyrics: Harvey Lasker
        staging: Harvey Lasker
        costumes: Phyllis Uzill
        choreography: Buster Burnell
Productions:
        (Off-Broadway) Opened November 5, 1962 for 16 performances
Reviews:
        New York Times page 36, Nov 5, 1962
                          page 39, Nov 6, 1962
        New Yorker 38:148, Nov 17, 1962

Old Dutch
        book: Edgar Smith

```
    music:              Victor Herbert
    lyrics:             George V. Hobart
    staging:            Ned Wayburn
Productions:
    Opened November 22, 1909 for 88 performances
Reviews:
    Dramatic Mirror 62:5, Dec 4, 1909
    Hampton 24:273-5, Feb 1910
    Harper's Weekly 54:24, Jan 29, 1910
    Life (New York) 54:854, Dec 9, 1909
    Metropolitan Magazine 31:820-1, Mar 1910
    Theatre Magazine 11:xi, Jan 1910
                       11:30, Jan 1910
```

The Old Town
```
    book:               George Ade
    music:              Gustav Luders
Productions:
    Opened January 10, 1910 for 171 performances
Reviews:
    Dramatic Mirror 63:5, Jan 22, 1910
    Green Book 8:382-3, Sep 1912
    Hampton 24:410, Mar 1910
    Leslie's Weekly 110:136, Feb 10, 1910
    Life (New York) 55:128, Jan 20, 1910
    Metropolitan Magazine 32:120-1, Apr 1910
    Pearson 24:93, Jul 1910
    Theatre Magazine 11:xv, Feb 1910
                       11:86, Mar 1910
```

The Oldest Trick in the World (with The Bible Salesman, billed
    as Double Entry)
```
    book:               Jay Thompson
    music:              Jay Thompson
    lyrics:             Jay Thompson
    staging:            Bill Penn
    sets:               Howard Becknell
Productions:
    (Off-Broadway) Opened February 20, 1961 for 56 performances
Reviews:
    New York Times page 40, Feb 21, 1961
    New Yorker 37:115-16, Mar 11, 1961
```

Oliver!
```
    book:               Lionel Bart, adapted from Charles Dickens'
                        Oliver Twist
    music:              Lionel Bart
    lyrics:             Lionel Bart
    staging:            Peter Coe
    sets:               Sean Kenny
    costumes:           Sean Kenny
Productions:
    Opened January 6, 1963 for 774 performances
```

Opened August 2, 1965 for 64 performances
Reviews:
    Commonweal 77:493, Feb 1, 1963
    Life 54:75-7, Jan 18, 1963
    New York Theatre Critics' Reviews 1963:397+
    New York Times page 34, Aug 8, 1962
                  page 32, Sep 27, 1962
                   page 27, Nov 2, 1962
                   VI, page 60, Dec 9, 1962
                   page 5, Jan 8, 1963
                   page 35, Aug 3, 1965
                   page 85, Nov 21, 1965
                   page 32, Feb 5, 1966
                   page 19, Sep 10, 1966
    New York Times Magazine page 60, Dec 9, 1962
    New Yorker 36:145, Oct 8, 1960
             38:85-6, Jun 2, 1962
             38:60, Jan 19, 1963
    Newsweek 60:87, Aug 20, 1962
            61:65, Jan 14, 1963
    Saturday Review 46:26, Jan 19, 1963
    Theatre Arts 46:19-20, Dec 1962
              47:10-11+, Feb 1963
    Time 81:52, Jan 11, 1963

On a Clear Day You Can See Forever

book:	Alan Jay Lerner
music:	Burton Lane
lyrics:	Alan Jay Lerner
staging:	Robert Lewis
sets:	Oliver Smith
costumes:	Freddy Wittop
choreography:	Herbert Ross

Productions:
    Opened October 17, 1965 for 272 performances
Reviews:
    Dance Magazine 39:138-9, Dec 1965
    Holiday 39:118+, Jan 1966
    Nation 201:398, Nov 22, 1965
    New York Theatre Critics' Reviews 1965:308
    New York Times page 44, Oct 18, 1965
                  page 53, Jun 7, 1966
                  page 40, Jun 8, 1966
    New Yorker 41:108, Oct 30, 1965
    Newsweek 66:84+, Nov 1, 1965
    Saturday Review 48:41-2, Nov 6, 1965
    Time 86:84, Oct 29, 1965

On the Town

book:	Betty Comden and Adolph Green, based on an idea by Jerome Robbins
music:	Leonard Bernstein
lyrics:	Betty Comden and Adolph Green

```
        staging:        George Abbott
        sets:           Oliver Smith
        costumes:       Alvin Colt
        choreography:   Jerome Robbins
Productions:
        Opened December 28, 1944 for 463 performances
        Opened October 31, 1971 for 73 performances
Reviews:
        America 125:428, Nov 20, 1971
        Catholic World 160:453, Feb 1945
        Commonweal 41:332, Jan 12, 1945
        Dance Magazine 33:22-3, Apr 1959
        Life 18:49-51, Jan 15, 1945
        Nation 160:48, Jan 13, 1945
                213:538-9, Nov 22, 1971
        New Republic 112:85, Jan 15, 1945
        New York Theatre Critics' Reviews 1944:45+
                                          1971:199
        New York Times page 11, Dec 29, 1944
                        II, page 1, Jan 7, 1945
                        II, page 5, Feb 4, 1945
                        II, page 1, Feb 18, 1945
                        II, page 2, Oct 17, 1945
                        page 36, Jan 16, 1959
                        II, page 1, Jan 25, 1959
                        page 15, Feb 14, 1959
                        page 30, May 31, 1963
                        page 52, Apr 14, 1971
                        page 14, Aug 13, 1971
                        page 46, Sep 1, 1971
                        II, page 1, Oct 31, 1971
                        page 54, Nov 1, 1971
                        II, page 1, Nov 7, 1971
                        II, page 26, Nov 14, 1971
                        page 27, Jan 4, 1972
        New Yorker 20:40, Jan 6, 1945
                   47:115, Nov 6, 1971
        Newsweek 25:72+, Jan 8, 1945
                 78:106, Nov 15, 1971
        Saturday Review 28:26-7, Feb 17, 1945
        Theatre Arts 29:133-4, Mar 1945
        Time 45:67-8, Jan 8, 1945
             98:51, Nov 15, 1971

On Your Toes
        book:           George Abbott
        music:          Richard Rodgers
        lyrics:         Lorenz Hart
        staging:        Worthington Miner
        sets:           Jo Mielziner
        costumes:       Irene Sharaff
        choreography:   George Balanchine
Productions:
```

Opened April 11, 1936 for 315 performances
Opened October 11, 1954 for 64 performances
Reviews:
America 92:163, Nov 6, 1954
Catholic World 143:340, Jun 1936
                180:228, Dec 1954
Commonweal 23:724, Apr 24, 1936
                61:166, Nov 12, 1954
Mademoiselle 40:142, Nov 1954
Nation 142:559, Apr 29, 1936
        179:390, Oct 30, 1954
New Republic 131:22-3, Nov 1, 1954
New York Times page 22, Mar 23, 1936
                page 14, Apr 13, 1936
                page 15, Feb 6, 1937
                page 21, Aug 3, 1937
                II, page 1, Oct 10, 1954
                page 24, Oct 12, 1954
New Yorker 30:84-6, Oct 23, 1954
Newsweek 7:28-9, Apr 25, 1936
        44:93, Oct 25, 1954
Theatre Arts 20:415, Jun 1936
            38:22-3+, Dec 1954
Time 37:56, Apr 20, 1936
    64:41, Oct 25, 1954
Vogue 124:100-1, Oct 15, 1954

Once Over Lightly
      book: Laszlo Halasz; adapted from Beaumarchais'
                       The Barber of Seville
      music: G. Rossini
      dialogues: Louis Garden and Robert Pierpont Forshaw
      solos: Louis Garden and Robert Pierpont Forshaw
      ensembles: George Mead
      staging: Robert H. Gordon
      sets: Richard Rychtarick
Productions:
      Opened November 19, 1942 for 6 performances
Reviews:
      New York Times page 26, Nov 20, 1942

Once upon a Mattress
      book: Jay Thompson, Marshall Barer, Dean Fuller
      music: Mary Rodgers
      lyrics: Marshall Barer
      staging: George Abbott
      sets: William and Jean Eckart
      costumes: William and Jean Eckart
      choreography: Joe Layton
Productions:
      Opened May 11, 1959 for 460 performances
      (Off-Broadway) Season of 1966-67 for 14 performances
        (Equity Theatre)

Reviews:
    America 101:397-8, May 30, 1959
    Nation 188:484, May 23, 1959
    New York Theatre Critics' Reviews 1959:309+
    New York Times page 40, May 12, 1959
                        II, page 1, May 17, 1959
                        II, page 3, May 8, 1960
                        page 14, Jul 1, 1960
                        page 43, Sep 21, 1960
                        page 55, Oct 11, 1960
    New Yorker 35:80-1, May 23, 1959
    Newsweek 53:78, May 25, 1959
    Saturday Review 42:26, May 30, 1959
    Time 73:50, May 25, 1959

One for the Money
    book: Nancy Hamilton
    music: Morgan Lewis
    lyrics: Nancy Hamilton
    staging: John Murray Anderson
    sets: Raoul Pene du Bois
    choreography: Robert Alton
Productions:
    Opened February 4, 1939 for 132 performances
Reviews:
    Catholic World 148:730, Mar 1939
    New York Times page 9, Feb 6, 1939
    Stage 16:11-12, Feb 1939

One Kiss
    book: Clare Kummer; from the French Ta Bouche by
                     Y. Mirande and A. Willemetz
    music: Maurice Yvain
Productions:
    Opened November 27, 1923 for 95 performances
Reviews:
    New York Times page 14, Nov 28, 1923

110 in the Shade
    book: N. Richard Nash, based on his play The Rain-
                     maker
    music: Harvey Schmidt
    lyrics: Tom Jones
    staging: Joseph Anthony
    sets: Oliver Smith
    costumes: Motley
    choreography: Agnes de Mille
Productions:
    Opened October 24, 1963 for 330 performances
Reviews:
    America 109:644, Nov 16, 1963
    New York Theatre Critics' Reviews 1963:218+
    New York Times page 33, Sep 12, 1963

page 37, Oct 25, 1963
New Yorker 39:93, Nov 2, 1963
Newsweek 62:63, Nov 4, 1963
Saturday Review 46:32, Nov 9, 1963
Theatre Arts 48:68, Jan 1964
Time 82:74, Nov 1, 1963

One Touch of Venus
    book: S. J. Perelman and Ogden Nash, suggested by
                     "The Tinted Venus" by F. Anstey (Thomas
                     Anstey Guthrie)
    music: Kurt Weill
    lyrics: Ogden Nash
    staging: Elia Kazan
    sets: Howard Bay
    costumes: Paul Du Pont, Kermit Love, Mainbocher
    choreography: Agnes de Mille
Productions:
    Opened October 7, 1943 for 567 performances
Reviews:
    Catholic World 158:185-7, Nov 1943
    Commonweal 39:14-15, Oct 22, 1943
    Life 15:61-4, Oct 25, 1943
    Nation 157:479, Oct 23, 1943
    New York Theatre Critics' Reviews 1943:264+
    New York Times page 14, Oct 8, 1943
                     II, page 1, Oct 17, 1943
                     II, page 1, Feb 20, 1944
    New Yorker 19:41, Oct 16, 1943
    Newsweek 22:86+, Oct 18, 1943
    Theatre Arts 27:703-7, Dec 1943
    Time 42:50, Oct 18, 1943
    Vogue 102:60-1, Nov 1, 1943

Only Fools Are Sad
    book: Dan Almagor; based on old Hassidic stories
                     and parables
    music: Derived from Hassidic songs
    lyrics: Translated by Robert Friend
    staging: Yossi Yzraely
    sets: Dani Karavan and Herbert Senn
    costumes: Helen Pond
Productions:
    Opened November 22, 1971 for 144 performances
Reviews:
    New York Theatre Critics' Reviews 1971:176
    New York Times page 59, Nov 11, 1971
                     page 53, Nov 23, 1971

The Only Girl
    book: Henry Blossom; adapted from Our Wives by
                     Frank Mandel
    music: Victor Herbert

staging: Fred G. Latham
Productions:
    Opened November 2, 1914 for 240 performances
    Opened May 21, 1934 for 16 performances
Reviews:
    Dramatic Mirror 72:8, Nov 11, 1914
                    73:1, Feb 24, 1915
    Dramatist 7:622-3, Oct 1915
    Leslie's Weekly 120:107, Feb 4, 1915
    Munsey 53:811, Jan 1915
           55:104, Jun 1915
    Musical Courier 106:10, May 27, 1933
    New York Dramatic News 60:19, Nov 7, 1914
    New York Times page 11, Oct 2, 1914
                    page 11, Nov 3, 1914
                    VII, page 8, Nov 15, 1914
                    page 28, May 22, 1934
    Theatre Magazine 20:263+, Dec 1914
                     20:303, Dec 1914

The Opera Ball
    book: Sydney Rosenfeld and Clare Kummer; adapted
                  from the German of Victor Leon and H. Von
                  Waldberg
    music: Richard Heuberger
Productions:
    Opened February 12, 1912 for 32 performances
Reviews:
    Dramatic Mirror 67:6-7, Feb 14, 1912
                    67:8, Feb 21, 1912
    Green Book 7:459-61+, Mar 1912
    Hampton 28:203, Apr 1912
    Theatre Magazine 15:xi, Mar 1912

The Opposite Side of Sonny
    book: Peter Copani
    music: John Roman and Peter Copani
    lyrics: Peter Copani
Productions:
    (Off-Off-Broadway) Season of 1973-74 (The People's Perform-
    ing Co.)
No Reviews.

The Optimists
    sketches: Clifford Grey, Greatrex Newman and Austin
                  Melford
    lyrics: Clifford Grey, Greatrex Newman and Austin
                  Melford
    staging: Melville Gideon
Productions:
    Opened January 30, 1928 for 24 performances
Reviews:
    Life 91:23, Mar 1, 1928

New York Times page 28, Jan 31, 1928

Orange Blossoms
    book: Fred deGresac, based on Fred deGresac and
                    Francis deCroisset's play The Marriage of Kitty
    music: Victor Herbert
    lyrics: B. G. De Sylva
    staging: Edward Royce
Productions:
    Opened September 19, 1922 for 95 performances
Reviews:
    New York Clipper 70:20, Oct 25, 1922
    New York Times page 18, Sep 20, 1922

Orchids Preferred
    book: Fred Herendeen
    music: Dave Stamper
    lyrics: Fred Herendeen
    staging: Alexander Leftwich
    sets: Frederick Fox
    choreography: Robert Sanford
Productions:
    Opened May 11, 1937 for 7 performances
Reviews:
    New York Times page 16, Aug 29, 1937
                    page 26, May 12, 1937

Oscar Brown, Jr.   (see Worlds of Oscar Brown, Jr.)

Our Miss Gibbs
    book: James T. Tanner
    music: Ivan Caryll and Lionel Monckton
    staging: Thomas Reynolds
Productions:
    Opened August 29, 1910 for 64 performances
Reviews:
    Cosmopolitan 47:628-32, Oct 1909
                50:70, Dec 1910
    Dramatic Mirror 64:6, Sep 10, 1910
    Hampton 25:674+, Nov 1910
    Leslie's Weekly 111:317, Sep 22, 1910
    Munsey 41:907, Sep 1909
    Theatre Magazine 12:101-2, Oct 1910
                   12:126, Oct 1910

Our Nell
    book: A. E. Thomas and Brian Hooker
    music: George Gershwin and William Daly
    lyrics: Brian Hooker
    staging: W. H. Gilmore, Edgar MacGregor, Julian
                    Mason
Productions:
    Opened December 4, 1922 for 40 performances

Out of this World

369

Reviews:
New York Clipper 70:20, Dec 13, 1922
New York Times page 24, Dec 5, 1922

Out of this World
    book: Dwight Taylor and Reginald Lawrence
    music: Cole Porter
    lyrics: Cole Porter
    staging: Agnes de Mille
    sets: Lemuel Ayers
    costumes: Lemuel Ayers
    choreography: Hanya Holm
Productions:
Opened December 21, 1950 for 157 performances
(Off-Broadway) Season of 1955-56
(Off-Broadway) Opened November 30, 1962 for 9 performances
  (Equity Library Theatre)
(Off-Off-Broadway) Opened March 8, 1973 (Equity Library
  Theatre)
Reviews:
Catholic World 173:69, Apr 1951
Christian Science Monitor Magazine page 9, Dec 30, 1950
Commonweal 53:349, Jan 12, 1951
New York Theatre Critics' Reviews 1950:166+
New York Times VI, page 62, Dec 10, 1950
                II, page 3, Dec 17, 1950
                page 17, Dec 22, 1950
                II, page 8, Jan 14, 1951
                page 35, Oct 13, 1955
                page 44, Nov 10, 1955
                page 39, Mar 12, 1973
New Yorker 26:44, Dec 30, 1950
           49:94, Mar 17, 1973
Newsweek 37:35, Jan 1, 1951
Theatre Arts 35:19, Feb 1951
Time 57:42, Jan 1, 1951

Over Here!
    book: Will Holt
    music: Richard M. Sherman and Robert B. Sherman
    lyrics: Richard M. Sherman and Robert B. Sherman
    staging: Tom Moore
    sets: Douglas W. Schmidt
    costumes: Carrie F. Robbins
    choreography: Patricia Birch
Productions:
Opened March 6, 1974 for 348 performances
Reviews:
America 130:262, Apr 6, 1974
Nation 218:410, Mar 20, 1974
New York Theatre Critics' Reviews 1974:347
New York Times page 51, Mar 7, 1974
                II, page 5, Mar 17, 1974

New Yorker 50:107, Mar 11, 1974
Newsweek 83:83, Mar 13, 1974
Time 103:66, Mar 18, 1974

Over the River
    book: George V. Hobart and H. A. DuSouchet; based
                   on The Man from Mexico
    music: John Golden
Productions:
Opened January 8, 1912 for 120 performances
Reviews:
    Blue Book 15:18-21, May 1912
    Dramatic Mirror 67:6, Jan 10, 1912
                 67:4, Jan 24, 1912
                 67:4, Feb 14, 1912
    Green Book 7:455-8+, Mar 1912
             7:566-7, Mar 1912
             8:1020-21, Dec 1912
    Hampton 28:117, Mar 1912
    Harper's Weekly 56:19, Feb 3, 1912
    Munsey 47:128, Apr 1912
    Theatre Magazine 15:xii, Feb 1912
                  15:40, Feb 1912
                  15:136, Apr 1912

Over the Top
    book: Philip Bartholomae and Sigmund Romberg
    music: Sigmund Romberg and Herman Timberg
    staging: J. C. Huffman
Productions:
Opened November 28, 1917 for 78 performances
Reviews:
    Dramatic Mirror 77:7, Dec 8, 1917
    New York Times page 11, Dec 3, 1917
    Theatre Magazine 27:89, Feb 1918

Oy Is Dus a Leben!
    book: Jacob Kalich
    music: Joseph Rumshinsky
    lyrics: Molly Picon
    staging: Jacob Kalich
    sets: Harry Gordon Bennett
    choreography: David Lubritzky and Lillian Shapero
Productions:
Opened October 12, 1942 for 139 performances
Reviews:
New York Times page 19, Oct 13, 1942

- P -

Pacific Paradise
    staging: Jack Regas

Productions:
    Opened October 16, 1972 for 7 performances
No Reviews.

Padlocks of 1927
        sketches: Paul Gerard Smith and Ballard Macdonald
        music: Lee David, Jesse Greer and Henry H. Tobias
        lyrics: Billy Rose
        staging: W. J. Wilson
Productions:
    Opened July 5, 1927 for 95 performances
Reviews:
    New York Times page 23, Jul 6, 1927
                    page 33, Sep 23, 1927

Paint Your Wagon
        book: Alan Jay Lerner
        music: Frederick Loewe
        lyrics: Alan Jay Lerner
        staging: Daniel Mann
        sets: Oliver Smith
        costumes: Motley
        choreography: Agnes de Mille
Productions:
    Opened November 12, 1951 for 289 performances
    (Off-Broadway) Opened February 24, 1962 for 9 performances
        (Equity Library Theatre)
Reviews:
    Catholic World 174:308, Jan 1952
    Commonweal 55:199, Nov 30, 1951
    Nation 173:484-5, Dec 1, 1951
    New Republic 126:22, Jan 7, 1952
    New York Theatre Critics' Reviews 1951:173+
    New York Times II, page 1, Nov 11, 1951
                    page 32, Nov 13, 1951
                    II, page 1, Nov 18, 1951
    New Yorker 27:67, Nov 24, 1951
    Newsweek 38:84, Nov 26, 1951
    Saturday Review 35:27, Jul 5, 1952
    School and Society 75:246, Apr 19, 1952
    Theatre Arts 36:72, Feb 1952
                    36:33-5, Dec 1952
    Time 58:87, Nov 26, 1951

The Pajama Game
        book: George Abbott and Richard Bissell, based on
                        Bissell's novel 7-1/2 Cents
        music: Richard Adler and Jerry Ross
        lyrics: Richard Adler and Jerry Ross
        staging: George Abbott and Jerome Robbins
        sets: Lemuel Ayers
        costumes: Lemuel Ayers
        choreography: Bob Fosse

Productions:
    Opened May 13, 1954 for 1, 063 performances
    Opened May 15, 1957 for 23 performances
    Opened December 9, 1973 for 65 performances
Reviews:
    America 91:306, Jun 12, 1954
    Business Week page 76+, Jun 5, 1954
    Catholic World 179:307-8, Jul 1954
    Life 36:125-6+, Jun 7, 1954
    Nation 178:470, May 29, 1954
    New York Theatre Critics' Reviews 1954:324+
                                          1973:152
    New York Times page 20, May 14, 1954
                    II, page 1, May 30, 1954
                    page 87, Jan 30, 1955
                    II, page 3, May 8, 1955
                    page 27, May 16, 1957
                    II, page 1, May 26, 1957
                    page 61, Oct 23, 1973
                    page 58, Dec 10, 1973
                    II, page 3, Dec 16, 1973
    New Yorker 30:68+, May 22, 1954
               49:56, Dec 24, 1973
    Newsweek 43:64, May 24, 1954
    Saturday Review 37:24-5, Jun 12, 1954
                  39:12, Sep 15, 1956
    Theatre Arts 38:14, Sep 1954
              38:18-19, Jul 1954
              41:17, Jul 1957
    Time 63:66, May 24, 1954

Pal Joey

    book: John O'Hara
    music: Richard Rodgers
    lyrics: Lorenz Hart
    staging: George Abbott
    sets: Jo Mielziner
    costumes: John Koenig
    choreography: Robert Alton
Productions:
    Opened December 25, 1940 for 374 performances
    Opened October 21, 1941 for 104 performances
    Opened January 3, 1952 for 540 performances
    Opened May 31, 1961 for 31 performances
    Opened May 29, 1963 for 15 performances
Reviews:
    Catholic World 152:598, Feb 1941
                  174:391, Feb 1952
    Commonweal 55:398-9, Jan 25, 1952
               74:379-80, Jul 7, 1961
    Dance Magazine 35:21, Jul 1961
    Life 10:44, Feb 17, 1941
        32:67-8+, Jan 21, 1952

Nation 152:81, Jan 18, 1941
New Republic 126:23, Jan 21, 1952
New York Theatre Critics' Reviews 1940:172+
                                  1941:442+
                                  1952:398+
New York Times page 22, Dec 26, 1940
                IX, page 8, Jun 8, 1941
                page 20, Sep 2, 1941
                page 17, Mar 7, 1949
                II, page 1, Dec 30, 1951
                page 17, Jan 4, 1952
                II, page 1, Jan 13, 1952
                II, page 13, Feb 17, 1952
                page 23, Jun 17, 1952
                II, page 3, Nov 23, 1952
                page 40, Apr 1, 1954
                II, page 2, Apr 11, 1954
                page 32, Jun 1, 1961
                page 21, May 30, 1963
New Yorker 27:38, Jan 12, 1952
Newsweek 17:42, Jan 6, 1941
         39:73, Jan 14, 1952
Saturday Review 35:28-9, Feb 2, 1952
School and Society 76:404, Dec 20, 1952
Stage 1:17, Dec 1940
      1:22-3, Feb 1941
Theatre Arts 25:95, Feb 1941
Time 37:41, Jan 6, 1941
     59:62, Jan 14, 1952

Panama Hattie
    book: Herbert Fields and B. G. De Sylva
    music: Cole Porter
    lyrics: Cole Porter
    staging: Edgar MacGregor
    sets: Raoul Pene du Bois
    costumes: Raoul Pene du Bois
    choreography: Robert Alton
Productions:
    Opened October 30, 1940 for 501 performances
Reviews:
    Catholic World 152:335, Dec 1940
    Commonweal 33:103, Nov 15, 1940
    Life 9:67-8, Oct 28, 1940
    Nation 151:513, Nov 23, 1940
    New York Theatre Critics' Reviews 1940:233+
                                      1941:460+
    New York Times page 28, Oct 4, 1940
                   page 28, Oct 31, 1940
                   IX, page 1, Nov 10, 1940
                   II, page 5, Dec 5, 1943
    Newsweek 16:60, Nov 11, 1940
    Stage 1:40-41, Nov 1940

Theatre Arts 25:12-13, Jan 1941
Time 36:65, Oct 28, 1940

Pansy
    book: Alex Belledna
    music: Maceo Pinkard
Productions:
Opened May 14, 1929 for 3 performances
Reviews:
    Life (New York) 93:28, Jun 7, 1929
    New York Times page 36, May 15, 1929
                   page 24, May 17, 1929
                   III, page 4, May 19, 1929
    Theatre Magazine 50:42, Jul 1929

Papa's Darling
    book: Harry B. Smith; based on Grenet d'Ancourt and
                  Maurice Vaucaire's Le Fils Surnaturel
    music: Ivan Caryll
    lyrics: Harry B. Smith
    staging: Julian Mitchell
Productions:
Opened November 2, 1914 for 40 performances
Reviews:
    Dramatic Mirror 72:8, Nov 11, 1914
                   72:2, Nov 18, 1914
    Green Book 13:377-8, Feb 1915
    New York Dramatic News 60:19-20, Nov 7, 1914
    New York Times I, page 7, Nov 4, 1914
    Theatre Magazine 20:314, Dec 1914

Parade
    sketches: Paul Peters, George Sklar, Frank Gabrielson,
                  David Lesan, Kyle Crichton
    music: Jerome Moross
    staging: Philip Loeb
    sets: Lee Simonson
    choreography: Robert Alton
Productions:
Opened May 20, 1935 for 40 performances
Reviews:
    Commonweal 22:160, Jun 7, 1935
    Nation 140:666+, Jun 5, 1935
    New Republic 83:106, Jun 5, 1935
    New York Times page 26, May 7, 1935
                   X, page 2, May 12, 1935
                   page 22, May 21, 1935
                   XI, page 22, May 26, 1935
    Newsweek 5:24-5, Jun 1, 1935
    Time 25:26+, Jun 3, 1935

Paradise Alley
    book: Charles W. Bell and Edward Clark

music: Carl Carlton, Harry Archer and A. Otvos
lyrics: Howard Johnson
Productions:
   Opened March 31, 1924 for 64 performances
Reviews:
   New York Times VIII, page 2, Mar 16, 1924
                   page 17, Apr 2, 1924
   Theatre Magazine 39:68, Jun 1924

Paradise Island
   book: Carmen Lombardo and John Jacob Loeb
   music: Carmen Lombardo and John Jacob Loeb
   lyrics: Carmen Lombardo and John Jacob Loeb
   staging: Francis Swann
   sets: George Jenkins
   choreography: June Taylor
Productions:
   (Off-Broadway) Opened June 22, 1961 for 75 performances
   (Off-Broadway) Opened June 27, 1962 for 68 performances
Reviews:
   America 105:532, Jul 15, 1961
   New York Times page 11, Jun 24, 1961
                   page 22, Jun 28, 1962

Pardon My English
   book: Herbert Fields
   music: George Gershwin
   lyrics: Ira Gershwin
   staging: George Hale
   sets: John Wenger
Productions:
   Opened January 20, 1933 for 46 performances
Reviews:
   New Outlook 161:48, Mar 1933
   New York Times IX, page 5, Dec 11, 1932
                   page 11, Jan 21, 1933

Pardon Our French
   sketches: Ole Olsen and Chic Johnson
   music: Victor Young
   lyrics: Edward Heyman
   sets: Albert Johnson
   costumes: Jack Mosser
Productions:
   Opened October 5, 1950 for 100 performances
Reviews:
   Catholic World 172:228, Dec 1950
   Commonweal 53:62, Oct 27, 1950
   New York Theatre Critics' Reviews 1950:254+
   New York Times page 22, Oct 6, 1950
   New Yorker 26:52+, Oct 14, 1950
   Newsweek 36:86, Oct 16, 1950
   Theatre Arts 34:12, Dec 1950

Time 56:54, Oct 16, 1950

Paris
> book: Martin Brown
> music: Cole Porter; additional words and music by
>   Ray Goetz and Walter Kollo
> lyrics: Cole Porter; additional words and music by
>   Ray Goetz and Walter Kollo
> staging: W. H. Gilmore

Productions:
Opened October 8, 1928 for 195 performances
Reviews:
Life (New York) 92:17, Oct 28, 1928
New York Times VIII, page 4, Apr 8, 1928
                page 34, Oct 9, 1928
Outlook 150:1124, Nov 7, 1928
Theatre Magazine 48:81, Dec 1928

Parisiana
> book: Vincent Valentini
> staging: Vincent Valentini

Productions:
Opened February 9, 1928 for 28 performances
Reviews:
New York Times page 26, Feb 10, 1928
Theatre Magazine 17:159, May 1913

Park
> book: Paul Cherry
> music: Lance Mulcahy
> lyrics: Paul Cherry
> staging: John Stix
> sets: Peter Harvey
> costumes: Peter Harvey
> choreography: Lee Theodore

Productions:
Opened April 22, 1970 for 5 performances
Reviews:
New York Theatre Critics' Reviews 1970:270
New York Times page 47, Apr 23, 1970

Park Avenue
> book: Nunnally Johnson and George S. Kaufman,
>   based on the story "Holy Matrimony"
> music: Arthur Schwartz
> lyrics: Ira Gershwin
> staging: George S. Kaufman
> sets: Donald Oenslager
> choreography: Helen Tamiris

Productions:
Opened November 4, 1946 for 72 performances
Reviews:
Catholic World 164:361, Jan 1946

Nation 163:629, Nov 30, 1946
New York Theatre Critics' Reviews 1946:275+
New York Times VI, page 26, Sep 22, 1946
                page 31, Nov 5, 1946
                II, page 3, Dec 15, 1946
New Yorker 22:59, Nov 16, 1946
Newsweek 28:98, Nov 18, 1946
Time 48:64+, Nov 18, 1946
Vogue 108:196, Nov 15, 1946

A Party with Betty Comden and Adolph Green
    music and
    lyrics: Betty Comden, Adolph Green, Andre Previn,
                     Leonard Bernstein, Morton Gould, Roger Edens,
                     Jule Styne and Saul Chaplin
    sets: Marvin Reiss
Productions:
    (Off-Broadway) Opened Season of 1958-59
    Opened December 23, 1958 for 38 performances
    Opened April 16, 1959 for 44 performances
Reviews:
    Nation 188:77, Jan 24, 1959
    New York Theatre Critics' Reviews 1958:159
    New York Times page 2, Dec 24, 1958
                    page 30, May 18, 1959
    New Yorker 34:70, Jan 10, 1959
    Newsweek 53:61, Jan 5, 1959
    Saturday Review 42:67, Jan 10, 1959
    Theatre Arts 43:67-8, Mar 1959
    Time 73:56, Jan 5, 1959

The Passing Show of 1913
    dialogue: Harold Atteridge
    music: Jean Schwartz and Al W. Brown
    special music: Melville Ellis
    lyrics: Harold Atteridge
    staging: Ned Wayburn
Productions:
    Opened July 24, 1913 for 116 performances
Reviews:
    Dramatic Mirror 70:7, Aug 6, 1913
    Munsey 50:90, Oct 1913
    New York Times page 7, Jul 25, 1913
    Theatre Magazine 18:83, Sep 1913
                     18:89, Sep 1913

The Passing Show of 1914
    dialogue: Harold Atteridge
    music: Harry Carroll and Sigmund Romberg
    special music: Melville Ellis
    lyrics: Harold Atteridge
    staging: J. C. Huffman
    costumes: Melville Ellis

    choreography: Jack Mason
Productions:
Opened June 10, 1914 for 133 performances
Reviews:
    Dramatic Mirror 71:8, Jun 17, 1914
    Munsey 53:92-4, Oct 1914
    New York Times page 11, Jun 11, 1914
    Theatre Magazine 20:37, Jul 1914
                        20:230, Nov 1914

The Passing Show of 1915
    dialogue: Harold Atteridge
    music: Leo Edwards, William F. Peters and J. Leubrie
                   Hill
    lyrics: Harold Atteridge
    staging: J. C. Huffman
    choreography: Jack Mason and Theodor Kosloff
Productions:
Opened May 29, 1915 for 145 performances
Reviews:
    Dramatic Mirror 73:8, Jun 2, 1915
                    73:2, Jun 30, 1915
                    74:4, Jul 7, 1915
    Green Book 14:221-3, Aug 1915
    Harper's Bazaar 50:49, Jul 1915
    Smart Set 46:146-8, Aug 1915
    Theatre Magazine 22:27, Jun 1915
                     22:39, Jun 1915
                     22:57, Aug 1915

The Passing Show of 1916
    book: Harold Atteridge
    music: Sigmund Romberg, Otto Motzan and George
                   Gershwin
    staging: J. J. Shubert, J. C. Huffman
    choreography: Allen K. Foster
Productions:
Opened June 22, 1916 for 140 performances
Reviews:
    Dramatic Mirror 76:8, Jul 1, 1916
                    76:4, Jul 8, 1916
                    76:2, Jul 15, 1916
                    76:4, Jul 22, 1916
    Green Book 16:422-3, Sep 1916
    New York Times page 9, Jun 23, 1916
    Theatre Magazine 24:63, Aug 1915
                     24:94, Aug 1915

The Passing Show of 1917
    dialogue: Harold Atteridge
    music: Sigmund Romberg and Otto Motzan
    lyrics: Harold Atteridge
    staging: J. C. Huffman

choreography: Allen K. Foster
Productions:
    Opened April 26, 1917 for 196 performances
Reviews:
    Dramatic Mirror 77:7, May 5, 1917
                    77:4, May 12, 1917
    Green Book 18:16+, Jul 1917
    Life (New York) 69:816, May 10, 1917
    New York Times page 9, Apr 27, 1917
    Theatre Magazine 25:344+, Jun 1917

The Passing Show of 1918
    dialogue: Harold Atteridge
    music: Sigmund Romberg and Jean Schwartz
    lyrics: Harold Atteridge
    staging: J. C. Huffman and J. J. Shubert
    sets: Watson Barratt
    choreography: Jack Mason
Productions:
    Opened July 25, 1918 for 124 performances
Reviews:
    Dramatic Mirror 79:193, Aug 10, 1918
                    79:683, Nov 9, 1918
    Forum 60:365, Sep 1918
    Green Book 20:582-6, Oct 1918
    New York Times page 9, Jul 26, 1918
    Theatre Magazine 28:144+, Sep 1918

The Passing Show of 1919
    conceived: Lee Shubert and J. J. Shubert
    book: Harold Atteridge
    songs: Jean Schwartz
    staging: J. J. Shubert
    sets: Watson Barratt
    costumes: Cora McGeachey and Homer Conant
Productions:
    Opened October 23, 1919 for 280 performances
Reviews:
    New York Times page 11, Oct 24, 1919

The Passing Show of 1921
    book: Harold Atteridge
    music: Jean Schwartz
    staging: J. C. Huffman and J. J. Shubert
    sets: William Weaver
    choreography: Max Scheck
Productions:
    Opened December 29, 1920 for 200 performances
Reviews:
    Nation 112:126, Jan 26, 1921
    New York Clipper 68:30, Jan 5, 1921
    New York Times page 16, Dec 30, 1920
    Theatre Magazine 33:165, Mar 1921

33:177-8, Mar 1921

The Passing Show of 1923
        book: Harold Atteridge
        music: Jean Schwartz and Sigmund Romberg
        lyrics: Harold Atteridge
        staging: J. C. Huffman
Productions:
        Opened June 14, 1923 for 118 performances
Reviews:
        Life (New York) 82:20, Jul 5, 1923
        New York Clipper 71:30, Jun 20, 1923
        New York Times page 24, Jun 15, 1923
        Theatre Magazine 38:15, Aug 1923

The Passing Show of 1924
        book: Harold Atteridge
        music: Sigmund Romberg and Jean Schwartz
        lyrics: Harold Atteridge and Alex Gerber
        staging: J. C. Huffman
Productions:
        Opened September 3, 1924 for 106 performances
Reviews:
        New York Times page 13, Sep 4, 1924
        Theatre Magazine 40:16, Nov 1924

Peace
        book: Tim Reynolds; based on the play by Aristophanes
        music: Al Carmines
        lyrics: Tim Reynolds
        staging: Lawrence Kornfield
        costumes: Nancy Christofferson
        choreography: Arlene Rothlein
Productions:
        (Off-Broadway) Opened January 27, 1969 for 192 performances
Reviews:
        Dance Magazine 43:23+, Apr 1969
        New York Theatre Critics' Reviews 1969:276
        New York Times page 49, Jan 28, 1969
                        II, page 10, Feb 16, 1969
                        II, page 1, Feb 23, 1969
                        page 22, Jul 11, 1969
        New Yorker 44:98-100, Feb 8, 1969

The Pearl Maiden
        libretto: Earle C. Anthony
        music: Harry Auracher
        staging: Al Holbrook
Productions:
        Opened January 22, 1912 for 24 performances
Reviews:
        Dramatic Mirror 67:7, Jan 24, 1912
        Green Book 7:1205, Jun 1912

The Pearl Necklace   381

Theatre Magazine 15:xv, Mar 1912

The Pearl Necklace
    book: Israel Bercovici; based on Jewish folk tales
    staging: Franz Auerbach
Productions:
(Off-Broadway) Opened September 21, 1972 for 8 performances
Reviews:
    New York Times page 35, Sep 22, 1972

The Peasant Girl
    book: Leo Stein; adapted by Edgar Smith
    music: Oskar Nedbal; additional numbers by Rudolph
                     Friml
    lyrics: Herbert Reynolds and Harold Atteridge
    staging: J. H. Benrimo
Productions:
Opened March 2, 1915 for 111 performances
Reviews:
    Dramatic Mirror 73:8, Mar 10, 1915
                     73:2, Mar 31, 1915
    Green Book 13:826, May 1915
               13:1144-5, Jun 1915
    Munsey 54:731, May 1915
    New York Dramatic News 60:17, Mar 13, 1915
    New York Times page 11, Mar 3, 1915
    Theatre Magazine 21:171, Apr 1915
                     21:192, Apr 1915
                     22:78, Aug 1915

Peg-o'-My-Dreams
    book: J. Hartley Manners
    music: Hugo Felix
    lyrics: Anne Caldwell
Productions:
Opened May 5, 1924 for 32 performances
Reviews:
    Life (New York) 83:18, May 29, 1924
    New York Times page 25, May 6, 1924
                     VIII, page 1, May 18, 1924

Peggy
    book: George Grosmith, Jr.
    music: Leslie Stuart
    lyrics: C. H. Bovill
    staging: Ned Wayburn
Productions:
Opened December 7, 1911 for 36 performances
Reviews:
    Blue Book 14:900-903, Mar 1912
    Dramatic Mirror 66:7, Dec 13, 1911
    New York Times page 8, Dec 8, 1911
    Theatre Magazine 15:xi, Jan 1912

Peggy-Ann
    book: Herbert Fields
    music: Richard Rodgers
    lyrics: Lorenz Hart
    staging: Robert Milton
Productions:
    Opened December 27, 1926 for 333 performances
Reviews:
    New York Times page 16, Dec 28, 1926
                     VII, page 2, Mar 27, 1927
                     VII, page 1, Jul 3, 1927
                     VIII, page 4, Jan 29, 1928

The Penny Friend
    book: William Roy; based on J. M. Barrie's A Kiss
                       for Cinderella
    music: William Roy
    lyrics: William Roy
    staging: Benno D. Frank
    sets: Ben Shecter
    choreography: Lou Kristofer
Productions:
    (Off-Broadway) Opened December 26, 1966 for 32 performances
Reviews:
    New York Times page 46, Dec 27, 1966

The Pepper Mill
    sketches: W. H. Auden, Klaus Mann, Erich Muhsam,
                       Ernst Toller, Erica Mann; English adaptation
                       by John Latouche and Edwin Denby
    music: Magnus Henning, Aaron Copland, Peter Krender,
                       Herbert Murril, Werner Kruse
    staging: Therese Giehse
    sets: Anton Refregier
Productions:
    Opened January 5, 1937 for 6 performances
Reviews:
    New York Times page 19, Jan 6, 1937
    Theatre Arts 21:6, Jan 1937

The Perfect Fool
    book: Ed Wynn
    music: Ed Wynn
    lyrics: Ed Wynn
    staging: Ed Wynn
Productions:
    Opened November 7, 1921 for (256) performances
Reviews:
    Dramatic Mirror 84:593, Oct 22, 1921
    Life (New York) 78:18, Dec 15, 1921
    New York Clipper 69:20, Nov 16, 1921
    New York Times page 28, Nov 8, 1921
                     VI, page 1, Nov 27, 1921

Theatre Magazine 35:32, Jan 1922

Peter Pan
     book: Richard Halliday, adapted from James M.
                        Barrie's play
     music: Mark Charlap and Jule Styne
     lyrics: Carolyn Leigh, Betty Comden, Adolph Green
     staging: Jerome Robbins
     sets: Peter Larkin
     costumes: Motley
     choreography: Jerome Robbins
Productions:
     Opened October 20, 1954 for 152 performances
Reviews:
     America 92:259, Nov 27, 1954
     Catholic World 180:225, Dec 1954
     Commonweal 61:223, Nov 26, 1954
     Dance Magazine 28:24-5, Dec 1954
     Life 37:109-10+, Nov 8, 1954
          38:97-100, Apr 4, 1955
     Look 18:54-5, Dec 14, 1954
     Nation 179:428, Nov 13, 1954
     New Republic 131:23, Nov 1, 1954
     New York Theatre Critics' Reviews 1954:273+
     New York Times page 15, Jul 20, 1954
                    II, page 1, Oct 17, 1954
                    page 30, Oct 21, 1954
                    II, page 1, Oct 31, 1954
     New York Times Magazine page 60, Oct 10, 1954
     New Yorker 30:66+, Oct 30, 1954
     Newsweek 44:60, Nov 1, 1954
     Saturday Review 37:29, Nov 20, 1954
     Theatre Arts 38:18-19+, Nov 1954
                  39:12-13+, Jan 1955
     Time 64:80, Nov 1, 1954
     Vogue 124:124, Dec 1954

Phoebe of Quality Street
     adapted: Edward Delaney Dunn; adapted from Sir James
                        M. Barrie's Quality Street
     music: Walter Kollo
     staging: W. H. Gilmore
Productions:
     Opened May 9, 1921 for 16 performances
Reviews:
     New York Times page 20, May 10, 1921

Phoenix '55
     sketches: Ira Wallach
     music: David Baker
     lyrics: David Craig
     staging: Marc Daniels
     sets: Eldon Elder

```
        costumes:      Alvin Colt
        choreography:  Boris Runanin
Productions:
        Opened April 23, 1955 for 97 performances
        (Off-Broadway)  Season of 1954-55 (Phoenix Theatre)
Reviews:
        America 92:545+, Feb 19, 1955
                93:191, May 14, 1955
        Catholic World 181:67-8, Apr 1955
                181:228, Jun 1955
        Commonweal 61:551, Feb 25, 1955
        Life 38:75-6+, Feb 21, 1955
             38:130, May 23, 1955
        Nation 180:430, May 14, 1955
        New York Theatre Critics' Reviews 1955:317+
        New York Times page 20, Apr 25, 1955
        New Yorker 30:52, Feb 5, 1955
                31:67-9, Apr 30, 1955
        Newsweek 45:72, Feb 7, 1955
                46:55, Jul 18, 1955
        Saturday Review 38:24, Feb 12, 1955
                39:12-13, Sep 15, 1956
        Theatre Arts 39:18-19+, Apr 1955
                39:86+, Jul 1955
        Time 65:50, Feb 7, 1955
```

Piaf, Edith (see Edith Piaf)

Pick a Number XV
```
        conceived:     Julius Monk
        sketches:      William F. Brown and others
        songs:         Clark Gesner, Claibe Richardson and others
        staging:       Julius Monk
        choreography:  Frank Wagner
Productions:
        (Off-Broadway)  Opened October 14, 1965 for 400 performances
No Reviews.
```

Pickwick
```
        book:          Wolf Mankowitz
        music:         Cyril Ornadel
        lyrics:        Leslie Bricusse
        staging:       Peter Coe
        sets:          Sean Kenny
        costumes:      Roger Furse and Peter Rice
        choreography:  Gillian Lynne
Productions:
        Opened October 4, 1965 for 55 performances
Reviews:
        America 113:509, Oct 30, 1965
        Dance Magazine 39:24, Nov 1965
        New York Theatre Critics' Reviews 1965:265
        New York Times page 5, Oct 6, 1965
```

page 57, Nov 16, 1965
New Yorker 41:195, Oct 16, 1965
Newsweek 66:114, Oct 18, 1965
Saturday Review 48:74, Oct 23, 1965
Time 86:75, Oct 15, 1965
Vogue 146:71, Nov 15, 1965

Piggy
    book: Daniel Kusell and Alfred Jackson; adapted from
                       Harry B. Smith and Ludwig Englander's The
                       Rich Mr. Hoggenheimer
    staging: William B. Friedlander
Productions:
Opened January 11, 1927 for 83 performances
Reviews:
    New York Times page 22, Jan 12, 1927
    Theatre Magazine 45:4, Mar 1927
(See also I Told You So)

Pimpernel!
    book: William Kaye; based on The Scarlet Pimpernel
                       by Baroness Orczy
    music: Mimi Stone
    lyrics: William Kaye
    staging: Malcolm Black
    sets: Lloyd Burlingame
    costumes: Sonia Lowenstein
    choreography: Sandra Devlin
Productions:
    (Off-Broadway) Opened January 7, 1964 for 3 performances
Reviews:
    New York Times page 26, Jan 7, 1964

The Pink Lady
    book: C. M. S. McLellan; adapted from the French
                       of Georges Berr and Marcel Guillemaud
    music: Ivan Caryll
    lyrics: C. M. S. McLellan
    staging: Herbert Gresham
    choreography: Julian Mitchell
Productions:
Opened March 13, 1911 for 312 performances
Reviews:
    Blue Book 13:4-8, May 1911
    Dramatic Mirror 65:7, Mar 15, 1911
                    65:2, Mar 22, 1911
                    67:14+, Jan 31, 1912
    Green Book Album 5:922-4, May 1911
    Hampton 27:524, Oct 1911
    Metropolitan Magazine 34:221, May 1911
    Munsey 45:284, May 1911
    New England Magazine 45:398, Dec 1911
    New York Dramatic News 57:5, Dec 28, 1912

Pearson 25:666+, May 1911
Red Book 17:379+, Jun 1911
Theatre Magazine 13:xii, Apr 1911
                    13:134, Apr 1911
                    15:iii, May 1912

Pink Ships on Parade
    book: Muni Diamond, Ben Ross, Kenneth Hunter and
                    Peter Martin
    music: Earl Robinson
    lyrics: Muni Diamond, Ben Ross, Kenneth Hunter and
                    Peter Martin
Productions:
    (Off-Broadway) Opened January 30, 1937
Reviews:
    New York Times page 14, Feb 1, 1937

Pins and Needles (1922)
    book: Albert de Courville, Wal Pink and Edgar Wallace
    music: James Hanley and Frederick Chappelle
    lyrics: Ballard MacDonald, Rupert Hazel and I. Caesar
Productions:
    Opened February 1, 1922 for 46 performances
Reviews:
    New York Times page 20, Feb 2, 1922
    Theatre Magazine 35:264+, Apr 1922

Pins and Needles (1937)
    book: Arthur Arent, Marc Blitzstein, Emanuel Eisen-
                    berg, Charles Friedman, David Gregory
    music: Harold J. Rome
    lyrics: Harold J. Rome
    staging: Charles Friedman
    sets: S. Syrjala
    choreography: Benjamin Zemach
Productions:
    Opened November 27, 1937 for 1,108 performances
Reviews:
    Catholic World 147:215, May 1938
                   150:86-7, Oct 1939
    Collier's 102:34+, Nov 12, 1938
    Independent Woman 17:52, Feb 1938
                      17:359, Nov 1938
    Life 3:52-3, Dec 27, 1937
    Literary Digest 125:34, Jan 1, 1938
    Nation 145:698, Dec 18, 1937
    New York Theatre Critics' Reviews 1940:497+
    New York Times page 24, Jun 15, 1936
                    page 18, Nov 29, 1937
                    XI, page 1, Jan 23, 1938
                    IX, page 3, Aug 21, 1938
                    page 27, Dec 6, 1938
                    X, page 3, Dec 11, 1938

                              page 16, Jan 24, 1939
                              page 26, Apr 21, 1939
                              page 19, Nov 21, 1939
        Scholastic 32:19F, Mar 5, 1938
        Stage 15:54-5, Feb 1938
        Theatre Arts 22:4, Jan 1938
                          23:403, Jun 1939
                          24:20, Jan 1940
        Time 31:32+, Mar 14, 1938

Pipe Dream
        book: Oscar Hammerstein II, based on John Steinbeck's
                         novel Sweet Thursday
        music: Richard Rodgers
        lyrics: Oscar Hammerstein II
        staging: Harold Clurman
        sets: Jo Mielziner
        costumes: Alvin Colt
Productions:
        Opened November 30, 1955 for 246 performances
Reviews:
        America 94:417-18, Jan 7, 1956
        Catholic World 182:388, Feb 1956
        Commonweal 63:331, Dec 30, 1955
        Nation 181:544, Dec 17, 1955
        New York Theatre Critics' Reviews 1955:198+
        New York Times II, page 1, Nov 27, 1955
                          page 44, Dec 1, 1955
                          II, page 5, Dec 11, 1955
        New Yorker 31:104+, Dec 10, 1955
        Newsweek 46:110, Dec 12, 1955
        Saturday Review 38:24, Dec 17, 1955
                        39:13, Sep 15, 1956
        Theatre Arts 40:12-13, Feb 1956
        Time 66:67, Dec 12, 1955

Pippin
        book: Roger O. Hirson
        music: Stephen Schwartz
        lyrics: Stephen Schwartz
        staging: Bob Fosse
        sets: Tony Walton
        costumes: Patricia Zipprodt
        choreography: Bob Fosse
Productions:
        Opened October 23, 1972 for 1,113* performances
Reviews:
        America 127:418, Nov 18, 1972
        Dance Magazine 49:90-1, Apr 1975
        Ebony 28:74-6+, May 1973
        Life 73:54-7, Nov 17, 1972
             73:30, Nov 24, 1972
        Nation 215:474-5, Nov 13, 1972

New York Theatre Critics' Reviews 1972:208
New York Times page 46, Feb 9, 1972
                page 37, Oct 24, 1972
                II, page 1, Oct 29, 1972
                II, page 1, Nov 5, 1972
                page 26, Nov 7, 1972
                II, page 27, Dec 3, 1972
                II, page 1, Jan 28, 1973
New Yorker 48:105, Nov 4, 1972
Newsweek 80:134-5, Nov 6, 1972
Saturday Review 55:92, Dec 2, 1972
Time 100:83, Nov 6, 1972

Pitter Patter
        book: Will M. Hough; based on W. Collier and G.
                           Stewart's Caught in the Rain
        music: William B. Friedlander
        lyrics: William B. Friedlander
Productions:
        Opened September 28, 1920 for 111 performances
Reviews:
        Dramatic Mirror page 621, Oct 2, 1920
        New York Clipper 68:28, Oct 6, 1920
        New York Times page 12, Sep 29, 1920

Plain and Fancy
        book: Joseph Stein and Will Glickman
        music: Albert Hague
        lyrics: Arnold B. Horwitt
        staging: Morton Da Costa
        sets: Raoul Pene du Bois
        costumes: Raoul Pene du Bois
        choreography: Helen Tamiris
Productions:
        Opened January 27, 1955 for 461 performances
        (Off-Off-Broadway) Opened February 23, 1964 for 8 per-
           formances (Equity Library Theatre)
Reviews:
        America 92:545+, Feb 19, 1955
        Catholic World 181:67-8, Apr 1955
        Commonweal 61:551, Feb 25, 1955
        Life 38:75-6+, Feb 21, 1955
        New York Theatre Critics' Reviews 1955:382+
        New York Times page 14, Jan 28, 1955
                        II, page 1, Feb 6, 1955
                        II, page 6, Feb 6, 1955
                        II, page 3, Feb 5, 1956
        New Yorker 30:52, Feb 5, 1955
        Newsweek 45:72, Feb 7, 1955
        Saturday Review 38:24, Feb 12, 1955
                        39:12-13, Sep 15, 1956
        Theatre Arts 39:18-19+, Apr 1955
        Time 65:50, Feb 7, 1955

Plain Jane
    book: Phil Cook and McElbert Moore
    music: Tom Johnstone
    lyrics: Phil Cook
Productions:
    Opened May 12, 1924 for (40) performances
Reviews:
    New York Times page 24, May 13, 1924
    Theatre Magazine 40:16, Aug 1924

Plantation Revue
Productions:
    Opened July 17, 1922 for 40 performances
Reviews:
    New York Times page 18, Jul 18, 1922

Pleasure Bound
    book: Harold Atteridge, Max and Nathaniel Lief
    music: Muriel Pollock
    lyrics: Harold Atteridge, Max and Nathaniel Lief
    staging: Lew Morton
    choreography: Busby Berkeley
Productions:
    Opened February 18, 1929 for 136 performances
Reviews:
    New York Times IX, page 2, Feb 10, 1929
                 page 22, Feb 19, 1929
                 X, page 4, Mar 17, 1929
    Theatre Magazine 49:47, Apr 1929

The Pleasure Seekers
    book: Edgar Smith
    music/lyrics: E. Ray Goetz
    staging: William J. Wilson
Productions:
    Opened November 3, 1913 for 72 performances
Reviews:
    Dramatic Mirror 70:11, Nov 5, 1913
    New York Times page 11, Oct 23, 1913
                 page 9, Nov 4, 1913
    Theatre Magazine 18:xx, Dec 1913

The Plot Against the Chase Manhattan Bank
    sketches: Carl Larsen, David Dozer, Ernest Leongrande,
                     Lawrence B. Eisenberg and Betty Freedman
    music: Richard R. Wolf
    lyrics: Frank Spiering, Jr.
    staging: Tom Gruenwald
    sets: Robert T. Williams
    costumes: Sylvia Kalegi
    choreography: Karen Kristen and Bick Goss
Productions:
    (Off-Broadway) Opened November 26, 1963 for 15 performances
Reviews:

New York Times page 29, Nov 27, 1963

La Plume de Ma Tante
    book: Robert Dhery
    music: Gerard Calvi
    lyrics: Ross Parker
    staging: Alec Shanks
    sets: Charles Elson
    choreography: Colette Brosset
Productions:
    Opened November 11, 1958 for 835 performances
Reviews:
    America 100:381, Dec 20, 1958
    Christian Century 75:1435, Dec 10, 1958
    Dance Magazine 33:16, Jan 1959
    Life 45:67-8+, Dec 8, 1958
    New York Theatre Critics' Reviews 1958:206+
    New York Times page 42, Nov 12, 1958
                    page 39, Nov 13, 1958
                    II, page 1, Nov 16, 1958
                    II, page 1, Sep 13, 1959
                    II, page 3, Dec 18, 1960
    New Yorker 34:99-100, Nov 22, 1958
    Newsweek 52:78-9, Nov 24, 1958
    Saturday Review 41:24, Nov 29, 1958
    Theatre Arts 43:11+, Jan 1959
    Time 72:80+, Nov 24, 1958
    Vogue 133:94-5, Jan 1, 1959

Policy Kings
    book: Michael Ashwood
    music: Sam Manning
    songs: James P. Johnson
    staging: Winston Douglas
Productions:
    (Off-Broadway) Opened December 29, 1938
Reviews:
    New York Times page 6, Dec 31, 1938

A Political Party
    sketches: Daniel Ruslander, Kurt Moss, C. D. Bryan
                   and others
    songs: Daniel Ruslander, Kurt Moss, C. D. Bryan
                   and others
    staging: Arch Lustberg
    costumes: Jean Anne
Productions:
    (Off-Broadway) Opened September 26, 1963 for 8 performances
Reviews:
    New York Times page 17, Sep 27, 1963

Polly
    book: Guy Bolton and George Middleton, based on

David Belasco's <u>Polly with a Past</u>
music: Herbert Stothart and Philip Charig
lyrics: Irving Caesar
staging: Jack Haskell
Productions:
Opened January 8, 1929 for 15 performances
Reviews:
Life (New York) 93:28, Jan 25, 1929
New York Times X, page 2, Nov 11, 1928
                page 28, Jan 9, 1929

Polly of Hollywood
    book: Will Morrissey
    staging: Will Morrissey
Productions:
Opened February 21, 1927 for 24 performances
Reviews:
New York Times page 22, Feb 22, 1927

Polonaise
    book: Gottfried Reinhardt and Anthony Veiller
    music: Frederic Chopin (Adaptations by Bronislaw
                Kaper)
    lyrics: John Latouche
    staging: Stella Adler
    sets: Howard Bay
    costumes: Mary Grant
    choreography: David Lichine
Productions:
Opened October 6, 1945 for 113 performances
Reviews:
Catholic World 162:167, Nov 1945
New York Theatre Critics' Reviews 1945:149+
New York Times page 20, Oct 8, 1945
               II, page 1, Oct 14, 1945
New Yorker 21:50, Oct 13, 1945
Newsweek 26:94, Oct 15, 1945
Theatre Arts 29:687, Dec 1945
Time 46:66, Oct 15, 1945

Poor Little Ritz Girl
    book: Lew Fields and George Campbell
    music: Richard Rodgers and Sigmund Romberg
    lyrics: Lorenz Hart and Alex Gerber
    staging: Ned Wayburn
Productions:
Opened July 27, 1920 for 119 performances
Reviews:
Dramatic Mirror page 23, Aug 4, 1920
New York Clipper 68:25, Jun 2, 1920
New York Times page 7, Jul 29, 1920
Theatre Magazine 32:187, Oct 1920

Pop
    book: Larry Schiff and Chuck Knull
    music: Donna Cribari
    lyrics: Larry Schiff and Chuck Knull
    staging: Allen R. Belknap
    sets: Pat Gorman
    costumes: Pat Gorman
    choreography: Ron Spencer
Productions:
    (Off-Broadway) Opened April 3, 1974 for one performance
Reviews:
    New York Times page 54, Apr 4, 1974

Poppy
    book: Dorothy Donnelly
    music: Stephen Jones and Arthur Samuels
    lyrics: Dorothy Donnelly
    staging: Dorothy Donnelly and Julian Alfred
Productions:
    Opened September 3, 1923 for (328) performances
Reviews:
    Life (New York) 82:18, Sep 20, 1923
    Nation 119:304, Sep 19, 1923
    New York Times page 14, Sep 4, 1923
                     page 14, Sep 6, 1924
    Theatre Magazine 38:19, Nov 1923

Porgy and Bess
    book: Du Bose Heyward, adapted from Du Bose and
                      Dorothy Heyward's play Porgy
    music: George Gershwin
    lyrics: Du Bose Heyward and Ira Gershwin
    staging: Rouben Mamoulian
    sets: Sergei Soudekine
Productions:
    Opened October 10, 1935 for 124 performances
    Opened January 22, 1942 for 286 performances
    Opened September 13, 1943 for 24 performances
    Opened February 7, 1944 for 16 performances
    Opened February 28, 1944 for 48 performances
    Opened March 10, 1953 for 305 performances
    Opened May 17, 1961 for 16 performances
    Opened May 6, 1964 for 15 performances
Reviews:
    America 88:687, Mar 21, 1953
             105:473, Jun 24, 1961
    Catholic World 142:340-1, Dec 1935
                 177:148-9, May 1953
    Commonweal 22:642, Oct 25, 1935
               57:624-5, Mar 27, 1953
    Etude 74:14-15, Mar 1956
    Good Housekeeping 141:17+, Oct 1955
    Life 12:65, Feb 23, 1942

Literary Digest 120:18, Oct 26, 1935
Look 17:17, May 19, 1953
Modern Music 19:195, Mar-Apr 1942
Musical America 73:33, Apr 15, 1953
Musical Courier 111:7, Oct 12, 1935
Nation 141:518-19, Oct 30, 1935
          176:272, Mar 28, 1953
New Republic 84:338, Oct 30, 1935
             128:30-1, Apr 6, 1953
New York Theatre Critics' Reviews 1942:373+
                                  1953:337+
New York Times IX, page 2, Sep 15, 1935
                   page 27, Oct 1, 1935
                   XI, page 3, Oct 6, 1935
                   page 30, Oct 11, 1935
                   X, page 1, Oct 20, 1935
                   X, page 7, Oct 20, 1935
                   page 25, Mar 17, 1936
                   page 16, Jan 23, 1942
                   IX, page 1, Feb 1, 1942
                   VIII, page 7, Nov 15, 1942
                   page 26, Sep 14, 1943
                   page 13, Feb 8, 1944
                   II, page 4, Jun 17, 1945
                   II, page 7, Nov 26, 1950
                   II, page 1, Sep 7, 1952
                   page 18, Sep 8, 1952
                   page 37, Sep 11, 1952
                   page 18, Sep 18, 1952
                   II, page 1, Sep 28, 1952
                   VI, page 20, Sep 28, 1952
                   page 29, Oct 31, 1952
                   page 21, Feb 17, 1953
                   page 25, Mar 10, 1953
                   II, page 1, Mar 15, 1953
                   page 42, Sep 23, 1954
                   page 36, Dec 17, 1954
                   page 30, Dec 22, 1954
                   page 19, Jan 21, 1955
                   page 22, Jan 31, 1955
                   page 23, Feb 8, 1955
                   page 26, Feb 16, 1955
                   page 23, Feb 23, 1955
                   page 20, Apr 22, 1955
                   page 14, Aug 5, 1955
                   page 38, Nov 22, 1955
                   page 29, Dec 27, 1955
                   page 36, Jan 11, 1956
                   II, page 3, Jan 15, 1956
                   page 40, May 18, 1961
                   page 53, Oct 20, 1965
New York Times Magazine page 58, Jan 30, 1955
New Yorker 29:71, Mar 7, 1953

29:62+, Mar 21, 1953
                38:175-6, Apr 14, 1962
Newsweek 6:23-4, Oct 19, 1935
                19:56, Feb 2, 1942
                40:68, Sep 22, 1952
                41:98, Mar 23, 1953
                47:43-4, Jan 9, 1956
Pictorial Review 37:4+, Nov 1935
Saturday Review 34:50-1, Sep 29, 1951
                35:44, Jun 28, 1952
                36:27, Mar 28, 1953
                39:38, Jan 14, 1956
                44:30, Jun 17, 1961
Stage 13:25-8, Oct 1935
        13:31-3, Nov 1935
        13:36-8, Dec 1935
Theatre Arts 19:853-9+, Nov 1935
                19:893-4, Dec 1935
                37:89, Jun 1952
                37:64-5, May 1953
                39:66-7+, May 1955
                45:10-11, Jul 1961
Time 26:49-50, Sep 30, 1935
        26:48-9, Oct 21, 1935
        39:45, Feb 2, 1942
        61:80, Mar 23, 1953
        65:83, Mar 7, 1955
Vanity Fair 45:68, Dec 1935

Porter, Cole (see Cole Porter)

Portofino
        book: Richard Ney
        music: Louis Bellson and Will Irwin
        lyrics: Richard Ney and Sheldon Harnick
        staging: Karl Genus
        sets: Wolfgang Roth
        costumes: Michael Travis
        choreography: Charles Weidman
Productions:
        Opened February 21, 1958 for 3 performances
Reviews:
        New York Theatre Critics' Reviews 1958:346+
        New York Times page 8, Feb 22, 1958
        New Yorker 34:58+, Mar 1, 1958

Pousse-Café
        book: Jerome Weidman; based on the film The Blue
                         Angel
        music: Duke Ellington
        lyrics: Marshall Barer and Fred Tobias
        staging: José Quintero
        sets: Will Steven Armstrong

    costumes: Patricia Zipprodt and Albert Wolsky
    choreography: Valerie Bettis
Productions:
    Opened March 18, 1966 for 3 performances
Reviews:
    Dance Magazine 40:24, May 1966
    New York Theatre Critics' Reviews 1966:326
    New York Times page 19, Mar 19, 1966
                   page 36, Mar 21, 1966
    New Yorker 42:120, Mar 26, 1966
    Newsweek 67:88, Mar 28, 1966

Power
    book: Peter Copani
    music: David McHugh
    lyrics: Peter Copani
Productions:
    (Off-Off-Broadway) Opened Season of 1973-74 (The Peoples'
    Performing Co.)
No Reviews.

Present Arms
    book: Herbert Fields
    music: Richard Rodgers
    lyrics: Lorenz Hart
    staging: Alexander Leftwich
Productions:
    Opened April 26, 1928 for 155 performances
Reviews:
    New York Times page 16, Apr 27, 1928
    Outlook 149:185, May 30, 1928
    Theatre Magazine 47:65, Jun 1928
    Vogue 71:74, Jun 15, 1928

The President's Daughter
    book: H. Kalmanov
    music: Murray Rumshinsky
    lyrics: Jacob Jacobs
    staging: Jacob Jacobs
    sets: Barry Arnold
    choreography: Henrietta Jacobson
Productions:
    Opened November 3, 1970 for 72 performances
Reviews:
    New York Times page 41, Nov 4, 1970

Pretty Mrs. Smith
    book: Oliver Morosco and Elmer Harris
    music: Henry James and Alfred Robyn
    lyrics: Earl Carroll
    staging: T. Daniel Frawley
Productions:
    Opened September 21, 1914 for 48 performances

Reviews:
    Dramatic Mirror 72:8, Sep 30, 1914
                    72:4, Oct 7, 1914
                    72:2, Oct 21, 1914
    Green Book 12:91+, Jul 1914
    New York Dramatic News 60:20, Jan 2, 1915
    New York Times page 11, Sep 22, 1914
    Theatre Magazine 20:206-7, Nov 1914

The Prince and the Pauper
    book: Verna Tomasson; based on the story by Mark
                       Twain
    music: George Fischoff
    lyrics: Verna Tomasson
    staging: David Shanstrom
    sets: Norman Womack
    costumes: Norman Womack
    choreography: Bick Goss
Productions:
    (Off-Broadway) Opened October 12, 1963 for 158 performances
No Reviews.

The Prince of Bohemia
    book: J. Hartley Manners
    music: A. Baldwin Sloane
    lyrics: E. Ray Goetz
    staging: Ned Wayburn
Productions:
    Opened January 13, 1910 for 20 performances
Reviews:
    Dramatic Mirror 63:6, Jan 22, 1910

The Prince of Liederkranz (see The Student Gypsy)

Princess April
    book: William Cary Duncan and Lewis Allen Browne;
                       adapted from a story by Frank R. Adams
    music: Carlo and Sanders
    lyrics: Carlo and Sanders
Productions:
    Opened December 1, 1924 for 24 performances
Reviews:
    New York Times page 23, Dec 2, 1924
    Theatre Magazine 41:16, Feb 1925

Princess Flavia
    book: Harry B. Smith; adapted from Anthony Hope's
                       The Prisoner of Zenda
    music: Sigmund Romberg
    lyrics: Harry B. Smith
    staging: J. J. Shubert
Productions:
    Opened November 2, 1925 for 152 performances

Reviews:
    New York Times page 34, Nov 3, 1925
                VIII, page 2, Nov 8, 1925
    Theatre Magazine 43:4, Jan 1926

Princess Virtue
    book: B. C. Hilliam and Gitz Rice
    staging: Leon Errol
Productions:
    Opened May 4, 1921 for 16 performances
Reviews:
    Dramatic Mirror 83:660, Apr 16, 1921
                 83:817, May 14, 1921
    New York Clipper 69:19, May 11, 1921
    New York Times page 20, May 5, 1921

Priorities of 1942
    assembled: Clifford C. Fischer
    music: Marjery Fielding and Charles Barnes
    lyrics: Marjery Fielding and Charles Barnes
    choreography: Marjery Fielding
Productions:
    Opened March 12, 1942 for 353 performances
Reviews:
    New Republic 106:430, Mar 30, 1942
    New York Theatre Critics' Reviews 1942:329
    New York Times page 23, Mar 13, 1942
                   VIII, page 1, Mar 29, 1942
                   VII, page 18, Apr 19, 1942
    Time 39:46, Mar 23, 1942

Promenade
    book: Maria Irene Fornes
    music: Al Carmines
    lyrics: Maria Irene Fornes
    staging: Lawrence Kornfield
    sets: Rouben Ter-Arutunian
    costumes: Willa Kim
Productions:
    (Off-Broadway) Opened June 4, 1969 for 259 performances
Reviews:
    Life 67:8, Aug 1, 1969
    Nation 208:837, Jun 30, 1969
    New York Theatre Critics' Reviews 1969:213
    New York Times page 56, Jun 5, 1969
                  page 32, Jun 6, 1969
                  II, page 1, Jun 15, 1969
    New Yorker 45:63, Jul 5, 1969
    Newsweek 73:107, Jun 16, 1969

Promises, Promises
    book: Neil Simon; based on the screenplay The Apart-
                  ment by Billy Wilder and I. A. L. Diamond

music: Burt Bacharach
lyrics: Hal David
staging: Robert Moore
sets: Robin Wagner
costumes: Donald Brooks
choreography: Harold Wheeler
Productions:
Opened December 1, 1968 for 1,281 performances
Reviews:
America 120:146, Feb 1, 1969
Dance Magazine 43:93-4, Jan 1969
Life 66:14, Jan 17, 1969
National Review 21:918, Sep 9, 1969
Nation 208:125, Jan 27, 1969
New York Theatre Critics' Reviews 1968:161
                                    1968:164
New York Times page 59, Dec 2, 1968
              page 52, Dec 3, 1968
              II, page 3, Dec 15, 1968
              page 26, Oct 4, 1969
              page 17, Jan 22, 1971
              page 21, Dec 29, 1971
New Yorker 44:139, Dec 7, 1968
Newsweek 72:114, Dec 16, 1968
Saturday Review 51:13, Dec 21, 1968
Time 92:81, Dec 13, 1968

Provincetown Follies
sketches: Frederick Herendeen, Gwynn Langdon, Barrie
                  Oliver, George K. Arthur
music: Sylvan Green, Mary Schaeffer, Arthur Jones,
                  Trevor Jones, Dave Stamper
lyrics: Frederick Herendeen, Gwynn Langdon, Barrie
                  Oliver, George K. Arthur
staging: Lee Morrison
choreography: Mary Read
Productions:
Opened November 3, 1935 for 63 performances
Reviews:
New York Times page 24, Nov 4, 1935

Prunella, or Love in a Garden
book: Laurence Housman and Granville Barker
music: Joseph Moorat
Productions:
Opened October 27, 1913 for 104 performances
Reviews:
American Mercury 77:33-4, Mar 1914
Bookman 38:363, Dec 1913
Current Opinion 56:24-8, Jan 1914
Dramatic Mirror 70:6, Oct 29, 1913
                70:2, Nov 12, 1913
                70:1, Dec 3, 1913

Everybody's 30:264, Feb 1914
Green Book 11:71-2, Jan 1914
                11:165-6, Jan 1914
Harper's Bazaar 49:37+, Mar 1914
International 7:364+, Dec 1913
Leslie's Weekly 117:495, Nov 20, 1913
Life (New York) 62:790-91, Nov 6, 1913
Literary Digest 47:944-5, Nov 15, 1913
Munsey 50:726-7, Jan 1914
New York Times page 11, Oct 17, 1913
                page 9, Oct 27, 1913
Theatre Magazine 18:174-5, Dec 1913
                18:197, Dec 1913

Prussian Suite
    book: Michael Smith
    music: John Smead
    staging: Michael Smith
Productions:
    (Off-Off-Broadway) Opened February 14, 1974 (Theatre Genesis)
No Reviews.

Pugh, Ted   (see An Evening with Sue and Pugh)

Purlie
    book: Ossie Davis, Philip Rose, Peter Udell; based
                   on the play Purlie Victorious by Ossie Davis
    music: Gary Geld
    lyrics: Peter Udell
    staging: Philip Rose
    sets: Ben Edwards
    costumes: Ann Roth
    choreography: Louis Johnson
Productions:
    Opened March 15, 1970 for 688 performances
    Opened December 27, 1972 for 14 performances
Reviews:
    America 122:510, May 9, 1970
    Dance Magazine 44:89-90, May 1970
    Life 68:18, Apr 24, 1970
    Nation 210:414, Apr 6, 1970
    New York Theatre Critics' Reviews 1970:340
    New York Times page 53, Mar 16, 1970
                    II, page 3, Mar 22, 1970
                    II, page 1, Apr 5, 1970
                    page 48, Apr 21, 1970
                    II, page 5, Nov 29, 1970
                    page 17, Apr 24, 1971
                    page 37, Nov 25, 1972
                    page 36, Dec 28, 1972
    New Yorker 46:81, Mar 28, 1970
    Newsweek 75:84, Mar 30, 1970
    Time 95:77, Mar 30, 1970

Put It in Writing
    staging: Bill Penn
    sets: Peter Harvey
    costumes: Audré
    choreography: Joyce Trisler
Productions:
    (Off-Broadway)   Opened May 13, 1963 for 24 performances
Reviews:
    New York Times page 31, May 14, 1963
    New Yorker 39:59, May 25, 1963
    Saturday Review 45:21, Aug 18, 1962
    Theatre Arts 47:12, Jul 1963

- Q -

The Quaker Girl
    book: James T. Tanner
    music: Lionel Monckton
    lyrics: Adrian Ross and Percy Greenbank
    staging: T. A. E. Malone
Productions:
    Opened October 23, 1911 for 240 performances
Reviews:
    Blue Book 14:472-4, Jan 1912
    Canadian Magazine 38:280, Jan 1912
    Dramatic Mirror 66:10, Oct 25, 1911
                 66:4, Nov 8, 1911
                  66:4, Dec 13, 1911
                  67:19, Jan 31, 1912
    Green Book 7:13-15+, Jan 1912
    Hampton 27:825, Jan 1912
    Munsey 46:430, Dec 1911
    Red Book 18:957-60, Mar 1912

A Quarter for the Ladies Room
    music: John Clifton and Arthur Siegel
    lyrics: Ruth Batchelor
    staging: Darwin Knight
    sets: David R. Ballou
    costumes: Miles White
Productions:
    (Off-Broadway)   Opened November 12, 1972 for one performance
Reviews:
    New York Theatre Critics' Reviews 1972:161
    New York Times page 47, Nov 13, 1972

Queen High
    book: Laurence Schwab and B. G. De Sylva; based
                  on E. Peple's A Pair of Sixes
    music: Lewis E. Gensler
    lyrics: B. G. De Sylva
    staging: Edgar McGregor and Sammy Lee

Productions:
   Opened September 8, 1926 for 378 performances
Reviews:
   Bookman 64:343, Nov 1926
   Life (New York) 88:23, Oct 7, 1926
   New York Times page 21, Sep 9, 1926
                    IX, page 1, Sep 19, 1926
   Theatre Magazine 44:66+, Nov 1926
                    44:21, Dec 1926
   Time 52:48, Oct 1930
   Vogue 68:91, Nov 1926

Queen of Hearts
   book: Frank Mandel and Oscar Hammerstein II
   music: Lewis Gensler and Dudley Wilkinson
   lyrics: Oscar Hammerstein II and Sydney Mitchell
   staging: Ira Hards
Productions:
   Opened October 10, 1922 for 39 performances
Reviews:
   New York Clipper 70:20, Oct 18, 1922
   New York Times page 22, Oct 11, 1922
   Theatre Magazine 32:31, Midsummer 1920
                    36:377, Dec 1922

The Queen of the Movies
   book: Glen Macdonough; based on Die Kino-Konigin by
                 Julius Freund and Georg Okonowski
   music: Jean Gilbert
   lyrics: Glen Macdonough
   staging: Herbert Gresham
   choreography: Julian Mitchell
Productions:
   Opened January 12, 1914 for 104 performances
Reviews:
   Dramatic Mirror 71:11, Jan 7, 1914
                   71:6, Jan 21, 1914
   Green Book 11:541-3, Apr 1914
              11:607-8, Apr 1914
              11:699-700, Apr 1914
   New York Times page 9, Jan 13, 1914
   Theatre Magazine 19:96, Feb 1914

- R -

Rain or Shine
   book: James Gleason and Maurice Marks
   music: Milton Ager and Owen Murphy
   lyrics: Jack Yellen
Productions:
   Opened February 9, 1928 for 356 performances
Reviews:

Life (New York) 91:23, Mar 8, 1928
                          96:18, Aug 29, 1930
New York Times page 26, Feb 10, 1928
                          VIII, page 1, Feb 19, 1928
Outlook 148:344, Feb 29, 1928
Theatre Magazine 48:38, Aug 1928
Vogue 71:140, Apr 1, 1928

Rainbow (1928)
    book: Laurence Stallings and Oscar Hammerstein II
    music: Vincent Youmans
    lyrics: Oscar Hammerstein II
    staging: Oscar Hammerstein II
    choreography: Busby Berkeley
Productions:
    Opened November 21, 1928 for 29 performances
Reviews:
    New York Times page 1, Nov 4, 1928
                          page 25, Nov 22, 1928
                          IX, page 1, Dec 16, 1928
    Theatre Magazine 49:60, Jan 1929

Rainbow (1972)
    book: James and Ted Rado
    music: James Rado
    lyrics: James Rado
    staging: Joe Donovan
    sets: James Tilton
    costumes: Nancy Potts
Productions:
    (Off-Broadway) Opened December 18, 1972 for 48 performances
Reviews:
    New York Times page 50, Dec 19, 1972
                          II, page 1, Jan 7, 1973
    New Yorker 48:47, Dec 30, 1972

The Rainbow Girl
    book: Rennold Wolf; based on a comedy by Jerome K.
                       Jerome
    music: Louis A. Hirsch
    lyrics: Rennold Wolf
    staging: Julian Mitchell and Herbert Gresham
Productions:
    Opened April 1, 1918 for 160 performances
Reviews:
    Dramatic Mirror 77:32, Dec 8, 1917
                          78:509, Apr 13, 1918
                          78:549, Apr 20, 1918
                          79:189, Aug 10, 1918
                          79:261, Aug 24, 1918
    Green Book 19:972+, Jun 1918
    Munsey 64:438, Jul 1918
    New York Times page 11, Apr 2, 1918

Theatre Magazine 27:277, May 1918
27:316, May 1918

Rainbow Jones
    book: Jill Williams
    music: Jill Williams
    lyrics: Jill Williams
    staging: Gene Persson
    sets: Richard Ferrer
    costumes: James Berton-Harris
    choreography: Sammy Bayes
Productions:
Opened February 13, 1974 for one performance
Reviews:
New York Theatre Critics' Reviews 1974:390
New York Times page 57, Feb 14, 1974

Rainbow Rose
    book: Walter De Leon; based on Zelda Sears' A Lucky
                    Break
    music: Harold Levey and Owen Murphy
    lyrics: Walter De Leon and Owen Murphy
    staging: Walter Wilson
Productions:
Opened March 16, 1926 for 55 performances
Reviews:
New York Times page 28, Mar 17, 1926
Theatre Magazine 43:15, May 1926

Raisin
    book: Robert Nemiroff and Charlotte Zaltzberg; based
                    on Lorraine Hansberry's A Raisin in the Sun
    music: Judd Waldin
    lyrics: Robert Brittan
    staging: Donald McKayle
    sets: Robert U. Taylor
    costumes: Bernard Johnson
    choreography: Donald McKayle
Productions:
Opened October 18, 1973 for 658* performances
Reviews:
America 129:392, Nov 17, 1973
Dance Magazine 49:90, Apr 1975
Ebony 29:74-6+, May 1974
Nation 217:508, Nov 12, 1973
New York Theatre Critics' Reviews 1973:218
New York Times page 49, May 31, 1973
              page 59, Oct 19, 1973
              page 20, Oct 27, 1973
              II, page 1, Oct 28, 1973
              II, page 3, Nov 4, 1973
New Yorker 49:107, Oct 29, 1973
Newsweek 82:67, Oct 29, 1973

Time 102:99, Oct 29, 1973

Rambler Rose
    book: Harry B. Smith
    music: Victor Jacobi
Productions:
    Opened September 10, 1917 for 72 performances
Reviews:
    Dramatic Mirror 77:31, Sep 8, 1917
                    77:7, Sep 22, 1917
                    77:5, Sep 29, 1917
    New York Dramatic News 64:7, Sep 15, 1917
    New York Times page 11, Sep 11, 1917
    Theatre Magazine 26:277, Nov 1917
                     26:281, Nov 1917

The Ramblers
    book: Guy Bolton, Bert Kalmar and Harry Ruby
    music: Bert Kalmar and Harry Ruby
    lyrics: Bert Kalmar and Harry Ruby
    staging: Philip Goodman
Productions:
    Opened September 20, 1926 for 289 performances
Reviews:
    Life (New York) 88:23, Oct 7, 1926
    New York Times page 32, Sep 21, 1926
    Theatre Magazine 44:15, Nov 1946
                     45:19, Jan 1927
    Vogue 68:106+, Nov 15, 1926

Rang Tang
    book: Kaj Gynt
    lyrics: Jo Trent
    staging: Charles Davis and Miller and Lyles
Productions:
    Opened July 12, 1927 for 119 performances
Reviews:
    Life (New York) 90:19, Aug 18, 1927
    New York Times page 20, Jul 13, 1927

Razzle Dazzle
    sketches: Mike Stewart
    music: Leo Schumer, Shelley Mowell, James Reed
                       Lawlor, Bernice Kroll, Irma Jurist
    lyrics: Mike Stewart
    sets: William Riva
    choreography: Nelle Fischer
Productions:
    Opened February 19, 1951 for 8 performances
Reviews:
    Commonweal 53:542, Mar 9, 1951
    New York Theatre Critics' Reviews 1951:339+
    New York Times page 21, Feb 20, 1951

Newsweek 37:83, Mar 5, 1951
Theatre Arts 35:21, Apr 1951

The Red Canary
    book: William Le Baron and Alexander Johnstone
    music: Harold Orlob
    lyrics: Will B. Johnstone
    staging: Ben Teal
Productions:
    Opened April 13, 1914 for 16 performances
Reviews:
    Dramatic Mirror 71:12, Apr 15, 1914
    New York Times page 11, Apr 14, 1914
                   page 13, Apr 15, 1914
    Theatre Magazine 19:319-20, Jun 1914

Red, Hot and Blue
    book: Howard Lindsay and Russel Crouse
    music: Cole Porter
    lyrics: Cole Porter
    staging: Howard Lindsay
    sets: Donald Oenslager
    costumes: Constance Ripley
    choreography: George Hale
Productions:
    Opened October 29, 1936 for 183 performances
Reviews:
    Catholic World 144:338-9, Dec 1936
    Nation 143:585, Nov 14, 1936
    New York Times page 28, Oct 8, 1936
                  X, page 3, Oct 11, 1936
                   page 26, Oct 30, 1936
                  X, page 1, Nov 8, 1936
    Newsweek 8:41, Nov 7, 1936
              34:88, Nov 14, 1949
    Photoplay 36:19, Dec 1949
    Stage 14:49, Oct 1936
    Time 28:21, Nov 9, 1936
         54:96, Nov 7, 1949

The Red Mill
    book: Henry Blossom
    music: Victor Herbert
    lyrics: Henry Blossom
    additional
      lyrics: Forman Brown
    staging: Billy Gilbert
    sets: Arthur Lonergan
    costumes: Walter Israel and Emile Santiago
    choreography: Aida Broadbent
Productions:
    Opened October 16, 1945 (Originally produced in 1906) for 531
    performances

Reviews:
Catholic World 162:262, Dec 1945
Life 19:75-8+, Nov 12, 1945
Nation 161:441, Oct 27, 1945
New York Theatre Critics' Reviews 1945:141+
New York Times page 16, Oct 17, 1945
                          II, page 1, Oct 28, 1945
                          II, page 1, Aug 11, 1946
                          VI, page 23, Dec 8, 1946
New Yorker 21:42+, Oct 27, 1945
Newsweek 26:90, Oct 29, 1945
Theatre Arts 29:687, Dec 1945
Time 46:62, Oct 29, 1945

Red Pepper
   book: Edgar Smith and Emily Young
   music: Albert Gumble and Owen Murphy
   lyrics: Howard Rogers and Owen Murphy
   staging: Frank Smithson
Productions:
Opened May 29, 1922 for (22) performances
Reviews:
New York Clipper 70:24, Jun 7, 1922
New York Times page 8, May 30, 1922
Theatre Magazine 36:95, Aug 1922

The Red Petticoat
   book: Rida Johnson Young
   music: Jerome D. Kern
   lyrics: Paul W. Herbert
   staging: Joseph W. Herbert
Productions:
Opened November 13, 1912 for 61 performances
Reviews:
Blue Book 16:912-14, Mar 1913
Dramatic Mirror 68:7, Nov 20, 1912
                 68:2, Dec 4, 1912
                 68:2, Dec 25, 1912
Green Book 9:183-4, Jan 1913
Harper's Weekly 56:19, Nov 30, 1912
Munsey 48:683-4, Jan 1913
New York Dramatic News 56:22, Nov 23, 1912

The Red Rose
   book: Harry B. and Robert B. Smith
   music: Robert Hood Bowers
   lyrics: Harry B. and Robert B. Smith
   staging: R. H. Burnside
   sets: Valeska Suratt
   costumes: Valeska Suratt
Productions:
Opened June 22, 1911 for 76 performances
Reviews:

Blue Book 13:684-7, Aug 1911
Dramatic Mirror 65:11+, Jun 28, 1911
Hampton 27:522, Oct 1911
Red Book 17:959, Sep 1911
Theatre Magazine 14:40-1+, Aug 1911

The Red, White and Black
book:	Eric Bentley
music:	Brad Burg
lyrics:	Eric Bentley
staging:	John Dillon and Eric Bentley
sets:	Bill Mikeulewicz
costumes:	Margaret Tobin

Productions:
(Off-Broadway) Opened March 30, 1971 for one performance
Reviews:
New York Times page 20, Mar 6, 1971
                 page 37, Mar 31, 1971

Red, White and Maddox
book:	Don Tucker and Jay Broad
music:	Don Tucker
lyrics:	Don Tucker
staging:	Jay Broad and Don Tucker
sets:	David Chapman
costumes:	David Chapman

Productions:
Opened January 26, 1969 for 41 performances
Reviews:
America 120:232, Feb 22, 1969
Nation 208:221, Feb 17, 1969
New Republic 160:29-30, Feb 22, 1969
New York Theatre Critics' Reviews 1969:379
New York Times page 27, Jan 27, 1969
                 II, page 3, Feb 2, 1969
                 page 33, Mar 4, 1969
                 page 29, Jul 25, 1968
                 page 71, Oct 5, 1968
                 VI, page 61, Nov 24, 1968
                 page 75, Feb 13, 1970
New Yorker 44:49, Feb 1, 1969
Saturday Review 51:32, Oct 26, 1968
                 52:33, Feb 1, 1969
Time 92:73, Nov 29, 1968
Vogue 153:42, Mar 15, 1969

The Red Widow
book:	Channing Pollock and Rennold Wolf
music:	Charles J. Gebest
lyrics:	Channing Pollock and Rennold Wolf
staging:	Frederick G. Latham

Productions:
Opened November 6, 1911 for 128 performances

Reviews:
    Blue Book 14:240-3, Dec 1911
    Dramatic Mirror 66:7, Nov 15, 1911
    Green Book 7:16-18+, Jan 1912
    Hampton 28:116, Mar 1912
    Munsey 46:586, Jan 1912
    New York Times page 13, Nov 7, 1911
    Theatre Magazine 14:xii, Dec 1911
                        14:186, Dec 1911

Redhead
    book: Herbert and Dorothy Fields, Sidney Sheldon,
                     David Shaw
    music: Albert Hague
    lyrics: Dorothy Fields
    staging: Bob Fosse
    sets: Rouben Ter-Arutunian
    costumes: Rouben Ter-Arutunian
    choreography: Bob Fosse
Productions:
    Opened February 5, 1959 for 452 performances
    (Off-Broadway) Opened January 12, 1968 for 15 performances
Reviews:
    America 100:671, Mar 7, 1959
    Catholic World 189:58-9, Apr 1959
    Dance Magazine 33:40-5, May 1959
    Life 46:81-3, Feb 23, 1959
    Nation 188:234, Mar 14, 1959
    New York Theatre Critics' Reviews 1959:384+
    New York Times page 21, Feb 6, 1959
                    II, page 1, Feb 15, 1959
                    II, page 1, Mar 20, 1960
    New Yorker 35:98+, Feb 21, 1959
    Newsweek 53:94, Feb 16, 1959
    Saturday Review 42:25, Feb 28, 1959
    Theatre Arts 43:10-11, Apr 1959
    Time 73:77, Feb 16, 1959

Reety in Hell
    book: Stephen Holt
    music: Don Arrington
    staging: Peter Schneider
Productions:
    (Off-Off-Broadway) Opened May 8, 1973 (Workshop of the
    Players' Art)
No Reviews.

Regina
    book: Marc Blitzstein, based on Lillian Hellman's
                     The Little Foxes
    music: Marc Blitzstein
    lyrics: Marc Blitzstein
    staging: Robert Lewis

<pre>
    sets: Horace Armistead
    costumes: Aline Bernstein
    choreography: Anna Abravanel
Productions:
    Opened October 31, 1949 for 56 performances
Reviews:
    American Mercury 70:172-3, Feb 1950
    Catholic World 170:228-9, Dec 1949
    Commonweal 51:238, Dec 2, 1949
    Musical America 69:9, Dec 1, 1949
                    73:5, Apr 15, 1953
    Nation 169:478, Nov 12, 1949
           177:118-19, Aug 8, 1953
           186:399, May 3, 1958
    New Republic 121:22, Dec 5, 1949
    New York Theatre Critics' Reviews 1949:237+
    New York Times II, page 1, Oct 30, 1949
                   page 32, Nov 1, 1949
                   II, page 1, Nov 13, 1949
                   VI, page 14, Dec 11, 1949
                   page 25, Jun 2, 1952
                   page 18, Apr 3, 1953
                   II, page 7, Apr 12, 1953
                   page 12, Oct 10, 1953
                   page 19, Apr 19, 1958
                   page 10, May 3, 1958
                   page 36, Apr 20, 1959
    New Yorker 25:56-8, Nov 12, 1949
               28:103-5, Jun 14, 1952
               29:113, Oct 17, 1953
               34:80, Apr 26, 1958
    Newsweek 34:84-5, Nov 14, 1949
             41:96, Apr 13, 1953
    Reporter 8:36-7, Jun 23, 1953
    Saturday Review 32:54-5, Nov 19, 1949
                    36:41-2, Apr 4, 1953
                    36:33, Apr 18, 1953
    School and Society 71:24-5, Jan 14, 1950
    Theatre Arts 34:12, Jan 1950
    Time 54:46, Nov 14, 1949
         61:79, Apr 13, 1953
</pre>

Religion
<pre>
    oratorio: Al Carmines
    staging: Al Carmines
Productions:
    (Off-Off-Broadway) Opened October 28, 1973 (Judson Poets'
    Theatre)
Reviews:
    New York Times page 37, Oct 30, 1973
</pre>

Reunion in New York
<pre>
    conceived by: Lothar Metzl and Werner Michel
</pre>

sketches: Carl Don, Richard Alma, Richard Holden, Hans
                 Lefebre
music: André Singer, Bert Silving, Berenece Kazouneff,
                 M. Cooper Paul
lyrics: David Gregory, Peter Barry, Stewart Arthur
staging: Herbert Berghof and Ezra Stone
sets: Harry Horner
costumes: Lester Polakov
choreography: Lotte Gosler
Productions:
Opened February 21, 1940 for 89 performances
Reviews:
New York Theatre Critics' Reviews 1940:388+
New York Times page 28, Feb 22, 1940
                 X, page 1, Mar 3, 1940
Theatre Arts 24:237, Apr 1940
Time 35:34, Mar 4, 1940

Revenge with Music
book: Howard Dietz and Arthur Schwartz, from the
                 Spanish fable "The Three Cornered Hat"
music: Arthur Schwartz
lyrics: Howard Dietz
staging: Komisarjevsky
sets: Albert Johnson
choreography: Michael Mordkin
Productions:
Opened November 28, 1934 for 158 performances
Reviews:
Catholic World 140:469, Jan 1935
Golden Book Magazine 21:32a, Feb 1935
New York Times page 33, Nov 29, 1934
                 IX, page 2, Dec 23, 1934
Time 24:50, Dec 10, 1934

Revue of 1924 (see Andre Charlot's Revue of 1924)

The Revue of Revues
produced by: The Shuberts
Productions:
Opened September 27, 1911 for 55 performances
No Reviews.

Rhapsody in Black
assembled by: Lew Leslie
music: Alberta Nichols
lyrics: Mann Holiner
staging: Lew Leslie
Productions:
Opened May 4, 1931 for 80 performances
Reviews:
New York Times page 33, May 5, 1931

Richard Farina; Long Time Coming and a Long Time Gone

material: Nancy Greenwald, adapted from the works of
                Richard Farina
staging: Robert Greenwald
sets: Richard Hammer and Patrick Sullivan
costumes: Joyce and Jerry Marcel

Productions:
(Off-Broadway) Opened November 17, 1971 for 7 performances
Reviews:
New York Times page 58, Nov 18, 1971

Ride the Winds

book: John Driver
music: John Driver
lyrics: John Driver
staging: Lee D. Sankowich
sets: Samuel C. Ball
costumes: Samuel C. Ball
choreography: Jay Norman

Productions:
Opened May 16, 1974 for 3 performances
Reviews:
New York Theatre Critics' Reviews 1974:266

The Right Girl

book: Raymond Peck
music: Percy Wenrich
lyrics: Raymond Peck
staging: Walter Wilson

Productions:
Opened March 15, 1921 for 98 performances
Reviews:
Dramatic Mirror 83:508, Mar 19, 1921
New York Clipper 69:19, Mar 23, 1921
New York Times page 12, Mar 16, 1921
Theatre Magazine 33:370, May 1921
                  33:421, Jun 1921

Right This Way

book: Marianne Brown Waters; additional dialogue by
                Parke Levy and Allen Lipscott; additional songs
                by Sammy Fain and Irving Kahal
music: Brad Greene and Fabian Storey
lyrics: Marianne Brown Waters
staging: Bertram Robinson and Alice Alexander
sets: Nat Karson
costumes: Miles White
choreography: Marjery Fielding

Productions:
Opened January 4, 1938 for 15 performances
Reviews:
New York Times VI, page 6, Oct 31, 1937
                  page 22, Jan 6, 1938

Rio Rita
    book: Guy Bolton and Fred Thompson
    staging: John Harwood
Productions:
    Opened February 2, 1927 for 494 performances
Reviews:
    Life (New York) 89:21, Feb 24, 1927
    New York Times page 18, Feb 3, 1927
                  VII, page 1, Feb 13, 1927
                  IX, page 2, May 13, 1928
                  page 25, May 21, 1928
    Theatre Magazine 46:16, Aug 1927
    Vogue 69:132+, Apr 1, 1927

Ripples
    book: William Anthony McGuire
    music: Oscar Levant and Albert Sirmay
    lyrics: Irving Caesar and Graham John
    staging: William Anthony McGuire
    choreography: William Holbrook
Productions:
    Opened February 11, 1930 for 55 performances
Reviews:
    Life (New York) 95:18, Mar 14, 1930
    New York Times VIII, page 2, Feb 2, 1930
                  page 26, Feb 12, 1930
                  page 31, Mar 18, 1930
    Outlook 154:512, Mar 26, 1930
    Theatre Magazine 51:46, Apr 1930
    Vogue 75:55+, Mar 29, 1930

The Rise and Fall of the City of Mahagonny (see Mahagonny)

The Rise of Rosie O'Reilly
    book: George M. Cohan
    staging: Julian Mitchell and John Meehan
Productions:
    Opened December 25, 1923 for 87 performances
Reviews:
    New York Times page 13, Dec 26, 1923
    Theatre Magazine 39:19, Mar 1924

Ritz Revue (see Hassard Short's Ritz Revue)

The Riviera Girl
    book: Guy Bolton and P. G. Wodehouse
    music: Emmerich Kalman
    lyrics: Guy Bolton and P. G. Wodehouse
Productions:
    Opened September 24, 1917 for 78 performances
Reviews:
    Dramatic Mirror 77:4-5, Oct 6, 1917
    New York Dramatic News 64:10, Sep 29, 1917

New York Times page 9, Sep 25, 1917
                    III, page 8, Sep 30, 1917
Theatre Magazine 26:265, Nov 1917
                    26:328, Nov 1917

Riverwind
      book: John Jennings
      music: John Jennings
      lyrics: John Jennings
      staging: Adrian Hall
      sets: Robert Soule
      costumes: Robert Soule
Productions:
      (Off-Broadway) Opened December 12, 1962 for 433 performances
      (Off-Off-Broadway) Opened May 3, 1973 (Equity Library Thea-
         tre)
Reviews:
      New York Times page 5, Dec 14, 1962
                       page 33, Jan 2, 1964
                       page 53, May 7, 1973
      New Yorker 38:66-7, Dec 22, 1962

The Roar of the Greasepaint--The Smell of the Crowd
      book: Leslie Bricusse and Anthony Newley
      music: Leslie Bricusse and Anthony Newley
      lyrics: Leslie Bricusse and Anthony Newley
      staging: Anthony Newley
      sets: Sean Kenny
      costumes: Freddy Wittop
      choreography: Gillian Lynne
Productions:
      Opened May 16, 1965 for 231 performances
Reviews:
      America 112:867-8, Jun 12, 1965
      Catholic World 201:151-2, May 1965
      Dance Magazine 39:22-3, Jul 1965
      New York Theatre Critics' Reviews 1965:326+
      New York Times page 46, May 17, 1965
      New Yorker 41:56, May 29, 1965
      Newsweek 65:76, May 31, 1965
      Reporter 32:45-6, Apr 8, 1965
      Saturday Review 48:38, Jun 5, 1965
      Time 85:83, May 28, 1965

Roberta
      book: Otto Harbach, adapted from Alice Duer Miller's
                       novel Gowns
      music: Jerome Kern
      lyrics: Otto Harbach
      staging: Hassard Short
      sets: Clark Robinson
      choreography: John Lonergan
Productions:

Opened November 18, 1933 for 295 performances
Reviews:
   Catholic World 138:733-4, Mar 1934
   Fortune 9:69-76+, May 1934
   New Outlook 163:43, Jan 1934
   New York Times page 18, Nov 20, 1933
             IX, page 3, Jan 13, 1935
             II, page 3, Aug 18, 1935
   Newsweek 2:32, Nov 25, 1933
   Review of Reviews 89:48, Mar 1934
   Stage 11:8-9+, Dec 1933
   Time 22:45, Nov 27, 1933

Robinson Crusoe, Jr.
   book: Harold Atteridge and Edgar Smith
   music: Sigmund Romberg and James Hanley
   lyrics: Harold Atteridge and Edgar Smith
   staging: J. C. Huffman
   choreography: Allen K. Foster
Productions:
   Opened February 17, 1916 for 139 performances
Reviews:
   Dramatic Mirror 75:8, Feb 26, 1916
                75:2, Mar 25, 1916
   Munsey 57:700, May 1916
   New York Dramatic News 62:17-18, Feb 26, 1916
   Theatre Magazine 23:196, Apr 1916
                  23:238, Apr 1916

Rock-a-Bye Baby
   book: Edgar Allan Woolf and Margaret Mayo
   music: Jerome Kern
   lyrics: Herbert Reynolds
   staging: Edward Royce
Productions:
   Opened May 22, 1918 for 85 performances
Reviews:
   Dramatic Mirror 78:608, Apr 27, 1918
                78:802, Jun 8, 1918
                78:873, Jun 22, 1918
   Green Book 20:202-3+, Aug 1918
   New York Times page 11, May 23, 1918
   Theatre Magazine 28:23, Jul 1918
                  28:31, Jul 1918

Roly-Boly Eyes
   book: Edgar Allan Woolf
   music: Eddy Brown and Louis Gruenberg
   lyrics: Edgar Allan Woolf
Productions:
   Opened September 25, 1919 for 100 performances
Reviews:
   Dramatic Mirror 80:1578, Oct 9, 1919

Musical Courier 79:39, Oct 2, 1919
New York Times page 11, Sep 26, 1919
Theatre Magazine 30:344, Nov 1919
            30:371, Dec 1919

Rondelay
   book: Jerry Douglass; based on Arthur Schnitzler's
                  La Ronde
   music: Hal Jordon
   lyrics: Jerry Douglass
   staging: William Francisco
   sets: Raoul Pene du Bois
   choreography: Jacques d'Amboise
Productions:
  (Off-Broadway) Opened November 5, 1969 for 11 performances
Reviews:
  New York Times page 55, Nov 6, 1969

Rosalie
   book: William Anthony McGuire and Guy Bolton
   music: George Gershwin and Sigmund Romberg
   lyrics: P. G. Wodehouse and Ira Gershwin
   staging: Florenz Ziegfeld, Seymour Felix, William A.
                  McGuire
Productions:
  Opened January 10, 1928 for 335 performances
Reviews:
  New York Times IX, page 2, Dec 18, 1927
               page 26, Jan 11, 1928
  Outlook 148:344, Feb 29, 1928
  Vogue 71:114, Mar 1, 1928

Rose, Billy (see Billy Rose)

The Rose Girl
   book: William Cary Duncan
   music: Anselm Goetzl
   lyrics: William Cary Duncan
   staging: Hassard Short
Productions:
  Opened February 11, 1921 for 110 performances
Reviews:
  Dramatic Mirror 83:328, Feb 19, 1921
  New York Clipper 69:23, Feb 23, 1921
  New York Times page 11, Feb 12, 1921
  Theatre Magazine 33:304, Apr 1921
               33:329, May 1921

Rose-Marie
   book: Otto Harbach and Oscar Hammerstein II
   music: Rudolf Friml and Herbert Stothart
   lyrics: Otto Harbach and Oscar Hammerstein II
   staging: Paul Dickey

     choreography: David Bennett
Productions:
     Opened September 2, 1924 for 311 performances
     Opened January 24, 1927 for 48 performances
Reviews:
     Canadian Magazine 64:164-6, Jul 1925
     New York Times VII, page 1, Aug 24, 1924
                        page 12, Sep 3, 1924
                        page 16, Mar 21, 1925
                        page 26, Dec 4, 1925
                        page 17, Apr 1, 1926
                        page 1, Sep 14, 1926
                        page 16, Sep 16, 1926
                        page 19, Jan 25, 1927
                        II, page 8, Apr 17, 1927
                        VII, page 2, May 8, 1927
                        page 15, Jul 17, 1927
                        page 23, Mar 31, 1928
                        IX, page 2, Apr 29, 1928
     Theatre Magazine 40:16, Nov 1924

The Rose of Algeria
     book: Glen MacDonough
     music: Victor Herbert
     lyrics: Glen MacDonough
     staging: Ned Wayburn
Productions:
     Opened September 20, 1909 for 40 performances
Reviews:
     Dramatic Mirror 62:7, Oct 2, 1909
     Leslie's Weekly 109:391, Oct 21, 1909
                     109:415, Oct 28, 1909
     Life (New York) 54:477, Oct 7, 1909
     Metropolitan Magazine 31:268-9, Nov 1909
     Theatre Magazine 10:v, Nov 1909
                      10:xiv, Nov 1909

The Rose of China
     book: Guy Bolton
     music: Armand Vecsey
     lyrics: P. G. Wodehouse
Productions:
     Opened November 25, 1919 for 47 performances
Reviews:
     Dramatic Mirror 80:1909, Dec 11, 1919
     Forum 63:113-14, Jan 1920
     Munsey 69:314, Mar 1920
     New York Times page 11, Nov 26, 1919
     Theatre Magazine 31:61, Jan 1920
                      31:99, Feb 1920

The Rothschilds
     book: Sherman Yellen; based on The Rothschilds by
                      Frederic Morton

music: Jerry Bock
lyrics: Sheldon Harnick
staging: Michael Kidd
sets: John Bury
costumes: John Bury
choreography: Michael Kidd
Productions:
Opened October 19, 1970 for 507 performances
Reviews:
America 124:125, Feb 6, 1971
Dance Magazine 45:77-8, Jan 1971
Nation 211:506, Nov 16, 1970
New York Theatre Critics' Reviews 1970:181
                                    1970:184
New York Times page 26, Aug 11, 1970
              page 60, Oct 15, 1970
              II, page 1, Oct 18, 1970
              page 40, Oct 20, 1970
              II, page 1, Nov 1, 1970
              II, page 17, Nov 15, 1970
              page 34, Nov 5, 1971
              page 26, Dec 22, 1971
              page 21, Dec 29, 1971
              page 29, Feb 7, 1972
              VII, page 4, Mar 5, 1972
New Yorker 46:101, Oct 31, 1970
Newsweek 76:104, Nov 2, 1970
Saturday Review 53:6+, Nov 28, 1970
Time 96:77, Nov 2, 1970

Round the Town
    assembled: Herman Mankiewiez and S. Jay Kaufman
Productions:
Opened May 21, 1924 for 13 performances
Reviews:
New York Times page 14, May 22, 1924

Rufus LeMaire's Affairs
    book: Ballard Macdonald; additional skits by Andy Rice
    music: Martin Broones
    lyrics: Ballard Macdonald
    staging: William Halligan, Jack Hascall and Albertina
                 Rasch
Productions:
Opened March 28, 1927 for 56 performances
Reviews:
New York Times page 22, Mar 29, 1927
              VIII, page 1, Apr 10, 1927
Theatre Magazine 45:24, Jun 27, 1927
Vogue 69:122, May 15, 1927

Rugantino
    book: Pietro Garinei and Sandro Giovannini, with

                            Festa Campanile and Franciosa; English version
                            by Alfred Drake
        music: Armando Trovaioli
        lyrics: Pietro Garinei and Sandro Giovannini; English
                            version by Edward Eager
        staging: Pietro Garinei and Sandro Giovannini
        sets: Giulio Coltellacci
        costumes: Giulio Coltellacci
        choreography: Dania Krupska
Productions:
        Opened February 6, 1964 for 28 performances
Reviews:
        Nation 198:204, Feb 24, 1964
        New York Theatre Critics' Reviews 1964:362+
        New York Times page 25, Jan 17, 1964
                            II, page 1, Feb 2, 1964
                            page 24, Feb 20, 1964
        New Yorker 39:113, Feb 15, 1964
        Newsweek 63:90-1, Feb 17, 1964
        Time 83:69, Feb 14, 1964

Ruggles of Red Gap
        book: Harrison Rhodes; from stories by Harry Leon
                            Wilson
        music: Sigmund Romberg
        lyrics: Harold Atteridge
        staging: J. H. Benrimo
Productions:
        Opened December 25, 1915 for 33 performances
Reviews:
        Dramatic Mirror 75:8, Jan 1, 1916
                            75:4, Jan 8, 1916
        Life (New York) 67:26-7, Jan 6, 1916
        Nation 101:786-7, Dec 30, 1915
        New York Dramatic News 62:17-18, Jan 1, 1916
        New York Times page 7, Dec 25, 1915
        Theatre Magazine 23:65-6, Feb 1916

Rumple
        book: Irving Phillips
        music: Ernest G. Schweikert
        lyrics: Frank Reardon
        staging: Jack Donohue
        sets: George Jenkins
        costumes: Alvin Colt
        choreography: Bob Hamilton
Productions:
        Opened November 6, 1957 for 45 performances
Reviews:
        New York Theatre Critics' Reviews 1957:188+
        New York Times page 42, Nov 7, 1957
        New Yorker 33:104+, Nov 16, 1957
        Newsweek 50:90, Nov 18, 1957

Theatre Arts 42:22, Jan 1958
Time 70:78, Nov 18, 1957

Runnin' Wild
    book: F. E. Miller and A. L. Lyles
    music: James Johnson and Cecil Mack
    lyrics: James Johnson and Cecil Mack
Productions:
    Opened October 29, 1923 for 213 performances
Reviews:
    New York Times page 17, Oct 30, 1923

Russell, Anna   (see Anna Russell's Little Show)

- S -

Sacco-Vanzetti
    book: Armand Aulicino
    music: Frank Gaskin Fields
    lyrics: Armand Aulicino
    staging: Allan Lokos
    choreography: Diane Adler
Productions:
    (Off-Broadway) Opened February 7, 1969 for 15 performances
Reviews:
    New York Times page 78, Feb 9, 1969
(See also The Shoemaker and the Peddler)

Sacred Guard
    conceived: Ken Rubenstein
    music: John Smead
    staging: Ken Rubenstein
Productions:
    (Off-Off-Broadway) Opened April 11, 1973 (La Mama Experi-
    mental Theatre Club)
No Reviews.

Sadie Thompson
    book: Howard Dietz and Rouben Mamoulian, adapted
                  from Rain, a drama by John Colton and
                  Clemence Randolph, based on a story by
                  Somerset Maugham
    music: Vernon Duke
    lyrics: Howard Dietz and Rouben Mamoulian
    staging: Rouben Mamoulian
    sets: Boris Aronson
    costumes: Motley and Azadia Newman
    choreography: Edward Caton
Productions:
    Opened November 16, 1944 for 60 performances
Reviews:
    Catholic World 160:357, Jan 1945

Collier's 115:12-13, Jan 6, 1945
Commonweal 41:174-5, Dec 1, 1944
Life 17:43-6+, Dec 11, 1944
Nation 159:698, Dec 2, 1944
New York Theatre Critics' Reviews 1944:84+
New York Times VI, page 28, Nov 12, 1944
                    page 25, Nov 17, 1944
                    II, page 1, Nov 26, 1944
New Yorker 20:46, Nov 25, 1944
Newsweek 24:100, Nov 27, 1944
Theatre Arts 29:12+, Jan 1945
Time 44:48, Nov 27, 1944

Safari 300
    book: Tad Truesdale
    staging: Hugh Gittens
    sets: Bob Olsen
    costumes: Lee Lynn
    choreography: Lari Becham and Phil Black
Productions:
    (Off-Broadway) Opened July 12, 1972 for 17 performances
Reviews:
    New York Times page 27, Jul 13, 1972

Sail Away
    book: Noel Coward
    music: Noel Coward
    lyrics: Noel Coward
    staging: Noel Coward
    sets: Oliver Smith
    costumes: Helene Pons and Oliver Smith
    choreography: Joe Layton
Productions:
    Opened October 3, 1961 for 167 performances
Reviews:
    Commonweal 75:154, Nov 3, 1961
    Dance Magazine 35:28, Nov 1961
    Nation 193:361, Nov 4, 1961
    New Republic 145:22, Nov 6, 1961
    New York Theatre Critics' Reviews 1961:251+
    New York Times page 17, Aug 10, 1961
                    II, page 1, Oct 1, 1961
                    page 48, Oct 4, 1961
                    page 14, Jun 23, 1962
    New Yorker 37:162+, Oct 14, 1961
    Newsweek 58:101, Oct 16, 1961
    Reporter 25:53, Oct 26, 1961
    Saturday Review 44:34, Oct 21, 1961
    Theatre Arts 45:10-11, Dec 1961
    Time 78:58, Oct 13, 1961

St. Louis Woman
    book: Arna Bontemps and Countee Cullen based on

                          Arna Bontemps' God Sends Sunday
    music: Harold Arlen
    lyrics: Johnny Mercer
    staging: Rouben Mamoulian
    sets: Lemuel Ayers
    costumes: Lemuel Ayers
    choreography: Charles Walters
Productions:
    Opened March 30, 1946 for 113 performances
Reviews:
    Catholic World 163:170, May 1946
    Commonweal 44:14, Apr 19, 1946
    Forum 105:937-8, Jun 1946
    Life 20:63-4, Apr 29, 1946
    Modern Music 23 no2:146, Apr 1946
    New York Theatre Critics' Reviews 1946:415+
    New York Times page 22, Apr 1, 1946
                    page 20, Jul 3, 1946
    New Yorker 22:46+, Apr 6, 1946
    Newsweek 27:84, Apr 15, 1946
    Saturday Review 29:24, Apr 27, 1946
    Time 47:47, Apr 8, 1946

The Saint of Bleecker Street
    book: Gian-Carlo Menotti
    music: Gian-Carlo Menotti
    lyrics: Gian-Carlo Menotti
    staging: Gian-Carlo Menotti
    sets: Robert Randolph
    costumes: Robert Randolph
Productions:
    Opened December 27, 1954 for 92 performances
    Opened September 29, 1965 for 2 performances
Reviews:
    America 92:434, Jan 22, 1955
    Catholic World 180:385, Feb 1955
    Commonweal 61:476-7, Feb 4, 1955
    Life 38:62-3, Feb 14, 1955
    Musical America 75:3+, Jan 15, 1955
    Nation 180:83, Jan 22, 1955
    New York Theatre Critics' Reviews 1954:199+
    New York Times page 21, Dec 28, 1954
                    II, page 1, Jan 2, 1955
                    II, page 1, Mar 6, 1955
                    page 26, May 9, 1955
                    page 76, Sep 18, 1955
                    page 26, Nov 1, 1955
                    page 38, Nov 22, 1955
                    page 78, Jun 10, 1956
                    page 40, Sep 4, 1957
    New Yorker 30:74-6, Jan 8, 1955
              30:77, Jun 2, 1955
    Newsweek 45:62, Jan 10, 1955

Reporter 12:40, Apr 7, 1955
Saturday Review 38:28, Jan 8, 1955
Theatre Arts 39:17+, Mar 1955
Time 65:42, Jan 10, 1955

Sally
    book: Guy Bolton
    music: Jerome Kern and Victor Herbert
    lyrics: Clifford Grey, additional lyrics by B. G.
                 De Sylva
    staging: Edward Royce
Productions:
    Opened December 21, 1920 for 570 performances
    Opened May 6, 1948 for 36 performances
Reviews:
    Catholic World 167:268, Jun 1948
    Dramatic Mirror page 1241, Dec 25, 1920
    New Republic 118:34, May 31, 1948
    New York Clipper 68:18, Dec 29, 1920
    New York Theatre Critics' Reviews 1948:271+
    New York Times page 16, Dec 22, 1920
                  page 20, Sep 11, 1921
                   page 20, Mar 30, 1922
                   page 31, May 7, 1948
    New Yorker 24:48+, May 15, 1948
    Newsweek 31:90, May 17, 1948
    Theatre Arts 32:14, Jun 1948
    Theatre Magazine 33:178, Mar 1921
    Time 51:88, May 17, 1948

Sally, Irene and Mary
    book: Eddie Dowling and Cyrus Wood
    music: J. Fred Coots
    lyrics: Raymond Klages
    staging: Frank Smithson
Productions:
    Opened September 4, 1922 for 312 performances
    Opened March 23, 1925 for 16 performances
Reviews:
    New York Clipper 70:20, Sep 27, 1922
    New York Times page 21, Sep 5, 1922

Saluta
    book: Will Morrissey, revised by Eugene Conrad and
                 Maurice Marks
    music: Frank D'Armond
    lyrics: Will Morrissey
    staging: William Morrissey and Edwin Saulpaugh
    sets: Hugh Willoughby
    choreography: Boots McKenna
Productions:
    Opened August 28, 1934 for 39 performances
Reviews:

New York Times page 13, Aug 29, 1934

Salvation
    book: Peter Link and C. C. Courtney
    music: Peter Link and C. C. Courtney
    lyrics: Peter Link and C. C. Courtney
    staging: Paul Aaron
    choreography: Kathryn Posin
Productions:
    (Off-Broadway) Opened September 24, 1969 for 239 per-
    formances
Reviews:
    Christian Century 86:1646-7, Dec 24, 1969
    Commonweal 91:534-5, Feb 13, 1970
    Dance Magazine 43:84, Nov 1969
    New York Theatre Critics' Reviews 1969:198
    New York Times page 53, Mar 13, 1969
                page 55, Sep 25, 1969
                page 24, Sep 27, 1969
                II, page 1, Oct 5, 1969
    New Yorker 45:114, Oct 4, 1969
    Newsweek 74:133, Oct 6, 1969
    Saturday Review 52:26, Oct 11, 1969

Sambo
    music: Ron Steward and Neal Tate
    lyrics: Ron Steward
    staging: Gerald Freedman
    sets: Ming Cho Lee and Marjorie Kellogg
    costumes: Milo Morrow
Productions:
    (Off-Broadway) Opened December 12, 1969 for 37 performances
    (Off-Broadway) Opened July 14, 1970 for 22 performances
Reviews:
    New York Theatre Critics' Reviews 1969:130
    New York Times page 42, Dec 22, 1969
                II, page 3, Jan 11, 1970
                page 24, Jul 23, 1970
                page 20, Jul 24, 1970
    New Yorker 45:43, Jan 3, 1970

Sancho Panza
    book: Melchior Lengyel; based on Cervantes' Don
                     Quixote de la Mancha
    music: Hugo Felix
    lyrics: Hugo Felix
Productions:
    Opened November 26, 1923 for 40 performances
Reviews:
    American Mercury 1:119, Jan 1924
    New York Times VIII, page 2, Oct 21, 1923
                page 23, Nov 27, 1923
                VIII, page 1, Dec 2, 1923

IX, page 2, Dec 16, 1923
Theatre Magazine 39:16, Feb 1924

Sandhog
    book: Earl Robinson and Waldo Salt; based on Theodore
                     Dreiser's St. Columba and the River
    music: Earl Robinson and Waldo Salt
    lyrics: Earl Robinson and Waldo Salt
    staging: Howard Da Silva
    sets: Howard Bay
    costumes: Toni Ward
    choreography: Sophie Maslow
Productions:
    Opened November 23, 1954 for 48 performances
Reviews:
    America 92:326, Dec 18, 1954
    Catholic World 180:308-9, Jan 1955
    Nation 179:518, Dec 11, 1954
    Newsweek 44:84, Dec 6, 1954
    New York Theatre Critics' Reviews 1954:239
    New York Times page 17, Nov 24, 1954
    New Yorker 30:86+, Dec 4, 1954
    Saturday Review 38:62, Jan 1, 1955
    Theatre Arts 39:76+, Feb 1955

The Sap of Life
    book: Richard Maltby, Jr.
    music: David Shire
    lyrics: Richard Maltby, Jr.
    staging: William Francisco
    sets: John Conklin
    costumes: John Conklin
Productions:
    (Off-Broadway) Opened October 2, 1961 for 49 performances
Reviews:
    New York Times page 44, Oct 3, 1961
                   page 15, Nov 4, 1961
                   page 48, Nov 6, 1961
    New Yorker 37:166, Oct 14, 1961

Saratoga
    book: Morton Da Costa, based on Edna Ferber's
                     Saratoga Trunk
    music: Harold Arlen
    lyrics: Johnny Mercer
    staging: Morton Da Costa
    sets: Cecil Beaton
    costumes: Cecil Beaton
    choreography: Ralph Beaumont
Productions:
    Opened December 7, 1959 for 80 performances
Reviews:
    America 102:594+, Feb 13, 1960

New York Theatre Critics' Reviews 1959:195+
New York Times page 59, Dec 8, 1959
                page 23, Feb 1, 1960
New Yorker 35:81, Dec 19, 1959
Newsweek 54:83, Dec 21, 1959
Saturday Review 42:25, Dec 26, 1959
Theatre Arts 44:17-21, Jan 1960
Time 74:34, Dec 21, 1959
Vogue 135:114-15, Feb 1, 1960

Saturday Night (see American Legend)

Say, Darling
    book: Richard Bissell, Abe Burrows, and Marian
                     Bissell, based on the novel by Richard Bissell
    music: Jule Styne
    lyrics: Betty Comden and Adolph Green
    staging: Abe Burrows
    sets: Oliver Smith
    costumes: Alvin Colt
    choreography: Matt Mattox
Productions:
    Opened April 3, 1958 for 332 performances
    Opened February 25, 1959 for 16 performances
    (Off-Broadway) Opened November 12, 1965 for 15 performances
Reviews:
    America 99:178, May 3, 1958
    Catholic World 187:225, Jun 1958
    Commonweal 68:351, Jul 4, 1958
    New York Theatre Critics' Reviews 1958:317+
    New York Times II, page 1, Mar 30, 1958
                    page 17, Apr 4, 1958
                    II, page 1, Apr 13, 1958
                    II, page 1, Jan 18, 1959
                    page 38, Feb 26, 1959
    New Yorker 34:67, Apr 12, 1958
    Newsweek 51:87, Apr 14, 1958
    Saturday Review 41:28, Apr 19, 1958
    Time 71:66, Apr 14, 1958

Say When (1928)
    book: Calvin Brown, based on Amelie Rives and
                     Gilbert Emery's Love in a Mist
    music: Jesse Greer
    lyrics: Raymond Klages
    staging: Bertram Harrison and Max Scheck
Productions:
    Opened June 26, 1928 for 24 performances
Reviews:
    Golden Book Magazine 21:30a, Feb 1935
    New York Times page 29, Jun 27, 1928
    Outlook 149:425, Jul 11, 1928

Say When (1934)
    book: Jack McGowan
    music: Ray Henderson
    lyrics: Ted Koehler
    staging: Bertram Harrison and Russell Markert
    sets: Clark Robinson
Productions:
    Opened November 8, 1934 for 76 performances
Reviews:
    New York Times page 24, Nov 9, 1934
    Stage 12:9, Dec 1934

Say When (1972)
    book: Keith Winter
    music: Arnold Goland
    lyrics: Keith Winter
    staging: Zoya Leporska
    sets: William James Wall
    costumes: Leilia Larmon
    choreography: Zoya Leporska
Productions:
    (Off-Broadway) Opened December 4, 1972 for 7 performances
Reviews:
    New York Times page 61, Dec 5, 1972

Scandals   (see George White's Scandals)

Sea Legs
    book: Arthur Swanstrom
    music: Michael H. Cleary
    lyrics: Arthur Swanstrom
    staging: Bertram Harrison
    sets: Mabel Buell
    choreography: Johnny Mattison
Productions:
    Opened May 18, 1937 for 15 performances
Reviews:
    New York Times page 26, May 19, 1937

Second Little Show
    assembled by: Dwight Deere Wiman
    music: Arthur Schwartz
    lyrics: Howard Dietz
    staging: Dwight Deere Wiman, Dave Gould, Monty
                       Woolley
Productions:
    Opened September 2, 1930 for 63 performances
Reviews:
    Life (New York) 96:16, Sep 19, 1930
    New York Times VIII, page 2, Aug 17, 1930
                    page 36, Sep 3, 1930
    Vogue 76:60+, Oct 27, 1930

The Secret Life of Walter Mitty
    book: Joe Manchester; based on the short story by
                    James Thurber
    music: Leon Carr
    lyrics: Earl Shuman
    staging: Mervyn Nelson
    sets: Lloyd Burlingame
    costumes: Al Lehman
    choreography: Bob Arlen
Productions:
    (Off-Broadway) Opened October 26, 1964 for 96 performances
Reviews:
    New York Times page 44, Oct 27, 1964
                    page 34, Dec 28, 1964

Seduction Scene from a Musical Play in Progress
    book: Stuart Richard Townsend
    music: John Wallowitch
    staging: Robert Haddad
Productions:
    (Off-Off-Broadway) Opened May 10, 1964 for 3 performances
    (Theatre 1964 Playwrights Unit)
No Reviews.

See-Saw
    book: Earl Derr Biggers; adapted from the novel Love
                    Insurance
    music: Louis A. Hirsch
    lyrics: Earl Derr Biggers
Productions:
    Opened September 23, 1919 for 89 performances
Reviews:
    Dramatic Mirror 80:1538, Oct 2, 1919
    New York Times page 21, Sep 24, 1919
    Theatre Magazine 30:371, Dec 1919

Seeniaya Ptitza (The Blue Bird)
    material: Yasha Yushua
Productions:
    Opened December 29, 1924 for 80 performances
Reviews:
    Life (New York) 85:18, Jan 15, 1925
    New York Times page 11, Dec 29, 1924

Seesaw
    book: Michael Bennett; based on the play Two for the
                    Seesaw by William Gibson
    music: Cy Coleman
    lyrics: Dorothy Fields
    staging: Michael Bennett
    sets: Robin Wagner
    costumes: Ann Roth
    choreography: Michael Bennett

Productions:
    Opened March 18, 1973 for 296 performances
Reviews:
    America 128:336, Apr 14, 1973
    Dance Magazine 47:58A-58C, Jun 1973
    Harper's 106:153, Mar 1973
    Nation 216:508, Apr 16, 1973
    New York Theatre Critics' Reviews 1973:324
    New York Times page 46, Mar 19, 1973
                 II, page 1, Mar 25, 1973
                  II, page 1, Apr 8, 1973
                  page 53, Sep 11, 1973
    New Yorker 49:74, Mar 24, 1973
    Newsweek 81:83, Apr 2, 1973
    Time 101:71, Apr 2, 1973

The Selling of the President
    book: Jack O'Brien and Stuart Hample; based on the
                    book by Joe McGinniss
    music: Bob James
    lyrics: Jack O'Brien
    staging: Robert H. Livingston
    sets: Tom John
    costumes: Nancy Potts
Productions:
    Opened March 22, 1972 for 5 performances
Reviews:
    Life 35:52-3, Sep 7, 1971
    New York Theatre Critics' Reviews 1972:351
    New York Times page 30, Jan 19, 1972
                 page 37, Feb 7, 1972
                 page 28, Mar 3, 1972
                 page 50, Mar 23, 1972
    Newsweek 77:121, Apr 12, 1971

Sensations
    book: Paul Zakrzweski; suggested by William Shake-
                    speare's Romeo and Juliet
    music: Wally Harper
    lyrics: Paul Zakrzweski
    staging: Jerry Dodge
    sets: William and Jean Eckart
    costumes: Jeanne Button
Productions:
    (Off-Broadway) Opened October 25, 1970 for 16 performances
Reviews:
    New York Times page 48, Oct 26, 1970
    New Yorker 46:135, Nov 7, 1970

The Serenade
    book: Harry B. Smith
    music: Victor Herbert
    staging: Milton Aborn

Productions:
    Opened March 4, 1930 for 15 performances
Reviews:
    New York Times page 23, Feb 20, 1930

The Seven Deadly Sins
    book: Bertolt Brecht
    music: Kurt Weill
    lyrics: Bertolt Brecht
Productions:
    (Off-Broadway) Opened Season of 1958-59 (City Center)
Reviews:
    Time 72:42, Dec 29, 1958

Seven Lively Arts
    assembled: Billy Rose
    sketches: Moss Hart, George S. Kaufman, Robert Pirosh,
                   Joseph Schrank, Charles Sherman, Ben Hecht
    music: Cole Porter and Igor Stravinsky
    lyrics: Cole Porter
    staging: Hassard Short
    sets: Norman Bel Geddes
    costumes: Mary Shaw and Valentina
    choreography: Anton Dolin
Productions:
    Opened December 7, 1944 for 183 performances
Reviews:
    Catholic World 160:356, Jan 1945
    Commonweal 41:253-4, Dec 22, 1944
    Life 17:24-6, Dec 25, 1944
    Nation 159:781, Dec 23, 1944
    New Republic 111:867, Dec 25, 1944
    New York Theatre Critics' Reviews 1944:62+
    New York Times page 26, Dec 8, 1944
                  II, page 5, Dec 10, 1944
                   II, page 3, Dec 17, 1944
    New Yorker 20:42+, Dec 16, 1944
    Newsweek 24:76+, Dec 18, 1944
    Saturday Review 28:26, Jan 20, 1945
                  28:19-20, Mar 10, 1945
    Theatre Arts 29:66+, Feb 1945
    Time 44:72+, Dec 18, 1944

Seventeen
    book: Sally Benson, based on Booth Tarkington's novel
    music: Walter Kent
    lyrics: Kim Gannon
    staging: Hassard Short
    sets: Stewart Chaney
    costumes: David Ffolkes
    choreography: Dania Krupska
Productions:
    Opened June 21, 1951 for 182 performances

(Off-Broadway) Opened May 5, 1962 for 9 performances (Equity
    Library Theatre)
Reviews:
    Catholic World 173:386, Aug 1951
    Commonweal 54:309, Jul 6, 1951
    Life 31:57-8, Jul 23, 1951
    Musical America 71:34, Jul 1951
    New York Theatre Critics' Reviews 1951:250+
    New York Times II, page 2, Jun 10, 1951
                    page 16, Jun 22, 1951
                    II, page 1, Jul 1, 1951
                    II, page 9, Jul 1, 1951
    New Yorker 27:39, Jun 30, 1951
    Newsweek 38:74, Jul 2, 1951
    Theatre Arts 35:6-7, Sep 1951
    Time 58:55, Jul 2, 1951

1776

book:	Peter Stone; based on a conception of Sherman Edwards'
music:	Sherman Edwards
lyrics:	Sherman Edwards
staging:	Peter Hunt
sets:	Jo Mielziner
costumes:	Patricia Zipprodt
choreography:	Onna White and Martin Allen

Productions:
    Opened March 16, 1969 for 1,217 performances
Reviews:
    America 120:512-14, Apr 26, 1969
    Dance Magazine 43:92-3, May 1969
    Nation 208:443-4, Apr 7, 1969
    National Review 21:919, Sep 9, 1969
    New York Theatre Critics' Reviews 1969:324
    New York Times page 46, Mar 17, 1969
                    page 38, Mar 18, 1969
                    II, page 1, Mar 23, 1969
                    II, page 1, Apr 6, 1969
                    page 1, Feb 23, 1970
                    page 54, Jun 18, 1970
                    page 17, Apr 3, 1971
                    II, page 9, Jan 30, 1972
                    page 23, Feb 8, 1972
    New Yorker 45:87, Mar 22, 1969
    Newsweek 73:105, Mar 31, 1969
    Reader's Digest 96:199-200+, Feb 1970
    Saturday Review 52:20, Apr 5, 1969
    Time 93:55, Mar 28, 1969
    Vogue 153:118-19, Jun 1969

The Seventh Heart

book:	Sarah Ellis Hyman
staging:	Edward Elsner

Productions:
   Opened May 2, 1927 for 8 performances
No Reviews.

Seventh Heaven
   book: Victor Wolfson and Stella Unger, based on
                       Austin Strong's play Seventh Heaven
   music: Victor Young
   lyrics: Stella Unger
   staging: John C. Wilson
   sets: Marcel Vertes
   costumes: Marcel Vertes
   choreography: Peter Gennaro
Productions:
   Opened May 26, 1955 for 44 performances
Reviews:
   America 93:298, Jun 11, 1955
   Catholic World 181:307-8, Jul 1955
   Commonweal 62:329, Jul 1, 1955
   Nation 180:510, Jun 11, 1955
   New York Theatre Critics' Reviews 1955:302+
   New York Times VI, page 19, May 15, 1955
                   II, page 1, May 22, 1955
                   page 16, May 27, 1955
   New York Times Magazine page 19, May 15, 1955
   Saturday Review 38:25, Jun 11, 1955
   Theatre Arts 39:18-19, Aug 1955
   Time 65:57, Jun 6, 1955

70, Girls, 70
   book: Fred Ebb and Norman L. Martin; adaption by
                       Joseph Masteroff
   music: John Kander
   lyrics: Fred Ebb
   staging: Paul Aaron
   sets: Robert Randolph
   costumes: Jane Greenwood
   choreography: Onna White and Martin Allen
Productions:
   Opened April 15, 1971 for 36 performances
Reviews:
   America 124:615-16, Jun 12, 1971
   Dance Magazine 45:81-2, Jun 1971
   Nation 212:570-1, May 3, 1971
   New York Theatre Critics' Reviews 1971:302
   New York Times page 28, Feb 16, 1971
                   page 29, Apr 16, 1971
                   II, page 1, Apr 25, 1971
   New Yorker 47:93-4, Apr 24, 1971

Sextet
   book: Harvey Perr and Lee Goldsmith
   music: Lawrence Hurwit

    lyrics: Lee Goldsmith
    staging: Jered Barclay
    sets: Peter Harvey
    costumes: Zoe Brown
    choreography: Jered Barclay
Productions:
    Opened March 3, 1974 for 9 performances
Reviews:
    New York Theatre Critics' Reviews 1974:352
    New York Times page 36, Mar 4, 1974

Shady Lady
    book: Estelle Morando, revised by Irving Caesar
    music and
     lyrics: Sam H. Stept, Bud Green, Jesse Greer, Stanley
                       Adams
    staging: Theodore Hammerstein
    sets: Tom Adrian Cracraft
    choreography: Jack Donohue
Productions:
    Opened July 5, 1933 for 30 performances
Reviews:
    New York Times page 26, Jul 26, 1933

Shangri-La
    book: James Hilton, Jerome Lawrence, Robert E. Lee,
                       based on James Hilton's novel Lost Horizon
    music: Harry Warren
    lyrics: James Hilton, Jerome Lawrence, Robert E. Lee
    staging: Albert Marre
    costumes: Irene Sharaff
    choreography: Donald Saddler
Productions:
    Opened June 13, 1956 for 21 performances
Reviews:
    America 95:330, Jun 30, 1956
    Catholic World 183:388, Aug 1956
    New York Theatre Critics' Reviews 1956:293+
    New York Times page 40, Jun 14, 1956
    Saturday Review 39:22, Jun 30, 1956
    Theatre Arts 40:16, Aug 1956
    Time 67:86+, Jun 25, 1956

Sharlee
    book: Harry L. Cort and George E. Stoddard
    music: C. Luckyeth Roberts
    lyrics: Alex Rogers
Productions:
    Opened November 22, 1923 for 36 performances
Reviews:
    New York Times page 20, Nov 23, 1923

She Loves Me

book: Joe Masteroff, based on Miklos Laszlo's play
                 Parfumerie
music: Jerry Bock
lyrics: Sheldon Harnick
staging: Harold Prince
sets: William and Jean Eckart
costumes: Patricia Zipprodt
choreography: Carol Haney
Productions:
    Opened April 23, 1963 for 301 performances
    (Off-Broadway) Opened April 18, 1969 for 15 performances
Reviews:
    Commonweal 78:225, May 17, 1963
    Life 55:49-50+, Jul 12, 1963
    New York Theatre Critics' Reviews 1963:330+
    New York Times page 39, Apr 24, 1963
                    II, page 1, May 5, 1963
                    page 20, Jan 10, 1964
    New Yorker 39:90, May 4, 1963
    Newsweek 61:83, May 6, 1963
    Saturday Review 46:26, May 11, 1963
    Theatre Arts 47:12-13, Jun 1963
    Time 81:76, May 3, 1963

Sheba
    book: Hazel Bryant
    music: Jimmy Justice
    staging: Helaine Head
    choreography: Milo Timmons
Productions:
    (Off-Off-Broadway) Opened April 19, 1974 (Afro-American
    Total Theater)
No Reviews.

Shelter
    book: Gretchen Cryer
    music: Nancy Ford
    lyrics: Gretchen Cryer
    staging: Austin Pendleton
    sets: Tony Walton
    costumes: Tony Walton
    choreography: Sammy Bayes
Productions:
    Opened February 6, 1973 for 31 performances
Reviews:
    New York Theatre Critics' Reviews 1973:370
    New York Times page 31, Feb 7, 1973
                    II, page 1, Feb 18, 1973
    New Yorker 48:79, Feb 17, 1973

Sherry!
    book: James Lipton; based on The Man Who Came to
                     Dinner by George S. Kaufman and Moss Hart

music: Laurence Rosenthal
lyrics: James Lipton
staging: Joe Layton
sets: Robert Randolph
costumes: Robert Mackintosh
choreography: John Morris
Productions:
Opened March 27, 1967 for 72 performances
Reviews:
America 116:736-7, May 13, 1967
Christian Century 84:870-1, Jul 5, 1967
Commonweal 86:208-10, May 5, 1967
Dance Magazine 41:27-8, May 1967
New York Theatre Critics' Reviews 1967:332
New York Times page 39, Mar 29, 1967
                  II, page 5, Apr 9, 1967
                  page 55, May 24, 1967
New Yorker 43:138, Apr 8, 1967
Newsweek 69:109, Apr 10, 1967
Vogue 149:142, May 1967

She's a Good Fellow
music: Jerome Kern
libretto: Anne Caldwell
lyrics: Anne Caldwell
staging: Fred G. Latham and Edward Royce
Productions:
Opened May 5, 1919 for 120 performances
Reviews:
Forum 61:755, Jun 1919
Life (New York) 73:904, May 22, 1919
New York Times page 16, May 6, 1919
Theatre Arts 29:343, Jun 1919
                  29:19, Jul 1919

She's My Baby
book: Bert Kalmar and Harry Ruby
music: Richard Rodgers
lyrics: Lorenz Hart
staging: Edward Royce
Productions:
Opened January 3, 1928 for 71 performances
Reviews:
Life (New York) 91:21, Jan 19, 1928
New York Times page 22, Jan 4, 1928

Shinbone Alley
book: Joe Darion and Mel Brooks, based on the
                  "archy and mehitabel" stories of Don Marquis
music: George Kleinsinger
lyrics: Joe Darion
sets: Eldon Elder
costumes: Motley

    choreography: Rod Alexander
Productions:
    Opened April 13, 1957 for 49 performances
Reviews:
    America 97:216, May 11, 1957
    Catholic World 185:228-9, Jun 1957
    Christian Century 74:762, Jun 19, 1957
    Commonweal 66:204, May 24, 1957
    New York Theatre Critics' Reviews 1957:292+
    New York Times page 23, Apr 15, 1957
                    II, page 1, Apr 28, 1957
    New Yorker 33:82+, Apr 20, 1957
    Newsweek 49:69-70, Apr 22, 1957
    Theatre Arts 41:15-16, Jun 1957
    Time 69:90, Apr 22, 1957

The Shoemaker and the Peddler
    book: Armand Aulicino; based on the story of Sacco
                     and Vanzetti
    music: Frank Fields
    lyrics: Armand Aulicino
    staging: Lee Nametz
    sets: David Ballou
    costumes: David Ballou
    choreography: Sophie Maslow
Productions:
    (Off-Broadway) Opened October 14, 1960 for 43 performances
Reviews:
    New York Times page 27, Oct 15, 1960
                    page 12, Nov 12, 1960
    New Yorker 36:92, Oct 22, 1960
(See also Sacco-Vanzetti)

Shoemaker's Holiday
    book: Ted Berger
    music: Mel Marvin
    lyrics: Ted Berger
    staging: Ken Costigan
    sets: Robert Conley
    costumes: Whitney Blausen
    choreography: Myrna Gallé
Productions:
    (Off-Broadway) Opened March 3, 1967 for 6 performances
Reviews:
    New York Times page 25, Mar 3, 1967
                    page 15, Mar 4, 1967
    New Yorker 43:127-8+, Mar 11, 1967

Shoestring Revue
    conceived: Ben Bagley
Productions:
    (Off-Broadway) Season of 1954-55 (President Theatre)
Reviews:

America 93:26, Apr 2, 1955
Catholic World 181:68, Apr 1955
Nation 180:294, Apr 2, 1955
New York Times page 22, Mar 1, 1955
New Yorker 31:67, Mar 12, 1955
Saturday Review 38:25, Apr 23, 1955
Theatre Arts 39:87, May 1955

Shoot the Works
    assembled by: Heywood Broun and Milton Raison
    contributors: Heywood Broun, H. I. Phillips, Peter Arno,
                   Sig Herzig, Edward J. McNamara, Michael H.
                   Cleary, Philip Charig, Jay Gorney, Dorothy
                   Fields, Ira Gershwin, Alexander Williams,
                   Robert Stolz, A. Robinson, Dorothy Parker,
                   Nunnally Johnson, E. B. White, Jack Hazzard,
                   Irving Berlin, Max Lief, Nathaniel Lief, E. Y.
                   Harburg, Jimmie McHugh, Vernon Duke, Her-
                   bert Goode, Walter Reisch
Productions:
    Opened July 21, 1931 for 87 performances
Reviews:
    Arts and Decoration 35:45+, Oct 1931
    Commonweal 14:346, Aug 5, 1931
    Nation 133:148, Aug 12, 1931
    New Republic 67:317-18, Aug 5, 1931
    New York Times page 19, Jul 22, 1931
                    VIII, page 2, Jul 26, 1931
                    VIII, page 2, Aug 16, 1931
                    page 35, Oct 6, 1931
    Outlook 158:437, Aug 5, 1931
    Saturday Evening Post 204:16-17+, Nov 14, 1931

Short, Hassard (see Hassard Short)

Show Boat
    book: Oscar Hammerstein II, adapted from Edna
                   Ferber's novel
    music: Jerome Kern
    lyrics: Oscar Hammerstein II
    staging: Florenz Ziegfeld and Zeke Cohan
    sets: Joseph Urban
    costumes: John Harkrider
    choreography: Sammy Lee
Productions:
    Opened December 27, 1927 for 572 performances
    Opened May 19, 1932 for 180 performances
    Opened January 5, 1946 for 418 performances
    Opened September 1948 for 15 performances
    Opened May 5, 1954 for 15 performances
    Opened April 12, 1961 for 14 performances
    Opened July 19, 1966 for 63 performances
Reviews:

America 91:227+, May 22, 1954
        95:351, Jul 7, 1956
        97:490, Aug 10, 1957
        115:140-1, Aug 6, 1966
Arts and Decoration 37:43+, Sep 1932
Catholic World 162:456, Feb 1946
                168:77, Oct 1948
                179:308, Jul 1954
                183:388, Aug 1956
                185:469, Sep 1957
Commonweal 74:379, Jul 7, 1961
Cosmopolitan 120:32-3+, Apr 1946
Dance Magazine 40:34+, Sep 1966
Life (New York) 91:21, Jan 12, 1928
Life 20:71-2+, Jan 28, 1946
Musical America 74:10, May 1954
Nation 134:660, Jun 8, 1932
        162:138, Feb 2, 1946
        178:390, May 1, 1954
        192:378, Apr 29, 1961
New Republic 119:38, Sep 27, 1948
New York Theatre Critics' Reviews 1946:496+
New York Times page 26, Dec 18, 1927
                VIII, page 1, Jan 8, 1928
                page 31, May 4, 1928
                page 9, May 5, 1928
                page 14, Dec 26, 1928
                VIII, page 4, Dec 30, 1928
                page 22, May 20, 1932
                VIII, page 5, May 29, 1932
                II, page 5, Jul 3, 1938
                page 17, Jan 7, 1946
                II, page 1, Jan 13, 1946
                II, page 1, Feb 24, 1946
                II, page 1, Jun 23, 1946
                VI, page 25, Sep 29, 1946
                VI, page 23, Dec 8, 1946
                page 33, Sep 9, 1948
                II, page 1, Sep 19, 1948
                page 19, Jun 6, 1952
                page 19, Apr 9, 1954
                page 72, Apr 18, 1954
                page 21, May 3, 1954
                page 44, May 6, 1954
                page 28, Oct 29, 1954
                page 27, Nov 1, 1954
                page 16, Jun 22, 1956
                page 30, Jun 28, 1957
                page 32, Apr 13, 1961
                II, page 1, Jul 17, 1966
                page 48, Jul 20, 1966
New Yorker 21:40+, Jan 12, 1946
        30:116, Apr 17, 1954

Newsweek 27:77, Jan 14, 1946
    43:52-3, Apr 19, 1954
Outlook 148:265, Feb 15, 1928
Saturday Review 29:30-2, Jan 26, 1946
    37:27, Apr 24, 1954
    49:34, Aug 6, 1966
Stage 9:4, Jul 1932
Theatre Arts 27:246, Apr 1943
    30:138, Mar 1946
Theatre Magazine 47:58, Feb 1928
    47:35, May 1928
Time 47:47, Jan 14, 1946
Vogue 71:122, Feb 15, 1928

Show Girl (1929)
    book: William Anthony McGuire, based on the novel
                     by J. P. McEvoy
    music: George Gershwin
    lyrics: Ira Gershwin and Gus Kahn
    staging: Florenz Ziegfeld, Bobby Connelly, Albertina
                     Rasch
Productions:
    Opened July 2, 1929 for 111 performances
Reviews:
    Life (New York) 94:22, Aug 30, 1929
    New Republic 59:262-3, Jul 24, 1929
    New York Times page 19, Jul 3, 1929
                    page 29, Aug 8, 1929
    Outlook 152:515, Jul 24, 1929
    Theatre Magazine 50:39, Sep 1929

Show Girl (1961)
    sketches: Charles Gaynor (additional sketches by Ernest
                     Chambers)
    music: Charles Gaynor
    lyrics: Charles Gaynor
    staging: Charles Gaynor
    sets: Oliver Smith
    costumes: Miles White
    choreography: Richard D'Arcy
Productions:
    Opened January 12, 1961 for 100 performances
Reviews:
    America 104:557, Jan 28, 1961
    New York Theatre Critics' Reviews 1961:394+
    New York Times page 37, Jan 13, 1961
                    II, page 1, Jan 29, 1961
                    page 27, Apr 3, 1961
    Newsweek 57:57, Jan 23, 1961
    Saturday Review 44:27, Jan 28, 1961
    Time 77:77, Jan 20, 1961

The Show Is On

    assembled by: Vincente Minnelli
    contributors: David Freedman, Moss Hart, Vernon Duke, Ted
                     Fetter, Howard Dietz, Arthur Schwartz, Richard
                     Rodgers, Lorenz Hart
    staging: Vincente Minnelli
    sets: Vincente Minnelli
    choreography: Harry Losee
Productions:
    Opened December 25, 1936 for 237 performances
    Opened September 18, 1937 for 17 performances
Reviews:
    Arts and Decoration 46:22-3, Jul 1937
    Catholic World 144:729-30, Mar 1937
    Nation 144:80, Jan 16, 1937
    New York Times page 22, Nov 9, 1936
                    XI, page 2, Nov 15, 1936
                    page 14, Dec 26, 1936
                    X, page 1, Jan 10, 1937
                    X, page 2, Feb 14, 1937
                    XI, page 8, Feb 28, 1937
                    page 18, Sep 20, 1937
                    X, page 3, Oct 31, 1937
    Newsweek 9:22, Jan 2, 1937
    Stage 13:33-5, Sep 1936
    Theatre Arts 21:97, Feb 1937
    Time 29:30-1, Jan 4, 1937
    Vogue 89:64, Feb 1, 1937

Show Me Where the Good Times Are
    book: Lee Thuna; based on Molière's The Imaginary
                     Invalid
    music: Kenneth Jacobson
    lyrics: Rhoda Roberts
    staging: Morton Da Costa
    sets: Tom John
    costumes: Gloria Gresham
    choreography: Bob Herget
Productions:
    (Off-Broadway) Opened March 5, 1970 for 29 performances
Reviews:
    America 122:398, Apr 11, 1970
    New York Times page 32, Mar 6, 1970
                    page 35, Mar 31, 1970
    New Yorker 46:122, Mar 14, 1970

The Show of Wonders
    book: Harold Atteridge
    music: Sigmund Romberg, Otto Motzan and Herman
                     Timberg
    lyrics: Harold Atteridge
    staging: J. J. Shubert, J. C. Huffman and Allen K.
                     Foster
Productions:

Opened October 26, 1916 for 209 performances
Reviews:
Dramatic Mirror 76:7, Nov 4, 1916
New York Dramatic News 63:10, Nov 4, 1916
New York Times page 7, Oct 27, 1916
           II, page 6, Nov 12, 1916
Theatre Magazine 26:357, Sep 1917

The Shrinking Bride
    book: Jonathon Levy
    music: William Bolcom
    lyrics: Jonathon Levy
    staging: Marvin Gordon
    sets: T. E. Mason
    costumes: Joseph G. Aulisi
Productions:
(Off-Broadway) Opened January 17, 1971 for one performance
Reviews:
New York Times page 28, Jan 18, 1971

Shubert Gaieties 1919
    words: J. J. Shubert and Lee Shubert
    music: J. J. Shubert and Lee Shubert
    staging: J. C. Huffman
Productions:
Opened July 17, 1919 for 87 performances
Reviews:
New York Times page 9, Jul 8, 1919

Shuffle Along
    book: Flourney E. Miller
    music: Eubie Blake
    lyrics: Noble Sissle
    staging: Walter Brooks
Productions:
Opened May 23, 1921 for 27 performances
Opened December 26, 1932 for 17 performances
Opened May 8, 1952 for 4 performances
Reviews:
Commonweal 56:197, May 30, 1952
National Magazine 51:244, Oct 1922
New Republic 27:171, Jul 6, 1921
New York Clipper 69:19, May 25, 1921
New York Theatre Critics' Reviews 1952:286
New York Times page 16, May 23, 1921
               page 11, Dec 27, 1932
               page 20, May 9, 1952
New Yorker 28:87, May 17, 1952
Theatre Magazine 34:98, Aug 1921
Time 59:83, May 19, 1952

Sidewalks of New York
    book: Eddie Dowling and Jimmy Hanley

music: Eddie Dowling and Jimmy Hanley
lyrics: Eddie Dowling and Jimmy Hanley
staging: Edgar MacGregor
Productions:
Opened October 3, 1927 for 112 performances
Reviews:
Life (New York) 90:23, Nov 3, 1927
New York Times page 33, Oct 4, 1927
Theatre Magazine 46:44, Dec 1927

Signs Along the Cynic Route
sketches: Will Holt and Dolly Jonah
music: Will Holt
lyrics: Will Holt
staging: Walt Witcover
Productions:
(Off-Broadway) Opened December 14, 1961 for 93 performances
Reviews:
Commonweal 75:389, Jan 5, 1962
New York Times page 49, Dec 15, 1961
                 page 29, Feb 28, 1962
New Yorker 37:68, Jan 20, 1962

Silk Stockings
book: George S. Kaufman, Leueen MacGrath, and Abe
                  Burrows, suggested by Melchior Lengyel's
                  Ninotchka
music: Cole Porter
lyrics: Cole Porter
staging: Cy Feuer
sets: Jo Mielziner
costumes: Lucinda Ballard and Robert Mackintosh
choreography: Eugene Loring
Productions:
Opened February 24, 1955 for 478 performances
Reviews:
America 93:109, Apr 23, 1955
Catholic World 181:67, Apr 1955
Commonweal 61:676, Apr 1, 1955
Life 38:93-4+, Mar 21, 1955
Look 19:66-8, Feb 8, 1955
Mademoiselle 40:142, Nov 1954
Nation 180:226, Mar 12, 1955
New York Theatre Critics' Reviews 1952:354+
New York Times page 17, Feb 25, 1955
                 II, page 1, Mar 27, 1955
New Yorker 31:68, Mar 5, 1955
Newsweek 45:85, Mar 7, 1955
Saturday Review 38:26, Mar 12, 1955
                 39:13+, Sep 15, 1956
Theatre Arts 39:18+, May 1955
Time 65:92, Mar 7, 1955
Vogue 125:124, Jan 1955

Silks and Satins
    book: Thomas Duggan
    music: Leon Rosebrook
    lyrics: Louis Weslyn
Productions:
    Opened July 15, 1920 for 53 performances
Reviews:
    New York Clipper 68:23, Jul 21, 1920
    New York Times page 19, Jul 1920
    Theatre Magazine 32:105, Sep 1920

Sillman, Leonard   (see Leonard Sillman)

Silver Queen
    book: Paul Foster
    music: John Braden
    staging: Robert Patrick
Productions:
    (Off-Off-Broadway) Opened April 11, 1973 (La Mama Experi-
    mental Theatre Club)
No Reviews.

The Silver Star
    book: Harry B. Smith
    staging: Herbert Gresham
    choreography: Julian Mitchell
Productions:
    Opened November 1, 1909 for 80 performances
Reviews:
    Dramatic Mirror 62:7, Nov 13, 1909
    Hampton 24:133-4, Jan 1910
    Leslie's Weekly 110:37, Jan 13, 1910
    Metropolitan Magazine 31:674-5, Feb 1910
    Theatre Magazine 10:xv, Dec 1909

The Silver Swan
    book: William S. Brady and Alonzo Price
    music: H. Maurice Jacquet
    lyrics: William S. Brady and Alonzo Price
    staging: Alonzo Price and Leroy J. Prinz
Productions:
    Opened November 27, 1929 for 21 performances
Reviews:
    New York Times IX, page 1, Nov 3, 1929
                    page 34, Nov 28, 1929

Simple Simon
    book: Ed Wynn and Guy Bolton
    music: Richard Rodgers
    lyrics: Lorenz Hart
    staging: Zeke Colvan
    choreography: Seymour Felix
Productions:

Opened February 18, 1930 for 135 performances
Opened March 9, 1931 for 16 performances
Reviews:
Life (New York) 95:18, Mar 28, 1930
New York Times VIII, page 2, Feb 2, 1930
                  page 22, Feb 19, 1930
                  page 23, Mar 10, 1931
Theatre Magazine 51:46, Apr 1930

Simply Heavenly
book:	Langston Hughes
music:	David Martin
lyrics:	Langston Hughes
staging:	Joshua Shelley
sets:	Raymond Sovey

Productions:
(Off-Broadway) Season of 1956-57
Opened August 20, 1957 for 62 performances
Reviews:
Catholic World 185:388-9, Aug 1957
Nation 185:230, Oct 5, 1957
New York Theatre Critics' Reviews 1957:264+
New York Times page 28, May 22, 1957
            II, page 1, Jun 2, 1957
           page 36, Jan 2, 1958
Saturday Review 40:24, Sep 7, 1957

Sinbad
dialogue:	Harold Atteridge
music:	Sigmund Romberg and Al Jolson
lyrics:	Harold Atteridge
staging:	J. C. Huffman and J. J. Shubert

Productions:
Opened February 14, 1918 for 164 performances
Reviews:
Dramatic Mirror 78:5, Mar 2, 1918
Life (New York) 71:343, Feb 28, 1918
New York Times page 7, Feb 18, 1918
Theatre Magazine 37:227, Apr 1918
                 37:316, May 1918

Sing for Your Supper
compiled by:	Harold Hecht
sketches:	Dave Lesan, Turner Bullock, Charlotte Kent, John Latouche
music:	Lee Wainer and Ned Lehak
lyrics:	Robert Sour
staging:	H. Gordon Graham and Harold Hecht
sets:	Herbert Andrews
costumes:	Mary Merrill
choreography:	Anna Sokolow

Productions:
Opened April 24, 1939 for 44 performances

Reviews:
> Catholic World 149:345-6, Jun 1939
> New York Times page 18, Apr 25, 1939
> Newsweek 13:22, May 8, 1939
> Theatre Arts 23:404, Jun 1939

Sing Israel Sing
book, music,
lyrics: Asaf Halevi, Moishe Broderson, M. M. War-
shavsky, Wolf Younin, M. Neu, Shlomo Weis-
fisch, Joel Chayes, E. Kishon and H. Kon
special
material: M. Nudelman
staging: Mina Bern and Felix Fibich
costumes: Judith Fibich
choreography: Felix and Judith Fibich
Productions:
> Opened May 11, 1967 for 14 performances
> Opened June 7, 1967 for 8 performances

Reviews:
> New York Times page 50, May 12, 1967
>   page 57, Jun 13, 1967

Sing Muse!
book: Erich Segal
music: Joseph Raposo
lyrics: Erich Segal
staging: Bill Penn
sets: Boyd Dumrose
Productions:
> (Off-Broadway) Opened December 6, 1961 for 39 performances

Reviews:
> New York Times page 52, Dec 7, 1961
> New Yorker 37:100+, Dec 16, 1961

Sing out Sweet Land
book: Walter Kerr
special music: Elie Siegmeister (other music folk and popular)
staging: Leon Leonidoff
sets: Albert Johnson
costumes: Lucinda Ballard
choreography: Doris Humphrey and Charles Weidman
Productions:
> Opened December 27, 1944 for 102 performances

Reviews:
> Catholic World 160:452, Feb 1945
> Collier's 115:22-3, Apr 7, 1945
> Commonweal 41:331, Jan 12, 1945
> Nation 160:52, Jan 13, 1945
> New Republic 112:85, Jan 15, 1945
> New York Theatre Critics' Reviews 1944:48+
> New York Times page 24, Nov 10, 1944
>   VI, page 14, Dec 24, 1944

page 24, Dec 28, 1944
II, page 1, Jan 7, 1945
II, page 1, Jan 14, 1945
II, page 5, Jan 21, 1945
New York Times Magazine pages 14-15, Dec 24, 1944
New Yorker 20:40, Jan 6, 1945
Newsweek 25:72, Jan 8, 1945
Theatre Arts 29:79, Feb 1945
29:134-6, Mar 1945
Time 45:67, Jan 8, 1945

Sing out the News
book: Harold Rome and Charles Friedman
music: Will Irwin
lyrics: Harold Rome
staging: Charles Friedman
sets: Jo Mielziner
costumes: John Hambleton
choreography: Ned McGurn, Dave Gould, Charles Walters
Productions:
Opened September 24, 1938 for 105 performances
Reviews:
Catholic World 148:214-15, Nov 1938
Commonweal 28:615, Oct 7, 1938
New Republic 96:271, Oct 12, 1938
New York Times page 12, Sep 26, 1938
IX, page 1, Oct 2, 1938
Stage 16:6+, Oct 1938
Theatre Arts 22:784, Nov 1938
Time 32:30, Oct 3, 1938

The Singing Rabbi
book: Bores and Harry Thomashefsky
music: J. Rumshinsky and Harry Lubin
staging: William E. Morris
Productions:
Opened September 10, 1931 for 4 performances
Reviews:
New York Times page 24, Sep 11, 1931

The Siren
book: Leo Stein and A. M. Willner; English version
by Harry B. Smith
music: Leo Fall
Productions:
Opened August 28, 1911 for 136 performances
Reviews:
Blue Book 14:19-21, Nov 1911
Dramatic Mirror 66:11, Aug 30, 1911
66:8, Sep 6, 1911
Everybody's 25:691, Nov 1911
Green Book Album 6:963-4, Nov 1911
6:999, Nov 1911

Life (New York) 58:430, Sep 14, 1911
Munsey 46:279-80, Nov 1911
New York Times page 7, Aug 29, 1911
                  I, page 4, Sep 10, 1911
Pearson 26:651, Nov 1911
Red Book 17:1140-42+, Oct 1911
Theatre Magazine 14:xii, Oct 1911
                  14:120, Oct 1911

Sissy
    book: Seth Allen
    music: Michael Meadows and Seth Allen
    staging: John Vaccaro
Productions:
    (Off-Off-Broadway) Opened November 9, 1972 (La Mama Ex-
    perimental Theatre Club)
No Reviews.

Sisters of Mercy
    conceived: Gene Lesser
    words: Leonard Cohen
    music: Leonard Cohen
    additional
      music: Zizi Mueller
    staging: Gene Lesser
    sets: Robert U. Taylor
    costumes: Carrie F. Robbins
Productions:
    (Off-Broadway) Opened September 25, 1973 for 15 per-
    formances
Reviews:
    New York Times page 46, Sep 26, 1973

Sitting Pretty
    book: Guy Bolton and P. G. Wodehouse
    music: Jerome Kern
    lyrics: P. G. Wodehouse
Productions:
    Opened April 8, 1924 for 95 performances
Reviews:
    New York Times VIII, page 2, Mar 30, 1924
                        page 24, Apr 9, 1924
    Theatre Magazine 39:19, Jun 1924

Six
    book: Charles Strouse
    music: Charles Strouse
    lyrics: Charles Strouse
    staging: Peter Coe
    sets: Richard Nelson
Productions:
    (Off-Broadway) Opened April 12, 1971 for 8 performances
Reviews:

New York Times page 29, Apr 13, 1971
New Yorker 47:95, Apr 24, 1971

Skating Vanities of 1942
Productions:
    (Off-Broadway) Opened June 1942
Reviews:
    New York Times VII, page 39, Apr 26, 1942

Sketch Book   (see Earl Carroll's Sketch Book)

Skits-oh-Frantics!
    words, music: Bernie Wayne; additional material by Charles
                    Naylor and Ken Welch
    staging: Hank Ladd
    sets: Carleton Snyder
    costumes: Eve Henriksen
    choreography: Frank Westbrook and Patti Karr
Productions:
    (Off-Broadway) Opened April 2, 1967 for 17 performances
Reviews:
    New York Times page 39, Apr 3, 1967

Sky High
    book: Harold Atteridge and Captain Harry Graham
    music: Robert Stolz, Alfred Goodman, Carlton Kelsey
                    and Maurie Rubens
    staging: J. J. Shubert
Productions:
    Opened March 2, 1925 for 80 performances
Reviews:
    Life (New York) 85:18, Mar 19, 1925
    New York Times page 21, Mar 3, 1925
    Theatre Magazine 41:34, May 1925

Skye
    book: Avery Corman and Dan Rustin
    music: Ben Finn
    lyrics: Avery Corman and Dan Rustin
    staging: James Curtan
Productions:
    Opened Season of 1970-71 (Equity Theatre Informal)
Reviews:
    New York Times page 29, Feb 4, 1971

A Skylark
    book: William Harris, Jr.
    music: Frank G. Dossert
    lyrics: William Harris, Jr.
    staging: Ben Teal
Productions:
    Opened April 4, 1910 for 24 performances
Reviews:

Dramatic Mirror 63:5, Apr 16, 1910
Leslie's Weekly 110:336, Apr 7, 1910
                    110:385, Apr 21, 1910
Theatre Magazine 11:xxvii, May 1910

Skyscraper
    book: Peter Stone; based on Elmer Rice's Dream Girl
    music: James Van Heusen
    lyrics: Sammy Cahn
    staging: Cy Feuer
    sets: Robert Randolph
    costumes: Theoni V. Aldredge
    choreography: Michael Kidd
Productions:
    Opened November 13, 1965 for 241 performances
Reviews:
    America 114:180, Jan 29, 1966
    Commonweal 83:316, Dec 1, 1965
    Dance Magazine 40:16, Jan 1966
    Holiday 39:118+, Jan 1966
    Life 60:90-2, Feb 4, 1966
    New York Theatre Critics' Reviews 1965:274
    New York Times page 48, Nov 15, 1965
                    page 57, Nov 16, 1965
                    page 31, Jun 3, 1966
                    page 50, Jun 6, 1966
    New Yorker 41:149, Nov 20, 1965
    Newsweek 66:91, Nov 29, 1965
    Saturday Review 48:76, Dec 4, 1965
    Time 86:67, Nov 26, 1965

Sleepy Hollow
    book: Russell Maloney and Miriam Battista, based on
                     Washington Irving's "The Legend of Sleepy Hol-
                     low"
    music: George Lessner
    lyrics: Russell Maloney and Miriam Battista
    staging: John O'Shaughnessy and Marc Connelly
    sets: Jo Mielziner
    costumes: David Ffolkes
    choreography: Anna Sokolow
Productions:
    Opened June 3, 1948 for 12 performances
Reviews:
    New Republic 118:29, Jun 21, 1948
    New York Theatre Critics' Reviews 1948:258+
    New York Times page 26, Jun 4, 1948
    New Yorker 24:44, Jun 12, 1948
    Newsweek 31:86, Jun 14, 1948
    Time 51:64, Jun 14, 1948

The Slim Princess
    book: Henry Blossom; adapted from a story of George Ade

music: Leslie Stuart
lyrics: Henry Blossom
staging: Austin Hurgon
Productions:
Opened January 2, 1911 for 104 performances
Reviews:
Dramatic Mirror 65:6, Jan 4, 1911
Green Book Album 5:471-3+, Mar 1911
Life (New York) 57:109, Jan 19, 1911
Munsey 44:864-6, Mar 1911
New York Dramatic News 56:3, Nov 30, 1912
New York Times page 12, Jan 3, 1911
                  I, page 2, Jan 22, 1911
Pearson 25:495, Apr 1911
Red Book 16:945+, Mar 1911
Theatre Magazine 13:x, Feb 1911

Small Wonder
sketches: Charles Spalding, Max Wilk, George Axelrod,
                  Louis Laun
music: Baldwin Bergersen and Albert Selden
lyrics: Phyllis McGinley and Billings Brown
staging: Burt Shevelove
sets: Ralph Alswang
costumes: John Derro
choreography: Gower Champion
Productions:
Opened September 15, 1948 for 134 performances
Reviews:
Catholic World 168:160, Nov 1948
New Republic 119:26-7, Oct 4, 1948
New York Theatre Critics' Reviews 1948:244+
New York Times page 33, Sep 16, 1948
                  II, page 1, Sep 26, 1948
New York Times Magazine pages 40-1, Sep 12, 1948
New Yorker 24:53, Sep 25, 1948
Newsweek 32:79, Sep 27, 1948
School and Society 68:302, Oct 30, 1948
Theatre Arts 33:17, Jan 1949
Time 52:63, Sep 27, 1948

Smile at Me
sketches: Edward J. Lambert
music: Gerald Dolin
lyrics: Edward J. Lambert
staging: Frank Merlin
sets: Karl Amend
costumes: Dorothy Van Winkle
choreography: Paul Florenz
Productions:
Opened August 23, 1935 for 27 performances
Reviews:
New York Times page 18, Aug 24, 1935

Smile, Smile, Smile
     book: Robert Russell
     music: Hugo Peretti, Luigi Creatore and George David
                        Weiss
     lyrics: Hugo Peretti, Luigi Creatore and George David
                        Weiss
     staging: Robert Simpson
     sets: Philip Gilliam
     costumes: Patricia McGourty
Productions:
     (Off-Broadway) Opened April 4, 1973 for 7 performances
Reviews:
     New York Times II, page 1, Feb 11, 1973
                        page 51, Apr 5, 1973

Smiles
     book: William Anthony McGuire
     music: Vincent Youmans
     lyrics: Clifford Grey, Harold Adamson, Ring Lardner
     staging: Ned Wayburn and William Anthony McGuire
Productions:
     Opened November 18, 1930 for 63 performances
Reviews:
     Life (New York) 96:18, Dec 12, 1930
     New York Times page 19, Nov 19, 1930

Smiling Faces
     book: Harry Clarke
     music: Harry Revel
     lyrics: Mack Gordon
     staging: R. H. Burnside
Productions:
     Opened August 30, 1932 for 33 performances
Reviews:
     Catholic World 136:84-5, Oct 1932

Smiling the Boy Fell Dead
     book: Ira Wallach
     music: David Baker
     lyrics: Sheldon Harnick
     staging: Theodore Mann
     sets: Herbert Senn and Helen Pond
     costumes: Theoni V. Aldredge
Productions:
     (Off-Broadway) Opened April 19, 1961 for 22 performances
Reviews:
     New York Times page 28, Apr 20, 1961
                        page 22, May 5, 1961
     New Yorker 37:94, Apr 29, 1961
     Theatre Arts 45:32, Jun 1961

Smith
     book: Dean Fuller, Tony Hendra and Matt Dubey

music:	Matt Dubey and Dean Fuller
lyrics:	Matt Dubey and Dean Fuller
staging:	Neal Kenyon
sets:	Fred Voelpel
costumes:	Winn Morton
choreography:	Michael Shawn

Productions:
Opened May 19, 1973 for 17 performances
Reviews:
New York Theatre Critics' Reviews 1973:265
New York Times page 43, May 21, 1973
New Yorker 49:54, May 26, 1973

So Long, Letty

book:	Oliver Morosco and Elmer Harris
music:	Earl Carroll
lyrics:	Earl Carroll
staging:	Oliver Morosco
choreography:	Julian Alfred

Productions:
Opened October 23, 1916 for 96 performances
Reviews:
Dramatic Mirror 76:7, Oct 28, 1916
                76:8, Nov 11, 1916
Life (New York) 68:767, Nov 2, 1916
New York Dramatic News 63:11, Oct 28, 1916
New York Times page 14, Oct 24, 1916
Theatre Magazine 24:355, Dec 1916

Some Night

book:	Harry Delf
music:	Harry Delf
lyrics:	Harry Delf
staging:	W. H. Post and Julian Mitchell

Productions:
Opened September 23, 1918 for 24 performances
Reviews:
Dramatic Mirror 79:507, Oct 5, 1918
New York Times page 11, Sep 17, 1918
                IV, page 1, Sep 29, 1918
Theatre Magazine 38:279, Nov 1918

Some Party

arranged:	R. H. Burnside
music:	Silvio Hein, Percy Wenrich and Gustave Kerker
staging:	R. H. Burnside

Productions:
Opened April 15, 1922 for 17 performances
Reviews:
New York Clipper 70:20, Apr 19, 1922
New York Times page 22, Apr 17, 1922

Somebody's Sweetheart

           book: Alonzo Price
           music: Antonio Bafunno
           lyrics: Alonzo Price
           staging: Arthur Hammerstein
       Productions:
           Opened December 23, 1918 for 224 performances
       Reviews:
           Dramatic Mirror 80:9, Jan 4, 1919
           Forum 61:248, Feb 1919
           New York Times page 7, Dec 24, 1918
           Theatre Magazine 29:78, Feb 1919
                             29:145, Mar 1919

Something for the Boys
           book: Herbert and Dorothy Fields
           music: Cole Porter
           lyrics: Cole Porter
           staging: Hassard Short
           sets: Howard Bay
           costumes: Billy Livingston
           choreography: Jack Cole
       Productions:
           Opened January 7, 1943 for 422 performances
       Reviews:
           Catholic World 156:601, Feb 1943
           Life 14:79+, Feb 8, 1943
           New York Theatre Critics' Reviews 1943:398+
           New York Times page 24, Jan 8, 1943
                             VIII, page 1, Jan 17, 1943
                             II, page 1, Apr 30, 1944
           New Yorker 18:32, Jan 16, 1943
           Theatre Arts 27:138-9, Mar 1943
           Time 41:58, Jan 18, 1943

Something More!
           book: Nate Monaster, based on Gerald Green's
                            Portofino P. T. A.
           music: Sammy Fain
           lyrics: Marilyn and Alan Bergman
           staging: Jule Styne
           sets: Robert Randolph
           costumes: Alvin Colt
           choreography: Bob Herget
       Productions:
           Opened November 10, 1964 for 15 performances
       Reviews:
           Dance Magazine 39:18-19, Jan 1965
           New York Theatre Critics' Reviews 1964:159+
           New York Times II, page 3, Oct 4, 1964
                             page 36, Nov 11, 1964
                             page 52, Nov 18, 1964
           Time 84:81, Nov 20, 1964

Sometime
    material: Rida Johnson Young and Rudolf Friml
Productions:
    Opened October 4, 1918 for 283 performances
Reviews:
    New York Times page 11, Oct 5, 1918
                 IV, page 2, Oct 13, 1918
    Theatre Magazine 38:346, Dec 1918

Somewhere Else
    book: Avery Hopwood
    music: Gustav Luders
    lyrics: Avery Hopwood
    staging: Frank Smithson
Productions:
    Opened January 30, 1913 for 8 performances
Reviews:
    Dramatic Mirror 69:7, Jan 22, 1913
    New York Dramatic News 57:25, Jan 25, 1913
    New York Times page 13, Jan 21, 1913

Songbook (see The Harold Arlen Songbook)

Songs and Impressions (see Maurice Chevalier in Songs and Impressions)

Sonny
    book: George V. Hobart
    music: Raymond Hubbell
    staging: George V. Hobart
Productions:
    Opened August 16, 1921 for 31 performances
Reviews:
    Dramatic Mirror 84:265, Aug 20, 1921
    New York Clipper 69:24, Aug 24, 1921
    New York Times page 12, Aug 17, 1921
    Theatre Magazine 34:236, Oct 1921

Sons o'Fun
    book: Ole Olsen, Chic Johnson, Hal Block
    songs: Jack Yellen and Sam E. Fain
    staging: Edward D. Dowling
    sets: Raoul Pene du Bois
    choreography: Robert Alton
Productions:
    Opened December 1, 1941 for 742 performances
Reviews:
    Catholic World 154:474, Jan 1942
    Life 11:44-5, Nov 17, 1941
    Nation 153:621, Dec 13, 1941
    New York Theatre Critics' Reviews 1941:193+
    New York Times page 20, Nov 1, 1941
               page 28, Dec 2, 1941

Time 38:73, Dec 15, 1941

Sons o'Guns
book: Fred Thompson and Jack Donahue
music: J. Fred Coots
lyrics: Arthur Swanstrom and Benny Davis
staging: Bobby Connelly
choreography: Albertina Rasch
Productions:
Opened November 26, 1929 for 295 performances
Reviews:
New York Times page 30, Nov 27, 1929
                  X, page 2, Dec 15, 1929
                  VIII, page 1, Jan 12, 1930
Theatre Magazine 51:49, Jan 1930

Soon
book: Joseph Martinez Kookoolis and Scott Fagan;
                   adapted by Martin Duberman
music: Joseph Martinez Kookoolis and Scott Fagan
lyrics: Scott Fagan
staging: Gerald Freedman
sets: Kert Lundell
costumes: David Chapman
choreography: Fred Benjamin
Productions:
Opened January 12, 1971 for 3 performances
Reviews:
New York Theatre Critics' Reviews 1971:393
New York Times page 29, Jan 13, 1971
                  page 43, Jan 14, 1971
New Yorker 46:66, Jan 23, 1971

Sophie
book: Phillip Pruneau
music: Steve Allen
lyrics: Steve Allen
staging: Jack Sydow
sets: Robert Randolph
costumes: Fred Voelpel
choreography: Donald Saddler
Productions:
Opened April 15, 1963 for 8 performances
Reviews:
New York Theatre Critics' Reviews 1963:344+
New York Times page 32, Apr 16, 1963
                  page 28, Apr 19, 1963
Newsweek 61:54, Apr 29, 1963
Theatre Arts 47:66, Jun 1963

The Sound of Music
book: Howard Lindsay and Russel Crouse, suggested
                   by Maria Augusta Trapp's The Trapp Family

Singers
music: Richard Rodgers
lyrics: Oscar Hammerstein II
staging: Vincent J. Donehue
sets: Oliver Smith
costumes: Lucinda Ballard
choreography: Joe Layton
Productions:
    Opened November 16, 1959 for 1,443 performances
    Opened April 26, 1967 for 23 performances
    (Off-Broadway) Opened July 8, 1971 (Jones Beach Marine
        Theatre)
Reviews:
    America 102:402, Jan 2, 1960
    Catholic World 191:19-22, Apr 1960
    Christian Century 76:1407-8, Dec 2, 1959
    Dance Magazine 41:38+, Jun 1967
    Life 47:137-46, Nov 23, 1959
    Musical America 79:15, Dec 1, 1959
    New Republic 141:25-6, Dec 28, 1959
    New York Theatre Critics' Reviews 1959:227+
    New York Times VI, pages 22-23, Nov 1, 1959
                    II, page 1, Nov 15, 1959
                    page 40, Nov 17, 1959
                    II, page 1, Nov 22, 1959
                    page 22, May 19, 1961
                    page 41, May 19, 1965
                    page 27, Jan 16, 1967
                    page 52, Apr 27, 1967
                    page 23, Jul 12, 1971
    New Yorker 35:106+, Nov 28, 1959
    Newsweek 54:100+, Nov 30, 1959
    Saturday Review 42:28-9, Dec 5, 1959
    Theatre Arts 44:65-9, Jan 1960
                 46:57-9+, Nov 1962
    Time 74:64, Nov 30, 1959

South Pacific
    book: Oscar Hammerstein II and Joshua Logan, based
                    on James A. Michener's Tales of the South
                    Pacific
    music: Richard Rodgers
    lyrics: Oscar Hammerstein II
    staging: Joshua Logan
    sets: Jo Mielziner
    costumes: Motley
    choreography: Joshua Logan
Productions:
    Opened April 7, 1949 for 1,925 performances
    Opened May 4, 1955 for 15 performances
    Opened April 24, 1957 for 23 performances
    Opened April 26, 1961 for 23 performances
    Opened June 2, 1965 for 15 performances

Opened June 12, 1967 for 104 performances
Reviews:
America 93:221+, May 21, 1955
    105:355, May 20, 1961
    117:63, Jul 15, 1967
    119:55, Jul 20, 1968
American Mercury 73:114-18, Dec 1951
Business World pages 96-8+, Jun 18, 1949
Catholic World 169:145-6, May 1949
Commonweal 50:69, Apr 29, 1949
Coronet 26:10-11, Jul 1949
    29:44-52, Mar 1951
Good Housekeeping 129:4+, Dec 1949
Harper's Bazaar 83:83, Jun 1949
Life 26:93-6, Apr 18, 1949
  30:63-5, Jan 29, 1951
Musical America 69:13, May 1949
Nation 168:480, Apr 23, 1949
New Republic 120:27-8, Apr 25, 1949
New York Theatre Critics' Reviews 1949:312+
New York Times II, page 1, Apr 3, 1949
      page 30, Apr 8, 1949
      II, page 1, Apr 17, 1949
      II, page 1, May 1, 1949
      II, page 1, Jun 5, 1949
      II, page 1, Jul 3, 1949
      page 26, Apr 25, 1950
      page 36, Apr 26, 1950
      page 1, May 2, 1950
      page 32, Oct 24, 1950
      page 30, Jul 10, 1951
      II, page 1, Sep 2, 1951
      II, page 3, Nov 11, 1951
      page 17, Jan 29, 1952
      page 9, Jan 31, 1952
      page 16, Sep 15, 1952
      II, page 3, Nov 2, 1952
      page 41, Dec 11, 1953
      page 83, Jan 17, 1954
      page 39, May 5, 1955
      II, page 1, Sep 23, 1956
      page 35, Apr 25, 1957
      page 26, Apr 27, 1961
      page 25, Jun 3, 1965
      page 56, Jun 13, 1967
      page 60, Sep 18, 1967
      page 54, Jun 30, 1968
New York Times Magazine pages 22-3, Mar 27, 1949
        page 56+, Nov 27, 1949
New Yorker 25:54+, Apr 16, 1949
    41:130+, Jun 12, 1965
Newsweek 33:78-9, Apr 11, 1949
Saturday Review 32:47-8, Mar 26, 1949

                          32:28-30, Apr 30, 1949
                          33:4, Jan 14, 1950
                          51:35, Jul 20, 1968
        Theatre Arts 33:15, Jun 1949
                          34:42-3, Jun 1950
                          41:16, Jul 1957
        Time 53:77, Apr 18, 1949
              65:91, Mar 28, 1955

A Space Oddity   (see 2, 008 1/2)

Speed Gets the Poppies
        book: Lila Levant
        music: Lorenzo Fuller
        lyrics: Lorenzo Fuller and Lila Levant
        staging: Charles Abbott
        sets: Milton Duke
        costumes: Milton Duke
        choreography: Charles Abbott
Productions:
        (Off-Broadway) Opened July 25, 1972 for 7 performances
Reviews:
        New York Times page 21, Jul 26, 1972

Spice of 1922
        book: Jack Lait
        staging: Allen K. Foster
Productions:
        Opened July 6, 1922 for 73 performances
Reviews:
        Life (New York) 80:18, Aug 3, 1922
        New York Clipper 70:20, Jul 12, 1922
        New York Times page 12, Jul 7, 1922
        Theatre Magazine 36:151+, Sep 1922

Spiro Who?
        book: William Meyers
        music: Phil Ochs
        staging: Bernard Barrow
        sets: Eldon Elder
        costumes: Winn Morton
Productions:
        (Off-Broadway) Opened May 18, 1969 for 41 performances
Reviews:
        New York Times page 55, May 19, 1969
                        II, page 3, Jun 15, 1969
                        page 35, Jun 20, 1969

Split Lip
        book: John Cromwell
        music: Lee Pockriss
        staging: Gene Frankel
        choreography: Doug Rogers

458   Spook Scandals

Productions:
    (Off-Off-Broadway) Opened May 14, 1974 (Gene Frankel Thea-
    tre Workshop)
Reviews:
    New York Times page 49, May 16, 1974

Spook Scandals
    conceived: Jerry Sylvon
    music: Sergio De Karlo
    staging: Jerry Sylvon
    choreography: Paul Haakon, Marta Nita and Paul Reyes
Productions:
    Opened December 8, 1944 for 2 performances
No Reviews.

Spring Is Here
    book: Owen Davis
    music: Richard Rodgers
    lyrics: Lorenz Hart
    staging: Alexander Leftwich
    choreography: Bobby Connelly
Productions:
    Opened March 11, 1929 for 104 performances
Reviews:
    Catholic World 129:205-6, May 1929
    Life (New York) 93:25, Apr 12, 1929
    New York Times page 26, Mar 12, 1929
    Outlook 151:508, Mar 27, 1929
    Theatre Magazine 49:47, May 1929
    Vogue 73:150, May 11, 1929

The Spring Returneth
    material: Alfred Allegro
    staging: William Vaughan
Productions:
    (Off-Broadway) Opened February 9, 1939 for 3 performances
No Reviews.

Springtime of Youth
    book: Based on the book by Bernhauser and Rudolph
                    Schanzer
    music: Sigmund Romberg and Walter Rollo
    lyrics: Harry B. Smith, Cyrus Wood, Matthew Wood-
                    ward
    staging: John Harwood
Productions:
    Opened October 26, 1922 for 68 performances
Reviews:
    New York Clipper 70:20, Nov 1, 1922
    New York Times page 15, Oct 27, 1922

Stag Movie
    book: David Newburge

```
        music:            Jacques Urbont
        lyrics:           David Newburge
        staging:          Bernard Barrow
        sets:             David Chapman
        costumes:         David Toser
        choreography:     Doug Rogers
```
Productions:
   (Off-Broadway) Opened January 3, 1971 for 88 performances
Reviews:
   New York Times page 39, Jan 4, 1971

Star and Garter
```
        assembled:        Michael Todd
        music and
          lyrics:         Irving Berlin, Al Dubin, Will Irwin, Harold
                          Rome, Lester Lee, Irving Gordon, Alan Roberts,
                          Harold Arlen, Frank McCue, Doris Tauber,
                          Dorival Caymmi, Jerry Seelen, Jerome
                          Brainin, Johnny Mercer, Sis Wilner, Al Stillman
        staging:          Hassard Short
        sets:             Harry Horner
        costumes:         Irene Sharaff
```
Productions:
   Opened June 24, 1942 for 609 performances
Reviews:
   Life 13:60+, Jul 27, 1942
   Nation 155:18, Jul 4, 1942
   New York Theatre Critics' Reviews 1942:262+
   New York Times page 26, Jun 25, 1942
                    VIII, page 1, Sep 13, 1942
   Newsweek 20:60, Jul 6, 1942
   Time 40:54, Jul 6, 1942

The Star Gazer
```
        book:             Cosmo Hamilton
        music:            Franz Lehar
        lyrics:           Matthew C. Woodward
```
Productions:
   Opened November 26, 1917 for 8 performances
Reviews:
   Dramatic Mirror 77:5, Dec 8, 1917
   New York Times page 14, Nov 27, 1917

Stars in Your Eyes (Swing to the Left)
```
        book:             J. P. McEvoy
        music:            Arthur Schwartz
        lyrics:           Dorothy Fields
        staging:          Joshua Logan
        sets:             Jo Mielziner
        costumes:         John Hambleton
        choreography:     Carl Randall
```
Productions:
   Opened February 9, 1939 for 127 performances

Reviews:
  Life 6:66-9, Feb 27, 1939
  Catholic World 149:88-9, Apr 1939
  Commonweal 29:525, Mar 3, 1939
  New York Times page 18, Feb 10, 1939
                  X, page 1, Mar 5, 1939
  Nation 148:245, Feb 25, 1939
  New Republic 98:102-3, Mar 1, 1939
  Stage 16:4+, Feb 1939
  Theatre Arts 23:242-3, Apr 1939
  Time 33:54-5, Feb 20, 1939

Stars on Ice
      assembled: Sonja Henie and Arthur M. Wirtz
      music: Paul McGrane and Paul Van Loan
      lyrics: Al Stillman
      staging: William H. Burke and Catherine Littlefield
      sets: Bruno Maine
      costumes: Lucinda Ballard
      choreography: Catherine Littlefield
Productions:
  Opened July 2, 1942 for 830 performances
Reviews:
  Catholic World 155:727, Sep 1942
  Commonweal 36:328, Jul 24, 1942
  New York Times page 12, Jul 3, 1942
                  page 13, Jun 25, 1943
                  II, page 2, Oct 10, 1943
  Newsweek 20:67, Jul 13, 1942
  Theatre Arts 26:630, Oct 1942

Stein, Gertrude   (see Gertrude Stein)

Step Lively, Boy
      book: Vinnette Carroll; based on a play by Irwin Shaw
      music: Micki Grant
      lyrics: Micki Grant
      staging: Vinnette Carroll
Productions:
  (Off-Off-Broadway) Opened February 7, 1973 (Urban Arts
  Corps.)
No Reviews.

Step This Way (The Girl Behind the Counter)
      book: Edgar Smith
      music: E. Ray Goetz and Bert Grant
      lyrics: E. Ray Goetz
      staging: Frank McCormack
      choreography: Jack Mason
Productions:
  Opened May 29, 1916 for 88 performances
Reviews:
  Dramatic Mirror 75:8, Jun 3, 1916

New York Times page 7, May 30, 1916
Theatre Magazine 24:11, Jul 1916

Stepping Stones
    book: Anne Caldwell and R. H. Burnside
    music: Jerome Kern
    lyrics: Anne Caldwell
    staging: R. H. Burnside
Productions:
    Opened November 6, 1923 for 241 performances
    Opened September 1, 1924 for 40 performances
Reviews:
    New York Times page 14, Nov 7, 1923
                  VI, page 8, Dec 16, 1923
                  page 8, Aug 20, 1924
    Theatre Magazine 39:58, Jan 1924

Stomp
    devised: The Combine
Productions:
    (Off-Broadway) Opened November 16, 1969 for 161 performances
Reviews:
    Commonweal 91:534-5, Feb 13, 1970
    Dance Magazine 44:93, Feb 1970
    New York Times page 32, Oct 31, 1969
                  page 60, Nov 17, 1969
                  II, page 1, Nov 23, 1969
                  page 23, Jan 24, 1970
    Newsweek 74:86+, Dec 1, 1969
               74:138-9, Dec 8, 1969

Stoones, Harry (see Another Evening with Harry Stoones)

Stop! Look! Listen!
    book: Harry B. Smith
    music: Irving Berlin
    lyrics: Irving Berlin
    staging: R. H. Burnside
Productions:
    Opened December 25, 1915 for 105 performances
Reviews:
    Dramatic Mirror 75:9, Jan 1, 1916
    Green Book 15:447-8, Mar 1916
    Life (New York) 67:26, Jan 6, 1916
    New York Dramatic News 62:18, Jan 1, 1916
    New York Times II, page 15, Dec 25, 1915
                  II, page 9, Mar 12, 1916
    Opera Magazine 3:29-31, Feb 1916
    Stage 15:41, Aug 1938
    Theatre Magazine 23:66, Feb 1916
                  23:180, Feb 1916

Stop the World--I Want to Get Off

    book: Leslie Bricusse and Anthony Newley
    music: Leslie Bricusse and Anthony Newley
    lyrics: Leslie Bricusse and Anthony Newley
    staging: Anthony Newley
    sets: Sean Kenny
    choreography: John Broome and Virginia Mason
Productions:
    Opened October 3, 1962 for 555 performances
Reviews:
    America 107:1231, Dec 8, 1962
    Catholic World 196:200, Dec 1962
    Commonweal 77:201, Nov 16, 1962
    Dance Magazine 36:24-5+, Dec 1962
    Life 53:117, Nov 30, 1962
    Nation 195:246-7, Oct 20, 1962
    New York Theatre Critics' Reviews 1962:260+
    New York Times page 39, Sep 17, 1962
                     page 45, Oct 4, 1962
                     VI, page 36, Oct 7, 1962
                     II, page 1, Oct 14, 1962
    New York Times Magazine page 36, Oct 7, 1962
    New Yorker 38:180, Oct 13, 1962
    Newsweek 60:68, Oct 15, 1962
    Reporter 27:42, Dec 20, 1962
    Saturday Review 45:37, Oct 20, 1962
    Theatre Arts 46:11, Nov 1962
    Time 80:67, Oct 12, 1962

La Strada
    book: Charles K. Peck, Jr.; based on the Federico
                       Fellini film
    music: Lionel Bart
    lyrics: Lionel Bart
    staging: Alan Schneider
    sets: Ming Cho Lee
    costumes: Nancy Potts
    choreography: Alvin Ailey
Productions:
    Opened December 14, 1969 for one performance
Reviews:
    New York Times page 40, Sep 23, 1969
                     page 63, Dec 15, 1969
                     page 56, Dec 16, 1969
    New Yorker 45:57, Dec 20, 1969

The Straw Hat Revue
    conceived by: Max Liebman
    assembled by: Max Liebman
    sketches: Max Liebman and Samuel Locke
    music: Sylvia Fine and James Shelton; special music
                       by Glenn Bacon
    lyrics: Sylvia Fine and James Shelton
    staging: Max Liebman

sets: Edward Gilbert
choreography: Jerome Andrews
Productions:
Opened September 29, 1939 for 75 performances
Reviews:
Catholic World 150:216, Nov 1939
Commonweal 30:563, Oct 13, 1939
New York Times page 10, Sep 30, 1939
                    IX, page 3, Oct 29, 1939
                    IX, page 8, Nov 12, 1939
Theatre Arts 23:860-2, Dec 1939
Time 34:49, Oct 9, 1939

Street Scene
book: Elmer Rice, based on his nonmusical play
                    Street Scene
music: Kurt Weill
lyrics: Langston Hughes
staging: Charles Friedman
sets: Jo Mielziner
costumes: Lucinda Ballard
choreography: Anna Sokolow
Productions:
Opened January 9, 1947 for 148 performances
(Off-Broadway) Season of 1958-59 (City Center)
Opened February 24, 1966 for 6 performances
Reviews:
Catholic World 164:453, Feb 1947
Commonweal 45:397, Jan 31, 1947
Life 22:78, Feb 24, 1947
Musical Courier 135:52, Feb 1, 1947
Musical America 79:3+, May 1959
                    79:29-30, Oct 1959
New Republic 116:40, Feb 10, 1947
New York Theatre Critics' Reviews 1947:490+
New York Times II, page 3, Jan 5, 1947
                    page 17, Jan 10, 1947
                    II, page 2, Jan 19, 1947
                    II, page 7, Jan 26, 1947
                    II, page 3, Feb 2, 1947
                    VI, page 28, Feb 2, 1947
                    II, page 1, May 4, 1947
                    page 24, May 12, 1947
New Yorker 22:44+, Jan 18, 1947
Newsweek 29:84, Jan 20, 1947
Saturday Review 30:24-6, Feb 1, 1947
Theatre Arts 31:12-13+, Mar 1947
Time 49:69, Jan 20, 1947

Street Singer
book: Cyrus Wood and Edgar Smith
music: John Gilbert, Nicholas Kempner, Sam Timberg
lyrics: Graham John

staging: Busby Berkeley
Productions:
Opened September 17, 1929 for 191 performances
Reviews:
New York Times page 35, Sep 18, 1929
Outlook 153:192, Oct 2, 1929
Theatre Magazine 50:72, Nov 1929

The Streets of New York
book: Barry Alan Grael; based on the play by Dion
                    Boucicault
music: Richard B. Chadosh
lyrics: Barry Alan Grael
staging: Joseph Hardy
sets: Howard Becknell
costumes: W. Thomas Seitz
choreography: Neal Kenyon
Productions:
(Off-Broadway) Opened October 29, 1963 for 318 performances
Reviews:
America 109:644, Nov 16, 1963
New York Times page 47, Oct 30, 1963
New Yorker 39:95-6+, Nov 9, 1963
Newsweek 62:72, Nov 18, 1963

Streets of Paris
sketches: Charles Sherman, Tom McKnight, Mitchell
                    Hodges, S. Jay Kaufman, Edward Duryea
                    Dowling, James LaVer, Frank Eyton, Lee Brody
music: James McHugh
lyrics: Harold J. Rome and Al Dubin
staging: Edward Duryea Dowling and Dennis Murray
sets: Lawrence L. Goldwasser
costumes: Irene Sharaff
choreography: Robert Alton
Productions:
Opened June 19, 1939 for 274 performances
Reviews:
Commonweal 30:278, Jul 7, 1939
Life 7:32+, Jul 17, 1939
Nation 149:110, Jul 22, 1939
New York Theatre Critics' Reviews 1940:484+
New York Times page 25, Jun 20, 1939
                    IX, page 1, Jun 25, 1939
                    IX, page 4, Dec 17, 1939
Newsweek 14:28, Jul 3, 1939
Time 34:42, Jul 3, 1939

Strike Me Pink
book: Ray Henderson and Lew Brown, additional
                    dialogue by Mack Gordon
music: Ray Henderson
lyrics: Lew Brown

```
        staging:        Ray Henderson and Lew Brown
        sets:           Henry Dreyfuss
        choreography:   Seymour Felix
Productions:
    Opened March 4, 1933 for 105 performances
Reviews:
    Nation 136:356, Mar 29, 1933
    New Outlook 161:46, Apr 1933
    New York Times page 16, Mar 6, 1933
                       IX, page 2, Apr 9, 1933
    Stage 10:19-22, Apr 1933
    Time 21:40, Mar 13, 1933
```

Strike up the Band
```
        book:           Morrie Ryskind, based on George S. Kaufman's
                        libretto
        music:          George Gershwin
        lyrics:         Ira Gershwin
        staging:        Alexander Leftwich
        choreography:   George Hale
Productions:
    Opened January 14, 1930 for 191 performances
Reviews:
    Christian Century 48:899-901, Jul 8, 1931
    Life (New York) 95:18, Feb 7, 1930
    Nation 130:226, Feb 19, 1930
    New York Times VIII, page 4, Dec 29, 1929
                       page 29, Jan 15, 1930
    Outlook 154:191, Jan 29, 1930
    Theatre Magazine 51:48, Mar 1930
    Vogue 75:106+, Mar 1, 1930
```

Strings
```
        book:           Samuel Taylor
        music:          Richard Rodgers
        lyrics:         Richard Rodgers
        staging:        Ric Michaels
        sets:           Billy Puzzo
        costumes:       Sally Krell
        choreography:   Lynn Gannaway
Productions:
    (Off-Broadway) Opened March 9, 1972 (Equity Library Theatre)
No Reviews.
```

Strip Girl
```
        book:           Henry Rosendahl
        music:          Harry Archer
        lyrics:         Jill Rainsford
        staging:        Jose Ruben
        sets:           Cirker and Robbins
Productions:
    Opened October 19, 1935 for 33 performances
Reviews:
```

New York Times page 22, Oct 21, 1935

The Student Gypsy, or The Prince of Liederkranz
    book: Rick Besoyan
    music: Rick Besoyan
    lyrics: Rick Besoyan
    staging: Rick Besoyan
    sets: Raoul Pene du Bois
    costumes: Raoul Pene du Bois
    choreography: Ray Harrison
Productions:
    Opened September 30, 1963 for 16 performances
Reviews:
    New York Theatre Critics' Reviews 1963:266+
    New York Times page 34, Oct 1, 1963
                    page 51, Oct 10, 1963
    Newsweek 62:77, Oct 14, 1963
    Theatre Arts 47:13, Dec 1963

The Student Prince
    book: Dorothy Donnelly
    music: Sigmund Romberg
    lyrics: Dorothy Donnelly
    staging: J. C. Huffman
Productions:
    Opened December 2, 1924 for 183 performances
    Opened January 29, 1931 for 42 performances
    Opened June 8, 1943 for 153 performances
    (Off-Broadway) Opened July 13, 1961 for 13 performances
Reviews:
    American Mercury 4:248-9, Feb 1925
    Commonweal 38:252, Jun 25, 1943
    New York Theatre Critics' Reviews 1943:320
    New York Times page 25, Dec 3, 1924
                    page 18, Jan 30, 1931
                    VIII, page 3, Feb 1, 1931
                    page 16, Jun 9, 1943
                    page 14, Jul 14, 1961
    Newsweek 21:104, Jun 21, 1943
    Theatre Magazine 41:14-15, Feb 1925

Subways Are for Sleeping
    book: Betty Comden and Adolph Green, suggested by
                    Edmund G. Love's novel
    music: Jule Styne
    lyrics: Betty Comden and Adolph Green
    staging: Michael Kidd
    sets: Will Steven Armstrong
    costumes: Freddy Wittop
    choreography: Michael Kidd and Marc Breaux
Productions:
    Opened December 27, 1961 for 205 performances
Reviews:

America 106:737, Mar 3, 1962
Dance Magazine 36:13, Mar 1962
New York Theatre Critics' Reviews 1961:135+
New York Times II, page 3, Dec 17, 1961
                    page 22, Dec 28, 1961
                    page 27, Jun 21, 1962
New Yorker 37:56, Jan 6, 1962
Newsweek 59:44, Jan 8, 1962
Theatre Arts 46:60, Mar 1962
Time 79:52, Jan 5, 1962

Sue, Dear
    book: Bide Dudley, Joseph Herbert and C. S. Montayne
    music: Frank H. Grey
    lyrics: Bide Dudley
    staging: Joseph Herbert and Jack Mason
Productions:
Opened July 10, 1922 for 96 performances
Reviews:
New York Clipper 70:20, Jul 12, 1922
New York Times page 16, Jul 11, 1922

Sue Lawless and Ted Pugh   (see An Evening with Sue and Pugh)

Sugar
    book: Peter Stone; based on the screen play Some Like
                    It Hot by Billy Wilder and I. A. L. Diamond
                    (based on a story by Robert Thoeren)
    music: Jule Styne
    lyrics: Bob Merrill
    staging: Gower Champion
    sets: Robin Wagner
    costumes: Alvin Colt
    choreography: Gower Champion
Productions:
Opened April 9, 1972 for 505 performances
Reviews:
America 126:462, Apr 29, 1972
Harper's 105:84, Mar 1972
Life 72:28, May 12, 1972
New Republic 166:35, Apr 29, 1972
New York Theatre Critics' Reviews 1972:320
New York Times page 47, Apr 10, 1972
                    II, page 1, Apr 16, 1972
                    II, page 1, Apr 23, 1972
New Yorker 48:109, Apr 15, 1972
Newsweek 79:50, Apr 24, 1972
Saturday Review 55:65, May 6, 1972
Time 99:66, Apr 24, 1972

Sugar Hill
    book: Charles Tazewell
    music: Jimmy Johnson

lyrics: Jo Trent
Productions:
Opened December 25, 1931 for 11 performances
Reviews:
New York Times page 15, Dec 26, 1931

Summer on Parade
    book: Arthur C. Leach
    music: Irving Bilbo and Jerry Lang
Productions:
(Off-Broadway) Opened January 22, 1934 (Group Players)
No Reviews.

The Summer Widowers
    words: Glen Macdonough
    music: A. Baldwin Sloan
    staging: Ned Wayburn
Productions:
Opened June 4, 1910 for 140 performances
Reviews:
Dramatic Mirror 63:6, Jun 11, 1910
Green Book Album 4:681, Oct 1910
                    5:304, Feb 1911
Hampton 25:526, Oct 1910
Metropolitan Magazine 32:678-9, Aug 1910
Theatre Magazine 12:3-4, Jul 1910

The Sun Dodgers
    book: Edgar Smith
    music: E. Ray Goetz and A. Baldwin Sloane
    lyrics: E. Ray Goetz and A. Baldwin Sloane
    staging: Ned Wayburn
Productions:
Opened November 30, 1912 for 29 performances
Reviews:
Blue Book 16:908-11, Mar 1913
Dramatic Mirror 68:6, Dec 4, 1912
                    68:2, Dec 18, 1912
Green Book 9:367, Feb 1913
Harper's Weekly 56:19, Dec 7, 1912
New York Dramatic News 56:19, Dec 7, 1912
Theatre Magazine 17:4, Jan 1913

Sun Showers
    staging: Frederick Stanhope
Productions:
Opened February 5, 1923 for 40 performances
Reviews:
New York Clipper 71:14, Feb 14, 1923
New York Times page 14, Feb 6, 1923

Sunday Night Varieties
    conceived: Nat Lichtman

sketches:	Berenice Kazunoff and Sylvia Fine
lyrics:	John La Touche and David Gregory
sets:	Nat Lichtman

Productions:
(Off-Broadway) Opened April 9, 1939
No Reviews.

Sunkist

book:	Fanchon and Marco
lyrics:	Fanchon and Marco

Productions:
Opened May 23, 1921 for (27) performances
Reviews:
New York Times page 20, May 24, 1921

Sunny

book:	Otto Harbach and Oscar Hammerstein II
music:	Jerome Kern
lyrics:	Otto Harbach and Oscar Hammerstein II

Productions:
Opened September 22, 1925 for 517 performances
Reviews:
New Republic 44:303, Nov 11, 1925
New York Times page 29, Sep 10, 1925
          page 22, Sep 23, 1925
          page 29, Dec 6, 1926
Theatre Magazine 42:16, Dec 1925

Sunny Days

book:	Clifford Grey and William Cary Duncan; adapted from M. Hennequin and P. Veber's A Kiss in the Taxi
music:	Jean Schwartz
lyrics:	Clifford Grey and William Cary Duncan
staging:	Hassard Short

Productions:
Opened February 8, 1928 for 101 performances
Opened October 1, 1928 for 32 performances
Reviews:
New York Times page 29, Feb 9, 1928
          VIII, page 2, May 20, 1928
          page 34, Oct 2, 1928
Theatre Magazine 47:41, Apr 1928

Sunny River

book:	Oscar Hammerstein II
music:	Sigmund Romberg
lyrics:	Oscar Hammerstein II
staging:	Oscar Hammerstein II
sets:	Stewart Chaney
costumes:	Irene Sharaff
choreography:	Carl Randall

Productions:

Opened December 4, 1941 for 36 performances
Reviews:
    Catholic World 154:474, Jan 1942
    New York Theatre Critics' Reviews 1941:186+
    New York Times page 28, Dec 5, 1941
    Newsweek 18:72, Dec 15, 1941

The Sunshine Girl
    book: Paul A. Rubens and Cecil Raleigh
    music: Paul A. Rubens
    staging: J. A. E. Malone
Productions:
Opened February 3, 1913 for 160 performances
Reviews:
    Blue Book 17:246-9, Jun 1913
    Dramatic Mirror 69:6, Feb 5, 1913
                  69:2, Feb 19, 1913
                  69:2, Mar 5, 1913
    Green Book 9:560-2+, Apr 1913
    Munsey 47:985, Sep 1912
           49:154, Apr 1913
    New York Dramatic News 57:13, Feb 8, 1913
    New York Times page 11, Feb 4, 1913
    Red Book 21:113+, May 1913
    Theatre Magazine 17:66-7, Mar 1913
                 18:24, Jul 1913
                 18:93, Sep 1913

The Sunshine Train
    conceived: William E. Hunt
    staging: William E. Hunt
    sets: Philip Gilliam
Productions:
    (Off-Broadway) Opened June 15, 1972 for 224 performances
No Reviews.

Surprise Package
    book: Tom Hill
    music: Frances Ziffer, Hortense Belson and Hardy
                  Wieder
Productions:
    (Off-Broadway) Season of 1952-53 (Originals Only)
No Reviews.

The Survival of St. Joan
    book: James Lineberger
    music: Hank and Gary Ruffin
    lyrics: James Lineberger
    staging: Chuck Gnys
    sets: Peter Harvey
    costumes: Peter Harvey
Productions:
    (Off-Broadway) Opened February 28, 1971 for 17 performances

No Reviews.

Surving Death in Three Acts
    book: Nancy Fales
    music: George Miller
    staging: Nancy Fales and Gail Julian
Productions:
    (Off-Off-Broadway) Opened May 7, 1973 (The Playwrights
    Cooperative)
No Reviews.

Susanna and the Elders (see Ballet Ballads)

Susanna, Don't You Cry
    book: Sarah Newmeyer and Clarence Loomis
    music: Melodies of Stephen Foster; special music by
                     Haus Spialek
    lyrics: Sarah Newmeyer and Clarence Loomis
    staging: Jose Ruben
    sets: Robert Edmund Jones
Productions:
    Opened May 22, 1939 for 4 performances
Reviews:
    Musical Courier 119:7, Jun 1, 1939
    New York Times X, page 7, Apr 16, 1939
                     page 27, May 23, 1939
    Newsweek 13:34, Jun 5, 1939

Suzette
    book: Roy Dixon
    music: Arthur Gutman
Productions:
    Opened November 24, 1921 for 4 performances
Reviews:
    New York Times page 18, Nov 25, 1921

Sweet Adeline
    book: Oscar Hammerstein II
    music: Jerome Kern
    lyrics: Oscar Hammerstein II
    staging: Reginald Hammerstein and Danny Dare
    choreography: Danny Dare
Productions:
    Opened September 3, 1929 for 234 performances
Reviews:
    Arts and Decoration 32:67, Nov 1929
    Catholic World 131:81, Apr 1930
    Commonweal 10:564, Oct 2, 1929
    Life (New York) 94:23, Sep 27, 1929
    Nation 129:310-11, Sep 18, 1929
    New York Times VIII, page 3, Aug 25, 1929
                    page 33, Sep 23, 1929
    Theatre Magazine 50:45, Nov 1929

Vogue 74:63+, Oct 26, 1929

Sweet and Low
    book: David Freedman
    music: Billy Rose
    lyrics: David Freedman
    staging: Alexander Leftwich
Productions:
    Opened November 17, 1930 for 184 performances
Reviews:
    Nation 131:632, Dec 3, 1930
    New York Times page 28, Nov 18, 1930

Sweet Charity
    book: Neil Simon; based on the screenplay Nights of
                    Cabiria by Federico Fellini, Tullio Pinelli and
                    Ennio Flaiano
    music: Cy Coleman
    lyrics: Dorothy Fields
    staging: Bob Fosse
    costumes: Irene Sharaff
    sets: Robert Randolph
    choreography: Bob Fosse
Productions:
    Opened January 29, 1966 for 608 performances
Reviews:
    America 114:452, Apr 2, 1966
    Commonweal 84:57, Apr 1, 1966
    Dance Magazine 40:24, May 1966
    Life 60:99-100, Mar 25, 1966
    Nation 202:248-9, Feb 28, 1966
    New York Theatre Critics' Reviews 1966:384
    New York Times page 22, Jan 31, 1966
                  II, page 1, Feb 6, 1966
                   page 29, Jun 30, 1967
                   page 13, Jul 1, 1967
                   page 17, Jul 21, 1967
                   page 34, Oct 13, 1967
    New Yorker 41:84, Feb 5, 1966
    Newsweek 67:88, Feb 14, 1966
    Saturday Review 49:44, Feb 12, 1966
    Time 87:46, Feb 4, 1966
    Vogue 147:58, Mar 15, 1966

Sweet Feet
    book: Dan Graham
    music: Don Brockett
    lyrics: Don Brockett
    staging: Don Brockett
    sets: James French
    costumes: Tom Fallon
Productions:
    (Off-Broadway) Opened May 25, 1972 for 6 performances

Reviews:
    New York Times page 17, May 26, 1972

Sweet Little Devil
    book: Frank Mandel and Laurence Schwab
    music: George Gershwin
    lyrics: B. G. De Sylva
Productions:
    Opened January 21, 1924 for 120 performances
Reviews:
    New York Times page 15, Jan 22, 1924
    Theatre Magazine 39:70, Mar 1924

Sweet Miami
    book: Stuart Bishop
    music: Ed Tyler
    lyrics: Ed Tyler
    staging: Louis MacMillan
    sets: Stuart Slade
    costumes: André
Productions:
    (Off-Broadway) Opened September 25, 1962 for 22 performances
Reviews:
    New York Times page 33, Sep 26, 1962
    New Yorker 38:183-4, Oct 13, 1962

Sweet Potato   (see Noel Coward's Sweet Potato)

The Sweetheart Shop
    book: Anne Caldwell
    music: Hugo Felix
    lyrics: Anne Caldwell
    sets: Edgar MacGregor
Productions:
    Opened August 31, 1920 for 55 performances
Reviews:
    Dramatic Mirror 82:782, Apr 24, 1920
                  page 420, Sep 4, 1920
    New York Clipper 68:27, Sep 15, 1920
    New York Times page 13, Sep 1, 1920
    Theatre Magazine 32:281, Nov 1920
                  32:334, Nov 1920

Sweetheart Time
    book: Harry B. Smith; based on Never Say Die
    music: Walter Donaldson and Joseph Meyer
    lyrics: Ballard Macdonald and Irving Caesar
Productions:
    Opened January 19, 1926 for 143 performances
Reviews:
    New York Times page 23, Jan 20, 1926
    Theatre Magazine 43:18, Apr 1926

Sweethearts
    book: Harry B. Smith and Fred De Gresac
    music: Victor Herbert
    lyrics: Robert B. Smith
    staging: Frederick G. Latham
Productions:
    Opened September 8, 1913 for 136 performances
    Opened January 21, 1947 for 288 performances
Reviews:
    Blue Book 18:221-4, Dec 1913
    Dramatic Mirror 69:2, Apr 9, 1913
                  69:1, Apr 30, 1913
                  70:7, Sep 10, 1913
                  70:2, Oct 1, 1913
    Green Book 10:870-71, Nov 1913
               10:967, Dec 1913
    Munsey Magazine 50:295-6, Nov 1913
    New Republic 116:44, Feb 3, 1947
    New York Dramatic News 58:20, Sep 13, 1913
    New York Theatre Critics' Reviews 1947:479
    New York Times page 7, Sep 9, 1913
                  II, page 2, Jan 19, 1947
                  page 31, Jan 22, 1947
                  II, page 1, Feb 2, 1947
                  II, page 1, Jul 6, 1947
                  page 39, Dec 9, 1947
    Newsweek 29:71, Feb 3, 1947
    Theatre Arts 31:24, Mar 1947
               31:17-18, Apr 1947
    Theatre Magazine 18:xii-xiii, Oct 1913
                 50:72, Nov 1929
    Time 49:72, Feb 3, 1947

Swing It
    book: Cecil Mack and Milton Reddie
    music: Eubie Blake
    lyrics: Cecil Mack and Milton Reddie
    staging: Cecil Mack and Jack Mason
    sets: Walter Walden and Victor Zanoff
    costumes: Maxine and Alexander Jones
Productions:
    Opened July 22, 1937 for 60 performances
Reviews:
    New York Times page 17, Jul 22, 1937

Swing to the Left (see Stars in Your Eyes)

Swingin' the Dream
    book: Gilbert Seldes and Erik Charell, based on
                  Shakespeare's A Midsummer Night's Dream
    music: Jimmy Van Heusen
    lyrics: Eddie de Lange
    staging: Erik Charell

    sets: Herbert Andrews and Walter Jageman, based
                    on Walt Disney cartoons
    choreography: Agnes deMille and Herbert White
Productions:
    Opened November 29, 1939 for 13 performances
Reviews:
    Catholic World 150:471, Jan 1940
    New York Times page 24, Nov 30, 1939
                    page 66, Dec 10, 1939
    Theatre Arts 24:93, Feb 1940
    Time 34:50, Dec 11, 1939

Sybil
    book: Max Brody and Frank Martos; English version
                    by Harry Graham
    music: Victor Jacobi
    staging: Fred G. Latham
Productions:
    Opened January 10, 1916 for 168 performances
Reviews:
    Dramatic Mirror 75:7, Jan 15, 1916
                    75:2, Jan 29, 1916
                    75:2, Feb 5,   1916
                    75:4, Mar 18, 1916
                    75:2, Apr 1,   1916
    Green Book 15:446, Mar 1916
    Munsey 57:500, Apr 1916
             58:315, Jul 1916
    New York Dramatic News 62:18, Jan 15, 1916
    New York Times page 11, Jan 11, 1916
    Theatre Magazine 23:125-6, Mar 1916
                    23:135, Mar 1916

                            - T -

Take a Bow
    music: Ted Murray and Benny Davis
    staging: Wally Wanger
    sets: Kaj Velden
    costumes: Ben Wallace
    choreography: Marjery Fielding
Productions:
    Opened June 15, 1944 for 12 performances
Reviews:
    New York Theatre Critics' Reviews 1944:167
    New York Times page 15, Jun 16, 1944

Take a Chance
    book: B. G. De Sylva and Laurence Schwab, additional
                    dialogue by Sid Silvers
    music: Herb Brown Nacio and Richard Whiting, addi-
                    tional songs by Vincent Youmans

lyrics: B. G. De Sylva
staging: Edgar MacGregor
sets: Cleon Throckmorton
choreography: Bobby Connelly
Productions:
Opened November 26, 1932 for 243 performances
Reviews:
New Outlook 161:47, Jan 1933
New York Times page 11, Nov 18, 1932
                III, page 2, Dec 4, 1932

Take It from Me
book: Will B. Johnstone
music: Will R. Anderson
lyrics: Will B. Johnstone
staging: Fred A. Bishop, Joe C. Smith and Joseph
                   Gaites
Productions:
Opened March 31, 1919 for 96 performances
Reviews:
Forum 61:30, May 1919
Life (New York) 73:663, Apr 17, 1919
New York Times page 9, Apr 1, 1919
Theatre Magazine 29:275-6, May 1919
                29:293, May 1919

Take It from the Top
staging: Maurice Edwards
sets: Duane Camp
Productions:
(Off-Broadway) Opened November 22, 1967 for 15 performances
No Reviews.

Take Me Along
book: Joseph Stein and Robert Russell, based on
                   Eugene O'Neill's Ah, Wilderness!
music: Robert Merrill
lyrics: Robert Merrill
staging: Peter Glenville
sets: Oliver Smith
costumes: Miles White
choreography: Onna White
Productions:
Opened October 22, 1959 for 448 performances
Reviews:
America 102:255, Nov 21, 1959
Commonweal 71:240, Nov 20, 1959
Dance Magazine 33:24-5, Dec 1959
Life 47:117-20, Nov 2, 1959
New York Theatre Critics' Reviews 1959:244+
New York Times page 22, Oct 23, 1959
                II, page 1, Nov 1, 1959
                page 50, Dec 14, 1960

New Yorker 35:134-5, Oct 31, 1959
Newsweek 54:94, Nov 2, 1959
Saturday Review 42:40, Nov 14, 1959
Theatre Arts 43:13, Dec 1959
Time 74:30+, Nov 2, 1959

Take the Air
    book: Anne Caldwell and Gene Buck
    music: Dave Stamper
    lyrics: Anne Caldwell and Gene Buck
    staging: Alexander Leftwich and Gene Buck
Productions:
    Opened November 22, 1927 for 206 performances
Reviews:
    Life (New York) 90:21, Dec 29, 1927
    New York Times page 28, Nov 23, 1927
                    VIII, page 4, Feb 12, 1928
    Vogue 71:70, Jan 15, 1928

Tales of Rigo
    book: Maurice V. Samuels; based on a story by
                     Hyman Adler
    music: Ben Schwartz
    lyrics: Ben Schwartz
    staging: Clarence Derwent
Productions:
    Opened May 30, 1927 for 20 performances
No Reviews.

Talk About Girls
    book: William Cary Duncan; based on a play by John
                     Hunter Booth
    music: Harold Orlob and Stephen Jones
    lyrics: Irving Caesar
    staging: John Harwood
Productions:
    Opened June 14, 1927 for 13 performances
Reviews:
    Life (New York) 80:19, Jun 30, 1927
    New York Times page 31, Jun 15, 1927
    Theatre Magazine 46:18, Aug 1927

Tambourines to Glory
    book: Langston Hughes, adapted from his novel
    music: Jobe Huntley
    lyrics: Langston Hughes
    staging: Nikos Psacharapoulos
    sets: John Conklin
    costumes: John Conklin
Productions:
    Opened November 2, 1963 for 24 performances
Reviews:
    New York Theatre Critics' Reviews 1963:207+

New York Times page 47, Nov 4, 1963
                page 46, Nov 12, 1963
                page 28, Nov 15, 1963
                page 43, Nov 22, 1963

Tangerine
    book: Philip Bartholomae
    music: Carlo Sanders
    lyrics: Howard Johnston
    staging: George Marion and Bert French
Productions:
Opened August 9, 1921 for 337 performances
Reviews:
    Dramatic Mirror 84:229, Aug 13, 1921
    Life (New York) 78:18, Aug 25, 1921
    New York Clipper 69:24, Aug 17, 1921
    New York Times page 8, Aug 10, 1921
                    page 16, Sep 5, 1921
    Theatre Magazine 34:213, Oct 1921
                     34:234, Oct 1921

Tantalizing Tommy
    book: Michael Morton and Paul Gavault
    music: Dr. Hugo Felix
    lyrics: Adrian Ross
    staging: George Marion
Productions:
Opened October 1, 1912 for 31 performances
Reviews:
    Blue Book 16:16-19, Nov 1912
    Dramatic Mirror 68:7, Sep 11, 1912
                    68:6, Oct 9, 1912
    Harper's Weekly 56:20, Oct 12, 1912
    Leslie's Weekly 115:411, Oct 24, 1912
    Munsey 48:525, Dec 1912
    New York Dramatic News 56:24-5, Oct 12, 1912
    Theatre Magazine 16:xv, Nov 1912
                     17:23, Jan 1913

Tattle Tales
    book: Frank Fay and Nick Copeland
    music and
    lyrics: Howard Jackson, Edward Ward, Leo Robin,
                   Ralph Rainger, George Waggoner, Willard
                   Robison, Edward Eliscu, Eddie Beinbryer,
                   William Walsh
    staging: Frank Fay
Productions:
Opened June 1, 1933 for 28 performances
Reviews:
    New Outlook 162:43, Jul 1933
    New York Times page 22, Jun 2, 1933

The Tattooed Countess
    book: Coleman Dowell; based on Carl Van Vechten's
                    novel
    music: Coleman Dowell
    lyrics: Coleman Dowell
Productions:
    (Off-Broadway) Opened Season of 1960-61
Reviews:
    New York Times page 40, May 4, 1961
                   page 27, May 6, 1961

Ted Pugh (see An Evening with Sue and Pugh)

Telemachus Friend
    book: Sally Dixon Wiener; based on the O. Henry
                    short story
Productions:
    (Off-Broadway) Opened April 17, 1972 (Theatre at Noon)
No Reviews.

The Telephone (Presented with The Medium)
    book: Gian-Carlo Menotti
    music: Gian-Carlo Menotti
    lyrics: Gian-Carlo Menotti
    staging: Gian-Carlo Menotti
    sets: Horace Armistead
    costumes: Horace Armistead
Productions:
    Opened May 1, 1947 for 212 performances
    Opened December 7, 1948 for 40 performances
    Opened July 19, 1950 for 110 performances
Reviews:
    Catholic World 165:265-6, Jun 1947
                   171:469, Sep 1950
    Musical Courier 135:16, Mar 1, 1947
                 138:5, Nov 15, 1948
    Nation 164:637, May 24, 1947
    New York Theatre Critics' Reviews 1947:379
                               1950:280
    New York Times page 28, May 2, 1947
                II, page 2, May 11, 1947
                page 26, Apr 30, 1948
                page 41, Dec 8, 1948
    New Yorker 23:50+, May 10, 1947
    Newsweek 29:76, Mar 3, 1947
    Saturday Review 30:22-4, May 31, 1947
    School and Society 66:66, Jul 26, 1947
                    69:86, Jan 29, 1949
    Theatre Arts 31:60, May 1947
    Time 49:65, Mar 3, 1947

Tell Her the Truth
    book: R. P. Weston and Bert Lee, adapted from

Frederick Isham and James Montgomery's
Nothing But the Truth
music: Jack Waller and Joseph Tunbridge
lyrics: R. P. Weston and Bert Lee
staging: Morris Green and Henry Thomas
Productions:
Opened October 28, 1932 for 11 performances
Reviews:
New York Times page 18, Oct 29, 1932
                page 20, Nov 7, 1932

Tell Me More
book: Fred Thompson and William K. Wells
music: George Gershwin
lyrics: B. G. De Sylva and Ira Gershwin
Productions:
Opened April 13, 1925 for 32 performances
Reviews:
Life (New York) 85:18, May 28, 1925
New York Times page 27, Apr 14, 1925
Theatre Magazine 42:16, Jul 1925

A Temporary Island
book: Halsted Welles
songs: Lorenzo Fuller
music: Lehman Engel
staging: Halsted Welles
sets: Lawrence Goldwasser
costumes: Mildred Sutherland
Productions:
Opened March 14, 1948 for 6 performances
Reviews:
New Republic 118:30, Mar 29, 1948
New York Times page 27, Mar 15, 1948
Theatre Arts 32:32, Spring 1948

Tenderloin
book: George Abbott and Jerome Weidman, based on
                the novel by Samuel Hopkins Adams
music: Jerry Bock
lyrics: Sheldon Harnick
staging: George Abbott
sets: Cecil Beaton
costumes: Cecil Beaton
choreography: Joe Layton
Productions:
Opened October 17, 1960 for 216 performances
Reviews:
America 104:354+, Dec 3, 1960
Christian Century 77:1382, Nov 23, 1960
Dance Magazine 34:33, Dec 1960
Nation 191:353, Nov 5, 1960
New York Theatre Critics' Reviews 1960:205+

New York Times page 47, Oct 18, 1960
                page 28, Nov 4, 1960
                page 30, Apr 13, 1961
New Yorker 36:86, Oct 29, 1960
Newsweek 56:84, Oct 31, 1960
Saturday Review 43:39, Nov 5, 1960
Theatre Arts 44:12, Dec 1960
Time 76:68, Oct 31, 1960

Texas, Li'l Darlin'
    book: John Whedon and Sam Moore
    music: Robert Edmund Dolan
    lyrics: Johnny Mercer
    staging: Paul Crabtree
    sets: Theodore Cooper
    costumes: Eleanor Goldsmith
    choreography: Al White, Jr.
Productions:
    Opened November 25, 1949 for 221 performances
Reviews:
    Catholic World 170:309, Jan 1950
    Commonweal 51:293, Dec 16, 1949
    New York Theatre Critics' Reviews 1949:214+
    New York Times page 10, Nov 26, 1949
                    page 19, Jul 11, 1951
    New Yorker 25:70-1, Dec 3, 1949
    Newsweek 34:84, Dec 5, 1949
    Theatre Arts 34:9, Feb 1950
    Time 54:66, Dec 5, 1949

That 5 A.M. Jazz
    music: Will Holt
    lyrics: Will Holt
    staging: Michael Kahn
    sets: Lloyd Burlingame
    choreography: Sandra Devlin
Productions:
    (Off-Broadway) Opened October 19, 1964 for 94 performances
Reviews:
    New York Times page 42, Oct 20, 1964
    New Yorker 40:129, Oct 31, 1964

That Hat!
    book: Adapted by Cy Young from the French farce
                    Le Chapeau de Paille d'Italie
    music and
     lyrics: Adapted by Cy Young
    staging: Dania Krupska
    sets: Bill Hargate
    costumes: Bill Hargate
    choreography: Dania Krupska
Productions:
    (Off-Broadway) Opened September 23, 1964 for 1 performance

Reviews:
    New York Times page 45, Sep 24, 1964
                  page 33, Sep 25, 1964

That's Entertainment
    music: Howard Dietz and Arthur Schwartz
    lyrics: Howard Dietz and Arthur Schwartz
    staging: Paul Aaron
    sets: David F. Segal
    costumes: Jane Greenwood
    choreography: Larry Fuller
Productions:
    Opened April 14, 1972 for 4 performances
Reviews:
    New York Theatre Critics' Reviews 1972:317
    New York Times page 19, Apr 15, 1972
    New Yorker 48:108, Apr 22, 1972

Theater Songs   (see Leonard Bernstein's Theater Songs)

There You Are
    book: Carl Bartfield
    music: William Heagney
    lyrics: William Heagney and Tom Connell
    staging: Horace Sinclair
Productions:
    Opened May 16, 1932 for 8 performances
Reviews:
    New York Times page 25, May 17, 1932

They Don't Make 'em Like That Anymore
    sketches: Hugh Martin and Timothy Gray
    music: Hugh Martin and Timothy Gray
    lyrics: Hugh Martin and Timothy Gray
    staging: Timothy Gray
    sets: Don Gordon
    costumes: E. Huntington Parker
Productions:
    (Off-Broadway) Opened June 8, 1972 for 32 performances
Reviews:
    New York Times page 44, Jun 12, 1972

The Thing Itself
    book: Arthur Sainer
    music: Jim Kurtz, Meredith Monk, Robert Cosmo
                  Savage and David Tice
    staging: Crystal Field
Productions:
    (Off-Off-Broadway) Opened November 30, 1972 (Theatre for
    the New City)
No Reviews.

The Third Little Show

assembled by: Dwight Deere Wiman
music: Noel Coward, Henry Sullivan, Michael Cleary,
             Morris Hamilton, Burton Lane, Herman Hup-
             feld, Ned Lehak, William Lewis, Jr.
lyrics: Noel Coward, Earle Crooker, Max and Nathaniel
             Lief, Grace Henry, Harold Adamson, Herman
             Hupfeld, Edward Eliscu, Ted Fetter
staging: Alexander Leftwich
Productions:
Opened June 1, 1931 for 136 performances
Reviews:
    Bookman 73:632-3, Aug 1931
    Catholic World 133:463, Jul 1931
    Commonweal 14:188, Jun 17, 1931
    Life (New York) 97:19, Jun 26, 1931
    New York Times VIII, page 2, May 10, 1931
                     page 34, Jun 2, 1931
    Outlook 158:219, Jun 17, 1931

13 Daughters
    book: Eaton Magoon (additional book material by Leon
                 Tokatyan)
    music: Eaton Magoon
    lyrics: Eaton Magoon
    staging: Billy Matthews
    sets: George Jenkins
    costumes: Alvin Colt
    choreography: Rod Alexander
Productions:
Opened March 2, 1961 for 28 performances
Reviews:
    New York Theatre Critics' Reviews 1961:350+
    New York Times page 17, Mar 3, 1961
                     page 30, Mar 23, 1961
    New Yorker 37:112, Mar 11, 1961

This Is the Army
    sketches: James McColl, based on the musical show
                 Yip, Yip, Yaphank
    music: Irving Berlin
    lyrics: Irving Berlin
    staging: Ezra Stone
    sets: John Koenig
    costumes: John Koenig
    choreography: Robert Sidney and Nelson Barclift
Productions:
Opened July 4, 1942 for 113 performances
Reviews:
    American Mercury 55:450-1, Oct 1942
    Catholic World 155:726, Sep 1942
    Collier's 110:14-15+, Oct 17, 1942
    Commonweal 36:303-4, Jul 17, 1942
    Life 13:72-5, Jul 20, 1942

484   Thoughts

New York Theatre Critics' Reviews 1942:256+
New York Times VIII, page 1, Jun 14, 1942
                page 28, Jul 5, 1942
                VII, page 1, Jul 12, 1942
                VII, page 6, Jul 12, 1942
                VIII, page 1, Aug 16, 1942
                VIII, page 8, Sep 13, 1942
New York Times Magazine pages 6-7, Jul 12, 1942
                        page 20, Nov 21, 1943
Newsweek 20:52+, Jul 13, 1942
Theatre Arts 26:546, Sep 1942
        26:608+, Oct 1942
Time 40:36, Jul 13, 1942

Thoughts
    book and
    music: Lamar Alford
    lyrics: Lamar Alford; additional lyrics by Megan Terry
                    and Jose Tapla
    staging: Michael Schultz
    sets: Stuart Wurtzel
    costumes: Joseph Thomas
    choreography: Jan Mickens
Productions:
    (Off-Broadway) Opened March 19, 1973 for 24 performances
Reviews:
    New York Times page 25, Feb 5, 1973
                    page 29, Mar 20, 1973
                    II, page 3, Apr 1, 1973
    New Yorker 49:77, Mar 31, 1973

Three Cheers
    book: Anne Caldwell and R. H. Burnside
    music: Raymond Hubbell
    lyrics: Anne Caldwell
    staging: R. H. Burnside
    choreography: Dave Bennett
Productions:
    Opened October 15, 1928 for 210 performances
Reviews:
    New York Times page 28, Oct 16, 1928
                    IX, page 1, Oct 21, 1928
    Outlook 150:1086, Oct 31, 1928
    Theatre Magazine 48:46, Dec 1928
    Vogue 72:146, Dec 8, 1928

3 for Tonight
    special
    material: Robert Wells
    music: Walter Schumann
    lyrics: Robert Wells
    staging: Gower Champion
Productions:

Opened April 6, 1955 for 85 performances
Reviews:
America 93:165, May 7, 1955
Catholic World 181:226, Jun 1955
Commonweal 62:105, Apr 29, 1955
Life 38:129-30+, Apr 25, 1955
Nation 180:354-5, Apr 23, 1955
New York Theatre Critics' Reviews 1955:337+
New York Times II, page 3, Apr 3, 1955
                page 23, Apr 7, 1955
                II, page 1, Apr 17, 1955
New Yorker 31:74+, Apr 16, 1955
Newsweek 44:90+, Dec 13, 1954
Saturday Review 38:25, Apr 23, 1955
Theatre Arts 39:20-1, 93, Jun 1955
Time 65:72, Apr 18, 1955
Vogue 125:122, Apr 1, 1955

Three Little Girls
        book: Herman Feiner and Bruno Hardt-Warden,
                        adapted by Marie Hecht and Gertrude Purcell
        music: Walter Kollo
        lyrics: Harry B. Smith
        staging: J. J. Shubert
Productions:
Opened April 14, 1930 for 104 performances
Reviews:
Life (New York) 95:18, May 2, 1930
New York Times page 29, Apr 15, 1930
Theatre Magazine 51:48, Jun 1930

The Three Romeos
        book: R. H. Burnside
        music: Raymond Hubbell
        lyrics: R. H. Burnside
        staging: R. H. Burnside
Productions:
Opened November 13, 1911 for 56 performances
Reviews:
Blue Book 14:469-71, Jan 1912
Dramatic Mirror 66:10, Nov 15, 1911
                66:2, Nov 22, 1911
                66:2, Dec 6, 1911
Life (New York) 58:902-3, Nov 23, 1911
New York Times page 13, Nov 14, 1911
Theatre Magazine 14:xv, Dec 1911

Three Showers
        book: William Cary Duncan
        music: Creamer and Layton
        lyrics: Creamer and Layton
Productions:
Opened April 5, 1920 for 48 performances

Reviews:
    Dramatic Mirror 82:681, Apr 10, 1920
    New York Clipper 68:14, Apr 14, 1920
    New York Times page 18, Apr 6, 1920
    Theatre Magazine 31:402, May 1920
                        31:407, May 1920

Three to Make Ready
        book: Nancy Hamilton
        music: Morgan Lewis
        lyrics: Nancy Hamilton
        staging: John Murray Anderson
        sets: Donald Oenslager
        costumes: Andre
        choreography: Robert Sidney
Productions:
    Opened March 7, 1946 for 327 performances
Reviews:
    Catholic World 163:72-3, Apr 1946
    Commonweal 43:572-3, Mar 22, 1946
    Life 20:67-70, Mar 25, 1946
    Musical Courier 133:14, Apr 15, 1946
    New York Theatre Critics' Reviews 1946:434+
    New York Times page 16, Mar 8, 1946
                    II, page 1, Mar 17, 1946
                    II, page 1, May 19, 1946
                    II, page 2, Oct 27, 1946
    New Yorker 22:44+, Mar 16, 1946
    Newsweek 27:92, Mar 18, 1946
    Theatre Arts 30:261-2, May 1946
    Time 47:56, Mar 18, 1946

Three Waltzes
        book: Clare Kummer and Rowland Leigh, adapted
                        from Paul Knepler and Armin Robinson's play
        music: Johann Strauss, Sr., Johann Strauss, Jr.,
                        Oscar Strauss
        lyrics: Clare Kummer, Edwin Gilbert
        staging: Hassard Short
        sets: Watson Barratt
        costumes: Connie dePinna
        choreography: Chester Hale
Productions:
    Opened December 25, 1937 for 122 performances
Reviews:
    Commonweal 27:300, Jan 7, 1938
    New York Times page 15, Nov 15, 1937
                    page 10, Dec 27, 1937
    One Act Play Magazine 1:849, Jan 1938
    Stage 15:51, Feb 1938
    Theatre Arts 22:100, Feb 1938
    Time 31:24, Jan 3, 1938

Three Wishes for Jamie
        book: Charles O'Neal and Abe Burrows, based on
                           Charles O'Neal's novel
        music: Ralph Blane
        lyrics: Ralph Blane
        staging: Abe Burrows
        sets: George Jenkins
        costumes: Miles White
        choreography: Ted Cappy, Herbert Ross, Eugene Loring
Productions:
    Opened March 21, 1952 for 91 performances
Reviews:
    Catholic World 175:148, May 1952
    Commonweal 56:14, Apr 11, 1952
    Life 32:119+, Apr 14, 1952
    New York Theatre Critics' Reviews 1952:332+
    New York Times page 9, Mar 22, 1952
    New Yorker 28:62, Mar 29, 1952
    Newsweek 39:84, Mar 31, 1952
    Saturday Review 35:27, Apr 5, 1952
    Theatre Arts 36:91, May 1952
    Time 59:69, Mar 31, 1952

The Threepenny Opera
        book: Marc Blitzstein; based on the play by Bertolt
                           Brecht
        music: Kurt Weill
        lyrics: Marc Blitzstein
Productions:
    (Off-Broadway) Opened March 1954 for 2,611 performances
    (Off-Off-Broadway) Opened October 13, 1972 (Workshop of the
        Players' Art)
Reviews:
    Catholic World 179:226, Jun 1954
    Commonweal 60:118, May 7, 1954
    Coronet 49:18, Dec 1960
    Musical America 74:14, Apr 1954
    Nation 178:265-6, Mar 27, 1954
    New Republic 153:35, Aug 7, 1965
    New York Times II, page 3, Mar 7, 1954
                       page 26, Mar 11, 1954
                       II, page 1, Mar 21, 1954
                       II, page 7, Apr 4, 1954
                       page 38, Sep 21, 1955
                       page 83, Feb 12, 1956
                       VI, page 24, Feb 16, 1958
                       page 32, Sep 14, 1959
                       page 13, Oct 10, 1959
                       page 44, Sep 15, 1960
                       page 46, Sep 20, 1960
                       page 15, Feb 4, 1961
                       page 30, Apr 13, 1961
                       page 41, Sep 21, 1961

page 58, Dec 6, 1961
page 33, Oct 24, 1972
New Yorker 30:62+, Mar 20, 1954
41:172-3, Mar 20, 1965
Newsweek 46:54, Oct 3, 1955
Saturday Review 37:22, Mar 27, 1954
37:21, Apr 17, 1954
39:47, Sep 15, 1956
41:64-5, Oct 25, 1958
48:22, Mar 27, 1965
Time 63:46, Mar 22, 1954

Three's a Crowd
    book: Howard Dietz
    music: Arthur Schwartz and others
    lyrics: Howard Dietz
    staging: Hassard Short
    choreography: Albertina Rasch
Productions:
Opened October 15, 1930 for 272 performances
Reviews:
Bookman 72:411-12, Dec 1930
Catholic World 132:721-2, Mar 1931
Life (New York) 96:21, Oct 31, 1930
Nation 131:480, Oct 29, 1930
New York Times page 28, Oct 16, 1930
IX, page 4, Oct 5, 1930
VIII, page 1, Oct 26, 1930
Theatre Magazine 53:42, Jan 1931
53:20, Feb 1931
Vogue 76:76+, Dec 8, 1930

Through the Years
    book: Brian Hooker, based on Jane Cowl's Smilin'
                  Through
    music: Vincent Youmans
    lyrics: Edward Heyman
    staging: Edgar McGregor
    choreography: Jack Haskell and Max Scheck
Productions:
Opened January 28, 1932 for 20 performances
Reviews:
New York Times VIII, page 3, Jan 3, 1932
page 23, Feb 13, 1932

Thumbs Up
    sketches: H. I. Phillips, Harold Atteridge, Alan Baxter,
                  Ballard McDonald, Earle Crooker
    music: James Hanley and Henry Sullivan
    lyrics: H. I. Phillips, Harold Atteridge, Alan Baxter,
                  Ballard McDonald, Earle Crooker
    staging: John Murray Anderson
    sets: Ted Weidhaas, James Reynolds, Raoul Pene

du Bois
choreography: Robert Alton
Productions:
Opened December 27, 1934 for 156 performances
Reviews:
Catholic World 140:723, Mar 1935
Commonweal 21:346, Jan 18, 1935
New York Times page 24, Dec 28, 1934
VIII, page 2, Feb 3, 1934
IX, page 1, Aug 18, 1934
Newsweek 5:26, Jan 5, 1935

Ti-Jean and His Brothers
book: Derek Walcott
music: Andre Tanker
lyrics: Derek Walcott and Andre Tanker
staging: Derek Walcott
sets: Edward Burbridge
choreography: George Faison
Productions:
(Off-Broadway) Opened July 20, 1972 for 15 performances
Reviews:
New York Times page 20, Jul 28, 1972
II, page 1, Aug 6, 1972

Tick-Tack-Toe
written: Herman Timberg
staging: Herman Timberg
Productions:
Opened February 23, 1920 for 32 performances
Reviews:
Dramatic Mirror 82:415-16, Mar 6, 1920
New York Clipper 68:19, Mar 1920
New York Times page 11, Feb 24, 1920
Theatre Magazine 31:273, Apr 1920

Tickets, Please!
sketches: Harry Herrmann, Edmund Rice, Jack Roche, Ted Luce
music and
lyrics: Lyn Duddy, Joan Edwards, Mel Tolkin, Lucille Kallen, Clay Warnick
staging: Mervyn Nelson
sets: Ralph Alswang
costumes: Peggy Morrison
choreography: Joan Mann
Productions:
Opened April 27, 1950 for 245 performances
Reviews:
Catholic World 171:227, Jun 1950
New Republic 122:20, May 15, 1950
New York Theatre Critics' Reviews 1950:300+
New York Times page 25, Apr 28, 1950

II, page 1, May 7, 1950
II, page 1, Aug 6, 1950
New Yorker 26:52, May 6, 1950
Newsweek 35:80, May 8, 1950
Theatre Arts 34:16, Jul 1950
Time 55:48, May 8, 1950

Tickle Me
book: Otto Harbach, Oscar Hammerstein II, Frank
                 Mandel
music: Herbert Stothart
lyrics: Otto Harbach, Oscar Hammerstein II, Frank
                 Mandel
staging: William Collier
choreography: Bert French
Productions:
Opened August 17, 1920 for 207 performances
Reviews:
Dramatic Mirror page 327, Aug 21, 1920
New York Clipper 68:19, Aug 25, 1920
New York Times page 12, Aug 19, 1920
Theatre Magazine 32:240, Oct 1920

La Tierra de la Alegria   (see The Land of Joy)

The Tiger Rag
book: Seyril Schochen; based on the Oedipus legend
music: Kenneth Gaburo
lyrics: Seyril Schochen
Productions:
(Off-Broadway) Opened Season of 1960-61
Reviews:
New York Times page 20, Feb 17, 1961

Tillie's Nightmare
book: Edgar Smith
music: A. Baldwin Sloane
staging: Ned Wayburn
Productions:
Opened May 5, 1910 for 77 performances
Reviews:
Dramatic Mirror 63:6, May 14, 1910
Leslie's Weekly 110:591, Jun 18, 1910
Life (New York) 55:922, May 19, 1910
Metropolitan Magazine 32:540-41, Jul 1910
Pearson 24:92, Jul 1910
          24:94-5, Jul 1910
Theatre Magazine 11:174, Jun 1910
          11:187, Jun 1910

A Time for Singing
book: Gerald Freedman and John Morris; based on
                 Richard Llewellyn's novel How Green Was My

Valley
music: John Morris
lyrics: Gerald Freedman
staging: Gerald Freedman
sets: Ming Cho Lee
costumes: Theoni V. Aldredge
choreography: Donald McKayle
Productions:
Opened May 21, 1966 for 41 performances
Reviews:
America 114:881-2, Jun 25, 1966
Commonweal 84:370, Jun 17, 1966
Dance Magazine 40:25, Jul 1966
New York Theatre Critics' Reviews 1966:305
New York Times page 48, May 23, 1966
              page 28, Jun 20, 1966
New Yorker 42:79, May 28, 1966
Newsweek 67:89, Jun 6, 1966
Saturday Review 49:34, Jun 11, 1966

Time, Gentlemen Please
staging: Don Gammell and Fred Stone
sets: Thea Neu
costumes: Reginald Woolley
choreography: Tony Bateman
Productions:
(Off-Broadway) Opened November 4, 1961 for 336 performances
No Reviews.

The Time, the Place, and the Girl
book: Will Morrissey, John Neff, William B. Fried-
                lander, based on the musical by Will M. Hough,
                Frank R. Adams, and Joe Howard, originally
                produced in Chicago in 1906
music: Joe Howard
lyrics: Will Morrissey, John Neff, William B. Fried-
                lander, based on the musical by Will M. Hough,
                Frank R. Adams, and Joe Howard, originally
                produced in Chicago in 1906
staging: William B. Friedlander
sets: Karl Amend
costumes: Paul DuPont
choreography: Carl Randall
Productions:
Opened October 21, 1942 for 13 performances
Reviews:
New York Theatre Critics' Reviews 1942:198+
New York Times page 24, Oct 22, 1942

Times Square Two   (see An Evening with the Times Square Two)

Timon of Athens
book: based on William Shakespeare's play

music: Jonathon Tunick
staging: Gerald Freedman
sets: Ming Cho Lee
costumes: Theoni V. Aldredge
choreography: Joyce Trisler
Productions:
(Off-Broadway) Opened June 25, 1971 for 19 performances
Reviews:
New York Times page 22, Jul 2, 1971
                 II, page 1, Jul 11, 1971

Tip-Toes
    book: Guy Bolton and Fred Thompson
    music: George Gershwin
    lyrics: Ira Gershwin
    staging: John Harwood
Productions:
Opened December 28, 1925 for 194 performances
Reviews:
New York Times page 20, Dec 29, 1925
                 page 27, Sep 1, 1926
Vogue 67:102+, Feb 15, 1926

Tip Top
    book: Anne Caldwell and R. H. Burnside
    music: Ivan Caryll
    lyrics: Anne Caldwell and R. H. Burnside
Productions:
Opened October 5, 1920 for 246 performances
Reviews:
Dramatic Mirror page 665, Oct 9, 1920
Life (New York) 76:724, Oct 21, 1920
New York Clipper 68:28, Oct 13, 1920
New York Times page 13, Oct 6, 1920
                 page 17, Apr 12, 1921
                 VI, page 1, Apr 17, 1921
Theatre Magazine 32:424, Dec 1920

'Tis of Thee
    assembled: Alfred Hayes
    sketches: Sam Locke
    music: Alex North and Al Moss, additional music and
                  lyrics by Peter Barry, David Gregory, Richard
                  Levine
    staging: Nat Lichtman
    sets: Carl Kent
    choreography: Esther Junger
Productions:
Opened October 26, 1940 for one performance
Reviews:
New York Theatre Critics' Reviews 1940:240+
New York Times page 21, Oct 28, 1940
Stage 1:20, Nov 1940

To Be or Not to Be--What Kind of a Question Is That?
        book: H. Ritterman and Zvi Reisel
        music: Eli Rubinstein
        lyrics: Max Meszel
        staging: Marvin Gordon
        sets: Ami Shamir
Productions:
        (Off-Broadway) Opened October 19, 1970 for 23 performances
Reviews:
        New York Times page 39, Oct 20, 1970

To Broadway with Love
        conceived: Morton Da Costa
        music: Philip J. Lang, Jerry Bock and Sheldon Harnick
        staging: Morton Da Costa
        sets: Peter Wolf
        costumes: Freddy Wittop
Productions:
        (Off-Broadway) Opened April 21, 1964 for 97 performances
        (New York World's Fair)
Reviews:
        America 111:55-6, Jul 11, 1964
        Dance Magazine 38:21+, Jul 1964
        Life 56:17, May 22, 1964
        Newsweek 63:60, May 11, 1964

To Live Another Summer, to Pass Another Winter
        book: Hayim Hefer
        music: Dov Seltzer; additional music by David Krivoshei,
                           Alexander Argov and Naomi Shemer
        lyrics: Hayim Hefer; additional lyrics by Naomi Shemer
        staging: Jonaton Karmon
        sets: Neil Peter Jampolis
        costumes: Lydia Pincus Gany
        choreography: Jonaton Karmon
Productions:
        Opened October 21, 1971 for 173 performances
Reviews:
        New York Theatre Critics' Reviews 1971:226
        New York Times page 29, Oct 22, 1971
                          II, page 3, Oct 31, 1971
                          page 41, Nov 3, 1971
                          page 7, Nov 7, 1971
        Time 98:95, Nov 1, 1971

To the Water Tower
        music: Tom O'Horgan
        staging: Paul Sills
        sets: Ralph Alswang
Productions:
        (Off-Broadway) Opened April 4, 1963 for 210 performances
Reviews:
        New Republic 148:28-9, May 11, 1963

Todd, Michael   (see Michael Todd)

'Toinette
    book: J. I. Rodale; based on Molière's The Imaginary
                     Invalid
    music: Deed Meyer
    lyrics: Deed Meyer
    staging: Curt Conway
Productions:
    (Off-Broadway)   Opened November 20, 1961 for 31 performances
Reviews:
    New York Times page 46, Nov 21, 1961
                   page 40, Nov 28, 1961
                   page 42, Nov 28, 1961
                   page 38, Dec 19, 1961
    New Yorker 37:121, Dec 2, 1961

Tonight's the Night
    book: Fred Thompson
    music: Paul Rubens
    staging: Austen Hurgon
Productions:
    Opened December 24, 1914 for 108 performances
Reviews:
    Current Opinion 58:98-9, Feb 1915
    Dramatic Mirror 72:8, Dec 30, 1914
                    73:2, Jan 13, 1915
                    73:2, Feb 3, 1915
                    73:2, Feb 17, 1915
    Munsey 54:543, Apr 1915
    Nation 99:783-4, Dec 31, 1914
    New York Times page 11, Dec 25, 1914
    Theatre Magazine 21:57+, Feb 1915

Too Many Girls
    book: George Marion, Jr.
    music: Richard Rodgers
    lyrics: Lorenz Hart
    staging: George Abbott
    sets: Jo Mielziner
    costumes: Raoul Pene du Bois
    choreography: Robert Alton
Productions:
    Opened October 18, 1939 for 249 performances
Reviews:
    Catholic World 150:338, Dec 1939
    Commonweal 31:96, Nov 17, 1939
    Life 7:78-80, Oct 23, 1939
    New Republic 101:16, Nov 8, 1939
    New York Theatre Critics' Reviews 1940:467+
    New York Times page 26, Oct 19, 1939
                   IX, page 1, Oct 29, 1939
    Theatre Arts 23:861, Dec 1939

Time 34:42, Oct 30, 1939

Toot Sweet
    music: Richard A. Whiting
    lyrics: Raymond B. Eagan
    staging: Will Morrissey
Productions:
Opened May 7, 1919 for 45 performances
Reviews:
    Life (New York) 73:904, May 22, 1919
    New York Times page 19, May 8, 1919
    Theatre Magazine 29:343-4, Jun 1919
                      30:17, Jul 1919

Toot-Toot
    book: Edgar Allan Woolf; adapted from Excuse Me by
                        Rupert Hughes
    music: Jerome Kern
    lyrics: Berton Braley
    staging: Edgar Allan Woolf and Edward Rose
Productions:
Opened March 11, 1918 for 40 performances
Reviews:
    Dramatic Mirror 78:32, Jan 5, 1918
                    78:5, Mar 23, 1918
                    78:4, Apr 6, 1918
    New York Times page 11, Mar 12, 1918
                    IV, page 10, Mar 24, 1918
    Theatre Magazine 27:220, Apr 1918
                     27:289, May 1918

Top Banana
    book: H. S. Kraft
    music: Johnny Mercer
    lyrics: Johnny Mercer
    staging: Jack Donohue
    sets: Jo Mielziner
    costumes: Alvin Colt
    choreography: Ron Fletcher
Productions:
Opened November 1, 1951 for 350 performances
Reviews:
    Catholic World 174:228, Dec 1951
    Commonweal 55:173-4, Nov 23, 1951
    Life 31:75-6+, Dec 3, 1951
    New York Theatre Critics' Reviews 1951:180+
    New York Times page 19, Nov 2, 1951
                    II, page 1, Nov 18, 1951
    New Yorker 27:64+, Nov 10, 1951
    Newsweek 38:92, Nov 12, 1951
    Theatre Arts 35:3, Dec 1951
                  36:81, Jan 1952
    Time 58:59, Nov 12, 1951

Top-Hole
    book: Eugene Conrad and George Dill; revised by
                         Gladys Unger
    music: Jay Gorney
    lyrics: Owen Murphy
Productions:
    Opened September 1, 1924 for 104 performances
Reviews:
    New York Times page 23, Sep 2, 1924
    Theatre Magazine 40:72, Nov 1924

Top-Notchers
    assembled: Clifford C. Fischer
Productions:
    Opened May 29, 1942 for 48 performances
Reviews:
    New York Times page 8, May 30, 1942
(Also see Keep 'em Laughing)

Top Speed
    book: Guy Bolton
    music: Harry Ruby
    lyrics: Bert Kalmar
    staging: John Harwood
    choreography: John Boyle
Productions:
    Opened December 25, 1929 for 102 performances
Reviews:
    Life (New York) 95:20, Jan 17, 1930
    New York Times IX, page 4, Nov 17, 1929
                       page 20, Dec 26, 1929
    Theatre Magazine 51:63, Feb 1930
    Vogue 75:122, Feb 15, 1930

Topics of 1923
    book: Harold Atteridge and Harry Wagstaff Gribble
    music: Jean Schwartz and Alfred Goodman
    lyrics: Harold Atteridge
    staging: J. C. Huffman
Productions:
    Opened November 20, 1923 for 143 performances
Reviews:
    New York Times page 23, Nov 21, 1923
    Theatre Magazine 39:16, Jan 1924

Toplitzky of Notre Dame
    book: George Marion, Jr.
    music: Sammy Fain
    lyrics: Jack Barnett
    staging: Jose Ruben
    sets: Edward Gilbert
    costumes: Kenn Barr
    choreography: Robert Sidney

Productions:
    Opened December 26, 1946 for 60 performances
Reviews:
    Catholic World 164:455, Feb 1947
    New York Theatre Critics' Reviews 1946:201+
    New York Times II, page 4, Dec 22, 1946
                    page 13, Dec 27, 1946
                    page 19, Feb 16, 1947
    New Yorker 22:48+, Jan 11, 1947
    Newsweek 29:64, Jan 6, 1947
    Theatre Arts 31:17, Mar 1947
    Time 49:56, Jan 6, 1947

Topsy and Eva
    book: Catherine Chisholm Cushing
    music: Duncan Sisters
    lyrics: Duncan Sisters
    staging: Oscar Eagle
Productions:
    Opened December 23, 1924 for 159 performances
Reviews:
    New York Times page 11, Dec 24, 1924
    Theatre Magazine 41:16, Mar 1925
                    42:31, Jul 1925

Touch
    book: Kenn Long and Amy Salz
    music: Kenn Long and Jim Crozier
    lyrics: Kenn Long
    staging: Amy Salz
    sets: Robert U. Taylor
Productions:
    (Off-Broadway) Opened November 8, 1970 for 422 performances
Reviews:
    Nation 211:542, Nov 23, 1970
    New York Times page 52, Nov 9, 1970
    New Yorker 46:132, Dec 12, 1970

Touch and Go
    sketches: Jean Kerr and Walter Kerr
    music: Jay Gorney
    lyrics: Jean Kerr and Walter Kerr
    staging: Walter Kerr
    sets: John Robert Lloyd
    choreography: Helen Tamiris
Productions:
    Opened October 13, 1949 for 176 performances
Reviews:
    Catholic World 170:228, Dec 1949
    Commonweal 51:159, Nov 11, 1949
    Life 27:52, Oct 24, 1949
    New York Theatre Critics' Reviews 1949:250+
    New York Times page 34, Oct 14, 1949

II, page 1, Oct 30, 1949
II, page 1, Nov 6, 1949
page 9, May 20, 1950
New Yorker 25:60+, Oct 22, 1949
Newsweek 34:84, Oct 24, 1949
Saturday Review 33:4-5, Jan 14, 1950
Theatre Arts 33:13, Dec 1949
Time 54:57, Oct 24, 1949

Tour de Four
    conceived: Tom Eyen
    sketches: John Aman, Larry Alexander, Gary Popkin and
           others
    music: John Aman, Larry Alexander, Gary Popkin and
           others
    lyrics: John Aman, Larry Alexander, Gary Popkin and
           others
    staging: Tom Eyen
    costumes: Edward Charles
Productions:
    (Off-Broadway) Opened June 18, 1963 for 16 performances
Reviews:
    New York Times page 41, Jun 19, 1963

Tovarich
    book: David Shaw, based on the play by Robert E.
           Sherwood and Jacques Deval
    music: Lee Pockiss
    lyrics: Anne Crosswell
    staging: Peter Glenville
    sets: Rolf Gerard
    costumes: Motley
    choreography: Herbert Ross
Productions:
    Opened March 18, 1963 for 264 performances
Reviews:
    America 108:651, May 4, 1963
    Commonweal 78:224, May 17, 1963
    National Review 14:535-7, Jul 2, 1963
    Nation 196:334, Apr 20, 1963
    New York Theatre Critics' Reviews 1963:308+
    New York Times page 5, Jan 23, 1963
                page 5, Mar 20, 1963
                page 40, Nov 11, 1963
    New Yorker 39:108+, Mar 30, 1963
    Newsweek 61:78, Apr 1, 1963
    Saturday Review 46:40, Apr 6, 1963
    Theatre Arts 47:14-15+, May 1963
    Time 81:46, Mar 29, 1963

Town Topics (see Ned Wayburn's Town Topics)

Treasure Girl

    book: Fred Thompson and Vincent Lawrence
    music: George Gershwin
    lyrics: Ira Gershwin
    staging: Bertram Harrison
    choreography: Bobby Connelly
Productions:
    Opened November 8, 1928 for 68 performances
Reviews:
    Life (New York) 92:11, Nov 12, 1928
    New York Times page 22, Nov 9, 1928
    Outlook 150:1195, Nov 21, 1928
    Vogue 72:82, Dec 22, 1928

A Tree Grows in Brooklyn
    book: Betty Smith and George Abbott, based on Betty
                     Smith's novel
    music: Arthur Schwartz
    lyrics: Dorothy Fields
    staging: George Abbott
    sets: Jo Mielziner
    choreography: Herbert Ross
Productions:
    Opened April 19, 1951 for 270 performances
    (Off-Broadway) Opened April 15, 1966 for 14 performances
Reviews:
    Catholic World 173:229, Jun 1951
    Commonweal 54:88, May 4, 1951
    Life 30:97-8+, May 7, 1951
    Musical America 71:34, Jul 1951
    Nation 172:403, Apr 28, 1951
    New Republic 124:20, May 14, 1951
    New York Theatre Critics' Reviews 1951:291+
    New York Times II, page 3, Apr 15, 1951
                    page 24, Apr 20, 1951
                    II, page 1, Apr 29, 1951
    New Yorker 27:56+, Apr 28, 1951
    Newsweek 37:53, Apr 30, 1951
    Saturday Review 34:23-4, May 5, 1951
    Time 57:89, Apr 30, 1951

The Trials of Oz
    book: Geoff Robertson
    songs: Buzzy Linehart, Mick Jagger, John Lennon and
                     Yoko Ono
    staging: Jim Sharman
    sets: Mark Ravitz
    costumes: Joseph G. Aulisi
Productions:
    (Off-Broadway) Opened December 19, 1972 for 15 performances
Reviews:
    New York Times page 51, Mar 14, 1972
                    page 54, Dec 20, 1972
                    II, page 1, Jan 7, 1973

Tricks
    book: Jon Jory; based on Molière's Les Fourberies
                     de Scapin
    music: Jerry Blatt
    lyrics: Lonnie Burstein
    staging: Jon Jory
    sets: Oliver Smith
    costumes: Miles White
    choreography: Donald Saddler
Productions:
    Opened January 8, 1973 for 8 performances
Reviews:
    New York Theatre Critics' Reviews 1973:391
    New York Times page 29, Jan 9, 1973
    New Yorker 48:59, Jan 20, 1973

A Trip to Japan
    book: R. H. Burnside
    music: Manuel Klein
    lyrics: Manuel Klein
    staging: R. H. Burnside
Productions:
    Opened September 4, 1909 for 447 performances
Reviews:
    Leslie's Weekly 109:415, Oct 28, 1909

Trois Jeunes Filles Nues
    book: Yves Mirande and Albert Willemetz
    music: Raoul
    lyrics: Yves Mirande and Albert Willemetz
Productions:
    Opened March 4, 1929 for 40 performances
Reviews:
    New York Times page 28, Mar 5, 1929
    Theatre Magazine 50:41, Jul 1929

Trouble in Tahiti (part of a bill titled All in One)
    book: Leonard Bernstein
    music: Leonard Bernstein
    lyrics: Leonard Bernstein
    staging: David Brooks
Productions:
    Opened April 19, 1955 for 47 performances
    (Off-Off-Broadway) Opened April 23, 1965 for 14 per-
        formances (Equity Library Theatre)
Reviews:
    America 93:192, May 14, 1955
    Catholic World 181:227, Jun 1955
    Commonweal 62:255, Jun 10, 1955
    Nation 180:410, May 7, 1955
    New Republic 132:22, May 2, 1955
    New York Theatre Critics' Reviews 1955:325
    New York Times page 40, Apr 20, 1955

II, page 1, Apr 24, 1955
New Yorker 31:69-71, Apr 30, 1955
Saturday Review 38:26, May 14, 1955
Theatre Arts 39:26, May 14, 1955
Time 65:78, May 2, 1955

Trumpets of the Lord
    book: Vinnette Carroll; based on James Weldon John-
                    son's God's Trombone
    music: Based on gospel hymns
    lyrics: Based on gospel hymns
    staging: Donald McKayle
    sets: Ed Wittstein
    costumes: Normand Maxton
Productions:
    (Off-Broadway) Opened December 21, 1963 for 160 performances
    Opened April 29, 1969 for 7 performances
Reviews:
    New York Times page 22, Dec 23, 1963
                  page 37, Apr 30, 1969
                  page 53, May 1, 1969
    New Yorker 39:60-1, Jan 4, 1964

Tumble In
    book: Otto Hauerbach; adapted from Mary R. Rinehart
                    and Avery Hopwood's Seven Days
    music: Rudolf Friml
    lyrics: Rudolf Friml
    staging: Bertram Harrison
Productions:
    Opened March 24, 1919 for 128 performances
Reviews:
    New York Times page 11, Mar 25, 1919
    Theatre Magazine 29:274, May 1919
                   29:277, May 1919

Tunes from Blackness (see Ain't Supposed to Die a Natural Death)

Twinkle, Twinkle
    book: Harlan Thompson
    music: Harry Archer
    lyrics: Harlan Thompson
    additional
      material: Bert Kalmar and Harry Ruby
    staging: Frank Craven, Julian Alfred and Harry Puck
Productions:
    Opened November 16, 1926 for 167 performances
No Reviews.

Two by Two
    book: Peter Stone; based on the play The Flowering
                    Peach by Clifford Odets
    music: Richard Rodgers

lyrics: Martin Charnin
staging: Joe Layton
sets: David Hays
costumes: Fred Voelpel
Productions:
Opened November 10, 1970 for 351 performances
Reviews:
America 124:124-5, Feb 6, 1971
Commonweal 93:397, Jan 22, 1971
Commentary 51:80, Feb 1971
New York Theatre Critics' Reviews 1970:160
New York Times page 52, Jun 16, 1970
                page 26, Aug 11, 1970
                II, page 1, Nov 8, 1970
                page 37, Nov 11, 1970
                page 52, Nov 12, 1970
                II, page 1, Nov 22, 1970
                II, page 8, Dec 20, 1970
                page 15, Jul 23, 1971
                II, page 27, Aug 15, 1971
New Yorker 46:103, Nov 21, 1970
Newsweek 76:137, Nov 23, 1970
Saturday Review 53:12, Nov 28, 1970
Time 96:100, Nov 23, 1970

Two for the Show
sketches: Nancy Hamilton
music: Morgan Lewis
lyrics: Nancy Hamilton
staging: John Murray Anderson
sets: Raoul Pene du Bois
costumes: Raoul Pene du Bois
choreography: Robert Alton
Productions:
Opened February 8, 1940 for 124 performances
Reviews:
Catholic World 150:731-2, Mar 1940
Commonweal 31:386, Feb 23, 1940
New York Theatre Critics' Reviews 1940:394+
New York Times page 14, Feb 9, 1940
                IX, page 1, Feb 18, 1940
                IX, page 2, Feb 18, 1940
Theatre Arts 24:237-8, Apr 1940

Two for Tonight
sketches: Ralph Berton and Mitchell Hodges
music: Eugene Berton, Ralph Berton, Bernice Kazounoff
                 and John Latouche
lyrics: Eugene Berton, Ralph Berton, Bernice Kazounoff
                 and John Latouche
Productions:
(Off-Broadway) Opened December 28, 1939
No Reviews.

Two Gentlemen of Verona
    adapted: John Guare and Mel Shapiro; based on the play
                   by William Shakespeare
    music: Galt MacDermot
    lyrics: John Guare
    staging: Mel Shapiro
    sets: Ming Cho Lee
    costumes: Theoni V. Aldredge
    choreography: Jean Erdman
Productions:
    Opened December 1, 1971 for 613 performances
    (Off-Broadway) Opened July 22, 1971 for 14 performances
Reviews:
    America 125:534-5, Dec 18, 1 971
    Commentary 53:85-7, Apr 1972
    Nation 213:668, Dec 20, 1971
    New York Theatre Critics' Reviews 1971:172
    New York Times page 40, Jul 29, 1971
                  II, page 1, Aug 8, 1971
                   II, page 3, Aug 22, 1971
                   page 65, Dec 2, 1971
                   page 30, Dec 3, 1971
                   II, page 3, Dec 12, 1971
                   II, page 1, Dec 26, 1971
                   II, page 1, Feb 27, 1972
                   II, page 21, Oct 8, 1972
    New Yorker 47:101, Dec 11, 1971
    Newsweek 78:114, Dec 13, 1971
    Saturday Review 55:38, Jan 8, 1972
                 54:18, Aug 21, 1971
    Time 98:48, Dec 13, 1971
    Vogue 158:124, Dec 1971

Two if by Sea
    book: Priscilla B. Dewey and Charles Werner Moore
    music: Tony Hutchins
    lyrics: Priscilla B. Dewey
    staging: Charles Werner Moore
    sets: John Doepp
    costumes: Julie Weiss
    choreography: Edward Roll
Productions:
    (Off-Broadway) Opened February 6, 1972 for 1 performance
Reviews:
    New York Times page 35, Feb 7, 1972

Two Is Company
    book: Edward A. Paulton and Adolf Philipp; from
                   Paul Herve's My Friend Emily
    music: Jean Briquet and Adolf Philipp
    staging: Adolf Philipp
Productions:
    Opened September 22, 1915 for 29 performances

Reviews:
  Dramatic Mirror 74:8, Sep 29, 1915
                 74:2, Oct 30, 1915
  Green Book 14:970-1, Dec 1915
  New York Dramatic News 61:19, Oct 2, 1915
  Opera Magazine 2:31, Nov 1915
  Theatre Magazine 22:224, Nov 1915
                   22:234, Nov 1915

Two Little Brides
  book: Arthur Anderson, James T. Powers and Harold
                 Atteridge; from the German of Willner and
                 Wilhelm, adapted by Gustave Kerker
  lyrics: Arthur Anderson, James T. Powers and Harold
                 Atteridge
  staging: J. C. Huffman
Productions:
  Opened April 23, 1912 for 63 performances
Reviews:
  Blue Book 15:686-9, Aug 1912
  Dramatic Mirror 67:6, May 1, 1912
  Green Book 8:12-14+, Jul 1912
            8:135, Jul 1912
  Life (New York) 59:975, May 9, 1912
  Red Book 19:764-5+, Aug 1912
  Theatre Magazine 15:x, Jun 1912
                   15:172, Jun 1912

Two Little Girls in Blue
  book: Fred Jackson
  music: Vincent Youmans and Paul Lannin
  lyrics: Arthur Francis (Ira Gershwin)
  staging: Ned Wayburn
Productions:
  Opened May 3, 1921 for 135 performances
Reviews:
  Dramatic Mirror 83:715, Apr 23, 1921
                  83:769, May 7, 1921
  New York Clipper 69:19, May 11, 1921
  New York Times page 10, May 4, 1921
  Theatre Magazine 34:30, Jul 1921

Two on the Aisle
  sketches: Betty Comden, Adolph Green, Nat Hiken,
                 William Friedberg
  music: Jule Styne
  lyrics: Betty Comden, Adolph Green, Nat Hiken,
                 William Friedberg
  staging: Abe Burrows
  sets: Howard Bay
  costumes: Joan Personette
  choreography: Genevieve Pitot
Productions:

Opened July 19, 1951 for 281 performances
Reviews:
    Catholic World 173:469-70, Sep 1951
    Commonweal 54:405-6, Aug 3, 1951
    Harper 203:100-1, Sep 1951
    Life 31:111-12, Sep 10, 1951
    Nation 173:78, Jul 28, 1951
    New Republic 125:21, Sep 17, 1951
    New York Theatre Critics' Reviews 1951:246+
    New York Times page 13, Jul 20, 1951
               II, page 1, Jul 29, 1951
               VI, page 14, Aug 5, 1951
    New York Times Magazine page 14, Aug 5, 1951
    New Yorker 27:48+, Jul 28, 1951
    Newsweek 38:47, Jul 30, 1951
    Theatre Arts 35:6, 22-3+, Sep 1951
    Time 58:47, Jul 30, 1951

2, 008-1/2 (A Space Oddity)
    book: Tom Eyen
    music: Gary William Friedman
    lyrics: Tom Eyen
    staging: Tom Eyen
Productions:
    (Off-Off-Broadway) Opened February 10, 1974 (New York Theatre Strategy)
Reviews:
    New York Times page 39, Feb 12, 1974

Two's Company
    sketches: Charles Sherman and Peter De Vries
    music: Vernon Duke
    lyrics: Ogden Nash and Sammy Cahn
    staging: John Murray Anderson
    sets: Ralph Alswang
    costumes: Miles White
    choreography: Jerome Robbins
Productions:
    Opened December 15, 1952 for 90 performances
Reviews:
    Catholic World 176:389, Feb 1953
    Colliers 130:20-1, Nov 29, 1952
    Commonweal 57:376-7, Jan 16, 1953
    Life 33:24, Dec 29, 1952
    Nation 175:613, Dec 27, 1952
    New York Theatre Critics' Reviews 1952:157+
    New York Times page 43, Dec 16, 1952
               II, page 3, Dec 21, 1952
    New Yorker 28:44, Dec 27, 1952
    Newsweek 40:40, Dec 29, 1952
    Saturday Review 36:52, Jan 3, 1953
    Time 60:54, Dec 29, 1952

- U -

Uhuruh
    book: Danny Duncan
    music: Danny Duncan
    lyrics: Danny Duncan
    staging: Danny Duncan
    costumes: Richmond Curry
    choreography: Danny Duncan
Productions:
    (Off-Broadway) Opened March 20, 1972 for 8 performances
Reviews:
    New York Times page 35, Mar 21, 1972

Under Many Flags
    book: Carroll Fleming
    music: Manuel Klein
    lyrics: Manuel Klein
    staging: Carroll Fleming
Productions:
    Opened August 31, 1912 for 445 performances
Reviews:
    Dramatic Mirror 68:11, Sep 19, 1912
    Munsey 48:347-9, Nov 1912
    Theatre Magazine 16:xv, Oct 1912

Under the Counter
    book: Arthur Macrae
    music: Manning Sherwin
    lyrics: Harold Purcell
    staging: Jack Hulbert
    sets: Clifford Pember
    costumes: Clifford Pember
    choreography: Jack Hulbert
Productions:
    Opened October 3, 1947 for 27 performances
Reviews:
    Catholic World 166:172, Nov 1947
    Nation 165:481, Nov 1, 1947
    New York Theatre Critics' Reviews 1947:320+
    New York Times II, page 3, Sep 28, 1947
                     page 10, Oct 4, 1947
    New Yorker 23:52, Oct 11, 1947
    Newsweek 30:81, Oct 13, 1947

Unfair to Goliath
    book: Ephraim Kishon
    music: Menachem Zur
    lyrics: Herbert Appleman
    staging: Ephraim Kishon and Herbert Appleman
    sets: C. Murawski
    costumes: Pamela Scofield
Productions:

(Off-Broadway) Opened January 25, 1970 for 73 performances
Reviews:
America 122:228, Feb 28, 1970
New York Times page 28, Jan 16, 1970
                 page 27, Jan 26, 1970
                 page 35, Mar 31, 1970
New Yorker 45:76, Feb 7, 1970

The Unsinkable Molly Brown
    book: Richard Morris
    music: Meredith Willson
    lyrics: Meredith Willson
    staging: Dore Schary
    sets: Oliver Smith
    costumes: Miles White
    choreography: Peter Gennaro
Productions:
    Opened November 3, 1960 for 532 performances
Reviews:
    America 104:353-4, Dec 3, 1960
    Christian Century 77:1441-2, Dec 7, 1960
    Dance Magazine 34:33, Dec 1960
    Life 49:141-3+, Dec 5, 1960
    Nation 191:421, Nov 26, 1960
    New York Theatre Critics' Reviews 1960:184+
    New York Times VI, page 41, Oct 23, 1960
                     page 28, Nov 4, 1960
    New Yorker 36:103, Nov 12, 1960
    Newsweek 56:61, Nov 14, 1960
    Saturday Review 43:38, Nov 19, 1960
    Theatre Arts 45:58-9, Jan 1961
    Time 76:84, Nov 14, 1960

Up and Down Broadway
    book: Edgar Smith
    music: Jean Schwartz
    lyrics: William Jerome
    staging: William J. Wilson
Productions:
    Opened July 18, 1910 for 72 performances
Reviews:
    Cosmopolitan 49:612, Oct 1910
    Dramatic Mirror 64:10, Jul 30, 1910
    Theatre Magazine 12:xiv, Sep 1910
                     12:85, Sep 1910

Up Eden
    book: Robert Rosenblum and Howard Schuman
    music: Robert Rosenblum; adapted from Mozart's
                     Cosi fan Tutte
    lyrics: Robert Rosenblum and Howard Schuman
    staging: John Bishop
    sets: Gordon Micunis

508   Up in Central Park

    costumes: Gordon Micunis
    choreography: Patricia Birch
Productions:
    (Off-Broadway) Opened November 27, 1968 for 7 performances
Reviews:
    New York Times page 42, Nov 27, 1968
    New Yorker 44:142, Dec 7, 1968

Up in Central Park
    book: Herbert and Dorothy Fields
    music: Sigmund Romberg
    lyrics: Herbert and Dorothy Fields
    staging: John Kennedy
    sets: Howard Bay
    costumes: Grace Houston and Ernest Schraps
    choreography: Helen Tamiris
Productions:
    Opened January 27, 1945 for 504 performances
    Opened May 19, 1947 for 16 performances
Reviews:
    Catholic World 160:549-50, Mar 1945
    Commonweal 41:448, Feb 16, 1945
    Harper's Bazaar 79:91, Feb 1945
    Life 18:41-2+, Feb 19, 1945
        18:80, Apr 9, 1945
    New York Theatre Critics' Reviews 1945:280+
    New York Times II, page 1, Jan 21, 1945
                    page 17, Jan 29, 1945
                    II, page 4, Feb 4, 1945
                    II, page 1, May 18, 1947
                    page 29, May 20, 1947
                    II, page 1, May 25, 1947
                    page 31, May 27, 1947
    New Yorker 20:40+, Feb 3, 1945
    Newsweek 25:83, Feb 12, 1945
    Theatre Arts 29:205+, Apr 1945
                  29:333, Jan 1945
                  29:651, Nov 1945
                  31:37, Jun 1947
    Time 45:60, Feb 5, 1945

Up She Goes
    book: Frank Craven; adapted from Too Many Cooks
    music: Harry Tierney
    lyrics: Joseph McCarthy
    staging: Frank Craven and Bert French
Productions:
    Opened November 6, 1922 for 256 performances
Reviews:
    New York Clipper 70:20, Nov 15, 1922
    New York Times page 14, Nov 7, 1922

Ups-a-Daisy

The Vagabond King   509

book: Clifford Grey and Robert A. Simon
music: Lewis E. Gensler
lyrics: Clifford Grey
staging: Edgar MacGregor and Earl Lindsey
```
Productions:
Opened October 8, 1928 for 64 performances
Reviews:
Life (New York) 92:21, Nov 2, 1928
New York Times page 34, Oct 9, 1928


- V -


## The Vagabond King
```
book: Brian Hooker and W. H. Post; based on J. H.
               McCarthy's If I Were King
music: Rudolf Friml
lyrics: Brian Hooker and W. H. Post
staging: Max Figman
```
Productions:
Opened September 21, 1925 for 511 performances
Opened June 29, 1943 for 56 performances
Reviews:
Catholic World 157:521-2, Aug 1943
New York Theater Critics' Reviews 1943:311
New York Times page 23, Sep 22, 1925
                VIII, page 2, Jan 17, 1926
                page 20, Jun 2, 1943
                page 24, Jun 30, 1943
Newsweek 22:66, Jul 12, 1943
Theater Magazine 47:44, Dec 1925
                48:13, Jan 1926
Woman's Home Companion 53:141, Feb 1926


## Valmouth
```
book: Sandy Wilson; based on the novel by Ronald
               Firbank
music: Sandy Wilson
lyrics: Sandy Wilson
staging: Vida Hope
sets: Tony Walton
costumes: Tony Walton
choreography: Harry Naughton
```
Productions:
(Off-Broadway) Opened October 6, 1960 for 14 performances
Reviews:
New York Times page 29, Oct 7, 1960
                page 46, Oct 18, 1960
New Yorker 34:168-9, Nov 1, 1958
                36:75-6, Oct 15, 1960


## The Vamp
```
book: John Latouche and Sam Locke, based on a story
```
```

```
                        by John Latouche
     music:             James Mundy
     lyrics:            John Latouche
     staging:           David Alexander
     sets:              Raoul Pene du Bois
     costumes:          Raoul Pene du Bois
     choreography:      Robert Alton
Productions:
     Opened November 10, 1955 for 60 performances
Reviews:
     Catholic World 182:310, Jan 1956
     Commonweal 63:285, Dec 16, 1955
     Look 19:108+, Nov 29, 1955
     New York Theatre Critics' Reviews 1955:210+
     New York Times II, page 1, Nov 6, 1955
                       page 30, Nov 11, 1955
     New Yorker 31:121, Nov 19, 1955
     Newsweek 46:68, Nov 21, 1955
     Saturday Review 38:26, Nov 26, 1955
     Theatre Arts 40:20-1, Jan 1956
     Time 66:110+, Nov 21, 1955
```

The Vanderbilt Revue
```
     assembled by:  Lew Fields
     sketches:      Kenyon Nicholson, Ellis O. Jones, Sig Herzig,
                    E. North
     music and
     lyrics:        Dorothy Fields, Jimmy McHugh, Jacques Fray,
                    Mario Braggiotti, E. Y. Harburg
     staging:       John E. Lonergan, Jack Haskell, Theodore J.
                    Hammerstein
Productions:
     Opened November 5, 1930 for 13 performances
Reviews:
     Bookman 72:409, Dec 1930
     New York Times VIII, page 3, Oct 26, 1930
                       page 22, Nov 6, 1930
```

Vanities   (see Earl Carroll Vanities)

Veils
```
     book:          Irving Kaye Davis
     music:         Donald Heywood
     staging:       Edward Elsner
Productions:
     Opened March 13, 1928 for 4 performances
Reviews:
     Theatre Magazine 47:40-41, May 1928
```

The Velvet Lady
```
     book:          Fred Jackson; adapted by Henry Blossom
     music:         Victor Herbert
     lyrics:        Henry Blossom
```

staging: Edgar MacGregor and Julian Mitchell
Productions:
Opened February 3, 1919 for 136 performances
Reviews:
Dramatic Mirror 80:48, Jan 11, 1919
New York Times page 11, Feb 4, 1919
Theatre Magazine 29:135, Mar 1919
                29:143, Mar 1919

Vera Violetta
    book: Leonard Liebling and Harold Atteridge; from
                      the German of Leo Stein
    music: Edmund Eysler
Productions:
Opened November 20, 1911 for 112 performances
Reviews:
Dramatic Mirror 66:7, Nov 22, 1911
Green Book 7:232-6+, Feb 1912

Very Good, Eddie
    book: Philip Bartholomae and Guy Bolton
    music: Jerome Kern
    lyrics: Schuyler Green
Productions:
Opened December 23, 1915 for 341 performances
Reviews:
Dramatic Mirror 75:8, Jan 1, 1916
Green Book 15:445-6, Mar 1916
New York Dramatic News 62:17, Jan 1, 1916
Opera Magazine 3:30-1, Mar 1916
Theater Magazine 23:64-5, Feb 1916

Very Warm for May
    book: Oscar Hammerstein II
    music: Jerome Kern
    lyrics: Oscar Hammerstein II
    staging: Oscar Hammerstein II and Vincente Minnelli
    sets: Vincente Minnelli
    choreography: Albertina Rasch
Productions:
Opened November 17, 1939 for 59 performances
Reviews:
Catholic World 150:470, Jan 1940
Commonweal 31:137, Dec 1, 1939
New York Times IX, page 2, Nov 12, 1939
                    page 23, Nov 18, 1939
Theatre Arts 24:19, Jan 1940
Time 34:60, Nov 27, 1939

Via Galactica
    book: Christopher Gore and Judith Ross
    music: Galt MacDermot
    lyrics: Christopher Gore

```
    staging:          Peter Hall
    sets:             John Bury
    costumes:         John Bury
Productions:
    Opened November 28, 1972 for 7 performances
Reviews:
    America 127:570, Dec 30, 1972
    New York Theatre Critics' Reviews 1972:174
    New York Times II, page 1, Feb 27, 1972
                     page 42, Sep 26, 1972
                     page 33, Nov 29, 1972
                     page 52, Nov 30, 1972
                     II, page 5, Dec 10, 1972
    New Yorker 48:109, Dec 9, 1972
    Opera News 37:24, Jan 20, 1973
```

Victor Borge's One-Man Show   (see Comedy in Music)

Vintage '60
```
    sketches:         Jack Wilson, Alan Jeffreys, Maxwell Grant
    additional        David Rogers, Mickey Deems, Mark Bucci,
    material:         Sheldon Harnick, David Baker, Phil Green,
                      Tommy Garlock, Fred Ebb, Paul Klein,
                      William Lanteau, Alice Clark, David Morton,
                      Lee Goldsmith, Michael Ross, Barbara Heller,
                      Fay DeWitt, Ronald Axe, William Link, Richard
                      Levinson
    staging:          Jonathan Lucas
    sets:             Fred Voelpel
    costumes:         Fred Voelpel
    choreography:     Jonathan Lucas
Productions:
    Opened September 12, 1960 for 8 performances
Reviews:
    New York Theatre Critics' Reviews 1960:247+
    New York Times page 41, Sep 13, 1960
                    page 44, Sep 21, 1960
    New Yorker 36:97, Sep 24, 1960
    Newsweek 56:109, Sep 26, 1960
    Theatre Arts 44:10, Nov 1960
```

Virginia
```
    book:             Laurence Stallings and Owen Davis
    music:            Arthur Schwartz
    lyrics:           Albert Stillman
    staging:          Leon Leonidoff
    sets:             Lee Simonson
    costumes:         Irene Sharaff
    choreography:     Florence Rogge
Productions:
    Opened September 2, 1937 for 60 performances
Reviews:
    Catholic World 146:86, Oct 1937
```

Commonweal 26:478, Sep 17, 1937
Nation 145:303, Sep 18, 1937
New York Times page 13, Sep 3, 1937
                XI, page 1, Sep 12, 1937
                page 29, Oct 5, 1937
Newsweek 10:25, Sep 13, 1937
Stage 14:34-5, Sep 1937
Theatre Arts 21:836-7, Nov 1937

Viva O'Brien
        book: William K. and Eleanor Wells
        music: Marie Grever
        lyrics: Raymond Leveen
        staging: Robert Milton
        sets: Clark Robinson
        costumes: John N. Booth, Jr.
        choreography: Chester Hale
Productions:
        Opened October 9, 1941 for 20 performances
Reviews:
        New York Theatre Critics' Reviews 1941:271+
        New York Times page 27, Oct 10, 1941

Vogues of 1924
        book: Fred Thompson and Clifford Grey
        music: Herbert Stothart
Productions:
        Opened March 27, 1924 for (92) performances
Reviews:
        American Mercury 2:118-19, May 1924
        New York Times page 14, Mar 28, 1924
                        page 18, Apr 12, 1924
                        page 9, Apr 22, 1924
        Theatre Magazine 39:14-16, Jun 1924

- W -

Wait a Minim!
        book: Leon Gluckman
        staging: Leon Gluckman
        sets: Frank Rembach and Leon Gluckman
        costumes: Heather MacDonald-Rouse
        choreography: Frank Staff and Kendrew Lascelles
Productions:
        Opened March 7, 1966 for 456 performances
Reviews:
        America 114:604, Apr 23, 1966
        Commonweal 84:154, Apr 22, 1966
        Dance Magazine 40:24, May 1966
        Life 61:26, Oct 14, 1966
        National Review 18:1062-5, Oct 18, 1966
        Nation 202:374, Mar 28, 1966

New York Theatre Critics' Reviews 1966:335
New York Times page 43, Mar 8, 1966
             page 46, Mar 9, 1966
             II, page 1, Mar 20, 1966
             page 54, Mar 30, 1967
New Yorker 42:160, Mar 19, 1966
Newsweek 67:98, Mar 21, 1966
Saturday Review 49:45, Mar 26, 1966
Time 87:80, Mar 18, 1966
Vogue 147:145, May 1966

Wake up and Dream
     book: J. H. Turner
     music: Cole Porter
     lyrics: Cole Porter
     staging: Frank Collins
     choreography: Tilly Losch, Jack Buchanan, Max Rivers
Productions:
     Opened December 30, 1929 for 136 performances
Reviews:
     Life (New York) 95:20, Jan 24, 1930
     Nation 130:106, Jan 22, 1930
     New York Times X, page 1, Apr 14, 1929
                    page 14, Dec 31, 1929
                    VIII, page 1, Jan 5, 1930
     Theatre Magazine 51:63, Feb 1930
     Vogue 75:122, Feb 15, 1930

Walk a Little Faster
     sketches: S. J. Perelman and Robert MacGunigle
     music: Vernon Duke
     lyrics: E. Y. Harburg
     staging: E. M. Woolley (Monty Wooley)
     sets: Boris Aronson
     choreography: Albertina Rasch
Productions:
     Opened December 7, 1932 for 119 performances
Reviews:
     New Outlook 161:47, Jan 1933
     New Republic 73:189, Dec 28, 1932
     New York Times page 24, Dec 8, 1932
     Vogue 81:56+, Feb 1, 1933

Walk Down Mah Street!
     music: Norman Curtis; special material by James
                    Taylor, Gabriel Levenson and the members of
                    The Next Stage Theater Company
     lyrics: Patricia Taylor Curtis
     staging: Patricia Taylor Curtis
     sets: Jack Logan
     costumes: Bob Rogers
Productions:
     (Off-Broadway) Opened June 12, 1968 for 135 performances

Reviews:
    New York Times page 54, Jun 13, 1968
    New Yorker 44:59, Jun 22, 1968

Walk with Music
    book: Guy Bolton, Parke Levy, Alan Lipscott, based
                       on Stephen Powys' Three Blind Mice
    music: Hoagy Carmichael
    lyrics: Johnny Mercer
    staging: R. H. Burnside
    sets: Watson Barratt
    costumes: Tom Lee
    choreography: Anton Dolin and Herbert Harper
Productions:
    Opened June 4, 1940 for 55 performances
Reviews:
    Catholic World 151:472, Jul 1940
    New York Theatre Critics' Reviews 1940:290+
    New York Times page 33, Jun 5, 1940

Walking Happy
    book: Roger O. Hirson and Ketti Frings; based on
                       Harold Brighouse's play Hobson's Choice
    music: James Van Heusen
    lyrics: Sammy Cahn
    staging: Cy Feuer
    sets: Robert Randolph
    costumes: Robert Fletcher
    choreography: Danny Daniels
Productions:
    Opened November 26, 1966 for 161 performances
Reviews:
    America 116:160, Jan 28, 1967
    Dance Magazine 41:76-7, Jan 1967
    Nation 204:29, Jan 2, 1967
    New York Theatre Critics' Reviews 1966:225
    New York Times page 47, Nov 28, 1966
                    II, page 3, Dec 11, 1966
                    II, page 3, Dec 18, 1966
                       page 35, Feb 7, 1967
    Newsweek 68:100, Dec 12, 1966
    Time 88:60, Dec 9, 1966

The Wall Street Girl
    book: Margaret Mayo and Edgar Selwyn
    music: Karl Hoschna
    lyrics: Hapgood Burt
    staging: Charles Winninger and Gus Sohlke
Productions:
    Opened April 15, 1912 for 56 performances
Reviews:
    Blue Book 14:692-5, Feb 1912
    Dramatic Mirror 67:7, Apr 17, 1912

67:7, Apr 24, 1912
Green Book 8:133, Jul 1912
Munsey 47:468, Jun 1912
New York Dramatic News 55:19, Apr 20, 1912
Red Book 19:766-8, Aug 1912
Theatre Magazine 15:xvi, May 1912

Wanted

book:	David Epstein
music:	Al Carmines
lyrics:	Al Carmines
staging:	Lawrence Kornfeld
sets:	Paul Zalon
costumes:	Linda Giese

Productions:
   (Off-Broadway) Opened January 19, 1972 for 79 performances
   (Off-Broadway) Opened Season of 1971-72 (Judson Poets'
      Theatre)
Reviews:
   New York Theatre Critics' Reviews 1972:339
   New York Times page 52, Jan 20, 1972
                  II, page 9, Jan 30, 1972
   New Yorker 47:74, Jan 29, 1972
   Newsweek 79:83, Jan 31, 1972

Wars of the World

conceived:	Arthur Voegtlin
music:	Manuel Klein
lyrics:	Manuel Klein
dialogue:	John P. Wilson
staging:	William J. Wilson

Productions:
   Opened September 5, 1914 for 229 performances
Reviews:
   Green Book 12:1065, Dec 1914
   Munsey 53:356, Nov 1914
   New York Dramatic News 60:33, Jan 2, 1915
   Theatre Magazine 20:151, Oct 1914
                     20:193, Oct 1914

Watch Your Step

book:	Harry B. Smith
music:	Irving Berlin
lyrics:	Irving Berlin
staging:	R. H. Burnside

Productions:
   Opened December 8, 1914 for 175 performances
Reviews:
   Dramatic Mirror 72:8, Dec 16, 1914
   Green Book 13:301, Feb 1915
             13:575-6, Mar 1915
   Munsey 55:99, Jun 1915
   New Republic 1:27, Jan 9, 1915

New York Dramatic News 60:18, Dec 19, 1914
New York Times page 13, Dec 1, 1914
Stage 15:41, Aug 1938
Theatre Magazine 21:9, Jan 1915
                21:67, Feb 1915
                22:78, Aug 1915

The Water Carrier
    book: Jacob Prayer
    music: Alexander Olshanetsky
Productions:
    (Off-Broadway) Opened December 24, 1936
No Reviews.

Waters, Ethel   (see At Home with Ethel Waters)

Wayburn, Ned   (see Ned Wayburn)

We Live and Laugh
    material: Alfred Kreymborg, J. L. Peretz and others
    staging: Judah Bleich and Zvee Scooler
Productions:
    Opened May 8, 1936 (Federal Theatre Project)
Reviews:
    New York Times page 9, May 10, 1936

The Wedding Night   (see Oh, I Say!)

Weill, Kurt   (see Kurt Weill)

We're Civilized?
    book: Alfred Aiken
    music: Ray Haney
    lyrics: Alfred Aiken
    staging: Martin B. Cohen
    sets: Jack H. Cornwell
    costumes: Sonia Lowenstein
    choreography: Bhaskar
Productions:
    (Off-Broadway) Opened November 8, 1962 for 22 performances
Reviews:
    New York Times page 30, Nov 9, 1962
    New Yorker 38:148, Nov 17, 1962

West Side Story
    book: Arthur Laurents
    music: Leonard Bernstein
    lyrics: Stephen Sondheim
    staging: Jerome Robbins
    costumes: Irene Sharaff
    choreography: Jerome Robbins and Peter Gennaro
Productions:
    Opened September 26, 1957 for 732 performances

Opened April 27, 1960 for 249 performances
Opened April 8, 1964 for 31 performances
Opened June 24, 1968 for 89 performances
Reviews:
America 98:90, Oct 19, 1957
          119:54, Jul 20, 1968
Catholic World 186:224-5, Dec 1957
Christian Century 75:561-2, May 7, 1958
Dance Magazine 31:14-19, Aug 1957
                 31:12-13, Nov 1957
                 39:35-8, Apr 1965
                 39:40-1, Nov 1965
                 42:18, Aug 1968
Good Housekeeping 145:40, Sep 1957
Life 43:103-4+, Sep 16, 1957
Musical America 77:11, Nov 1, 1957
Nation 185:250-1, Oct 12, 1957
New Republic 137:21, Sep 9, 1957
New York Theatre Critics' Reviews 1957:252+
                                   1960:275+
New York Times VI, page 28, Aug 25, 1957
                VI, page 60, Sep 8, 1957
                page 14, Sep 27, 1957
                II, page 1, Oct 6, 1957
                II, page 9, Oct 13, 1957
                II, page 15, Oct 27, 1957
                page 31, Apr 28, 1960
                II, page 1, May 8, 1960
                II, page 5, Dec 11, 1960
                page 24, Apr 9, 1964
                page 50, Nov 18, 1964
                page 12, Dec 31, 1964
                page 32, Jun 25, 1968
                II, page 20, Sep 1, 1968
                II, page 5, Sep 8, 1968
New York Times Magazine pages 60-1, Sep 8, 1957
New Yorker 33:64, Oct 5, 1957
Newsweek 50:102, Oct 7, 1957
          52:28, Dec 29, 1958
Reporter 17:38, Nov 14, 1957
Saturday Review 40:22, Oct 5, 1957
                 51:41+, Jul 13, 1968
Theatre Arts 41:22-3, Sep 1957
              41:16-17, Dec 1957
Time 70:48-9, Oct 7, 1957

Wet Paint
     staging: Michael Ross
     sets: David Moon
     costumes: Mostoller
     choreography: Rudy Tronto
Productions:
     (Off-Broadway) Opened April 12, 1965 for 16 performances

Reviews:
    New York Times page 33, Apr 13, 1965
    New Yorker 41:85-6, Apr 24, 1965

What a Killing
        book: Fred Hebert
        music: George Harwell
        lyrics: George Harwell and Joan Anania
Productions:
    (Off-Broadway) Opened Season of 1960-61
Reviews:
    New York Times page 41, Mar 28, 1961

What Makes Sammy Run?
        book: Budd and Stuart Schulberg, based on the novel
                           by Budd Schulberg
        music: Ervin Drake
        lyrics: Ervin Drake
        staging: Abe Burrows
        sets: Herbert Senn and Helene Pons
        costumes: Noel Taylor
        choreography: Matt Mattox
Productions:
    Opened February 27, 1964 for 540 performances
Reviews:
    America 110:465, Mar 28, 1964
    Life 57:30, Sep 25, 1964
    New York Theatre Critics' Reviews 1964:328+
    New York Times II, page 3, Feb 9, 1964
                    page 19, Feb 28, 1964
    Saturday Review 47:34, Apr 11, 1964
    Time 83:50, Mar 6, 1964

What's in a Name?
        book: John Murray Anderson, Anna Wynne O'Ryan
                           and Jack Yellen
        music: Milton Ager
        lyrics: John Murray Anderson, Anna Wynne O'Ryan
                           and Jack Yellen
Productions:
    Opened March 19, 1920 for 87 performances
Reviews:
    Dramatic Mirror 82:576, Mar 27, 1920
    Life (New York) 75:664, Apr 8, 1920
    New York Clipper 68:14, Mar 24, 1920
    New York Times page 14, Mar 20, 1920
    Theatre Magazine 31:405, May 1920
                     31:460, May 1920
                     32:375, Dec 1920

What's Up
        book: Alan Jay Lerner and Arthur Pierson
        music: Frederick Loewe

lyrics: Alan Jay Lerner and Arthur Pierson
staging: George Balanchine and Robert H. Gordon
sets: Boris Aronson
costumes: Grace Houston
Productions:
Opened November 11, 1943 for 63 performances
Reviews:
Catholic World 158:395, Jan 1944
Commonweal 39:144, Nov 26, 1943
New York Theatre Critics' Reviews 1943:229+
New York Times page 24, Nov 12, 1943
               II, page 1, Nov 21, 1943

When Claudia Smiles
     book: Anne Caldwell; based on a play by Leo Ditrich-
                      stein
     songs: Anne Caldwell
Productions:
Opened February 2, 1914 for 56 performances
Reviews:
Dramatic Mirror 71:2, Feb 18, 1914
               71:7, Dec 4, 1914
Life (New York) 63:318-19, Feb 19, 1914
Munsey Magazine 51:584-5, Apr 1914
New York Times page 9, Feb 4, 1914
Theatre Magazine 19:115, Mar 1914

When Dreams Come True
     book: Philip Bartholomae
     music: Silvio Hein
     lyrics: Philip Bartholomae
     staging: Frank Smithson and Philip Bartholomae
Productions:
Opened August 18, 1913 for 64 performances
Reviews:
Blue Book 17:441-4, Jul 1913
Dramatic Mirror 70:6, Aug 20, 1913
               70:2, Oct 1, 1913
Green Book 10:8-9, Jul 1913
               10:120, Jul 1913
Munsey Magazine 50:94-5, Oct 1913
New York Dramatic News 58:21-2, Aug 23, 1913
New York Times page 9, Aug 19, 1913
Theatre Magazine 18:xi, Aug 1913
               18:101, Sep 1913
               18:xiii-xiv, Oct 1913
               18:117, Oct 1913

When Sweet Sixteen
     book: George V. Hobart
     music: Victor Herbert
     lyrics: George V. Hobart
     staging: R. H. Burnside

Productions:
    Opened September 14, 1911 for 12 performances
Reviews:
    Blue Book 13:19-21, May 1911
    Dramatic Mirror 66:10, Sep 20, 1911
    Green Book Album 5:928, May 1911
    New York Times page 9, Sep 15, 1911

When the Owl Screams
    music: Tom O'Horgan
    staging: Paul Sills
    sets: Ralph Alswang
Productions:
    (Off-Broadway) Opened September 12, 1963 for 141 per-
    formances
No Reviews.

When You Smile
    book: Tom Johnstone and Jack Alicoate
    music: Tom Johnstone
    lyrics: Phil Cook
    staging: Oscar Eagle
Productions:
    Opened October 5, 1925 for 49 performances
Reviews:
    New York Times page 31, Oct 6, 1925

Where's Charley?
    book: George Abbott, based on Brandon Thomas's
                    Charley's Aunt
    music: Frank Loesser
    lyrics: Frank Loesser
    staging: George Abbott
    sets: David Ffolkes
    costumes: David Ffolkes
    choreography: George Balanchine and Fred Danielli
Productions:
    Opened October 11, 1948 for 792 performances
    Opened January 29, 1951 for 48 performances
    Opened May 25, 1966 for 15 performances
Reviews:
    Catholic World 168:242, Dec 1948
    Collier's 122:26-7, Dec 11, 1948
    Commonweal 49:94, Nov 5, 1948
    Dance Magazine 40:27, Jul 1966
    Life 25:85-8, Nov 8, 1949
        60:18, Jun 17, 1966
    Nation 167:503, Oct 30, 1948
    New Republic 119:28, Nov 1, 1948
    New York Theatre Critics' Reviews 1948:197+
    New York Times II, page 1, Oct 10, 1948
                    page 33, Oct 12, 1948
                    II, page 1, Oct 24, 1948

II, page 2, Apr 3, 1949
II, page 3, Nov 20, 1949
II, page 1, Aug 20, 1950
page 57, May 26, 1966
New Yorker 24:52, Oct 23, 1948
Newsweek 32:87, Oct 25, 1948
Saturday Review 31:26-7, Nov 6, 1948
Theatre Arts 33:17, Jan 1949
Time 52:63, Oct 25, 1948
Vogue 112:154, Dec 1948

The Whirl of New York
  book: Hugh Morton and Edgar Smith
  music: Gustav Kerker, Al Goodman and Lew Pollack
  lyrics: Hugh Morton and Edgar Smith
  staging: Lew Morton
Productions:
Opened June 13, 1921 for (3) performances
Reviews:
  New York Clipper 69:20, Jun 22, 1921
  New York Times page 18, Jun 14, 1921
  Theatre Magazine 34:126, Aug 1921
                   34:169, Aug 1921

Whirl of Society
  book: Harrison Rhodes
  music: Louis A. Hirsch
  lyrics: Harold Atteridge
  staging: J. C. Huffman
Productions:
Opened March 5, 1912 for 136 performances
Reviews:
  Blue Book 15:697-700, Aug 1912
  New York Dramatic News 55:13, Mar 16, 1912

The Whirl of the World
  dialogue: Harold Atteridge
  music: Sigmund Romberg
  lyrics: Harold Atteridge
  staging: William J. Wilson
Productions:
Opened January 10, 1914 for 161 performances
Reviews:
  Dramatic Mirror 71:22, Jan 14, 1914
  New York Dramatic News 60:4, Nov 7, 1914
  New York Times II, page 15, Jan 11, 1914
  Theatre Magazine 19:100, Feb 1914

Whispers on the Wind
  book: John B. Kuntz
  music: Lor Crane
  lyrics: John B. Kuntz
  staging: Burt Brinckerhoff

White, George

```
    sets:              David F. Segal
    costumes:          Joseph G. Aulisi
Productions:
    (Off-Broadway) Opened June 3, 1970 for 15 performances
Reviews:
    New York Times page 50, Jun 4, 1970
    New Yorker 46:90+, Jun 13, 1970
```

White, George   (see George White)

White Eagle
```
    book:              Brian Hooker and W. H. Post, based on Edwin
                       Milton Royle's The Squaw Man
    music:             Rudolf Friml
    lyrics:            Brian Hooker and W. H. Post
    staging:           Richard Boleslavsky
Productions:
    Opened December 26, 1927 for 48 performances
Reviews:
    New York Times page 24, Dec 27, 1927
                       VIII, page 4, Jan 1, 1928
    Theatre Magazine 47:62, Mar 1928
```

White Horse Inn
```
    book:              Hans Mueller, suggested by Oskar Blumenthal
                       and G. Kandelburg, adapted by David Freedman
    music:             Ralph Benatsky
    lyrics:            Irving Caesar
    staging:           Erick Charell
    sets:              Ernst Stern
    costumes:          Irene Sharaff
    choreography:      Max Rivers
Productions:
    Opened October 1, 1936 for 223 performances
Reviews:
    Catholic World 144:215, Nov 1936
    Collier's 98:64-6, Nov 7, 1936
    Commonweal 34:590, Oct 16, 1936
    Literary Digest 122:31-2, Oct 17, 1936
    New Republic 88:314, Oct 21, 1936
    New York Times X, page 1, Aug 16, 1936
                       page 28, Oct 2, 1936
                       X, page 2, Oct 11, 1936
    Newsweek 8:28-9, Oct 10, 1936
    Theatre Arts 20:848-9, Nov 1936
    Time 28:53, Oct 12, 1936
```

White Lights
```
    book:              Paul Gerard Smith and Leo Donnelly
    music:             J. Fred Coots
    lyrics:            Al Dubin and Dolf Singer
Productions:
    Opened October 11, 1927 for 31 performances
```

Reviews:
    New York Times page 30, Oct 12, 1927
    Theatre Magazine 46:43, Dec 1927

White Lilacs
    book: Harry B. Smith, based on the life of Frederic
                       Chopin from the German original by Sigurd
                       Johannsen
    music: Karl Hajos, based on melodies by Chopin
    lyrics: Harry B. Smith
    staging: J. J. Shubert and George Marion
Productions:
    Opened September 10, 1928 for 136 performances
Reviews:
    New York Times page 31, Sep 11, 1928
                    X, page 5, Oct 14, 1928
                    page 25, Oct 22, 1928
    Theatre Magazine 48:80, Nov 1928

White Nights
    book: Paul Zakrzewski; based on the short story by
                       Dostoyevsky
    music: Wally Harper
    lyrics: Paul Zakrzewski
    staging: Paul Zakrzewski
Productions:
    (Off-Off-Broadway) Opened February 6, 1974 (Theatre of the
    Riverside Church)
No Reviews.

Who Cares
    sketches: Edward Clarke Lilley, Bertrand Robinson,
                       Kenneth Webb, John Cantwell
    music: Percy Wenrich
    lyrics: Harry Clarke
    staging: George Vivian, Edward Clarke Lilley, William
                       Holbrook
Productions:
    Opened July 8, 1930 for 32 performances
Reviews:
    Life (New York) 96:16, Aug 1, 1930
    New York Times page 27, Jul 9, 1930
    Theatre Magazine 52:26, Aug 1930

Who Did It?
    book: Stephen Gardner Champlin
Productions:
    Opened June 9, 1919 for 8 performances
Reviews:
    New York Times page 13, Jun 10, 1919
                    page 22, Jun 18, 1919
    Theatre Magazine 30:81, Aug 1919

Whoop-Up
book: Cy Feuer, Ernest H. Martin, and Dan Cushman,
                   based on "Stay Away Joe" by Dan Cushman
music: Moose Charlap
lyrics: Norman Gimbel
staging: Cy Feuer
sets: Jo Mielziner
costumes: Anna Hill Johnstone
choreography: Onna White
Productions:
Opened December 22, 1958 for 56 performances
Reviews:
America 100:558-9, Feb 7, 1959
Catholic World 188:506, Mar 1959
Dance Magazine 33:18, Feb 1959
New York Theatre Critics' Reviews 1958:161+
New York Times page 2, Dec 23, 1958
                   II, page 1, Feb 8, 1958
New Yorker 34:50+, Jan 3, 1959
Saturday Review 42:67, Jan 10, 1959
Theatre Arts 43:9, Mar 1959

Whoopee
book: William Anthony McGuire, based on Owen
                   Davis's The Nervous Wreck
music: Walter Donaldson
lyrics: Gus Kahn
staging: William Anthony McGuire and Seymour Felix
Productions:
Opened December 4, 1928 for 379 performances
Reviews:
New York Times X, page 2, Nov 11, 1928
                 X, page 4, Dec 9, 1928
                 page 18, Sep 23, 1929
Outlook 152:434, Jul 10, 1929
Theatre Magazine 49:50, Feb 1929

Whores, Wars, and Tin Pan Alley
songs: Kurt Weill
Productions:
(Off-Broadway) Opened June 16, 1969 for 72 performances
Reviews:
New York Times page 37, Jun 17, 1969

Who's Who
assembled by: Leonard Sillman
sketches: Leonard Sillman and Everett Marcy
music: Baldwin Bergerson, James Shelton, Irving
                   Graham, Paul McGrane
lyrics: June Sillman, Irvin Graham, James Shelton
staging: Leonard Sillman
sets: Mercedes
costumes: Billy Livingston

Productions:
   Opened March 1, 1938 for 23 performances
Reviews:
   New York Times page 16, Mar 2, 1938
                   page 24, Mar 20, 1938

Who's Who, Baby?
   book: Gerald Frank; based on Guy Bolton and P. G.
                       Wodehouse's Who's Who?
   music: Johnny Brandon
   lyrics: Johnny Brandon
   staging: Marvin Gordon
   sets: Alan Kimmel
   costumes: Alan Kimmel
   choreography: Marvin Gordon
Productions:
   (Off-Broadway) Opened January 29, 1968 for 16 performances
Reviews:
   New York Times page 28, Jan 26, 1968
                   page 36, Jan 30, 1968
                   page 38, Feb 10, 1968
   New Yorker 43:90-1, Feb 10, 1968

Why Do I Deserve This?
   sketches: Kay and Lore Lorentz, Eckart Hachfeld and
                       Martin Morlock
   music: Werner Kruse, Emil Schuchardt and Fritz
                       Maldener
   lyrics: Wolfgang Franke and Mischa Leinek
   staging: Kay Lorentz
   sets: Fritz Butz
   costumes: Fritz Butz
Productions:
   (Off-Broadway) Opened January 18, 1966 for 12 performances
Reviews:
   New York Times page 31, Jan 19, 1966

The Wife Hunters
   book: Edgar Allan Woolf
   music: Anatol Friedland and Malvin Franklin
   lyrics: David Kempner
   staging: Ned Wayburn
Productions:
   Opened November 2, 1911 for 36 performances
Reviews:
   Dramatic Mirror 66:7, Nov 8, 1911
                   66:4, Nov 29, 1911
   Green Book 7:19-22+, Jan 1912
   Theatre Magazine 14:xiii, Dec 1911
                   14:187, Dec 1911

Wild and Wonderful
   book: Phil Phillips

```
    music and       Bob Goodman; from an original work by Bob
    lyrics:         Brotherton and Bob Miller
    staging:        Burry Fredrik
    sets:           Stephen Hendrickson
    costumes:       Frank Thompson
    choreography:   Ronn Forella
Productions:
    Opened December 7, 1971 for one performance
Reviews:
    New York Theatre Critics' Reviews 1971:170
    New York Times page 71, Dec 8, 1971
                    page 64, Dec 9, 1971
```

The Wild Rose
```
    book:           Otto Harbach and Oscar Hammerstein II
    music:          Rudolf Friml
    lyrics:         Otto Harbach and Oscar Hammerstein II
    staging:        William J. Wilson
Productions:
    Opened October 20, 1926 for 61 performances
Reviews:
    New York Times page 23, Oct 21, 1926
    Theatre Magazine 45:16, Jan 1927
```

The Wildcat (1921)
```
    book:           Manuel Penella
    staging:        Manuel Penella
Productions:
    Opened November 26, 1921 for 74 performances
Reviews:
    Dramatic Mirror 84:809, Dec 3, 1921
    New York Clipper 69:20, Nov 30, 1921
    New York Times page 16, Nov 28, 1921
    Theatre Magazine 35:99, Feb 1922
```

Wildcat (1960)
```
    book:           N. Richard Nash
    music:          Cy Coleman
    lyrics:         Carolyn Leigh
    staging:        Michael Kidd
    sets:           Peter Larkin
    costumes:       Alvin Colt
    choreography:   Michael Kidd
Productions:
    Opened December 16, 1960 for 171 performances
Reviews:
    America 104:546, Jan 21, 1961
    Coronet 49:16, Apr 1961
    Nation 191:531, Dec 31, 1960
    New York Theatre Critics' Reviews 1960:134+
    New York Times page 20, Dec 17, 1960
                    page 39, Feb 7, 1961
    New Yorker 36:38, Dec 24, 1960
```

Newsweek 56:53, Dec 26, 1960
Saturday Review 43:28, Dec 31, 1960
Theatre Arts 45:9-10, Feb 1961

Wildflower
    book: Otto Harbach and Oscar Hammerstein II
    music: Herbert Stothart and Vincent Youmans
    lyrics: Otto Harbach and Oscar Hammerstein II
    staging: Oscar Eagle
    choreography: David Bennett
Productions:
Opened February 7, 1923 for 477 performances
Reviews:
    Life (New York) 81:18, Mar 1, 1923
    New York Clipper 71:14, Feb 14, 1923
    New York Times page 17, Feb 8, 1923
    Theatre Magazine 38:16, Aug 1923

Will the Mail Train Run Tonight
    book: Malcolm L. La Prade; based on a play by Hugh
                     Nevill
    music: Alyn Hein
    lyrics: Malcolm L. La Prade
    staging: Jon Baisch
    sets: Gene Czernicki
    costumes: Joe Crosby
    choreography: Lynne Fippinger
Productions:
(Off-Broadway) Opened January 9, 1964 for 8 performances
Reviews:
New York Times page 18, Jan 10, 1964

Willie the Weeper   (see Ballet Ballads)

The Wings of the Dove
    book: Ethan Ayer, based on Henry James' novel
    music: Douglas Moore
    lyrics: Ethan Ayer
    staging: Christopher West
    sets: Donald Oenslager
    costumes: Patton Campbell
    choreography: Robert Joffrey
Productions:
(Off-Broadway) Opened October 12, 1961 for 3 performances
No Reviews.

A Winsome Widow
    book: Raymond Hubbell; based on A Trip to Chinatown
                     by Charles H. Hoyt
    music: Raymond Hubbell
    lyrics: Raymond Hubbell
Productions:
Opened April 11, 1912 for 172 performances

Reviews:
    Blue Book 15:452-7, Jul 1912
    Dramatic Mirror 67:6, Apr 17, 1912
                67:2, May 1, 1912
                67:2, May 8, 1912
                67:4, Jun 19, 1912
    Green Book 8:4-7+, Jul 1912
             8:136, Jul 1912
             8:326-7, Aug 1912
    Leslie's Weekly 115:760, Jul 4, 1912
    Munsey Magazine 47:467-8, Jun 1912
    New York Dramatic News 55:18, Apr 20, 1918
    Red Book 19:574-6, Jul 1912
    Theatre Magazine 15:140, May 1912

Wish You Were Here
    book: Arthur Kober and Joshua Logan, based on
                    Arthur Kober's play Having Wonderful Time
    music: Harold Rome
    lyrics: Harold Rome
    staging: Joshua Logan
    sets: Jo Mielziner
    costumes: Robert Mackintosh
    choreography: Joshua Logan
Productions:
    Opened June 25, 1952 for 598 performances
Reviews:
    Catholic World 175:388, Aug 1952
    Commonweal 56:366-7, Jul 18, 1952
    Life 33:79-80, Jul 21, 1952
    Nation 175:18, Jul 5, 1952
    New York Theatre Critics' Reviews 1952:266+
    New York Times VI, page 22, Jun 15, 1952
                    II, page 1, Jun 22, 1952
                    page 26, Jun 26, 1952
                    II, page 1, Aug 31, 1952
                    II, page 1, Feb 22, 1953
                    II, page 1, Jul 12, 1953
                    page 83, Oct 11, 1953
                    II, page 3, Oct 18, 1953
    New Yorker 28:45, Jul 5, 1952
                28:56, Dec 20, 1952
    Newsweek 40:70, Jul 7, 1952
    Saturday Review 35:24, Jul 12, 1952
                   35:5, Aug 16, 1952
    Theatre Arts 36:14, Jul 1952
               36:28-9, Aug 1952
    Time 60:60, Jul 7, 1952

The Wonder Bar
    book: Irving Caesar and Aben Kandel; adapted from
                    the German of Geza Herczeg and Karl Farkas
    music: Robert Katscher

staging: William Mollison
Productions:
   Opened March 17, 1931 for 76 performances
Reviews:
   Bookman 73:408-9, Jun 1931
   Drama 21:6+, May 1931
   Life (New York) 97:20, Apr 17, 1931
   New York Times VIII, page 3, Mar 8, 1931
                    VIII, page 1, Mar 22, 1931
                    page 35, Jun 2, 1931
   Theatre Arts 15:366-7+, May 1931
   Vanity Fair 36:52, Jun 1931

Wonderful Town
   book: Joseph Fields and Jerome Chodorov, based on
                    the play My Sister Eileen by Joseph Fields and
                    Jerome Chodorov and the stories of Ruth McKen-
                    ney
   music: Leonard Bernstein
   lyrics: Betty Comden and Adolph Green
   staging: George Abbott
   sets: Raoul Pene du Bois
   costumes: Raoul Pene du Bois
   choreography: Donald Saddler
Productions:
   Opened February 25, 1953 for 559 performances
   Opened March 5, 1958 for 16 performances
   Opened February 13, 1963 for 16 performances
   Opened May 17, 1967 for 23 performances
Reviews:
   America 88:661, Mar 14, 1953
   Catholic World 177:67-8, Apr 1953
   Commonweal 57:603-4, Mar 20, 1953
   Dance Magazine 32:15, Apr 1958
                  41:70-1, Jul 1967
   Life 34:134-5, Mar 16, 1953
   Look 17:84-5, Mar 10, 1953
   Nation 176:232, Mar 14, 1953
   New York Theatre Critics' Reviews 1953:344+
   New York Times II, page 1, Feb 22, 1953
                    page 22, Feb 26, 1953
                    II, page 1, Mar 8, 1953
                    II, page 1, Apr 5, 1953
                    II, page 7, May 10, 1953
                    II, page 1, May 9, 1954
                    page 33, May 17, 1955
                    page 32, Mar 6, 1958
                    page 10, Feb 15, 1963
                    page 56, May 18, 1967
   New Yorker 29:59, Mar 7, 1953
   Newsweek 41:59, Mar 9, 1953
   Saturday Review 36:36, Mar 14, 1953
                   36:6, May 9, 1953

Theatre Arts 37:16-17, May 1953
              37:18-21, Aug 1953
    Time 61:96+, Mar 9, 1953
         61:40-2+, Mar 30, 1953

Woof, Woof
    book: Estelle Hunt, Sam Summers, Cyrus Wood
    music: Edward Pola and Eddie Brandt
    lyrics: Edward Pola and Eddie Brandt
    staging: Leonide Massine
Productions:
    Opened December 25, 1929 for 45 performances
Reviews:
    New York Times page 20, Dec 26, 1929
    Theatre Magazine 51:63, Feb 1930

Words and Music (1917)
    by: E. R. Goetz and R. Hitchcock
    staging: Leon Errol
Productions:
    Opened December 24, 1917 for 24 performances
Reviews:
    Dramatic Mirror 78:5, Jan 5, 1918
    New York Times page 13, Dec 25, 1917
    Theatre Magazine 27:88, Feb 1918

Words and Music (1974)
    words: Sammy Cahn
    music: various composers
    lyrics: Sammy Cahn
    staging: Jerry Adler
    sets: Robert Randolph
Productions:
    Opened April 16, 1974 for 128 performances
Reviews:
    America 130:344, May 4, 1974
    Nation 218:666-7, May 25, 1974
    New York Theatre Critics' Reviews 1974:307
    New York Times page 35, Apr 17, 1974
                   II, page 1, Apr 28, 1974
                   page 20, Aug 1, 1974
    New Yorker 50:63, Apr 29, 1974

The World of Charles Aznavour
    music: Charles Aznavour
    lyrics: Charles Aznavour
    sets: Ralph Alswang
Productions:
    Opened October 14, 1965 for 29 performances
Reviews:
    New York Times page 49, Oct 15, 1965
    Time 86:102+, Oct 22, 1965

The World of Kurt Weill in Song
    written: Will Holt
    music: Kurt Weill
    staging: Will Holt
Productions:
    (Off-Broadway) Opened June 6, 1963 for 245 performances
Reviews:
    Saturday Review 48:38, Jan 23, 1965

A World of Pleasure
    book: Harold Atteridge
    music: Sigmund Romberg
    lyrics: Harold Atteridge
    staging: J. C. Huffman
    choreography: Jack Mason and Theodore Kosloff
Productions:
    Opened October 14, 1915 for 116 performances
Reviews:
    Dramatic Mirror 74:8, Oct 23, 1915
                   74:2, Nov 13, 1915
    Green Book 15:70-72, Jan 1916
    Life (New York) 66:808, Oct 28, 1915
    New York Dramatic News 61:17, Oct 23, 1915
    Theatre Magazine 22:282, Dec 1915

Worlds of Oscar Brown, Jr.
    created: Oscar Brown, Jr.
    performed: Oscar Brown, Jr.
Productions:
    (Off-Broadway) Opened February 18, 1965 for 55 performances
Reviews:
    New York Times page 25, Feb 19, 1965

The Would-Be Gentleman
    book: Bobby Clark; adapted from Molière's Le
                   Bourgeois Gentilhomme
    music: Jerome Moross; adapted from the original by
                   Lully
    staged: John Kennedy
    sets: Howard Bay
    costumes: Irene Sharaff
Productions:
    Opened January 9, 1946 for 77 performances
Reviews:
    Nation 162:108, Jan 26, 1946
    New York Theatre Critics' Reviews 1946:490
    New York Times II, page 1, Jan 6, 1946
                   page 29, Jan 10, 1946
                   page 18, Jan 18, 1946
                   II, page 1, Jan 20, 1946
    Newsweek 27:87, Jan 21, 1946
    Saturday Review 29:28-30, Feb 9, 1946
    Theatre Arts 30:137+, Mar 1946

Time 47:79, Jan 21, 1946
Vogue 107:100, Feb 15, 1946

Wynn, Ed   (see Ed Wynn)

- Y -

The Yankee Girl
    book: George V. Hobart
    music: Silvio Hein
    lyrics: George V. Hobart
    staging: Ned Wayburn
Productions:
Opened February 10, 1910 for 92 performances
Reviews:
Theatre Magazine 11:xi, Mar 1910

The Yankee Princess
    book: William Le Baron; adapted from Die Bajadere by
                  Julius Brammer and Alfred Grunwald
    music: Emmerich Kalman
    lyrics: B. G. De Sylva
    staging: Fred G. Latham and Julian Mitchell
Productions:
Opened October 2, 1922 for 80 performances
Reviews:
New York Clipper 70:20, Oct 11, 1922
New York Times page 22, Oct 3, 1922
Theatre Magazine 36:377, Dec 1922

Yeah Man
    book: Leigh Whipper and Billy Mills
    music: Al Wilson, Charles Weinberg, Ken Macomber
    lyrics: Al Wilson, Charles Weinberg, Ken Macomber
    staging: Walter Campbell
Productions:
Opened May 26, 1932 for 4 performances
Reviews:
New York Times page 27, May 27, 1932

The Yearling
    book: Herbert Martin and Lore Noto; based on the
                  novel by Marjorie Kinnan Rawlings
    music: Michael Leonard
    lyrics: Herbert Martin
    staging: Lloyd Richards
    sets: Ed Wittstein
    costumes: Ed Wittstein
    choreography: Ralph Beaumont
Productions:
Opened December 10, 1965 for 3 performances
Reviews:

New York Theatre Critics' Reviews 1965:221
New York Times page 19, Aug 27, 1965
              page 25, Dec 11, 1965
              page 55, Dec 13, 1965

Yes, Yes, Yvette
    book: James Montgomery and William Cary Duncan;
                   based on a story by Frederick S. Isham
    music: Philip Charig and Ben Jerome
    lyrics: Irving Caesar
    staging: H. H. Freeze
Productions:
Opened October 3, 1927 for 40 performances
Reviews:
    New York Times page 32, Oct 4, 1927
                  page 25, May 14, 1927

Yip Yip Yaphank
    words: Irving Berlin
    music: Irving Berlin
Productions:
Opened August 19, 1918 for 32 performances
Reviews:
    Dramatic Mirror 79:301, Aug 31, 1918
    Green Book 19:398-9+, Mar 1918
    New York Times page 7, Jul 27, 1918
                  page 7, Aug 20, 1918
                  page 12, Sep 11, 1918
    Stage 15:40, Aug 1938
    Theatre Magazine 28:222-3, Oct 1918

Yokel Boy
    book: Lew Brown and Charles Tobias
    music: Sam Stept
    lyrics: Lew Brown and Charles Tobias
    staging: Lew Brown
    sets: Walter Jagemann
    costumes: Frances Feist and Veronica
    choreography: Gene Snyder
Productions:
Opened July 6, 1939 for 208 performances
Reviews:
    New York Theatre Critics' Reviews 1940:481+
    New York Times page 12, Jul 12, 1939
                  page 16, Aug 17, 1939
    Time 34:66, Jul 17, 1939

You Never Know
    book: Rowland Leigh, adapted from the original by
                   Robert Katscher, Siegfried Geyer, Karl Farkas
    music: Cole Porter
    lyrics: Cole Porter
    staging: Rowland Leigh

        sets: Watson Barratt and Albert Johnson
        choreography: Robert Alton
Productions:
    Opened September 21, 1938 for 78 performances
    (Off-Broadway) Season of 1969-70 (Stage Directors and Chore-
        ographers Workshop)
    (Off-Broadway) Opened March 12, 1973 for 8 performances
Reviews:
    Catholic World 148:215, Nov 1938
    New York Times page 16, Mar 4, 1938
                     page 26, Sep 22, 1938
                     page 31, Mar 13, 1973
    Theatre Arts 22:783, Nov 1938
    Time 31:38, Apr 11, 1938

You Said It
        book: Jack Yellen and Sid Silvers
        music: Harold Arlen
        lyrics: Jack Yellen
        staging: John Harwood and Danny Dare
Productions:
    Opened January 29, 1931 for 192 performances
Reviews:
    Life (New York) 97:18, Feb 6, 1931
    New York Times page 21, Jan 20, 1931

You'll See Stars
        book: Herman Timberg
        music: Leo Edwards
        lyrics: Herman Timberg
        staging: Herman Timberg and Dave Kramer
        choreography: Eric Victor
Productions:
    Opened December 29, 1942 for 4 performances
Reviews:
    New York Theatre Critics' Reviews 1942:122+
    New York Times page 26, Jan 1, 1943

Young Abe Lincoln
        book: Richard N. Bernstein and John Allen
        music: Victor Ziskin
        lyrics: Joan Javits and Arnold Sungaard
Productions:
    (Off-Broadway) Season of 1960-61
Reviews:
    New York Times page 36, Apr 26, 1961
                     page 27, May 6, 1961

The Young Turk
        book: Aaron Hoffman
        music: Max Hoffman
        lyrics: Harry Williams
        staging: Herbert Gresham

Productions:
    Opened January 31, 1910 for 32 performances
Reviews:
    Dramatic Mirror 63:8, Feb 12, 1910
    Theatre Magazine 11:xii, Mar 1910

Your Own Thing
    book: Donald Driver; suggested by William Shake-
                       speare's Twelfth Night
    music: Hal Hester and Danny Apolinar
    lyrics: Hal Hester and Danny Apolinar
    staging: Donald Driver
    sets: Robert Guerra
    costumes: Albert Wolsky
    choreography: Charles Schneider
Productions:
    (Off-Broadway) Opened January 13, 1968 for 933 performances
Reviews:
    Commonweal 87:623-4, Feb 23, 1968
    Dance Magazine 42:26-7, Apr 1968
    Mademoiselle 67:116-17, Jun 1968
    Nation 206:220, Feb 12, 1968
    New York Theatre Critics' Reviews 1968:270
    New York Times page 33, Jan 15, 1968
                    II, page 3, Jan 28, 1968
                    II, page 7, Feb 25, 1968
                    page 23, Feb 8, 1969
                    page 39, Mar 29, 1969
    New Yorker 43:86, Jan 27, 1968
    Saturday Review 51:39, Feb 10, 1968
    Time 91:45, Jan 26, 1968
    Vogue 151:46, Apr 15, 1968

You're a Good Man, Charlie Brown
    book: Clark Gesner; based on the comic strip
                       "Peanuts" by Charles M. Schulz
    music: Clark Gesner
    lyrics: Clark Gesner
    staging: Joseph Hardy
    sets: Alan Kimmel
    costumes: Alan Kimmel
Productions:
    (Off-Broadway) Opened March 7, 1967 for 98 performances
    Opened June 1, 1971 for 32 performances
Reviews:
    Christian Century 84:1561, Dec 6, 1967
    National Republic 19:976-8, Sep 5, 1967
    Nation 204:444-5, Apr 3, 1967
    New York Theatre Critics' Reviews 1971:255
    New York Times page 51, Mar 8, 1967
                    page 44, Mar 9, 1967
                    II, page 1, Apr 9, 1967
                    II, page 1, Sep 3, 1967

                              page 46, Mar 8, 1968
                              page 13, Feb 13, 1971
                              page 16, May 1, 1971
                              page 48, May 6, 1971
                              page 33, Jun 2, 1971
                              page 56, Jun 23, 1971
        New Yorker 43:121-3, Mar 18, 1967
        Newsweek 69:109, Mar 20, 1967
        Saturday Review 50:42, Apr 1, 1967
        Time 89:62, Mar 17, 1967

You're in Love
        book: Otto Hauerbach and Edward Clark
        music: Rudolf Friml
        lyrics: Otto Hauerbach and Edward Clark
        staging: Edward Clark
Productions:
        Opened February 6, 1917 for 167 performances
Reviews:
        Dramatic Mirror 77:5, Feb 10, 1917
                        77:7+, Feb 17, 1917
                        77:4, Mar 3, 1917
        New York Dramatic News 63:27, Dec 16, 1918
        New York Times page 11, Feb 7, 1917
        Theatre Magazine 25:151-2, Mar 1917
                         25:231, Apr 1917

Yours Truly
        book: Clyde North
        music: Raymond Hubbell
        lyrics: Anne Caldwell
        staging: Paul Dickey and Ralph Reader
Productions:
        Opened January 25, 1927 for 129 performances
        Opened March 12, 1928 for 16 performances
Reviews:
        Life (New York) 89:21, Feb 24, 1927
        New York Times page 16, Jan 26, 1927
        Theatre Magazine 45:19, Apr 1927

Yves Montand   (see An Evening with Yves Montand)

Yvette
        book: Benjamin Thorne Gilbert
        music: Frederick Herendeen
        lyrics: Frederick Herendeen
        staging: M. Ring
Productions:
        Opened August 10, 1916 for 4 performances
Reviews:
        Dramatic Mirror 76:8, Aug 19, 1916
        New York Times page 7, Aug 11, 1916
                        page 9, Aug 12, 1916

- Z -

Ziegfeld Follies of 1910
    book: Harry B. Smith
    music: Gus Edwards
    staging: Julian Mitchell
    sets: John H. Young and Ernest Albert
    costumes: Crage, Berlin, Tappé and W. H. Matthews, Jr.
Productions:
    Opened June 20, 1910 for 88 performances
Reviews:
    Leslie's Weekly 111:11, Jul 7, 1910
                    111:31, Jul 14, 1910
                    111:55, Jul 21, 1910
    Metropolitan Magazine 32:674-5, Aug 1910
    Theatre Magazine 12:35+, Aug 1910

Ziegfeld Follies of 1911
    book: George V. Hobart
    music: Maurice Levi, Raymond Hubbell, Jerome Kern,
                       and Irving Berlin
    staging: Julian Mitchell
    sets: Ernest Albert and Unitt and Wickers
    costumes: Matthews and Tryce
Productions:
    Opened June 26, 1911 for 80 performances
Reviews:
    Blue Book 13:1124-9, Oct 1911
    Dramatic Mirror 65:14, Jun 28, 1911
                    66:9, Jul 12, 1911
                    66:4, Jul 19, 1911
    Green Book Album 6:452-7, Sep 1911
    Red Book 17:955, Sep 1911
    Stage 13:56+, Aug 1936
    Theatre Magazine 14:40, Aug 1911
                    14:46+, Aug 1911

Ziegfeld Follies of 1912
    book: Harry B. Smith
    music: Raymond Hubbell
    lyrics: Harry B. Smith
    staging: Julian Mitchell
    sets: Ernest Albert
    costumes: Callot of Paris, Schneider and Anderson
Productions:
    Opened October 21, 1912 for 88 performances
Reviews:
    Blue Book 16:452-7, Jan 1913
    Dramatic Mirror 68:6, Oct 23, 1912
    Green Book 9:18-20+, Jan 1913
    Harper's Weekly 56:20, Nov 2, 1912
    Munsey 48:528-9, Dec 1912
    New York Dramatic News 56:21, Oct 26, 1912

Ziegfeld Follies of 1913
```
    book:            George V. Hobart
    music:           Raymond Hubbell, Gene Buck, and Dave Stamper
    lyrics:          George V. Hobart
    staging:         Julian Mitchell
    sets:            John H. Young, Gates and Morange, Ernest
                     Albert
    costumes:        Schneider and Anderson
```
Productions:
    Opened June 16, 1913 for 96 performances
Reviews:
    Blue Book 17:868-71, Sep 1913
    Dramatic Mirror 70:2, Jul 2, 1913
    Green Book 10:373-75, Sep 1913
              10:430-32, Sep 1913
              11:212-18, Feb 1914
    Munsey 50:92, Oct 1913
    New York Times page 11, Jun 17, 1913

Ziegfeld Follies of 1914
```
    book:            George V. Hobart
    music:           Raymond Hubbell and David Stamper
    lyrics:          George V. Hobart; additional lyrics by Gene
                     Buck
    staging:         Florenz Ziegfeld, Jr. and Leon Errol
    sets:            John H. Young and Ernest Albert
    costumes:        Cora McGeachey and W. H. Matthews, Jr.
```
Productions:
    Opened June 1, 1914 for 112 performances
Reviews:
    Dramatic Mirror 71:8, Jun 3, 1914
    Green Book 12:322-5, Aug 1914
    Munsey 53:90-92, Oct 1914
    New York Times page 11, Jun 2, 1914
    Theatre Magazine 20:37, Jul 1914

Ziegfeld Follies of 1915
```
    book:            Channing Pollock, Rennold Wolf and Gene Buck
    music:           Louis Hirsch and David Stamper
    lyrics:          Channing Pollock, Rennold Wolf and Gene Buck
    staging:         Julian Mitchell and Leon Errol
    sets:            Joseph Urban
    costumes:        Lucille and Tappé
```
Productions:
    Opened June 21, 1915 for 104 performances
Reviews:
    Dramatic Mirror 73:8, Jun 23, 1915
    Green Book 14:388-403, Sep 1915
              14:874-5, Nov 1915
    Harper's Bazaar 50:48, Jul 1915
    New Republic 3:366, Jul 31, 1915
    New York Times page 15, Jun 22, 1915
    Strand 50:208-15, Sep 1915

Theatre Magazine 22:66, Aug 1915

Ziegfeld Follies of 1916
   book: George V. Hobart and Gene Buck
   music: Louis Hirsch, Jerome Kern and Dave Stamper
   lyrics: George V. Hobart and Gene Buck
   staging: Ned Wayburn
   sets: Joseph Urban
   costumes: Lucille
Productions:
Opened June 12, 1916 for 112 performances
Reviews:
   Dramatic Mirror 75:8, Jun 17, 1916
   Green Book 16:418-19, Sep 1916
   New York Times page 9, Jun 13, 1916
   Theatre Magazine 24:11+, Jul 1916
                    24:71, Aug 1916

Ziegfeld Follies of 1917
   book: Gene Buck and George V. Hobart
   music: Raymond Hubbell and Dave Stamper
   lyrics: Gene Buck and George V. Hobart
   additional
     sketches: Ring Lardner
   staging: Ned Wayburn
   sets: Joseph Urban
   costumes: Lucille, Callot of Paris, Bendel
Productions:
Opened June 12, 1917 for 111 performances
Reviews:
   Dramatic Mirror 77:5+, Jun 23, 1917
                    77:7, Jun 23, 1917
   New Republic 11:278, Jul 17, 1917
   New York Times page 11, Jun 13, 1917
                   VIII, page 5, Jun 17, 1917
   Theatre Magazine 26:55, Jul 17, 1917
                    26:87, Aug 1917

Ziegfeld Follies of 1918
   book: Rennold Wolf and Gene Buck
   music: Louis A. Hirsch, Victor Jacobi, Dave Stamper,
                     Irving Berlin
   lyrics: Rennold Wolf and Gene Buck
   staging: Ned Wayburn
   sets: Joseph Urban
   costumes: Lucille
Productions:
Opened June 18, 1918 for 151 performances
Reviews:
   Dramatic Mirror 78:921, Jun 29, 1918
   Green Book 20:388-99, Sep 1918
   New York Times page 9, Jun 19, 1918
   Theatre Magazine 28:112, Aug 1918

Ziegfeld Follies of 1919

book:	Gene Buck, Dave Stamper, Rennold Wolf
music:	Victor Herbert, Harry Tierney, Joseph J. McCarthy, and Irving Berlin
lyrics:	Gene Buck, Dave Stamper, Rennold Wolf
staging:	Ned Wayburn
sets:	Joseph Urban
costumes:	Lucille and Mme. Frances

Productions:
   Opened September 1919 for 171 performances
Reviews:
   Arts and Decoration 11:302, Oct 1919
   Theatre Magazine 30:77, Aug 1919
                   30:81, Aug 1919
                   30:159, Sep 1919

Ziegfeld Follies (1920)

sketches:	W. C. Fields, George V. Hobart, James Montgomery
music and lyrics:	Irving Berlin, Dave Stamper, Gene Buck, Joseph McCarthy, Harry Tierney, Victor Herbert
staging:	Edward Royce

Productions:
   Opened June 22, 1920 for 123 performances
Reviews:
   New York Clipper 68:14, Mar 17, 1920
   New York Times page 14, Jun 23, 1920

Ziegfeld Follies (1921)

book:	Willard Mack, Raymond Hitchcock, Channing Pollock, Ralph Spence
music:	Victor Herbert, Rudolf Friml, Dave Stamper
lyrics:	Gene Buck, B. G. De Sylva, Brian Hooker
staging:	Edward Royce

Productions:
   Opened June 21, 1921 for 119 performances
Reviews:
   Life (New York) 78:18, Jul 14, 1921
   New York Clipper 69:20, Jun 29, 1921
   New York Times page 8, Jun 17, 1921
                   page 10, Jun 22, 1921
   Theatre Magazine 34:168, Sep 1921

Ziegfeld Follies of 1922

book:	Ring Lardner, Gene Buck and Ralph Spence
music:	Victor Herbert, Louis A. Hirsch and Dave Stamper
staging:	Ned Wayburn
sets:	Joseph Urban and Herman Rosse
costumes:	James Reynolds, Cora McGeachey, Alice O'Neil, Ben Ali Haggin, Tappé, and Charles LeMaire
choreography:	Michel Fokine

Productions:

Opened June 5, 1922 for 333 performances
Reviews:
    Bookman 55:601-2, Aug 1922
    Life (New York) 79:18, Jun 29, 1922
    New York Clipper 70:20, Jun 14, 1922
    New York Times page 18, Jun 6, 1922
    Theatre Magazine 36:95, Aug 1922
                        36:135, Sep 1922

Ziegfeld Follies (1923)
    sketches: Eddie Cantor and Gene Buck
    music: Victor Herbert, Rudolf Friml, Dave Stamper
    lyrics: Gene Buck
    staging: Ned Wayburn
Productions:
Opened October 20, 1923 for 233 performances
Reviews:
    Dial 76:618, Dec 1923
    Life (New York) 82:18, Nov 8, 1923
    New York Times page 17, Oct 22, 1923
                    VIII, page 1, Oct 28, 1923
                    page 25, Mar 18, 1924
    Theatre Magazine 38:19, Dec 1923

Ziegfeld Follies of 1924
    book: Will Rogers and William Anthony McGuire
    music: Victor Herbert, Raymond Hubbell, Dave
                    Stamper, Harry Tierney, and Dr. Albert Sirmay
    lyrics: Gene Buck and Joseph J. McCarthy
    staging: Julian Mitchell
    sets: Joseph Urban and John Wenger
    costumes: Erté of Paris, James Reynolds, Alice O'Neill
Productions:
Opened June 24, 1924 for 401 performances
Reviews:
    Life (New York) 84:18, Jul 17, 1924
    New York Times page 25, Jun 19, 1924
                    page 17, Jun 22, 1924
                    page 26, Jun 25, 1924
                    page 19, Mar 11, 1925
                    page 9, Jun 6, 1925
    Theatre Magazine 40:15, Sep 1924
    World's Work 48:595, Oct 1924

Ziegfeld Follies (1927)
    sketches: Harold Atteridge and Eddie Cantor
    music: Irving Berlin
    lyrics: Irving Berlin
    staging: Florenz Ziegfeld, Sammy Lee, Zeke Colvan
Productions:
Opened August 16, 1927 for 167 performances
Reviews:
    Independent 119:362, Oct 8, 1927

Life 90:21, Sep 1, 1927
New York Times VII, page 1, Aug 7, 1927
                page 27, Aug 17, 1927
                VII, page 1, Aug 28, 1927
                VII, page 2, Sep 18, 1927
Vogue 70:96, Oct 15, 1927

Ziegfeld Follies, 1931
    assembled by: Florenz Ziegfeld
    contributors: Gene Buck, Mark Hellinger, J. P. Murray,
                   Barry Trivers, Ben Oakland, Walter Donaldson,
                   Dave Stamper, Hugo Reisenfeld, Mack Gordon,
                   Harry Revel, Dmitri Tiomkin
    staging: Florenz Ziegfeld and Gene Buck
    choreography: Bobby Connelly and Albertina Rasch
Productions:
Opened July 1, 1931 for 165 performances
Reviews:
New Republic 67:262-3, Jul 22, 1931
New York Times page 30, Jul 2, 1931
                VIII, page 2, Aug 16, 1931
Outlook 158:343, Jul 15, 1931

Ziegfeld Follies (1934)
    sketches and Vernon Duke, Samuel Pokrass, Billy Hill,
    songs: H. I. Phillips, Fred Allen, Harry Tugend,
                  Ballard McDonald, David Freedman
    lyrics: E. Y. Harburg
    staging: Edward C. Lilley
    sets: Watson Barratt and Albert R. Johnson
    choreography: Robert Alton
Productions:
Opened January 4, 1934 for 182 performances
Reviews:
Commonweal 19:441, Feb 16, 1934
Nation 138:310, Mar 14, 1934
New Outlook 163:48, Feb 1934
New York Times X, page 1, Jan 21, 1934
                IX, page 1, Nov 11, 1934
Review of Reviews 89:40, Feb 1934
Time 23:40, Jan 15, 1934
Vanity Fair 42:38-9, Mar 1934

Ziegfeld Follies (1936)
    book: Ira Gershwin and David Freedman
    music: Vernon Duke
    lyrics: Ira Gershwin and David Freedman
    staging: John Murray Anderson
    sets: Vincente Minnelli
    costumes: Vincente Minnelli
    choreography: Robert Alton
Productions:
Opened January 30, 1936 for 115 performances

Reviews:
    Nation 142:231, Feb 19, 1936
    New York Times page 10, Dec 31, 1935
                    IX, page 3, Jan 5, 1936
                    page 17, Jan 31, 1936
    Time 27:47, Feb 10, 1936

Ziegfeld Follies of 1936-1937
    book: Ira Gershwin and David Freedman
    music: Vernon Duke
    lyrics: Ira Gershwin and David Freedman
    staging: John Murray Anderson
    sets: Vincente Minnelli
    costumes: Vincente Minnelli
    choreography: Robert Alton
Productions:
    Opened September 4, 1936 for 112 performances
Reviews:
    New York Times page 37, Sep 15, 1936

Ziegfeld Follies (1943)
    sketches: Lester Lee, Jerry Seelen, Bud Pearson, Les
                    White, Joseph Erens, Charles Sherman, Harry
                    Young, Lester Lawrence, Baldwin Bergersen,
                    Ray Golden, Sid Kuller, William Wells, Harold
                    Rome
    music: Ray Henderson and Dan White
    lyrics: Jack Yellen and Buddy Burston
    staging: John Murray Anderson
    sets: Watson Barratt
    costumes: Miles White
    choreography: Robert Alton
Productions:
    Opened April 1, 1943 for 553 performances
Reviews:
    New York Theatre Critics' Reviews 1943:338+
    New York Times page 16, Apr 2, 1943
                    II, page 1, Apr 11, 1943
    Newsweek 21:84, Apr 12, 1943
    Theatre Arts 27:331, Jun 1943

Ziegfeld Follies (1957)
    sketches: Arme Rosen, Coleman Jacoby, David Rogers,
                    Alan Jeffreys, Maxwell Grant
    music and   Jack Lawrence, Richard Myers, Howard Dietz,
    lyrics: Sammy Fain, David Rogers, Colin Romoff,
                    Dean Fuller, Marshall Barer, Carolyn Leigh,
                    Philip Springer
    staging: John Kennedy
    sets: Raoul Pene du Bois
    costumes: Raoul Pene du Bois
    choreography: Frank Wagner
Productions:

Opened March 1, 1957 for 123 performances
Reviews:
America 97:311, Jun 8, 1957
Catholic World 185:147-8, May 1957
Commonweal 66:36, Apr 12, 1957
Life 42:89-90+, Mar 18, 1957
Nation 184:242, Mar 16, 1957
New York Theatre Critics' Reviews 1957:327+
New York Times page 19, Mar 2, 1957
New Yorker 33:64, Mar 9, 1957
Newsweek 49:66, Mar 11, 1957
Theatre Arts 41:18, May 1957
Time 69:80, Mar 11, 1957

Ziegfeld Midnight Frolic
        music: Gene Buck and Dave Stamper
        lyrics: Gene Buck and Dave Stamper
        staging: Leon Errol
Productions:
Opened November 17, 1921 for 123 performances
Reviews:
New York Times page 11, Nov 19, 1921

Ziegfeld Midnight Frolic, Second Edition
        music: Dave Stamper
        lyrics: Gene Buck
        staging: Ned Wayburn
Productions:
Opened October 2, 1919 for 88 performances
Reviews:
New York Clipper 68:14, Mar 24, 1920
New York Times page 15, Oct 4, 1919
Theatre Magazine 32:106, Sep 1920
                     32:334, Nov 1920

Ziegfeld's American Revue of 1926 (see No Foolin')

Zizi
        sketches: Roland Petit
        songs: Jean Ferrat, Michael Legrand, and others
        staging: Roland Petit
        costumes: Yves Saint-Laurent
        choreography: Roland Petit
Productions:
Opened November 21, 1964 for 49 performances
Reviews:
Dance Magazine 39:19, Jan 1965
New York Theatre Critics' Reviews 1964:135
New York Times page 51, Nov 23, 1964
Newsweek 64:93, Nov 30, 1964
Saturday Review 48:32, Jan 2, 1965

Zorbá

book: Joseph Stein; adapted from Zorba the Greek by
                   Nikos Kazantzakis
music: John Kander
lyrics: Fred Ebb
staging: Harold Prince
sets: Boris Aronson
costumes: Patricia Zipprodt
choreography: Ronald Field
Productions:
Opened November 17, 1968 for 305 performances
Reviews:
America 119:632, Oct 14, 1968
Dance Magazine 43:93, Jan 1969
New York Theatre Critics' Reviews 1968:174
New York Times page 58, Nov 4, 1968
              page 58, Nov 18, 1968
              II, page 1, Nov 24, 1968
              page 28, Aug 5, 1969
              page 43, Nov 12, 1969
New Yorker 44:124+, Nov 23, 1968
Newsweek 72:105, Dec 2, 1968
Saturday Review 51:36, Dec 7, 1968
Time 92:71, Nov 29, 1968

The Zulu and the Zayda
book: Howard Da Silva and Felix Leon; based on a
                   story by Dan Jacobson
music: Harold Rome
lyrics: Harold Rome
staging: Dore Schary
sets: William and Jean Eckart
costumes: Frank Thompson
Productions:
Opened November 10, 1965 for 179 performances
Reviews:
New York Theatre Critics' Reviews 1965:278
New York Times page 59, Nov 11, 1965
              page 36, Apr 6, 1966

LONG RUN MUSICALS

Performances	Show	Season
6,281*	(OB) The Fantasticks	1959-1960
3,242	Fiddler on the Roof	1964-1965
2,844	Hello Dolly!	1963-1964
2,717	My Fair Lady	1955-1956
2,611	(OB) The Threepenny Opera	1953-1954
2,328	Man of La Mancha	1965-1966
2,212	Oklahoma	1942-1943
1,925	South Pacific	1948-1949
1,847	(OB) Jacques Brel Is Alive and Well and Living in Paris	1967-1968
1,750	Hair	1967-1968
1,684*	(OB) Godspell	1970-1971
1,508	Mame	1965-1966
1,443	The Sound of Music	1959-1960
1,417	How to Succeed in Business Without Really Trying	1961-1962
1,404	Hellzapoppin	1938-1939
1,375*	Grease	1971-1972
1,375	The Music Man	1957-1958
1,348	Funny Girl	1963-1964
1,314	Oh, Calcutta!	1969-1970
1,281	Promises, Promises	1968-1969
1,246	The King and I	1950-1951
1,217	1776	1968-1969
1,200	Guys and Dolls	1950-1951
1,165	Cabaret	1966-1967
1,147	Annie Get Your Gun	1945-1946
1,143	(OB) Little Mary Sunshine	1959-1960
1,114	(OB) El Grande de Coca-Cola	1972-1973
1,113*	Pippin	1972-1973
1,108	Pins and Needles	1937-1938
1,070	Kiss Me, Kate	1948-1949
1,065	Don't Bother Me, I Can't Cope	1971-1972
1,063	The Pajama Game	1953-1954
1,019	Damn Yankees	1954-1955
964	A Funny Thing Happened on the Way to the Forum	1961-1962
933	(OB) Your Own Thing	1967-1968
931	(OB) Curley McDimple	1967-1968
924	Bells Are Ringing	1956-1957

896	Applause	1969-1970
892	Can-Can	1952-1953
890	Carousel	1944-1945
889	Hats Off To Ice	1944-1945
888	Fanny	1954-1955
882	Follow the Girls	1943-1944
873	Camelot	1960-1961
871	(OB) The Mad Show	1965-1966
861	No! No! Nanette! (Also see 321 perf.)	1970-1971
849	Comedy in Music	1953-1954
835	La Plume De Ma Tante	1958-1959
830	Stars On Ice	1942-1943
795	Fiorello!	1959-1960
792	Where's Charley?	1948-1949
774	Oliver!	1962-1963
742	Sons O'Fun	1941-1942
740	Gentlemen Prefer Blondes	1949-1950
734	Call Me Mister	1945-1946
732	West Side Story (Also see 249 perf.)	1957-1958
728	(OB) Dime A Dozen	1962-1963
727	High Button Shoes	1947-1948
725	Finian's Rainbow	1946-1947
720	Jesus Christ Superstar	1971-1972
719	Carnival!	1960-1961
705	Company	1969-1970
702	Gypsy	1958-1959
700*	(OB) Let My People Come	1973-1974
693	Li'l Abner	1956-1957
688	Purlie	1969-1970
676	The Most Happy Fella	1955-1956
658*	Raisin	1973-1974
654	Bloomer Girl	1944-1945
644	Call Me Madame	1950-1951
620	(OB) The Game Is Up	1964-1965
613	Two Gentlemen of Verona	1971-1972
609	Star and Garter	1942-1943
608	Sweet Charity	1965-1966
607	Bye Bye Birdie	1959-1960
604	Irene (1973)	1972-1973
600	Flower Drum Song	1958-1959
600	A Little Night Music	1972-1973
598	Wish You Were Here	1952-1953
592	Blossom Time	1921-1922
586	The Me Nobody Knows (Also see 208 perf.)	1970-1971
583	Kismet	1953-1954
581	Brigadoon	1946-1947
580	No Strings	1961-1962
575	(OB) Dames at Sea	1968-1969
572	Show Boat (Also see 418 perf.)	1927-1928
570	Sally	1920-1921
568	Golden Boy	1964-1965
567	One Touch of Venus	1943-1944

559	Wonderful Town	1952-1953
555	Jamaica	1957-1958
555	Stop the World--I Want to Get Off	1962-1963
553	Ziegfeld Follies (1943)	1942-1943
551	Good News	1927-1928
547	Let's Face It	1941-1942
543	Milk and Honey	1961-1962
540	Pal Joey (Also see 374 perf.)	1951-1952
540	What Makes Sammy Run?	1963-1964
532	The Unsinkable Molly Brown	1960-1961
531	The Red Mill	1945-1946
524	Irma La Douce	1960-1961
521	Follies (1971)	1970-1971
519*	Candide	1973-1974
518	Lew Leslie's Blackbirds of 1928	1927-1928
517	Sunny	1925-1926
511	Half a Sixpence	1964-1965
511	The Vagabond King	1925-1926
509	The New Moon	1928-1929
507	The Rothschilds	1970-1971
505	Sugar	1971-1972
504	Up in Central Park	1944-1945
503	Carmen Jones	1943-1944
501	Panama Hattie	1940-1941
494	Rio Rita	1926-1927
492	Maytime	1917-1918
485	The Boy Friend	1954-1955
485	(OB) The Last Sweet Days of Isaac	1969-1970
481	Mexican Hayride	1943-1944
478	Silk Stockings	1954-1955
477	Wildflower	1922-1923
472	Destry Rides Again	1958-1959
471	The Desert Song	1926-1927
469	(OB) Baker's Dozen	1963-1964
469	(OB) The Boys from Syracuse (Also see 235 perf.)	1962-1963
463	The Apple Tree	1966-1967
463	Oh, Boy	1916-1917
463	On the Town	1944-1945
461	Everything	1918-1919
461	Plain and Fancy	1954-1955
460	Lend An Ear	1948-1949
460	Once Upon A Mattress	1958-1959
456	Cheer Up	1917-1918
456	Good Times	1920-1921
456	Wait a Minim!	1965-1966
(453)	Little Jesse James	1923-1924
452	Happy Days	1919-1920
452	Redhead	1958-1959
448	Take Me Along	1959-1960
447	A Trip to Japan	1909-1910
445	Around the World (1911)	1911-1912
445	Under Many Flags	1912-1913

444	Louisiana Purchase	1939-1940
441	Of Thee I Sing	1931-1932
440	Earl Carroll Vanities (1926-27)	1926-1927
440	Music Box Revue (1921)	1921-1922
438	Good Evening	1973-1974
433	(OB) Riverwind	1962-1963
431	New Girl in Town	1956-1957
430	Howdy, Mr. Ice of 1950!	1948-1949
429	Make Mine Manhattan	1947-1948
428	(OB) Mixed Doubles	1966-1967
427	By Jupiter	1941-1942
427	George M!	1967-1968
426	(OB) Bits and Pieces XIV	1964-1965
425	The Big Show	1916-1917
425	Hip-Hip-Hooray	1915-1916
424	George White's Scandals (1926)	1925-1926
422	The Gingham Girl	1922-1923
422	Icetime of 1948	1946-1947
422*	The Magic Show	1973-1974
422	Something for the Boys	1942-1943
422	(OB) Touch	1970-1971
420	Anything Goes	1934-1935
420	As the Girls Go	1948-1949
418	A Connecticut Yankee	1927-1928
418	Show Boat (Also see 572 perf.)	1945-1946
413	Hold Everything	1928-1929
412	Happy Hunting	1956-1957
411	Artists and Models (1925)	1925-1926
410	(OB) ... And in This Corner	1963-1964
409	Better Times	1922-1923
409	The Girl Friend	1925-1926
408	DuBarry Was A Lady	1939-1940
406	Howdy, Mr. Ice!	1948-1949
403	Follow Thru	1928-1929
401	Ziegfeld Follies of 1924	1924-1925
400	As Thousands Cheer	1933-1934
400	Do Re Mi	1960-1961
400	Earl Carroll's Sketch Book (1929)	1929-1930
400	(OB) Pick a Number XV	1965-1966
399	Inside U.S.A.	1947-1948
395	The Cat and the Fiddle	1931-1932
395	(OB) Just for Openers	1965-1966
390	Earl Carroll Vanities (1925)	1925-1926
386	It Happens On Ice	1941-1942
383	Golden Rainbow	1967-1968
383	Mr. Wonderful	1955-1956
382	Early to Bed	1943-1944
379	Whoopee	1928-1929
378	Queen High	1926-1927
377	The Cocoanuts	1925-1926
375	High Spirits	1963-1964
374	Pal Joey (Also see 540 perf.)	1940-1941
365	New Faces of 1952	1951-1952

364	Honeymoon Lane	1926-1927
360	America	1913-1914
358	Me and Juliet	1952-1953
357	Flying High	1929-1930
356	The Blue Paradise	1915-1916
356	Rain or Shine	1927-1928
353	The Better 'Ole	1918-1919
353	Priorities of 1942	1941-1942
352	Hit the Deck	1926-1927
351	Going Up	1917-1918
351	Two By Two	1970-1971
350	(OB) National Lampoon's Lemmings	1972-1973
350	Top Banana	1951-1952
348	Over Here!	1973-1974
342	Music in the Air	1932-1933
341	Very Good, Eddie	1915-1916
338	I Married An Angel	1937-1938
337	Tangerine	1921-1922
336	(OB) Time, Gentleman Please	1961-1962
335	Rosalie	1927-1928
334	Here's Love	1963-1964
333	The International Cup, the Ballet of	
	Niagra and the Earthquake	1910-1911
333	Peggy-Ann	1926-1927
333	Ziegfeld Follies of 1922	1922-1923
332	Coco	1969-1970
332	Say Darling	1957-1958
330	110 in the Shade	1963-1964
330	Lady Be Good	1924-1925
(328)	Poppy	1923-1924
327	Three to Make Ready	1945-1946
326	Best Foot Forward	1941-1942
325	Ain't Supposed to Die a Natural Death	1971-1972
321	The Little Show (1929)	1928-1929
321	Lorelei	1973-1974
321	No! No! Nanette! (Also see 861 perf.)	1925-1926
320	Dark of the Moon	1944-1945
319	Louie the 14th	1924-1925
318	Countess Maritza	1926-1927
318	George White's Scandals (1920)	1920-1921
318	Illya Darling	1966-1967
318	The Streets of New York	1963-1964
315	Allegro	1947-1948
315	On Your Toes	1935-1936
312	Artists and Models (1923)	1923-1924
312	My Maryland	1927-1928
312	The Pink Lady	1910-1911
312	Sally, Irene and Mary	1922-1923
311	Baker Street	1964-1965
311	Rose-Marie	1924-1925
310	(OB) The Believers	1967-1968
308	Miss Liberty	1949-1950
307	Leave It To Me	1938-1939

305	Lady in the Dark	1941-1942
305	Porgy and Bess (Also see 286 perf.)	1952-1953
305	Zorbá	1968-1969
301	She Loves Me	1962-1963
300	Angel in the Wings	1947-1948
300	I Can Get It For You Wholesale	1961-1962
298	The Great Waltz	1934-1935
296	Seesaw	1972-1973
295	Chin-Chin	1914-1915
295	Roberta	1933-1934
295	Sons O'Guns	1929-1930
294	(OB) Oh, Coward!	1972-1973
293	Halleujah, Baby!	1966-1967
290	I'd Rather Be Right	1937-1938
289	Babes in Arms	1936-1937
289	Paint Your Wagon	1951-1952
289	The Ramblers	1926-1927
(288)	Battling Buttler	1923-1924
288	The Dollar Princess	1909-1910
288	Sweethearts	1946-1947
286	Dearest Enemy	1925-1926
286	(OB) Graham Crackers	1962-1963
286	Porgy and Bess (Also see 305 perf.)	1941-1942
285	The Happy Time	1967-1968
283	Sometime	1918-1919
281	Two On the Aisle	1951-1952
280	Five O'Clock Girl	1927-1928
280	The Passing Show of 1919	1919-1920
278	Earl Carroll Vanities (1931)	1931-1932
278	Michael Todd's Peep Show	1950-1951
274	Streets of Paris	1939-1940
273	(OB) The Decline and Fall of the Entire World as Seen Through the Eyes of Cole Porter	1964-1965
273	Lost in the Stars	1949-1950
273	Music Box Revue (1922)	1922-1923
273	Music Box Revue (1923)	1923-1924
272	Girl Crazy	1930-1931
272	Listen Lester	1918-1919
272	On a Clear Day You Can See Forever	1965-1966
272	Three's A Crowd	1930-1931
271	Fade Out--Fade In	1963-1964
270	By the Beautiful Sea	1953-1954
270	A Tree Grows in Brooklyn	1950-1951
269	The Consul	1949-1950
267	Are You With It?	1945-1946
265	Good Morning Dearie	1921-1922
265	Jack O'Lantern	1917-1918
265	Mr. President	1962-1963
264	Manhattan Mary	1927-1928
264	Tovarich	1962-1963
261	Artists and Models (1924)	1924-1925
260	The Band Wagon	1930-1931

260	(OB) The Establishment (1963-64)	1963-1964
259	Buddies	1919-1920
259	(OB) Promenade	1969-1970
257	Little Me	1962-1963
256	Apple Blossoms	1919-1920
256	Oh, Kay	1926-1927
(256)	The Perfect Fool	1921-1922
256	Up She Goes	1922-1923
255	Experience	1914-1915
255	Fine and Dandy	1930-1931
254	Fifty Million Frenchmen	1929-1930
254	Monte Cristo, Jr.	1918-1919
249	Too Many Girls	1939-1940
249	West Side Story (Also see 732 perf.)	1959-1960
248	Gay Divorce	1932-1933
(248)	Little Nellie Kelly	1922-1923
248	Oh! Oh! Delphine	1912-1913
246	Pipe Dream	1955-1956
246	Tip Top	1920-1921
245	Tickets, Please!	1949-1950
245	(OB) The World of Kurt Weill in Song	1963-1964
244	Funny Face	1927-1928
243	Take A Chance	1932-1933
241	(OB) Man With a Load of Mischief	1966-1967
241	Skyscraper	1965-1966
241	Stepping Stones	1923-1924
240	The Only Girl	1914-1915
240	Quaker Girl	1911-1912
239	(OB) Anything Goes (Also see 420 perf.)	1961-1962
239	(OB) Salvation	1969-1970
237	Life Begins at 8:40	1934-1935
237	The Show Is On	1936-1937
235	The Boys from Syracuse	1938-1939
235	Good Boy	1928-1929
234	Sweet Adeline	1929-1930
233	Jumbo	1935-1936
233	Laffing Room Only	1944-1945
233	Ziegfeld Follies (1923)	1923-1924
232	Alma, Where Do You Live?	1910-1911
232	Bajour	1964-1965
232	Greenwich Village Follies (1919)	1919-1920
232	The Lady in Ermine	1922-1923
232	The Lady of the Slipper	1912-1913
(231)	Honeydew	1920-1921
231	The Laugh Parade	1931-1932
231	Madame Sherry	1910-1911
231	The Roar of the Greasepaint--The Smell of the Crowd	1964-1965
230	George White's Scandals (1928)	1928-1929
229	John Murray Anderson's Almanac	1953-1954
229	Wars of the World	1914-1915
228	(OB) The Game Is Up (New Edition)	1965-1966
228	Irene (1919)	1919-1920

224	Americana (1926)	1926-1927
224	(OB) Best Foot Forward (Also see	
	326 perf.)	1962-1963
224	The Little Whopper	1919-1920
224	Miss Springtime	1916-1917
224	Somebody's Sweetheart	1918-1919
224	(OB) The Sunshine Train	1972-1973
223	White Horse Inn	1936-1937
222	A Night in Spain (1927)	1927-1928
221	Texas, Li'l Darlin'	1949-1950
220	Do I Hear A Waltz?	1964-1965
220	Flo-Flo	1917-1918
220	Hitchy-Koo, 1917	1917-1918
220	How Now, Dow Jones	1967-1968
220	Katinka	1915-1916
220	New Faces of 1956	1956-1957
219	Bombo	1921-1922
219	Hot Chocolates	1929-1930
219	Mary	1920-1921
219	Oh, Lady! Lady!	1917-1918
216	Greenwich Village Follies (1922)	1922-1923
216	Tenderloin	1960-1961
215	Ben Franklin in Paris	1964-1965
215	Earl Carroll Vanities (1930)	1930-1931
214	(OB) Money	1963-1964
213	High Jinks	1913-1914
213	May Wine	1935-1936
213	Runnin' Wild	1923-1924
212	The Medium	1946-1947
212	The Telephone	1946-1947
211	Garrick Gaieties (1925)	1924-1925
210	Three Cheers	1928-1929
210	(OB) To the Water Tower	1962-1963
209	The Show of Wonders	1916-1917
208	(OB) Absolutely Free	1966-1967
208	Bagels and Yox	1951-1952
208	Chu Chin Chow	1917-1918
208	(OB) Joy	1969-1970
208	(OB) The Me Nobody Knows (Also see	
	586 perf.)	1969-1970
208	Yokel Boy	1939-1940
207	Earl Carroll Sketch Book (1935)	1934-1935
207	Murder at the Vanities	1933-1934
207	Tickle Me	1920-1921
206	Criss Cross	1926-1927
206	Take the Air	1927-1928
205	Subways Are for Sleeping	1961-1962
204	Earl Carroll Vanities	1923-1924
204	The Fireman's Flame	1937-1938
203	Vanities (1928)	1928-1929
202	George White's Scandals (1931)	1931-1932
200	The Century Girl	1916-1917

| 200 | Hooray for What! | 1937-1938 |
| 200 | The Passing Show of 1921 | 1920-1921 |

*Still Running on June 1, 1975

(OB) Off-Broadway production

(performances) Closing date not available. Show may have run longer.

PULITZER PRIZE MUSICALS

1931-1932	Of Thee I Sing
1949-1950	South Pacific
1959-1960	Fiorello!
1961-1962	How to Succeed in Business Without Really Trying

NEW YORK DRAMA CRITICS' CIRCLE AWARD MUSICALS

First award for "Best Musical Production" granted in 1945-1946.

1945-1946	Carousel
1946-1947	Brigadoon
1947-1948	no award
1948-1949	South Pacific
1949-1950	The Consul
1950-1951	Guys and Dolls
1951-1952	Pal Joey
1952-1953	Wonderful Town
1953-1954	The Golden Apple
1954-1955	The Saint of Bleecker Street
1955-1956	My Fair Lady
1956-1957	The Most Happy Fella
1957-1958	The Music Man
1958-1959	La Plume de Ma Tante
1959-1960	Fiorello!
1960-1961	Carnival
1961-1962	How to Succeed in Business Without Really Trying
1962-1963	no award
1963-1964	Hello Dolly!
1964-1965	Fiddler on the Roof
1965-1966	Man of La Mancha
1966-1967	Cabaret
1967-1968	Your Own Thing
1968-1969	1776
1969-1970	Company
1970-1971	Follies
1971-1972	Two Gentlemen of Verona
1972-1973	A Little Night Music
1973-1974	Candide

INDEX OF AUTHORS, COMPOSERS, LYRICISTS

557

INDEX OF DIRECTORS, DESIGNERS, CHOREOGRAPHERS

INDEX OF ORIGINAL WORKS AND AUTHORS

WITHDRAWAL